THE SPY WHO WOULD BE T

CW00818778

Michal Goleniewski was one of the Cold War's most important spies but has been overlooked in the vast literature on the intelligence battles between the Western Powers and the Soviet Bloc. Renowned investigative journalist Kevin Coogan reveals Goleniewski's extraordinary story for the first time in this biography.

Goleniewski rose to be a senior officer in the Polish intelligence service, a position which gave him access to both Polish and Russian secrets. Disillusioned with the Soviet Bloc, he made contact with the CIA, sending them letters containing significant intelligence. He then decided to defect and fled to America in 1961 via an elaborate escape plan in Berlin. His revelations led to the exposure of several important Soviet spies in the West including the Portland spy ring in the UK, the MI6 traitor George Blake, and a spy high up in the West German intelligence service. Despite these hugely important contributions to the Cold War, Goleniewski would later be abandoned by the CIA after he made the outrageous claim that he was actually Tsarevich Alexei Nikolaevich of Russia – the last remaining member of the Romanov Russian royal family and therefore entitled to the lost treasures of the Tsar. Goleniewski's increasingly fantastical claims led to him becoming embroiled in a bizarre *demi-monde* of Russian exiles, anti-communist fanatics, right-wing extremists and chivalric orders with deep historical roots in America's racist and antisemitic underground.

This fascinating and revelatory biography will be of interest to students and researchers of the Cold War, intelligence history and right-wing extremism as well as general readers with an interest in these intriguing subjects.

Kevin Coogan was a veteran investigative journalist. His previous books include *Dreamer of the Day: Francis Parker Yockey and the Postwar Fascist International* (1999).

THE SPY WHO WOULD BE TSAR

The Mystery of Michal Goleniewski and the Far-Right Underground

Kevin Coogan

LONDON AND NEW YORK

First published 2022
by Routledge
2 Park Square, Milton Park, Abingdon, Oxon OX14 4RN

and by Routledge
605 Third Avenue, New York, NY 10158

Routledge is an imprint of the Taylor & Francis Group, an informa business

© 2022 Ellen Coogan

British Library Cataloguing-in-Publication Data
A catalogue record for this book is available from the British Library

Library of Congress Cataloging-in-Publication Data
Names: Coogan, Kevin, author.
Title: The spy who would be tsar : the mystery of Michal Goleniewski and the
far-right underground / Kevin Coogan.
Description: Abingdon, Oxon ; New York, NY : Routledge, 2021. |
Includes bibliographical references and index.
Identifiers: LCCN 2020057013 (print) | LCCN 2020057014 (ebook) |
ISBN 9780367506636 (hardback) |
ISBN 9780367506650 (paperback) | ISBN 9781003051114 (ebook)
Subjects: LCSH: Goleniewski, Michal, 1922-1993. | Intelligence service--Poland. |
Cold War. | Spies--Poland--Biography. | Defectors--Poland--Biography. |
Defectors--United States--Biography. | Right-wing extremists--Biography.
Classification: LCC DK4435.G65 C66 2021 (print) | LCC DK4435.G65 (ebook) |
DDC 327.124380092 [B]--dc23
LC record available at https://lccn.loc.gov/2020057013
LC ebook record available at https://lccn.loc.gov/2020057014

ISBN: 978-0-367-50663-6 (hbk)
ISBN: 978-0-367-50665-0 (pbk)
ISBN: 978-1-003-05111-4 (ebk)

DOI: 10.4324/9781003051114

Typeset in Bembo
by Taylor & Francis Books

CONTENTS

ACKNOWLEDGEMENTS

I had been interested in the strange pseudo-chivalric 'Shickshinny Knights' for many years. In the early 1980s, a friend and I drove to Shickshinny and met Charles Pichel. We simply knocked on his door. It was around three in the afternoon. Pichel, a very old man, was in his pyjamas watching TV. We chatted for a bit and then left. If Charles Pichel were a secret master of the universe, he disguised his role brilliantly. The only thing I really remember about the encounter was that Pichel had displayed an award from some rightist group in Asia in his living room.

My interest in the Knights led me to the fantastic tale of Michal Goleniewski. I had known about Goleniewski as a minor character in books on the CIA and James Jesus Angleton in particular. That fact alone aroused my curiosity. Why did a top Eastern Bloc defector suddenly declare he was the Tsar of Russia? I was also acquainted with the writer Peter Tompkins. A former member of the wartime intelligence organization, the Office of Strategic Services (OSS), Tompkins wrote exotic books about the secret history of the pyramids and the hidden life of plants. Tompkins had met Goleniewski. He told me that he didn't think Goleniewski was the Tsar, but that he could be very convincing in person.

A few years ago, I first heard about Leszek Pawlikowicz's 2004 book *Tajny Front Zimnej Wojny: Uciekinierzy z Polskich Służb Specjalnych 1956–1964* (Secret Front of the Cold War: Refugees from the Polish Special Services 1956–1964). Pawlikowicz's study of Cold War defectors was made possible by the opening up of Polish intelligence service archives to qualified scholars. Pawlikowicz included a long section on Goleniewski in his study.

I then took the 7 subway train seven stops until I reached one of the most remarkable institutions in the world, the Central Research Division of the New York Public Library on 42nd Street and Fifth Avenue. Naturally, Pawlikowicz's book was in its incredible collection. Without that book and that library, I would never have attempted, much less written, *The Spy Who Would Be Tsar*.

As far as I know, my book is the first scholarly study of Goleniewski, although I draw on both Guy Richards' and Pierre de Villemarest's earlier portraits.[1] As part of that study, I also turned to the librarians and archivists at Boston University, who graciously helped guide me through the relevant sections of the Edward Jay Epstein and Tennent Bagley collections.

The research for the book led me down many strange rabbit holes. For that reason, I am eternally grateful for Professor Michael Hagemeister's help. One of the world's leading experts on the history of the *Protocols of the Elders of Zion*, Professor Hagemeister's advice (along with his own published studies) proved invaluable. I am most grateful, however, to my editor Craig Fowlie for his friendship and his willingness to take a chance on a slightly eccentric Yank.

After writing a book about such compulsive shapeshifters as spies, I hope this book will help open a new conversation about Goleniewski as there is clearly much more to be learned. For this reason, I would like to conclude by especially thanking whoever declassified (I suspect mistakenly) Goleniewski's January 1960 'Sniper' letter, which proved so invaluable for my research.

Kevin Coogan, New York City, February 2020

Note

1 As I was finalising sending this manuscript to the publisher, I became aware of a forth-coming book on Goleniewski by the British journalist Tim Tate. We have had no contact with each other so these should be regarded as entirely separate parallel investigations. Tate's book is listed as forthcoming in my bibliography.

PUBLISHER'S FOREWORD

Kevin Coogan passed away on 27 February 2020 in his beloved New York City.

Kevin sent me a letter, that I received after his death, with instructions to publish this book (which was already under contract) and another manuscript then under review called *The Secret History of the Japanese Red Army*. That manuscript is currently being edited by Japanese politics scholar Professor Claudia Derichs and will be published in 2022.

I sought advice and approval from Kevin's sister Nell, and she shared my desire to honor Kevin's memory by proceeding with the publication of both manuscripts. I am extremely grateful to Nell for her invaluable and unstinting support in helping me to see both these manuscripts through to publication.

Although we had corresponded before then, I first met Kevin Coogan in person in New York City (NYC) in 2012. I had greatly admired his 1999 book *Dreamer of the Day: Francis Parker Yockey and the Postwar Fascist International* and a mutual acquaintance put us in touch with each other. Our first meeting was in the Routledge office – then on Third Avenue – and we went out that evening for drinks and dinner. That was the start of a friendship that lasted until his untimely death.

Kevin and I shared a great interest in political history, in the extremes of right and left, in fringe cultural movements, and in 'deep politics', the murky clandestine underworld where intelligence agencies, organized crime, terrorists and other extremists conspire and collaborate to influence political outcomes. We corresponded frequently about these topics, his research and writing projects and my publishing programme, as well as our shared passions for books, music and films. This book emerged from those conversations.

I used to visit the Routledge NYC office every few months and always made time to see Kevin. Occasionally we went to talks at the Tamiment library at New York University (Kevin was a regular attender of talks and events in NYC's busy intellectual scene and would often e-mail me afterwards with his thoughts on the speakers). Sometimes Kevin would act as my tour guide and we'd explore on foot some of the offbeat parts of that wonderful city while Kevin would regale me with his exceptional knowledge of the history of NYC. He was always a brilliant dinner companion – a genuine polymath who was exceptionally knowledgeable about so many different subjects and we shared a similar sense of absurdist, and occasionally dark, humour. So, while we would spend hours in conversation on weighty historical, political and cultural topics, there was also lots of laughter.

Kevin was extremely generous with his time and knowledge, happy to help other researchers with insights, material and sources. When news of his death became public, as well as expressing their grief, this was one of the topics frequently mentioned by journalists, scholars and anti-fascist researchers. In tribute to his generosity of spirit, and the breadth and depth of his scholarship, we have also added a bibliography of all his writings and research at the end of this book.

Kevin sent me his manuscript just days before he died, and it is that manuscript which is the basis for the book you are holding. I have edited and formatted the manuscript, making corrections to typos and grammatical mistakes, removing some repetition, reordering some of the content and adding the occasional detail when the meaning was unclear. I have also checked, and occasionally updated, the references and bibliography (updates to the references are marked [CF]). I decided on a final title as we had not resolved this earlier. I'm sure Kevin would have polished the final manuscript better than I have but as Bob Dylan would sing a month after Kevin's death, 'it is what it is'.

Kevin once told me that in writing the Yockey book, he started with a biography and ended up with a film noir. And there is a similar feel to this book which branches out from Goleniewski's, already strange biography, to explore dozens of other obscure, fringe, extremist and underground individuals, organizations, publications and events. As in *Dreamer*, the manuscript takes some strange tangents into areas that are related only distantly to a conventional narrative biography.

Kevin told me often that when you are researching, similar to when you are exploring a city on foot, it's the smaller unexplored pathways, the offbeat side alleys, the subterranean arcana and even the trap streets that are often the most interesting places to explore. We always then envisaged that the final book would stay true to this, rabbit holes, digressions, mysteries and all. So I've made no effort to cut sections or over-simplify the narrative. I've also retained Kevin's penchant for posing questions but not resolving them when the available evidence does not support this.

What you will read are Kevin's words and in the final form that I believe he wanted them to be. This is his book and it is my privilege to be able to assist in its publication. Although it will always be tinged with sadness that Kevin will never get to see it.

I am writing this at home during the pandemic lockdown. I would love to have had a chance to talk with Kevin about that, the recent global Black Lives Matter protests and a pivotal US Presidential campaign. He would, as he always did, have had illuminating things to say about all of them.

In conclusion, I hope that publishing this volume is the most appropriate tribute that can be paid to Kevin's extraordinary research, analysis and writing.

Bella Ciao, old friend. We'll always have the Algonquin.

Craig Fowlie, Global Editorial Director for
Social Science Books, Routledge
Autumn/Fall 2020

PREFACE

If you ask people in Poland interested in espionage who was the greatest Polish defector in the Cold War, they might likely reply with a name almost unheard of in the rest of the world: Ryszard Kuklinski.[1] From the early 1970s to the eve of the declaration of martial law in December 1981, Colonel Kuklinski, a staff officer for the Polish General Staff, provided the CIA with somewhere between 35–40,000 pages of highly classified documents outlining everything from tank designs to Warsaw Pact maneuvers before he and his family defected to the USA.

Yet another top defector from Polish intelligence, Lt. Colonel Michal Goleniewski, however, remains obscure even in his native land. On 4 January 1961, Goleniewski entered the US Consulate in West Berlin and announced he was 'Sniper,' the name he first used in April 1958 when he began sending the CIA secret intelligence reports. His defection, some two decades earlier than Kuklinski's, doomed him to a certain obscurity, especially after he was marginalized by the CIA. Nor was he a Polish nationalist hero. Goleniewski even claimed he was not Polish but Russian.

Today Goleniewski is best remembered (when remembered at all) for his startling claim that he was 'H.I.H. [His Imperial Highness] Alexei Nikolaevich Romanoff, The Heir to the All-Russian Imperial Throne, Tsarevich and Grand Duke of Russia, Head of the Russian Imperial House, etc. and August Ataman etc. etc.'[2] Put more simply, he claimed that he was the hemophilic son of Nicholas II, born in 1904 and long believed murdered by the Bolsheviks with the rest of his family in the Siberian city of Yekaterinburg in July 1918.

Some years ago, Goleniewski became a bit better known. On 20 April 2005, Poland's public TV channel ran a documentary entitled *Czlowiek cien* (Man of Shadows). One consultant to the program was Leszek Pawlikowicz, who teaches history at Rzeszow University in southeast Poland. In 2004, Professor Pawlikowicz published *Tajny Front Zimnej Wojny: Uciekinierzy z Polskich Sluzb Specjalnych 1956–1964* (*Secret Front of the Cold War: Refugees from the Polish Special Services 1956–1964*). He devoted close to one hundred pages on Goleniewski with the most important section taken from a formerly secret investigation and trial of Goleniewski conducted by the Sad (Court) of the Warsaw Military District (*Warszawskiego Okregu Wojskowego*/WOW), which on 18 March 1961 sentenced Goleniewski to death in absentia. Pawlikowicz's study reignited my long-standing curiosity about Goleniewski.[3]

Michal Goleniewski was one of the Cold War's most important spies. Such an assertion may sound quite strange since for decades in mainstream espionage books Goleniewski has been relegated to the same one or two set paragraphs ritualistically repeated.[4] Yet it was the CIA's legendary counterintelligence chief James Angleton who told the journalist Edward Jay Epstein that Goleniewski was the most complicated defector case the CIA had ever seen.

In January 1975 Michal Goleniewski launched *Double Eagle*, his crudely produced amateur personal newsletter. It appeared in the wake of his remarkable claim that Henry Kissinger, Richard Nixon's former National Security Advisor and the then-current US Secretary of State, was a secret Russian agent. His charges were first announced in a 20 March 1974 article in the John Birch Society (JBS) weekly publication *Review of the News*. The author was Goleniewski's friend Frank Capell, an associate editor of the *Review*. He was best known, however, as the long-time publisher of an anti-communist newsletter called *Herald of Freedom*.

In the late 1970s, Capell became the 'Grand Prior' of a far-right pseudo-chivalric organization known as the Knights of Malta. Capell and his fellow Knights began their collaboration with Goleniewski in the early 1960s. They even proclaimed him as 'Grand Master' of their Order, which they claimed had its roots dating back to Catherine the Great's son Tsar Paul I.

Before beginning any investigation of Goleniewski, it is necessary to address the elephant in the room, the one wearing the tin foil hat. A significant part of Goleniewski's story sounds flat out crazy, some of it obviously is. When Edward Jay Epstein interviewed Goleniewski in the early 1980s he found him lucid on all matter espionage related. He only veered into 'crazy' when discussing his royal claims. Nor was Epstein's experience unique.

James Angleton was not even convinced that Goleniewski was mad. Former CIA officer Tennent 'Pete' Bagley reports that 'JA' didn't believe Goleniewski was insane but that he used insanity 'as a way out.'[5] Bagley, however, disagreed. In his book *Spy Wars*, he writes about Goleniewski: 'It was a great loss to our side when, all too soon after his defection, this sharpest of counterintelligence minds slipped into delusion and his information became confused and misleading.'[6] Yet Bagley remained convinced that Goleniewski had provided critical clues to the existence of a covert Soviet–Nazi spy network *Die Hacke* that supposedly flourished at the height of the Cold War.

The far-right French former spy and espionage author Pierre de Villemarest published a 1984 biography of Goleniewski entitled *Le Mystérieux Survivant d'Octobre*. He personally encountered Goleniewski's bizarre behavior when Villemarest arrived in New York on 11 May 1981 to interview him. Goleniewski refused to see him even though Villemarest had written him a month earlier announcing his impending visit.[7] In his book *Le Dossier Saragosse*, Villemarest reflected:

The disinformation services of Spetsnaz preformed marvelously and even succeeded this time to penetrate the yet restricted circle of the American friends of Goleniewski. No need to physically intervene against him. Moscow knew that worn out by years of playing a triple game in which he constantly risked his life, weakened by his hemophilia, in constant terror that the protection assured him by the FBI through the years no longer existed, stunned to find that the climate of rapprochement with the USSR intensified with each passing year, Goleniewski began losing his mind.[8]

The intelligence professionals who dealt with Goleniewski tried hard to distill gold from the shattered alembic of his mind. In much the same way, we will do so as well, keeping in mind that it is just this infuriating mix of illumination and delusion that makes Goleniewski's story so challenging.

Yet Goleniewski is not the only strange character in this study. As a result, his trail leads down some very twisted paths from an obscure pseudo-chivalric order in Pennsylvania, to a huge run-down mansion in Staten Island, to a notorious SS General, who reportedly lived in Eastern Europe after World War II. And did I mention the US Army Colonel who said he saw a real-life UFO and believed in Roswell conspiracy theories? Or the former CIA official who was convinced that Heinrich Himmler was living in Washington?

Structure

That said, I have organized the book in a fairly straightforward way. The introduction provides a brief summary of the 'labyrinth' of Goleniewski's life. The first chapters of Part I ('Sniper') provide some background on Goleniewski and his family as well as his life inside Polish intelligence up to his defection in early January 1961.

Chapters 4 and 5 explore the impact of Goleniewski's revelations on both American and British intelligence. In the US chapter the focus is on the CIA and its legendary Chief of Counterintelligence James Jesus Angleton. The chapter explores the complications arising from the competing claims of a series of defectors such as Goleniewski, Anatoliy Golitsyn and Yuri Nosenko. In the UK chapter I examine how Goleniewski helped to expose a number of Soviet spies including MI6 traitor George Blake and the 'Portland spy ring.' Both chapters explore the paranoid and debilitating 'molehunts' – based in part on evidence from Goleniewski – as MI5 and the CIA searched for further potential traitors within their own ranks.

In Part II, 'Hacke', I examine Goleniewski's claim that the Soviet Union had established a postwar intelligence network in both Eastern and Western Europe with high-ranking 'former' Nazis. I also reveal how information from Goleniewski led to Heinz Felfe, a senior counterintelligence officer in the West German Federal Intelligence Service BND, being exposed as a Soviet spy.

This section further focuses on the mysterious history of a leading SS General named Heinrich Müller, whose fate fascinated not just Goleniewski but some top figures inside the CIA, especially James Angleton. I follow Müller's trail to Prague, Czechoslovakia,[9] before concluding my investigation.

In Part III, 'King of Queens'. I examine Goleniewski's break with the CIA and his links to well-established conservative, far-right and anti-communist networks in Washington that hoped to use him for their own political purposes. When Goleniewski next publicly declared that he was the rightful heir to the Romanov throne, a new cast of characters takes center stage starting with an obscure New York City publisher named Robert Speller and the former UK Liberal Party MP Richard Bessell. I conclude by looking at how these far-right networks combined to promote Goleniewski's shocking claim that Secretary of State Henry Kissinger was a Soviet agent code-named 'Bor.'

Finally, in Part IV of the study 'Knights of Malta', I depart from the roughly chronological depiction of Goleniewski's life. Our labyrinth goes further back in time before reconnecting this organizational and ideological history to the final decades of Goleniewski's life. It looks at a bizarre group called the Knights of Malta which claimed it was the direct successor of the legendary knightly order founded during the Crusades. I first examine the complicated role various White Russian exiles played in working with such figures as Henry Ford to lay the basis for a new radical right underground dedicated to promoting the *Protocols of the Elders of Zion*. This same network in both the USA and Europe closely cooperated with the early Nazi Party thanks to an obscure organization named Aufbau. The results of this collaboration helped spawn a new radical right network in the USA centered on the sinister figure of Boris Brasol, and an utterly strange White Russian political operative named General Arthur Count Cherep-Spiridovich, who, in turn, would be found dead, under mysterious circumstances, in a vast mansion in Staten Island.

While these organizations largely operated *sub-rosa*, they maintained close ties with Grand Duke Kirill Vladimirovich, the most prominent claimant to the Romanov throne and his wife Grand Duchess Victoria, Queen Victoria's granddaughter. Kirill and Victoria were early Hitler supporters while also enjoying access to New York's high society elite.

This constellation of far-right and antisemitic Russians and their American collaborators included 'Leslie Fry,' author of *Waters Flowing Eastward*, a defense of the *Protocols of the Elders of Zion* and her allies such as Henry Ford. This world laid the basis for a pro-Nazi and pro-White Russian organization named Blue Lamoo, out of which a far-right chivalric order the Shickshinny Knights would emerge in the mid-1950s. A few years later, Goleniewski would become involved with the Knights and this same group would become the most vocal advocates of Goleniewski's claim to the Romanov throne.

I conclude Part IV with a closer examination of the Shickshinny Knights and the group's somewhat astonishing links to sections of the American military as well as at least one former official of the CIA who became a Goleniewski enthusiast.

Finally, in my conclusion 'Imaginary Castle', I try to provide an overview of the ongoing questions surrounding Goleniewski's strange life and try to make sense of his incredible story. To ease the reader's path through the labyrinth of

Goleniewski's life and the related subjects I explore, there is a 'Cast of characters' and a 'Chronology' of his life in Poland at the end of the book

My hope then is that this study will finally shed some light on one of the most mysterious figures ever to emerge out of the shadows of the Cold War.

Notes

1 On Kuklinski, see Weiser (2019).
2 So Goleniewski describes himself in his 1984 publication *White Book*. The old-fashioned spelling of his name, with the use of 'Romanoff' instead of 'Romanov,' was his choice. As for Goleniewski, the name is pronounced 'Gole-nyef-ski.'
3 For this study, I have either translated directly or summarized Polish language texts. I have employed multiple on-line translators and dictionaries as well as a print Polish dictionary. I have further included the original Polish text in footnotes for critical passages.
4 In two relatively recent well researched biographies of the controversial former CIA official James Angleton, for example, Goleniewski's name does not appear in the index. See the Angleton biographies by Holzman (2008) and Morley (2017).
5 Tennent Bagley Archives, Box 11.
6 Bagley (2007), 49.
7 Villemarest (1984), 185.
8 Villemarest (2002), 111–12 (translated by author).
9 I refer to Czechoslovakia deliberately as these events preceded the separation of the Czech Republic and Slovakia.

ABBREVIATIONS, ACRONYMS AND AGENCY NAMES

ACI	Anti-Communist International. (Small US-based far-right group)
Aufbau	'Reconstruction'. (Far-right grouping of anti-Bolshevik White Russians and German Nazis)
AW	Foreign Intelligence Agency (Poland 2002–present)
BBC	British Broadcasting Corporation
BfV	Federal Office for the Protection of the Constitution. Domestic security agency (Germany)
BND	Federal Intelligence Service (Germany)
CHEKA	Secret Police (Bolshevik Russia 1917–1922)
CE	Counter Espionage
CIA	Central Intelligence Agency (USA 1947–present)
CIC	Counter Intelligence Corps
CP	Communist Party
CPCS	Communist Party of Czechoslovakia
CPSU	Communist Party of the Soviet Union
DAC	Defenders of the American Constitution (Postwar far-right group based in USA)
DDR	German Democratic Republic aka East Germany
FBI	Federal Bureau of Investigation (USA)
FRG	Federal Republic of Germany aka West Germany
GEE	The Government Employees' Exchange (Fringe anti-communist leak sheet, USA)
Gestapo	Secret State Police (Nazi Germany 1933–1945)
GRU	Military Intelligence Service (Soviet Union 1942–1991)
GZI	Main Directorate of Information (of the Polish Army)
HUAC	House Un-American Activities Committee (USA)
IS	Intelligence Service

JBS	John Birch Society. Anti-communist organization (USA 1958–present)
JTA	Jewish Telegraphic Agency
Kds. BP	Committee for Public Security (Poland)
KGB	Secret Service (Soviet Union 1954–1991)
KPP	Communist Party (Poland)
LWP	Polish People's Army, the Communist controlled army in World War II
MBP	Ministry of Public Security (Poland)
MGB	Ministry of State Security (Soviet Union)
MI5	Security Service (UK)
MI6	Secret Intelligence Service (UK)
MON	Ministry of National Defense (Poland)
MSW	Ministry of the Interior (Poland)
MUBP	City (Municipal) Office of Public Security (Poland)
NKVD	Secret Service (Soviet Union 1934–1943)
NSC	National Security Council (USA 1952–present)
NSDAP	National Socialist German Workers' Party (Nazi Germany 1920–1945)
NYJA	New York Journal-American
NYT	New York Times
OCB	Operations Coordinating Board (Executive to coordinate covert action, USA 1953–1961)
OGPU	Secret Service (Soviet Union 1922–1934)
OKHRANA	Secret Police (Tsarist Russia 1881–1917)
OSS	Office of Strategic Studies (WW2 intelligence agency and forerunner to CIA, USA 1942–1945)
OUN	Organization of Ukrainian Nationalists
PRC	People's Republic of China
PRL	Polish People's Republic
PUBP	District Office of Public Security (Poland)
PZPR	Polish United Workers Party (name of the Polish Communist Party after 1948)
ROCOR	The Russian Orthodox Church Outside Russia
RSHA	'Reich Main Security Office' (Secret Police/Intelligence Agency, Nazi Germany 1939–45)
SIG-I	Senior Interagency Group-Intelligence (CIA)
SIS	Secret Intelligence Service aka MI6 (UK)
SMERSH	Military Counterintelligence (Soviet Union 1942–1946)
SOSJ	Sovereign Order of Saint John of Jerusalem (a fringe US chivalric order)
SD	Intelligence agency (Nazi Germany 1931–1945)
SS	Paramilitary organization (Nazi Germany 1925–1945)
SSD	State Security Service aka 'Stasi' (East Germany 1950–1990)
StB	State Security (Czechoslovakia)

TN	Tennessee
Trust	Name for operation by Bolshevik secret service to create a fake Monarchist organization
UB	Security Service (Poland)
UBP	(Regional) Office of Public Security for the MBP (Poland)
USIA	United States Information Agency
VFC	Volunteer Freedom Corps (American-backed anti-communist émigrés)
WiN	Freedom and Independence (Polish anti-Communist resistance organization)
WOP	Border Protection Army/Border Guards (Poland)
WOW	Court of the Warsaw Military District (Poland)
WSW	Polish Military Internal Service
WUBP	Provincial Office of Public Security (Poland)

Author Photograph

INTRODUCTION

Labyrinth

On 1 April 1958, April Fool's Day, the United States Embassy in Bern, Switzerland, received a mysterious envelope addressed to Ambassador Henry J. Taylor. Enclosed in a second envelope was a single-spaced typewritten letter in German addressed to FBI Director J. Edgar Hoover. The letter's author offered to provide Hoover information on Soviet and East Bloc espionage operations under the strict understanding that the relationship between the source and the FBI would exclude the CIA. The note was cryptically signed 'Heckenschütze' ('Sniper'). Following protocol, Taylor promptly turned the mysterious missive over to the CIA.[1]

'Sniper' proved the cover name for a Polish Lieutenant Colonel named Michal Goleniewski.[2] Symbolic of Goleniewski's future troubled relations with the CIA, an even earlier overture of his to the United States was botched because the CIA couldn't understand what he was talking about. In 2005, a retired CIA agent named Ted Shackley wrote a memoir entitled *Spymaster: My Life in the CIA*. Shackley, who served in the CIA's Berlin station in the late 1950s, recalled the station receiving an odd communique from a 'mail intercept program' and signed by a name he recalled as 'Heckenschuss.'[3] As the text was filled with 'an impenetrable form of double talk,' it was simply filed away.

Berlin station was later contacted by a high-ranking CIA official named Howard Roman. A gifted linguist and close friend of CIA director Allen Dulles, Roman had formerly headed the CIA's Polish desk. He now inquired whether Berlin had received a cryptic message recently and was overjoyed when he learned about the peculiar dispatch.[4] Thus began one of the strangest stories of Cold War espionage.

In the early evening of 4 January 1960, the CIA finally met the man they knew only as Sniper when Goleniewski and his mistress Irmgard Kampf walked into the American Consulate in West Berlin. After an initial debrief in Frankfurt, Goleniewski was flown by military aircraft on 12 January 1961 to America. He now

DOI: 10.4324/9781003051114-1

underwent an extensive interrogation by the CIA, first at a Maryland safe house and later in Virginia.

On 16 September 1961 the Agency and Goleniewski signed a contract that provided financial support, protection, and medical help for him for one year. On 5 March 1962, the CIA relocated Goleniewski and his now wife Irmgard to New York City. The CIA then renewed Goleniewski's contract for another year on 16 June 1962.

In 1963, however, Goleniewski began writing letters to President Kennedy and other government officials complaining about his treatment by the Agency. On 17 October 1963, the CIA and Goleniewski agreed on yet another written agreement. CIA debriefings with the former spy continued until 14 December 1963 when Goleniewski declared he was finished and broke contact with the Agency. The CIA then cancelled his newly negotiated contract on 14 January 1964.

During his tumultuous time in Virginia, Goleniewski met CIA Director Allan Dulles in a short formal meeting in Dulles's office. Goleniewski's stormy relationship to the Agency continued under Dulles's successor, John McCone. The CIA's historian David Robarge writes of this time:

> Goleniewski had psychological problems, however, that emerged fully after he defected – notably his fanciful claim to be the last Russian tsarevich and heir to the Romanov name and fortune. Seized by this delusion and resentful at the treatment CIA officers had given him, Goleniewski stopped cooperating with debriefers in 1963, holed up in his New York apartment, refused to return a handgun the Agency had given him, and began writing long rambling letters to US government officials – among them the chairman of the House Immigration Subcommittee, the president, the attorney general, the FBI director, and the DCI. CIA renegotiated Goleniewski's contract in his favor in October 1963, and, when that incentive failed, took the opposite tack and suspended it in early 1964.[5]

As we will see, Goleniewski's post-CIA life was spent in the company of a range of figures on the far right of American politics. Not untypically for the far-right fringe, it was also filled with feuds, sectarianism and paranoia, as former friends became foes and often the targets of vitriolic screeds, rants and invective. He also willingly embraced and then published the most outlandish conspiracy theories and flights of fancy. Yet despite the increasingly unhinged nature of his public statements, Goleniewski was also capable of occasional moments of lucidity and rationality, particularly when discussing espionage and intelligence. In exploring his life, the contradictions and tensions between these two extremes are a constant feature.

Until his death on 2 July 1993 in Manhattan's Lenox Hill hospital, Goleniewski, his wife Irmgard, and their daughter Tatiana ('Tati') lived in a CIA-provided high-rise apartment building at 125–10 Queens Boulevard and 82nd Road, in Kew Gardens, just across from the Queens County Criminal Court. It remains a placid middle-class neighborhood with a Long Island Rail Road (LIRR) connection just a few blocks away.

From his apartment sanctuary, the 'King of Queens' in 1975 began issuing a truly bizarre monthly newsletter entitled *Double Eagle*.[6] Shoddily produced, often type-written with cross outs and corrections written in by hand, and at times even hard to read, it remains utterly obscure, so obscure that WorldCat lists exactly three libraries in the world that even retain copies of *Double Eagle*.[7]

Double Eagle's obscurity is understandable since in its pages Goleniewski enumerated some truly bizarre claims. One of the most notorious concerned Guy Richards, a former *New York Journal-American* (NYJA) reporter. In March 1964, Richards penned a series of front-page articles about Goleniewski. After interviewing Goleniewski, in 1966 Richards published a sympathetic book on him entitled *Imperial Agent: The Goleniewski–Romanov Case*. By the time the book came out, Goleniewski had had a bitter falling out with Richards.

Goleniewski's most incredible attack on Richards appeared in the August 1976 issue of *Double Eagle* under the title *'Double Eagle* versus SS Order under Death's Head.' Here Goleniewski *proves* via 'photographic evidence' that Guy Richards was Reinhard Heydrich, the Nazi leader assassinated in Prague in June 1942. Goleniewski claimed the assassination was faked and that Heydrich had secretly been brought to the United States. Heydrich was now living as 'Guy Richards.' Goleniewski later explained:

> In result of my first few contacts with Guy Richards in 1964, I had been warned by some knowledgeable individuals in the United States to be vigilant in cooperation with Richards because in reality he was the defector from Hitler's SS, Chief of Staff of the Security Main Office of the Third Reich (RSHA), the SS General Reinhard Heydrich. ... Since 1975, I published in my Bulletin *Double Eagle* a series of reports concerning SS General Heydrich and other Nazi criminals hiding in the United States by Soviet-British arrangement and protection. In result of my justified attacks against 'Richards,' he undertook steps which had been planned to coax me into silence forever ... on May 10, 1976 (i.e., 3 years before he died), Guy Richards filed with the Criminal Court of the City of New York a Complaint against me, as Editor and Publisher of the Bulletin *Double Eagle*.[8]

In another issue of the *Double Eagle*, Goleniewski devotes most of the text to a glowing review of an obscure 1980 book entitled *The New Dark Ages Conspiracy* published by the Lyndon LaRouche cult.[9] Fulsomely praising the book's expose of a vast British conspiracy to destroy world civilization, Goleniewski's review was entitled 'Britain's Plot to Destroy Civilization.' Goleniewski also used yet more 'photographic evidence' to demonstrate that 'Jack the Ripper' was really the Duke of Clarence. Instead of dying in 1892, the Duke was secretly taken to Germany where he now became the person we know as Adolf Hitler. Jack/Adolf safely returned to England in 1945; in 1980 he was still alive at the ripe old age of 126!

Goleniewski had been on the Ripper's case at least since 1977 when his writings proved too much for a far-right pundit named Revilo P. Oliver who now mocked him (anonymously) in the April 1977 issue of the racist journal *Instauration*.[10] A classics professor who taught Indo-European languages, Oliver was a hard-core antisemite. A founding member of the anti-communist John Birch Society (JBS), Oliver was expelled from the organization in the mid-1960s for his extremist views.[11] Because the Birchers embraced Goleniewski's claim that Henry Kissinger was employed by the KGB, Oliver used Goleniewski's ramblings to expose JBS leader Robert Welch as a buffoon. Oliver returned to Goleniewski in the January 1991 issue of the far-right publication *Liberty Bell*. Here he recalled of *Double Eagle*: 'The periodical was chiefly noteworthy for the phenomenal credulity of its subscribers.' From Oliver's *Liberty Bell* examination of *Double Eagle*:

> That wicked man, Adolf Hitler, weren't no German or Austrian. As his handwriting shows, he was an Englishman, none other than the man who was famous in 1888 as Jack the Ripper, and, what is more, he was probably the Duke of Clarence, eldest son of King Edward VII. This is proved by a photograph of Queen Elizabeth II, whose features show shock and horror, according to His Imperial Highness, at the mere mention of the dastardly Duke of Clarence. Now if this identification is correct, Hitler was eighty-one at the time of his (faked?) death in Berlin, but, as his Imperial Highness explains, his wickedness enabled him to retain his vim and vigor to an advanced age, so that he could advance Sir Francis Bacon's scheme for a 'Pagan British Empire.'

Nor was the outlaw Jesse James safe from Goleniewski:

> If you think that Jesse James was just an American bandit, that shows how ignorant you are. He was a high officer of 'the Rosicrucians' Order under the Death's Head,' an early version of the German S.S. Having been taught 'second sight' and how to 'go out of Body' separating his astral body from his physical body by a 'gifted' Negress owned by his parents, he joined the 'British Secret Intelligence Service' and advanced Francis Bacon's 'Divine Plan for a Pagan British Empire' by becoming one of the richest men in the world, and living 'seventy-three incredible lives' under as many different names, for which lack of space forces me to refer you to His Imperial Highness. I need not add that the assassination of Jesse James in 1882 was just another hoax staged by the International Bankers. Whether Jesse is still flourishing, the Czar coyly sayeth not. Come to think of it, he may be Nelson Rockefeller.[12]

Goleniewski believed Queen Elizabeth and Lord Mountbatten sabotaged his claim to the Russian throne. In the November 1980 issue of *Double Eagle*, he quotes from an article he first published in February 1976. Entitled 'British Bandits, Thieves, and Prostitutes,' it contained 'a short report about the Task of Bankers' Magicians: To Make U.S. Disappear' that read:

there is a long way during this century in the task of the British oligarchy and of the Bankers' magicians to abolish the United States Constitution and to dissolve the Great Republic. It is a process during which for six decades humanity has been suffering the horrors of Marxian Communism, the dialectical anti-thesis of which, indeed, National Socialism was and is. This infamous system of repression as the Bankers' vehicle to conquer the World and to establish a global tyranny is without a doubt the most inimical and criminal system that man has known for thousands of years of dramatic history.

Yet Goleniewski remained capable of rational discourse when discussing the world of espionage. In September 1980, the same month Goleniewski propounded his unique brand of Ripperology alongside his encomium to the LaRouchies, the well-known journalist and espionage author Edward Jay Epstein introduced him to the readers of the *New York Times* magazine in a famous article entitled 'Spy Wars.'

In his 28 September 1980 story, Epstein framed Goleniewski's saga as part of a larger CIA debate over Soviet 'moles' and 'false defectors,' especially one Soviet defector named Yuri Nosenko. It was here that Epstein wrote: 'Goleniewski had been the most productive agent in the entire history of the CIA, revealing more than a dozen Soviet moles....'

The article proved a first draft for Epstein's 1989 book *Deception: The Invisible War between the KGB and CIA*. Epstein's 1978 book *Legend* explored Lee Harvey Oswald's possible ties to the KGB.[13] While researching *Legend*, Epstein met James Angleton, the CIA's former head of Counterintelligence who led Epstein even more deeply into the mirror world of spies and traitors.

With his advance for *Deception*, Epstein opened a research office at 217 Broadway not far from City Hall that he dubbed the Center for Research on International Deception. He now began interviewing former spies and defectors, including Goleniewski, whom he saw on a regular basis.[14] In May 1981, some seven months after 'Spy Wars,' Epstein published a long profile on Goleniewski syndicated through the Independent News Alliance. Epstein presented him in a sympathetic light even while acknowledging his claim to be the Czar.[15] Epstein's true interest, however, was in Goleniewski's spook world past.

Epstein's profile marked the last serious press coverage of Goleniewski, who again sank into near total obscurity. When 'Alexei' finally died in 1993, the only mention of his name in the *New York Times* was a small paid obituary notice, surely a curious end for someone who single-handedly destroyed Polish intelligence, exposed Soviet control over West Germany's spy service, and saved Britain's MI6 spy agency from certain catastrophe.

Notes

1 One CIA official who served as 'desk officer' in Washington for the Sniper letters was Richards Heuer, then a member of the CIA's Operations Directorate. See Heuer (1987), 389. Heuer recalls (413), 'I had been the Headquarters desk officer on the Goleniewski

case at the time we received both of his reports, the one on the penetration of CIA and the one that led to identification of Felfe as a KGB penetration of West German intelligence. I had also seen firsthand how much damage a well-placed penetration, such as Goleniewski, could do to an opposition service.'

2 Martin (1980), 95. Martin misdates the letter's composition to March 1959; the CIA's Tennent ('Pete') Bagley copies Martin when he writes in *Spy Wars* that Goleniewski's first letter arrived in 'April 1959.' Bagley (2007), 48. Bagley later corrected his error. See Bagley (2015), 21.

Other reports say the letter was postmarked in Zurich. See Massie (1996), 149; Bagley (2007), 48. William J. Gill claims that the first contact began 'early in 1958 when a packet of letters was tossed over the wall of the US embassy in Berne, Switzerland.' See Gill (1969), 211.

3 'Heckenschütze' literally means something like 'shooting behind a hedge/hedgerow,' with the notion of shooting from a concealed position.

4 Shackley (2005), 26. During his time in the Polish secret service, Goleniewski frequently visited Berlin. He tried to contact the US there. When that failed, he next reached out to Bern. Goleniewski's would-be biographer Guy Richards reports, as does no one else, that Goleniewski first sent a telegram to Taylor in Bern 'to be on the lookout' for an important 'Heckenschütze' communique. Next, 'the finished produce was then delivered to the US Consulate in West Berlin with the request that it be forwarded by diplomatic courier to Bern. An employee in the consulate gave assurances that it would be.' Was this a different version of the incident Shackley mentioned? Richards (1966), 134.

5 Robarge (2015), 320.

6 The first issue appeared in January 1975. See Confidential Intelligence Report of the *Herald of Freedom*, March 1975 p. 4 which was produced by Goleniewski supporter Frank Capell. *Double Eagle's* 'mission statement' in each issue was 'DOUBLE EAGLE IS A MONTHLY BULLETIN focusing on selected matters from the past and present. It is the only self-edited publication issued under the auspices of H.I.H., the Heir to All-Russian Imperial Throne, Tsarevich and Grand Duke Aleksei Nicholaevich Romanoff of Russia, the August Ataman and Head of the Russian Imperial House of Romanoff; also known under the cover-identity of Colonel 'Michael M. Goleniewski', renowned for his support of the national security of the United States and its Western allies.'

7 I managed to locate about ten issues myself.

8 Goleniewski, *White Book*, 82.

9 *Double Eagle*, September 1980, 6/9; White (1980). For more on LaRouche, see 'Hylozoic Hedgehog' and Sweet (2019).

10 Anonymous (1977). The article was later reproduced with Oliver named as the author in other extreme-right publications. See *National Vanguard*, 19 September 2015.

11 For a standard scholarly history of JBS, see Mulloy (2014). See also the valuable resources and analysis collected by independent researcher Ernie Lazar https://sites.google.com/site/ernie124102/home

12 Goleniewski drew on an obscure 1975 self-published book by Del Schrader entitled *Jessie James Was One of His Names: The Greatest Cover Up in History by the Famous Outlaw Who Lived 73 Incredible Lives.* Also see https://www.genealogy.com/forum/surnames/topics/james/36329/.

13 On *Legend*, also see Coogan (2015).

14 Goleniewski, however, is only mentioned in *Deception* in a brief research acknowledgment.

15 Epstein's article, for example, was picked up in 17 May 1981 issue of *The Washington Star* and the 29 May 1981 *Hartford Courant*.

PART I
Sniper

1

GRAVE SECRETS

Paper trail

Michal Goleniewski is universally portrayed as a Polish intelligence officer. But just how Polish was he? He was born on 16 August 1922 in Nieswiez, a city that was Polish only as a result of the 1919–1922 Polish–Soviet War. The family then migrated to Poland's Western border with Germany where he was raised. In 1995, British author William Clarke published *The Lost Fortune of the Tsars*. For background on Goleniewski, Clarke turned to Malgorzata Stapinska, a professor of English at Krakow's Jagellonian University. She confirmed Goleniewski's story that his father (also named Michal) was buried in a cemetery in the small town of Wolsztyn, near Poznan, the largest city in western Poland. His father and mother lived in the small village of Ciosaniec in the Lubusz Voivodeship (Province), some 14 miles from Wolsztyn. After his death, the body was brought to the cemetery in Wolsztyn. Stapinska also confirmed that Goleniewski's father died on 17 May 1952 at age 69.[1]

Using birth records and other documents, Stapinska learned that Michal, Sr., had been born in Russia on 29 September 1883. Parish records list his parents as Antoni and Marcela (née Buczynska or Bieczynska). Stapinska also found a discrepancy: his tombstone in the Wolsztyn cemetery lists his birth as 29 September 1893 (not 1883), which would have made him 59 at the time of his death.

From *Lost Fortune of the Tsars*:

> The grave was certainly there. It was found in the main aisle of the graveyard, to the left of the main entrance. Made of stone, with a headstone and a stone surround with soil filling in between, the grave had been covered by evergreen branches as though someone had recently been caring for it. Two glass jars stood beside each other, one empty, the other containing plastic flowers and some dead leaves. Behind one of the jars, the inscription on the marble

DOI: 10.4324/9781003051114-3

headstone read: s.p. Michal Goleniewski, ur. 29.9.1893 zm. 17.5.1952 that is 'The late Michal Goleniewski, Born September 29, 1893, Died May 17, 1952.' It looked as though someone had tried to scratch out the '52' with a sharp instrument, or at least to leave that impression.[2]

Stapinska, however, found Michal, Sr.'s, death certificate in the small town of Slawa, a village a few miles south of Ciosaniec. It confirmed that he was born on 29 September 1883.

As for Goleniewski's mother Janina, the Central Registry of Inhabitants listed her maiden name as Turynska.[3] She may have been born in Russia, but it is unclear from the records. Goleniewski claimed that after 'the Imperial family' fled Russia, they first traveled under the name 'Turynski' before changing it to 'Goleniewski.' After 'his mother's death' in 1924, the family relocated from Warsaw to a rural area outside of Poznan in the area of Wolsztyn.[4]

Located on the Warta River, until 1918 Poznan (then Posen) had been part of the German empire since the Second Partition of Poland in 1793. It passed into Polish hands following a 1918–1919 uprising against the Germans. The city was incorporated into what became the Polish Second Republic in the Treaty of Versailles. On 1 January 1920, the German town of Wollstein formally became Wolsztyn.[5]

The only glimpse of Goleniewski's father comes from *Lost Fortune*:

> One of the elderly people interviewed, who had a horse carriage, remembered going hunting with him for hares. 'He usually joked and argued over the hares and when my dog brought one back, Michal would try to convince me that he had shot it.' He was on extremely good terms with the local farmers and, it was said, they would visit him in his flat in the distillery to play cards. One of the couples interviewed recognized him from the picture shown to them from Guy Richards' book *The Hunt for the Czar*. They did not recognize the son (Colonel Goleniewski) and had not seen him in Ciosaniec, though the other couple remembered him attending the funeral.[6]

At the time of his death, Michal had been the manager of an alcohol distillery factory, and one older couple said they believed he died after falling down steps in the factory. His widow Janina was reportedly five or six years younger than her husband. In a report to Polish intelligence shortly before his defection, however, Goleniewski said his mother was 61 at the time of his father's death, which would make her born in 1891. Janina then would have been eight years younger than her husband who, as the records indicate, was most likely born in 1883.

As for Goleniewski, Stapinska uncovered his birth record which was given as 6 September 1922 in Poland's Central Register of Inhabitants. Goleniewski, however, stated he had been born on 16 August 1922 when he applied for US citizenship. His Polish intelligence files list his birthday as 16 August 1922 as well. Polish reports say he was born in the city of Nieswiez (in Poland), south of Minsk and today a city in Belarus known as Nesvizh. In World War I the city had been captured from Russia by the Germans, briefly incorporated into the Soviet Union, and then claimed by Poland from 1919 to 1939.[7]

Goleniewski later asserted that after being smuggled out of Russia and traveling through Turkey, Greece, and Austria, the Romanovs relocated to Poland because of the number of Russians living there. He claimed that when the family first arrived in Poland, Marshall Pilsudski assigned two Polish colonels named Alexander Prystow (Aleksander Prystor) and Waclaw Szalewicz to provide them with false papers as the Turynski family.[8] He said they lived in an apartment on Rynek Nowomiejski Street until 17 February 1924 when they relocated to Karpicko, also near Wolsztyn.[9] His father entered Poland as 'Raymond Turynski' and then changed the name first to 'Michal Goleniowski' and then Goleniewski.[10]

In a 17 August 1964 interview with Phillipa Schuyler for the *Manchester Union Leader* ('Russia's Czar Lives'), Goleniewski said that his father 'Czar Nicholas II' went with Polish and Russian troops fighting the Bolsheviks during the 1919–1921 Russo-Polish War, which at one point saw Polish forces occupy Kiev. Goleniewski's father also had links to 'a special advisory group that was close to General Weigand.' General Maxime Weygand was a member of the Second Interallied Mission to Poland during the 1920 war with the Soviet Union.

On 17 February 1924, the family moved to a village near Poznan (Poland's fourth largest city), and close to the German border. He claimed that England's de jure recognition of the Soviet Union in February 1924 – and the planned arrival of the new Soviet Ambassador 'Piotr Voikov' (Pyotr Voykov) that same year – made the family decide to abandon Warsaw. Goleniewski stated that his mother, 'the Empress Aleksandra Feodorovna' died in Warsaw in the autumn of 1924. He adds that her 'cover name' was 'Marie A. Kaminski.'[11]

About the new Soviet Ambassador, Goleniewski writes that he had been 'also involved in RUSSIAN IMP. FAMILY's imprisonment in EKATERINBURG, PIOTR VOIKOV (who was executed by RUSSIAN IMP. UNDERGROUND in POLAND on JUNE 7, 1927 publicly with regard to his attempts to investigate the fate of RUSSIAN IMP. FAMILY).'[12] Voykov, who became the Soviet Ambassador to Poland on 8 November 1924, was shot to death in the Warsaw Central Train Station three years later by Boris Kowerda, a teenage White Russian living in stateless exile in Poland. A monarchist, he was given the gun used to kill Voykov from another White Russian exile. In retaliation, the Soviets arrested hundreds of monarchists and carried out summary executions of some of them while claiming the murder of Voykov was a British conspiracy.

Pierre de Villemarest writes that the family lived first in a modest home in Wolsztyn. They next relocated to the small town of Karpicko, near Wolsztyn until they decided to move even closer to Poznan.[13] Whatever the exact sequence, it seems clear they lived in the Wolsztyn area. Polish intelligence files also state that Goleniewski was enrolled in a gymnasium in Wolsztyn in 1939 when World War II began. Polish records also report that the family lived in Ciosaniec, and Goleniewski's parents did live there after the war.

Finding out anything about the family was not easy. Stapinska examined the records of the Central Register of Inhabitants, the key archive for genealogical research and the source for Goleniewski's birthday as well as the name of his parents. The Central Register, however, only listed him from 1953 on when he was living in Gdansk. It also gave his local address. Yet when Stapinska checked the Register of Inhabitants of Gdansk and its surrounding regions, there was no mention of his name, although from other records we know he did live in Gdansk at this time.

Goleniewski's absence from the Central Registry records raises the possibility that the family was registered, but that they either employed a variant spelling of their name or used a different name when first registering. Given that the family employed the names 'Turynski' and 'Goleniowski,' her failure may be less surprising.

As for Ciosaniec, it had been the German village of Schussenze; after 1937 it was renamed Ostlinde.[14] After the German defeat (and finalized in the Potsdam Agreement), the town became Ciosaniec. The few elderly Polish residents in Ciosaniec who spoke to Stapinska said they did not remember the family before the late 1940s. From *Lost Fortune of the Tsars*:

> The locals were quite sure that the Goleniewskis were not in the area before the war. One of them who arrived in 1948 was certain that the Goleniewskis must have arrived 'before, in or just after 1950.' They assumed that they had come from further east, perhaps from Lvov, but were not certain. 'He liked singing songs about Lvov,' they recalled. Certainly Michal Goleniewski [Sr.] seemed to them to have a strong 'eastern' accent, indicating someone from around Lvov. But my researcher [Stapinska] thinks that this could easily have been confused with a Russian accent by the locals. They are quite similar.[15]

Goleniewski's parents, then, most likely relocated to Ciosaniec after the war when his father became the head of the distillery. The available evidence suggests that starting sometime in the early 1920s they lived in the Karpicko–Wolsztyn–Ciosaniec area. For now, the best we can say is that Goleniewski's family seems to have been most likely ethnic Russians. During the turmoil of the Russian Civil War and the Polish–Soviet War, they fled to western Poland, literally to Poland's border with Germany. As a result, Goleniewski spoke both Russian and German flawlessly along with Polish.

Reichsland

Michal Goleniewski grew up a sickly child. He most likely had polio because later in life he walked with a slight limp that appeared to be the result of wearing braces as a child. More mysteriously, he claimed he was a hemophiliac. Lacking any independent scientific verification of his claim, it is impossible to know. In a July 1966 broadcast by the rightwing radio host Richard Cotten (and reprinted in transcript form for Cotten's *Conservative Viewpoints* journal on 16 July 1966), Goleniewski ('Mr. Romanoff') stated:

Now, the second problem regarding my hereditary blood disease – the expression 'Hemophilia' is not exactly the right expression because my hereditary blood disease is stranger, i.e. more rare than hemophilia. Now the development of the hematology knowledge from that time was going pretty quick – and even from the point of my blood disease and from some damages done by this blood disease – from this point there is no question that it is very definitely the right identification.[16]

Whatever health issues Goleniewski may have suffered from as a child remain as murky as the rest of his early life. Nor is there any discussion of his health in the WOW investigation.[17] Yet the WOW files on Goleniewski's early years are meager, so much so that Pawlikowicz cites Stapinska's research to fill in his childhood years.

In theory, Polish intelligence should have known a good deal about Goleniewski's past as it was standard practice to research family genealogy back three generations when contemplating the hiring of potential spies.[18] This policy, however, may only have been implemented when the security services became more established. In the immediate chaos following the end of World War II, this may have proven impossible. In any event, Pawlikowicz just cites a summary report that in one line describes the social origins of the family as '*intelligencja pracujaca*' (working intelligentsia).

Nor did the WOW investigation show any interest in how Goleniewski spent his youth from age 17 in 1939 to age 23 in 1945. All we learn is that in 1939 at the time of the invasion, he had been arrested by the German authorities, charged with membership in an unnamed illegal organization, and then released. Goleniewski was a 4th level student in a local gymnasium in Wolsztyn, but with the outbreak of war he apparently never graduated school, although some sources say he did get a diploma.

The files next report that Goleniewski became employed as an office worker ('*pracownik umyslowy*') for a German firm called Reichsland (the *Reichsgesellschaft für Landbewirtschaftung*) that is often described as a property estates management firm. Another Polish WOW report states that Goleniewski's father worked in 1939 as an accountant (*ksiegowy*) in Wolsztyn.[19] The journalist Piotr Gontarczyk describes his father's pre-war position as a revenue officer ('*urzednikiem skarbowym*'). It may be that the father worked for the government until the war and then obtained employment as an accountant. Goleniewski told Guy Richards that while his father was a bookkeeper for a merchant during the war, he 'worked as an administrative assistant on a large farm.' As for his arrest, Goleniewski reported that he had spent six months in jail due to an unspecified conflict with an 'overseer.'[20] Goleniewski spoke impeccable German and could converse in several German dialects.[21] His linguistic skills, most likely due to a childhood spent on the border, may have facilitated his position at Reichsland.

But what was Reichsland?

Bluntly put, the firm managed property forcibly taken from the Poles for the benefit of German colonists.[22] On 28 February 1940, the German Ministry of Agriculture established the *Ostdeutschen Landbewirtschaftungsgesellschaft mbH* (Ostland) also known as the *Reichsgesellschaft für Landbewirtschaftung in den eingegliederten Ost-gebieten mbH* ('Reichsland') or the Reich Association to Manage the Captured Polish Territories. The firm was run by a long-time Nazi named Waldemar Kraft, who later became a Cabinet Minister in the Adenauer government as well as a prominent leader of the All German Bloc of Expellees.

Reichsland was charged with, among other things, the '*Zwangsverwaltung*' (receivership/forced administration) of Polish property, the resettling of German colonists in Polish lands, food supply for the German military, and the employment of forced labor in the agricultural sector. Once France fell, the corporation dropped the word '*Ostland*' from its title. Headquartered in Berlin where it had two main offices, it managed some 82 branches throughout occupied Europe.

Reichsland's local operations would have taken place in two new Western administrative 'Gaus' (districts) in territories now annexed to Germany. The first, Reichegau Danzig-Westpreussen, was run by Albert Foerster (Förster), the long-time Nazi Gauleiter of the Free City of Danzig. The second Gau was initially called Reichsgau Posen; it was later renamed Reichsgau Wartheland or Warthegau for short. Named after the river Warthe, Warthegau was administered by Arthur Greiser. Some 44,000 square kilometers in size, Warthegau had a population of around 4.5 million people, almost all of them Poles and Roman Catholics. The area, however, did include the Lodz ghetto – the second largest in occupied Poland. Greiser helped organize an early extermination camp at Chelmno where Jews were systematically murdered.

During the 1930s, Greiser had been the head of the Senate of the Free City of Danzig when Foerster was Gauleiter. Foerster and Greiser were bitter political enemies and their rivalry never went away. Greiser's major sponsor was Himmler while Foerster enjoyed the support of Rudolf Hess and later Martin Bormann. Once the war began, Himmler appointed Greiser to run the area south of Poznan in the newly created Warthegau.

Although Foerster had no hesitation when it came to killing Jews, he made it relatively easy for Polish citizens to claim Germanic background and not be stripped of their property. The only real requirement for Poles to become 'German' was a reasonable proficiency in speaking the language. Greiser, however, insisted that any Pole claiming a German identity first had to submit elaborate genealogical proofs. As Gauleiter of Warthegau, Greiser was extremely brutal when it came to Poles as well as Jews. He spearheaded a policy of 'Germanization' by new settlers from the Reich as well as ethnic Germans from the East (now under Soviet control following the division of Poland by the two powers in 1939). These newcomers could now take over Polish farms 'ethnically cleansed' by Greiser.[23]

Goleniewski's proficiency in German may have saved him. As an employee of Reichsland, he must have witnessed its role in 'purifying' Warthegau. The WOW proceedings, however, show no interest in this period of his life. Had he been a victim of German aggression? Or a witting collaborator? Did he fight in the underground against the occupation? The court records remain mute.

Goleniewski told Guy Richards and Pierre de Villemarest that 'after V-E day' the family planned to flee Poland for Portugal, but that because he suffered a case of 'protracted food poisoning' dating back to 1944, they failed to make good their escape.[24] He added that he belonged to a mysterious intelligence group dubbed 'the Secret Circle' during the war. Following the war's conclusion, he decided to enter Poland's security service on behalf of the Secret Circle's resistance to Communist rule.

There is no mention that Goleniewski belonged to any pro or anti-Nazi group in the WOW proceedings. Nor would it seem to make much sense that as a resistance fighter, he and his family would plan to flee to the Salazar dictatorship in Portugal. If Goleniewski were an anti-communist Polish nationalist, he had many options to choose from, that included fighting in the Polish Home Army (the *Armia Krajowa*/AK). Enlisting in the Russian-run Polish security forces in August 1945 shortly after the fall of Berlin does not sound like something an anti-communist Polish resistance fighter would do.

The peasants interviewed by Malgorzata Stapinska recalled that at Michal's funeral in 1952 no priest was present, which led them to assume he must have been a member of the Communist Party. It is certainly possible he did join the Polish Communist Party after the war. It is also possible that there was no priest because the family was either Russian Orthodox or not religious. Or it may have been that a religious funeral would not reflect well on their son, who was then moving up the ranks of Polish intelligence.

The Metelmann mystery

In 1990 a former German soldier who fought on the Eastern Front named Henry Metelmann published a memoir entitled *Through Hell for Hitler*. A convinced Nazi at age 18 when he joined the Wehrmacht, Metelmann came from a working-class background. When Metelmann was sent to the Eastern Front, he kept a detailed illegal diary (illegal because it could fall into Russian hands) and other notes that decades later helped him reconstruct his story. His book is also filled with personal photos of his time in Russia.

Wounded multiple times, Metelmann ended the war as a POW in the hands of the Americans: he even spent time in an American camp in Arizona. He later worked as a POW on an English farm and stayed in England where he married and raised a family. Disgusted by his experience on the Russian front, Metelmann became a supporter of the British Communist Party who worked for the Campaign for Nuclear Disarmament (CND) and similar groups while holding a job as a railroad signalman. His war memoir became a minor classic; in 2003 the BBC devoted a documentary to his story.[25]

Metelmann's background is important because of one astonishing paragraph from his war memoir. He reports that when his unit first headed to the Russian front, they stopped in Lemberg/Lwow/Lviv; the different spellings reflect its stormy geopolitical history. He and his friends visited a *Soldatenheim* (soldier's hostel and restaurant) across the road from the train station. While they were eating:

A couple of elderly transport soldiers joined us at our table, and we got into conversation. They told us that to the northwest of Lemberg, somewhere near the town of Radom [about 210 miles from Lviv], lived an old Polish land-owner on a large estate, guarded by the SS. His name was Goleniewski and he was no other, they claimed, than the Russian Tsar Nicholas II himself, who with his family was supposed to have been murdered by the Bolsheviks in the Siberian town of Ekaterinburg shortly after the Revolution. Though it was true that no physical evidence had ever been produced to establish the Tsar's death, we did not believe any of the soldiers' story and laughed, thinking they were having us on. But then some others joined us and said that it was true. One claimed that without eliminating the Tsar from the minds of the largely illiterate Russian peasants of the time, the Russian Revolution would have fallen to pieces. Of course, we knew that ex-Kaiser Wilhelm II had been quarantined on his estate across the Dutch border near the town of Doorn, and had also, until his death the previous summer, been closely guarded by the SS. The strange thing about this was when about three years later, being driven out of Russia through the Lemberg region, we heard the same story about Panje Goleniewski again.[26]

Metelmann's book appeared in 1990. If his comments had been inserted on behalf of Soviet intelligence for some reason – a distinct possibility given Metelmann's Communist affiliations – it is hard to imagine why. Goleniewski was an old man who would die just three years later.

But what if Metelmann accurately reported what he had heard at that restaurant? Was there a 'Panje Goleniewski' who enjoyed the protection of the SS? In the 1920s, there also were strange rumors that another one of the supposed Romanov survivors lived in the remote east of Poland near the Russian border.[27]

For his part, Goleniewski claimed that 'German intelligence' knew about his family. From *Imperial Agent*:

If the Romanovs lived so long in Poland, doesn't it seem likely that some of their Polish neighbors would have got wind of their real identities, even though they lived under assumed names?

ANSWER: Yes, some Poles did know, according to Goleniewski. He believes that German intelligence was aware also, for certain things took place during the German occupation of Poland which hinted along these lines. Remember, he hasn't told everything he knows.[28]

Goleniewski's family lived close to the German border and nowhere near Radom in the East where Metelmann places the compound. Some of the peasants inter-viewed by Stapinska, however, said that his father spoke with a strong 'eastern' or even Russian accent. Goleniewski also once claimed that during World War II, he worked for a Polish resistance group that had its network in ByeloRussia as well as in the western half of Ukraine.[29]

If Metelmann's recollection has even a glimmer of truth, it raises the rather remarkable possibility that there was someone called Goleniewski who may have had some odd Imperial connection. Without further information, it's impossible to say much more.

'Mela' and the Duchess

Goleniewski's father Michal was not Nicholas II, and his mother Janina was not Princess Alexandra. Janina's maiden name was 'Turynska.' On 11 November 1960, Polish Colonel Witold Sienkiewicz submitted a report that included a statement from Goleniewski about his mother. Goleniewski said that after his father's death in 1952, his 61-year-old mother Janina ('61 late matka Janina') for a time moved in with Goleniewski and his then wife and family. Because his wife suffered severe mental problems, she made it impossible for Janina to live with them, so his mother relocated to Warsaw.[30]

Goleniewski claimed that while his mother the Empress died in 1924, he did have an older sister, the 'Grand Duchess Maria Nicolaevna.' Born in Russia in 1899, she was now living in Warsaw. In the early 1970s a woman claiming to be the Grand Duchess – as well as Goleniewski's sister – was interviewed in Warsaw by at least two people. Stapinska, however, searched in vain local records for a sister of Goleniewski. She also checked national records and again found nothing.

How then to explain the mysterious woman in Warsaw?

In their 1976 book *The File on the Tsar*, Tony Summers and Tom Mangold relate a strange encounter one of their researchers had with this woman. The mystery began in 1972 when the authors, both *Times of London* reporters, met Robert Speller, Sr., the head of a New York-based small publishing firm and a long-time supporter of Goleniewski who we will feature more prominently later in this book. Although Summers and Mangold had spoken with Goleniewski on the phone and met him briefly, it was Speller who assured them that the 'Grand Duchess Maria' was living in Poland; he even provided them with her Warsaw address. In his 1984 Goleniewski biography *Le Mystérieux Survivant d'Octobre*, Pierre de Villemarest reprints a photograph of the woman. He indicated that the picture was taken in 1968 in Warsaw by an 'enquêteur américain,' working on behalf of Guy Richards.

A researcher for Summers and Mangold now contacted the woman at the address given by Speller. She did indeed claim to be Goleniewski's sister, the Grand Duchess Maria. Next, she:

> produced a photograph of her father – 'Nicholas II' – which she said had been cut from his passport after his death in 1952. The picture showed an old man with a beard in working clothes and had allegedly been taken while the ex-czar was working as a tram-driver in Poland. We showed it to Scotland Yard experts, who compared it with pictures of the real Nicholas. It came as no surprise that they said it could not be the tsar but could very well be a Polish tram-driver.[31]

When was the photo taken? We know that Goleniewski's father managed an alcohol distillery at the time of this death and was not a tram-driver. During the war he worked as an accountant; before that he was connected to the government's tax department. Was the man in Warsaw Janina's own elderly father Raymond Turynski? Recall that in late 1963 Goleniewski claimed that the 'Imperial family' first entered Poland under the Turynski name, and that Nicholas II traveled as 'Raymond Turynski.' Was the man in the Warsaw photo Goleniewski's maternal grandfather?

In *Mystérieux Survivant*, Villemarest reprints a photo given him by Goleniewski that purportedly shows Goleniewski, his father, and 'Grand Duchess Maria' taken in Poland in 1942. She is in the center of the photo with her arms around two men, one younger and one rather old, both of whom are dressed in suits, not tram worker garb.[32] In the *White Book*, Goleniewski says the photo was taken 'May 6/19 1942 in Poland (German Occup.)' and that the photographer was 'E. v. Veber.'[33] He claims the image is of the 'Grand Duchess Maria Nicholaevna,' with her arms around himself and Nicholas II. He adds in his caption:

> They lived during World War II under the cover of Polish Nationality and remained Slavs under the German occupation. For reasons of cover, the Imperator was obliged at 74 years of age to do the hard work of a simple wood-cutter. The Imperator and the Tsarevich in exile and underground in Poland and during the German occupation fought in the underground against Bolshevism: RED AND BROWN [Communism & Fascism][34]

In my view, the picture most likely shows Goleniewski's mother Janina with her arms around her husband and her father.[35]

Villemarest states that Maria was first contacted through Guy Richards, who sent an envoy to Poland to meet her. In his 1970 book *The Hunt for the Czar*, Richards said that, in the wake of *Imperial Agent*, a group calling itself the 'Three G's' (or 'Goleniewski Go-Gos') formed to investigate the spy's claims. An unnamed envoy from the 'Three G's' visited Warsaw to speak with 'Maria.'

In his August 1976 *Double Eagle* article attacking Guy Richards, Goleniewski claimed that his mother was never interviewed. Yet it seems highly likely she was because she was interviewed again a few years later. Tellingly, Goleniewski reports that Richards said 'Maria' told friends that she was Goleniewski's mother, not his sister. To cover himself, Goleniewski now said that his 'sister' (the 'Grand Duchess Maria Nikolaevna Romanoff') lived in Poland under the names 'Janina Turynski' and 'Janina Goleniewski.' When 'Maria' was interviewed again by a researcher for *The File on the Tsar*, she claimed that her father was buried in Warsaw and not Wolsztyn, a claim in line with her assertion that 'Nicholas II' worked on a Warsaw tram and the fact that her husband was buried in Wolsztyn.

For his part, Villemarest (who never met her) states that Maria, '*une femme de bientôt 70 ans*,' and weary despite her dynamism ('*lassée malgré son dynamisme*') died not long after this second interview; she would have been around 80 in 1971. He said that Goleniewski was convinced she had been killed by the Polish authorities and that for many years she had been denied a temporary visa to visit him. Villemarest added that 'Maria' had been arrested, interrogated at length, and jailed in the wake of Goleniewski's defection. Goleniewski, however, said he doubted she had been arrested or that anything else had happened to her beyond routine questioning. When Villemarest pressed him on this point, as on many others, he refused to answer and said he was reserving the right to tell all in his planned memoir.[36]

It seems obvious that 'Grand Duchess Maria' was Janina Goleniewska (neé Turynska), and that Goleniewski's mother posed as his sister to help her son. A further clue comes from an obscure book entitled *The Conspirator who Saved the Romanovs*, written in 1973 by Gary Null.[37] Goleniewski told Null that after the Tsarina Alexandra died in 1924, his 'sister' Maria pretended to be his mother, a deception made possible by his then-small stature and boyish appearance due to a medical condition related to his blood disease.

In the spring of 2015, Pawel Zietara published a scholarly article in *Polish American Studies* entitled 'Troubles with 'Mela.'' 'Mela' was the Polish secret service code-name for a Polish American journalist named Leopold Dende, who worked off and on for Polish intelligence for decades. Dende ran various businesses in the United States, including newspapers and a travel agency for American visitors to Poland.

In the early 1960s, Major Jan Slowikowski, Deputy Chief of the Operations Division for the USA and Canada in Polish intelligence, served as Dende's handler. In 1962 Slowikowski gave Dende a picture of Goleniewski – dubbed 'Technik' (Technician) by the Poles – and asked him to find out where he lived. As Zietara put it, 'The idea was to give 'Technik' a clear signal that his former colleagues in the Department were still interested in him.' As Piotr Gontarczyk explains:

> After Goleniewski's escape, the First Department of the Ministry of the Interior established the operational issue of 'Teletechnik.' It involved surveillance of the deserter's closest family, especially his mother, in the hope that her son would like to contact her. His son Jerzy, guitarist of the band Breakout, had his passport troubles. The security service also selected and trained agents who could make contact with the fugitive in the USA. Rumors and slanders were rumored about him (including the fact that he was a Nazi agent), hoping that he would reveal himself and respond to the charges.[38] This was to give the PRL intelligence 'new operational possibilities.' In the departmental slang, it could mean an attempt to physically liquidate the fugitive, only that he could not be 'tracked.'[39]

Dende again got tangled up in Goleniewski matters when in the summer of 1967 he met eight times with members of Polish intelligence to discuss 'Teletechnik.' Once more, they wanted him to contact Goleniewski. Things took an even stranger turn in 1969. Dende's former travel business partner Jan Pargiello recalled that in 1969 Dende 'was involved in bringing Goleniewski's mother, then living in Poland, to the US.'[40] From 'Troubles with 'Mela'':

In a conversation with an officer of the Polish communist secret service held in Warsaw, Pargiello revealed that, in connection with his visit to the country, Dende had asked him to arrange Janina Goleniewska's trip to the United States. He provided him with the relevant invitation and a check to cover the cost of travel. He also asked him to visit Goleniewska in order to clear up the matter of her passport. A visa for her to visit the United States was supposed to have been issued already. As Dende observed, this could have been an event even 'more notable than the defection of Stalin's daughter.' Pargiello, having considered this 'a dirty business,' limited his activity to arranging the plane ticket for Goleniewska on KLM.[41]

Zietara comments: 'I have not yet found any evidence concerning her departure.' She never left. Polish intelligence, it seems clear, was playing psychological manipulation games with Goleniewski by dangling the possibility of a family reunion. The report also bolsters Goleniewski's statement, as reported by Villemarest, that 'Maria' had been trying to get a visa to leave Poland to visit him for years but that she had ultimately been denied it.

Further confirmation that something curious was going on between Polish intelligence and Goleniewski can be found in the memoir of one of the highest officials in postwar Polish intelligence named Franciszek Szlachcic. A top Communist official and Brigadier General of the Civic Militia, Szlachcic served as Minister of Internal Affairs in 1971. Inside the security apparatus, Szlachcic ran a group dubbed 'the Franciscans' committed to ridding the service of Jewish officers. He backed Gomulka's successor Edward Gierek, but he fell from power in 1973 after he was accused of creating a ring to spy on Gierek.

Szlachcic's memoir *Gorzki smak wladzy* (*The Bitter Taste of Power*) appeared in 1990, the year he died. Szlachcic briefly discusses Goleniewski in a very curious way. He mistakenly claims that Goleniewski defected on a routine business trip to West Germany in 1955, and that 'after a few months he revealed himself as a military officer of the US intelligence service.'[42] Szlachcic presents Goleniewski less as a defector and more as a foreign-trained intelligence operative. Goleniewski's personal files, however, showed that he was born and raised in Poland.[43] Szlachcic then adds: 'Through studies have, however, undermined this data.[44] Actually, it was not known who he really was. Beyond any doubt, he was a US intelligence agent.'[45]

How could Polish intelligence not know who Goleniewski really was?

Later, Szlachcic writes, 'After considering the matter, I was tempted to believe that Goleniewski was first sent to the USSR, and later to Poland, as a US intelligence agent.'[46] Does Szlachcic wish to imply that Goleniewski was first 'planted' on the Soviets, and then sent to Poland, all the time while working as an agent of American intelligence? Or was he really saying, perhaps in an Aesopian way, that Goleniewski's family was Russian?

Following his defection, Polish intelligence may have planned to kill Goleniewski if they could find him. On 27 October 1960, the body of Wladyslaw Mroz, a Polish intelligence officer living as an illegal in France, was discovered in a forest area outside Paris. Mroz had been murdered by Warsaw after it was discovered that he was cooperating with French intelligence.[47] Szlachcic also states that in 1969 'one of our intelligence officers' was sent to America and Brazil to cross paths with Goleniewski but that he failed in his mission.[48] Leszek Pawlikowicz suggests Szlachcic was implying that the Poles were still hoping to assassinate him even then.[49]

Goleniewski was so worried about retribution that in 1963 he convinced the CIA to supply him with a legal handgun. After Goleniewski went public with his Russian throne claim, the journalist Piotr Gontarczyk believes Warsaw adopted a different approach to make the CIA look ridiculous for relying on information from a madman. Yet both approaches are not mutually exclusive.

Following Goleniewski's 1964 Romanov proclamation, Polish intelligence arranged for the distribution of information about his family still living in Poland. Piotr Gontarczyk reports that in 1965

> Through a paid Austrian journalist, a richly documented series of articles about Goleniewski was prepared with information about his wife and children in Poland. The hero – as a cheat and bigamist – was discredited inside Russian communities and disappeared from public life....[50]

The articles were almost certainly timed to coincide with Goleniewski's 2 February1965 public declaration to a Hamburg court adjudicating the Anna Anderson 'Anastasia' case in which he proclaimed himself Tsar.

A former Colonel in Polish intelligence named Henryk Wendrowski recalled:

> To neutralize the damage to the results of this defection, they [Polish intelligence] invented a lot of stories about him and 'sold' them to the West. Our information implied that the Americans had 'bought' disinformation. We were helped in this [when the] same fugitive started submitting a claim to the Russian throne. But even if you did not 'buy' it, there still was a lot of confusion in United States intelligence. By the end it was not sure what's really going on. Personally, I met many CIA employees who believed that in the case of Goleniewski [the CIA] may deal with the obvious misinformation of our secret services....[51]

Polish intelligence's ongoing interest in Goleniewski can be further seen in remarks by Marceli Wieczorek. A former Polish intelligence agent who enjoyed diplomatic cover, Wieczorek maintained an operational interest in Goleniewski. In 1967–68, Wieczorek was stationed in New York City before being reassigned to the Polish Consulate in Chicago. Wieczorek said Polish intelligence organized an elaborate surveillance operation on Goleniewski that involved 'technical' devices, presumably bugs, phone taps, and other listening equipment.[52]

Whatever was bubbling under the surface, when both 'the three G's' envoy and Summers and Mangold's researcher spoke with the mysterious 'Grand Duchess

Maria,' the meetings surely would have occurred under the watchful eyes of the Polish secret service. Yet Maria/Janina did speak to outside visitors. Was this because she was cooperating with the secret police in the false hope of finally obtaining a visa?

Notes

1 Clarke (1995), 139–40. Stapinksa's research can be found in Clarke (1995), 139–43.
2 Ibid., 139.
3 The 'a' at the end of Janina's last name indicates that she was female.
4 By 'his mother,' Goleniewski meant Empress Alexandra, Nicholas II's wife.
5 There was also a plebiscite in 1919. Although most of the region became Polish, districts with majority German inhabitants remained German.
6 Clarke (1995), 140.
7 The Soviet Union briefly reoccupied the city in 1920.
8 Villemarest (1984), 228. Alexander Prystor was Prime Minister of Poland from 1931–1933. During the Polish–Soviet war, he was a close aide to Marshall Pilsudski. Waclaw Szalewicz was a famous Polish military officer.
9 Goleniewski, *White Book*, 237.
10 See the March 1978 issue of Frank Capell's Confidential Intelligence Report of the *Herald of Freedom* reprinted in the *White Book*, 263; Richards (1966), 79.
11 Goleniewski, *White Book*, 237.
12 Ibid.
13 Villemarest (1984), 230. Guy Richards writes that in early 1924 the family 'set up housekeeping in humble towns like Wolsztyn and Karpicko.' Richards (1966), 78.
14 During the war the village had a 'work camp' where some Jews were sent.
15 Clarke (1995), 141.
16 Goleniewski reprints the interview in *The White Book*. He also reprints a photo taken of him by Cotten on 15 July 1966 showing Goleniewski in a leather coat and sporting a large walrus mustache. He is also seen wearing a tiepin made of platinum with a profile of Nicholas II in gold. The tiepin, which he said he had in platinum, sapphire, and rubies, was said to be the symbol of 'the Russian National Secret Army' that he claimed to lead. See Philippa Schuyler, 'Russia's Czar Lives!' 17 August 1964 *Manchester Union Leader* and reprinted in *The White Book*. Schuyler had childhood polio, and she felt sure he had experienced something similar as a child.
17 *Warszawskiego Okregu Wojskowego*/WOW was the court of the Warsaw Military District which, following his defection to the West, sentenced Goleniewski to death in absentia on 18 March 1961.
18 Kochanski (1979), 52.
19 Pawlikowicz (2004), 222.
20 Richards (1966), 82.
21 Siemiatkowski (2006).
22 Witak (2014), 57.
23 After escaping to Austria at the end of World War II, Greiser was picked up by the American Army in Salzburg on 17 May 1945 and promptly transported back to Poland. On 21 July 1946, he was hanged before a large crowd in the last public execution in Poland. See Breitman and Goda (2011), and Epstein (2010).
24 Richards (1966), 84; Villemarest (1984), 231.
25 It can be seen on YouTube at https://www.youtube.com/watch?v=UCM4gJM-Qjk.
26 Metelmann (1990), 31. 'Panje' is the name of a Polish work horse used on farms and Metelmann seems to be having fun with the idea that an old Polish farmer could be the Tsar.
27 For more, see Appendix II: A weird Yank in Warsaw.

28 Richards (1966), 237.

29 Villemarest (1984), 22.

30 Pawlikowicz (2004), 222.

31 Summers and Mangold (1976), 195.

32 Villemarest (1984), 136. The picture first appeared on page 15 of the 16 July 1966 edition of Richard Cotton's *Conservative Viewpoints* issue devoted to Goleniewski.

33 The 'May 6/19' date is because Goleniewski uses both Russian Old and New Calendar dates quite frequently.

34 Goleniewski, *White Book*, 164.

35 See the *White Book* for photos of Goleniewski taken in 1939 (206), in a military uniform in 1955 (208), and in his 1961 Alien Registration Card taken in Virginia (204).

36 Villemarest (1984), 263–64.

37 Unblemished by footnotes, this short book proports to tell the story of Aaron Simanovitsch, Rasputin's Jewish secretary, who wrote a book on Rasputin that was translated into English as *Rasputin: The Memoirs of His Secretary*. Null argues that Simanovitsch organized the escape of the Imperial Family. One chapter is devoted to an interview with Goleniewski. Goleniewski said that the Simanovitsch book was a fake. Simanovitsch may have been a minor jeweler to the Tsar, but he was never Rasputin's secretary. He said that his book *Rasputin: der allmächtige Bauer* (Rasputin: The All-Powerful Peasant) first published by Hensel & Company in Berlin in 1928 was part of an attempt by the Nazis to blame the death of the Romanovs on the Jews, and that Hensel was a pro-Nazi publishing house.

38 Recall that Goleniewski was still living undercover in New York under a false name and a new CIA-supplied identity. He only went 'public' in August 1964, when he appeared on a New York radio show. Even then, he was highly secretive, not surprising given that he had been sentenced to death.

39 Gontarczyk (2013).

40 Zietara (2015), 36.

41 Ibid., 36–37.

42 Szlachcic (1990), 116. '*W 1955 roku ze służbowego wyjazdu do RFN nie wrocil do kraju. Po kilku miesaiacach ujawnit sie jako oficer wojskowegeo wywiadu USA.*' Szlachcic most likely just confused the date when he should have written 1960.

43 Ibid. '*Z akt personalnych wynikalo ze byl Polakiem, urodzil sie w Polsce i przez caly czas przebywal w kraju.*'

44 '*Wnikliwe*' can also be translated as 'in-depth' or 'insightful' as well as 'through.'

45 Ibid. '*Wnikliwe badania podwazyly jednak te dane. Wlasciwie nie bylo wiadomo, kim byl naprawde. Ponad wszelka watpliwosc byl agentem wywiadu usa.*'

46 Ibid. '*Po przewertowaniu sprawy sklonny bylem wierzyc ze Goleniewski byl naslanym najpierw do ZSRR, a pozniej do Polski, agentem wywiadu USA.*'

47 Wolton (1986), 78–80.

48 Szlachcic (1990), 116. '*W 1969 roku oficer naszego wywiadu trafil w usa i brazylii na slad 'carewicza' Goleniewskiego. Nie udalo sie jednak do niego dotrzec*' ('In 1969, our intelligence officer arrived in the USA and Brazil in the direction of Tsarevich. However, he did not manage to reach him.') To reach him' (*do niego dotrzec*) can also have a sinister implication of 'to hit him' as '*dotrzec*' can mean 'hit,' 'get,' and 'get at,' along the lines of a 'mafia hit.'

49 Pawlikowicz (2004), 300 (fn. 1052).

50 Gontarczyk (2013) writes: '*Poprzez oplaconego dziennikarza austriackiego spreparowano bogato udokumentowany cykl artykulow o Goleniewskiego z informacjami o jego zonie i dzieciach w Polsce. Bohater – jako oszust i bigamista – zostal skompromitowany wobec srodowisk rosyjskich i znikal z zycia publicznego …*'

51 Pawlikowicz (2004), 293.

52 Piecuch (1997), 268–69.

2

TIGHTROPE WALK

On the inside

Goleniewski began his career in Polish intelligence in 1945 as a camp guard. By 1950 he held the rank of captain. He was next reassigned from the Poznan region to the port city of Gdansk (formerly Danzig). Quickly promoted to major, in 1955 he achieved the rank of lieutenant colonel. In a 2013 essay on Goleniewski's career, the journalist Piotr Gontarczyk remarks:

> Michał Goleniewski … from the very beginning did not quite match the standards in force in security. He volunteered for the service at the County Public Security Office in Zielona Góra, with a high school degree obtained before the war from a lyceum in Wolsztyn. Here he survived the occupation: for five years he worked as an accountant in the German management of landed estates taken away from the Poles. He did not drink alcohol and joined the UB as a member of the People's Party, not the PPR.[1] Interestingly, his father was a tax official before the war, which in the eyes of the communists was an aggravating factor. Nevertheless, Goleniewski's career ran quickly. He started in 1945 as a guard and then became the head of the County Public Security Office (PUBP) after two years.[2]

Goleniewski was a guard (*wartownik*) in the town of Nowy Tomysl, not far from Poznan. He was officially employed by the *Powiatowy Urzad Bezpieczenstwa Publicznego*/PUBP (District Office of Public Security), more commonly known as the UB (*Urzad Bezpieczenstwa*/Security Police). The UB functioned under the umbrella of the *Ministerstwo Bezpieczenstwa Publicznego* (MBP), the Polish Ministry of Public Security.

DOI: 10.4324/9781003051114-4

Goleniewski caught the attention of Colonel Stefan Antosiewicz. Trained in espionage by the Russians during the war, Colonel Antosiewicz recalled: 'I approved of Goleniewski to work in Poznan. This was around 1947. He directed the Provincial UBP. Goleniewski was still a young man in his late twenties. When I met him, he worked as a guard for the PUBP in Nowy Tomysl.' Piotr Gontarczyk claims that Goleniewski:

> was intelligent, zealous and brutal. He became famous for torturing the soldiers of the Polish underground with a baton of braided wires covered with leather. In official opinions, his conceit and pride were often emphasized, but he was considered one of the most effective heads of the district UB in the voivodship.[3]

For his part, Goleniewski said he began as a recruit in the Army's supply section, and 'was soon shunted to the supply echelons of the counter-intelligence branch.'[4] By 1947, he led PUBP operations in Zielona Gora.

In 1949 Goleniewski transferred to Poznan, where he worked for the *Wojewodzki Urzad Bezpieczenstwa Publicznego* (Security Office of the Province/Voivodeship of Poznan/WUBP), an important office where he functioned as chief (*naczelnik*) for the Poznan municipality. He then was reassigned to Gdansk where he served as director of Department I of the WUBP branch from early1950 to 1953.[5] In Gdansk, he held the position of director of Department I of the WUBP office there and reportedly lived on Okopowa Street, until 1954.[6]

Despite Goleniewski's lack of formal education, Antosiewicz said he helped Goleniewski's rise 'because after the war, the country suffered the lack of educated people.' Therefore:

> I hired him as to become a referent [clerk] in the WUBP in Poznan. He did well so when I was promoted to the directorate of Department I [responsible for counterintelligence], I brought him to the ministry. In 1951 [1953] I appointed him head of the newly-formed Department of Studies [*Wydzialu Studiow*/Department IX], where he dealt with confronting and evaluating information. Following the dissolution of MBP, he went into the [civilian] secret service, where he was responsible for collecting information about military-industrial technologies.[7]

Antosiewicz's decision to reassign Goleniewski from Gdansk to Warsaw and place him in charge of the MBP's Department/Section IX of Department 1 taught – now Major – Goleniewski an enormous amount about the craft of counter-intelligence. Although Goleniewski oversaw just a three-person unit, Antosiewicz modeled Section IX on the pre-war counterintelligence unit that formed part of '*Oddzial*-II' ('Section II'), the famed intelligence division of the Polish General Staff.[8] Prewar Polish counterintelligence was headed by Colonel Stefan Meyer, who supervised the military's Cypher Bureau that famously decrypted German

Enigma transmissions before World War II. While running Section IX, Goleniewski played an important role in a devastating Polish counterintelligence operation dubbed 'Spiders' (Pajaki) aimed at destroying one wing of the Ukrainian OUN (Organization of Ukrainian Nationalist) known as the Melnyk faction (OUN-M), directly financed after the war by the CIA.[9]

Operation Spiders followed in the wake of the phenomenal success of Polish intelligence in completely fooling both the CIA and MI6 in the WiN operation. Freedom and Independence (*Zrzeszenie Wolność i Niezawisłość*/WiN) had been a Polish anti-Communist resistance organization that the Soviets and Poles managed to infiltrate and subvert starting in 1945. By 1947, the Polish secret service even convinced the CIA and MI6 to covertly finance WiN, which, in turn, sent false reports back to the West about conditions in Poland. The CIA and MI6 continued to finance and supply WiN right up to 27 December 1951 when Polish radio exposed the entire operation as an intelligence trap. The WiN deception, one of the greatest victories of East Bloc intelligence, called to mind the Soviet creation in the 1920s of a false monarchist organization, dubbed 'the Trust' that Soviet intelligence used to destroy anti-Communist networks in Russia.[10]

Goleniewski's career track that he told Guy Richards loosely corresponds with the Polish archives. After joining the Army in 1945, Richards writes:

> For the first six months of his Army career he was a sergeant under indoctrination. He was also in poor health. By the end of 1945, however, he had become deputy commander of a 60-man field office in the counter-intelligence branch. By the end of 1948, he was a field officer chief. He was then moved to Poznan, the largest city in his area of operations. Then, in 1950, in far better health and spirits, life was made more interesting for him. He was promoted to captain and transferred to one of the most colorful cities in Northern Europe, the old Free City of Danzig.[11]

Goleniewski was also decorated with the Bronze Cross of Merit in 1946.

On 15 March 1955, two years after relocating to Warsaw, Goleniewski was appointed vice-director of the Section II (counterintelligence) of Department I of the Committee for Public Security/KdsBP (*Komitet do Spraw Bezpieczenstwa Publicznego*). On 14 December 1955, he became a director of the GZI (*Glowny Zarzad Informacji*) in the Polish Ministry of National Defense (*Ministerstwo Obrony Narodowej*/MON) which, in turn, operated under the overall direction of the KdsBP.

When Goleniewski first contacted the US consulate in West Berlin, he said that through December 1957 he acted as 'Deputy Chief' of the GZI responsible for 'military counter-intelligence.'[12] Other reports say he shifted into civilian intelligence in February 1957. In any event, sometime in 1957 he took responsibility for organizing scientific and industrial spy operations in the West, a position he held until his defection.

Poland's intelligence service at the time of Goleniewski's rise enjoyed spectacular success with operations such as the WiN and Spider deceptions. Yet it also suffered major disruptions. On 5 December 1953, the Polish security apparatus was shaken to the core when one of its top officials, Józef Swiatlo, defected to the West. Swiatlo fled Poland following the purge of the intelligence network around The People's Commissariat for Internal Affairs' (*Naródnyy Komissariát Vnútrennikh Del*/NKVD) boss and Politburo member Lavrenty Beria, and Beria's subsequent execution. In November 1954 Swiatlo broadcast embarrassing facts about the corrupt inner workings of Poland's communist leaders over the airwaves of Radio Free Europe (RFE).[13]

Swialto's revelations proved so damaging that the Ministry of Public Security was abolished. Its functions were taken over by two separate organizations, a new Committee for Public Security (*Komitet do Spraw Bezpieczenstwa Publicznego*/KdsBP) on the one hand and a new Ministry of the Interior (*Ministerstwo Spraw Wewnetrznych*/MSW) on the other. Polish Army Intelligence and Counter-intelligence functioned under the military's Main Intelligence Directorate (*Glowny Zarzad Informacji*/GZI) which now was folded into the KdsBP.

Poland was shaken yet again in 1956 when a political uprising almost triggered a Soviet military invasion. The crisis broke out in the wake of the 20th Congress of the Communist Party of the Soviet Union (CPSU)following Soviet leader Nikita Khrushchev's 25 February 1956 speech denouncing Stalin. His speech shocked Poland's top Communist leaders, all avowed Stalinists. Boleslaw Bierut, the head of the Polish Communist Party, was in a Moscow hospital being treated for pneumonia when he got a copy of the speech. He then had a heart attack and died.[14]

As word of Khrushchev's speech spread, a worker protest over wages and living conditions at the Poznan Stalin Works locomotive plant (ZISPO) broke out on 28–29 June 1956. Known as the Poznan Uprising (*Poznanski Czerwiec*), it led to the killing of several dozen demonstrators (and the wounding of hundreds more) in a crowd of some 100,000 protesters by some 10,000 soldiers and 400 tanks, all following the orders of a Polish-Russian General. Some of the protesters attacked Poznan's UB's offices in a blunt challenge to state power.[15]

In the wake of the revolt, the Polish Communist Party moved to dismiss Bieurt's successor Edward Ochab and replace him with Wladyslaw Gomulka, a move dubbed the 'Polish October.' Purged from his leadership position in the Communist Party (which in 1948 changed its name to the Polish United Workers Party (*Zjednoczona Partia Robotnicza*/PZPR)), Gomulka had been jailed by his former comrades. Now back in power, he demanded the removal of a Russian Marshall named Konstantin Rokossovskii, whom the Kremlin had imposed on Poland as its Defense Minister.

Tensions grew so bad that when Khrushchev demanded to come to Poland to discuss the situation, the new government refused to invite him. On 19 October 1956, with Ochab on the way out and Poland on the brink of a possible Russian invasion, Khrushchev landed at Warsaw Airport. Meanwhile both Soviet and Polish military forces began mobilizing in anticipation of an invasion. The historian Anne Applebaum reports that when Khrushchev arrived in Warsaw he also ordered Soviet troops based elsewhere in Poland to start marching toward Warsaw immediately. According to several accounts, Gomulka responded with his own threats. He became 'rude,' he blamed Soviet officers in the Polish army for creating public anger, and he declared that if put in charge he could easily control the army without Soviet interference. More importantly, he also ordered Interior Ministry troops and other armed groups who were loyal to him, and not to the Soviet-dominated army, to take up strategic positions around Warsaw where they prepared to defend him and his new government. A violent clash pitting Polish troops loyal to Gomulka against Polish troops loyal to Soviet commanders – the latter backed up by the Red Army – suddenly seemed possible.

Khrushchev blinked first. ... He decided reconciliation was the best policy and eventually agreed to recall Rokossovskii, his deputy, and several other Soviet officers. In return, Gomulka promised loyalty to Moscow in matters of foreign policy and swore not to withdraw from the Warsaw Pact.[16]

The Polish security services were yet again badly shaken by the larger crisis. Janusz Kochanski, a Polish intelligence agent who later defected to the West, recalled:

In the wake of the popular demonstrations that restored Wladyslaw Gomulka to power, the Russians were kicked out of the Polish Intelligence Service completely. They left their offices without even cleaning out their desks. During a meeting of the Department I unit of the Polish Communist Party, things got so bad that the Russians were told to leave the building. They promptly did so. Moreover, they were afraid to come back, particularly since one of the department's deputy directors had decided to give all of the Polish staffers arms from our storage supply.

(He was later expelled from the service for this, but that was two years after the fact in 1958.)[17]

The 1956 revolt led to yet another bureaucratic shuffle in the security agencies. All intelligence operations were now placed under the direct control of the MSW, the Polish Ministry of the Interior. During the crisis, Goleniewski was seemingly nowhere to be found. As *Imperial Agent* puts it: 'Lt. Col. Goleniewski kept his nose pretty much to the grindstone of his Army duties during the winter of 1956–57.'[18]

Section VI

In 1957 Michal Goleniewski became head of the intelligence branch of the MSW for scientific and technical information (*naukowo-technicznego*), known as Section VI of Department I.[19] Goleniewski enjoyed no special scientific expertise or training. When the CIA tried to debrief him on scientific developments in Poland during his time as Section VI director, he proved incapable of erudite discussion on issues like rocket telemetry and missile launch systems. Goleniewski's inability to discuss scientific ideas in depth greatly frustrated Herbert 'Pete' Scoville who, under the name 'Peter Skov,' tried to debrief him.[20] If Scoville couldn't get anything of real scientific value out of Goleniewski, why had Goleniewski been placed in charge of Section VI in the first place?

One possible answer may stretch back to Goleniewski's three years in the famed port city of Gdansk. During the Cold War, smugglers played a key role for both sides in transporting goods and information through the Iron Curtain. While in Gdansk, *Imperial Agent* reports that Goleniewski

> served in the technical and scientific branch whose function was to spot those trying to ferret out technological secrets of the state ranking from weaponry to aircraft design. Then he was assigned to the analysis and inspection branch. Here his job was to see that equipment for the Army was maintained at a high standard, that deliveries were prompt and servicing proper.[21]

Goleniewski's involvement in this cut-throat world surfaced in one of his 'Heckenschütze' letters. Howard Roman, a leading CIA official assigned to read the mysterious letters, recalled that 'Sniper'

> wrote at great length about a notorious black marketer who smuggled watches to the Soviet military officers in Warsaw and undertook occasional spy missions for both the Russians and the Poles. 'I remember one letter which Sniper said he had sent us at great personal risk, warning us that this black marketer was making a trip to Vienna wearing a wig,' Roman said. Sniper urged the CIA to take an adjoining room in his hotel, drill a hole through the wall, pump some anesthetizing gas into his room, and spirit the scoundrel away. 'This was the kind of stuff that took up a lot of room in his letter,' Roman said.[22]

After being reassigned from Gdansk to Warsaw, Goleniewski also undertook new intelligence assignments outside Poland. *Imperial Agent* reports that Goleniewski now

> began a number of assignments … in Czechoslovakia, East Germany and Poland … and on February 8, 1957, he was transferred from counterintelligence to military intelligence. Ostensibly his new assignment would involve him in the matters of industrial processes, chemistry, manufacturing technology and advances in electronics, aeronautics and weaponry. In actual fact, however, it placed him more directly on the orbit of foreign agents of the highest sophistication who were on the trail of the prize technological breakthroughs. In his first post he was in charge of a branch employing 68 staff officers. From there on his travels and range of operations covered many cities.[23]

Goleniewski's skills in dealing with smuggling and technology transfer issues first homed in Gdansk may have recommended him for the science/technology directorship, an important post in Gomulka's Poland. To understand why, some context is needed.

In the mid-1950s Polish intelligence operations in the United States and England were in a sad state. In the winter of 1955, an internal report entitled *Zakres dzialania I structura Departamentu I* (The range of the First Department's activity and structure) revealed that Polish intelligence employed only five agents each in the United States and Canada and just nine in England. One year later, Polish intelligence yet underwent another reorganization under the new Gomulka regime with the establishment of the Interior Ministry (the MSW) that housed Department I. Department I also had a new powerhouse boss. On 28 November 1956, the Lithuanian-born Colonel Witold Sienkiewicz took over as chief of Department I and its 12 sub-sections or branches. Sienkiewicz's closeness to the Russians fueled speculation that he may have been a KGB agent.

Under Gomulka's leadership, and as part of the larger Cold War 'thaw,' Poland now opened many more commercial contacts with the West as scientific exchanges increased. In 1958 the *Komitet do Wspolpracy Naukowo-Technicznej z Zagranica* (the Committee for Scientific-Technical Cooperation with Abroad) was established by the Council of Ministers. Komitet coordinated its activities with a host of Polish government ministries from the Defense Department to the Ministries of Mining and Energy. Komitet helped organize commercial scientific and technology transfers from the West in coordination with Department I's Section VI. Komitet was the scientific 'brain' behind Section VI.

In the late 1950s Section VI underwent a major reorganization. Before then, the desks had been arranged by geography. Now Section VI was broken down into new sub-sections organized around desks for nuclear energy, chemistry, machinery, metallurgy, electricity and so on. When Goleniewski became head of Section VI, it still only had eight overseas representatives in Berlin, Paris, Vienna, Brussels and London. From Andrezej Paczkowski's overview of Polish intelligence in the 1950s:

> Specialists from scientific-technical intelligence worked only in several European resident posts, and the scientific-technical division did not have a single officer in the USA.... On the other hand, significant progress had been achieved not only due to organizational changes (the territorial sections in the technological division had been replaced by a 'branch' structure, i.e. nuclear energy or chemistry sections) but also predominantly, by contacts between Polish scientists and representatives of industry and the West, which had grown rapidly since 1957. The head of the Department planned considerable expansion, the employment of new officers, and enlarging the cooperation with the research institutes and the industry. The Committee of the Scientific-Technical Cooperation with Abroad prepared as many as 340 intelligence tasks for the 1960–1963 period.[24]

Goleniewski's appointment as Section VI's boss came at a time when there was tremendous pressure to deliver more and better-quality consumer goods and to modernize Poland's industries that had suffered dreadfully under both the Germans and the Russians. Nor had Gomulka forgotten that the Poznan uprising began as a protest over wages, working conditions, and lack of consumer goods. Goleniewski's role, then, was not just restricted to military and spy-related concerns but industrial technology issues as well.

Section VI's importance was underscored by the choice of Goleniewski's Russian advisor, KGB Colonel Andrey Ivanovich Raina.[25] Raina had worked in America from 1942 to 1946 as part of the 'X Line' charged with scientific and intellectual espionage in America generally and with the Manhattan project more specifically. Back in Moscow in the early 1950s, Raina played a major role in Soviet damage control operations following exposes of Soviet atomic espionage rings on US soil.[26] Goleniewski's belief in the FBI's competence may have stemmed from his conversations with Raina, who worked against the Bureau in New York and who said that Hoover ran a first-rate counterintelligence operation.

In the notes from Edward Jay Epstein's taped conversations with Goleniewski, there is also a mention that Raina had been formerly involved with someone spelled in the note as 'Chevchenko.' 'Chevchenko' was almost certainly Andrei Shevchenko, known under his code name as ARSENJI in the Venona files. Shevchenko first came to Buffalo, New York, in June 1942 as part of a Soviet Purchasing Commission delegation; his real mission was to gather information especially as it related to military aircraft. Bell Aircraft's factory in Niagara Falls proved of special interest.

In the course of its investigation into Shevchenko's spy network, the FBI managed to 'double' two of its agents after the Bureau received an anonymous tip in a letter that identified a score of NKVD operatives on US soil. Raina's ties to Andrei Shevchenko may have been especially close. In a 2009 symposium on cryptological history, John Earl Haynes and Harvey Klehr examined Soviet spy cover names. They report that 'Arseny,' a cover name that appears in *The Vassiliev Notebooks*,

> was identified in the Venona decryptions as KGB officer Andrey Ivanovich Shevchenko, who worked on aviation intelligence in upstate New York. Shevchenko may be the pseudonym used in the US by KGB officer Andrey Ivanovich Raina.[27]

Wielkiego Brata

Goleniewski's rise from an obscure camp guard to head of Section VI obviously stemmed from his own talent and drive. But there was another factor at play as well, his remarkably close connections to the Soviet 'advisors,' whom the Poles ironically dubbed '*Wielkiego Brata*' or 'Big Brother.' There seems little doubt that Goleniewski served as a Russian agent inside Polish intelligence. One German study of Polish intelligence describes him as a '*Vertrauensmann des KGB im Polen.*'[28] One of the first things Goleniewski said after he entered the US Consulate in Berlin was that he was the KGB's man inside Polish intelligence!

While there is virtually unanimous agreement that Goleniewski enjoyed an extremely close relationship with the KGB, it remains a mystery just why that should have been the case. It was true that he spoke perfect Russian, his first wife was Russian, and he would later identify as the Tsar of Russia which is about as Russian as you can get. Still, this does not clarify his special relationship with the Soviets. Equally mysterious is the reason why the Russians trusted him so deeply. Rumors began circulating that perhaps he really was not Polish at all. Others wondered whether he might not have been secretly trained in Russia by the NKVD during World War II.

The KGB's trust in Goleniewski resulted in Goleniewski's exposing a top Russian agent inside Germany. In 1958 General Oleg Mikhailovich Gribanov, the head of the KGB's Second Chief Directorate (SCD) who ran KGB counterintelligence, gave a speech to a group of Warsaw Pact intelligence and security chiefs in Moscow. Dubbed 'the Little Napoleon' by one of his KGB peers, Gribanov reportedly bragged that the Russians had so successfully penetrated Western intelligence that when a delegation of six West German Federal Intelligence Service (*Bundesnachrichtendienst*/BND) leaders visited Washington in 1956, two of them were Russian agents. Goleniewski sent this critical information to the CIA in a March 1959 Heckenschütze letter.[29] His report led to the unmaking of Heinz Felfe, a member of the delegation to the DC meeting.[30]

Gribanov also reportedly made an extraordinary proposal at the same gathering. From Tennent Bagley's 2007 book *Spy Wars*:

> In 1958, in one of his periodically convened meetings of chiefs of Warsaw Pact counterintelligence services, Gribanov proposed a joint operation. All at the same time, each of these services would expose publicly (on one pretext or another) a lot of Western spies they had caught and turned or whom they themselves had planted. This, Gribanov thought, would sow dismay and confusion in Western intelligence services, inhibit further spying, and tie them up in time-consuming and useless investigations.
>
> Gribanov's proposal was not adopted. It caused (unspoken) outrage among the Eastern European chiefs because they, not the KGB, were to make the bulk of the sacrifices and because they doubted it would have long-term effect.[31]

Realizing how incredible all this must sound, Bagley added this footnote: 'Two of the Eastern European participants confirmed to me this conference that Michal Goleniewski had reported in his "Sniper" correspondence.'[32]

The story of the 1958 meeting remains contested. *Battleground Berlin*, co-written in part by former CIA Berlin station chief David Murphy and former KGB Berlin station chief Sergei Kondrashev, states that the 1958 conclave was the second gathering of the East Bloc CI chiefs, the first having taking place in 1956. They report that Gribanov organized it primarily to secure support for 'active measures' against West Germany. They say that Goleniewski 'first heard the statement by Gribanov' in his 1958 speech. In other words, they seem to imply that Goleniewski attended the talk in person. They then add:

> As he did in other cases, Goleniewski, who was also a KGB spy within the Polish service, elicited confirmation of the brief Gribanov statement from a Soviet adviser in 1960 during a discussion.[33]

In Edward Jay Epstein's 17 May 1981 *Washington Star* article, however, Goleniewski states that Colonel Raina, his Soviet advisor in Section VI, first told him about the two Soviet moles in the 1956 BND delegation to Washington. In his 'Spy Wars' piece in the *New York Times* magazine, Epstein writes:

> 'Heckenschütze' reported in 1959 that he had been told by a high-ranking KGB officer that the BND had been thoroughly infiltrated by Soviet intelligence, and that many of its top officials had been blackmailed by the KGB into cooperating with it. He stated that of the six BND officers who had visited CIA headquarters in Washington in 1956, and Allen Dulles met with, two were KGB moles.

Epstein's report almost certainly was right.

Goleniewski first reported on Gribanov's claim in a March 1959 Sniper letter after he heard the story from Raina. By 1957 Goleniewski no longer worked in counterintelligence and there would be no reason for him to attend the Moscow gathering. The most logical sequence is that Colonel Raina heard about Gribanov's boast from a Russian colleague. Sometime later, he told Goleniewski about Gribanov's brag about the BND.

By the late 1950s Goleniewski was on a roll. Not only was he chief of Section VI, he clearly was trusted by his Soviet colleagues. Yet with all this – and with an even brighter future assured should he succeed at Section VI – he now decided to risk his life and begin sending his Sniper missives to the American Embassy in Switzerland.

Notes

1 The People's Party, also known as the Peasants Party, was a social-democratic group that entered a coalition with the Communists only to be crushed by them.
2 Gontarczyk (2013).
3 A voivodeship is an area administered by a Governor (*voivode*) over several districts and counties. It is somewhat like a duchy, but it functioned in postwar Poland as a large administrative district.
4 Richards (1966), 85.
5 It was during his time in Gdansk that Goleniewski's father died.
6 Clarke (1995), 142. A scholarly study of Polish security personnel in postwar Gdansk reportedly mentions Goleniewski. See Weglinski (2010).
7 Pawlikowicz (2004), 223.
8 Ibid., 281–82.
9 Bury (2017), 264–65. For a fascinating look at the OUN, see Plokhy (2016).
10 For WiN, see the article by former CIA officer Robert D. Chapman (2006). For the CIA's account of *The Trust* see Simpkins and Dyer (1989).
11 Richards (1966), 86.
12 Pawlikowicz (2004), 221.
13 See Gluchowski (1999).
14 Fitzpatrick (2015), 246.
15 On the crisis in Poznan and the confrontation with Russia, see Granville (2002), 659–63, 674–79.

16 Applebaum (2012), 457.
17 Kochanski (1979), 98–99.
18 Richards (1966), 124.
19 Some reports date his entry into Section VI as 1 February 1957. Other reports say he took the position in the fall. It may be that he was transferred to civilian intelligence in February, but that Section VI began operations later.
20 Scoville served as the CIA's Assistant Director of Scientific Intelligence and Deputy Director for Research until 1963.
21 Richards (1966), 88.
22 Martin (1980), 96.
23 Richards (1966), 104.
24 Paczkowski (2007), 7.
25 Epstein (1981). As far as I can tell, Epstein first identified Colonel Raina by name based on an interview he conducted with Goleniewski. Epstein, however, gives his name as 'Ivan Andreievich Raina' when it is almost certainly 'Andrej Ivanovich Raina.'
26 Haynes, Klehr, and Vassiliev (2010), 131.
27 See http://www.johnearlhaynes.org/page102.html. In the Venona decrypt, 'Shevchenko's' name is coded as ARSENIJ. For more on 'Shevchenko,' see Haynes and Klehr (1999). They report (294) that the FBI wanted to arrest and either try or deport Shevchenko. The State Department objected on the grounds that it might hurt US–Soviet relations during the war.
28 Sikora (2014), 572. About Section VI, Sikora writes:

> Der erste Wendepunkt war das Jahr 1961, als ein sehr erfahrener polnischer Geheimdienst-funktionär und seit 1958 Leiter der Abteilung VI, Oberstleutnant Michał Goleniewski (der auch als Vertrauensmann des KGB im Polen galt), in die Vereinigten Staaten floh und dort dem CIA das polnische Spionage – netz im Westen offenbarte, was selbstverständlich einen völligen Umbau der polnischen Geheimdienstorganisation im Allgemeinen und des WTA im Besonderen veranlasste.

Translating 'Vertrauensmann' in this context as 'confidant' is also a bit misleading because in espionage jargon, the term means more like 'confidential agent/informer/information agent.'
29 See the CIA document entitled 'KGB Exploitation of Heinz Felfe,' https://www.cia.gov/readingroom/docs/FELFE%2C%20HEINZ%20%20KGB%20EXPLOITATION%20OF%20HEINZ%20FELFE_0001.pdf, pp. 115–16 for the date of the Sniper letter. Felfe is discussed in more detail in Chapter 6.
30 Murphy, Kondrashev, and Bailey (1997), 509. The CIA was unable to determine the second agent's identity.
31 Bagley (2007), 234.
32 Ibid., 302.
33 Murphy, Kondrashev, and Bailey (1997), 509. They report in a footnote on page 497 that on 4 January 1964, the CIA issued a memorandum entitled 'Goleniewski's Work with the Soviets' and cite as their source, CIA-HRP. I could not find the report on the CIA's Historical Review Program website.

3

CROSSING OVER

Irmgard Kampf

Even as he continued his rise inside Polish intelligence, Goleniewski's personal life bordered on the disastrous. At issue was the collapse of his marriage. Colonel Stefan Antosiewicz, a former director of civilian counterintelligence who know Goleniewski well and helped mentor him, recalled that Goleniewski's first wife, Anna, had been deported from Russia to work as a slave laborer in the Greater Reich. Here she met her first husband, a Pole, and they had a child together, a daughter named Halina. After the war, they settled in the town of Nowy Tomysl in Western Poland near both Poznan and Wolsztyn, but her husband soon died of illness. She next married Goleniewski and together they raised three children.[1] Goleniewski may have met her while he was at the Nowy Tomysl camp.

Over time Anna began to develop a severe form of mental illness that was believed to be caused in part by the horrors of the war.[2] His wife's emotional problems made it impossible for Goleniewski's mother Janina to live with them following her husband's death.[3]

Goleniewski said Anna suffered from schizophrenic delusions and at one point experienced a complete collapse. Thanks to treatment from two psychiatrists, she recovered somewhat but she still had to cope with the delusions. Yet for all his marital woes, Goleniewski never received a formal divorce.[4]

During a November 1960 investigation by Polish intelligence, Goleniewski described his painful personal life this way:

> Because of an incurable mental illness of my wife Anna (schizophrenia of a delusional nature) that began some six years after we married, my marriage completely collapsed. My fourfold attempts to treat my wife not only were

DOI: 10.4324/9781003051114-5

without any result; she says that the treatment offered for her persecution mania is yet one 'proof' on my part to 'destroy' her, 'poisoning' her and so forth.

Two prominent psychiatrists, who treated my wife about three years ago, concluded that she suffers from the so-called quiet schizophrenia covering delusions about some phenomena of life (persecution mania, morbid suspicion, morbid jealousy) in principle, but that her personality in the sense of living life is intact, i.e., she leads the household and she has a very good attitude to children whom she loves and for whom she cares for.... On the advice of a doctor ... one and one-half years ago I moved out of the house – more precisely I was driven out because of my wife's delusions and I lived jointly with my mother. I left her and the family the house along with the furniture.

I could have taken advantage, it is true, of the possibility of 'a long treatment' of my wife in a psychiatric hospital. Yet to isolate her from life was too inhumane a step, in light of the fact of attachment to her children and the preservation of her personality beyond the elements covered by delusions, the center of which is focused against me.

I continued for a long time without the difficulty of getting a formal divorce which does not change the reality of the end of the marriage.... In January 1957, my wife, while staying with a family in the Soviet Union, expressed her serious intention to repatriate to the USSR and taking with her a daughter, Halina, from her first marriage. She intended to again become a citizen of the USSR and use her maiden name.[5]

In 1964 Goleniewski issued a public notice that offered more information. He related that in a 19 April 1963 conversation with CIA Legal Counsel John Warner in Goleniewski's Queens apartment, he told Warner that he had two sons, Dmitrii and Jerzy. Dmitrii was born in 1946 in Zielona Gora, southwest of Wolsztyn. His other son, and future rock musician, Jerzy was born in 1950. He added that his wife had a daughter named Halina Malinowski, who was born in 1944 in Swiebodzin, northwest of Wolsztyn, and that his wife Anna's original name was Sofia Diatchechtov.[6]

Anna/Sophia was of Russian-Ukrainian nationality and had been born in 1924 in Poltava. Her family still lived in Russia. Hanna was her daughter with her first husband who died in the war. Goleniewski said that when his wife became mentally ill, he obtained an annulment. He added that his wife's mental problems were partly based on stress she suffered in 1944 living underground and hiding from the Nazis and that she and their children lived in Warsaw.

In 1958, as head of Section VI, Goleniewski began visiting East Berlin on a regular basis. During the WOW proceedings, Henryk Sokolak, the then-deputy director of Department I, explained that when Goleniewski first became active in foreign intelligence operations as head of Section VI, he rarely traveled abroad. Starting in 1958, however, he began visiting East Berlin more frequently.[7] On one of these visits, Goleniewski met Irmgard Margareta Kampf. In November 1960, Goleniewski told his Warsaw bosses: 'During one of my business trips in Berlin in

1958, I accidentally met a DDR German citizen named Irmgard Kampf (IK) born 6 January 1929, in Berlin, a woman office worker in East Berlin. Anyway, the introduction came from my initiative.'[8]

Goleniewski's first Sniper letter reached the US Embassy in Bern on 1 April 1958. If Ted Shackley's memory is correct, Goleniewski initially attempted to contact the US Consulate in Berlin some weeks earlier. Whether Goleniewski decided to contact the West before or after meeting Kampf is hard to say, but both events most likely occurred sometime in the spring of 1958, although it is possible that he met her earlier.

Goleniewski said he followed standard precautions to make sure Kampf wasn't an enemy agent. He first told her he was 'Jan Roman … a journalist, who deals with cooperation with GDR [East German] journalists, writes articles for newspapers, comments, etc. IK adopted the legend without any reservations,' convinced that 'Roman' was 'a citizen of People's Republic [of Poland] of Jewish origin.' Kampf told 'Roman' that 'she very much liked Jews,' and that before the war her mother had worked in a shop as a seamstress (presumably alongside Jewish workers). He continued:

> Meeting with IK during my stays in Berlin … I determined that IK is the daughter of Berlin workers and lived with her parents at the address Wolli-nerstr. 54 East Berlin, N. 58. Since the beginning of the organization of the municipality of the GDR in Berlin, she works in medium schools as a secretary, a class affiliated with the regime of the GDR. [IK] is completely devoid of religious superstition, she has no shadow chauvinism, she looks after and is dedicated to her parents, she likes her work, she holds a critical attitude to the conditions of life in West Berlin….

In short, 'the hypotheses that she could be the "enemy" after a few months completely vanished as well as any suspicion of IK as an agent for the NDR [DDR/East German] authorities.'[9]

As they grew more intimate, Goleniewski revealed his main cover name, Roman Tarnowski, also the name on his passport:

> At the beginning of acquaintance with IK, I operated under the name ROMAN, JAN … After some time because of the passport [I explained] the cover name TARNOWSKI, ROMAN. I explained the affair in this way: with the war under the name ROMAN, JAN I was hiding and working for some time against German fascists in the underground, now I just use it as a literary pseudonym. My true name is Tarnowski. My real name IK does not know….[10]

Polish intelligence's interest in Kampf apparently arose sometime in the fall of 1960, or just a few months before Goleniewski's defection. Either Goleniewski informed his superiors of their relationship or Polish intelligence discovered it independently.

Goleniewski had successfully concealed aspects of his affair for almost two years and used operational money to buy gifts for his mistress, who believed her boyfriend worked as a journalist for a Polish news agency. It is possible that Goleniewski first called attention to Kampf when he may have asked his superiors for permission to marry her. Whatever the exact sequence, the issue seems simple: Goleniewski had been less than forthcoming about his relationship with Kampf.

In 1961, Stasi head Erich Mielke sent a report on Kampf to the Polish Minister of the Interior Wladyslaw Wicha. The document was largely based on an interview with the female director of 13 Oberschule Berlin-Mitte, Koppenplatz 12, where Kampf worked as a secretary. The director and Kampf knew each other for four years. She told Stasi investigators that sometime in 1957 (Goleniewski said 1958), Kampf met the journalist 'Roman Tarnowski' at the HO-Gaststätte 'Melodie' in the East Berlin Friedrichstrasse district.[11] Tarnowski told Kampf that during World War II, he had served as a 'reserve officer' for the Polish partisans and that his entire family (with the sole exception of his mother) had been murdered. After about a year's courtship, Kampf said that they became engaged.

After Goleniewski defected, it was discovered that he had been sending money on a regular basis into Kampf's bank account. He also supplied her with a TV, jewelry from Switzerland, furs from Paris, and clothes from England.[12] Kampf said that the money in the account was meant to be savings for their upcoming marriage. As the date for the wedding approached, Kampf grew worried when she found out the Polish authorities were trying to hinder it.

As for Tarnowski, Kampf said he did not visit Berlin for a long time and told her it was because his mother was sick. Finally, at the end of December 1960, Tarnowski sent Kampf a telegram reporting he would be in Berlin from 3–8 January 1961. The Stasi report concludes with the director saying that none of Kampf's colleagues detected any hint that she was planning to leave for the West.[13] It seems quite possible that Kampf didn't know she would defect until the man she knew as Roman Tarnowski convinced her that if they wanted to stay together, it was now or never.

When Warsaw discovered Goleniewski's relationship with Kampf, his superiors were furious but not because they suspected that he was involved in some subversive operation. Nor is there any evidence that Kampf was used for any espionage purpose by Goleniewski or that she had links to the Stasi, BND, or any other foreign service. Goleniewski may have been attracted to Kampf precisely because she had no connection to the treacherous world of espionage. Or maybe he just enjoyed leading a double life.

In 1959 Goleniewski would be awarded the Knight's Cross of the prestigious Order *Oprodzenia Polski* (Order of the Rebirth of Poland). The odd man with the slight limp proved himself a trusted operator. And yet he had deceived his superiors about his personal life. Piotr Gontarczyk analyses Goleniewski's troubles this way:

> In contrast, the personal affairs of the young lieutenant colonel were terrible. His wife never recovered after her dramatic war experiences that in the 1950s caused her mental illness. The family did not really exist. Goleniewski

established relations with Irmgard Kampf, who lived in eastern Berlin, and after a few years he submitted to his superiors a comprehensive elaboration in this matter, asking for permission for a divorce, and marrying anew. However, the first superiors found it difficult from the legal point of view, and the second, in the case of an intelligence officer – even though the candidate was from the GDR – was considered inadvisable. What's more, the management of Department I scrupulously looked at the justifications of his foreign trips to Germany and began to issue negative decisions in this matter. Goleniewski responded the following way: a letter on the next 'operationally important' trip was sent not to the director of Department I Colonel Witold Sienkiewicz, only directly to the head of the Ministry of Internal Affairs Mieczyslaw Moczar. He agreed.[14]

When Goleniewski was grilled about his relationship, he argued that this was purely a personal matter. Goleniewski's portrait of Kampf to his Department I superiors bordered on the poignant. He states that her 'agreeable appearance'

> was associated in her with positive traits – refined behavior, modesty, honesty, attachment to the family, readiness to help, cleanliness, care and economy. She said that she came from a poor, working-class family but nonetheless she was raised well and despite her age she is still subject to her parent's demands.
>
> It is an unusual thing that a 28-year-old single woman considers it her duty, because of her parents, to be home by midnight at the latest…. As to the question of why she is not yet married, she declared that at a young age she survived personal tragedy because her fiancé broke up with her because of the large dowry of another girl. Since then she decided to deal with her elderly parents, who always treat her more like a small child. Since their attitude towards her will not be based on her personal qualities and character, she will spend her life an old maid. Since the beginning of our acquaintance, she insisted that material values do not interest her. She is interested only in sincere human feelings.[15]

Desperate to return to Berlin, Goleniewski said that if it was a problem that he was close to a German girl or if any other matter related to Kampf troubled his superiors, he would choose the service and forego any connection with her. His Department I chiefs decided he had to break off his relationship with his mistress. But how? And when? Would they even permit him to tell Kampf personally that it was all over?

The then-vice director of Department I, Colonel Sokolak, was not a particularly sentimental type. Born in 1921, he was captured by the Germans in 1940. He spent the rest of the war in Buchenwald, where he helped lead the resistance organization. After Colonel Sienkiewicz, the long-time head of Department I, was dismissed in June 1961 in the wake of Goleniewski's defection, Sokolak would run Department I until 1969. Sokolak said that Goleniewski should not be allowed back to East Berlin.

Colonel Sienkiewicz argued that Goleniewski should return and be allowed to resolve this 'private matter.' As head of Department I, Sienkiewicz faced some pressing realities. Goleniewski helped run ongoing intelligence operations for Section VI out of Berlin, and his skills were needed in the field. If he had to take a weekend off to end things with Kampf, it seemed a small price to pay. With Department I divided and Goleniewski still pressing his case, the final decision was left to Mieczyslaw Moczar, who at the time oversaw foreign intelligence from his position as a high-ranking official in the Ministry of the Interior. General Moczar now green-lighted Goleniewski's trip.

Vanishing act

On 4 January 1961, at exactly 6:06 p.m., a West Berlin taxi pulled up to the front of the American Consulate in West Berlin. Goleniewski and Kampf exited the vehicle carrying small bags. A short time later, the CIA's Berlin Station sent an urgent message to Washington that read in part:

1. SUBJ IS LT COL MICHAL GOLENIEWSKI DOB 16 AUGUST 1922 IN NIESWIERZ [Nesvizh/Nieswiez] (FORMER PART USSR). THROUGH DECEMBER 1957 DEPUTY CHIEF MAIN OFFICE (STELLVERTR-ETER DES HAUPTAMTES) IN MILITARY COUNTER INTELLI-GENCE (GZI). TO PRESENT ASSERTS HE DEPUTY DIRECTOR INDEPENDENT SCIENTIFIC BRANCH IN MINISTRY OF INTER-NAL AFFAIRS. AT SAME TIME ACTS FOR KGB IN UB. WILL CLARIFY STATUS IN LATTER ROLE.
2. SUBJ CALLED 1730 AND INFORMED ___ TO EXPECT HIM IN HALF HOUR. AGAIN ASKED THAT SPECIAL ATTENTION BE PAID TO WIFE.
3. SUBJ APPEARED 1800. ENTERED CONSULATE GREETED BY ___.[16]

David Murphy, head of the CIA's Berlin Station, wrote an eyewitness description of that night in *Battleground Berlin*.[17] He recalled that Goleniewski first approached the CIA as 'Herr Kowalski.' Under that name, he contacted the Consulate some months earlier because Murphy recalls the CIA arranged a dead-drop in Berlin for 'materials' – presumably camera equipment – for him to take back to Warsaw.

Because Goleniewski had made the call as 'Kowalski,' Murphy said that Goleniewski told them that Kampf only knew him as 'Kowalski,' although, as we have seen, she also knew him both as 'Jan Roman' and 'Roman Tarnowski.' It seems more likely that Murphy greeted the couple as 'Herr und Frau Kowalski' as Goleniewski said he was bringing his wife. Goleniewski then admitted that Kampf was his mistress. He feared the CIA would not bring her to the United States because they were not married, but the Agency agreed to do so once it confirmed that he was 'Sniper.' (Goleniewski and Kampf were officially married in a civil ceremony in the USA a few days after they arrived.[18])

At the consulate, Goleniewski was welcomed by someone described by Murphy as a CIA officer 'who had just flown in from West Germany to act as Washington's "special representative."'[19] Goleniewski said that Howard Roman was his case officer along with a 'Robert Hegebai' or 'Hegenbart' in Washington, which is the way the name is spelled in a transcript in the Edward Jay Epstein archive file on Goleniewski.[20] Howard Roman finally met Goleniewski in Wiesbaden, where the USA had a large military base.[21]

Goleniewski's last tightrope walk between East and West began on the evening of 26 December 1960 when he left Warsaw by train for East Berlin. On 27 December, Goleniewski met MSW officers in Berlin to begin his assigned duties.[22] On 31 December during a conversation with Colonel Wladyslaw Michalski, the head of MSW's Berlin section, he unexpectedly asked for added financial support.[23] On 3 January he was scheduled to meet with a contact, but he shifted the scheduled encounter to 6 January.

On the evening of 3 January, just hours before he would defect, Goleniewski again appeared in the MSW's office and arranged to receive more money, possibly under the pretext of needing it for the 6 January meeting. He now convinced his Department I colleagues to supply him with some 16,300 West German marks, 600 East German marks, and 300 American dollars. It would be one last act of betrayal. He then reserved 4–5 January for 'personal business,' namely, his pledge in Warsaw to end his relationship with Kampf. Instead, he used the time to coordinate their escape.

Piotr Gontarczyk recounts Goleniewski's last days in Berlin this way:

> According to an earlier plan, on December 26, 1960, Roman Tarnowski once again crossed the border and went to East Berlin. Here he appeared in the residency of the Polish People's Republic (*Polska Rzeczpospolita Ludowa*/PRL) intelligence, demanding from its boss, Colonel Władysław Michalski ... several thousand marks for operational purposes. Since he never collected such high amounts, Michalski agreed to give him 5,000, but in a few days, with the consent of the headquarters. The money was collected on January 3, 1961. It was the last meeting of Goleniewski with his colleagues from PRL intelligence. Then they stopped hearing from him, and contact was lost. Today, rich American literature allows you to recreate what happened to him later. On the same afternoon, 'Roman Tarnowski' got into the car and went to the apartment of Kampf. Both of them went peacefully to the zone controlled by the Western Allies (the wall was built only six months later). Here, Goleniewski went to the telephone booth and called the US consulate. He gave an agreed password.[24]

On 6–7 January, Goleniewski was scheduled to return to work in the MSW's Berlin office that housed Department I before returning to Warsaw on 8 January. Only after he failed to appear for the 6 January scheduled operation did the Poles realize they had a problem.

By that time Goleniewski was long gone from Berlin.

Secrets of Kuibyshev?

Goleniewski's defection devastated Polish intelligence. From Piotr Gontarczyk:

> The activities of the Department VI have been completely paralyzed. The services of all agents had to be abandoned because it was not known whether even those who had not been arrested were not recruited. This assumption was the most correct, because before the flight of Goleniewski, the Americans identified over 30 agents of the Department and the Ministry of the Interior, some of whom were recruited.
>
> 'Sniper' has exposed over 100 officers under cover in diplomatic and consular posts of the People's Republic of Poland. Department I estimated that he knew about 90 percent of the intelligence officers working abroad. Thousands of documents were found in the hands of Americans regarding the structure, objectives and methods of operation of the entire Department and Ministry of the Interior. In turn, Department II (counterintelligence), in which Goleniewski served until 1955, assessed that the escapee knew the identity of about 70 of his secret collaborators, half of whom were then abroad. He also had a great knowledge of the methods of penetration of foreign representations and recognized methods of operational activity of foreign special services in Poland.
>
> Morale in the PRL intelligence weakened considerably, depression and discouragement were visible. A death sentence imposed in absentia on Goleniewski may have improved someone's mood, but it did not reduce the size of the disaster.[25]

As head of Section VI, Goleniewski could examine files from other branches of Department I on the pretext of trying to identify potential new recruits. Along with the microdots he sent the CIA in his letters, Goleniewski microfilmed many more pages that he hid in a tree. Once he was safely in the West, a Warsaw-based CIA operative safely retrieved the film. Among other gems, the documents included the Polish secret service analysis and evaluation of the WiN deception operation that now allowed the CIA to better understand just how the Poles pulled off such a stunning intelligence coup.

Following Goleniewski's death, however, reports appeared in the Polish press suggesting that Goleniewski might not be all that he seemed. On 8 July 1993, a journalist named Jacek Kalabinski wrote an article entitled 'Smierc Superszpiega' ('Death of a Superspy') for the prestigious Warsaw paper *Gazeta Wyborcza*. One month later, on 10 August 1993, the paper published a letter commenting on the story by Henryk Bosak. Born in 1931, Bosak entered the MSW in 1956 and served in Rabat, Paris, Geneva, Belgrade, and Budapest before retiring in 1990. He then churned out a series of popular books on the Polish spy service.[26] Bosak claimed that during World War II, Goleniewski joined the Red Army and was sent to the NKVD school in Kuibyshev that trained security cadre for future Soviet rule in Eastern Europe.

Located in a bend on the Volga river south of Kazan, Kuibyshev (renamed Samara after 1991) served as the temporary seat for Soviet government ministries following Moscow's evacuation.[27] In the autumn of 1940 following the Soviet annexation of territory in eastern Poland, the NKVD first set up a base in the city of Gorky to train security cadre from a select group of recruits from Poland, Ukraine, and Belorussia. The outbreak of the June 1941 war put the plan on hold.

In January 1944, the NKVD established a new training camp in Kuibyshev where some two hundred new recruits were brought for basic ideological and intelligence training. They became known as the 'Kuibyshev gang' (the '*Kujbyszewiaey*'), the 'founding fathers' of the Polish security services. Their training ended abruptly that July when Soviet forces occupied sections of once-German controlled Poland. The training camp was now reconstituted on Polish soil.[28]

Following his alleged graduation that July, Bosak claimed Goleniewski was assigned to the intelligence (information) section of the Communist-controlled Polish People's Army (the *Ludowe Wojsko Polskie*/LWP).[29] And that's it. There is no documentation and no detailed description or explanation of how Bosak knew all this.[30] Yet if it were true, would Goleniewski have begun his espionage career as a low-level prison camp guard in 1945?

How then are we to interpret Bosak's claim about Goleniewski's NKVD past? Or that a former head of post-Soviet Polish intelligence named Zbigniew Siemiatkowski would repeat Bosak's story about Kuibyshev? A politician as well as an academic, Siemiatkowski served as Polish Minister of Internal Affairs from 1996 to 1997 and in 2001–2002 as Secretary of State. That same year he switched over to run Poland's intelligence service, the Agencja Wywiadu (AW), until 2004.

In a 3 June 2006 article in *Gazeta Wyborcza* entitled 'Agenci I dezerterzy,' Siemiatkowski critiqued Pawlikowicz's *Tajny Front*, and suggested that Pawlikowicz may have been too dependent on official records.[31] Echoing Bosak, Siemiatkowski states that Goleniewski's former colleagues in Polish intelligence were convinced that he had spent time in Russia not just because of his excellent Russian but also because witnesses saw him in the Kuibyshev camp ('*a takze swiadkowie pamietajacy go ze szkoly NKWD w Kuibyszewie*').[32]

Siemiatkowski then states something even more stunning: '*towarzysze radzieccy*' (Russian advisors) in Department I actually stood up when Goleniewski entered the room:

[Goleniewski] spoke German perfectly, including several dialects. Instantly promoted. His former colleagues associate this with the support that the Soviet comrades gave him. My friends remembered that in the presence of Goleniewski, Soviet advisers in the Department I stood at attention. During numerous stays in Berlin, Goleniewski disappeared for hours. It was widely believed that he was staying with his friend Irmgard Kampf. He was also seen at the NKVD school in Kuibyshev [where colleagues] remembered him.[33]

Siemiatkowski further notes that the WOW court described Goleniewski as an especially trusted man who actively informed the Russian KGB from inside the MSW. Goleniewski's visits to East Berlin also included regular private meetings with the KGB there.[34]

The assumption at the heart of both Bosak's and Siemiatkowski's discussion was that Michal Goleniewski owed his allegiance to Russia and not to Poland. As a protected Soviet asset – if not an outright 'illegal' (*nielegalem*) – his rapid rise in Polish intelligence came, at least in part, courtesy of the Kremlin. He was a '*potrojny agent*' or 'triple agent' for the Poles, the Russians, and the Americans. Yet even if Bosak and Siemiatkowski got some critical facts wrong, they were right in calling attention to Goleniewski's close ties to Russia.

The most remarkable suggestion that Goleniewski's defection may have been a planned KGB operation came from his old boss Colonel Witold Sienkiewicz, who was fired from Department I a few months after Goleniewski hopscotched from East to West.[35] A Polish defector named Janusz Kochanski, who joined Department I in the mid-1950s, describes Sienkiewicz this way:

> A blond, slightly balding, good-looking man with intense blue eyes, he stood about five feet, eleven inches tall and weighed about 200 pounds. Sienkiewicz had been Poland's master spy since 1951. In that year he had replaced his predecessor, General Komar, after Komar fell into party disfavor and was arrested. Sienkiewicz had been secretary of the Communist party in Lodz, a relatively minor post. His background was obscure; rumor had it that he might have been of Lithuanian origin and may at one time have been leader of the Communist youth movement in Lithuania....
>
> Witold Sienkiewicz was, as you would say in the States, the epitome of cool. He could have two drinks or twenty drinks and never get drunk. He never said anything that he would regret. When he looked at you with his cold blue eyes, you felt that he was able to read your mind. And you knew that whatever you were discussing had to be his way. Tough as he was, you respected him. And he was capable at times of a dry sense of humor.

Sienkiewicz also knew how to make an impression at a party:

> Once we had a New Year's Eve party. Sienkiewicz was at the head of the top officers' table with his wife. A slightly drunk guest started going around and the leaders' table asking each of the wives in turn to dance. Sienkiewicz told the fellow to bug off. The fellow said no. Sienkiewicz hit the fellow so hard he could not get up.[36]

Sienkiewicz discussed Goleniewski in a 1987 interview with Henryk Piecuch. A former high-ranking official in the Polish Border Guards (*Wojska Ochrony Pogranicza/ WOP*), Piecuch churned out numerous books on the Polish espionage service. Sienkiewicz's comments appeared in Piecuch's 1997 book *Imperium Sluzb Specijalnych od Gomulki do Kani* (*Secret Service Imperium from Gomulka to Kania*). (Sienkiewicz died on 13 January 1990.) In his interview, Sienkiewicz told Piecuch:

> The Goleniewski affair was supposed to be a special combined operation carried out by the secret service of the MSW in common with the intelligence service of the Soviet Union.[37]

After claiming Goleniewski was neither more nor less crazy than anyone else in Department I, Sienkiewicz said that simply dismissing him as crazy didn't explain anything. He then pondered:

> Or was he an associate of the CIA and we did not know? He was an associate, but we knew that. Because he told us about it. When he received a suggestion of cooperation [with the CIA] he came and reported it. I talked with him personally about the matter. Only later we learned that the Russian advisors received advice to look for contacts from the CIA as he had to do this in such a way that it looked like the Americans themselves had caught him. As you know, he managed it perfectly. The next step was supposed to be the defection of Goleniewski and the spectacular performance of investigating his rights to the Russian throne.[38]

Sienkiewicz claimed the deception operation involved the invention of another false Anastasia (presumably Eugenia Smith): 'A dame was created, which had to help him in this effort.'[39] Sienkiewicz's statement, however, does not correspond to any known facts about the case or, for that matter, to remarks he made at the time of Goleniewski's defection. Sienkiewicz may have been telling the truth and the Russians later explained to him that it was all some incredibly elaborate operation. Or was he deliberately laundering disinformation about Goleniewski to the West?

Sienkiewicz's claim that Goleniewski had been approached by the CIA on one of his trips outside Poland and that he reported the contacts back to headquarters may, for all we know, be true. The KGB may even have agreed to a plan to have Goleniewski 'recruited' as an asset by the CIA. Yet Goleniewski wanted to deal with the FBI, the one American intelligence agency he believed free of KGB infiltration.

Yet at the time of Goleniewski's defection, Colonel Sienkiewicz held a far less conspiratorial explanation of what happened and which to me sounds right. Zbigniew Siemiatkowski reports that former Department I agents remember Sienkiewicz joking at the time, 'That's how romance ends with agents. First romance, later pregnancy, and finally betrayal.'[40]

As someone who knew Goleniewski well, Sienkiewicz was aware of the collapse of his first marriage. Sienkiewicz also seemed to believe that Kampf was pregnant; she was not.[41] Was this one last Goleniewski aria, a plea for personal time in Berlin to break the news to his pregnant mistress that they were done, and perhaps even help arrange an abortion?

In his interview with Piecuch decades later, Sienkiewicz opined, 'Besides, the whole game with the Romanovs seemed very crude. I was convinced that Americans believe, because in the West, they like great historical figures, and Russian in particular. Even so, I was against the game.'[42]

But just what was the game?

Almost no one in America believed Goleniewski was the Tsar. Just the opposite; his royal claim obliterated his credibility. Nor did Colonel Sienkiewicz have a clue as to the purpose of the supposed game:

> Unfortunately, I don't know, further beyond the development of the affair since I was released from the Ministry [MSW].[43] Goleniewski defected and behind the scenes there was much intelligence noise on this matter. If, however, it achieved its operational target is difficult to say.[44]

It is not just 'difficult' but almost impossible to imagine an 'operation' that would allow, for example, the exposure of George Blake, a top MI6 officer whom the Russians valued so highly that for two years they refused to make any changes in their East Berlin communications network they knew the CIA and MI6 tapped in 'Operation Gold' because they wanted to protect Blake from suspicion. What 'operation' further justified the capture of a leading Soviet illegal network in England, the uncovering of top Russian spies in the BND, the near destruction of Polish intelligence, and the countless other cases opened after Goleniewski's microfilms showed just how many NATO secrets the East Bloc services had managed to pilfer?

If Goleniewski's aim were to burrow deep into the FBI or CIA, his quixotic quest for the Romanov throne insured his almost total marginalization by Western intelligence. Yet behind all the rumors and claims one fact seems clear: Goleniewski remained as mysterious to his former colleagues as he did to everyone else.

What, then, are we to make of Kuibyshev?

As far as the known evidence goes, Goleniewski joined the security services in 1945 as a lowly border guard. But as someone who came from a middle-class family and whose father had a background in accounting, he had management skills. Add to that his training at Reichsland. Goleniewski was literate and good with numbers at a time when Poland had just lost close to five million people. Much of Poland's pre-war educated classes no longer existed. The country was in chaos and hovering on the brink of famine as armed bands roamed the countryside. It was a time when the new government needed someone educated like Goleniewski. By all accounts, he was by temperament autocratic, dictatorial, a bully, and a high functioning workaholic. There seems no serious proof that he trained in Kuibyshev, just rumors by anonymous colleagues. But it is not difficult to see the NKVD side of his personality, the Kuibyshev in his soul.

Did the Russians see this as well?

From Piotr Gontarczyk's profile:

During the transformations of security in 1956, Goleniewski was taken away from the army and sent to the Department I of the Ministry of the Interior … where for four years he was the head of Department VI (scientific and technical). On the one hand, he was considered a megalomaniac who treated subordinates badly and was able to attribute his achievements to himself, and on the other he was seen to be hard-working and achieved his own successes. Although he was in a managerial position, he himself recruited and managed the agents, leaving for intelligence missions to the West, usually as a journalist of the Polish Press Agency Roman Tarnowski.[45]

Now we come to the final puzzle, the report that Russian advisors stood up when Goleniewski entered the room. Goleniewski really was trusted by the Russians. One of the first things he boasted about is encapsulated in a line from the 4 January 1961 CIA Berlin Station telegram announcing his defection: 'at same time acts for KGB in UB. Will clarify status in later role.' But why did the Russians trust him? Was it because he was himself Russian?

We end our examination of Goleniewski's time in Poland with that jubilant CIA communication announcing that the man they called 'Sniper' (and whose official cryptonym was BE/VISION) had quite literally come in from the cold. On that night Goleniewski had every reason to feel elated. He had done the impossible: for nearly three straight years he not only fooled his Polish colleagues, but he also double-crossed the mighty KGB as well. Now his daring tightrope walk between East and West had come to an end. He had crossed over.

Yet on that same night he now learned that the Americans had betrayed him. Instead of his reports going straight to J. Edgar Hoover, the Americans had lied to him. His life had been entrusted to the traitors and incompetents in the CIA, the same CIA whose agents now greeted him with open arms on the Consulate's steps.

Goleniewski certainly knew the German saying '*immer schlimmer*' meaning 'worse and worse.' From that night on, his life in the land of the free would become '*immer schlimmer*.' Or, as he summed up his experience years later: 'I came with a lot of goodwill and I was received like a dog.'[46]

A former Polish agent named Janusz Kochanski also recalled how Goleniewski's colleagues in Polish intelligence reacted when the news got out that he crossed over. In his memoir *Double Eagle*, Kochanski remembered when

the chief of the Scientific Department of the Polish Intelligence Service, Col. Goleniewski, failed to return to Poland from one of his foreign trips. Goleniewski traveled abroad quite often, mainly to meet our agents working for Scientific Intelligence. We suspected that Goleniewski had become a traitor, that he had disappeared somewhere in West Germany, and was in the hands of the CIA. Goleniewski would surely have been assassinated by his former colleagues in the UB if they could have got their hands on him, but they could not.[47]

Notes

1 One child, Jerzy, born on 11 January 1950, later played bass guitar from 1973 to 1975 for Poland's premier blues rock band Breakout and was on the band's most famous album entitled *Blues*. He died in 1989.
2 Pawlikowicz (2004), 239.
3 Ibid., 222.
4 Ibid., 240.
5 Ibid., 239–40. All translations from Polish in this chapter have been done by the author.
6 Swiebodzin was the former German town of Schwiebus. Its name changed after the war.
7 Pawlikowicz (2004), 231.
8 Ibid., 234.
9 Ibid., 234–35.
10 Ibid., 241.
11 HO stands for the East German Handelsorganization (trading organization) which, among other things, ran hotels.
12 Pawlikowicz (2004), 242–44.
13 A copy of the Stasi report is in the Tennent Bagley Files, Box 11.
14 Gontarczyk (2013).
15 Pawlikowicz (2004), 240–41,
16 Murphy, Kondrashev, and Bailey (1997), 346.
17 Ibid., 343.
18 Murphy also writes that Goleniewski's first 'Sniper' letter 'had been received in the West in March' making it sound as if the first contact occurred in March 1960. I think Murphy may be indirectly confirming Ted Shackley's memory that Goleniewski first tried to contact the Consulate in March 1958, but that the exchange was botched. Ibid., 343.
19 Ibid., 344. In *Wilderness of Mirrors* (97), David Martin says that when Goleniewski first called and signaled his intention to defect, Howard Roman 'and one other officer' were dispatched from Washington to meet him.
20 Edward Jay Epstein file on Goleniewski, Box 26. 'Hegebai' or 'Hegenbart' may be a confused rendition of the name of a CIA official named Richards Heuer, who served as the CIA desk officer in Washington for the Sniper/Goleniewski case. See Heuer (1987), 413.
21 Martin (1980), 97. Martin says that when Goleniewski signaled his intention to defect, Howard Roman 'and one other officer' were dispatched from Washington to meet him.
22 Tennent Bagley's summary of Goleniewski's last days in 'Ghosts of the Spy Wars' (2015, 23) reads: 'For some suspenseful weeks, he sought an opportunity and finally, while his (suspicious) UB superior was away on Christmas vacation, Goleniewski got, from a temporary replacement, the necessary approval for an official trip to Berlin.' In fact, his trip was cleared through General Moczar.
23 Gontarczyk (2013).
24 Ibid.
25 Ibid.
26 Bosak died in 2015.
27 The embassy of the Polish exile government in London, for example, was based in Kuibyshev until the summer of 1943 when it relocated back to Moscow.
28 On the importance of Kuibyshev, see Applebaum (2012), 69–72.
29 From the Bosak letter:

> *Michal Goleniewski w czasnie II wojny swiatowej wstapil do Armii Czerwonej i z niej zostal skierowany do osrodka NKWD w Kujbyszewie, szkolacego pierwsza kadre sluzby bezpieczenstwa i kotrawywiadu dla krajow Europy Wschodniej. Po jej ukonczeniu, w 1944 roku zostal skierowany do Informacji LWP, osiagajac stanowisko zastepcy szefa Glownego Zarzadu Informacji [GZI] WP.*

Cited in Pawlikowicz (2004), 215. Clarke (1995, 144–45) translates the first section of the passage:

> Goleniewski originally enlisted himself in the Red Army some time during the Second World War and was sent to the Kuybyshew (Kuibyshev) center of the NKVD for top-level intelligence training. Because of his background, he was then appointed to Polish Military Intelligence and graduated in 1944.

Another translation reads:

> During the Second World War, Michal Goleniewski joined the Red Army and was sent to a NKVD center in Kuibyshev, [that was] training the first cadre of security and ideology for the countries of Eastern Europe. After its completion, in 1944 he was directed to the LWP Information, reaching the position of the deputy head of the Central Board of Information [GZI] of the Polish Army. ('Information' means 'intelligence.')

30 Bosak believed that Goleniewski was a genuine defector. Yet he strangely asserts that Irmgard Kampf (whom he calls 'Inge') worked for both the Poles and the West German BND spy service, of which there is no evidence. Bosak, however, claimed in 1959 Polish intelligence in Berlin attracted 'a beautiful German' named 'Inge' [sic], and a few months later Goleniewski took over her case. (Goleniewski met Irmgard Kampf sometime in 1957 or 1958.) 'Inge' persuaded him to defect and put him in contact with the BND. What led Bosak down this rabbit hole is hard to know. See Pawlikowicz (2004), 233–34.

31 Available online at https://archive.fo/20150317131858/wyborcza.pl/1,75402,3391404.html

32 Bosak's claim in his 10 August 1993 letter to *Gazeta Wyborcza* came from older Polish officers as Bosak was eight years old when war broke out.

33 Siemiatkowski (2006) wrote:

> *Posługiwał się perfekcyjnie językiem niemieckim, w tym kilkoma jego dialektami. Błyskawicznie awansował. Jego dawni koledzy wiążą to z poparciem, jakiego udzielali mu towarzysze radzieccy. Koledzy zapamiętali, że w obecności Goleniowskiego doradcy radzieccy w Departamencie I stawali na baczność. Podczas licznych pobytów w Berlinie Goleniewski znikał na całe godziny. Powszechnie sądzono, że przebywał wówczas u swej przyjaciółki Irmgard Kampf. Widywano go też na pamiętające go ze szkoły NKWD w Kujbyszewie.*

34 Siemiatkowski bizarrely asserts that Irmgard Kampf was an MI6 agent! (Bosak just had her working for the BND.) *'Przyjęto założenie graniczace z pewnoscia, ze Goleniewski do wspolpracy z wywiadem brytyjskim sklonila jego berlinska przyjaciolka Kampf – agentka brytyjskiego MI6.'*

35 Col. Witold Sienkiewicz left his post on 31 June 1961 and landed a patronage job running a sports club. A famous 'courier scandal' a few years later further ripped through Department I. On 23 March 1962, Zbigniew Dybala, the deputy director of Department I, committed suicide in his office. The main blow, however, fell on the Polish Ministry of Foreign Affairs (MSZ). The scandal involved black market smuggling. See Bagieriski (2014).

36 Kochanski (1979), 49–50.

37 *'Sprawa Goleniewski miata byc specjalna kombinacja operacyjna przeprowadzana przez wywiad MSW wspolnie z wywiadem Zwiazku Radzieckiego,'* Piecuch (1997), 247.

38 *Czy byl wspolpracownikiem CIA, a mysmy o tym nie wiedzieli? Bo sam nam o tym powiedzial. Gdy otrzymal propozycie wspolpracy, przyszedl I zameldowal. Rozmawialum z nim osobiscie na ten temat. Dopiero pozniej sie dowiedzialem, ze od towarzyszy radziekich otrzymal rade, aby szukal kontatow z CIA, mial to robie w taki sposob, aby wygladalo, ze Amerykanie sami go*

zlowili. Jak wiadomo, udalo mu sie to doskonale. Nastepnym krokiem miala byc dezercja Gole-niewskinego i odegranie spektaklu z dochodzeniem praw do tronu rosyjskiego. Ibid., 247–48.

39 '*Szykowano nawat jakas dame, ktora miala mu w tych staraniach pomagnc.*' Ibid., 248. On 31 December 1963, Smith first met Goleniewski. He proclaimed Smith his older sister Anastasia; she proclaimed him her younger brother Alexi.

40 '*Tak koncza sie romanse z agentkami. Najpierw romans, potem ciaza, a na koncu zdrada.*'

41 The couple would only have their one and only child Tatiana in 1964.

42 '*Poza tym, cala gra w Romanowow wydawala mi sie bardzo prostacka. Przekonywano mnie, ze Amerykanie uwierza, gdyz na Zachodzie bardzo lubia wielkie postaci historyczne, a rosyjskie w szczegolnosci. Mimo to, bylem przeciwny grze.*' Piecuch, 248.

43 Sienkiewicz was dismissed from the MSW around June 1961, six months after Goleniewski's defection.

44 '*Niestety, nie wiem, jak dalej rozwijala sie ta sprawa, albowiem zostalem zwolniony z resortu. Goleniewski zdezerterowal, w kuluarach bylo duzo szumu informacyjnego na ten temat. Czy jednak osiagnieto zakladane cele operacyjne, trudno powiedziec.*' Piecuch (1997), 247–48.

45 Gontarczyk (2013)

46 In the taped transcript of the 'Burg-Anastasia' conversation released by Robert Speller on 17 February 1965 there is this exchange: 'ANASTASIA: All you would like I will do for you…. BURG: I came with a lot of good will and I was received like a dog.' See the *White Book*, 172.

47 Kochanski (1979), 147.

4

'SICK THINK'

The Bryn defection

One possible clue to Goleniewski's rocky relations with the CIA had nothing directly to do with him. It involved a Polish diplomat and former spy named Jerzy Bryn, whom the CIA wrongly concluded was a false defector. Goleniewski, however, told the CIA that Bryn was sincere. In his 25 January 1960 Sniper letter, he wrote:

> The case against BRYN is being zealously prepared. They have almost completely broken BRYN by showing him that the places where he was allegedly in your imprisonment were invented and that his descriptions do not fit the way the places actually are. They undertook through the KGB, through special officers of O-II and through the Chinese intelligence service, an exact check on BRYN's statements which has proved even more the falsity of BRYN's statements.[1] In connection with the cases of MONAT, BRYN, and the Czech attaché, preparations are being made here [Prague] and in Poland to remove all Jews from the intelligence services.[2] Thus, in the immediate future around 30 Jews from Department I will be dismissed under various excuses. In O-II the 'purging' action has been almost completed. (There are still two Jews left.) In the military CE [Counter espionage, Polish Military Internal Service (*Wojskowa Służba Wewnętrzna*/WSW] ... the purge is in full swing.[3]

From late August 1958 to early April 1959, Jerzy Bryn, the First Secretary in the Polish Embassy in Tokyo, defected to the West and was flown to an American military base in Okinawa for questioning. Before becoming a diplomat, Bryn served as a colonel in Polish military intelligence where he helped run an illegal spy

DOI: 10.4324/9781003051114-6

network in France from 1948 to 1952. After a stint in the General Staff, Bryn joined the diplomatic corps in 1957.

Bryn had been recalled to Warsaw from his Tokyo post in August and was scheduled to fly to Israel for a brief vacation before returning to Poland. (Bryn had emigrated to Palestine in 1935 and only returned to Poland in 1947.) Bryn later claimed the CIA had kidnapped him during a stop-over in Manila, but that he eventually escaped and made his way back to the Tokyo Embassy. The Poles, however, concluded that after arriving in Tel Aviv, he defected to the Israelis who then passed him on to the CIA.[4]

Sometime in the summer of 1958 the US began interrogating Bryn in Okinawa. Because of his ability to speak Polish, the CIA's Ted Shackley was temporarily reassigned from Berlin to Japan to assist in the debrief. As David Corn tells the story:

> Several officers in headquarters suspected the Pole was a fake, that he was posing as a defector for a devilish purpose, possibly to plant bad information on the CIA or to discover what the CIA knew of Polish operations. After arriving in Okinawa, Shackley joined Ed Juchniewicz, a CIA case officer based in Tokyo, in interrogating the Pole. They spent months with him and concluded that he was a bona fide defector. But messages whizzed back and forth, as officers in Washington continued to question the Pole's desire to defect.[5]

Goleniewski sent his first Heckenschütze letter in April 1958; Bryn approached the Agency that August. Given reports that Angleton and Helms thought 'Sniper' was fake, did they believe that Goleniewski and Bryn were pawns in some elaborate deception operation? Considering how badly the CIA had been taken in by WiN and related deception games by the Poles, theirs was not an entirely irrational concern. Shackley and Juchniewicz, however, insisted that Bryn was for real even if the defector

> did not help his own case. During his sessions ... he refused to discuss certain portions of his past. There were discrepancies in his cover story. He also was reluctant to talk about his wife, who was a Polish spy still stationed in Paris. Shackley and Juchniewicz ... believed that the Pole was holding back either to protect his wife or to save information for later bargaining. But the two case officers could not take him in unless he was entirely forthcoming. Assessing the Pole became moot. In the midst of the security review, the Pole bolted. Shackley and Juchniewicz had failed to hold on to him. The Pole rushed back to his intelligence service.[6]

Yet after returning to Poland, Bryn failed to convince Warsaw that he was not a traitor. Goleniewski was well aware of the case as Colonel Witold Sienkiewicz, the head of Department I, took part in Bryn's interrogation. Sentenced to death, Bryn was later given life imprisonment; he reportedly died in prison in 1978.

Bryn's treatment was a source of conflict between Goleniewski and the CIA. We have one indication of this in Edward Jay Epstein's 17 May 1981 syndicated article when he writes[7]:

The information he provided in the case of one Col. Bryn was particularly shocking.... American counterintelligence [Angleton] ... did not accept him as a bona fide defector and after interning him in a prison in the Philippines and questioning him, the CIA decided that he was providing them with misleading information and was ordered by the KGB to defect as part of a grander deception. Subsequently Bryn was released in Paris and, in a state of despair and confusion, returned to Poland.[8]

Now, Goleniewski added some very unsettling facts to the case. He stated that not only was Bryn a legitimate defector but had access to critically important information about KGB espionage operations all over Europe. His defection ... had raised fears in the KGB that these clandestine networks would soon be blown. Goleniewski was therefore amazed to find out, when he was vice-chairman of Polish intelligence, that the Americans had released Bryn and allowed him to return to Poland.[9]

Did the CIA use drugs on Bryn? Given the Agency's fascination with MK-ULTRA as an interrogation tool, it is certainly possible. In any event, Epstein continues:

Bryn claimed that the CIA had administered drugs to him and tortured him while he was in the Philippines. Goleniewski concluded by saying that Bryn was immediately arrested in Warsaw, interrogated, and sentenced to death for attempted defection.

If the CIA accepted Goleniewski's inside account, it meant that they had made a tragic error in judging Bryn a false defector. In a sense, the CIA officers involved had signed his death warrant by allowing him to return to Poland. Moreover, they had lost forever valuable information about the KGB underground in Europe.

Clearly the CIA had made a colossal blunder. Yet if Epstein is right, Sniper too was labeled suspicious because the CIA was protecting another mysterious asset:

It was especially difficult to believe that such a gross error had been made in the Bryn case because the CIA had received information from a very important source suggesting that Bryn was a fake. Was this source not to be discredited?

This mysterious source, if there really was one, remains unknown. Yet justifying the CIA source's bona fides meant that Goleniewski's debriefing may have gone off the rails if what Goleniewski next told Epstein is at all true:

Goleniewski's credentials were intensively re-examined. He later recalled that he was mistreated and found himself progressively isolated from his case officer. He claimed that at one point he was drugged into unconsciousness. He recalled being in a state of 'full narcosis.'

When Epstein questioned Angleton about what happened, the former CI chief told his journalist friend: 'The Goleniewski case was the most complicated defection we had ever dealt with in the CIA … no one knew what to believe.' Yet for years Angleton's defenders would rationalize his actions based on claims that Goleniewski was a Soviet 'plant.' As David Martin notes in *Wilderness of Mirrors*:

Angleton still maintained that Goleniewski was a Soviet provocation agent. If that was the case, then the Soviets had deliberately blown [top Soviet spy George] Blake as part of some larger operation. At first blush, Angleton's scenario was almost too callous and byzantine to contemplate. It means that the Soviets had given up not only Blake but also Lonsdale [the Soviet illegal in England] and his entire network as well. And that was not all. A third Soviet spy, Heinz Felfe of West Germany's Federal Intelligence Agency (BND), had also been captured through leads supplied by Goleniewski.[10]

Martin quotes one CIA agent as saying that Goleniewski was 'the best defector the US ever had.' Yet with his inexorable logic

Angleton maintained that Goleniewski was a Soviet provocation, a KGB trick designed to lead the CIA into some devilish trap. What could possibly be worth the loss of three such well-placed spies? 'It's hard for me to answer that without knowing the value of what they were trying to protect,' a counter-intelligence officer responded.[11]

Angleton's defenders now developed an elaborate explanation to justify his suspicion:

The temptation was to dismiss Angleton's thesis, but a subsequent analysis concluded that Goleniewski had unwittingly allowed himself to be used by the Russians as a conduit for passing selected intelligence to the West. 'The key to the Goleniewski case,' a counterintelligence officer explained, 'is that the Soviets became aware that somebody was writing these letters. There was a feedback in Goleniewski's later letters of things he'd learned from the Soviets which reflected things he'd already told us…. The Soviets began inserting corrections into his previous information.'[12]

Was this brilliant counter-intelligence analysis? Or a textbook example of what Angleton's CIA critics labeled yet more evidence of Angleton's 'sick think' that had so crippled the Agency?

According to the CIA's Howard Roman, a close read of the Sniper material showed that

> the general content had at first concerned Polish cases but that the focus had gradually shifted to intelligence picked up from the Soviets. 'He had been dropped as an agent by the Soviets and this was one thing that was eating at him when he turned to us,' a counterintelligence officer said of Goleniewski. 'He was out of favor, but in fairly short order after he began writing to us, they picked him up again, and the content turned around to things the Soviets were telling him particularly about the British.'[13]

As the Polish records make clear, none of this is true. Far from being on the out with the Russians when he first reached out to the USA in the spring of 1958, Goleniewski had been promoted to head of Section VI of Department I of Polish intelligence. As for the Russians, they viewed him as a top KGB informant inside Polish intelligence. Yet Martin continues:

> Viewed from that perspective, Angleton's conviction that, wittingly or unwittingly, Goleniewski was a Soviet provocateur agent appeared much more plausible than it had at first. Not all the information Goleniewski included in his letters was necessarily fed to him by the KGB for CIA consumption. Some of his most important leads might well have reflected information he had learned before he came under Soviet control. Only the Felfe lead looked like a deliberate plant.... There were elements of the case that suggested that once Goleniewski had delivered the Felfe lead, the KGB decided the game was no longer worth all the damage he was doing on his own.

None of this makes sense. Why would the CIA think the lead on Felfe was a 'deliberate plant' by the KGB to ruin one of its top agents inside West German intelligence? It was Goleniewski's information, after all, that led the CIA to finally catch Felfe.

Martin's source next claims that the KGB made a rather odd decision:

> In what looked like a deliberate attempt to get him out of its hair, the KGB ordered his travel restricted and enlisted his aid in searching for a penetration agent who he knew could only be himself. Terrified that the KGB was on to him, Goleniewski fled.[14]

Again, none of this seems rooted in fact, although it does follow the script that Angleton fed sympathetic journalists.

As for *Wilderness of Mirrors*, it is worth pointing out the controversy surrounding it. In the 18 May 1980 *New York Times Book Review*, Edward Jay Epstein subjected Martin to a devastating attack. Epstein pointed out that Martin's key source, Clare Edward Petty, a former member of Angleton's staff, had left the SIG (Special

Investigations Group) some months before it was shut down. Petty did so after he concluded that Angleton, his longtime boss, was himself a Soviet 'mole.' By concealing that rather important fact, Martin had done his readers a major disservice.

However, as should be clear, the passages I am selecting from *Wilderness* are those aimed at defending Angleton's attacks on Goleniewski dating back to the Sniper period. Howard Roman's defense of Angleton and Helms, for example, sounds like a long-standing Angleton 'party line.' Did the fact that Roman's wife Jane was a veteran OSS X-2 counterintelligence officer who served as a top official in Angleton's CI staff influence his view?

Decades later Goleniewski again made clear his view of the CIA:

> It is a matter of fact that the most difficult, complicated and dangerous discovery on my part was about an existence in the CIA of KGB agents, who betrayed Colonel Popov and Colonel Penkovskii, and my activities too, and who through disinformation caused the death of two genuine defectors, Colonel Bryn, Polish military intelligence O-II Staff Section, and Major Mroz, illegal resident of Polish intelligence department who defected in 1959 in France. Two days after my arrival in Frankfurt in West Germany, I already in a very detailed manner debriefed the representatives of the CIA 'Bleeke,' 'HONA …' and 'Robert' about all the facts and information finger pointing the existence of KGB penetration of CIA.[15] While this information was completely satisfactory to neutralize said penetration (-s??), nothing was done; in result of my insisting 'Howard' did have with me another session concerning the Soviet penetration in CIA, and again nothing had been undertaken in said matter of real Counter-Intelligence Measures, and this status quo is continuing during last more than 20 years.[16]

Popov was a Major in the Soviet Foreign Military Intelligence service, the GRU, and the first Russian after World War II to collaborate with the CIA. He supplied information to the CIA from 1953 to 1958. He was arrested in 1959, although the reasons for his arrest remain disputed, and executed by the Soviets in 1960.[17] Penkovsky was a colonel in the GRU who passed documents to the British and American intelligence services and is credited with supplying crucial information to defuse the Cuban Missile Crisis. He was captured by the Soviets, again in mysterious circumstances, and later executed in 1963.[18]

But who were these mysterious CIA agents who supposedly betrayed Popov and Penkovsky? And how would Goleniewski even know their names? Much like Angleton, Goleniewski did not offer any solid evidence, much less names, to support his allegations.

'Monster plot'

By the late 1970s, Goleniewski had drifted even deeper into the twilight world of *Double Eagle*. Except for one brief flicker, the world had heard the last from him.

On 24 November 1979, UPI reported Goleniewski's claim that the Ayatollah Khomeini was a Russian agent who was recruited in the early 1950s. One of five top Soviet agents in Iran, Goleniewski claimed that Khomeini reported to an Iraqi official, who passed the information to the KGB through its agent in Warsaw.[19]

No one cared.

Yet, astonishingly, just a few months later Goleniewski suddenly made the news again, not in obscure rightist publications but in the *New York Times* and *The Times* of London. Even more strange, Goleniewski owed it all to James Angleton. As we will see, the Angleton network tried to use Goleniewski in the hope that he would endorse their claim that former MI5 Director Sir Roger Hollis was a Soviet spy.

The 'Goleniewski revival' was the by-product of a bitter dispute in the CIA led by Angleton, who was forced out of the Agency in late December 1974.[20] Angleton was convinced the CIA had been taken in by a massive Soviet deception operation. The Russians had sent a string of false defectors to manipulate the West, all the while protecting a presumed Soviet mole high up in CIA, most likely in the Soviet Bloc Division. The operation supposedly ran as a cybernetic information feedback loop with the false defectors and the mole carefully calibrating and recalibrating the core deception message. Ironically, it was Angleton's promotion of the theories of one Soviet defector named Anatoliy Golitsyn that led him to his startling conclusions.

Our story begins some 11 months after Goleniewski crossed over to West Berlin when on 15 December 1961 Golitsyn, a KGB officer from the Soviet Union's Embassy in Helsinki, Finland, defected.[21] In the view of one CIA official who spoke for many, Golitsyn was 'a highly egocentric individual with an extremely conspiratorial turn of mind; after his defection, he became certifiably paranoid.'[22] Whether Golitsyn really was 'certifiable' is hard to know; what seems certain is that he shared Goleniewski's buzz saw personality. Golitsyn even claimed that in 1952 he and another KGB officer secretly sent a letter to the Soviet Central Committee criticizing the spy agency and proposing changes. Stalin then personally invited Golitsyn and his friend to a meeting where they convinced Uncle Joe of the correctness of their views.[23] In his 1984 book *New Lies for Old*, Golitsyn recalls: 'In connection with this proposal, he [Golitsyn] attended a meeting of the Secretariat chaired by Stalin and a meeting of the Presidium chaired by Malenkov and attended by Khrushchev, Brezhnev, and Bulganin.'[24]

Few believed him. From a 2011 CIA analysis of Golitsyn:

> It is not clear whether any independent corroboration of this incident was ever obtained. On the face of it, it seems highly unlikely that Golitsyn, at the time a 26-year-old junior officer in the KGB, would have gotten an audience with Stalin, much less been able to convince Stalin to reinstate banished KGB leaders.[25]

Goleniewski found Golitsyn's claim hilarious. He commented that it 'is a matter of great entertainment in various KGB and GRU schools in the Soviet Union and among some of the knowledgeable Chiefs of Western Security and

Counter-Intelligence Agencies (Netherlands, France, etc.)' that 'the US Government approved as true publication' of Golitsyn's claims. In fact, the US government never approved 'as true' Golitsyn's far-fetched claims.

Goleniewski said that he was even asked by the CIA what he made of Golitsyn:

> I was debriefed about Golitsyn's past and status in the structure of the KGB that was based on Golitsyn's own information. Because Golitsyn without any reason offended the Chief of the SU [Soviet Bloc] Division of CIA, who was one of the most appreciated and brilliant men in this Agency, and also requested a payment of $1,000,000 for information which he still kept to himself, 'Norman,' as well as other representatives of FBI and CIA – who discussed with me this case – expressed concern that this seemed to be a clever and well calculated Soviet KGB provocation.[26]
>
> Despite the fact that during the last 20 years Golitsyn produced many examples supporting aforesaid theory, he found in CIA and especially in British Secret Intelligence Service (SIS) strong support and promotion, and the continuous tolerance of Golitsyn's information about the Communist Strategy of Deception and Disinformation, being written by a KGB officer who was Security Officer (SK) in the third grade Embassy in Helsinki, is elevating Golitsyn to a prominence and authority on matters which he never understood and is not understanding.[27]

Golitsyn was also not short on bold theories: the Sino-Soviet split was a deception as was Khrushchev's de-Stalinization program, the Cuban Missile Crisis, the Yugoslavian-Soviet split, the Romanian-Soviet split, the Albanian–Soviet split, Prague Spring, and even Polish Solidarity which, Golitsyn argued, was secretly controlled by the Polish government, WiN style.

Golitsyn began articulating his KGB 'Master Plan' (or, as a CIA skeptic named John Hart dubbed it, 'Monster Plot') almost as soon as he landed in America.[28] He demanded personal meetings with both President Kennedy and J. Edgar Hoover to explain his recommendations for changes in US–Soviet policy. Astonishingly, he met twice with Attorney General Robert F. Kennedy and a remarkable 11 times with CIA Director John McCone, demonstrating how much support Golitsyn enjoyed inside the CIA and clearly spearheaded by Angleton. In a December 1962 meeting with McCone, Golitsyn explained that the 1956 Soviet invasion of Hungary was a deception operation meant to convince the West that the East Bloc was divided, an argument McCone rejected.

The attempt by the CIA and MI6 to 'sell' Golitsyn was also done at Goleniewski's expense. On 26 April 1968, for example, *Life* magazine ran a huge cover story highlighting the role a top Soviet defector codenamed 'Martel' (Golitsyn) played in unraveling a Soviet spy ring in France.[29] The feature came with a two page insert by John Barry, identified as a correspondent for the *The Sunday Times* of London, who said his paper was now working on its own 'Martel' story. According to Barry, 'Martel' played the key role in exposing the BND's Heinz Felfe and Hans Clemens, the Swedish GRU spy Stig Wennerström, British spy John Vassall, and a French

Defense Agency official named Georges Pâques. Goleniewski's name never appeared in the piece, even though Goleniewski was actually responsible for all these exposes.

To appreciate just how calculated the Barry article was, here is how Edward Jay Epstein discusses Goleniewski's role in catching Pâques in his 'Spy Wars' story:

> A large number of documents that Goleniewski had left for the CIA in the tree trunk in Warsaw contained information stolen from the NATO command. There was, for example, a top-secret June 1960 report on intelligence objectives elaborated by the commanding staff of NATO. Goleniewski claimed that some of these documents had come from a French source married to a Communist. Who had once been associated with the French war college.
>
> In August 1963, French intelligence photographed a NATO official passing an attaché case full of NATO documents to a Soviet Embassy official. He was Georges Pâques, a former director of studies at the war college who had been an aide to the French ministers. During his interrogation, he confessed that he had been spying for the Soviet Union for some 20 years.

'Martel' had done little to expose Pâques. The CIA and MI6 simply padded Golitsyn's resume with Goleniewski's contributions.

As David Martin notes in *Wilderness of Mirrors*, when Golitsyn defected his 'tantalizing information had produced little results' particularly when 'compared to Goleniewski's information, which had led swiftly to the arrests of George Blake, Heinz Felfe, Gordon Lonsdale, and a multitude of accomplices.'[30] The CIA's 2011 assessment of Golitsyn was even more damning:

> During this period, Golitsyn made no claim to having information regarding KGB penetration of CIA beyond Sasha.[31] In his early debriefings, he asserted that Western intelligence was well penetrated by the KGB, but he said nothing about the CIA. In fact, at one point, he said that he 'excluded the possibility that the KGB had any agent placed as high as a country desk in CIA.'
>
> Golitsyn did provide leads to other American agents of the KGB, but none of these was new or timely. He identified William Weisband as a KGB penetration agent of the US Army Security Agency, but Weisband had already been identified and arrested in 1950.
>
> Oddly, in light of his later conspiracy theories, in August 1962, Golitsyn reportedly told debriefers that the Sino–Soviet split was real. However, in discussing the matter with Golitsyn, one of the debriefers speculated on the possibility that the Sino–Soviet split might be a sophisticated Soviet disinformation operation. Not long after, Golitsyn began to espouse that position.[32]

In 1968, the year the *Life* story appeared, Angleton yet again accused Goleniewski of being a Soviet agent. MI5 official Peter Wright recalls traveling to Washington that year to brief the CIA on the investigation of Goleniewski's claim about a 'middling level' agent in MI5. He recalled:

After we left Helms, Angleton said he wanted to discuss with me the question of Goleniewski's being a plant. … Angleton and Helms already suspected that Goleniewski had fallen back under Russian control shortly before he defected. Repeated analysis of the intelligence he provided showed a distinct change in its character from Polish to Russian matters, as if the Russians were deliberately feeding out barium meals of their own intelligence in order to isolate the leak. This analysis was shared by MI5….[33]

Was catching George Blake a 'barium meal' designed to isolate what leak? The only leak was Goleniewski! From almost the first Sniper letter on, top CIA officers like Richard Helms and Angleton, presumably with Dulles's approval, tried to discredit Goleniewski, just as they tried to prove that Jerzy Bryn was a false defector.

Goleniewski aside, how did Golitsyn describe the KGB's master plan? The answer, it turned out, was that the KGB itself was a deception. KGB Chairman Alexander Shelepin had designed a better mousetrap, a new KGB inside the KGB, not unlike a series of Matryoshka dolls. This 'inner' KGB was hermetically sealed off from rest of the organization. The 'outer' KGB functioned as a front controlled by the 'inner' KGB. But what was this separate inner KGB? It was essentially Department D, the KGB's deception unit, on steroids. As we will see, Golitsyn again piggybacked off Goleniewski, who first informed Allen Dulles about Department D's existence.

In December 2011, the CIA's in-house journal *Studies in Intelligence* published an anonymous article entitled 'James J. Angleton, Anatoliy Golitsyn, and the "Monster Plot": Their Impact on CIA Personnel and Operations.' 'Monster Plot,' a takedown of Angleton and Golitsyn based on new archival research, notes that

> Golitsyn's analysis flowed from a 1959 presentation by the then-new KGB director Alexander Shelepin in which Shelepin laid out an initiative to politically attack the West through KGB disinformation operations. (Another source [Goleniewski] had reported similar information previously.) From that, Golitsyn reasons that a super-secret powerful disinformation department had been created to carry out these policies. Also created, he suggested, was a super-secret COMINTERN organization that included as members, among others, Nikita Khrushchev and Che Guevara.
>
> Golitsyn contended that the KGB had sent out multiple provocation agents to carry out this plan. Further, such provocations could not be successful unless there were penetration of the target services to provide feedback on the effect of the efforts. Thus, it was not a question of whether the KGB had penetrated CIA but rather of identifying the penetrations that were certain to exist.[34]

Goleniewski, in contrast, emphatically denied the existence of two KGBs. On 2 July 1980, Edward Jay Epstein interviewed Goleniewski for Canadian TV. Goleniewski first said that the idea that the practice of disinformation was somehow invented in the late 1950s was absurd; disinformation games had been going on for decades. Goleniewski then explained to Epstein that the Soviets employed two types of disinformation. The first, strategic disinformation (or what he said the Soviets called 'Inspiration'), is when a foreign service is provided with a false 'big picture.' A hypothetical example would be the claim that the Soviet elite was badly split between 'hawks' and 'doves.' In the context of 'Inspiration,' this idea would be deliberately disseminated into Western circles from academia to the media to government policy makers to intelligence analysts to encourage a more conciliatory policy designed to 'strengthen' the doves. This would be strategic or conceptual deception as opposed to the kind of tactical deception such as the WiN plot that so bamboozled the CIA and MI6.

Epstein pressed Goleniewski and said that the CIA's Tennent Bagley believed that the KGB's Second Chief Directorate, the counterintelligence operation led by General Oleg Gribanov (Moriarty to Angleton's Holmes), operated as a separate unit apart from the KGB.[35] Goleniewski, however, again dismissed this as nonsense and said that the KGB always functioned as one unified organization. The claim that the KGB had undergone a major reorganization in 1958–1959 was equally erroneous.

In a 12 August 1980 interview with Epstein, Goleniewski claimed that Golitsyn had been sent over by the KGB with a mix of information that the KGB fed him from the likes of Bryn, Mroz, and himself since they had already defected. Moreover, both Mroz and Bryn were military intelligence officers whose service was allied with the GRU. There was no way a KGB functionary like Golitsyn could independently access information on GRU-centered operations.

Goleniewski also vigorously rejected all charges against MI5's Sir Roger Hollis as a Soviet mole. As Epstein writes in his 17 May 1981 *Washington Star* article:

> I ended our lunch by asking Romanoff about Sir Roger Hollis who had been head of MI5 at the time of his defection. Did he think Sir Roger might be a KGB mole?
>
> 'I don't think it would have been possible,' he said. He then ticked off very precisely all the Soviet agents whom MI5 had captured due to the information he personally provided. 'If the KGB had had a mole at the head of MI5, you can be sure all those men would somehow have escaped,' he said.
>
> He suggested that the report that Sir Roger was a mole was quite likely itself a piece of disinformation being circulated by the KGB now in order to discredit British intelligence.

When Goleniewski agreed to meet regularly with Epstein, he presumably knew of his reputation as a literary factotum for Angleton. Did he use his time with Epstein as a way of debunking Angleton? In his 'SELECTED EXAMPLES OF DIS-SEMINATION,' he writes that Golitsyn had maintained a low profile for some years but that 'since approximately 2–3 years some of Soviet agents and dupes, often masquerading as "reporters," "authors," etc., began to elevate Golitsyn again ....'[36] For his part, when Epstein published his 1989 book *Deception*, all mention of

Goleniewski vanished except for a brief acknowledgement that he offered insight into the WiN deception operation in Poland.

The bitterness inside the CIA over Angleton and Golitsyn spilled into a review of *Deception* by Cleveland Cram. In 1975, towards the end of a long career that included the prestigious post of deputy-chief of the CIA's London station, Cram was tasked with writing a history of Angleton's role in the CIA. After six years' work, he turned in a 12-volume study entitled *History of the Counterintelligence Staff 1954–1974.*[37] The still-classified opus excoriated Angleton for the damage he had caused the Agency.

In October 1993, the CIA's Center for the Study of Intelligence published Cram's monograph *Of Moles and Molehunters: A Review of Counterintelligence Literature, 1977–92.* Reviewing *Deception*, Cram writes: 'This is but one of many errors and misinterpretations in the book. Like *Legend* [Epstein's book on Lee Harvey Oswald], it is propaganda for Angleton and essentially dishonest.' In Cram's view, *Deception* 'is one of many bad books inspired by Angleton after his dismissal that have little basis in fact.' On page eight of his monograph, Cram cites Epstein's talks with Goleniewski:

> Some months later Epstein managed to interview Michel Goleniewski, a defector who had become convinced he was the last of the Romanovs but otherwise remained a sensible person. Epstein asked if Goleniewski thought Hollis was a KGB mole, an idea supposed by Angleton. The defector replied in the negative and then listed the Soviet agents MI5 had apprehended from the information he had provided, adding: 'If the KGB had had a mole at the head of MI5, you can be sure all these men would somehow have escaped.'

Cram states that Golitsyn never even outlined the notion of an 'inner' and 'outer' KGB in any of his debriefings. He then adds: 'Moreover, no other Soviet source or defector has ever reported the existence of two KGBs, including the most senior defector of recent times, Oleg Gordievsky.'[38] The 2011 CIA 'Monster Plot' article suggests that Tennent Bagley developed the notion of the 'inner' and 'outer' KGB on his own or simply echoed Angleton. From 'Monster Plot':

> To operate thus [as two KGBs] and to manage CIA penetrations, Bagley would later explain, required a highly secret KGB element independent of the known First and Second Chief Directorates. This would have to be run by a KGB deputy chairman. In order to support and protect Soviet penetrations, KGB and GRU provocations would be dispatched to volunteer to CIA with information designed to cover the penetrations.[39]

Whatever one thinks of Cram's evaluation, his comments underscore the bitter feelings inside the Agency decades after Angleton left the CIA.

In April 1985 Goleniewski issued his own statement, the relentless all cap title of which reads in full: 'SELECTIVE EXAMPLES OF SOVIET DISSEMINATION

THROUGH WESTERN PUBLICATIONS IN RESULT OF ARRANGE-
MENTS, PARTICIPATION AND/OR MALFEASANCE ON THE PART OF
THE UNITED STATES GOVERNMENT (ETC.).' In it, he wrote:

> To my astonishment, I learnt in the meantime, that it was Golitsyn who
> 'learnt' about KGB agents in the CIA, and even the chief of counter-
> intelligence Angleton gave Golitsyn for review personal papers of officers of
> CIA, to enable Golitsyn to identity the KGB agent among the officers of the
> Central Intelligence Agency.

One year earlier in the May 1984 issue of *Double Eagle* (X/5), Goleniewski
remarked:

> It could be proven before US District Court that it was not Golitsyn who
> supplied the US Government with information and documentary evidence,
> concerning the Soviet agents: Wennerstrom, Philby, Blunt, and the still
> undetected KGB top agent in CIA (now retired), who eventually used Golit-
> syn for his own protection through distracting and misleading the
> investigations.

It was not hard to guess who the 'now retired' CIA agent was.

Tennent Bagley

When Albert Einstein used the term 'spooky action at a distance' to criticize the
Copenhagen interpretation of quantum theory, he was speaking about two elec-
trons and not Michal Goleniewski and Tennent 'Pete' Bagley. Yet 'spooky action
at a distance' is not a bad way of describing their relationship.

When Goleniewski was working for Polish intelligence, Bagley helped run the
Polish desk at the CIA with Howard Roman. When Goleniewski sent his first Sniper
letter to Bern, Bagley was a CIA officer in the Embassy operating under diplomatic
cover. As such, it was Bagley who first read the letter. Long after he retired from the
CIA, Bagley, as we shall see later in this study, went to great lengths to try and confirm
Goleniewski's belief about a secret post-war Soviet–Nazi intelligence network.

When Goleniewski spoke of a CIA agent he met in Germany after he defected,
the name he spells in quotes (meaning phonetically) is 'Bleeke.' I assumed this was
Bagley. Bagley, however, said he never met Goleniewski. In an 8 January 1997
letter to Pierre de Villemarest, Bagley wrote: 'I considered him to have had the
sharpest, most sophisticated C-I mind that ever became available to Western
intelligence from the other side. He caused more damage to Soviet Bloc intelligence than any single defector before or since.' After noting that 'I handled his
early anonymous correspondence,' Bagley added that by the time he became the
head of counterintelligence for the CIA's Soviet division, Goleniewski 'was almost
impossible to deal with and I never met him.'[40]

Bagley's admiration for Goleniewski reflected the feelings of other CIA officers who spent years tracking down his leads. One led to a high-ranking Swedish defense official named Stig Wennerström. For years Wennerström served as military attaché at the Swedish Embassy in Washington, all the while in the employ of the GRU. As historian J. J. Widen reports:

> In his capacity as military attaché to Moscow (1949–51) and Washington (1952–57), as well as Air Force Section Chief, Office of the Joint Services Staff, Ministry of Defense (1957–61), and military advisor to the Foreign Ministry on arms control issues (1961–63), Wennerström used his excellent connections with Western diplomats and attachés for espionage purposes, not only against Sweden, but also the United States and other NATO countries, thus serving Soviet military intelligence for almost 15 years.[41]

Swedish intelligence had been tipped off to Wennerström by Arthur Martin, who headed MI5's Soviet counter-espionage section. Martin acted in response to a Sniper letter in which Goleniewski described 'a senior Swedish Air Force officer who had once been a CIA agent, who had been recruited by the Russians when serving in Moscow as the Swedish Air Attaché.'[42] Even in 2006, however, the effect of the CIA and MI6 attempt to discredit Goleniewski still lingered. As Widen writes:

> But other less likely candidates have also been named. In a book of French intelligence written by Roger Faligot and Pascal Krop, they describe the revelations of a Soviet defector named Anatole Golitsyn, who told the CIA that the Soviets had a Swedish colonel in the Air Force working for them. According to [espionage writer Nigel] West and based on his own research and recent discussions with Golitsyn himself, the latter did not contribute to Wennerström being captured. Documents in the archives of Swedish military intelligence also indicated that Golitsyn had little to do with the case being solved.[43]

Faligot and Krop, respected writers on French intelligence, were most likely misled by the April 1968 *Life* puff piece on 'Martel.'

Another astonishing revelation from Goleniewski focused on 'Israel Beer,' one of Israel's foremost military experts, a professor of military history at Tel Aviv University, and a close friend of Israeli Prime Minister David Ben-Gurion. Thanks to Sniper's information, Beer was arrested in April 1961 and quickly confessed that he was a Russian spy. Beer even knew ahead of time about the 1956 Israeli plan to attack Egypt. He passed the information to his handlers, but when the Russians warned Nasser about the impending assault, he refused to believe them.[44] Beer also used his position as a military expert to develop connections into European intelligence agencies; he even had a personal meeting with BND head General Reinhard Gehlen.

Beer claimed to have been born in Vienna in 1912 and to have joined the Austrian Socialist Party and its Socialist Defense Corps (the Shutzbund) to defend against fascist attacks. He later fought in the Spanish Civil War as a member of the International Brigades. Israeli intelligence discovered his entire story was a lie. There was someone named Israel Beer, but he died in the Spanish Civil War. Using his papers, the NKVD fabricated their spy's past. The spy who called himself Israel Beer died in prison in May 1966; his real identity was never established. The Beer and Wennerström arrests were two of the most prominent cases triggered by Goleniewski's revelations. Many others we still know almost nothing about.[45]

Bagley's admiration for Goleniewski then is not surprising and suggests he never fully shared (or later abandoned) Angleton's attempt to discredit Goleniewski. Bagley became close to Angleton after Bagley was appointed head of the counterintelligence section for the CIA's Soviet Division in the early 1960s. Although his post was separate from Angleton's counter-intelligence unit, they now joined forces, no more so than over the 'false defector' controversy that effectively destroyed Bagley's career, the infamous 'Nosenko affair.'

In late May 1962, a KGB agent named Yuri Nosenko approached the CIA from his post in Switzerland, where he was on temporary assignment. Bagley personally helped recruit Nosenko, who officially defected to the USA on 4 February 1964 not long after the assassination of President Kennedy. Angleton, however, soon convinced Bagley that Nosenko was a 'false defector.'

At one point in the Nosenko affair, Goleniewski claimed that he was approached by the CIA for help on the case. From SELECTED SAMPLES OF DISSEMINATION:

> It is a matter of fact that from the beginning, Nosenko was accepted by senior officials of CIA as genuine defector, and as late as in 1968, the Security Chief of CIA Howard Osborn offered a consultation employment in his Security office (with salary of $24,000 a year), [to me] to handle special matter such as Nosenko's 'whom the professionals do not understand to handle properly during many years ...' (Osborn's statement). At that time despite all other evidence Osborn was convinced that Nosenko was loyal and that his person had been ill-treated by the competent CIA officers who did not understand the importance of Nosenko's information. To the surprise of Osborn, I refused his proposition, and our friendly relation was ended in that way.

The story of the Nosenko defection has padded many a journalist's expense account and there is no need to regurgitate it here, except to say that the CIA has long argued that Nosenko was a legitimate defector and that Bagley and Angleton were wrong. For our purpose, the important point is that at no time did Bagley – at least to my knowledge – suggest that Goleniewski was a false defector. It is even more ironic, then, that a few lines from one Sniper letter would lead one of Angleton's Special Intelligence Group (SIG) stalwarts, Clare Edward Petty, to accuse Bagley of being the dreaded CIA 'mole'!

Angleton long claimed that the most likely Soviet penetration was in the CIA's Soviet Division. Bagley left Switzerland in the fall of 1962 to serve first as chief of counterintelligence in the Soviet Bloc Division and then as its Deputy Chief. With the CIA bitterly split over Nosenko, CIA Director Richard Helms approved a form of harsh interrogation of the defector, who was in effect held as a prisoner for months. Nosenko, however, refused to break. With the investigation at an impasse, Helms reshuffled the deck. Bagley now was put out to pasture as CIA Station Chief in Brussels. He would remain there until he officially retired from the Agency in 1972.

As a young CIA officer in Switzerland, Bagley worked with the Agency's REDCAP program to recruit Soviet and other East Bloc intelligence officers. One of Bagley's operations targeted a Polish intelligence officer named Jan Switala. An apparent passing reference in a Sniper letter to the Switala operation would be used over a decade later to 'prove' that Bagley was the traitor. From *Wilderness of Mirrors*: "'A letter Goleniewski wrote us when he was still in Warsaw provided specific evidence that the Soviets knew of our intention to take a specific operational step,' a CIA officer said.' The source continued: 'For it to get into Goleniewski's letter, the Russians had to have told him about it within two weeks of its formulation in Washington.' In fact, the CIA plan to recruit the Polish officer 'could scarcely have been more tightly held.' Who in Washington leaked it to the Russians?[46] Petty thought he knew the answer: Tennent Bagley!

In his 1981 *Washington Star* profile of Goleniewski, Edward Jay Epstein tells a similar tale. Epstein wanted to promote the idea of the mole. He, however, omitted the fact that his friend Bagley was Petty's chief suspect. Nor could Epstein resist citing as his source the suspiciously chatty KGB Colonel Raina:

> On one occasion, for example, Col. Raina warned that the CIA would attempt to recruit a Polish diplomat in Switzerland. He gave the approximate time and place that the CIA approach would be made. How did Raina know the CIA plans? Romanoff deduced from such tidbits of information that the KGB had indeed succeeded in placing one or more 'moles' in the CIA.

Did Goleniewski really say this to Epstein? Or did Epstein hear what he wanted to hear? In fact, it was far more likely that Polish intelligence learned about the CIA approach directly from its Bern Station Chief. Nor would Raina, a consultant to Department VI, likely be concerned about a REDCAP operation that had nothing to do with his role as an advisor to Goleniewski.

Years later, Bagley spoke with Washington journalist David Wise about the accusation for Wise's book *Molehunt* and explained what he believed really happened:

> Now Bagley himself became a target of Angleton's mole hunters. Ed Petty, a member of the SIG, began digging into his background. Petty fastened on an episode that had taken place years earlier, when Bagley had been stationed in

Bern, handling Soviet operations in the Swiss capital. At the time, Bagley was attempting to recruit an officer of the UB, the Polish intelligence service, in Switzerland. Petty concluded that a phrase in a letter from Michal Goleniewski ... suggested that 'two weeks after approval of the operation by headquarters,' the KGB had advance knowledge of the Swiss recruitment attempt – advance knowledge that could only have come from a mole in the CIA.

Bagley said it proved nothing of the sort. 'I was running the correspondence phase of Sniper in Switzerland,' he said. 'We wrote a letter to a Polish security officer when I was in Bern station.' The letter, an attempt to recruit the Pole to work for the CIA, 'mentioned the man's boss. Sometime later, Goleniewski wrote again, mentioning the name of the UB chief in Bern, "whose name you already know," which meant that Goleniewski knew of our letter. But that doesn't mean there was a mole in CIA. It means the target turned the letter in to his service and our guy [Sniper] was high up enough to know it.'

Bagley said that Petty had interpreted the episode to mean that 'the UB knew of the recruitment attempt in advance, which is quite different.' Petty, nevertheless, wrote an analysis of the Swiss recruitment episode, and of Bagley's file, and concluded that 'Bagley was a candidate to whom we should pay serious attention.'[47]

After Petty wrote a lengthy report arguing that Bagley, one of Angleton's staunchest defenders inside the Agency, was the mole, he waited eagerly for a reply. Finally, Angleton spoke: 'Pete is not a Soviet spy.' At that moment, Petty realized that Bagley was not the mole: Angleton was![48]

Of course, if Bagley *had* been the mole, it seems obvious the first letter Sniper sent to the US Embassy in Bern would have been his last. There would have been spooky action, to be sure, but not at a distance.

Notes

1 'O-II' means 'Oddzial-II' or Branch/Section II as *'oddzial'* can mean branch, section, department in Polish.
2 'MONAT' was Colonel Pawel Monat, who served as Polish military attaché in Washington from 1955–1958. He defected in November 1959. He was also Jewish. Gomulka used his defection to appoint General Kazimierz Witaszewski as Deputy Chief of Staff in charge of Intelligence for the Polish Army. A pro-Soviet hardliner and member of the 'Natolin' group, Witaszewski had been bitterly opposed to Gomulka during the 1956 crisis.
3 The 'Sniper' letter is available online at https://www.cia.gov/readingroom/docs/BORMANN%2C%20MARTIN%20%20%20VOL.%202_0004.pdf
4 Jerzy Bryn is the subject of a forthcoming book by University of Toronto professor Leszek Gluchowski entitled *A Jew Lost in the Cold War* based on Polish archive documents. Gluchowksi has Bryn defecting in Israel. Other reports have him defecting in Japan.
5 Corn (1994), 56–57.
6 Ibid., 57–58. Corn devotes only a few paragraphs to the case and does not mention Bryn by name.
7 Epstein (1981).

8 Bryn first showed up at the Polish Embassy in Tokyo saying he had been kidnapped. He later may have gone to Paris to see his wife.

9 Goleniewski was never 'vice chairman of Polish intelligence.'

10 Martin (1980), 103.

11 Ibid., 104.

12 Ibid.

13 Ibid., 104–05.

14 Ibid., 105

15 Goleniewski wrote on a cheap typewriter and some of the letters in my copy are hard to read. The name could be 'HOHA' or 'HONA' or 'NONA' or even 'WIONA.'

16 From Goleniewski's April 1985 'SELECTED EXAMPLES OF DISSEMINATION' text.

17 For a summary of the Popov case, see Hart (1997).

18 For a detailed account of the Penkovksy case, see Duns (2014).

19 The story aimed to generate publicity for Goleniewski's proposed memoir that never appeared. It cites an attorney named Howard Lipton from the Beverly Hills law firm Kaplan, Livingston, Goodwin, Berkowitz & Selvin that was negotiating with Bantam Books. A former senior editor of *Look* named David Aldrich was reportedly editing the text.

20 There are now several books on Angleton. Besides Mangold (1991), Holzman (2008), and Morley's (2017) biographies, see Epstein (2014). For a critical but sympathetic read of Angleton, see Robarge (2003).

21 Anonymous (2011).

22 Heuer (1987), 390.

23 Technically speaking, the KGB did not exist until 1954. In the post-war period, the NKVD was changed to the MGB (Ministry of State Security) headed by SMERSH's Victor Abakumov until he fell from power. When Beria took over, the spy agency was reorganized once more. It was still the MGB but now had the internal security service (the MVD/Ministry of Internal Affairs) folded into it.

24 Golitsyn (1984), xiv.

25 Anonymous (2011), 44. For his part, Goleniewski claimed he had a long meeting with Leonid Brezhnev when Brezhnev was serving as CP Commissar to the Soviet Armed Forces. Richards (1966), 144.

26 I think the name is 'Norman.' It could be 'Herman' or some other name. Capital letters did not come out very clearly on Goleniewski's old typewriter.

27 Goleniewski (1985).

28 Hart wrote a very critical study of Angleton that was dubbed the 'Monster Plot' report.

29 The main article was written by a former French intelligence agent who had crossed over to the CIA named P. L. Thyraud de Vosjoli.

30 Martin (1980), 149–50.

31 'Sasha' turned out to be a low-level agent named Igor Orlov, who worked as a reported CIA contract agent against the Russian émigré community in Munich. The CIA stopped using him in 1961. Anonymous (2011), 45.

32 Ibid.

33 Wright (1987), 304. We can see Wright echo Howard Roman.

34 Anonymous (2011), 49.

35 Bagley and Epstein at one point discussed jointly writing a book on Soviet defectors.

36 Goleniewski was particularly upset by an article written by a long-time right-wing journalist and private spook named John Rees for the March 1984 issue of the John Birch Society journal *American Opinion*. Rees wrote an article praising Golitsyn.

37 For more on Cram and Angleton, see Morley (2017).

38 Cram (1993), 60.

39 Anonymous (2011), 49.

40 Bagley Archive, Box 13. It is possible that Bagley lied to de Villemarest and 'Bleeke' was Bagley. I think Bagley was most likely telling the truth as he only read the early Sniper communiques as management of Sniper shifted to Washington.

41 Widen (2006), 931–32.

42 Ibid., 938.
43 Ibid.
44 17 April 1961 JTA report available at https://www.jta.org/1961/04/17/archive/high-isra
    eli-military-expert-confesses-spying-for-Russia-israel-stunned.
45 In the March 1976 article in *American Opinion*, for instance, Goleniewski is cited as
    helping expose 'Blekingberg in Denmark and Bytonski in France.' Einar Blechingberg
    was an important diplomat who served as a Commercial Councilor in the Danish
    Embassy in Bonn. After being compromised by Polish intelligence, he provided the
    Poles with 11 documents that included a report on a NATO meeting in Copenhagen.
    He was sentenced to eight years in jail. A 21 February 1959 AP story reported his
    conviction in what AP said was the first major espionage trial in Denmark's history.
        As for Bytonski, in the September 1983 *Double Eagle*, Goleniewski writes (11): 'By
    the way, Sokolnicki's associate, a certain "Polish" leader Bytonski, operating in Benelux
    and France, as an agent of Division V of the Polish Intelligence Department, had been
    sentenced for his espionage and subversive activities by the Supreme Court to 10 years
    in jail in 1962.' 'Sokolnicki' was the British-based 'Count' Juliusz Nowina-Sokolnicki
    who claimed to be the president of the Polish Government in Exile, a claim few
    recognized. He was backed, however, by a famous Polish military officer and Resistance
    hero named Antoni Jozef Zdrojewski.
46 Martin (1980), 106.
47 Wise (1992), 234–35.
48 Ibid., 235.

5

SAVING SIX

Hunting Harry

Michal Goleniewski almost singlehandedly saved British intelligence from disaster when he helped unmask George Blake, a top KGB spy at the heart of MI6. He further exposed a high-level Soviet spy ring that led to the capture of the counterintelligence version of a unicorn – a top Soviet 'illegal' who went by the name 'Gordon Lonsdale.'[1] Goleniewski's information also led to the arrest of yet another Soviet spy in the British Admiralty named William John Vassall. New counterintelligence probes ignited by his testimony may have led to Kim Philby's decision to flee to Moscow.

MI5 first learned about Goleniewski, the spy they code-named LAVINIA, sometime in April 1959 reports MI5's Peter Wright.[2] Wright recalls that a CIA officer named 'Harry Roman' [Howard Roman] filled the Brits in on Sniper's claims that there were two Soviet moles inside British intelligence dubbed 'Lambda 1' and 'Lambda 2.' Goleniewski reported that 'Lambda 2' had been recruited by Polish intelligence while working at the British Embassy in Warsaw in the early 1950s.

In 1952, Harry Houghton, a clerk for the British naval attaché in Warsaw who dabbled in the black market, volunteered to sell secrets to the Poles.[3] Houghton was recruited by Lt. Tadeusz Dialowicki of Polish intelligence in January 1952. That September, Soviet General Yevgeni Pitovranov ordered Houghton to be run by the Russians. He was Lambda 2.

After Houghton was reassigned to England, he landed a job in the British naval facility in Portland called the Admiralty Underwater Weapons Establishment. He then recruited his girlfriend Ethel Gee, a file clerk at the base, to spy with him. Houghton began supplying the Russians with naval secrets, including the design plans for the all-important new sonar radar system for the British nuclear submarine fleet. Moscow now assigned one of the Soviet Union's top 'illegals' named Konon Molody, who passed himself off as a Canadian businessman named 'Gordon

DOI: 10.4324/9781003051114-7

Lonsdale,' to support the operation.[4] As a child, Molody lived in America and had little trouble passing himself off as either American or Canadian. Two other ring members were a husband and wife team who ran a secret radio transmitter. They called themselves the Krogers, and their cover was as owners of an antiquarian bookstore. Their real names were Morris and Lona Cohen. Members of the Rosenberg spy ring, Lona smuggled atomic bomb plans out of Los Alamos. With Molody and the Cohens, the KGB had sent its A-Team of illegals to England.

When MI5 proved unable to discover who the British diplomat was, the CIA pressed Goleniewski for more details. Then:

> In March 1960, Sniper suddenly sent further information about Lambda 2. His name was something like Huiton, and Sniper thought he had been taken over and run illegally by the Russians when he returned to London to work in Naval Intelligence. Only one man fitted Sniper's description: Harry Houghton, who was working in the Underwater Weapons Establishment at Portland, Dorset, and had served in Warsaw in 1952 before joining Naval Intelligence.[5]

Goleniewski knew nothing about the Portland ring. Instead, he provided a list of some 99 documents from the British naval attaché's office in Warsaw that the Poles had obtained as well as the name that began with an H and sounded like 'Huiton.' Now it took just six days to determine that Houghton was the spy. MI5 then placed Harry and Ethel Gee under intense surveillance and uncovered their connections to both 'Lonsdale' and the 'Krogers.'[6]

Decades later, MI5's great counterintelligence success would be used by James Angleton's stalwarts in British intelligence such as Peter Wright to suggest that former MI5 Director General Sir Roger Hollis was a Soviet spy! The far-right intelligence writer Robert Moss reported in a 1980 *Daily Telegraph* story that Goleniewski was informed by Colonel Raina that there was a 'pig' (i.e. a mole) in Polish intelligence spying for the West in March 1960, the same month MI5 got hold of LAVINIA's new information.[7] It seems likely that Moss's source wished to suggest there had been a tip-off in 1960 from a top MI5 official (presumably Hollis), who must have tipped off the Russians that there was some leak in Warsaw. Although the CIA still had no idea who Sniper was, it was obvious that he was an official inside Polish intelligence.

MI5's Peter Wright, however, dates the 'pig' talk to 'the last week of July' 1960. He does so to suggest this was when the Russians knew their spy ring had been blown.

> One fragment of his [Goleniewski's] story seemed devastating in the context of the thread of ambiguity which ran through the Lonsdale case. He told the CIA that in the last week of July a senior officer in the UB told him the Russians knew there was a 'pig' (a spy) in the organization. Goleniewski said that initially he was deputed to assist in the search for the spy, but eventually, by Christmas, realized he himself was falling under suspicion, so he defected.

'The last week in July.' I read the CIA account of Sniper's debriefing. It started out at me from the page. It seemed so innocuous a phrase. I checked back. Lonsdale was first seen by MI5 meeting Houghton on July 2. He was positively identified on the 11th. We began following him on the 17th. Allow a week for the news to filter through to the Russians. A day to get across to the UB. That takes you to the last week in July![8]

It is first worth noting that Moss claimed Colonel Raina told Goleniewski about the 'pig' in March, while Peter Wright has a Polish UB official told Goleniewski 'in July' that there was a Western spy in the intelligence service.

Wright is emphatic that the supposed leak occurred 'in the last week of July' since that date is pivotal to his larger argument. Both Wright and Moss employed different dates and sources to cast suspicion on Hollis. Yet the CIA's sharing of Sniper intelligence with MI5 either in later March/early April 1960 and the ability of both services to successfully maintain secrecy obviously suggests there were no leaks.

On 7 January 1961, three days after Goleniewski defected, the British arrested the Portland spy ring. They acted out of fear that Goleniewski's disappearance would alert the Russians, who would tip off their network and the illegals would disappear. Yet the Russians had no idea that Goleniewski's defection threatened the Portland spies. Nor could they. Goleniewski knew nothing about the Portland spies. Goleniewski only uncovered Houghton by studying old files and identifying Houghton's initial recruitment in Warsaw years before the Portland ring formed.[9]

Most importantly, the Portland arrests suggest that from April 1959 (when the CIA first mentioned Lambda 2 to MI5) to March–April 1960 (when the CIA shared Sniper's even more detailed information), to 4 January 1961 (when Goleniewski crossed over), and finally to 7 January when the spies were arrested, there was no 'mole' in either Washington or London able to tip off the Russians that the ring was under investigation. Even after Goleniewski defected, the KGB still had between 48 and 72 hours to save their top illegals like Molody and the Cohens, all of whom had emergency escape plans. Yet when they were arrested, all were taken by surprise. The Cohens were sentenced to 20 years in prison but they were released in a 1969 prisoner exchange for the British lecturer Gerald Brooke who had been imprisoned by the Soviets in 1965 for distributing illegal emigré material.[10] Konon Molody was jailed for 25 years but then released in a prisoner swap for British businessman Greville Wynne in 1964.[11]

Their successful arrest and imprisonment casts significant doubt on the suggestion that there were moles in British or American intelligence with access to active investigations. If the 'illegals' had detected even a hint of trouble, the Cohens, for example, would have destroyed their microfilms and microdots. They did not have the chance to do so and MI5's recovery of them now led to the unveiling of another Soviet spy named John Vassall.

The Vassall Affair

The Portland ring investigation led to the September 1962 arrest of John Vassall, yet another spy in the British Admiralty. A homosexual, Vassall had been compromised while serving on the clerical staff of the Naval Attaché in the Moscow Embassy. From 1954–1955, Vassall supplied the Russians with several thousand pages of classified documents on topics like radar systems, torpedoes, and anti-submarine equipment. In Vassall's case, both Anatoliy Golitsyn and Yuri Nosenko did provide critical clues that helped the British catch him, although exactly why they did so is in dispute.

Goleniewski claimed that microfilms and other documents discovered by the Portland spy investigation helped catch Vassall, and he may well be right. From the 6 December 1996 *New York Times* obituary for Vassall:

> His downfall came after the British arrested a group of spies in January 1961 and found microfilm of documents that could only have come from the Admiralty. Even so, it was more than a year before British investigators focused on Mr. Vassall and six more months before he was arrested.

In his autobiography, Vassall recalled that when the Portland arrests were announced, his KGB handler told him 'I was to cease operations altogether until further notice.' It was only around Christmas 1961 that Vassall was given the go-ahead from the Russians to resume spying. The Portland arrests put his spying on hold for a year.[12]

On 16 June 1973, Goleniewski received a letter from Father Ian McLean of the Norbertine Canons, which ran the Our Lady of England Priory in Sussex.[13] After being released from prison, Vassall, a devout Anglo-Catholic, lived at the Priory while working on his autobiography. Father McLean contacted Goleniewski in the hope of learning more background to the arrest so that Vassall could add it to his memoir. Goleniewski believed that Vassall must have come across his name either in a court trial document or at the Vassall Tribunal, a 1963 public inquiry organized by the British government.

In SELECTED EXAMPLES OF DISSEMINATION, Goleniewski writes in response to claims that Anatoliy Golitsyn 'broke the case':

> This [Vassall] case is especially ugly because the competent officers of CIA including its former Chief of CI Staff Angleton and his Deputy James Hunt (whom I learnt [he means met] in person by Director Dulles during my visit to H.Q. of CIA in 1961), knew that already in January of 1961 (Jan. 9 or 10), when I was in Frankfurt a/Main, in accordance with request of CIA representative Bleeke based on the fact that by Lonsdale's residentura had been found microfilm indicating Vassall (and some other persons) to be Soviet-recruited agents, informed him that I knew that Houghton made a list of candidates for agents including Vassall and other data.

It seems clear that Goleniewski's information came from conversations with CIA officials about the Portland ring. It also appears that Houghton recorded Vassall's name as a potential target for Russian recruiters, without knowing that Vassall had been compromised by Moscow years earlier. Because his name was on Houghton's list, MI5 now began watching Vassall and other suspects.

Enter Anatoliy Golitsyn. After Golitsyn defected in mid-December 1961, he offered key clues about Vassall's identity. British espionage writer Chapman Pincher claimed that Golitsyn told MI5's Arthur Martin about

> the recruitment in 1955 of a man in the Naval Attaché's office in the British Embassy in Moscow.... During his service in Moscow the spy had kept the KGB informed about documents passing through his office, as he was a competent photographer. Then, after returning to London, he had held a much more productive post in Naval Intelligence. Golitsyn believed that the spy was still active, being run by KGB agents posing as diplomats in the Soviet Embassy.[14]

As it so happened, Vassall had once studied to be a photographer.

At the very time Golitsyn was handing MI5 Vassall on a plate, Vassall's KGB controllers 'around Christmas' suddenly ordered him to resume his espionage activities. Remarkably, the Brits still could not catch him. Then in late May 1962 Yuri Nosenko passed on still more information to the CIA's Tennent Bagley in Geneva. Nosenko told Bagley that the spy was 'a pederast and had been acquired by homosexual blackmail.' In *Spy Wars*, Bagley describes his first meeting in Geneva when Nosenko put him onto Vassall:

> I filled his glass and was turning to hand it to him when I heard him say to George [Kisevalter], 'We recruited a member of the British naval attaché's office.'[15]
>
> I sat down, picked up my pad, and leaned forward. 'Tell us what you can.'
>
> 'Our guys recognized him as a homosexual and gave him a "friend" who worked for us. They threatened to expose him and got him to agree to work for us. It was a firm recruitment.'
>
> 'Do you know the name, any details at all?'
>
> 'All I know is it happened about five years ago, maybe a bit more. But you can find him. He's in touch with the residentura in London. He's working in the Admiralty.'
>
> 'Who told you?'
>
> 'I don't remember. Someone in the British Department.'[16]

As MI5 had Vassall under close surveillance, it knew he was gay. Thanks to Nosenko, Vassall now became MI5's top suspect; a few months later he was caught. His apartment was filled with incriminating evidence. After his arrest, Vassall willingly confessed to being a Soviet spy.

Chapman Pincher adds that Nosenko said that the spy

'had access to the highest level in the British Navy and gave us all NATO secrets, including documentation which had to do with a Lord.' By that time surveillance had revealed that Vassall was a practicing and promiscuous homosexual, with various partners, including MPs, visiting his flat. As he also worked in the office of the Civil Lord of the Admiralty, he quickly became the prime suspect. He might still have escaped prosecution but for the fact that he had suddenly been instructed by his controller … to resume spying on an even bigger scale. He had been given back his special camera and told to produce as much secret material as possible, as Vassall has confirmed to me personally.[17]

Bagley later became convinced that Nosenko deliberately leaked information on Vassall because

the KGB already knew Vassall to be compromised by Golitsyn's defection. They even played a game to build up Nosenko in Western eyes: after Golitsyn's defection, against all logic, they restored their contact with Vassall, which they had suspended while the British investigated an Admiralty lead from an earlier source.[18]

Although Bagley does not mention him, that 'earlier source' was Goleniewski.

Goleniewski argued that the information that both Golitsyn and Nosenko contributed was provided by the KGB to make them look like legitimate defectors. Both Goleniewski and Bagley thought the KGB was practically begging the British to arrest Vassall. But was there some deeper plot? Later events suggest it was possible that Vassall's arrest was intended to topple the Macmillan government in a new sex scandal and/or to send a threat to other Soviet agents in England that they could be compromised any time the Russians felt like it.

After Vassall was convicted, he was placed in Wormwood Scrubs prison. There he became friends with Colin Jordan, the British tabloid's favorite neo-Nazi. Jordan was serving time for leading an illegal paramilitary group called Spearhead.[19] After a series of extended conversations with Vassall, Jordan wrote British Prime Minister Harold Macmillan and said he wanted to offer a 'shocking picture of a still operative homosexual network of corruption, involving Members of Parliament, high civil servants, and even intelligence officers themselves.'[20]

After Jordan's letter somehow became known, Macmillan was questioned about Jordan in Parliament on 9 July 1963 by an MP named Frederick Bellinger.[21] The Prime Minister now issued a statement saying that Jordan had been interviewed in jail about his allegations, and that there was no substance to his charges. Not to be stopped, Jordan, a Cambridge graduate, penned an article in *National Socialist* to warn about 'a network of homosexual politicians, high civil servants, and others of grave power and prominence, gravely endangering our security.'[22]

Why, of all people, did Vassall decide to confide in Colin Jordan?

For years Vassall played an important role in upper-crust London's homosexual *demi-monde*. He undoubtedly provided the KGB with a gold mine of compromise information for Soviet spies looking to blackmail new targets. One of the leading figures in Vassall's sexual underground was Lord Robert Boothby, a longtime leading Conservative MP and friend of fascist leader Oswald Mosley.[23] Lord Boothby was a bisexual kink-friendly political operative of the highest order, connoisseur of gay brothels, holder of a KBE, and good pal of the notorious Kray Twins gangsters, particularly Ronnie (who was also gay).[24] Boothby also maintained a long-running affair with Macmillan's wife Dorothy.

The London *Sunday Mirror* now ran a story on the ties between Boothby and the Krays that MI5 believed had been given to the newspaper by a rival gang. After the 12 July 1964 story appeared, Boothby sued and won a £40,000 settlement. MI5's Sir Roger Hollis also met with Home Secretary Henry Brooke to assure him that since Boothby had no access to government secrets, there was no threat of a new Profumo Scandal.[25] Yet the *Sunday Mirror* revelations were largely true and it was obvious that the Boothby story was just one of a potentially devastating series of revelations as declassified MI5 files revealed decades later.[26] From a 23 October 2015 *Daily Telegraph* article entitled 'The Spy Files: Lord Boothby's sordid sex parties with Ronnie Kray revealed in MI5 files':

> MI5 interviewed fascist Colin Jordan, a former Wormwood Scrubs inmate, who claimed Boothby went to a 'homosexual brothel' on 'more than one occasions looking for "chickens"… understood to be homosexual parlance for young boys.' Jordan was said to have made a note… after conversations with fellow inmate John Vassall, a 'Russian spy'….[27]

From the KGB's standpoint, Vassall's decision to tell all to Colin Jordan may have been a signal sent to make it clear that Vassall could ruin anyone in the social/ sexual underground his masters chose to attack. If so, the messages delivered by both Golitsyn and Nosenko may even have been designed to force MI5 to arrest Vassall. In such a scenario, the bona fides of the two defectors would be enhanced even as Vassall was deliberately exposed as part of a much larger operation.

In February 1963, not long after Vassall's arrest, Golitsyn decamped to England where he told MI5 that British Prime Minister Harold Wilson was a KGB agent and that the KGB poisoned British Labour Party leader Hugh Gaitskell to bring Wilson to power. Goleniewski found Golitsyn's UK adventure exasperating, writing in the September 1984 issue of *Double Eagle*:

> The question must arise why experienced men from the British Security Service ever believed that Soviet low-ranking KGB officer Golitsyn, who was Security Officer (SK) of the Soviet Embassies in Vienna and Helsinki, using the cover of visa-clerk could obtain any information about top Soviet agents … which could be known on the level of Directors of the Main Directorate or Directorate of KGB.

Decades later Tennent Bagley also returned to the intrigue surrounding Vassall. Bagley was asked:

In December 1961 KGB officer Golitsyn changed sides to the CIA. He soon began providing intelligence about dozens of Soviet agents operating in the West, including an unnamed traitor, perhaps two, working in the UK's Admiralty. One of those was John Vassall. Nosenko later confirmed Vassall was a Soviet spy, but it has been suggested he 'gave up' Vassall to help conceal the second and even more important asset in the Admiralty. Is this possible?

Bagley replied:

Certainly. I gather that British counterintelligence had indications of another KGB source in the Admiralty, though I don't know how their investigation turned out. As for Vassall, Golitsyn gave precise descriptions of secret Admiralty documents that some unknown spy had given the KGB. This enabled MI5 to narrow down the list of candidate suspects to about three, of whom one was Vassall. So Vassall would have been caught without the extra detail that Nosenko later added that pinpointed him.

By the way, here's a fascinating insight into KGB trickery, showing that the KGB did, indeed, sacrifice Vassall – at least to build up Nosenko in our eyes and perhaps also, as you suggest, to hide yet another source in the Admiralty.

Our secret source inside Polish State Security, Michal Goleniewski, had uncovered an important KGB spy in the Admiralty, Harry Houghton. When Goleniewski defected to the West at the end of 1960, the KGB, realizing that he had known about Houghton, saw that the British would now investigate the Admiralty – and possibly stumble upon other mole or moles there. To protect Vassall the KGB took the standard precaution of suspending contact with him. They put the case temporarily 'on ice' as the expression goes.

Then, in late 1961, Anatoly Golitsyn defected. The KGB knew he was aware of Vassall's reporting to the KGB – but chose this unimaginable moment to reverse its normal practice and restored its suspended London contact with Vassall. Then they sent out Nosenko with information that pinpointed Vassall. This guaranteed that MI5 surveillance of Vassall would confirm his contact with the KGB – and make Nosenko look good in Western eyes.[28]

George Blake

After a leading MI6 official named George Blake was arrested in London in April 1961 and accused of being a Soviet spy; he immediately confessed. His capture remains Goleniewski's masterpiece, his espionage Mona Lisa. A Kim Philby in the making, Blake famously betrayed Operation Gold, the CIA's project to tap all Soviet and East Bloc telephone lines by digging a secret tunnel into East Berlin. He further betrayed every MI6 agent he ever met. By catching Blake, Goleniewski literally saved 'Six' from yet another devastating Soviet penetration and dealt the KGB a truly devastating blow.[29]

As Sniper, Goleniewski sent the CIA documents that he said proved Soviet intelligence had a mole in MI6. MI6, however, insisted Sniper had to be wrong. Finally, in January 1961 Goleniewski sat down with two leading MI6 officials and convinced them that he was right. Blake (code-named DIAMOND by the KGB) was arrested three months later.

Goleniewski provided the CIA with three MI6 documents that led to Blake's capture.[30] The first was a Watch List for MI6's Warsaw station listing possible targets for British recruitment. In *Spymaster*, Tennent Bagley claims that a KGB advisor in Warsaw 'apparently in a misplaced desire to help, had ignored standing orders to clear through FCD [KGB First Chief Directorate] Deputy Chief Tiskov any use of information from "Diomid."' Acting on his own, the Russian 'had given the Poles a list of MI6 recruitment targets in Poland.' In a Sniper letter, Goleniewski said that the Poles received the list from the KGB.[31] The second document from the Warsaw MI6 station was a review of its operations. Finally, Goleniewski sent a copy of a MI6 annual report circulated to its stations detailing the spy service's scientific and technical research.

MI5 identified ten individuals from its stations in Berlin and Warsaw who might have had access to the documents, including Blake. MI6, however, decided that none of them was the spy. Instead, it said:

> The best evidence was a burglary of an MI6 station safe in Brussels, which had taken place two years before. Unfortunately, there was no accurate record of the contents of the safe before the burglary. There was evidence that one, and possibly two, of the documents seen by Sniper had been in the safe, but no certainty that all three had been there. In spring 1960, when all ten MI6 officers had been cleared, MI5 and MI6 officially told the Americans that the burglary was the source of Sniper's Lambda I.[32]

As Edward Jay Epstein tells the story in 'Spy Wars':

> 'Heckenschütze' also provided a document that caused serious embarrassment at the British Secret Service – a purported list of 26 Polish officials compiled by British agents in Warsaw as potential targets for recruitment.... When Bagley and other CIA officers evaluated the list, the question arose: How could the KGB have obtained such a sensitive document unless it had a mole inside the British Secret Service?
>
> The British intelligence asserted that the names could have been taken out of the Warsaw telephone directory. The denials were so heated that even the usually suspicious Angleton was prepared to believe that the anonymous mole was a dispatched agent attempting to sow discord between the American and British services.[33]

Epstein then reports:

> to everyone's astonishment, a researcher in the CIA's Eastern European Division discovered that British intelligence had sent essentially the same list to the CIA a year or so earlier. It now became clear to the CIA officers handling the case that the list had not been lifted from the Warsaw phone book, but from the secret files of British intelligence. Allen Dulles, then the Director of Central Intelligence, presented this evidence to his British counterpart, and, after several months of investigating those who had access to the list, British intelligence traced the probable leak to the safe of George Blake.... During his interrogation, Blake admitted that he had spied for the Soviet Union since 1952 and that he had passed virtually every important document the British Secret Service had in its files to the KGB.[34]

The turning point only came a few weeks after Goleniewski defected. On 16 January 1961, he answered detailed questions from MI6's Maurice Oldfield and Harold Shergold. They met Goleniewski just a week after the arrest of the Portland spies. They now learned that before he became head of Section VI, Goleniewski worked in counterintelligence. In such a position, it was not surprising that he would have seen a list of potential targets drawn up for possible recruitment by MI6's Warsaw station. Based on both their conversations and seeing other documents now retrieved from the microfilm he had stashed in Warsaw, Oldfield and Shergold became convinced the burglary explanation could not stand up.[35]

Blake was finally arrested a few months later after returning from Beirut – where he was studying Arabic – to what he thought would be a routine meeting in London. Like the members of the Portland ring, he had no idea he was under suspicion. Once again, there was no advance warning to him from a supposed mole in either Washington or London.[36]

After being found guilty at his trial, Blake received a punitive sentence of 42 years and was imprisoned in Wormwood Scrubs prison. He later escaped from prison in 1966 with the help of a petty criminal Sean Bourke, and two peace activists Michael Randle and Pat Pottle – the trio had befriended Blake in jail. After breaking out of Wormwood Scrubs, he was smuggled to Berlin and then taken by the Soviets to Moscow. Blake died, aged 98, in Russia in December 2020.[37]

The revelations of Blake's betrayal coming on the heels of the Portland arrests so shocked the CIA and MI6 that they now felt compelled to reopen the Philby case:

> The depth of this KGB penetration into British intelligence stunned the CIA ... The Philby case was now reopened. Then, after Blake's confession, Anthony Blunt, a former officer in the British security service (MI5) who had retired at the end of the war, was confronted by British interrogators and, in return for a grant of immunity, admitted that he had served as a Soviet mole.[38]

In 1968 a team of reporters from *The Times* of London published *The Philby Conspiracy*, considered a classic in espionage literature. In it, they write that 'Colonel Michael Goleniewski who Philby knew was also in a position to betray him. It was worth the risk to wait and see if Goleniewski had, in fact, done so, but in the meantime Philby must have activated an emergency plan.'[39]

Goleniewski said he labeled Philby as 'Lambda 3' in his Sniper letters. In the Epstein Archive there is a 20 March 1963 letter by Goleniewski to 'Paul' from the CIA requesting that they meet.[40] It was written shortly after Philby fled to Moscow. Goleniewski wrote that he was 'really surprised' that 'Lambda 3' was able to flee some two years after Goleniewski said he reported on him.[41] In SELECTED EXAMPLES, he writes something similar:

> I had supplied information and commentary evidence which resulted in detecting anew the activities for the Soviets on the part of their top agent in Philby, who in result of delayed in time investigations on the part of SIS, despite my insisting and warning, was able to make a flight to Soviet Union and his subagents could freely continue to work for the Soviets, and some from MI6 could not be arrested. During 1962 at no time did Golitsyn have any knowledge about real activities of Philby, and 'information' which he discovered that he 'knew' during his stay in England in 1963, are classic and supporting his disinformation – fabrications.

In the May 1984 issue of *Double Eagle*, Goleniewski said:

> During December 13–14, 1963, this editor had debriefed in New York City a British representative Col. Lipton about information and leads concerning penetration of the British security service in London. Because of relations of this KGB agent with the British Royal House, this information had been neglected during investigations and generally suppressed.

The agent Goleniewski referred to was Anthony Blunt. What is most interesting, however, is the name 'Col. Lipton,' as this was almost certainly the Labour MP Colonel Marcus Lipton. Lipton famously questioned then Foreign Secretary Harold Macmillan in 1955 about Philby as the 'third man' in league with Guy Burgess and Donald MacLean. Goleniewski also said he was given a George III silver tankard made in London in 1777 by the famed craftsman John Kentenber as an expression of gratitude by British intelligence. (A picture of the tankard is in the *White Book*.) On 8 April 1963, a letter of appreciation from 'H.B.M. SECURITY SERVICE. H.Q. LONDON was sent to the CIA regarding Goleniewski.'[42] The text reads:

> Dear ____
> I think that this may be an appropriate moment at which to put on record our appreciation of the services rendered to the British Security Service by ____.
> Some cases of spies who have been detected and arrested as a result of leads

supplied by him received a great deal of publicity and ___ himself must be aware of how the value of his information has been appreciated and what effective action has been taken. There is, however, a large mass of information which he has provided which is less spectacular and of which he sees no end result.

In fact, often where he has indicated agents or operational targets of Section 6 [of Polish intelligence], we have been able to take effective preventive action which receives no publicity ___. The mass of data which he has provided about individual Intelligence Officers and the organizations and methods of the Polish Intelligence Service has been of inestimable and continuing value. He is still a copious source of information and an invaluable point of reference. We are always impressed by his outstanding expertise, his grasp of detail and his encyclopedic memory.

I hope you will arrange for a suitable message of appreciation to be conveyed to ___ together with our gratitude for the unvarying helpful way in which he replies to the innumerable questions which we have referred to him. At the same time I hope he will accept a George III silver tankard as a token of our appreciation.

On 24 October 1963, Goleniewski received the tankard at his home in Queens from a representative of the CIA named Clemens and witnessed by an FBI official named Joseph Marszalck. The ceremony no doubt helped smooth the way for MI5 Polish expert George Leggett's visit in November (not mentioned by Goleniewski) and Colonel Lipton's follow-up the next month.[43]

Did Philby fear Goleniewski? Were *The Philby Conspiracy* authors right? What seems beyond dispute is that Goleniewski's expose of George Blake and the Portland ring helped push the CIA and the British to take a new look at Philby. Before then, Philby's defenders, including James Angleton, still clung to the belief that Philby was a victim of McCarthyism.[44]

Was there some more specific reason for Philby to fear Goleniewski? John Vassall was arrested on 12 September 1962. Philby vanished from Beirut on 23 January 1963 with British intelligence pressuring him to confess. At the same time, the British were combing through Blake's past. Clearly Goleniewski's revelations forced a re-examination of the Philby affair. But was there something specific linked to Goleniewski's revelations that particularly panicked him? Why did the authors of *The Philby Conspiracy* state that 'Philby knew Goleniewski was in a position to betray him' even as Goleniewski claimed that he raised the Philby case with the CIA before Philby's decision to flee?

'HARRIET' and the Molehunt

When MI5 presented Goleniewski with his George III tankard, little could it have guessed it would receive a poison chalice in return, one that haunted MI5 for years.[45] Goleniewski said he told Colonel Lipton that he believed there was a 'mid-level' Soviet agent in MI5:

I discovered that the Soviets maintained up to 1954/55, on medium level of the British Security Services – an agent of more technical profile who was not directly involved in MI5's operations. Told MI5 representative Lipton this in Dec. 1963 when Lipton arrived to express his deep gratitude of the British government.

Goleniewski's claim touched off an intense investigation of any agent who had spent time in Poland during that period and who could speak Polish or had some connection to Poland. The probe focused on a fast-rising official named Michael Hanley, who at one time ran MI5's Polish desk. After an intense inquiry, Hanley (code-named HARRIET in the probe) was cleared of all charges; in 1972 he became MI5 Director General and would lead the service until 1978.

Was Goleniewski telling the truth? Or was he now engaged in a clever disinformation effort to drive a wedge between the US and British services? The British espionage writer Chapman Pincher implied as much when he wrote:

> An analysis of how Goleniewski's espionage for the CIA had leaked to the KGB prior to his defection – the tip about the existence of a 'pig' – was conducted separately by the CIA and MI5. The MI5 analysis concluded that while there is strong evidence that Goleniewski eventually came under strong KGB pressure in the US and may have been forced into acting as a disinformation agent from 1963 onwards, he was genuine before the time of his defection and for some time afterwards.[46]

Still, even Pincher accepted the validity of Goleniewski's earlier reports. Because Pincher separates MI5's view from that of the CIA, is he referring to Angleton's claim (as cited in *Wilderness of Mirrors*) that Goleniewski had been under KGB control not long after the first Sniper letters arrived in Bern? Given that Peter Wright was Pincher's main source, this could well be the case. But why would Goleniewski suddenly morph into a KGB disinformation agent just two years after defecting?

Wright wondered whether Goleniewski's claim that MI5 had a potential 'middling level agent' was part of an elaborate plot to sow dissension inside the service. Although he didn't think Goleniewski 'was a conscious false defector' as Angleton seemed to believe, Wright opined that he was 'part of a systematic attempt to rupture the all-important Anglo-American intelligence alliance,' a somewhat ironic claim given how much disruption and dissent would be caused by Wright's own allegations against Hollis and others.[47]

Pincher, perhaps thanks to Wright, singles out 1963 as the key date. Was it because Goleniewski was first interviewed by George Leggett, as a representative from MI5, that November? In the *White Book*, Goleniewski says he spoke to Colonel Lipton in December; but he was interviewed first by George Leggett in November. It may be that Lipton's visit was a follow-up to Leggett.[48] As Peter Wright reports:

The 'middling-grade agent' story began in November 1963. Goleniewski, Sniper as he was previously known, finally agreed to meet MI5 to clarify some of the details of the allegations he had made in anonymous letters from Poland. Previously Goleniewski was unwilling to meet anyone directly from MI5 because of our failure to catch Lambda 1, George Blake. But with Blake in jail, Goleniewski was seen by the head of the Polish section, who was himself half Polish by descent.[49]

Goleniewski wrote that he first told Colonel Lipton about the MI5 spy in December and not November, when Leggett met him. It is possible that Goleniewski hinted something about the spy in November to Leggett and that MI5 arranged a follow up with Lipton the next month, as Goleniewski trusted Lipton. To make matters even more murky, we shall later see that it would be towards the end of December 1963 that Goleniewski took the first steps to make public his claim to the Romanov throne.

Angleton contended that if Goleniewski were a KGB plant, and that he only gave information to British intelligence in 1963 that led to the investigation of Hanley, then the KGB must have had an inside source in MI5 to feed Goleniewski material to pull off the potential frame. Angleton concluded, 'with his position, the only person who could acquire' the needed information on Hanley was Sir Roger Hollis.[50] Wright said Goleniewski first told Leggett ('Gregory Stevens') that he believed there was a 'middling-grade agent' in MI5:

> Goleniewski said he knew about the middling-grade agent because he, a friend, and his former superior, had a serious discussion in the 1950s about whether to defect to the West. Deciding between Britain and the USA was difficult. All three agreed that Britain was the better place to live because of the large Polish émigré community, but MI6 was obviously impossible to approach because of Lambda 1 [Blake]. Goleniewski suggested to the other two that they try to contact MI5 through the émigré community in London, which he knew was monitored extensively by D Branch. Goleniewski's chief said that this plan was equally dangerous since he knew the Russians also had a spy inside MI5.
>
> The spy had been recruited by the Third Chief Directorate of the KGB, responsible for the armed services. The Third Chief Directorate had been allowed to keep the agent because he was so important to them, and he was not transferred to the First Chief Directorate, which was the usual practice. The agent had served in the British Army and held rank as a British officer when he was recruited. Goleniewski thought the recruitment had taken place in Eastern Europe and named the Russian KGB colonel who had carried it out. The spy had provided the Russians with valuable Polish counterintelligence, probably because he worked in the Polish section of MI5.[51]

Was this accurate? It is hard to believe such a candid conversation could have taken place, especially given Goleniewski's close relations with the KGB at the time.

Why would anyone risk talking to him? And why would someone as cautious as Goleniewski speak so directly?

Wright next reported:

> There was one other detail. In the mid-1950s the British successfully exfiltrated the Polish premier, Hanke, to the West. This had resulted in an inquiry in Warsaw, which General Serov, then head of the KGB, conducted himself. For some reason the KGB had failed to get advance warning of the exfiltration, and Goleniewski learned that this was because the middling-grade agent was 'on ice,' either because he was under suspicion or because he was abroad and out of contact, or perhaps simply because his nerve was shaky. The spy was apparently on ice for two or three years before resuming work in the Polish section in the late 1950s. Later, when Goleniewski was in Moscow in 1959, he asked a friend in the Third Chief Directorate who was responsible for recruiting the agent, if the operation was still active. His friend expressed surprise that he even knew of the affair and advised him to remain quiet.
>
> 'This is a very dark affair,' he said, 'and I advise you to forget all about it.'[52]

If Wright is to be believed, 'Angleton's doubts about Goleniewski ensured that the story did not have the dramatic impact it might otherwise have had, and in fact only served to strengthen Anglo-American suspicions of both Goleniewski and Hollis.'[53] But was Goleniewski even in Moscow in 1959? Again, only a full declassification of the Sniper letters may provide some hint. According to Chapman Pincher:

> The MI5 management was informed that the Polish defector, Goleniewski, had told the CIA that there was an extremely well-placed KGB agent still inside MI5 headquarters in London. He gave such precise details that they could apply to only one man – Michael Hanley ... then the 45-year-old Director of Protective Security, the branch mainly concerned with preventing the penetration of secret departments by Soviet spies and which had once been run by Hollis.[54]

What may have happened is that Goleniewski sometime in 1963 informed someone in the CIA or FBI about his suspicions. His claim may have gotten back to London and led to the first meeting with George Leggett in November 1963 and the follow-up by Colonel Lipton in December. The George III tankard may even have been given by MI5 to encourage Goleniewski to talk more freely, perhaps by playing on his obsession with royalty.[55]

To add to the sheer strangeness of all this, we are told that when Goleniewski first gave Leggett or Lipton this information, it was ignored. Pincher says that Hollis refused any investigation of Hanley; it was only after Hollis retired at the end of 1965 that MI5 felt free to act on Goleniewski's information.[56] According to Peter Wright:

Goleniewski's allegation was extraordinarily detailed, but because of the overload in Counterintelligence from late 1963 onward, and because of the doubts about Goleniewski's credibility, the allegations were not investigated properly until FLUENCY began sitting. We divided the allegation up into its seven separate indicators, and allotted marks to every candidate who fulfilled each of the criteria. Eight people in MI5 partially fitted Goleniewski's middling-grade agent, but one fitted every single part of it exactly. His name was Michael Hanley, the Director of C Branch.... Solely because he was the proverbial 'perfect fit,' FLUENCY unanimously recommended that Hanley be investigated in connection with Goleniewski's allegation, and he was given the code-name HARRIET.[57]

Hanley now had to face a dramatic inquisition led by MI5 Director Sir Martin Furnival Jones. Again from Wright:

> Throughout the first day, F.J. took Hanley through his life. Hanley was scrupulously honest, sometimes painfully so. He ducked no questions, hid no details of his life or his inner feelings. On the second day, he was given the details of Goleniewski's allegations. He was not shaken in any way. He agreed that he was a perfect fit, but calmly stated he was not a spy, had never been, and had never at any stage been approached by a Russian or anyone else, although at least once a week in Budapest he had met the Russian officer who was alleged to have made the approach.

Watching the interrogation, Wright experienced a kind of epiphany:

> Hanley's interrogation proved that while secret service is a profession of deceit and intrigue, many of its practitioners are men of exceptional character. Here was a proud man, who cherished his achievements and those that he felt might be his to come. One morning he is invited to undergo a trial by ordeal and is stripped apart, year by year, until his soul is bare. All the while he knows that faceless colleagues have dogged his every step, listening at home, listening at the office, listening now. The strain must have been more than most men could bear. No one listening could doubt for one moment that this was an honest man. Hanley was tough, and he showed the system could work. He walked through the fire and emerged unscathed.
>
> That night F.J., Patrick Stewart and I went to my club, the Oxford and Cambridge, to discuss the interrogation. F.J. settled down into a corner with a large Scotch. His eyes were inched, as they were when he was stressed.
> 'Are you satisfied?' he asked dully.
> 'He's in the clear,' I agree.
> Patrick nodded silently.
> 'You'll inform FLUENCY, of course...?' said F.J.

At that moment, Hanley himself walked in unexpectedly. He and I shared the same club, and occasionally ran into each other, but I never expected he would come there so soon after his ordeal. We were in a quiet corner, and he walked past without noticing us, dragging his feet slightly, as if in shock. His normally florid face was white as a sheet.[58]

After Hanley was cleared, MI5 still remained stuck with Goleniewski. MI5 also had to appease Washington:

> After the investigation was closed down, F.J. asked me to visit the CIA and inform them that MI5 considered Hanley cleared of the Goleniewski allegations. It was a job of enormous sensitivity. The CIA were already up in arms ... and were themselves aware of Goleniewski's allegations, and the fact that Hanley was a near-perfect fit.[59]

But why would the CIA take anything Goleniewski said seriously? After all, wasn't he insane? And working for the KGB either shortly after his first Sniper letter or sometime later in 1963? In any case, Wright continues, 'It was essential for the preservation of the alliance that they be left in no doubt about the veracity of our conclusion.' So, the 'preservation of the alliance' depended on how MI5 resolved Goleniewski's claim?

The investigation then shifted from Hanley to another leading MI5 official, a Russia and East Europe expert named George Leggett whose mother was Polish. Leggett had previously recruited David Cornwell (better known as John Le Carré) into MI5. Leggett was interviewed by Peter Wright and would be forced to retire under murky circumstances at age 50 in 1971, as recounted in Wright's book *Spycatcher*.[60] Le Carré's biographer Adam Sisman claims that Wright's account was 'misleading' and 'inaccurate' and that Leggett was 'deeply upset at his treatment after thirty years' loyal service with MI5.' Le Carré would later employ him as a fact checker for his novels.[61] What is not in dispute is that Leggett was unceremoniously forced out of MI5, even though he was the head of the Polish section of counterintelligence and one of its top experts on Soviet and East European affairs.[62]

As for Goleniewski, far from destabilizing MI5, he became its defender. He said that MI5 and the FBI were the only two Western intelligence organizations that the Russians feared. As he put it in a September 1984 *Double Eagle* article entitled 'British Apostles and Angels':

> Indeed, only two Security Agencies in the Western World were even feared and respected by the chiefs of the Soviet KGB and GRU Intelligence Services: MI5 and the FBI. Now, due to various public signals and other information, it appears clearly that the KGB decided through disinformation and subversion, caused by defection, to destabilize both these Western Security Agencies, which since a half a century are terrifying the Soviet agents.

'HARRIET,' Sir Michael Hanley, was elevated to MI5 Director General by Tory Prime Minister Edward Heath in 1972. Heath did so on the recommendation of Lord Victor Rothschild, a former World War II MI5 member, a scientist with a genius IQ, and one of Heath's shadow advisors. Lord Victor was a member of the Cambridge 'Apostles' secret society, and he personally knew some of the Cambridge spies. During World War II, Anthony Blunt and Guy Burgess regularly stayed at Rothschild's London flat.

Part of the Angleton coterie in British intelligence, Lord Victor Rothschild funded both Peter Wright and Chapman Pincher for Pincher's *Their Trade is Treachery*, presumably in a foolhardy attempt to clear his name. He even set up a private bank account for Wright. Pincher would never have written his book without Wright's help; he never would have received it except for Rothschild. Pincher and Wright first met at Rothschild's home in Cambridge. Faced with a legal action to prevent the publication of his memoir *Spycatcher*, Wright revealed in court Lord Rothschild's secret role in the creation of *Their Trade is Treachery*. In so doing, he reignited long-simmering suspicions that Lord Victor had been a Soviet spy. Outraged, Rothschild wrote a 4 December 1986 letter to the *Daily Telegraph* demanding the government clear his name:

> Since at least 1980 up to the present time there have been innuendoes in the press to the effect that I am 'the Fifth Man,' in other words a Soviet agent. The Director-General of MI5 should state publicly that he has unequivocal, repeat, unequivocal, evidence, that I am not, and never have been, a Soviet agent. If the 'regulations' prevent him from making such a statement, which in the present climate I doubt, let him do so through his legal adviser or through any other recognizably authoritative source. I am constrained by the Official Secrets Act, but I write this letter lest it be thought that silence would be an indication of anything other than complete innocence.[63]

In Parliament the next day, Mrs. Thatcher stated for the record:

> I have considered more fully Lord Rothschild's letter to the *Daily Telegraph* yesterday, in which he referred to innuendoes that he had been a Soviet agent. I consider it important to maintain the practice of successive governments of not commenting on security matters. But I am willing to make an exception on the matter raised in Lord Rothschild's letter. I am advised that we have no evidence that he was ever a Soviet agent.[64]

The allegation that Rothschild was the 'Fifth Man' was made in a book published in 1994 by Australian journalist Roland Perry and was based largely on his interviews with former KGB officers.[65] But its conclusions were disputed by Yuri Modin, the KGB controller of the Cambridge Five, who identified John Cairncross as the Fifth Man.[66] Subsequent investigations by other intelligence experts and historians have also identified Cairncross as the 'Fifth Man.'[67]

Notes

1 An illegal is defined by former KGB Archivist Vasili Mitrokhin (2002), 74 as, 'A specially trained individual (an intelligence officer or agent) who lives under instructions from Intelligence, and with the help of Intelligence, in a specific country with identity documents containing new assumed identifying particulars, generally in order to conceal from the authorities and the people around him his national and state affiliation, his true surname, and biographic particulars, thereby creating the conditions for conducting intelligence from illegal positions.' See also Riehle (2020).

2 Wright (1987), 128 states that the Sniper letters began 'earlier in the year' when the source 'began sending letters to the CIA, written in German, detailing information about Polish and Soviet intelligence operations.' The Sniper letters began in April 1958.

3 Houghton wrote a memoir entitled *Operation Portland*. Chapter two is called 'Black Market, Warsaw.' Houghton thrived in shady environments. Although his role as a spy in Warsaw is overshadowed by the Portland affair, he provided the Russians with high-grade intelligence while in Poland. See West and Tsarev (1998), 256–71.

4 See Corera (2018) for more details.

5 Wright (1987), 128–29.

6 Andrew (2009), 484–88.

7 Moss (1980). For Moss' own career as a far-right activist, see Beckett (2002), 187–89.

8 Wright (1987), 142.

9 The Security Services files on the Portland Spy Ring were declassified and released to the UK National Archives in September 2019. They revealed that Houghton's wife had alerted the Admiralty to his treachery in 1955 but that her complaints were written off as a domestic dispute. See https://www.theguardian.com/uk-news/2019/sep/24/portla nd-spy-ring-could-have-been-stopped-four-years-earlier-files-say. [The NA files form the basis for Trevor Barnes' book on the case published in September 2020. See Barnes (2020). CF.]

10 See Platt (2010) and Carr (2016) for more details.

11 Andrew and Mitrokhin (2000), 532–37. Corera (2018).

12 Vassall (1975), 133–36.

13 Father McLean's letter is reprinted in *The White Book* but with deletions for Vassall's name. Also, the way it is copied it is impossible to read McLean's signature. An unredacted copy of the letter, however, is in the Epstein Archive, Box 26.

14 Pincher (1984), 277.

15 Kisevalter, the same CIA official who dealt with Goleniewski.

16 Bagley (2007), 14.

17 Pincher (1984), 279.

18 Bagley (2007), 179.

19 Macklin (2020), 286.

20 Jackson (2017), 121.

21 See https://api.parliament.uk/historic-hansard/people/mr-frederick-bellenger/index.html.

22 Jackson (2017), 121.

23 Macklin (2020), 286.

24 See Pearson (2002).

25 23 October 2015 BBC News at https://www.bbc.com/news/uk-34612729.

26 The Security Service Files on Boothby are available at the UK National Archives, KV 2/ 4096; KV 2/4097. [A full-length study of Boothby including material on his relationship with Kray is now available. See Smith (2020) CF.]

27 The article is available at https://www.telegraph.co.uk/news/uknews/11948323/lord-boothby-sex-parties-ronnie-kray-mi5-documents.html.

28 *Eye Spy* Interview of Bagley, 53 (January 2008) at https://www.iwp.edu/docLib/ 20131119_BagleyT.H.InterviewEyeSpy.pdf.

29 For more on Blake, see Hermiston and Blake's own account, Blake. For more on Blake and the Berlin Tunnel, see Vogel. For Goleniewski and Blake's capture, see Vogel 344–364.

30 In *Spy Wars*, Bagley writes (2007, 291), 'I … had been the case officer of the CIA operation that uncovered Blake.' It is not clear to me if Bagley means he read the Sniper correspondence or that he had been tasked by the CIA specifically to investigate Blake. Or both.

31 Bagley (2013), 97–98.

32 Wright (1987), 128–29. 'Lambda I' was the term Goleniewski used in his Sniper letters to describe the MI6 mole who turned out to be Blake.

33 Epstein (1980).

34 Ibid.

35 West (1988), 134–35.

36 Blake phoned his KGB contact when he was summoned back to the UK, but they assured him there was nothing to worry about. Hermiston (2014), 222–23.

37 For details of the escape, see Bourke (1970); Hermiston (2014); Randle and Pottle (1989). Belatedly, Randle and Pottle were found not guilty of helping Blake escape in 1991.

38 Epstein (1980). For Blunt, see Carter (2001).

39 Page, Leitch, and Knightly (1968), 188.

40 In his 1985 SELECTED EXAMPLES OF DISSEMINATION text, Goleniewski identifies Paul as 'assistant of chief of EE Division at that time.' I think 'EE' stands for Eastern Europe.

41 In the letter Goleniewski also said that in 1962 he alerted Howard [Roman], Pete, Herman, Paul and others (including in the FBI) about France. He said he was assured by Howard and Herman that the case of Mroz (the defector killed outside Paris by Polish intelligence) would be reviewed 'with me' but that nothing happened. He then said the CIA ignored 'the Tartar Group,' ODRA, WiN, and the KGB Third Directorate and that he wanted Paul to visit him. (Epstein archive, box 26.)

42 Reprinted in the *White Book*, 96.

43 On the tankard, see Goleniewski, *White Book*, 87–90. The Spellers' Transglobal News Service in January 1965 put out a press release as well. This was probably done to bolster Goleniewski's credibility because of an impending legal battle with Eugenia Smith, an incident discussed later in this book. The *White Book* reprints an affidavit from Goleniewski dated 21 November 1969 on the tankard where he discusses Lipton (87–90), whom he says was accompanied by a representative of the US government (90). A copy was sent to J. Walter Yeagley of the Internal Security Division of the Department of Justice. (Yeagley was an Assistant Attorney General at the time.)

44 Angleton argued that Philby had simply been duped by his friend Burgess. Mangold (1991), 66–67.

45 The molehunts form the basis of the 2019 spy novel *Witchfinder* by Andrew Williams.

46 Pincher (1984), 255.

47 Wright (1987), 305–06.

48 In *Spycatcher*, Wright refers to Leggett as 'Gregory Stevens' and says he interviewed Goleniewski in 1963. Wright says as well that in 'late 1963' Goleniewski first mentioned the 'middling' MI5-linked agent.

49 Wright (1987), 271.

50 Ibid., 303–04.

51 Ibid., 294.

52 Ibid., 295.

53 Ibid., 306.

54 Pincher (1984), 402.

55 Indeed, in late December Goleniewski would approach the New York publisher Robert Speller to more openly promote his royal claim as we shall soon see.

56 Pincher (1984), 402–03.

57 Wright (1987), 295.

58 Ibid., 302.

59 Ibid., 279.

60 Wright (1987), 294–305, 320–23.

61 Sisman (2015), 358–59.
62 Leggett would later publish an academic study of the Bolshevik's secret police, *The Cheka*.
63 West (1987), 170.
64 Ibid.
65 Perry (2018). For a summary of the case for and against Rothschild see Riley and Dorril (1988) as well as the overview of his career in Dorril and Ramsay (1991), 218–23.
66 The other four in the 'Ring of Five' were obviously Donald Maclean, Guy Burgess, Kim Philby and Anthony Blunt. See Philipps (2018), Lownie (2015), MacIntyre (2015), Carter (2001) and Davenport-Hines (2019) for the latest in a long line of biographies. For Modin's rebuttal, see https://www.independent.co.uk/news/uk/home-news/roth schild-spied-as-the-fifth-man-1444440.html. For his own account, see Modin (1994).
67 Andrew and Gordievsky (1990), 216. See Cairncross (1997) for his own account and later biographies by Andrews (2020) and Smith (2019).

PART II
Hacke

6

RED SWASTIKA

Echoes from the Führerbunker

On 25 January1960, 'Heckenschütze' sent an astonishing report to the CIA.[1] In it, he warned about a secret Nazi–Soviet network he dubbed Hacke.[2] He wrote in his introduction to the Hacke section: 'I warn you very seriously about this dangerous conglomeration of brown–red Fascists who unexpectedly one day can cause enormous damage and who are an acute danger to the free world and to peace.'

Goleniewski's Sniper letter was declassified as part of a Congressional law forcing the CIA to make public all documents relating to the Agency's involvement with Nazi war criminals. Because the letter was anonymous, it is not clear that the declassification panel even knew that Goleniewski was the author. My suspicion is that the letter was declassified by mistake because it was anonymous.

The text of the letter runs to some 20 single-spaced pages; the section on Hacke begins on page 8 and ends on page 13.[3] Throughout the Hacke section, there are at times mistakes when it comes to dates. I cannot tell if this is a mistake in the original (Goleniewski was at times recalling events from almost a decade ago) or whether there are translation errors and/or typos.[4]

I will begin with Goleniewski's overall revelation about Hacke and then focus on one very prominent figure in the Hacke saga, SS Gruppenführer (Major General) Heinrich 'Gestapo' Müller, one of the highest-ranking members in SS intelligence (the RSHA/Reichssicherheitshauptamt).[5]

From the 25 January 1960 letter:

> The fire of Fascist AKTION is being unfolded at present on the political level.[6] It is supposed to be constantly accelerated up to the Summit Conference.[7] The fire of Fascist hate in the Federal Republic, into which the KGB knows how to pour gasoline through its own channels, is supposed to take on

DOI: 10.4324/9781003051114-9

an anti-American accent in the near future as well as be connected with strikes and demonstrations planned by the KPD.[8] As soon as AKTION transfers to the realm of intelligence, it can be connected to the 'fact' that the AIS is well informed about the activity of the Fascists and in fact has an interest in such activity.[9]

I have learned the following: 1) a Nazi cadre organization, which is 'inspired' and 'directed' by RIS penetration agents, has been active for years. This organization, which works out of the darkness above all through 'inspiration,' has various bases in the Federal apparatus and also 'inspires' various legal, radical political organizations in the Federal Republic such as the DRP.[10] The Federal government took advantage – for tactical political reasons – of legal possibilities, but these were intercepted by the KGB and puffed up and stretched out in a compromising fashion. The propaganda agitation to date has also been further artificially developed by the KGB and SSD through illegal members of the KPD as well as IS agents (above all in respect to 'painting').[11]

Beginning in late 1959 and continuing into 1960, a wave of swastika paintings on graves in Jewish cemeteries mysteriously appeared in Germany.[12] Goleniewski told the CIA that the KGB through its agents (and indirectly through far-right groups 'inspired' by the Russians) were behind the attacks. Confessions in various memoirs by former spies as well as the release of files in Russian and East German archives has confirmed that the KGB and Stasi vandalized Jewish cemeteries as part of a campaign to discredit West Germany by promoting the idea that the FRG was riddled with ex-Nazis who were once more on the rise.[13]

The letter continues:

I would now like to clarify and make as concrete as possible the allegations which were already mentioned in Report 9 of November 1959.[14] I unfortunately cannot make any overall statements and there is little likelihood that I will be able to do this in the future. In the following I would like to report to you succinctly various 'mosaic' pieces which I have been able to learn over a long period. At the same time, I would like to emphasize expressly that a number of these are based only on one source and have not been checked by me. The matter, however, is too serious to omit even the smallest thing which could be of the greatest importance. I will therefore sort out the information about the Nazi cadre organization and give it the code word 'HACKE.' It may be that I will be able to learn further details.

But exactly what was Hacke?

'HACKE': Historical introduction. At the end of 1943, in view of the approaching defeat of the Third Reich, the Nationalsozialistische Deutsche Arbeiterpartei (NSDAP/National Socialist German Workers' Party) boss, BORMANN, began to build up a secret Nazi cadre organization unknown to

HITLER and other Nazi bosses. This organization was set up according to the organizational plan of a Free Mason lodge in that there were strict 'secret circles.' The highest secret circle was formed by BORMANN with four other unidentified Nazi leaders; the organization was further set up according to the 'V' pattern (five persons). Members of one 'V' became leaders of further Vs, and the leadership was anonymous to the lower circles. For security reasons BORMANN spread the tale in the lower Vs that HIMMLER was behind 'HACKE.' He succeeded in this because MUELLER, the Chief of Department IV of the RSHA (Gestapo), was on his side because he could foresee the coming defeat.

The first reports were received by MUELLER, who at the beginning of 1944 (or even earlier) had been appropriately influenced by the RIS – and later doubled – in the course of a CE [counterespionage] game run through the chief Gestapo office in Danzig, directed by [Jakob] LÖLLGEN. This case of importance for the Soviet Union was run personally by General ABAKU-MOV, who was shot after the death of Stalin. Only a few people in the RIS and RIS-CE knew about his mysterious matter. One of these was General BESBORODOV, a former advisor of the MGB in Warsaw and a personal friend of ABAKUMOV.

According to BORMANN's plan, HACKE was supposed to be very restrictive in the number of its members (allegedly only 35 persons up to 1944), was to be expanded in accordance with the existing situation, and above all was to be active through the 'inspiration' (of others). For security reasons HACKE bases were built up abroad in order to be able to operate freely and securely after the defeat. The main bases were set up by the end of 1944, especially in Spain, Portugal, Argentina, Japan, and Italy. An enormous organizational capital in gold, jewelry and cash (all from concentration camp 'booty') of an approximate total value of half a billion dollars. Only a few members of the RSHA and SS knew about HACKE because of a deep conflict between BORMANN and HIMMLER.

As soon as the RIS got wind of it, it immediately recognized its importance and did everything to control and also 'inspire' HACKE for as long-range a purpose as possible. The exploitation of HACKE as a take-off point ('glacis') for IS activity by the Soviet Union was self-evident. Without waiting for the end of the war, ABAKUMOV recruited a few members of HACKE by blackmail in view of the imminent defeat as well as with threats of denunciation to HITLER and HIMMLER. ABAKUMOV was not getting sufficient information from the Gestapo Chief MUELLER, who was exploited but not completely trusted by BORMANN. Therefore, after the war the MGB did what it could to learn everything as thoroughly as possible. According to present information, the RIS allegedly succeeded almost completely in this. The KGB evaluates this affair so highly that the various information which is learned through HACKE is not, for example, exploited in counter-espionage operations.

Postwar period: After the war the MGB worked on HACKE in two directions primarily: the maximum investigation of it and the maximum infiltration of MGB agents. HACKE expanded organizationally around 1947–1948 and this opportunity was exploited. The case was all the more important to the MGB because HACKE kept alive the old Nazi slogan, 'Fight the Jews and plutocrats in the USA,' and had as a goal the founding of a Fourth Reich, and this was always hostile to America as well and remained so.

This netherworld alliance of Russian spies and top Nazis would be symbolized by alleged cooperation at the highest level between the Russians and SS General Heinrich Müller, Hitler's Gestapo chief and one of the highest-ranking SS intelligence officers in World War II. As such, Müller helped lead Himmler's Reich Security Main Office, the Reichssicherheitshauptamt (RSHA).

Although few Americans have ever heard of General Müller, millions of Russians knew his name thanks to a TV mini-series entitled *Seventeen Moments of Spring*. A masterpiece of espionage suspense, it became one of the most famous Soviet television series of all time when it debuted in August 1973. The series was written by a KGB-connected journalist and espionage writer named Yulian Semyonov, who was very interested in the postwar Nazi diaspora. He even landed an extremely rare 1974 interview with the infamous former SS Lieutenant-Colonel Otto Skorzeny in Madrid.[15]

Seventeen Moments depicts a Berlin-based Soviet agent working undercover as 'Max von Stierlitz' in SS intelligence towards the very end of the war, where he worked closely with Müller and SD intelligence chief Walter Schellenberg. Stierlitz's assignment, straight from Stalin, is to investigate secret negotiations between SS General Karl Wolff and Allen Dulles, the head of the Office of Strategic Studies (OSS)in Bern, Switzerland.[16] Müller is portrayed brilliantly in the series as being both peasant folksy (he is especially fond of apples) and utterly ruthless, a lovable granddad from hell.[17]

Goleniewski framed Hacke in the larger context of a murky war inside Russian intelligence over the former head of SMERSH, General Victor Abakumov, at one time one of the most powerful men in the Soviet Union. Established in 1942, SMERSH coordinated three separate Red Army counter-intelligence units. With an estimated 150,000 agents, SMERSH operated on a 2,400-mile front. As Abakumov's personal fief, SMERSH was 'hors des organismes "classique" qu'étaient le NKVD et le GRU.'[18] After the war, Abakumov took control of the MGB, the Ministry for State Security, the successor organization to the NKVD that, in turn, would later be replaced by the KGB.

In 1951, the wheel turned yet again. Abakumov was arrested and brutally tortured after one of his subordinates told Stalin that Abakumov had ignored the 'Jewish Doctors' Plot' to murder the Soviet leader.[19] Even after Stalin's death in March 1953 – and the collapse of the 'Doctors' Plot' allegation – Abakumov remained in jail; he was executed on 19 December 1954, ostensibly for his role in the 1949 'Leningrad Affair' and the resulting death of two Politburo members. Nikita Khrushchev particularly loathed Abakumov and it was he who ordered his death.[20]

In the summer of 1951, in the midst of the power struggle in Moscow, Goleniewski said he reportedly uncovered the first inklings of Hacke via his interrogation of Albert Foerster, the former Gauleiter of Danzig. Born in Bavaria in 1902, Foerster was an early member of the NSDAP, and his connections with Hitler and Rudolf Hess dated back to the Beer Hall Putsch.[21] Hitler and Hess also served as witnesses at the wedding of Foerster and Gertrud Deetz.[22]

In 1930 Foerster became the Nazi Gauleiter in Danzig. He would later clash with Himmler over the rate and implementation of the SS 'Germanization' policy of ethnically cleansing Poles from towns and villages in Poland and replacing them with Germans.[23] Foerster then allied himself with Martin Bormann, Himmler's main rival inside the Nazi Party and the man who replaced Rudolf Hess as Deputy Führer in his role as Chief of the Nazi Party Chancellery.

After fleeing Poland for Germany at the close of the war, Foerster was arrested in the British sector in Hamburg on 27 May 1945; in July 1946 he was identified as the former Gauleiter. In August 1946, the British returned him to Warsaw for war crimes prosecution. Foerster was sentenced to death in 1948, but his execution was postponed until 28 February 1952 when, at age 49, he was hanged.[24]

In his letter, 'Sniper' said Foerster broke under pressure from a Polish interrogator named Colonel Jozef Rozanski:

> In 1950 [1948] in Danzig (Poland) the former Gauleiter FOERSTER was sentenced to death as a war criminal. The sentence, however, was not carried out up to 1952. According to ['Gestapo'] MUELLER's reports, FOERSTER was a member of HACKE. Representatives of the MGB as well as representatives of the former MBP interrogated FOERSTER continuously after his death sentence (above all the notorious chief of the Investigative Department Colonel [Jozef] ROZANSKI, who was sentenced in 1957) in order to squeeze out of FOERSTER information about HACKE among other things. FOERSTER did not withstand the pressure of imminent death which lasted almost two years (a few times he was led out to his execution which then did not take place) and told everything he knew. Immediately after he began to talk about the middle of 1952 [1951], he was taken out of the Danzig prison by special representatives of the MGB from Moscow and was taken to Moscow in a special plane. Since that time all traces of FOERSTER have vanished and it is not clear whether he still lives today, or was executed, or 'escaped' from the Soviet Union as an MGB agent in order to play his role in HACKE.

> At the time of the trial of the former Gauleiter KOCH in Warsaw, General [Mieczyslaw] MOCZAR learned that KOCH had been kept so long in the Soviet Union in order to squeeze information about HACKE out of him too, but this did not fully succeed so they tried to put pressure on KOCH by means of the trial. It allegedly turned out that KOCH actually knew something about HACKE but he himself was not a member.

Goleniewski stated that although he never personally met Müller, he learned from his KGB friends that sometime between 1950 and 1952 Müller had been brought to Moscow for further interrogations. From a report by the US Nazi War Crimes Interagency Working Group:

> The January 1961 defection and interrogation of a Polish intelligence officer brought Western counterintelligence tips that led to several Soviet and Polish agents active in the West.... The defector surely was Lt. Col. Michal Goleniewski, the Deputy Chief of Polish Military Counterintelligence until 1958, who had also operated as a mole for the KGB in the Polish service. In recounting his work as an interrogator of captured German officials in Poland from 1948 to 1952, Goleniewski revealed information about the fate of some Nazi intelligence officials, including Gestapo Mueller. Goleniewski had not actually met Mueller. However, he had heard from his Soviet supervisors that sometime between 1950 and 1952 the Soviets had picked up Mueller and taken him to Moscow.[25]

When Goleniewski came to the USA in early 1961, he continued to insist on the importance of Hacke. Now, however, he added some even more startling twists.

Memo for UPHILL

Not long after Goleniewski's defection, a delegation from West Germany's Bundesnachrichtendienst (Federal Intelligence Service/BND) came to interview him. Colloquially known as the 'Gehlen Org' after the name of its founder General Reinhard Gehlen, its CIA cryptogram was UPHILL. As a result of preparations for the visit, we now have a more detailed record of Goleniewski's views of Hacke in a four-page document dated 10 May 1961.[26] It summarizes CIA debriefs with Goleniewski on 8, 18, and 24 April when Goleniewski discussed Hacke in more detail. Most striking is Goleniewski's claim that it was he (not Rozanski) who got Foerster to discuss Hacke. The fact that Goleniewski radically changed one aspect of his story does not necessarily discredit it. Recall that in the Sniper letters, he tried to preserve his identity so that not even the CIA knew who he really was. By shifting the focus away from Rozanski in the letter, Goleniewski may have been more concerned with protecting his own identity.

From the UPHILL memo:

1. [Goleniewski] was asked to give a background of reference material in preparation for the UPHILL visitors who visited Washington during the week of April 24. On the above-mentioned dates, he reviewed the history of his connections with Nazi and neo-Nazi affairs which is given in condensed form below.

2. It should be noted at the outset that the name HACKE is a code name which ___ invented for one of his reports. ___ used this code name to refer to a high-level neo-Nazi conspiracy with particular emphasis on clandestine Soviet control of this conspiracy. To the best of his knowledge the KGB had no

code name for the neo-Nazi conspiracy itself, nor for their controlling operations over it. He also does not know of any name which the German members of the neo-Nazi conspiracy had for their organization.

3.   It should also be stated at the outset that the lengthy debriefing of ___ on this subject did not essentially reveal any further facts concerning the identity of Germans who belonged to HACKE or those over whom the Russians had control.

With these caveats out of the way, the text continues:

1.   ___ began his story by relating that while he was stationed in Poznan with the UB as CE [Counter Espionage] Chief in the period 1948–49, he was given the special mission by the Soviet Advisor to the Poznan UB Station, MAJOROW, to carry out the interrogation of various high-level Nazis who had been stationed in the Poznan area during the war. The persons ___ interrogated at this time were: JAEGER who had been GAULEITER of Poznan,[27] HEPPNER who had been Chief of the SD in Poznan, STRICKNER who had been HEPPNER's Special Assistant for Germanization in the WARTHEGAU and various other purely military figures.[28] From none of these did ___ get any information on the subject of HACKE, although ___ later realized (see below) that the chief purpose of the detailed interrogation requested by the Soviets of these top Nazis was to try to get facts on the secret conspiracy set up by BORMANN at the end of the war.

Was Goleniewski chosen as an interrogator because of his past with Reichsland since it played a key role in 'Germanization in the Warthegau'? In any case, the memo continues:

1.   When ___ was transferred to Danzig in 1950, again as Chief of CE in the UB Station there, he was surprised to find that the former German GAULEITER of Danzig, FOERSTER, was being held in the UB jail. ___ learned in time that Col. [Jozef] ROZANSKI from the UB Headquarters in Warsaw frequently came to Danzig for the purpose of interrogating FOERSTER although for a long time ___ could not learn what the purpose of the interrogation was and how ROZANSKI was proceeding.[29] At that time the KGB Advisor in Danzig was SHUBAJEV and the Chief KGB Advisor in Warsaw was [Colonel Semyon] DAVYDOV. At the same time as DAVYDOV was replaced by BESBORODOV, SHUBAJEV in Danzig was replaced by Major SKLAR.

2.   Some tine early in 1951, SKLAR invited ___ into his office and introduced him to General BESBORODOV who was visiting Danzig at that time. BESBORODOV spoke to ___ about a special mission for him and swore him to secrecy before revealing what it was. BESBORODOV then explained that the special mission had to do with FOERSTER whom the Russians

were most anxious to bring to a point where he would talk of his relations with the Nazi hierarchy towards the end of the war. BESBORODOV confided to ___ that ROZANSKI who had been entrusted with this task had failed utterly to get FOERSTER's cooperation and was being relieved of the case. ___ later learned that ROZANSKI had used every kind of threat and brutality on FOERSTER from having him led out of the prison to his supposed execution, to beating him up personally, but had still not succeeded in getting him to talk. BESBORODOV informed ___ that he was responsible only to SKLAR in this matter and was to confide in no one else, including his superiors in his own service.

3.   ___ read all available files on FOERSTER, discovered that his wife was the sister of Rudolf HESS, and that FOERSTER had personally known Hitler exceedingly well and had belonged to the inner circle of top Nazis. For six months, according to ___'s story, he sat and talked to FOERSTER in the prison cell trying only to restore FOERSTER's psychic balance which had been severely disturbed by ROZANSKI's treatment. ___ did all this on his own time after office hours, mostly late in the evening. His visits to FOERSTER were kept secret from his colleagues, and the prison officials who knew of his visits had no idea what the nature of his discussions with FOERSTER was. All of the conversations he had with FOERSTER were tape-recorded although FOERSTER did not know this. The tapes were handed personally by ___ to SKLAR whose secretary transcribed them and translated them into Russian.

4.   In the spring of 1952 [1951], after ___ had been talking to FOERSTER for six months, he succeeded in getting FOERSTER to tell of certain historical events which were brand new to ___ at the time and which created a serious problem for him because these were all matters which, if true, shed light on a number of diabolic plots which he did not think the Russians would be happy to have him know about. These were: How Stalin wiped out the pre-war Polish Communist Party, the role HEYDRICH had played in inspiring the original Soviet distrust of the Polish Communist Party, the story behind the TUKACHEVSKY conspiracy, and, finally the true story behind the KATYN massacre. The Soviets were tremendously upset when ___ reported these matters and handed over the tapes and claimed vigorously that these stories were all a diabolic provocation on FOERSTER's part. Nevertheless, they told ___ to continue. Evidently in the attempt to convince ___ that FOERSTER's stories were provocations but that in any case ___ must not even mention them to anyone, he was invited to be interviewed by [General Roman] ROMKOWSKI on one occasion and on another occasion was seen again, this time in Warsaw, by BESBORODOV.[30] Despite Soviet high-level assurances ___ states that he felt there was much truth to FOERSTER's contentions and that he ___ first had his faith in the communist system and the Soviets shaken by these revelations.[31]

The UPHILL memo continues:

1. Around May or June of 1952 [1951] ___ in his chronological pursuit of Nazi history with FOERSTER, had finally reached the point of the German defeat at Stalingrad. ____ in drawing FOERSTER out on the topic of how the top Nazi command at the time had begun to face the possibility of total defeat after Stalingrad, noticed that FOERSTER gave some indication of knowledge of Nazi plans first conceived at that time to prepare for a post-war continuation of their efforts, underground if necessary. When ___ reported this to SKLAR, the latter, who had been exceedingly patient throughout the whole period of interrogation of FOERSTER, suddenly came to life and prevailed upon ___ to do everything possible to get FOERSTER talking about this subject.

2. One evening shortly after this, when FOERSTER was in a particularly good mood, ___ sprang the question on him concerning the preparations BORMANN might have made for a secret conspiracy of top Nazis who would continue working after a possible German defeat. FOERSTER was at first frightened by the question and didn't talk. Then ____ suggested that he might prefer talking to some other interrogator about this subject, after which be left. SKLAR, when ____ reported this, seemed upset and ordered ____ to get back to FOERSTER as soon as possible and to press with every means he could to get FOERSTER talking.

3. At the next session FOERSTER said, that he would refuse to talk to anyone else besides ___ and would be willing to tell him a little in answer to his question. This little turned into an all-night session. Once FOERSTER began to talk he evidently was anxious to relieve himself after the pressures he had been under for so many years and he delivered to ___ the information contained in the latter's report #1/60.[32] After telling all this, FOERSTER appeared sorry he had done so. ___ on his side felt that now that FOERSTER had opened up, ___ could keep him revealing further facts about the neo-Nazi conspiracy.

4. When early the next morning he reported the results of his interrogation to SKLAR, the latter immediately called BESBORODOV in Warsaw; thereupon [presumably Sklar] reported to Warsaw personally, and returned to Danzig the next day with a Soviet Lt. Col. and a Soviet Major who had evidently come straight from Moscow and who removed FOERSTER from the Danzig prison and took him back with them to Moscow on a special plane which had been ordered for the purpose. ___ never heard anything about FOERSTER again. ___ later learned from SKLAR that the Russians had secured permission from [Polish Communist leader Boleslaw] BIERUT to remove FOERSTER from Poland since FOERSTER had been waiting there under the death sentence which had been continuously commuted only, as it turned out, for the purpose of continuing interrogations.

5. 10. A few days after these events, BESBORODOV visited Danzig and personally thanked ___ for his achievement. Shortly after this ___ was promoted to the rank of Major, almost a year ahead of expected time, and was told by

SKLAR that this was out of gratitude for his work beyond the line of duty with FOERSTER. On this occasion SKLAR again swore him to secrecy.

The 25 January 1960 letter and the UPHILL memo form the basis for Goleniewski's claims about Hacke. They also allow us to compare them with Goleniewski's later far less believable accounts. On page 84 of Villemarest's *Le Mystérieux Survivant*, for example, the story mutates this way. After hearing about Hacke from Foerster, Goleniewski personally flew the former Gauleiter to Moscow. Instead of being met by his Russian boss at the airport, Goleniewski encountered an enraged General Abakumov, who warned him not to poke his nose in things he didn't understand. Abakumov then whisked Foerster away while Goleniewski returned to Poland alone. In his original CIA debrief, however, Goleniewski says a Soviet major and lieutenant-colonel from Moscow took Foerster back with them; there was no dramatic airport encounter with Abakumov.

Hacke references are also scattered in other CIA documents. One CIA text on SS General Müller that clearly draws from Goleniewski reads:

> In May 1961 __ said revelations on the neo-Nazi conspiracy agreed with information which the KGB already had from (various) sources. One of these sources was Heinrich MUELLER, former chief of Amt IV of the RSHA (Gestapo) whom the Soviets had under their control early in 1945 and had brought to Moscow later that year … At one time (it was) explained to (him i.e., ___) that MUELLER was close to BORMANN and along with others constituted a faction in opposition to HIMMLER, KALTEN-BRUNNER and associates. BORMANN did not intend, in setting up his conspiracy to include RSHA personnel or to give the conspiracy the shape or spirit of a secret police outfit. On the other hand, he wanted to use MUELLER's experience in shaping the conspiratorial frame of his organization….[33]

Goleniewski was questioned as well on 4–6 March 1961. He stated that 'the Russian police' had 'picked up Mueller … and took him to Russia.' He further claimed that a high-ranking German diplomat stationed in Hong Kong was a member of Hacke and that another diplomat in Cairo had an SS pedigree. He added that he only learned about another spy named Rogal not in Danzig/Gdansk but later in Warsaw in 1952 when he was 'Chief of the Analysis Section of Department II' (counterintelligence). He noted that Rogal worked for the KGB against British operations in Lithuania.[34]

But how did the CIA view Goleniewski's claims? Were they dismissed as the ravings of a madman?

In a 12 April 1978 CIA report entitled 'KGB Exploitation of Heinz Felfe: Successful KGB Penetration of a Western Intelligence Service,' Goleniewski's information is evaluated as follows:

The HACKE story is regarded by many knowledgeable persons as an important backdrop to understanding postwar German security problems, and particularly to an understanding of Soviet penetration of German intelligence and security services as illustrated by the Felfe case. It shows how early in the game and with what apparent success the Soviets moved to penetrate and exploit the various formal and informal groupings of former Nazis. Former SS and SD officers were particularly vulnerable to Soviet blackmail, as the Soviets systematically sought out and exploited the evidence of their war crimes guilt. In this group for which conspiracy had become a way of life, the Soviets could also make an ideological appeal – continued hatred of the United States combined with respect for authoritarian Soviet power. Many of these former Nazi officers, including some with a record of hushed-up war crimes, obtained important or sensitive positions in the West German government. This group exercised a particularly fatal attraction on the renascent West German intelligence and security services, which had an obvious need for experienced personnel to counter the growing threat of Soviet espionage.[35]

'Peter and Paul'

In March 1959, Goleniewski sent a 'Heckenschütze' report to the CIA that would throw German intelligence into chaos. In his letter (still not declassified), Goleniewski offered crucial leads that would expose one of General Gehlen's top aides and close personal friends Heinz Felfe as a Soviet double agent codenamed 'Paul' by the KGB. As head of BND counterintelligence, Felfe occupied the equivalent position to James Angleton in the CIA. Both men were tasked by their respective services to catch Soviet spies.

A recent homage to Felfe by Russia's Sputnik News gives a sense of his importance to the Russians:

> According to historians of intelligence services, the name of Felfe is on a par with legendary members of the British 'Cambridge Five' led by Kim Philby as well as the Soviet intelligence agents who helped extract information about the US Manhattan Project.

Felfe joined the Hitler Youth as a teenager and the SS in 1936 at age 17. He became a commissioned SS officer in 1943.[36] Sputnik, however, begins its narrative when Felfe 'took part in military operations against Poland' in 1939, where he apparently contracted pneumonia, returned to Berlin, and was demobilized. Next, reports Sputnik:

> Felfe received secondary education and joined the security police of the Main Directorate of Imperial [Reich] Security (RSHA). He was subsequently sent to study law at the University of Berlin. In August 1943, Felfe was transferred to

the Sixth Directorate of the RSHA, engaged in external intelligence and led by Walter Schellenberg. After a while, Felfe was promoted to head the RSHA's Switzerland department.

In May 1945, he was taken prisoner by the British, but was released in the autumn of 1946. At this time, his political views began to change. He realized that Soviet foreign policy was aimed at making sure that Germany remained a single and neutral state. The idea did not sit well with the West, which advocated the creation of a pro-American zone of occupation and the partition of Germany.

From 1947 to 1950 the British employed Felfe to spy on Communist activity in Cologne but dropped him due to suspicions he was working for the Soviets.[37] A native of Dresden, Felfe would later claim he was so morally outraged by the Allied bombing of the city that he decided to work for Russia.[38] In any event, Hans Clemens (the KGB's 'Peter'), a fellow Dresden native who worked for Walter Schellenberg's Department (Amt) VI of the RSHA began collaborating with the Russians in 1949. After Clemens approached him, Felfe agreed to spy for the Russians. He was then instructed to join the new Gehlen Org with Clemens. Now Moscow hit the proverbial jackpot:

> during his years as a Soviet intelligence agent Heinz Felfe handed more than 15,000 classified documents and information about more than a hundred CIA moles over to Moscow.... For his outstanding contribution to strengthening the security of the Soviet Union, and his longtime and fruitful cooperation with Soviet intelligence, Heinz Felfe was awarded the Order of the Red Banner and Red Star as well as the badge of 'Honorary Officer of the Committee for State Security' bestowed on him by the heads of the Soviet KGB.[39]

Repeated failures in BND operations led the CIA to suspect a high-level Soviet mole. In 1954 one of the heads of KGB operations in Vienna named Peter Deriabin defected to the West. Deriabin told his CIA debriefers that the Russians dubbed their two top moles inside the Gehlen Org 'Peter and Paul.' A CIA officer named Clare Edward Petty, who worked in Germany with the BND, guessed that Felfe was the likely mole simply because he seemed too good at catching East Bloc agents.[40] Petty, however, lacked solid evidence to back his hunch. To make matters more awkward, Felfe and General Gehlen were the best of friends. It took Goleniewski to finally convince the Agency to take a hard look at Felfe, who was finally arrested on 6 November 1961.

Goleniewski's identification of Felfe was pure luck. In the spring of 1959, Colonel Raina, Goleniewski's Russian adviser in Section VI, discussed a talk given in Moscow in 1958 by KGB General Oleg Gribanov, head of the KGB Second Main Directorate in charge of counterintelligence. In his speech before the heads of other East Bloc counterintelligence sections, Gribanov boasted that when six leaders of the BND visited Washington in 1956 and were given a tour of the CIA,

two of them were working for the KGB. When 'Sniper' reported this in one of his letters, the CIA checked its files and discovered that Felfe had been on that trip.[41]
From a declassified CIA report entitled 'KGB Exploitation of Heinz Felfe':

> The security situation continued to fester quietly [over CIA suspicions of Felfe] in this way until early 1959 when, finally, a report from a high-level penetration source shot us into action. In March 1959, Michal Goleniewski, a senior officer in the Polish Intelligence Service, reported to us that the KGB had had two agents in the BND group which visited the US in September 1956. The KGB also had an agent, Goleniewski reported, who was in position to obtain information on a joint American–BND office running operations against the Soviet Embassy in Bonn and against the Soviets traveling in the West. The KGB had guidance papers used by this office and prepared by the Americans in 1956. The original source of this information was the highest level of KGB: Gen. Gribanov, the Chief of the Internal Counterintelligence Directorate, who revealed this information in a briefing of the assembled satellite chiefs.[42] On the basis of this information and several other leads from Goleniewski, and despite some questions concerning Goleniewski's bona fides, CIA began a quiet, closer investigation of suspect KGB agents in the BND. This investigation concentrated on Felfe.... The BND was not immediately informed because of the extreme sensitivity of the source, Goleniewski, who was still in place.[43]

The CIA's intense investigation of Felfe now caught him red-handed providing secrets to the Russians. The arrests of both 'Peter and Paul' also set off a chain reaction inside the BND of suicides, arrests, and ruined careers.

On 7 February 1963, David E. Murphy, the head of the CIA's Eastern European Section (and coincidentally the CIA agent who first met Goleniewski in the US Consulate in West Berlin when Goleniewski defected), sent then CIA Deputy Director of Plans Richard Helms, a memo entitled 'Heinz FELFE Damage Assessment' that read:

1. This memorandum is for your information and requires no action. It represents a synopsis of the detailed damage assessment attached covering the activity of Heinz FELFE, a KGB penetration of the West German Intelligence Service (BND) from 1951 to 1961.
2. From June 1959 until his arrest on 6 November 1961, Heinz FELFE was the most knowledgeable of all BND officials on CIA operations against the Soviet targets in East and West Germany. With already some 8 years of experience as a KGB penetration of the BND, considerably more as a counter-intelligence officer, and a high degree of native intelligence and cunning, the KGB could only have evaluated his agent performance from that date as of the highest caliber. From the time of his entry on duty with the BND in November 1951, FELFE began to build with KGB assistance a reputation within the

German Service as a Soviet operations expert. This reputation grew as he rose in BND ranks until he was able to so deeply ingratiate himself with the BND that he attained a position whereby he could initiate, direct, or halt any BND operations and later some of CIA's to the ultimate advantage of the Soviets.

3. As a result, the degree of compromise of operations, personnel and facilities in Germany has been very heavy. The details of more than 65 CIA REDCAP and LCIMPROVE operations and a few of the REDSKIN type are known to the opposition as is much of their related M/O. The extent and depth of our liaison relationships with West German intelligence and police organs is known to the Soviets. FELFE has provided the KGB with information which makes both CIA and the BND vulnerable to intensive CA attacks from the East. Over 100 CIA staffers were exposed in either true name or alias. The damage is not confined to the approximately 15,000 recorded individual items of known or possible compromise, but includes the more difficult to document loss occasioned by FELFE's manipulation of certain operations on behalf of the KGB in either the planning stage or during actual execution. His influence on some members of the BND was of such degree as to permit him at times to dictate liaison policy vis-à-vis the Americans with respect to Soviet operations.

4. FELFE became so intimately concerned with CIA/BND operations against the Soviet installations and personnel in Bonn, Cologne, and Karlshorst that he was able to keep the Soviets sufficiently current on CIA strengths and weaknesses to allow the KGB wide latitude in countering most of our efforts. Frankfurt Operations Base formalized its joint operations with the BND in June 1959 for the primary purpose of obtaining BND support for audio-surveillance operations in the Federal Republic. Success should have been realized in a fair number of the many audio ventures, however, FELFE's timely reporting to the KGB and occasional blocking of planned action resulted either in their complete failure or a worthless product. Berlin Base entered into joint Karlshorst operations with the BND in July 1959 under a system which would have provided BOB [the CIA's own codename for the CIA] with reasonable control over BND activity and maximum security for the Base's own assets. Again, FELFE was able to provide the KGB with such extensive data on CIA Karlshorst targets, intentions, and M/O that in time the Base suffered virtual neutralization of its efforts in Karlshorst.

5. CIA's losses were not confined to the period after June 1959 although they did reach their peak from that date until Spring 1961 when the FELFE investigation became intense. For several years prior to the inception of the joint operations for which FELFE was the responsible BND officer, he had received periodic briefings and CIA reports on the Soviet Intelligence Services and their activities in East and West Germany. He had been privy to several operations on a case by case basis. FELFE had also been the guest of CIA at Headquarters for a week's briefings and a tour of the United States in September 1956. It does appear, however, that the earlier stages of his hostile career were devoted primarily to the collection of data on the BND and other West German governmental agencies with which he was in liaison.

6. Damage to the BND caused by FELFE's betrayals is of the broadest scope because of his deep insight into BND operations, policy, and administrative procedures. Here he was assisted by his fellow KGB agent and BND colleague, Hans CLEMENS. Although he has failed to admit much of what both CIA and the BND believe he compromised, what is known indicates that all major BND CE operations were compromised. To this must be added the compromise of all key BND headquarters personnel as well as a relatively high number of field officers.

7. FELFE easily crossed BND compartmentation lines using the weapon of elicitation with skill to obtain information not exclusive to the Soviet sphere. Munich Liaison Base received an 'off the record' report from a responsible BND officer that the BND front office is convinced the majority of the Service's tactical sources in East Germany were compromised and under hostile control as a result of FELFE's activities. BND officers were warned that these East Zone sources may possibly be used as channels for Eastern deception operations. MLB was also informed unofficially that a number of BND agents reporting with high speed transmitters had been lost in recent months and others determined beyond reasonable doubt to be under hostile control.

8. Although admittedly intangible, the psychological damage within the BND created by the arrest of a co-worker is significant. It may become difficult to restore esprit de corps at all levels. FELFE's treachery likewise, and possibly more significant, created a confirmed distrust on the part of outsiders both within the German government and foreign services which presumably will manifest itself in official transactions.

9. As one of the senior and most active BND liaison officers in contact with almost all West German Internal Security and Police services and several Federal Republic ministries and departments, the KGB in effect also gained through FELFE a valued penetration of these groups inflicting considerable damage on most of them. The American military intelligence services also suffered losses particularly in the revelation of operational interest in individuals traced with the BND and brought to FELFE's direct attention.

10. The assessment makes no attempt to gloss over the extensive damage done to CIA and the BND by FELFE. Continued investigation of leads to possible additional penetrations and follow-up on all aspects of the damage report now occupies most of the time of our Liaison Staff in Munich.

11. Despite this evidence of serious compromise, we cannot withdraw from liaison with the BND. It remains the Foreign Intelligence Service of the Federal Republic of Germany and as such provides us with a valuable channel to the German Government and a means for monitoring the attitudes, concepts and plans of that Government, particularly with respect to foreign and security policies. We intend to shape our liaison in the future with this in mind while conducting ourselves in a way which will avoid the depth of operational involvement and personnel compromise which characterized much of the past relationship.[44]

Another observer of the BND named David Cornwell was an MI6 agent then operating under diplomatic cover out of the British Embassy in Bonn when Felfe was arrested. He later became better known as John Le Carré. In his memoir *The Pidgeon Tunnel*, he writes about Felfe and the BND in an essay entitled 'The Legacy':

> The case of Heinz Felfe speaks for many. In 1961, when he was finally arrested – I happened to be in Bonn at the time – Felfe, a son of Dresden, had spied for the Nazi SD, Britain's MI6, East Germany's Stasi and the Soviet KGB in that order – oh, and of course for the BND, where he was a prized player in games of cat-and-mouse against the Soviet intelligence services. And well he might be, since his Soviet and East German paymasters fed him any spare agents they had on their books for their star man inside the Org to unmask and claim the glory. So precious indeed was Felfe to his Soviet masters that they set up a dedicated KGB unit in East Germany solely to manage their agent, process his intelligence and further his brilliant career inside the Org.
>
> By 1956 … Felfe and a fellow conspirator named Clements, also a son of Dresden and a leading player in the BND, had supplied the Russians with the BND's entire order of battle, including the identities of ninety-seven field officers serving under deep cover abroad, which must have been something like a grand slam. Gehlen, always a poseur and something of a fantasist, contrived to sit tight until 1968, at the end of which time 90 percent of his agents in East Germany were working for the Stasi, while back home in Pullach sixteen members of his extended family were on the BND payroll.
>
> Nobody can do corporate rot more discreetly than the spies. Nobody does better mission creep. Nobody knows better how to create an image of mysterious omniscience and hide behind it. Nobody does a better job of pretending to be a cut above a public that has no choice but to pay top price for second-rate intelligence whose lure lies in the gothic secrecy of its procurement, rather than its intrinsic worth. In all of which, the BND, to say the least, is not alone.[45]

Notes

1   Of course, Goleniewski believed he was actually writing to the FBI. The full letter can be accessed at https://www.cia.gov/readingroom/docs/BORMANN%2C%20MARTIN%20%20%20VOL.%202_0004.pdf. I am dating the letter 25 January 1960. It is an English translation of a letter originally written in German. All quotes from the letter come from this source.
2   *Die Hacke* is German for axe, hoe, or pickaxe.
3   In the letter Goleniewski either writes something like __ January 1960 and either leaves the date absent or the translator left the date out. There is a hand-written '15' to make it read '15 January 1960.' On page 2 of the letter, however, Goleniewski writes 'I am informing you that I have received no mail from you up to the 25th of January.' I assume that the letter was sent either on 25 January or shortly after and that the person who wrote in hand '15' should have written '25.' There is also a handwritten note: 'Received 5 Feb 1960.'

4 In the text, for example, I have transcribed 'Besbaradow' as Colonel Mikhail Besborodov. Note that in the text, Goleniewski called him 'General BESBARADOW' but he
made his remarks in January 1960. During the period Goleniewski is discussing, he was
still a Soviet Colonel. Besborodov (or Bezborodov) served as Soviet Senior Security
Advisor from 17 March 1950 to 10 April 1953. I have corrected other names as well.
Lorigen is Jakob Löllgen; Rudl is Karl Radl; and Davidow is Colonel Semyon Davidov
(or Davydov). (Davidov served as Soviet Senior Security Advisor from 1946 to 17
March 1950.) I have added first names in brackets when they are absent. Note also that
Mueller can be spelled 'Müller' or just 'Muller' in English texts, and Foerster can be
spelled 'Förster' and just 'Forster.' Löllgen can be spelled 'Loellgen' and even 'Lölgen.'
See https://www.cia.gov/readingroom/docs/LOELGEN%2C%20JAKOB_0005.pdf.

5 For Goleniewski's analysis of another famous Nazi, Otto Skorzeny, see Appendix III.

6 AKTION is described in a CIA note as 'Special operation against Western Intelligence
Services in the Federal Republic of Germany. Directed by 'RIS.' RIS is shorthand for
Russian Intelligence Service.

7 The 16 May 1960 Summit Conference held in Paris between Eisenhower and Khrushchev, a meeting that collapsed in the wake of the U-2 affair on 1 May 1960.

8 *Kommunistische Partei Deutschlands*/The West German Communist Party.

9 AIS means 'American Intelligence Service.'

10 The Deutsche Reichspartei as noted by the translator. This was a small far-right party in
Germany active 1950–1965.

11 The 'SSD' (for 'Staatssicherheitsdienst' or 'State Security Service') is an abbreviation for
the East German intelligence agency better known as Stasi.

12 Shekhovtsov (2018), 14–15.

13 The KGB carried out similar racist disinformation campaigns in the USA as well. See
Kalugin and Montaigne (1994), 103. [See Rid (2020), 123–32 for a detailed overview,
CF.]

14 This report has not been declassified.

15 There are several biographies of Skorzeny, the most recent one by Smith (2018).

16 This was codenamed 'Operation Sunrise' by the American OSS.

17 On the novel and film, see Jens (2017).

18 Villemarest (2002), 18.

19 Abakumov was replaced as head of the MGB by Semyon Ignatiev, who took over on 9
August 1951.

20 Parrish (1996), 255–83.

21 Schenk (2000).

22 There is a rare color photograph of Hitler and Gertrud Deetz laughing at a banquet at
Hitler's retreat in Berghof in Obersalzberg along with Eva Braun and other guests. https://
www.dailymail.co.uk/news/article-1315155/Hitler-home-Rare-photographs-Nazi-leader-
relaxed-waged-war.html.

23 Mazower (2009), 84–85.

24 Schenk (2000).

25 See RG 263 *Detailed Report, Heinrich Mueller, Record Group* 263: Records of the Central
Intelligence Agency at https://www.archives.gov/iwg/declassified-records/rg-263-cia-
records/rg-263-mueller.html. This was part of a group selected to examine the CIA's
relationship with various Nazis and included historians Timothy Naftali, Norman Goda,
Richard Breitman and Robert Wolfe. It was later republished in an academic journal, see
Naftali et al. (2001).

26 The UPHILL document can be found at https://www.cia.gov/readingroom/docs/
MUELLER%2C%20HEINRICH%20%20%20VOL.%201_0034.pdf.

27 This was August Jäger, who worked as Arthur Greiser's administrative lieutenant. He
later became Gauleiter in the Warthegau. At the end of the war he was captured in the
British zone and returned to the Poles. He was reportedly executed on 17 June 1949 in
Poznan.

28 'Heppner' was Rolf-Heinz Höppner. He was handed over to Poland for war crimes trials in 1947 and sentenced to death on 15 March 1949. Other reports say he was sentenced to life imprisonment in Poznan. In 1957, he was released from jail and allowed to return to West Germany where he lived in Cologne.

29 Rozanski was one of the most notorious interrogators in postwar Poland. After the death of Stalin, he was arrested for his role in torturing prisoners, including members of the Communist Party, and was sentenced to five years in jail. Due to some improprieties in the case, he was prosecuted a second time. In 1957 he was sentenced to 15 years in prison. He was released from jail in 1964. See Wrobel, 269–70.

30 Misspelled 'Ronkowski' in the original. Romkowski was General Roman Romkowski. Also notorious as a torturer, Romkowski was jailed in 1956 and sentenced to 15 years in prison. Romkowski was tried along with Rozanski and another Polish security official named Anatol Fejgin. See Wrobel (2014), 268.

31 Although these last lines can be easily overlooked, this is the one (and only) example I have seen that suggests Goleniewski was once a Communist.

32 This is the 25 January 1960 letter. Goleniewski referred to his letters as reports so 1/60 means his first report for 1960.

33 See https://www.cia.gov/readingroom/docs/MUELLER%2C%20HEINRICH%20% 20%20VOL.%201_0055.pdf.

34 See https://www.cia.gov/readingroom/docs/MUELLER%2C%20HEINRICH%20% 20%20VOL.%202_0027.pdf.

35 See https://www.cia.gov/readingroom/docs/FELFE%2C%20HEINZ%20%20KGB% 20EXPLOITATION%20OF%20HEINZ%20FELFE_0001.pdf.

36 For a brief overview of Felfe, see Norman Goda, 'CIA Files Relating to Heinz Felfe, SS Officer and KGB Spy,' at https://fas.org/sgp/eprint/goda.pdf.

37 Ibid., 2.

38 It is a curious claim given that the Russians pushed the Allies to bomb the city.

39 Sputnik News. 'Master Spy and Good Friend: Soviet Union's Master Spy in West German Intel Remembered,' 18 March 2018 at https://sputniknews.com/military/ 201803181062663769-intelligence-agent-tribute/.

40 Petty would join Angleton's staff in 1966.

41 The CIA never could determine to its satisfaction who the second spy was on the trip.

42 This was at a 1958 meeting in Moscow.

43 Available at the CIA's HRP website at https://www.cia.gov/readingroom/docs/FELFE %2C%20HEINZ%20%20KGB%20EXPLOITATION%20OF%20HEINZ%20FELFE_ 0001.pdf. Claire Edward Petty, who was the CIA expert on Felfe and helped unmask him, most likely wrote the report, which includes an appendix on 'Hacke.' For Gole-niewski's information, see 115–16.

44 See https://www.cia.gov/readingroom/docs/FELFE%2C%20HEINZ%20%20KGB% 20EXPLOITATION%20OF%20HEINZ%20FELFE_0001.pdf. This is a cover letter for a long CIA damage assessment of Felfe's operations.

45 Le Carré (2016), 57–58.

7

THE SEARCH FOR 'GESTAPO' MÜLLER

The men from SMERSH

For biographical background on Müller, the historians who worked on the Nazi war crimes interagency working group, Timothy Naftali, Norman J.W. Goda, Richard Breitman and Robert Wolfe, provide a good summary:

> Mueller was born in Munich on April 28, 1900. After serving as a pilot in World War I, he joined the police in Munich, soon acquiring a reputation as a skilled anti-communist investigator who did not feel bound by legal norms of police investigation. As such, he would draw the attention of Heinrich Himmler and Reinhard Heydrich, leaders of Hitler's SS. Following Hitler's rise to power in 1933, Himmler and Heydrich consolidated German regional police units while creating a national political police, the *Geheime Staatspolizei* (Gestapo). Mueller entered the SS in 1934 and quickly rose through the ranks of that organization as a police official. In September 1939, when the Gestapo and other police organizations were consolidated into the Reich Main Security Office (RSHA), Mueller was made the Chief of RSHA Amt IV – the Gestapo.
>
> As Gestapo chief, Mueller oversaw the implementation of Hitler's policies against Jews and other groups deemed a threat to the state. The notorious Adolf Eichmann, who headed the Gestapo's Office of Resettlement and then its Office of Jewish Affairs, was Mueller's immediate subordinate. Once World War II began, Mueller and Eichmann planned key components in the deportation and then extermination of Europe's Jews.[1]

The story of Hacke discussed in the previous chapter was intimately tied to one of the enduring mysteries of the Cold War, the fate of Müller whose body was never definitively identified in the ruins of Berlin. Although a fanatical Nazi in his actions

DOI: 10.4324/9781003051114-10

against the perceived enemies of the regime, Müller was also thought by some to be sympathetic to the Soviets. In his autobiography, the chief of the Nazi Foreign Security Service, Walter Schellenberg, recalls a drunken conversation with Müller where the Gestapo boss expressed his admiration for communism:

> National Socialism is nothing more than a sort of dung on this spiritual desert. In contrast to this, one sees that in Russia a unified and really uncompromising spiritual and biological force is developing. The Communists' global aim of spiritual and material world revolution offers a sort of positive electrical charge to Western negativism.[2]

Schellenberg also claimed that Müller established contact with the Russian secret service in 1943, joined the Communists in 1945 and died in Moscow in 1948.[3]

Unsurprisingly, the CIA were aware of these claims. From the CIA's 'KGB Exploitation of Heinz Felfe' report:

> Mueller was well-known as a student and admirer of the NKVD, and this apparently led him to general sympathy with the Soviet cause. In his memoires, Gen. Walter Schellenberg, a senior SS and SD officer, quotes Mueller as saying in Spring 1943: 'I cannot help it; I incline more and more to the conviction that Stalin is on the right road. He is immensely superior to the Western heads of State, and if I had anything to say about it, we would very quickly come to an agreement with him.' It was not long after this that Mueller apparently did make his own personal accommodation with the Soviets. The Soviet contact to him was reportedly arranged by Maj. Loelgen, the Gestapo chief in Danzig, who had been recruited by the Soviets sometime in 1943. Mueller's post-war whereabouts is a much-debated mystery. It was first believed that he died in the siege of Berlin, but there have been a number of reports that he escaped successfully to the Soviet Union.[4]

To try to unravel at least part of the mystery, we begin with Kostyantyn Boho-mazov, a famous Soviet intelligence officer who died on 24 May 2017 at age 98.[5] Assigned to SMERSH during World War II, the Ukrainian-born Bohomazov later worked alongside future KGB director Ivan Serov in the ruins of Berlin to determine Hitler's fate.[6] Their investigation led them to Colonel Walter Nicolai, a fluent Russian speaker whom Bohomazov described (possibly erroneously) as the Intelligence Advisor to the Nazi Party. Born in 1873, Nicolai began his career in intelligence in 1906 and was head of the German secret service between 1913 and 1919. He died in Moscow where he had been taken for further questioning on 4 May 1947.[7] (His papers went to Moscow as well.) Bohomazov later recalled of questioning Nicolai:

> Who would not be interested to hear straight from the horse's mouth how the German Intelligence Service in April 1917 ensured the safe passage from

Switzerland to Russia via the German territory for Bolsheviks-emigrants headed by Lenin? Or the details of preparation and discussion of the Molotov–Ribbentrop Pact in 1939, one of the authors of the idea of which was Walter Nicolai. Or about the investigation in 1943 (on Hitler's order) of Nicolai's activities on suspicion of his being sympathetic to the Soviet Union, and about the closing of the case by the Gestapo Chief Mueller.[8]

The 1939 Hitler–Stalin Pact established a tense understanding between the two totalitarian powers over Poland. Although the Pact was largely tactical, there were proponents on both sides who viewed it as a potential overture to a larger strategic alliance.[9] To make matters yet more complicated, some key German officials may have been long-term Soviet agents sent into the NSDAP in the 1920s and early 1930s.

The full extent of Soviet intelligence penetration into Nazi Germany remains unknown, but it may have been extraordinary. German General Franz Halder, who headed the German Army's High Command (the OKH) from 1938 until his dismissal by Hitler in 1942, thought so. Halder was convinced that 'nearly all the plans of the High Command were revealed to the Russians as soon as they were drawn up – even before they got to my desk.'[10] There were even persistent rumours that Martin Bormann, Chief of the Nazi Party Chancellery and a key figure in Hitler's inner coterie, might have been a Soviet agent.

The CIA's interest in Müller was heightened by comments made by Adolf Eichmann, a close associate of Müller, during his interrogation in Israel. Eichmann told the Israelis that he believed the Gestapo chief survived World War II.[11] From a section of a declassified CIA report on the hunt for Müller entitled 'Goleniewski and Eichmann Blame the Soviets':

In 1960 and early 1961 two events occurred which stimulated a sudden and powerful revival of interest in MUELLER. A Polish intelligence officer-defector, Michael GOLENIEWSKI, stated that he had learned while in the Polish service and in intimate contact with Soviet officers that MUELLER had defected to the Soviets. He had allegedly been reached through a contact established via one Jakob LOELLGEN, a friend of MUELLER's who had been chief of the Gestapo in Danzig and also an RIS agent. According to GOLENIEWSKI, MUELLER had worked with the RIS leader ABAKUMOV and had helped him in his efforts to gain control of the new Nazi underground.

At about the same time this was going on, the Israeli intelligence service was interrogating its prize catch Adolf EICHMANN who declared that MUELLER was to blame for everything, that he had survived the war, and was probably in Russian hands. The EICHMANN affair generated spectacular press repercussions. Simon WIESENTHAL, Chief of the Jewish Documentation Center in Vienna, who had been claiming apparently unmerited credit for the apprehension of EICHMANN and other war criminals and enjoyed an excellent press, rushed into print with assertions that he knew MUELLER was alive and working for the

Russians, etc. The German Special Commission for finding and punishing war criminals at Ludwigsburg, Baden-Wuerttemberg, was galvanized into belated action and began sending out investigative requests to Berlin and Bavarian police authorities. The Bavarian police conducted an intensive investigation, including technical coverage, of the MUELLER family, Barbara HELLMUTH (MUELLER's former secretary) et al. The results were all negative.[12]

The CIA never recovered the files of the RSHA, the SS intelligence service. The great fear was that the Russians had captured them. Such files were stored in bunkers and other secure locations built to survive bombing and fires. With both the SS archive and someone like Müller to help guide them through it, the Soviets would have a tremendous ability to blackmail and recruit former Nazis inside Germany. As a 9 December 1971 CIA memorandum put it: 'If SMERSH actually seized MUELLER and the best part of the RSHA records, Soviet capabilities to control important Germans and some other Europeans would far exceed those heretofore attributed to them.'[13]

But did the Soviets really have Müller?

Losing Löllgen

In his 25 January 1960 Sniper letter, Goleniewski identified a former Polish-based SS Major named Jacob Löllgen as a key go-between for the Soviets and Hacke. Löllgen, in turn, recruited a fellow agent named Jan Kaszubowski. The former head of the Danzig Gestapo, Kaszubowski later 'aryanized' his name to 'Kassner' and used the cover-name 'Larsen.' From Goleniewski's letter:

Circa 1947, the former Department I (now II) and Department VII (now I) recruited in West Germany the veteran Abwehr and Gestapo officer [Jan] KASZUBOWSKI, a/k/a LARSEN.[14] LARSEN had been spotted by the ABAKUMOV agent, the chief of the main STAPO office (Stapoleitstelle) in Danzig, Major LÖLLGEN, who had been 'doubled' by the RIS around 1943 and formerly was a close collaborator of LARSEN.

The agent KASZUBOWSKI a/k/a LARSEN was run with great success for a long time by (OMEGA) who is now in the Polish Ministry in Bern, Switzerland.[15] However, in this connection an action took place which is typical for the activity of the red IS. KASZUBOWSKI a/k/a LARSEN build [sic] up such a good position in West Germany because of his earlier Gestapo activity which he had been awarded with the Iron Cross 1st Class that he was considered for the leading position in the BfV which was being organized at that time.[16]

This was contrary to the plans of ABAKUMOV who had already prepared and pushed forward his own agent (who belonged to HACKE) for this post. This agent (whose name is unknown but who can be easily identified by you) is supposed to have had even greater 'merits,' to have been more intelligent than K. and in ABAKUMOV's opinion to be more secure than K.

Goleniewski then shed light on bitter in-fighting between Soviet and Polish intelligence which, not surprisingly, the Russians won:

An argument broke out between the MGB and the MBP.[17] At that time the MGB was naturally stronger and therefore because of pressure by BERIA and General BESBORODOV, K. was arrested around 1951 (approximate, another source says 1952) at a contact with ROGULSKI in Berlin, was transferred to Warsaw and was locked in a prison there as a war criminal.[18] He was allegedly in prison for about 5 years without a trial, was released around 1956 or 1957 and repatriated to West Germany. In this way, the agent of ABAKUMOV had a free path – without competition from the other agent who had been planned for the leading position in the BfV [but] could not get the job (but other MGB agents did succeed in this).

Before KASZUBOWSKI's release, the Russians tried to re-win him for further activity in the Federal Republic, but he laughed at them. Therefore Poles (Department II) negotiated with him and after a long hither and yon, KASZU-BOWSKI said he was ready to continue working for Poland but in no case for the Russians. Thus K. is still as CE agent of Department II but, in reality, directed by the KGB Chief Directorate II of General GRIBANOV. After K., who is a most experienced CE officer, has become acclimatized and has proved by his activity that he is secure, the KGB plans to steer him towards HACKE and to exploit him there. This is naturally a hypothetical plan which is supposed to take place after a long time. In my opinion it is not difficult to work on K. and to interrogate him. He undoubtedly has a complex because he knows that he was kept practically innocent in prison for years upon the orders of the Soviets. In case he may have reported fragmentarily after his return to West Germany. Please don't allow yourselves to be led astray because this could have been by instruction of Department II for the purpose of 'winning confidence.'

After the scandal with K., Major ROGUSKI tendered his resignation, was released from Department VII and entered the diplomatic service. According to my investigation, he is not active now as an intelligence officer. Formerly, however, he ran very important agents (also in the US) and therefore it would be useful to investigate him in respect to counterespionage. The information about KASZUBOWSKI has been checked by me.[19]

The CIA now sought to backtrack Goleniewski's story by examining the fate of SS *Sturmbannführer* (Major) Jacob Löllgen. The Agency drew on a 17 January 1945 US intelligence report that includes this description of him:

A keen Nazi.... Strongly built and rather fat. Pale face, straight nose, blue-grey eyes. Hair thin and parted in the middle. Wears gold-rimmed spectacles. Well shaved. Numerous gold fillings in his teeth. Married with two children (twins, boy and girl, aged about 10.) Lives in Zoppot.[20]

Shortly after Goleniewski's encounter with 'UPHILL,' the BND put a trace on Löllgen. It did not take long to locate him since he was already a BND informant! After returning to West Germany, Löllgen headed the Trier police force until he was pensioned off in 1957. He next worked in a Cologne-based private detective agency called IW founded by a 'Dr. Hans Schmitz,' who encouraged the BND to recruit Löllgen. From a 6 August 1963 CIA report on someone code-named CASTROP:

> CASTROP explained that SCHMITZ had been the tipper who recommended LOELLGEN to UPHILL. WALZ was sent to recruit LOELLGEN as a spotter for stay-behind agents. LOELLGEN had been most unproductive and apparently never made any efforts to get further into the UPHILL fold. It therefore seems unlikely that LOELLGEN has any RIS mission to penetrate UPHILL unless he has other UPHILL contacts as yet undiscovered.[21]

Some of Löllgen's other Danzig cronies worked for IW. On 10 July 1961, the BND confirmed that Löllgen had been connected to 'Johannes Kassner' via the IW detective company, and that Kassner was none other than Kaszubowski (a/k/a 'Larsen' and 'Herbert Skrypiets'). A 1958 report from the BfV (the Bundesamt für Verfassungsschutz/the Federal Office for the Protection of the Constitution) stated that both Löllgen and Kassner were in contact with yet another mysterious German born in Poland named Alarich Bross.[22] Arrested by the British in 1945, Bross worked for the RSHA Amt VI in Finland. He used at least ten aliases. Yet another suspect was a German named Hans Joachim Leyer. Born in Danzig in November 1908, Leyer served as Löllgen's deputy there.[23]

Recall that Goleniewski told the CIA about Kassner's handler Rogulski. Their connection was now confirmed to the CIA's satisfaction. A 12 March 1971 one-page CIA report (really a series of notes) on the Löllgen file states at the bottom of the page, 'A later murdered defector _____ confirmed the ROGULSKI/ KASZUBOWSKI.'[24]

A 10 February 1971 CIA report includes a comment that Goleniewski's claim that Abakumov wanted Kassner moved to the BfV 'seems to me unfounded.' It continues, 'I have an Army report on KASSNER which pretty well shows he was trapped by the Soviets because they wanted him out of the way but suggests no such reason.'[25]

What was true is that after the war KASSNER relocated to West Germany but sometime in late 1951 or early 1952 he was lured to East Berlin and disappeared.[26] The CIA report continues: 'About 1959, KASSNER was released and returned to West Germany.[27] In the interim ABAKUMOV's scheme to put his own man [here a footnote reads 'possibly Friedrich Wilhelm HEINZ'] in the BfV had failed and he himself [Abakumov] had been liquidated.'[28]

A 9 February 1971 CIA memo entitled 'Review of File: Jakob LÖLLGEN' states, 'By mid-July 1961, BND was promoting an operation to end in the arrest of LOELLGEN, KASSNER and LEYER. (Of course, FELFE investigation was also then in full swing).' In other words, the BND seemed about to break a possible Russian cell centered around a network of ex-Danzig SS officers. Then, seemingly overnight, the investigation was abandoned. A 10 February 1971 CIA memorandum on Löllgen, entitled 'The Man Who Probably Knows What Became of Heinrich (Gestapo) Mueller,' reported that although the BND followed leads on Löllgen, it claimed that the Felfe investigation so overwhelmed its resources that it could no longer pursue the investigation!

The BND apparently decided to abandon the Löllgen probe sometime in mid-July 1961. Its excuse, on the face of it, makes little sense. What if there were links between Felfe and Löllgen? From the 10 February 1971 CIA memo:

1. Up to mid-July 1961, the BND, which was receiving the information provided by GOLENIEWSKI from us, had shown a lively interest in this trio of Russian agents. The BND was, however, preoccupied with the FELFE investigation and hinted that there was not enough evidence to arrange for a round-up of LOELLGEN, KASSNER, and LEYER, not to mention one Alarich BROSS, born 23 March 1904, another special BND connection who was also involved with these three men. The file ends at that point, evidently because no further action was taken by the BND.

2. Clearly, LOELLGEN did something which caused the RIS to repose great confidence in him. Otherwise they would never have let him go back to West Germany. Clearly also, LOLLEGEN must have an interesting tale to tell about what happened to Heinrich MUELLER and how the RIS operation to penetrate the Nazi stay-behind operation fared. These are all matters of considerable importance in the assessment of what has been going on in West Germany. Can any way be found to get LOELLGEN to talk before it is too late, if it is not already too late?

Löllgen, however, found himself back in the news in April 1966 when he and a fellow Danzig Gestapo officer named Horst Eichler were acquitted for war crimes committed in the city of Bydgoszcz in the newly formed Reichsgau Danzig–West Pomerania under the control of Albert Foerster. From a 1 April 1966 AP story datelined Munich:

> Two former Nazi police officials were acquitted today of charges of having aided and abetted the 1939 mass murder of 349 intellectuals in central Poland. The court said there was insufficient evidence to convict Jakob Lölgen [sic], 69 years old, and Horst Eichler, 55. The prosecution had asked the court to sentence Lölgen to four years in prison and to acquit Eichler, a former lieutenant colonel in the Nazi SS (elite guard). Lölgen, who was director of the political division of an occupation police unit, told the court he had only transmitted orders from higher authorities.[29]

As far as the CIA paper trail goes, it appears that not just the BND, but the CIA abandoned the Löllgen hunt in mid-1961. But why?

Angleton's game?

Sometime in 1969–1970, the Müller case that lay dormant for almost a decade sprang back to life. The new probe was spearheaded by James Angleton and his Counter-Intelligence (CI) staff. The National Archives RG 263 Report on General Müller states that in reviewing the history of Goleniewski and the CIA, CI now 'found fault with how Goleniewski's leads had been handled in 1961.' But what were Angleton's views of Goleniewski?

What seems clear is that from the beginning, Angleton and then-CIA Deputy Director Richard Helms suspected 'Sniper' was a double agent (either witting or not) and claimed the Soviets had caught on to the Heckenschütze letters within some six weeks after they began. The Russians now began feeding Sniper fake information, or so they claimed.

Why would they make such a claim in the first place? What lay at the core of their reasoning? Nor were their arguments shared inside the Agency. Just the opposite according to author Thomas Powers: 'Inevitably, the Polish branch of the DDP [Deputy Directorate of Plans] and the case officers who dealt with Gole-niewski in the field disagreed – the beginning of bad blood between the CI Staff and the rest of the clandestine services.'[30]

Angleton and Helms' argument collapsed after Goleniewski's defection and subsequent debriefing. There could now be little doubt in both the CIA and British intelligence that his contribution had been enormous given the exposure of Blake, Houghton, Felfe etc. But if Angleton mellowed after Goleniewski came to America, there is no indication of it.[31] In fact, just the opposite as Angleton turned to Anatoliy Golitsyn as his defector of choice while marginalizing Goleniewski.

Yet it would be Angleton who relaunched the probe into Hacke and Müller. As to why, the RG 263 Müller report identifies a Czech intelligence officer named Ladislav Bittman, who defected to the West in 1968, as responsible for the probe. A 'disinforma-tion specialist,' Bittman claimed that a January 1964 article in the German magazine *Stern* by journalist Peter Stähle about Müller had been planted by Czech intelligence to combat rumors that Müller had been living in Prague. The document continues:

> These comments caught the attention of the CIA's Counter-Intelligence (CI) Staff, headed by the legendary James Angleton. If Mueller really had been in the USSR or elsewhere in Eastern Europe, and if he had taken RSHA central files with him (many of which had indeed vanished after the war), then numerous leading West Germans (presumably on the political right) could still be compromised. It was crucial to discover what had happened, not necessarily to Mueller, who well might have been dead in any case, but to the files. Angleton also had a special interest in Soviet disinformation. The CI Staff undertook a thorough-going inquiry of Mueller starting in late 1970.[32]

Although reports of General Müller's survival were plentiful, Angleton ignored them until Bittman's defection. The obvious question to Bittman would have been why the Czechs took such claims seriously enough to place an article in a major German magazine such as *Stern*. The author of the story, the West German journalist Peter Stähle, specialized in intelligence stories.[33] In the 16 August 1964 issue of *Stern*, he published a piece entitled 'Die Spur führt nach Südamerika' ('The trail leads to South America').[34] Stähle had written an earlier article in the January 1964 *Stern* entitled 'Gestapo-Müller Lebt in Albanien,' in which he claimed his information came from a secret service.

In his first story, Stähle said Müller used Albania to direct intelligence operations against the West after earlier living in both Russia and Hungary. According to the story, Müller 'was in Moscow from 1945 to 1955 and was active under Stalin, Beria, and Malenkov.' Following Stalin's death and Beria's downfall, Müller remained highly valued as an expert on security affairs, but he lost his political influence. He relocated to Budapest, and spent some 15 months working to orga- nize the Hungarian security services, but the 1956 revolt made him pack his bags and head for Albania. Here he worked under Mehmet Shehu, whom he reportedly first met in Hungary. Shehu had been Albania's Prime Minister in 1954; long Enver Hoxha's right-hand man, he was the second most powerful figure in Tirana.

In his August 1964 follow-up, Stähle claimed that Müller had reportedly con- verted to Islam and operated in Tirana as 'Abedin Bekir Nakoschiri.'[35] After the Israeli secret service caught on to him, Müller apparently fled Albania for Latin America via Romania and Turkey, where he linked up with a network of former SS men. From there he supposedly stopped off in South Africa before finally landing in Latin America.

In his second *Stern* story, Stähle reported that Müller had lived in Moscow and other Russian cities. Müller also sought to recruit German prisoners of war as Russian agents.[36] Stähle cites the testimony of a former German prisoner of war named Karl-Rudolf Harz, who was an employee of a Stuttgart hotel when Stähle interviewed him. During the war, Harz worked for Müller in the RSHA; he later wound up in a Soviet labor camp in Vorkuta. Harz said that in 1952 he was brought to Moscow and interrogated by the Russians for four straight weeks. During this time, he met Müller who asked him to spy for the Soviets, an offer Harz refused.[37] The CIA, for its part, was convinced Harz was lying. He apparently tried to sell his story to the Agency in the 1950s, but he failed to mention meeting Müller in Moscow.[38] From a CIA report on the *Stern* story:

> When Staehle's January 1964 article appeared in the *Stern* magazine, the German [CIA] station attempted to identify his source. After a thorough run- down, it was found that the authenticity is very suspect. In fact, the BND claims it is a complete fabrication. The BND said that they know that Staehle was connected with the Israeli IS and they suspect that he got the MUELLER information from the Israelis.[39]

The follow-up story in the August 1964 issue of *Stern* was apparently not checked out by the station. But in November 1964, we received an inquiry from the BfV concerning the authenticity of an allegation that after WW II MUELLER had fled to Argentina and organized 'Peron's Gestapo.' When Peron was ousted, MUELLER supposedly fled to Cuba where he was being protected by Castro.[40] The BfV received this information from a source who received it from Paul APOLD, Peron's former press chief, who also had fled from Cuba, but later returned to Argentina illegally. We did not authenticate this story.[41]

Trying to make sense of Angleton's inquiry into Müller is not easy. Did he not ask his friends in Israeli intelligence whether Stähle's article was inspired by them, as the BND believed? Why would Czech intelligence, a Soviet satrap, plant a story in a major German publication stating that the Russians protected a former SS General? What kind of Soviet disinformation ploy would such a story serve, unless the real purpose of the story was to convince ex-Nazis that it was fine to work with the Russians.

In any case, Angleton's Special Investigations Group (SIG) proved unable to unravel the pieces of a puzzle that stretched back decades, one littered with false clues and imaginary sightings of the mysterious Herr Müller. In the end, Angleton upheld the long-standing BND contention that Müller died in Berlin in 1945. This was also the conclusion of the historians who worked on the Nazi war crimes interagency working group.

But speculation persisted and fueled a publishing boom in lurid books about Nazi survival.[42] No less a figure than BND chief Reinhard Gehlen claimed in his 1971 memoir that Martin Bormann, a Nazi leader even more powerful than Müller, was a top Soviet agent and advisor on Soviet postwar German policy. Bormann, according to Gehlen, escaped from the Führerbunker, and only died in the Soviet Union in the late 1960s![43] The discovery of Bormann's body in Berlin in 1972 and subsequent confirmation of his identity by DNA testing in 1998 perhaps suggests a more prosaic explanation.[44]

Yet if the CIA/BND consensus now further validated by Angleton was that Müller died in the rubble of Berlin, it was an opinion very much not shared by one former top CIA officer and Angleton ally: Tennent 'Pete' Bagley.

Prague December

Tennent Bagley, as we have seen, had a strange relationship to the Goleniewski saga. Recall that in April 1958, when Goleniewski's 'Sniper' letter first came to the Bern Embassy, Bagley was a CIA officer under diplomatic cover there. As such, he was perhaps the first person in the Agency to see the Sniper material. Before coming to Bern, he had helped run the CIA's Polish desk in Washington.

A highflier inside the Agency from a distinguished military family and who was thought to be in the running for future CIA chief, Bagley's career was wrecked by the Nosenko affair. He retired as CIA station chief in Brussels in 1972 and made his home in the Belgian capital before dying at age 88 in February 2014. All that time, Bagley insisted that Nosenko was a fake. He also did something else rather extraordinary: in the late 1980s he launched his own private hunt for SS General Müller!

Bagley's decision to pursue Müller was not made casually; he may well have been thinking about it for decades. In 1954, Bagley scored his first major coup when as a young CIA case officer on his first overseas assignment, he helped engineer the defection of a former SMERSH and KGB officer named Peter Deriabin [Deryabin]. At the time of his defection, Deriabin served as KGB Chief of Counterintelligence in Vienna. On 15 February 1954, Deriabin walked into an American military complex in Vienna and announced he wanted to defect. Bagley now organized the exfiltration operation that smuggled Deriabin out of Austria first to Germany and then America. Recall that Deriabin correctly reported that there were two top Soviet moles in the West German BND, whom he only knew by their KGB code names 'Peter' and 'Paul.' It would take Goleniewski's information to expose Felfe and Clement. Deriabin also told the CIA in 1954 that General Müller was in Moscow.

In an 18 November 1971 statement, Deriabin supported Goleniewski's claims that Müller was in Soviet hands.[45] In fact he expanded on them. Goleniewski only said that Abakumov and SMERSH had recruited Müller, but not that Müller was living in Moscow in 1952.[46] Deriabin, however, reported that in the summer of 1952 he was working for the First Chief Directorate (FCD) of the MGB (soon to become the KGB) in its Austro-German Department.[47] He recalled, 'I remember that I read a few excerpts of the debriefing and interrogation of MÜLLER. At that time in 1952 he was held in Vladimir MGB prison' in Moscow.

In the CIA's 'KGB Exploitation of Heinz Felfe' report, Deriabin's knowledge of Müller is referenced as well. Here Deriabin recalled that:

> the voluminous files on Abakumov's wartime operations against high level Nazis were known in the KGB as 'Abakumov's legacy,' and that they read like a novel. There was renewed interest in these files about November 1952 ... at that time the files were removed from the Austro-German Section to a separate location, and a high degree of compartmentation was put into effect with regard to all files pertaining to former Nazi officials.[48]

Deriabin's assistant Valentina Orlek often served as an interpreter for Müller and other top Nazis in Vladimir Prison. They included Hans Pieckenbrock, formerly a high-ranking Abwehr official.[49] Deriabin personally read transcripts of Müller's interrogation, and added that Colonel Vasily Ilich Bulda, Captain Yuri Litovkin, and Boris Nalivaiko would know more.[50] He also recalled seeing Müller being discussed in a file on the actress Olga Chekhova.[51] Deriabin, in short, independently bolstered Goleniewski's claims about Müller.

Was Goleniewski, then, also right about Hacke?

In the early 1990s when Bagley took up the hunt for Müller, he did so without Deriabin who died in 1992. Instead, he joined forces with Pierre Faillant de Villemarest, who in 1984 published his Goleniewski biography *Le Mystérieux Survivant d'Octobre*. A hero of the French Resistance and holder of the Croix du guerre, Villemarest was a bitter anti-Communist, extreme rightist, and former member of French intelligence (Service de Documentation Extérieure et de Contre-Espionnage/SDECE). For decades he ran his own Centre Européen d'Information (CEI) focusing on intelligence issues.

Villemarest first encountered Goleniewski in 1975. At the time Villemarest wrote on intelligence matters for a French publication called *L'Aurore*. In one article, Villemarest expressed a belief that he had held since 1947 when he was Nazi hunting for French intelligence. At that time, he concluded that Martin Bormann and General Müller survived World War II and that they both had reached 'arrangements' with Moscow. Goleniewski now wrote Villemarest and included information supposedly 'confirming' his view.[52] Some years later, a contact of Villemarest's at the *International Journal of Intelligence and Counterintelligence* suggested he contact Bagley because both men were exploring postwar Nazi–Soviet connections.[53]

Bagley also was eager to interview Marcus Wolf, the former head of Stasi foreign intelligence, although it is not clear if they ever met. Goleniewski had said that while visiting Warsaw in June 1960, Wolf had a meal with Colonel Henrik Sokolak, still then the Vice-Director of Department I, at the restaurant W Z. During the meal, Wolf supposedly remarked ironically, 'On a bien roulé les Occidentaux avec Bormann et ses réseau nazis-communistes' ('We got one over the Westerners with Bormann and his Nazi-Communist network').[54]

On 2–4 December 1993, Bagley accompanied Villemarest to Prague to interview a former high ranking Czech Communist intelligence official named Rudolf Barak (who is discussed in detail later in the chapter). Villemarest's *Le Dossier Saragosse: Martin Bormann et Gestapo-Müller après 1945* and Bagley's *Spymaster: Startling Cold War Revelations of a Soviet KGB Chief as Revealed to His Ex-CIA Friend* both report on their conversations with Barak.[55]

Villemarest recalled he had been contacted out of the blue by a letter from Pavel Barak, Rudolf Barak's son, who said he wished to discuss Villemarest's book on the GRU, the Soviet military intelligence service.[56] When they met, Pavel said his father wanted to discuss the Müller affair as in his GRU book Villemarest expressed his belief that Müller survived the war.

Rudolf Barak, who died in 1995, headed the Czech Interior Ministry from 1953 to 1961; he was also a member of the Politburo before his dramatic fall from power in the early 1960s. Barak now told Bagley and Villemarest about a fantastic-sounding plot that he said he organized to capture Müller and return him to Moscow. Barak claimed he did so at the behest of KGB boss Ivan Serov, the same man who accompanied Kostyantyn Bohomazov in trying to determine Hitler's fate in Berlin.

Recall that Deriabin said that Müller was in Moscow in the early 1950s. In Barak's version of the Müller saga, by 1954–1955 the former SS General was living in the Corrientes province of Argentina, in or around the city of Cordoba. Barak claimed that Serov approached him in the summer of 1954 and asked him to have Czech intelligence kidnap Müller and return him alive to Prague.[57]

From Tennent Bagley's chapter 'The KGB–Nazi Underground' in *Spymaster*:

> By 1952 Müller was back in Russia, in jail and under KGB interrogation. This was the time of the 'Abakumov affair,' when the security service was aggressively investigating all of Abakumov's activities. After Stalin's death in March 1953, most of the arresters, although not Abakumov himself, were freed and returned to work. Apparently, Müller was too.[58]

In 1955 (Villemarest has it in 1954), Serov told Barak

> that Müller was living and working for the KGB in the Cordoba region of northern Argentina, not far from the Paraguayan border. The former Gestapo chief had become unresponsive to KGB direction, failing to appear at scheduled meetings with his KGB Illegal handling officer and not responding to messages. Now Serov wanted to get him back to shake him up and restore discipline. Because Czechoslovakia had more trade and industrial interests with better possibilities for cover and moving people and supplies in that part of Argentina than the Soviets did, Serov asked Barak to do the job for them.[59]

After a year of planning, Müller was supposedly kidnapped and brought to Prague's Ruzyne prison in 1955.

In a 17 July 1995 interview shortly before his death, the 82-year-old Barak discussed the alleged Müller kidnapping with a reporter named Josef Hufelschulte for the German magazine *Focus*.[60] Barak told *Focus* that Serov wanted the Czechs as they had the best Eastern Bloc agent network in Argentina thanks to Czech agricultural experts who were helping the Argentinians build breweries and sugar refineries. Barak said that while Müller was in a pub eating with Czech technicians, he was drugged and driven to an airport where he was put in a crate of machinery and flown to Prague. On board the plane were four KGB agents.

In Prague, Müller was supposedly met by Aleksandr Korotkov, dubbed 'the King of the Illegals' and a legend inside the Soviet security services for his work in France and Germany during World War II.[61] Korotkov reportedly had helped in the recruitment of Müller. According to Villemarest, Korotkov used the cover name 'Alexander Erdberg' to regularly meet with Müller in Berlin from 1938 to 1941. At the same time, Korotkov helped organize the famed Soviet spy operation known as the Red Orchestra.[62]

When Müller realized that he was to be dealing with Korotkov, he suddenly cheered up and the two men flew back to Moscow. Barak said that in 1958 he met Korotkov in Sochi. Korotkov thanked him for Müller's capture but said nothing else. It seems, however, that information leaked to other East European services who now wanted to question Müller, a leak that greatly angered Serov.

Had Barak for some reason, either impish or for financial gain, decided to make up wild stories about Müller and try to sell them to two professional intelligence operatives? Surprisingly, however, the CIA had picked up Czech intelligence rumors about Müller in Prague dating back at least to the 1960s.

On 9 December 1970, a CIA memo was addressed to CI/TRCO 'in response to your memorandum of 19 November 1970.'[63] CI/TRCO was interested in, of all things, Yulian Semyonov's famed TV miniseries *Seventeen Moments of Spring*, then being serialized in *Komsomolskaya Pravda* in the winter of 1979 before being published as a book. CI/TRCO was especially interested that in the story the Soviet agent inside the RSHA knew 'Gestapo' Müller. This may have been because CI thought that the lead Soviet spy in the story could have loosely been based on Korotkov.[64] Another CI/TRCO memo in December 1970 focuses on Müller, but this time it also includes Barak and Czech intelligence.

Some background: In February 1962, Rudolf Barak was arrested in a power struggle with Antonin Novotny, the ardent Czech hardliner who was finally deposed by Alexander Dubcek in 1968. Barak was given a 15-year sentence on corruption charges for supposedly embezzling a large amount of government funds. His supporters saw his arrest and jailing as an attempt to stifle a more reform-oriented regime. During the Prague Spring, he was released from prison when the government decided he did not have a fair trial.

As for the December 1970 memo, it draws on two sources who were recent defectors from the StB (*Statni Bezpecnost*), Czech intelligence. I believe the first may be Josef Frolik while the second is almost certainly Ladislav Bittman.[65] From the two-page memo:

1. Source commented that he had previously mentioned the fate of SS General Heinrich MUELLER in his report on former Minister of Interior Rudolf BARAK (see raw report dated 13 May 1970). Following is a quotation from this report:

    I heard from Major Frantisek BENES @ BENISEK that after the arrest of BARAK (1961), a secret prisoner was found in the Ruzyne prison, allegedly a former high functionary of the RSHA, who had been personally interrogated by BARAK. No one knew who he was; he refused to divulge his identity and BARAK refused to comment on his presence there. However, it was rumored that this was a former SS Obergruppenfuehrer and Police General, H. Mueller, whom the CIS had sought out and kidnapped. Perhaps the imaginations of some people went beyond the bounds of reality, but the secret prisoner was discussed officially at party meetings after BARAK's arrest. Probably the only persons who know his identity are BARAK himself and Colonel Jaroslav MUELLER, former Chief of Intelligence, who was ousted from his post shortly after BARAK's arrest.

2. Source added that BENES, who had interrogated Colonel MUELLER, above, as well as other high-level personnel in the Foreign Intelligence Directorate (CIS), still was not certain at all that this prisoner was General MUELLER.

3. BENES also told Source that around this time the Foreign Intelligence Directorate initiated an 'active measures' operation and arranged for publication of the story that General MUELLER was living in asylum in Tirana.[66] However, according to BENES, the 'political circles' were afraid that the truth would leak out, that the world would learn (or. think) that MUELLER had been kidnapped by the CIS, that he was not sentenced as a war criminal but had been exploited by the CIS for the sake of intelligence operations.

4. Source added that it is generally known in the HSR (Main Directorate for Intelligence, known as the Foreign Intelligence Directorate prior to the June 1969 reorganization of the MV) that the KGB used Nazi war criminals for operational purposes. It also is common knowledge that a large number of Nazi archives were captured by the Russians and exploited mainly with operational aims. Source could provide no concrete examples but noted that he had provided several 'stories' about Gestapo agents in high level Communist Party circles in the CSSR which should serve to confirm the thesis.

On page two of the memo, there appears to be a second source, whom I suspect is Bittman, who for most of his career worked against West Germany. Bittman's first wife was Jewish and that reason alone might have led him to be denied knowledge of certain operations. In any event, this page reads:

1. [__] recalls that according to *STERN* in West Germany about five or six years ago, a West German tourist in Albania supposedly recognized MUELLER there, alive and well, etc.

2. [__] recalls that there had been stories for some time about the possibility that various hidden Nazis were being found and blackmailed into service for the KGB but [__] is certain that he never heard anything official along these lines regarding either MUELLER or any other old Nazi.

3. [__] doubts personally that any of these stories are true.

4. In any event, having been employed in various. aspects of work against West Germany through most of his thirteen years with the Foreign Intelligence Directorate, [__] is certain that at least among the Czechs, there was no official operation mounted by the German Department to locate, kidnap, expose, or blackmail hidden Nazis. [__] hastened to place this in context by contrasting this fact with the well-known fact that the Czechs certainly did not hesitate to make propaganda whenever an exposed ex-Nazi could plausibly be spotlighted.[67]

According to Barak's account, Müller's stay in Ruzyne prison only lasted a short time before he was flown back to Moscow. If so, who was the German mystery man in the prison and why did people think it might be Müller, even to the extent that Czech intelligence felt compelled to plant stories that Müller was living in Albania of all places?

The 'Müller Diaries'

As we have seen, the saga of Heinrich 'Gestapo' Müller's alleged survival after World War II has given rise to a bevy of bizarre-sounding claims. With Bagley (*Spymaster*) and Villemarest (*Le Dossier Saragosse*), we seem at last to arrive at the end of a very twisted trail.[68]

Or have we?

In Box 8 of the Bagley archives, there is a translation of an article by Lev Bezymenskii in the well-known Russian journal *Novoye Vremya* (*New Times*) entitled 'Müller's Three Lives.'[69] A former intelligence officer, Bezymenskii was a leading Soviet expert on Hitler's last days, having served under Marshall Zhukov when the Russians captured Berlin. As Russia's leading 'Nazi hunter,' he was best known in the West for his 1966 book *Tracing Martin Bormann* that claimed Martin Bormann escaped Berlin in 1945.[70]

Bezymenskii's article debunked the 2000 publication by the Russian house 'Collection Top Secret' of *Shef Gestapo: Genrikh Myuller Verbovochnyye besedy: iz sekretnykh dos'ye tsru,* ('Gestapo Chief: Henrich Müller Recruitment Conversations: From the Secret Files of the CIA'). The text is a purported interrogation of Müller conducted by US intelligence in Switzerland in the late summer and early fall of 1948.[71]

The Russian book was a translation of a 1995 English language opus by one Gregory Douglas entitled *Gestapo Chief: The 1948 Interrogation of Heinrich Müller.* Douglas reports that he obtained a copy of an 800-page CIA interrogation of which *Gestapo Chief* merely highlights the most important excerpts. He said all of Müller's personal files entered private hands in Switzerland, but that in 1980 a Swiss dealer sold them to an American collector who barely looked at them.[72] After the collector died in 1994, Douglas gained access to them.

Bagley may have first learned of Douglas from the Bezymenskii article. After debunking *Gestapo Chief* as an absurd hoax and lamenting the gullibility of the Russian publisher, Bezymenskii added that there was yet another claim by a former Czech communist official (obviously Barak) that Müller wound up in Moscow.

It is also not hard to see why Bezymenskii made his comment. In the afterword to *Gestapo Chief*, Douglas cites the *Focus* article. Douglas also reprints a 16 July 1995 AP story datelined Bonn and entitled 'Gestapo chief nabbed in '56, Czech claims' that reported on the *Focus* story.[73] Douglas may have added the *Focus* and AP articles to imply the Soviets were issuing disinformation about Müller to discredit his own findings, although one would think Moscow would be quite happy to link the former Gestapo head to the CIA.

For his part, Bagley seemed to believe that Bezymenskii wrote his review of the Douglas/Müller book hoax largely to discredit the appendix citing Barak. Bagley apparently viewed both the Douglas book and the Bezymenskii review as a Russian disinformation campaign against Barak. In *Gestapo Chief*, for example, 'Müller' states that 'I believe' Martin Bormann died in Berlin, but that Hitler managed to fly safely to Spain while his double was executed. When asked if he had spoken to any Russians, Müller replies he had not since the end of the war and that the only Russians he knew were captured agents interrogated by the Gestapo. Müller further reports that the CIA wanted to stash him in the Virgin Islands to protect him from Russian assassins and kidnappers. All these claims, from Bagley's point of view were designed to hide the truth. Bagley further believed he had uncovered irrefutable proof that Douglas was a Russian asset and had been one for decades.

In *Spymaster*, Bagley claims that Peter Stähle ('Stahl' in Bagley's spelling), who penned the two *Stern* articles on Müller, wrote (or 'lent his name to') *Gestapo Chief*! From *Spymaster*:

> Then as the West became increasingly aware that Müller might still be alive, for example, by finding other bones in what was labeled as Müller's grave, the Soviets planted stories in the press to deflect attention toward Western use of Nazi war criminals. A Soviet-connected freelance journalist using the pen name Peter Stahl began peddling articles in Germany in 1963 showing that Müller was hiding in various countries. One or two were published a year later in a wide-circulated magazine.[74]

What was Bagley talking about?

First, the *Stern* journalist was 'Peter Stähle' and this was his real name. Peter Stähle was an editor at *Stern* as well as a reporter. In 1965 Stähle was sentenced to four months in jail by a German court for an article he wrote on sexual harassment of women in the German judiciary. In a *Der Spiegel* article on the case, he was identified as a *Stern* editor.[75] (Stähle had earlier worked for *Der Spiegel*.)[76] Bagley mistakenly assumed that Peter Stähle/'Peter Stahl' was behind the latest Müller hoax. To add to this Theater of the Absurd, it was, after all, Bagley and Villemarest who promoted the views of a former head of Czech communist intelligence who seemingly confirmed Stähle's 1964 *Stern* stories about Müller having worked for the Russians.

In any case, Bagley writes in *Spymaster*:

> But that was not enough. In the 1980s, Stahl lent his name, or rather another of his pseudonyms, 'Gregory Douglas,' to a fabrication and detailed biography of Müller. Finally published only after the collapse of the Soviet Union, its four elaborate volumes by their very existence testify to the depths of Soviet concern to obfuscate the fact that they had protected and used the most wanted of war criminals.[77]

He concludes:

> Purportedly based on a 1948 CIA interrogation of Müller in Switzerland – which could never have happened – the book 'revealed' that the American CIA took Müller to Washington to help American Intelligence in the Cold War, giving him the status of brigadier general in the US Army.[78]

Bagley adds in a footnote that the Müller text was:

> ostensibly composed by 'Gregory Douglas' (another alias of 'Peter Stahl,' whose original name may be Norwood Burch). Soviet involvement in its fabrication has never been proven, as far as I know, but only the KGB – terribly compromised by their own involvement and use of Müller – would have a reason to invest such long and painstaking efforts to produce a huge work of no historical value and no prospect of profitable sales.[79]

Bagley may have stumbled upon the name 'Norwood Burch' through the website of controversial far-right British writer David Irving. Fluent in German and with an acknowledged expertise of a sort when it comes to Nazi archives, Irving published several books with mainstream publishers on the Nazi era, but his work moved from evincing historical revisionism to outright Holocaust denial. His reputation was ruined in court in 2000. Irving had sued historian Deborah Lipstadt and her publisher Penguin for libel after her 1993 book *Denying the Holocaust* accused Irving of Holocaust denial. Irving lost the case and was shown in court to have 'for his own ideological reasons persistently and deliberately misrepresented and manipulated historical evidence.'[80]

Despite his own strained relationship with historical accuracy, Irving had for years attacked Gregory Douglas as a notorious forger of fake German documents. Irving reported that 'Gregory Douglas' was born Norwood Burch in March 1930, and that one of the many aliases was 'Peter Stahl.'[81] Bagley apparently became convinced that the American-born Norwood Burch/Gregory Douglas/Peter Stahl must also be the *Stern* journalist Peter Stähle. This erroneous claim was then offered as Bagley's 'smoking gun' proof of Russian 'active measures' mischief, since he associated Peter Stähle with a Czech intelligence plot.

No matter how one views the text, Gregory Douglas's elaborate concoction has blossomed into at least three volumes and possibly four. Not only did Douglas obtain the 'Müller' interrogation by the 'CIA,' he also discovered Müller's remarkable Washington 'diaries.' In *The CIA Covenant: Nazis in Washington*, Douglas publishes a smattering of excerpts from the diaries. We learn, for example, that Müller held a very private dinner at his plush Georgetown home for President Harry Truman where the former Gestapo chief 'wore all of his Third Reich and Imperial decorations.' And from Müller's 12 December 1949 diary: 'Today I inspected my new offices at the CIA headquarters at the Naval Hospital complex over on "E" and 23rd Streets.' Müller, however, held a dim view of his CIA coworkers: 'I have never met so many educated people in my life who are as empty of brains as a ladle.... I have to be bored with their incessant cigarette smoking, long and alcoholic lunches, and very dirty conversation dealing with private parts and fecal matter.' If the Douglas/Müller/Stahl/Norwood Birch volumes are made-in-Moscow fabrications, Russian spooks have a surprisingly quirky sense of humor.

On 4 January 2014, Tennent Bagley posted his only known Amazon review. It dealt with Douglas's *Müller Journals: 1948–1950, The Washington Years, Volume One*. It was not flattering:

> I refer readers to my recently published book *Spymaster*, of which chapter 10 entitled 'The KGB's Nazi Underground' tells Mueller's real story as known to the chiefs of the Soviet KGB. In fabricating these so-called journals, 'Gregory Douglas' alias Peter Stahl alias Norwood Burch was doing the KGB's work of hiding their own disgraceful use of Mueller in a false-flag operation. (It was managed by KGB General Aleksandr Korotkov unbeknownst to the rank and file of the KGB.) The CIA, where I worked for many years, never knew where the much-hunted Mueller was after the war but figured out that he was still alive and in Soviet hands.[82]

Did the CIA really believe that Müller 'was still alive and in Soviet hands' after the war? Did Bagley's friend Angleton think so?

In a 10 February 1995 letter to Pierre de Villemarest, who was then researching *Le Dossier Saragosse*, Bagley wrote: 'As you know, I tend to believe Goleniewski's reports about Bormann's activity in connection with "Hacke."'[83] Whatever the fates of both Bormann and Müller, Bagley believed Goleniewski because his claims corroborated information from Peter Deriabin, from high-ranking Czech defectors, and from what Rudolf Barak personally told Bagley and Villemarest in Prague in December 1993.

The Barak Affair

In the wake of the 1968 Soviet invasion, Czech intelligence suffered a series of high-level defections.[84] One of the best-known defectors was Ladislav Bittman, who helped lead 'Department D,' the Czech counterpart to the KGB disinformation branch first reported to the CIA by Goleniewski.[85] One of Department D's most brilliant initiatives was 'Operation Neptune.' The Czechs sank a hoard of old Nazi-era files (some reportedly doctored) that had outlived their usefulness in a lake and then arranged for them to be 'discovered,' thus generating worldwide publicity and reinforcing the notion that West Germany was populated by ex-Nazis.

In his 1972 book *The Deception Game*, Bittman revealed that in 1957 Czech intelligence created a fake neo-Nazi organization known as the Kämpferbund für Unabhängiges Deutschland.[86] As for the East Germans, Bittman explained:

> The possibility of blackmail based on compromising material from the Nazi period are among the factors facilitating East German infiltration of the German Federal Republic.... East Germany also tries to recruit former Nazis who had concealed their roles in Hitler's designs after the end of World War II. Nazi settlements and individuals in Latin America, the Arab countries, black Africa, and of course, West Germany are traced, and their pasts painstakingly

researched with the help of extensive East German archives. Those who agree to collaborate are given oral guarantees that they will not face prosecution for their wartime offenses. The East German intelligence service is probably now the largest satellite intelligence organization and may even be the most effective.[87]

As interesting as Bittman's book is, even more remarkable revelations were to come. A relatively obscure book appeared in London in 1975 entitled *The Frolik Defection*. It was the memoir of Josef Frolik, another Czech intelligence officer who defected to the West in 1969. An early chapter in Frolik's memoir entitled 'Barak!' discusses Rudolf Barak, who headed Czech intelligence in the 1950s and the man whom Bagley and Villemarest met decades later. Frolik reports that Barak supported de-Stalinization: thanks to his efforts, 'the torturers and murderers were quietly dismissed or jailed, and those who had ordered them to carry out their foul deeds soon followed.'[88] Morale in the service now skyrocketed.

But Barak had one strange quirk, 'his obsession with the part his fellow countrymen had played in the war.' Barak especially wanted to learn just who collaborated with the Nazis. Frolik says that Barak even persuaded Khrushchev to return to Prague a 'notorious double agent' named Nachtmann.[89] During the war Nachtmann, a leader in the Prague Gestapo and an anti-communist 'expert,' ordered the deaths of countless Czech patriots, all the while serving as a Soviet spy.[90]

Barak's big score, however, was tracking down Johann Siebert, an ex-member of the German SD then serving a life sentence in Moscow's Leopoldov Prison. Barak managed to get him sent back to Prague where he was given surgery, a new name, and a new apartment. Frolik reported that Siebert 'was not only a walking index of wartime Czech and German agents within the country,' but Siebert believed the payroll list of collaborators still existed, given the German reluctance to destroy financial documents: 'Immediately a search is instituted and within three weeks the files were found in the archives of Prague's National Bank. They contained 70,000 names – and what names they were!'[91] Frolik continues, 'Lastly, Barak gave an even more extraordinary example of his obsession with a past that most people in Czechoslovakia only wanted to forget. He issued orders that a man whom most people had thought long dead, be found.' That man was 'Gestapo' Müller.

From *The Frolik Defection*:

> According to my informant within Czech intelligence, this is what happened. In 1955, Müller was discovered living under an assumed name in South America. Instead of informing the South American authorities or the Germans ... Barak determined to kidnap Müller off his own bat and bring him to Czechoslovakia. An agent living in France was given the job and, just as the Israelis kidnapped Eichmann, Müller was smuggled aboard a ship heading for Szczecin (Stettin). From there he was transferred to a jail in Czechoslovakia where he was allowed special privileges on the undertaking that he wouldn't breathe a word about his real identity, even to the chief jailer. He didn't speak Czech anyway.[92]

Frolik continues: 'Thus, if my informant was correct, Barak now had three key Nazis at his disposal, complete with comprehensive records of nearly all known German agents within Czechoslovakia. But why?'[93]

Frolik explains that Barak saw his list of Nazi collaborators as a potential gold mine. He now had the goods on top officials in the Czech Politburo who collaborated with the Germans during the war, not least of all President Antonin Novotny. Barak could show that during the war Novotny – who had been sent to the Mauthausen concentration camp – became a Kapo there. This was a position obtained by spying on other inmates.

According to Frolik, Barak now prepared a coup against Novotny, and he hoped to use his collaborator list to intimidate other Politburo members into silence. Novotny, however, struck first. After Barak left a key Central Committee meeting, Novotny immediately convened an emergency session without him. Here he accused Barak of illegal money activities. Frolik says that Novotny even planted money in Barak's safe to make the charges stick. Barak was then arrested and thrown into jail. He would not see freedom until Prague Spring. By then, he was 'a broken man' who reportedly worked as 'a filling station attendant in some obscure suburban garage.'[94]

In 1984 yet another defector from Czech intelligence named Frantisek August published *Red Star Over Prague*. Born in 1928, August's anti-Nazi father survived a concentration camp. Having served Czech intelligence in top foreign postings in London and Beirut, August backed Prague Spring; in 1969 he defected from his post in Beirut.[95] In a chapter entitled 'The Case of Rudolf Barak,' August portrays Barak as a highly cautious reformer of the security services who maintained close ties to KGB head Ivan Serov.

From his appointment as Minister of the Interior in September 1953 to his arrest in February 1962, August writes that Barak was obsessed with uncovering Nazi operations during World War II and unmasking their Czech collaborators. He did so with support from high-ranking officials in Moscow. August believed Barak had been encouraged to topple Novotny, but that his Moscow supporters were themselves either outmaneuvered or changed their minds. As August puts it:

> Equally unresolved was the precise degree of Soviet involvement with the Barak case. At first, Moscow had seemed to support Mr. Barak's bid for power.... But eventually, Moscow had clearly assented to Barak's liquidation by Mr. Novotny. In this context, it was generally known in the Ministry of the Interior during 1960–61 that Mr. Barak was in agreement with Khrushchev's political line.[96]

In 1956, in the wake of the Khrushchev revelations about Stalin, August recalled, Barak was warned by the Russians against 'rehabilitating' Rudolf Slansky, the Jewish former Secretary General of the Czech Communist Party who was murdered in a Stalin-sponsored purge in 1952:

Mr. Bohumil Molnar [deputy director of the StB], who told friends during 1956 that 'our Soviet friends' had clearly told Mr. Barak that they supported freedom and democracy for the worker, 'but they would never consent to having Jewish intellectual radicals getting the upper hand.' Mr. Molnar, himself a KGB man, and an anti-Semite, continued to emphasize the 'Zionist conspiracy' right up to 1968.[97]

Disputes over the 'Jewish question' were not unique to the Czechs. When Gomulka introduced a more 'nationalist' form of rule in Poland, his move brought with it new tensions. There were those who looked to de-Stalinization as an opening to the West and a broader liberalization of society. They were often identified with the intelligentsia and 'cosmopolitan' thinking. In contrast, more 'nationalist' Polish Communists, who embraced a more 'ethnic' and less 'cosmopolitan' identity, used the 'nationalist' turn to remove Jewish members of the security service whom they believed could not be trusted.[98]

This sub-rosa war did not go unnoticed by Goleniewski. In his 25 January 1960 Sniper letter, he writes:

In connection with the case of MONAT, BRYN and the Czech attaché, preparations are being made here [Prague] and in Poland to remove all Jews from the intelligence services (GND). Thus in the immediate future about 30 Jews from Department I will be dismissed under various excuses. In G-II the 'purging' action has been almost completed. (There are still two Jews left.) In the military CE (WSW) … the purge is in full swing.

The CIA assumed that Goleniewski mentioned 'Prague' as an attempt in his Sniper letter to conceal the fact that he was a Polish official. Goleniewski, however, extensively traveled in the East Bloc and it is quite possible that he did write his letter from Prague. In any case, he was clearly aware of the similarities between the 'anti-Jewish' networks in both intelligence services.

In the power struggle in Czechoslovakia, however, Barak appeared on the offensive, in part because of his willingness to use 'the enormous amount of compromising material on high Party officials he had uncovered during his reign as Interior Minister,' material that led straight back to the Nazi era. From August:

After the war the former head of Slovakian State Security Centre (USB), Mr. Jozef Vicen, had fled to Austria, taking the most important USB files with him. Around 1958, Czechoslovakian intelligence kidnapped Mr. Vicen and transported his security files back to Prague. The value of these files was enormous. On their basis, Czechoslovak Intelligence was able to infiltrate the organization of Slovak separatists abroad and to discover collaborators of the fascist Hlinka Guard, and the Slovakian USB. The perpetrators of the mass murders at Kremnicka, in Slovakia, carried out under Father Tiso's fascist regime, were also discovered.[99]

August referenced a series of massacres primarily against Jews that took place in the Slovak town of Kremnicka between 1944 and 1945. The killings were carried out by the fascist Hlinka Guard working in collaboration with the SS Einsatzgruppe H's Einsatzkommando 14 unit. During this investigation, it emerged

> that the men responsible for the Kremnicka massacre were now high officials of the Communist Party. Some of them were sentenced to death, and their detection unnerved other Communist officials who had a dubious past in the Nazi era. Many people who had collaborated with the Gestapo, and who had been certain that this collaboration remained unknown, were now understandably alarmed.
>
> Most of the abovementioned files dealt with Slovakia, but it was also known that many Czechs had also collaborated with the SD and the Gestapo. Mr. Barak now issued orders that all incriminating documents were to be delivered to him personally and that all research in connection with the Nazi past must be authorized by him. He became an expert on all Nazi security activities in wartime Czechoslovakia. In particular Mr. Barak sought to find Nazi SD and Gestapo informers who were serving on the Central Committee or in the apparat.[100]

During the 1960 investigation, code-named 'Operation Karel,' the Czechs discovered

> A cache of material relating to the payment of the Gestapo agent network in Czechoslovakia during the war. Much of the material was found by member of the Fourth Administration (Economic Counterintelligence) of the Ministry of the Interior, in the vaults of the Czechoslovak State Bank in Prague. These Nazi informers were cited by name, along with the details of amounts paid by the Germans.[101]

August continues:

> At Mr. Barak's orders, processing of these documents was undertaken by a special group at the Ministry, members of which had to sign a special oath of secrecy. These files showed that many of these Czechoslovak agents of the Nazis had been in contact with a Gestapo officer named Mr. Nachtman.[102] As we have seen earlier, Mr. Nachtman was also a double agent of the NKVD. He had been taken to the Soviet Union after the war and was now married to a Soviet woman doctor. Some reports stated that he had been imprisoned by the Soviets. At Mr. Barak's personal request, the Soviet KGB now sent Mr. Nachtman back to Prague for further interrogation by Mr. Barak's security experts. The Nazi legacy lived on.[103]

Among the 'well known Party and Government officials' who had been on the Nazi payroll were:

Mr. Ladislav Kopriva: Former Minister of State Security at the time of the 1950s purges, and former Politburo member.

Mr. Vratislav Krutina: A former member of the Communist Party of Czecho-slovakia (CPCS) Central Committee, and a deputy in the National Assembly.

Mr. Jindrich Kotal: Former Deputy Minister of the Interior and an officer of the CPCS.

Mr. Josef Kavan: Head of the Seventh Administration of the Ministry of the Interior, in charge of suspect surveillance.

Mr. Vladimir Koucky: Until 1968, a member of the CPCS Politburo. Appointed ambassador to Moscow, and in 1970 ambassador to Belgium.

Mr. Karel Mestek: Deputy Minister of Agriculture. A member of the CPCS Central Committee in the 1970s.

Mr. M Moucka: A former member of the People's Militia who became head of the Ministry of the Interior Investigation Administration at Ruzyne Prison.[104]

August then adds:

During interrogation at Ruzyne, a former Nazi SD member, Mr. Vondracek, mentioned Mr. Moucka as a Gestapo informer. The investigating officer forgot that there was a monitoring microphone in Mr. Moucka's office and asked the former SD man to write out a full statement for forwarding to the CPCS. The next morning the interrogator was found dead, gassed in unex-plained 'accidental circumstances.' Mr. Barak later called this murder and associated it with Mr. Moucka.[105]

Was the strange placement of Gestapo and SD collaborators inside the Czech CP unknown to the Soviets? Given that the Russians penetrated SD intelligence in Prague so deeply, how could they not know?

Was the Czech situation unique? Or was there a deeper network of Gestapo-connected operators throughout the East Bloc? Were both Goleniewski's Hacke report and Barak's investigations both trying to highlight the same phenomenon? Did the 'Hacke network' operate both in Eastern and Western Europe? In a looking-glass reflection of *The Spy Who came in from the Cold*, was Rudolf Barak a real-life Czech Josef Fiedler?

Finally, there is Josef Swialto's testimony. As discussed earlier, he had defected to the CIA in 1953. He became best known for his 1954 broadcasts into Poland exposing corruption inside the Polish CP and security services, Swialto told the CIA much more. Recall that Tennent Bagley in the mid-1950s helped run the CIA's Poland Desk. One of the things he learned from Swialto was the hidden history of an NKVD operation to destroy Polish anti-Nazi resistance networks. Swialto said that the Polish communists created a special cell 'with an incredible mission – to collaborate with the Gestapo to destroy non-Communist Polish resistance.' The NKVD parachuted an agent named Marceli Nowotko into Poland to create the cell. When he contacted a Polish Communist named Molojec to organize the project, Molojec decided that Nowotko must have been a Gestapo plant and killed him. The NKVD still went ahead with the mission and parachuted a radio-equipped agent to maintain contact with Moscow. Bagley says that according to Swialto:

> The cell infiltrated an agent into an AK [Home Army]-related anti-Nazi resistance organization called 'Sword and Plow' (*Miecz i Plug*). The NKVD furnished Boguslaw Hrynkiewic, a leading agent of Soviet Intelligence, with falsified 'evidence' that the organization's two leaders were Gestapo agents, to give him the pretext to shoot them both. Then, taking command himself, he led 'Sword and Plow' into *real* contact with the Gestapo, using as his channel an NKVD agent within the Gestapo. In Gestapo uniforms he and three men raided an apartment in Warsaw where they knew the Home Army was storing its archives. They found the names of its members and *turned them over to the Gestapo*.
>
> All of these Gestapo collaborators later became party functionaries in the postwar Communist Polish regime, even the Gestapo man who adopted a Polish name. The Soviet invaders installed the overseer of the 'disinformation cell,' Boleslaw Bierut, a longtime NKVD agent, as president of Poland.[106]

Reflections of shadow

Was there a postwar Nazi network that embraced the slogan: 'Fight the Jews and plutocrats in the USA'? Had the Russians created another 'Trust' operation that this time opened the floodgates to Soviet penetration into the far right? In short, did Hacke exist?

In one obvious way it did not since Goleniewski invented the name. Yet a case can be made that something like Hacke not only did exist but had roots that stretched back to World War I. During that war, the Russian Social Democrats were split between two bitter factions. The majority followed George Plekhanov, who from his Paris exile fully supported the Entente. From his perch in Zurich, Lenin fervently hoped Russia would lose the war for an obvious reason: Russia's defeat in the Russo-Japanese War helped spark the October 1905 Revolution.

While the Entente powers helped the aged Plekhanov return to Russia to prop up the Kerensky regime, German intelligence reportedly funneled support to the Bolsheviks. Under Lenin, the Russians and Germans signed the 1922 Rapallo Treaty normalizing diplomatic relations. Behind the scenes, both militaries now worked together to undermine the Versailles system. Seen from the Kremlin, the most serious threat to Soviet rule came from victorious London and not vanquished Berlin. A Soviet foreign policy designed to encourage a more nationalistic East-oriented Deutschland was by no means an irrational geopolitical option.

Some radical right Germans, however, may have viewed close cooperation with Russia as key to breaking Entente encirclement once and for all. What Goleniewski saw as Hacke may have been a postwar extension of a network that put down roots decades earlier. If Martin Bormann and SS General Müller really were

'Soviet agents,' they may have been so precisely because they were extreme nationalists who saw the capitalist Entente powers, and England in particular, as Germany's true enemy.

When SMERSH entered Berlin in 1945, it may have reconnected with old friends not because they were secret Communists but because they were radical National Socialists. They may well have considered Bismarck's policy of alliance with Russia as the realpolitik key to Germany's future and viewed Stalin as just another Czar. Besides, hadn't the Entente powers and the USA allied with Stalin when they had the chance? Germany's famed General Karl Haushofer also maintained a complex geopolitical view of Russia as a potential ally against British power.[107]

The CIA's James Angleton presents a different kind of puzzle. He reportedly became interested in Müller only after Ladislav Bittman told him that the Peter Stähle story in *Stern* was a Czech Department D operation. Bittman defected in 1968; Frolik and August followed one year later. They clearly briefed both the CIA and MI6 about the 'Nazi question' inside Czech intelligence. In 1967–1968, the 'Partisan' faction in the Polish security services also began to openly employ anti-Jewish conspiracy theory dressed up in 'anti-Zionist' rhetoric. At a minimum, would not both the CIA and MI6 now reexamine Goleniewski's claims about Hacke?

Yet the only person in the CIA who seems to have bothered was Angleton, who despised Goleniewski. Angleton's SIG-I, however, conducted a strikingly limited probe into the Müller affair. But why? Was Angleton's limited investigation of Müller (perhaps forced by the Czech defections) designed to fail from the start? The CIA's relationship with the SS diaspora, after all, remains highly murky. Angleton and Helms' boss Allen Dulles, for example, went to considerable trouble to make sure that SS Obergruppenführer Karl Wolff, Himmler's closet personal aide, avoided war crimes prosecution.[108] The Dulles–Wolff negotiations at the end of World War II even formed the premise for *Seventeen Moments in Spring*.

Finally, it is entirely possible that the SIG/CI conducted a highly competent investigation and concluded that Müller most likely died in Berlin. The problem with this view is that it ignores all the other evidence of postwar Soviet–Nazi collaboration served up on a platter to the CIA and MI6 by the Czech defectors, evidence that echoed claims Goleniewski made a decade earlier, and which Peter Deriabin also raised with specific regard to SS General Müller. Had the SIG run a superficial investigation to prevent a real one?

Goleniewski ended the section on Hacke in his January 1960 Sniper letter this way:

> I also have various facts of a lesser format but have to analyze them thoroughly before I give them to you. Otherwise the danger exists that you will again take me for a dealer in 'canards.' I will do everything within my capabilities to make possible further reports about HACKE. It is, however, for me as well as for you, no easy field of investigation. However, I warn you very seriously about this dangerous conglomeration of brown–red Fascists who unexpectedly one day can cause enormous damage and who are an acute danger to the free

world and to peace. It is indeed regrettable that outside of HACKE itself so many potential HACKE ideologists are running around today in West Germany and who are only waiting for the opportunity to transform the old Hitler slogans into reality. In my opinion, American politicians are in many cases much too decent to recognize the slyness, deceit, hypocrisy and true aims of such bloodhounds. In my opinion this can be learned only from objective and hard counterintelligence work. I am prepared to support you in this respect as far as I can. This is undoubtedly a very difficult and complicated affair.

I ask you urgently to exploit the HACKE information with the greatest caution. The circle of the appropriately 'initiated' is very limited. In no case do I want to make you mistrustful of your partners. I have, however, definite reasons to state that if you were to use the BfV for the investigation of this matter you would be making a watchdog out of a wolf. This is a 'Trojan Horse' in which only the devil knows what is going on. When too many foreign agents and collaborators are in such an organization naturally nothing good comes out of it. By this is meant not only the Eastern agents, but also the English, French, Dutch, Belgian agents, etc. HACKE too has a strong sphere of influence.

I have various clues at present about agent activity in the BfV. I will take pains, however, to get down to concrete facts in the near future. I am afraid that these concrete facts will not be very gratifying. You can unquestionably throw my warning in the waste paper basket. In spite of such an eventuality, I see myself duty bound to urge the greatest caution in intelligence contacts on the territory of the Federal Republic. If you take my warning seriously, you will be protected from unexpected and unpleasant surprises. It may be that it is not at all necessary to convince you of this so strongly. This would be gratifying.

In *Imperial Agent*, Goleniewski was far more bitter. He told Guy Richards that after he came to America, the CIA showed a 'strange lack of interest' in drawing him out about

The affairs of the Bolshevik Cover Political Action via the Nazi movement by the KGB and the GRU as well as by the Red Chinese secret services. This movement was created during 1943–1944 by Martin Bormann and other Nazi leaders in the underground with the realization that Germany was going to lose the war.

This movement was taken over, in a covert manner, by the Soviets, and has been developed after many years of inspiration and underground operations into a powerful instrument of Bolshevik 'modus operandi' in the West. My first introductory reports on this subject were transmitted to the US Government during 1958–59 (that is, my anti-Bolshevik activities in the East).

In 1961, Mr. Howard E. Roman, CIA representative, discussed this report with me in a superficial way. Since that time no one from the CIA has shown the slightest initiative to discuss the most important aspects of this report in a profound or through way, or even to seek more knowledge on the subject.

In September 1961, Mr. Peter Skov, a CIA representative, informed me that the agency had checked with the British Secret Service and found that several important facts in my report were proved to be correct and true. This strange lack of interest by the CIA in pursuing further aspects of the report is most interesting because I informed the CIA that, on my own knowledge, not only Martin Bormann, but Gestapo Chief Heinrich Müller and SS Chief Gottlob Berger, and Reichs' SS Leader Heinrich Himmler are alive and working in this Nazi–Bolshevik underground movement.[109]

The evidence about the reality of a Hacke Nazi–Soviet network, and of Müller's alleged survival, is fragmentary, occasionally contradictory and ultimately inconclusive but Goleniewski's own engagement with the far right in America would become much clearer and that is the next stop on our journey through the labyrinth.

Notes

1 See Timothy Naftali, Norman Goda, Richard Breitman and Robert Wolfe, RG 263 *Detailed Report, Heinrich Mueller, Record Group* 263: Records of the Central Intelligence Agency, https://www.archives.gov/iwg/declassified-records/rg-263-cia-records/rg-263-mueller.html. Hereinafter RG 263.
2 Schellenberg (1971), 315.
3 Ibid., 318.
4 See. https://www.cia.gov/readingroom/docs/FELFE%2C%20HEINZ%20%20KGB%20EXPLOITATION%20OF%20HEINZ%20FELFE_0002.pdf.
5 In the 1950s, while working for the KGB, he was an 'adviser' to the Polish intelligence service.
6 Serov's allegiance was to Beria and the NKVD and not Abakumov. Serov was officially attached to the Berlin staff of Marshall Zhukov. For their rivalry while investigating Hitler's death, see Brisard and Parshina (2019), 194–98.
7 Campbell (2009).
8 See http://szru.gov.ua/index_en/index.html%3Fp=1502.html.
9 See Moorhouse (2014) for an overview.
10 Stephan (2004), 110.
11 See the 1971 CIA Directorate of Plans report 'The Hunt for "Gestapo Mueller,"' available at https://www.cia.gov/readingroom/docs/MUELLER%2C%20HEINRICH%20%20%20VOL.%201_0026.pdf.
12 Ibid., 33–34.
13 RG 263
14 For more on Kaszubowski, see https://pl.wikipedia.org/wiki/Jan_Kaszubowski.
15 In a note for readers added to the end of the document, OMEGA is said to be a cryptogram for 'RIS activity in Switzerland, including mounting illegal agents through Switzerland, OJEJNICZAK, MORACH.'
16 The BfV is the Federal Office for the Protection of the Constitution, roughly the German version of the FBI.
17 The MGB was the Soviet Ministry of State Security; the MBP was the Polish Ministry of Public Security.

18 Most likely Stanislaw Rogulski who in the mid-1960s was Poland's Ambassador to Albania. Rogulski served in diplomatic posts from 1945 to 1950 and later from 1956 to 1968. He was dismissed from the diplomatic service in 1968 during an upsurge of antisemitism. He relocated first to France and then Sweden. Some of his time in the Foreign Ministry may have been diplomatic cover for intelligence gathering. On Rogulski and Albanian operations in Poland, see 'Warsaw Charges Albanians who Helped Gomulka Opponent Flee,' 24 February 1966, *New York Times*.
19 https://www.cia.gov/readingroom/docs/BORMANN%2C%20MARTIN%20%20% 20VOL.%202_0004.pdf.
20 Now the Polish city of Sopot. https://www.cia.gov/readingroom/docs/LOELGEN% 2C%20JAKOB_0001.pdf.
21 The report adds that UJDRYROT [Kassner?] was in the KRIPO with Löllgen in Danzig 'from 1921 to 1934' and they were both in Trier after the war.
22 On Bross, see https://www.cia.gov/readingroom/docs/BROSS%2C%20ALARICH% 20ALFONS%20JOHANN_0140.pdf.
23 See https://www.cia.gov/readingroom/docs/LOELGEN%2C%20JAKOB_0007.pdf.
24 Here the text ends either because of deletions or a second page that was not made available, so it is impossible to learn more of what the source said.
25 https://www.cia.gov/readingroom/docs/MUELLER%2C%20HEINRICH%20%20% 20VOL.%202_0005.pdf.
26 Another CIA report on Alarich Bross says that in February 1952, Bross visited a certain Ursula Warno (or Warmo) in West Berlin, who told him that 'her friend Hans [Johannes] Kassner, who also was one of the contact men for Bross, disappeared in the east sector of Berlin. Bross was not sure whether Kassner was a double agent or just unfortunate to fall into the hands of the Soviets.' See https://www.cia.gov/readin groom/docs/BROSS%2C%20ALARICH%20ALFONS%20JOHANN_0086.pdf.
27 A 3 July 1961 CIA report states that Kassner returned in June 1959 and was 'debriefed' by the BND. See https://www.cia.gov/readingroom/docs/LOELGEN%2C% 20JAKOB_0003.pdf.
28 Heinz headed the Friedrich-William-Heinz-Dienst meant to be a competitor West German intelligence service to the Gehlen Organization. Heinz-Dienst apparently had support from American intelligence. The BfV seemingly helped to undermine the Heinz-Dienst. See Meinl and Krüger (1994).
29 The 2 April 1966 *New York Times* ran the AP story but only the first two sentences.
30 Powers (2004), 128–30. Powers also says that one Goleniewski letter claimed that Stepan Bandera, the Ukrainian émigré leader murdered in Munich on 15 October 1959, had been poisoned at a lunch by a Soviet agent. The letter, per Powers, was dated '1961.' Goleniewski defected to the West on 4 January 1961 and could not have written the purported letter. Presumably Powers made a typo. For Goleniewski's interpretation of the Bandera assassination, see https://www.cia.gov/readingroom/ docs/BANDERA%2C%20STEFAN_0081.pdf. This is a 22 April 1976 CIA review of the Bandera killing; pp. 14–15 deal with Goleniewski. For a detailed account of Bandera's murder, see Plokhy (2016).
31 In *Mystérieux Survivant* (1984, 238), however, Villemarest says that out of John McCone's four deputies, Angleton was the only one sympathetic to Goleniewski as his information showed the extent of Soviet infiltration into the West.
32 RG 263
33 'Staehle' in the CIA's spelling.
34 See https://www.cia.gov/readingroom/docs/MUELLER%2C%20HEINRICH%20% 20%20VOL.%201_0052.pdf.
35 https://www.cia.gov/readingroom/docs/MUELLER%2C%20HEINRICH%20%20% 20VOL.%201_0042.pdf.
36 From the article: '*Gestapo-Müller hat im Jahre 1952 in Moskau sowie in einer anderen Stadt der Sowjetunion deutsche Kriegsgefangene verhört und im Auftrage des sowjetischen Staatssi- cherheitsdienst versucht sie als Spione gegen das westliche Ausland zu gewinnen.*'

37 https://www.cia.gov/readingroom/docs/MUELLER%2C%20HEINRICH%20%20%20VOL.%201_0052.pdf.

38 https://www.cia.gov/readingroom/docs/MUELLER%2C%20HEINRICH%20%20%20VOL.%202_0013.pdf.

39 In his August 1964 story, Stähle cites Simon Wiesenthal as someone who had not abandoned the search for Müller. This may be one reason why the BND believed the Israelis were behind the article.

40 In 2012, the BND released a report showing that Fidel Castro tried to recruit former Nazis as mercenaries during the 1962 Cuban Missile Crisis.

41 From a CIA report, available at https://www.cia.gov/readingroom/docs/MUELLER%2C%20HEINRICH%20%20%20VOL.%201_0054.pdf.

42 See Rosenfeld (2019), 191–240. For a popular history account of the search for Müller, see Whiting (2000).

43 Gehlen (1972), 70–1. The authors Heinz Höhne and Hermann Zolling claim that Gehlen based his comments about Bormann's survival on an image from a newsreel of a figure in the crowd at a sporting event in Moscow in 1946 or 1947. See Höhne and Zolling (1972), xx–xi.

44 Daly-Groves (2019), 119–20. Although this hasn't stopped some authors suggesting that the bones were 'planted' in Berlin after Bormann died in Paraguay!

45 See https://www.cia.gov/readingroom/docs/MUELLER%2C%20HEINRICH%20%20%20VOL.%202_0023.pdf.

46 The RG 263 Report says, however, that Goleniewski 'had heard from his Soviet supervisors that sometime between 1950 and 1952 the Soviets had picked up Mueller and taken him to Moscow.' In his 4–6 March 1961 statement to the CIA, Goleniewski said the Russians had picked up Müller, but this was just after the war.

I have been unable to find any statement where Goleniewski states that Müller had been taken to Moscow between 1950 and 1952. However, it is also possible that the RG 263 authors are confusing Deriabin with Goleniewski. In *Le Mystérieux Survivant* (86), it is reported that Müller was in Vladimir Prison in 1951, but the source is given as Deriabin and not Goleniewski. It is also possible that the report confused Goleniewski's comments about Albert Foerster being brought to Moscow with Deriabin's comments about Müller.

47 The FCD was the KGB's foreign intelligence directorate.

48 https://www.cia.gov/readingroom/docs/FELFE%2C%20HEINZ%20%20KGB%20EXPLOITATION%20OF%20HEINZ%20FELFE_0001.pdf.

49 Tennent Bagley's Boston University Archive (Box 8) provides more detail about what Deriabin said about Müller that I am incorporating into this section.

50 In Deriabin's 18 November 1971 report to the CIA on Müller, the names are spelled 'Captain Gregory Litovkin' and 'Nalivayko.'

51 For a look at Chekhova, see Beevor (2004). In his 18 November 1971 CIA report, Deriabin said that Abakumov's secretary and investigator Lt. Col. Broverman, a Russian Jew who spoke perfect German, had the Chekhova's file that mentioned Müller.

52 Villemarest (1984), 84–85.

53 Villemarest (2002), 112.

54 Ibid., 108.

55 The most detailed discussion of Barak's story can be found in *Dossier Saragosse*, which summarizes numerous conversations Villemarest had with Barak and his son Pavel. Villemarest (2002), 215–25. (The book includes a photo of Rudolf Barak taken by Villemarest.)

56 Villemarest and Kiracoff (1988).

57 Villemarest (2002), 215.

58 Bagley (2013), 147–48.

59 Ibid., 149.

60 See http://www.deseretnews.com/article/428242/EX-NAZI-MAY-HAVE-BEEN-KIDNAPPED.html.

61 Haslam (2015), 108–12.
62 For Korotkov's role in the Red Orchestra, see Brysac (2000).
63 While CI stands for 'counterintelligence,' I believe TRCO may be a reference to training courses CI designed to expose its agents to difficult cases.
64 Others have claimed the central figure was based on legendary Soviet spy, Richard Sorge. Matthews (2019), 351.
65 After he came to America in 1968, he changed his name to Lawrence Martin-Bittman. See his obituary in the 21 September 2018 *New York Times*.
66 This is clearly a reference to the *Stern* article.
67 See https://www.cia.gov/readingroom/docs/MUELLER%2C%20HEINRICH%20%20 20%20VOL.%201_0062.pdf.
68 Villemarest's book was translated into English with an introduction by Vladimir Bukovsky. A Polish version was published in 2012.
69 Bezymenskii (2000).
70 Bezymenskii (1966).
71 The Douglas text claims the interrogations were arranged through an intermediary named Willi Krichbaum, who worked for Reinhard Gehlen. After Heinz Felfe's arrest, the BND suspected that Krichbaum might have been spying for the Russians. See his German Wiki at https://de.wikipedia.org/wiki/Wilhelm_Krichbaum. Krichbaum served under Müller in the RSHA.
72 It's possible that the 'Swiss dealer' may have been a reference to François Genoud, a Swiss far-right activist who traded in Nazi memoirs. See Coogan (1999), 584–89.
73 The AP article comes with a comment by Nazi hunter Serge Klarsfeld, who called the Barak story 'absurd' and said that Müller 'would have been no use to the KGB except for propaganda purposes.' For coverage of the story, see the JTA archive, 18 July 1995, and available at https://www.jta.org/1995/07/18/archive/ex-czech-official-tells-m edia-gestapo-leader-given-to-KGB.
74 Bagley (2013), 151. In 2013 German historian Professor Johannes Tuchel claimed to have found proof that 'Mueller did indeed die in Berlin in 1945, was first buried in a provisional grave in a garden in Luftwaffe headquarters and then consigned to a mass grave in a Jewish cemetery in the city.' See https://www.reuters.com/article/us-germa ny-gestapo-idUSBRE99U0XY20131031.
75 See *Der Spiegel*, 13/1967 where Stähle is identified as a *Stern* 'Redacteur.'
76 On Stähle, see Koch (2011).
77 Bagley (2013), 151.
78 Ibid.
79 Ibid., 281, fn. 22.
80 Irving v. Penguin Books Limited, Deborah E. Lipstadt [2000] EWHC QB 115 (11th April, 2000). http://www.bailii.org/ew/cases/EWHC/QB/2000/115.html. See also Evans (2001), and Lipstadt (2005).
81 See the many reports on Douglas/Stahl at David Irving's web site at http://www.fpp. co.uk/docs/Irving/RadDi/2002/100602.html.
82 See https://www.amazon.com/gp/profile/amzn1.account.AFDVPMTEWNKKU DAXTIUMOUBFL7VA/ref=cm_cr_arp_d_gw_btm?ie=UTF8.
83 Bagley Archives, Box 8. Villemarest says in *Le Dossier Saragosse* (109) that Bormann died in Paraguay in 1959 and was buried in the city cemetery at Ita. Three or four years later, the cemetery guard was bribed, and the skeleton taken to Berlin and placed in an area scheduled for construction so it could be found. Villemarest argued that no one wanted to arrest Bormann because the Soviets had made a deal with him, and the West wanted some of the enormous sums of money he still controlled.
84 Czech intelligence was called *Statni Bezpecnost* (State Security) and abbreviated as StB.
85 Recall that Bittman led James Angleton to became concerned with General Müller after Bittman said the Czechs were responsible for 'planting' the 1964 Peter Stähle story in *Stern*.
86 Bittman (1972), 31–33.

87   Ibid., 145.
88   Recall that something similar happened in Poland following Stalin's downfall and the removal of Stalinist hard liners in the wake of the Swialto affair.
89   Jaroslav Nachtmann. He apparently first returned to Czechoslovakia in 1955. On his incredibly complicated past, see Axis History Forum at https://forum.axishistory.com/viewtopic.php?t=119289.
90   Frolik (1975) adds that his own research showed that another top Prague Gestapo officer named Commissar Leimer was a Soviet agent. For his actions, Leimer became a NKVD Colonel after the war. (This was Willi Leimer.) Stalin reportedly personally awarded Leimer the Order of Lenin. As an NKVD agent, he reportedly infiltrated the Gestapo as far back as 1933.
91   Frolik (1975), 20–21.
92   Ibid., 22.
93   And why, we might add, was the story Frolik's informant told different from the one Barak gave to Bagley and Villemarest decades later?
94   Frolik (1975), 28.
95   Frolik and August also provided British intelligence highly detailed information on Czech operations in England in the early to mid-1960s.
96   August and Rees (1984), 100.
97   Ibid., 94.
98   In 1968, this network tried to blame student protests in Warsaw on a larger Jewish conspiracy orchestrated from Tel Aviv.
99   August and Rees (1984), 96–97.
100   Ibid., 97.
101   Ibid. Clearly this is a reference to the Siebert case.
102   Or 'Nachtmann' in Frolik's spelling.
103   August and Rees (1984), 97.
104   Ibid., 97–98.
105   Ibid., 98.
106   Bagley (2007), 119–20. In March 1955 (4/3), *News from Behind the Iron Curtain* published Swialto's revelations from his RFE broadcasts. Swialto singled out Polish Marshal Rola Zymierski for his collaboration with the Gestapo under the direction of Zymierski's Russian controller, Colonel Szklarenko. For an overview of the Swialto affair, see Gluchowksi (1999).
107   See Coogan (1999), 65–69.
108   On the SS and the CIA, see Lingen (2008) and (2013).
109   Richards (1966), 181–82.

PART III

King of Queens

8

WASHINGTON MERRY-GO-ROUND

Red scare redux?

> 'US Secret Agencies Penetrated by Reds.'
> '4 US Envoys Linked to Red Spy Sex Net.'

These two massive headlines dominated the front pages of the 2–3 March 1964 issues of the *New York Journal-American* (*NYJA*), the Hearst newspaper empire's tabloid New York paper. Written by the *Journal-American* editor Guy Richards, the first story began: 'A defector from the Soviet Secret Police has informed US officials that Moscow has placed active "cells" in the Central Intelligence Agency and the State Dept. in Washington and overseas.' Goleniewski was now frontpage news as he now found himself in the middle of a complex war between factions of American intelligence that even led back to Poland.

In September 1958, the USA and the People's Republic of China (PRC) resumed high-level diplomatic talks in Warsaw. The resumption of diplomatic negotiations came in the wake of the Second Taiwan Straits Crisis that began on 23 August 1958 when Communist forces began shelling Quemoy, an island controlled by the Nationalist government in Taiwan. Warsaw was chosen as the place for talks between US Ambassador Jacob Beam and Chinese envoy Wang Bingnan.[1] It would remain a key meeting ground for the two powers until January 1968.

The US Embassy now became an especially enticing target for a joint KGB–MSW counterintelligence operation. Otto Otepka, the State Department's Deputy Director of Office of Security, was told by the CIA in the summer of 1959 that the Agency had an informant who provided evidence of extensive Soviet penetration of the Embassy.[2] The CIA briefers 'stated that action to remove the security risks from the embassy should be done slowly and with a great deal of caution, for any unusual activity might alert the KGB to the fact that they had a spy in their ranks.'[3]

DOI: 10.4324/9781003051114-12

A Washington-based publication entitled *The Government Employees' Exchange* later claimed that after Goleniewski was debriefed by the CIA, a State Department electronic expert named Elmer Dewey Hill visited Warsaw in April 1962. Hill reportedly discovered listening devices both in the old Embassy as well as in bricks sent from Yugoslavia for the new Embassy. Thanks to these devices, the Soviets supposedly:

> recorded the reading of the texts of American top secret and secret codes by the code clerks while doing the encoding and decoding. Subsequently by comparing these with the transmitted messages, the Soviet Union broke the codes. This resulted in the breaking also of the major codes of the United States in messaging being sent to Germany, Italy, France, England and Japan. Central Intelligence Agency telegrams and communications were 'broken' in the same manner by the Soviet Union, the source revealed.[4]

The penetration of Eastern Bloc intelligence into the Embassy – from attractive Polish girls befriending Marines guards to a mid-level US diplomat turned Russian spy – also fueled fears over laxness in security.

The Warsaw revelations sharpened an on-going argument in Washington over the perceived liberalism of the new Kennedy regime. The State Department's Otto Otepka, a senior civil servant seen as a holdover from the McCarthy era, had become a focus of the new administration's wrath after Otepka tried to block certain top Kennedy appointees from entering government service for security reasons. The Kennedy brothers forced out Otepka from his post, an act that made Otepka a conservative *cause célèbre*. It was in this larger political context that Goleniewski was viewed as one more weapon to be used against Kennedy and perceived doves in State and CIA with the sensational *Journal-American* accusations.

In April 1964, a month after Guy Richards began his syndicated series on Goleniewski, the CIA retaliated by playing the 'Tsar card.' The Agency leaked news to columnist Drew Pearson that Goleniewski:

> has been in constant fear of his life and the strain may have been too much for him. For example, last summer he described himself as a Romanoff, a member of the Russian royal family, although he is a Pole. Then he began claiming that Communist agents had infiltrated the CIA. He spun a yarn about how $1,000,000 in CIA funds had fallen into KGB hands, half of which had been pumped back into the U.S. to finance Communist operations.... The CIA has tried to persuade Goleniewski to visit a psychiatrist, but he has refused on the ground that this may be a plot to silence him.[5]

In the 21 April 1964 *Allen-Scott Report*, the conservative syndicated columnists exposed the CIA's backroom takedown of Goleniewski:

> A major effort is being made by a group of State Department and Central Intelligence Agency authorities to whitewash, cover up and ridicule the

disclosures made by Polish defector Colonel Michal Goleniewski since they involve treason in both agencies. It is a well-organized campaign, with CIA officials making personal contact with members of Congress and newsmen and telling them Goleniewski is under heavy nervous tension.

But how did Goleniewski find himself in the spotlight in the first place?[6]
The answer begins with the CIA trying to do him a favor.
After Goleniewski defected, he and his now-wife Irmgard would not be legally eligible for US citizenship until 1968. Goleniewski, however, insisted on early citizenship. In the summer of 1963, a private congressional bill known as HR 5507 was introduced to Congress by the CIA to do just that.[7] The CIA acted after Goleniewski had written CIA Director John McCone a letter on 26 April 1963 'complaining about his treatment and threatening to tell the White House about his situation.'[8]
In its report on Goleniewski to the House Subcommittee on Immigration and Nationality, the CIA also volunteered some details about the defector. The Agency stated that Goleniewski was born on 16 August 1922 in Nieswiez, and that he graduated from a Gymnasium in 1939. It added that he spent three years studying for a law degree at the University of Poznan, and in 1956 he received an MA in political science from the University of Warsaw.[9] Yet Malgorzata Stapinska, William Clarke's researcher, could find no evidence of Goleniewski attending the University of Warsaw in 1956. If he did study at the University of Poznan, presumably it would have been when he worked for the security service in that city. Yet there is no mention of Goleniewski ever receiving a college degree in the WOW court proceedings.
The Acting Chairman of the House Subcommittee on Immigration and Nationality was Michael A. Feighan (pronounced FEE-an), a long-time Democratic Congressman from Cleveland and a fierce foe of Communism.[10] Feighan's father John, a banker and former owner of the Cleveland Indians baseball team, was made a Knight of St. Gregory by Pope Pius XII.[11] Michael, a Princeton and Harvard Law School grad, was first elected to Congress in 1942; he served for 28 years in the House until he was defeated in 1971. During that time, Feighan cultivated especially close relations with 'Captive Nations' émigré organizations in both America and Europe. A hawk's hawk, Feighan told one interviewer that 'peaceful coexistence between the East and West is impossible, nor can any diplomatic agreements short of complete surrender be reached with Soviet Communists.'[12]
Inside the Beltway, Feighan was known for his bitter feud with the syndicated columnist Drew Pearson. Pearson reported, for example, that in October 1963 (shortly before President Kennedy's assassination), Feighan went on a Congressional junket to Geneva. On the trip, Feighan was vocal about his hatred for President Kennedy's civil rights bill; he even labeled Eleanor Roosevelt a 'nigger lover.'[13] For his part, Feighan gave a speech in the House of Representatives in which he claimed that Pearson 'was acting as an agent of a foreign power, the Communist regime of Yugoslavia and its dictator, Tito.'[14]

Feighan's hatred for Robert Kennedy proved equally robust. One of Goleniewski's supporters named Frank Capell in 1964 wrote a 70-something page pamphlet entitled *The Strange Death of Marilyn Monroe*, in which Capell claimed that Robert Kennedy was personally responsible for her death. Pearson reported that Feighan put Capell in contact with Jimmy Hoffa's Teamsters Union, but not even Hoffa wanted anything to do with Capell's pamphlet.[15]

That Feighan was head of the Subcommittee on Immigration when Goleniewski's citizenship hearing was scheduled was accidental. The Subcommittee's Chairman, Pennsylvania Congressman Francis Walter, would have rubber-stamped the CIA's request without demanding Goleniewski's appearance. Walter, however, died on 31 May 1963, making Feighan, the next ranking member. The Subcommittee's new boss, Feighan had heard rumors about Goleniewski and he demanded to see Goleniewski in person.

Goleniewski appeared before the full Subcommittee on 27 May 1963 and testified for 20 minutes. The questions were translated, and he replied in Polish, although he said he understood English but not perfectly.[16] Goleniewski, however, still remained upset even after his hearing; he sent a registered letter to President Kennedy on 15 June 1963 listing his ongoing grievances with the CIA.[17]

Goleniewski's brief encounter with Feighan at his naturalization hearing proved significant when Feighan also received a letter from Goleniewski. He told Feighan that his problems with the CIA first began in Wiesbaden: 'After 33 months of my anti-Soviet efforts in the East for the United States of America,' he wrote, "Howard" [Roman] and "Bleeke" made the first contact with me by lying and making small distortions.'[18] Feighan received the letter in June, but put it out of his mind until Goleniewski followed up with another letter that July, this one to Feighan's home address. Goleniewski claimed that he had urgent information and went so far as to suggest that his life was in grave danger.[19]

On 2 August 1963, Feighan made a special trip to Queens. He brought with him two trusted aides, Colonel Philip J. Corso and Dr. Edwin O'Connor.[20] Corso had retired from the US Army in early 1962, and he officially worked for the far-right South Carolina Senator Strom Thurmond. Colonel Corso knew O'Connor from the NSC Operations Coordinating Board (OCB), on which both men served in the Eisenhower administration. The OCB included the head of the CIA, the Deputy Director of the Pentagon, the Undersecretary of State, and the President's special assistant for Psychological Warfare named C. D. Jackson among others.

As for O'Connor, in 1948 he served as US Commissioner for Displaced Persons (DPs) under Truman; in 1951 he helped draft the Displaced Persons Act enabling thousands of DPs to more freely emigrate to America. O'Connor then worked on the NSC staff from 1951 to 1960, and then as staff director of the Joint Congressional Committee on Immigration Policy. Feighan had been deeply involved in Displaced Persons issues since at least 1947. All three men stressed the importance of bringing émigrés from 'Captive Nations' to America; they helped ensure the Captive Nation refugees would be viewed favorably by immigration authorities.[21]

In the summer of 1954, Feighan attended European hearings of the House Committee on Communist Aggression headed by Wisconsin Republican Representative Charles Kersten (popularly referred to as the 'Kersten Commission').[22] The Committee was responsible for the passage of the 'Kersten Amendment' to the 1951 Mutual Security Act which authorized an appropriation

> not to exceed $100,000,000 ... for any selected persons who are residing in or escapees from the Soviet Union, Poland, Czechoslovakia, Hungary, Romania, Bulgaria, Albania, Lithuania, Latvia, Estonia, or the Communist-dominated or Communist-occupied areas of Germany or Austria, and any other countries absorbed by the Soviet Union either to form such persons into elements of the military forces supporting the NATO or for other purposes, when it is ... determined by the President that such assistance will contribute to the defense of ... and to the security of the US.[23]

When Feighan and his aides knocked on Goleniewski's door, they were more than curious to hear what he had to say. While Irmgard brought the trio refreshments, Goleniewski reportedly 'greeted them with a cultivated English accent slightly tinctured with German.... They soon learned that their host was perfectly at ease not only in English, but in Russian, Polish, German, and French.'[24] One of the men who met the chain-smoking Pole that night later told Guy Richards that 'my first impression was that of a creature who probably doesn't exist at all – a dashing, highly literate British cavalry officer.'[25]

Once pleasantries were exchanged, they got down to the business at hand, namely Goleniewski's claims that:

1. the Russians had hoaxed the CIA into passing over $1,200,000 in cash to support some imaginary American operatives and that the money had been split up in thirds for the KGB, the Italian Communist Party, and the American Communist Party.
2. Three top American scientists were on the KGB's payroll.
3. There were KGB informants inside the State Department including some in the code and communications sections.
4. Several CIA men were KGB or GRU agents.
5. The KGB managed to compromise four US diplomats in the Warsaw Embassy.
6. One of the top Soviet spies in the Embassy was a long-time US Foreign Service officer named Edward Symans and that Symans was allowed to resign from the State Department in 1961 to avoid a larger scandal.
7. The Russians had gotten a leak that an informer had been telling the US about Russian penetration into the Embassy and that this led the Russians to begin their own hunt for the leaker, a hunt that forced Goleniewski to flee to the West before it was too late.
8. How the US CIA reacted positively to Goleniewski's leads on Soviet moles abroad but how the CIA refused to investigate his claims about Americans

working for the KGB and how the CIA had prevented him from taking his information to the FBI and J. Edgar Hoover personally.[26]

During the meeting, Goleniewski reportedly tried to discuss his claim to the Romanov throne only to be brushed aside by Colonel Corso, who requested him to focus on espionage matters.[27]

Back in Washington, Feighan met CIA Director John McCone to discuss Goleniewski. Colonel Corso returned to New York for further detailed discussion with Goleniewski about alleged subversives. Corso also brought a subpoena from the Senate Internal Security Subcommittee, and asked Goleniewski if he wished to testify. Goleniewski 'immediately expressed his willingness to accept the subpoena and testify in an executive session of the Senate panel provided there was ample security and protection against photographers at the door.'[28] A tentative date for his testimony was also set.

The idea that Goleniewski would testify before the Internal Security Sub-committee so infuriated the CIA that it persuaded a high-ranking member of the Subcommittee to revoke the subpoena. This was almost certainly Republican Congressman Leslie C. Arends, who served as a strong CIA defender during the debates.[29] Colonel Corso came under attack as well. The CIA reportedly pressured the military to have Corso charged with 'making use of information gained on active duty' and 'for masquerading as an intelligence officer.'[30]

A strange Washington dance now began with Goleniewski's supporters pushing for him to testify, while the CIA and its allies tried to shut him down. On one or two occasions when Goleniewski was slated to appear, he himself postponed the appointment saying that his wife was ill and needed an operation.[31] Time and again, Goleniewski seemed on the brink of testifying. Yet he never did.

Guy Richards

After months of back-room political ping-pong, Goleniewski's Congressional backers decided to break the stalemate. In mid-February 1964, Frank Capell, editor of the rightwing newssheet *Herald of Freedom*, reached out to a longtime New York newspaper man named Guy Richards to tell him about Goleniewski and to set in motion Richards' *Journal-American* March expose. Capell was also close to Colonel Corso, both men being members of a pseudo-chivalric group that called itself the Knights of Malta. From his first conversation with Capell until his death at age 73 in 1979, Richards became engrossed in both Goleniewski and the fate of the Romanovs, and wrote three books on the topic.[32]

Born in 1905 and descended from a Dutch family that arrived in 'New Amsterdam' in the 1630s, Richards was educated at Yale.[33] After college, he joined the Whitney South Sea Expeditions (WSSE) sponsored by the American Museum of Natural History. Financed by Harry Payne Whitney, WSSE employed a 75-ton schooner named *France* to explore the South Seas. For over a decade, WSSE crews visited hundreds of islands collecting birds, plants, and other animals as well as anthropological information. In 1927–1928 Richards' group visited different Polynesian islands, including the Santa Cruz islands, the Solomon Islands, and Papua, New Guinea. In World War II, Richards served as an Assistant R-2 (intelligence) officer in the South Pacific with the rank of Colonel in the First Marine Corps; he would maintain a strong connection to the Marines after leaving the service. Back in New York, Richards wrote for various papers before becoming city editor on the conservative *New York Journal-American*.

In 1997 a former Polish intelligence officer turned pop espionage author named Henryk Piecuch published *Imperium Sluzb Specjalnych od Gomulki do Kani* (Secret Service Imperium from Gomulka to Kani) where he interviewed a former Colonel in the Polish secret service named Marceli Wieczorek. Born in February 1934, Wieczorek was assigned to New York City from 1967–1968. From 1969–1971 he worked out of the Polish Consulate in Chicago. Wieczorek said that one Saturday in July 1969, while at the Chicago Consulate, he received a phone call from a lawyer named Robert Samborski, whom Wieczorek assumed had some relationship to American intelligence.[34] In *Hunt for the Czar*, Richards describes Samborski as a Chicago lawyer who loved the mystery surrounding the Romanovs. Samborski was also a friend of John Fred Schlafly, a lawyer who lived in Alton, Illinois, and who was married to the well-known conservative activist Phyllis Schlafly. Both men helped Richards with his Goleniewski research.

Wieczorek recalled that he first met Guy Richards in Bob Samborski's company at the Hotel Drake on Lake Shore Drive to talk about Goleniewski. At the meeting, Richards asked him if Polish intelligence could supply him with documents on Goleniewski's past. Wieczorek kept up a friendship of sorts with Richards, whom he described not as a newspaper editor but as a professor and Naval Commander at the Naval Postgraduate Institute in Monterrey, California, where he helped train future CIA officers.

As Guy Richards was a well-known New York newspaper man with a book on Goleniewski, Wieczorek's claim made little sense. After World War II, however, Richards (a Major in the US Marine Corps Reserve) wrote articles on military topics such as a 1949 text entitled 'The Riddle of Combined Arms,' and it is possible that he may have lectured on specialized military topics (such as amphibious landing planning) for the Navy in the late 1940s. It seems more likely, however, that Wieczorek or Piecuch simply garbled Richards' back story.[35]

Richards also had a special interest in Russia. In 1956 he published his one novel, *Two Rubles to Times Square*. 'Alexis Mihalovich Ketov,' the book's hero of a sort, is born in western Russia in the early 1900s to parents of the minor nobility, his father being a colonel in the Russian cavalry. After joining the Red Army and fighting in World War II, Ketov, now a general, decides to destroy the Soviet system. *Two Rubles* is an odd 'Mouse that Roared' tale of a sneak military invasion and occupation of lower Manhattan by Ketov's secret army of Russian soldiers, who think they are on a Soviet mission. In one climatic moment, Ketov explains the real purpose of his sham attack:

'I hoped to convince you Americans ... that you are not the people to liberate everyone on earth. I hoped to convince you that it is the Russians who should work on the Russians, the Poles on the Poles, Czechs on the Czechs, Asians on the Asians, and Africans on the Africans.'

'After convincing you of that,' he continued, 'I hoped to get American backing for a Foreign Legion founded on that principle. I mean a legion made up partly of escapees who have suffered under the Kremlin's regime, the people who have no place to come to these days. A legion capable of inspiring a lot more than armed uprising. One whose way of life, whose very existence in being, would be a threat to the gangster governments of the countries whose people belonged to it.'[36]

At the time Richards wrote his book, hardline factions in the military and Congress were fighting for the creation of just such a US-sanctioned foreign legion made up of European displaced persons and émigrés to be called the Volunteer Freedom Corps (VFC). One of the proposal's strongest advocates was Colonel Corso, who worked on the project while on the OCB. In the early 1950s US intelligence flirted with the creation of 'Operation Crowbar' to raise a force of up to 50,000 displaced Russians with military experience. Thanks to the Kersten Amendment, there was up to $100 million dollars available to build such an army.

Was Richards chosen by Capell because he shared the same commitment to creating an émigré 'foreign legion'? In a 30 March 1964 radio interview with Barry Farber to discuss his Goleniewski series, Richards noted:

> I have a good many friends in the city that go back over my lifetime in the newspaper business. One of them is a man that I respect highly, a fellow called Frank Capell, who gets out a very fine publication called the *Herald of Freedom*. Now Frank had given me a good number of tips, some of which I'd found a little bit slanted in the sense that were – they were accurate but slanted ideologically speaking to the right.

Capell clearly played the go-between with his friends in Congress to set the stage for Goleniewski to testify in public. Did Capell's selection of Richards reflect the journalist's own intelligence connections as well?

Fiasco

Guy Richards' stories and Goleniewski's proposed Congressional appearance were designed as a dramatic opening gambit for a broader attack on the State Department and CIA. In his 3 March 1964 'U.S. Envoys Linked to Red Spy Sex Net' story, Richards opened the campaign by citing the case of Joseph Farland, a highly conservative former US Ambassador to Panama who resigned from his post in the summer of 1963. A lawyer, Farland had first worked for the FBI, but he then moved into the private sector as president of various coal companies. First appointed Ambassador to the Dominican Republic in 1957, Farland became Ambassador to Panama in 1960. According to Richards, 'for months before his resignation … Ambassador Farland had called the turn – and filed reports on – the widespread sabotage and revolutionary plots of Castro agents throughout the Caribbean, including Panama.' The article continues:

> In the Feb. 25th issue of the *Congressional Record*, Mr. Farland is quoted as follows:
>
> When I arrived home in August and the State Dept. circulated its customary notice to appropriate agencies listing returned ambassadors available for consultation, a man in the White House went to work. His name is Ralph Dungan. On whose authority he acted I do not know. But Mr. Dungan phoned the various agencies, including the Pentagon, that I was not to be invited for consultation.
>
> The *Congressional Record* also quotes Mr. Farland as having been taken in hand on an earlier visit to Washington in the Fall of 1962 by Edwin Martin, then Assistant Secretary of State for Latin American Affairs. 'Mr. Martin,' Mr. Farland reported, 'literally ordered me to have no contact with top CIA executive and Congressional leaders.'
>
> And Congress now is going to page Mr. Martin and Mr. Ralph Dungan, the mystery man who phoned from the White House.[37]

On the heels of Richards' articles, Ohio Republican Congressman John Ashbrook, a member of the House Un-American Activities Committee (HUAC), publicly defended Goleniewski. Ashbrook said he hoped HUAC also would call Goleniewski before it.[38] Ashbrook added that he had recently introduced a bill into Congress 'calling for an investigation of the State Department.'[39]

In his 4 March 1964 *NYJA* article entitled 'CIA Hiding Red Defector from Probers,' Richards quotes Ashbrook:

> 'I am flying up to see you for information on the whole story which obviously can't be given over the phone.' With these words, Rep. John Milan Ashbrook (R–Ohio) announced his arrival later today in the offices of the *N.Y. Journal-American*. His purpose, he said, was to learn all the details and background about the sensational disclosures by Soviet secret police defector and former high-ranking official, Lt. Col. Michal Goleniewski, and related stories published in this newspaper.
>
> Rep. Ashbrook, a member of the House Un-American Activities Committee, added: 'I want to get every particle of information I can get about Goleniewski's charges of KGB agents in the State Dept. and Central Intelligence Agency. I note that the Federal agencies are already engaged in the classic maneuver they used on Povl Bang-Jensen, trying to imply that Col. Goleniewski has gone off his rocker....[40]
>
> 'It is vitally important,' Rep. Ashbrook continued, 'that Col. Goleniewski appear before my committee. It is high time the whole State Dept. and its

policies be brought to account. It has continually lied about such Communist penetration as those made in Warsaw, Washington, and elsewhere.'

Ashbrook's desire for a larger investigation was fueled by the dismissal of the former head of the State Department's Office of Security Otto Otepka for reportedly leaking documents to Jay Sourwine, lead counsel for the Internal Security Subcommittee of the Senate Judiciary Committee, the Senate's version of HUAC.

Yet when Congressman Ashbrook and an investigator from HUAC came to New York, 'Ashbrook was told by Goleniewski's associates that the defector had gone to the Pittsburgh area. Upon his return to Washington … Ashbrook said an "intermediary" for the Central Intelligence told him the agency would prefer for him not to pursue the case any further.'[41]

But what about Goleniewski's other assertions, such as his supposed attack on unnamed pro-Russian American scientists? Otto Otepka's conservative biographer William Gill reports that these accusations had a stale feel:

> Most of the individuals named already had substantial amounts of questionable information in their security files long before anyone ever heard of Michal Goleniewski. Several had previously been identified as possible Soviet agents by other more ostensibly reliable sources. At least two of the scientists have openly espoused Communist causes or policies that have served the USSR's purposes.[42]

Goleniewski's claim that the CIA was fooled into supplying the Communist Parties of Italy, the USA, and the KGB with money also died on the vine. Recall that Goleniewski was reported as saying some $1.2 million in CIA funds 'in Vienna' was passed on to the Communists, with one-third going to the KGB, one-third to the Italian CP, and one-third to the US CP.[43] This assertion then disappeared from the headlines.[44]

What is most intriguing in the Richards' 2 March 1964 story mentioning the mysterious $1.2 million is one word: 'recently.' Richards writes: 'Approximately $1.2 million of CIA funds in Vienna recently was passed secretly to the Communists….' How would Goleniewski know about a 'recent' event in Vienna since he had defected three years earlier. One obvious possible answer is that Colonel Corso and company simply fed Goleniewski these stories, which is what the CIA thought. A comment originating from the CIA and appearing in the 3 March 1964 edition of the *Los Angeles Times* said as much. From 'Information from Polish Defector Helps Nab Red Spies Outside U.S.':

> It was learned on highest authority, however, that the newspaper account [in the *NYJA*] was considered not only inaccurate, but inconsistent with information Goleniewski has provided American officials over the past several years. There also was some suggestion here that the published account had not come from the defector himself, but rather from Congressional sources.

In response to the statement clearly coming from the CIA that Goleniewski had never informed it about KGB agents inside either the CIA or State, Richards wrote that 'Col. Goleniewski said the reason high CIA officials may not have received the information was that it had been quashed before reaching them by some of its own agents.'[45] Goleniewski would later claim that 'neo-Stalinists' in the CIA plotted against him.

By this time, however, Goleniewski had begun to fade from public view, in large part because his claim to the Russian throne so poisoned his credibility. From the CIA's standpoint, he was at best yesterday's paper. And with his mind-bending public radio announcement in the late summer of 1964 that he was really Aleksei, Tsar of Russia, Goleniewski clearly had moved on as well.

Allen Dulles and Department D

Defectors are often extremely complex characters with highly difficult personalities. It was not as if the CIA hadn't tried hard to reach an understanding with Goleniewski. It put up with his eccentricities, dictatorial commands, and abrasive personality. The CIA's Howard Roman also recalled that 'Goleniewski got into quite a psychological tizzy during his interrogations. He used to play Victrola records of old European songs at top volume and drink booze.'[46]

The Agency assigned a highly experienced case officer named George Kisevalter to handle the pesky Pole. Born in St. Petersburg in 1910, Kisevalter's father was a munitions expert who came to the USA in 1915 as part of an arms buying mission. The Bolshevik Revolution forced the family to remain in America. In World War II, Kisevalter worked on the Russian Lend–Lease program and as an army intelligence officer. He next joined the CIA and helped run a top in-place Soviet defector named Peter Popov as well as being involved with the case of one of the West's most important agents, GRU Colonel Oleg Penkovsky.[47] But even he could do nothing to stem Goleniewski's deteriorating relationship with the CIA. Goleniewski even labeled him a 'neo-Stalinist.' In one of his statements explaining why he stopped talking to his CIA debriefers, Goleniewski wrote: 'Because I could just contact by phone one of the no-satisfactory official of CIA, GEORGE, who knew me from the time of the RUSSIAN IMPERIUM, I was forced to refuse any further contacts with this – or similar to him gentlemen.'[48]

The CIA now told one and all that Goleniewski had been a highly valued defector, but under the strain of his double life had gone crazy, so crazy that he now claimed he was emperor of Russia. Former CIA officer Tennent Bagley summed up Langley's view when he noted: 'It was a great loss to our side, when, all too soon after his defection, this sharpest of counterintelligence minds slipped into delusion and his information became confusing and misleading.'[49] Former MI5 official Peter Wright also reports: 'By the time MI5 saw Goleniewski the CIA suspected he was going clinically insane. He began to have delusions that he was descended from the Tsar, but despite that, his recall of intelligence remained remarkably accurate.'[50] A former CIA agent who twice met Goleniewski recalled:

'I went up to see if I could pour oil on troubled waters. It was no use; he was around the bend. But I will say this: the material he provided us was very good indeed. There was no nonsense. It was not the product of a fevered imagination. It was the real stuff.'[51]

Goleniewski's supporters in Congress now hastily abandoned their plan to use him. As Jay Sourwine of the Senate Internal Security Subcommittee put it:

> The Subcommittee was unanimous in deciding not to put Colonel Goleniewski on the stand in a public hearing, after Colonel Goleniewski advised the Sub-committee that if called he would insist upon discussing first his claim to be the heir to the throne of Russia. The committee did not feel that its hearing table was a proper forum for the advancement of such a claim.[52]

The CIA took other aggressive actions. In April 1963 it helped Goleniewski obtain a legal permit to carry a gun in New York. As a high-ranking defector sentenced to death by a Polish military court, Goleniewski's desire to own a legal weapon was not surprising. In 1964, however, the CIA refused to extend the carry permit and demanded that he return the gun. The CIA may have acted out of genuine concern for Goleniewski's mental stability, but he viewed it as part of a plot by the CIA to ensure that the KGB would be able to kill him.

Financial pressure was put on Goleniewski as well. The CIA's historian David Robarge in his profile of John McCone writes that 'CIA renegotiated Goleniewski's contract in his favor in October 1963, and, when that incentive failed, took the opposite tack and suspended it in early 1964.' The move came after Goleniewski declared in December 1963 that he would refuse to meet any more debriefers. Goleniewski seemed particularly taken with the notion that the CIA – along with British intelligence – had known through their own separate investigations that he was the rightful Tsar, but they deliberately refused to acknowledge this fact. He was especially concerned to retrieve his original Polish passport and claimed that it carried key microdots that would prove his claim. In *Imperial Agent*, Richards quotes Goleniewski as saying:

> A short time after I arrived in the United States, I deposited my Polish documents with the CIA representative, Mr. Howard E. Roman – my Polish passport, my Polish officer-identification book and my Polish Intelligence Service identifica-tion card. For my personal security in Poland and in my travels outside Poland, my Polish passport always contained microfilmed photocopies of about forty documents which in an absolutely necessary situation could be and can be used to prove my real identity as the Czarevich Alexi Nicholaevich of Russia.[53]

All the CIA would do is give him a xeroxed copy of the document.

The Agency terminated Goleniewski's contract completely in late 1965 but continued to pay him a small annual annuity, a sum Goleniewski bitterly com-plained about as insufficient to support him, his wife, and his new daughter

Tatiana. In a 10 January 1965 letter to Congressman Feighan begging for help, Goleniewski's wife Irmgard wrote:

> I have to ask you also for immediate help. Ultimately I want just to tell you that we are still forced since January 1964, i.e. 3 months after the new U.S. Contract of CIA with my husband of October 7, 1963 (by your support) was signed – to continue our life now with our in the meantime-born daughter for $500 per month, here in New York City, without any health and life insurance, without any legal protection from part of CIA and also without any other remunerations contained in the U.S. Contract of October 7, 1963, and promised to us in the name of the U.S. Government.[54]

Goleniewski's clash with the CIA occurred under two Agency directors, Allen Dulles and John McCone. When Goleniewski arrived in America in January 1961, Dulles was at the height of his power. On 30 September 1961, Goleniewski and Dulles met in the latter's office in the CIA's old headquarters. Also present were Howard Roman, 'Mr. Skov' (Herbert Scoville), and James Hunt, deputy chief of James Angleton's counterintelligence staff. During the hour-long ceremonial encounter, Dulles avoided serious conversation and talked a good deal about his pipe collection. He worried that after the Agency move to Langley, he might not have enough room to have all the pipes he wanted put on display.[55] Dulles, however, was dismissed as CIA Director by President Kennedy just a short time later on 29 November 1961.

In 1963 the now-retired Dulles published *The Craft of Intelligence*. Dulles sent Goleniewski a signed copy that read 'Best Regards, Allen Dulles.'[56] When Goleniewski read the book, he was furious. Wasn't Dulles now claiming credit for things the Agency knew nothing about until he told them?

Goleniewski first told the CIA about the creation of a new 'Department D' inside the KGB's First Chief Directorate (FCD) devoted to 'disinformation.' Founded in 1959, Department D was led by a top KGB officer named Ivan Agayants, an Armenian-born Chekist who spoke Turkish, Persian, French, Spanish, and English and was a holder of the Order of Lenin. From longtime CIA official Richards Heuer's article 'Nosenko: Five Paths to Judgment':

> Goleniewski was the first CIA source to report in detail on its [Department D's] anticipated functions and significance. He stated that one of the many objectives of KGB disinformation was the protection of Soviet agents by means of actions designed to mislead Western security services. He listed among specific objectives and types of disinformation operations those designed to discredit accurate information of significance received by the opposition through sources not under Soviet control, such as defectors, thus casting doubt on the veracity of the source of the true information. Goleniewski stated further that, in extreme cases, the KGB would be willing to sacrifice some of its own agent assets to enhance the reputation of an agent penetration of a Western intelligence service. Golitsyn confirmed

Goleniewski's reporting on Department D and added that a KGB or GRU defector's file would be sent to this new unit.[57]

David Robarge also explains:

CIA first heard about the KGB disinformation unit from Polish intelligence officer Michal Goleniewski – a walk-in source of the CIA's beginning in 1959 [sic] – who had dealt with the KGB on dezinformatsiya matters since 1953.[58] Although he was not the first Agency asset to refer to the practice of disinformation, Goleniewski was the first to emphasise the role that Soviet counterintelligence officers played in disseminating it.[59]

In *The Craft of Intelligence*, Dulles drew on Goleniewski's revelations about Department D as if they were independently discovered by a crackerjack US intelligence agency. If blatantly stealing from him wasn't bad enough, Goleniewski said the information in the book would further inflame the Russians, as they would recognize Goleniewski as the real source. The book only placed his life in yet more danger. The idea that Dulles might have thought Goleniewski would be pleased to see his information made public never crossed his mind.

On 10 March 1964, Guy Richards appeared on Barry Farber's radio talk show to promote his Goleniewski series. A few days earlier, Allen Dulles was asked about Richards' articles on a Washington TV show. He responded by calling them 'hot air.' In his radio interview, Richards commented:

Now this is interesting because I have a man who had spoken to Goleniewski at great length, underlined those passages from Mr. Dulles' magazine article which preceded his book. There are some 700 words which are directly traceable to Goleniewski's testimony. If he was good enough to make Mr. Dulles' book, and good enough without name however, to get a letter from Mr. Dulles thanking him personally for the help that he rendered, it's extraordinary to me that now the same man's information suddenly becomes hot air.[60]

Goleniewski appeared on the Barry Farber show in August 1964 to announce his claim to the throne. On 17 August 1964, Philippa Schuyler, a journalist for the right-wing *Manchester Union Leader*, also wrote a front-page story entitled 'Russia's Czar Lives!' to promote his claim. Schuyler noted that when her paper asked Dulles for a comment about whether Goleniewski really was the Tsar, he would only reply, 'The story may all be true, or it may not be.'

'Telsur'

As the CIA struggled with Goleniewski, Polish intelligence tried to capitalize on the Agency's discomfort. In his 2013 article on 'The Agent who would be Tsar,' Polish journalist Piotr Gontarczyk reports:

So when in 1965 in Congress a special commission for the operation of the American secret services began to operate, there was a chance to discredit the CIA with Goleniewski's case by proving that the agency works on the basis of information given to it by a crazy and notorious imposter. Polish and Soviet services began discreetly supporting left-wing journalists and congressmen (typical 'useful idiots') in their attacks on the CIA, among others by sending disinformation materials and inspiring press articles on one of the most important sources of the Agency, currently 'Tsarevich Aleksei.' Through a paid Austrian journalist, a richly documented series of articles about Goleniewski was prepared with information about his wife and children in Poland. The hero – as a crook and bigamist – was discredited against Russian circles and disappeared from public life.[61]

As the Poles schemed, the CIA struggled, and the Tsar stewed, the FBI now entered the fray in an oblique way. From April 1958 on, Goleniewski fixated on FBI Director J. Edgar Hoover as the answer to all his prayers. As soon as he arrived in Washington, Goleniewski pushed for a private one-on-one meeting with Hoover. In the August 1976 issue of *Double Eagle*, Goleniewski recalled that on 20 December 1961, two months after meeting Allen Dulles, he received a tour of the FBI building and met FBI Assistant Director Alan Belmont. Yet he was still denied the direct access to Hoover he so desperately craved. After sending a personal letter to Hoover begging for an audience, 'he got back … a polite letter' and 'an autographed copy of Hoover's book.'[62]

One Goleniewski sighting on the FBI's radar stemmed from his association with super-patriot and Knight of Malta Frank Capell. Before relocating to Zarephath, New Jersey, in the early 1960s, Capell ran an employment bureau in Staten Island, where he and his wife Adele also raised seven children. His real passion, however, was anti-communism. *Herald of Freedom* (whose first issue appeared in February 1963) served as a leak sheet not just for conservatives in Congress and the Washington security establishment, but for local police intelligence units as well.

In the 11 February and 25 March 1966 issues of *Herald of Freedom*, Capell ran a two-part series entitled 'The Strange Case of "Col." Goleniewski,' based on talks with the defector. The series was the most detailed report on Goleniewski before *Imperial Agent*. Given Goleniewski's acidic personality, however, things did not go entirely smoothly with Capell. On 9 December 1966, Goleniewski took out a notice in the *New York Times* that criticized both Capell and Guy Richards. As for Capell, Goleniewski wrote:

With regard to the books of KNIGHT of SOVEREIGN ORDER OF ST. JOHN of JERUSALEM, FRANK A. CAPELL titled 'TREASON IS THE REASON' published by the HERALD OF FREEDOM … I have never supplied FRANK A. CAPELL with any information, nor were he or other persons authorized to make any reference in said book to my person, my activities, my support for the national security of USA, etc. He misrepresented in his book my person and my activities through distortion of facts and left the impression that I am the source in certain cases re: the affiliations of various high US officials to questionable activities. He hid my real identity and misused my assumed identity of M. M. GOLENIEWSKI.

Goleniewski was referring to a 1965 book by Capell titled *Treason is the Reason: 847 Reasons for Investigating the State Department*, a minor hit on the far right that enjoyed a second edition in 1966.[63] The text largely rehashed charges dating back to the 1950s against various alleged traitors in Washington and elsewhere. Capell wrote:

> Col. Michael Goleniewski was a Polish-Soviet intelligence officer who had 15,000 agents [sic] under his command. He defected and is in the U.S. He supplied the names of many Soviet agents in our employ plus others who have been compromised. Not a single one of these was ever prosecuted or even fired. One was asked to resign when it was learned he had been a KGB agent for 18 years – but even he was quietly rehired and then pensioned off. Some of the Soviet agents listed in this book have been named by Col. Goleniewski.[64]

Goleniewski's comment underscored the fact that his defection was intended to be used by the right in Congress to launch an attack on its perceived enemies in the CIA and State Department.

While Capell fumed over the government's inability to track down security risks, the FBI opened a security investigation on one potential risk: Frank Capell. On 4 April 1965, W. Raymond Warnell, who led the FBI's intelligence division, wrote a report on Capell. Warnell said that in three instances Capell was in unauthorized possession of classified material. Capell apparently had obtained 'derogatory information' about State Department employees in a loyalty investigation. Capell also identified a Soviet official as working for the KGB. Capell's source, Warnell believed, was in the State Department. Since Capell was unwilling to name his source and not publish the information, Warnell said:

> We should try to eliminate this security threat and dry up his source. We have asked State Department to conduct administrative inquiry to see if the source is a State Department employee. The best way for us to receive the identity of Capell's source is through a technical surveillance. Newark on 4/15/65 advised full security assured for technical surveillance (telsurs) on subject's residence and place of business.

Some of the information the FBI worried about apparently appeared in *Treason is the Reason* because a copy was sent to Washington.

On 11 May 1965, telephone wiretaps were installed on Capell's personal phone and the office phone for *Herald of Freedom*. On 28 May 1965, the FBI's Newark Bureau reported that the taps had picked up a discussion between Capell and someone who clearly had just spoken to Goleniewski. In the redacted FBI document, Capell's conversation partner is called 'the Colonel,' quite likely a reference to Capell's friend and fellow Knight of Malta Colonel Corso. It concerned Goleniewski's view that the Communists had infiltrated the postwar Nazi diaspora at the highest level.[65] In short, it was a conversation about 'Hacke.'

Ironically, just as Capell and Goleniewski were in communication about 'subversives' in the American government, the FBI was wiretapping Capell. As we shall see, one former State Department employee also enjoyed a strange connection to the Goleniewski saga. His name was Otto Otepka.

Warsaw whispers?

How did the KGB supposedly discover that there was a 'pig' (a traitor) in Warsaw? Seven years after Goleniewski's defection, new claims surfaced that purported to answer that question. In early 1968, a highly obscure Washington-based publication called *The Government Employees' Exchange* (*GEE*) published an article asserting that the tipster was the US Ambassador to Poland Jacob Beam!

A down-at-the-heels sheet, *GEE* was run for decades by its editor and publisher Sidney Goldberg and his wife Barbara out of a two-room office. It apparently had no other staff.[66] The paper's legal owner appears to have been a company called GEX (Government Employees Exchange) located at 7000 Veterans Memorial Highway, Metairie, Louisiana. GEX was a members-only department store open to the military and some labor union members.[67]

GEX's Louisiana location may be important since articles from Goldberg's *GEE* were regularly inserted into the *Congressional Record* by Judge John Rarick, the far-right Congressman from Louisiana. Whether there was a special tie to Congressman Rarick via GEX or not, *GEE* regularly ran stories with a far-right conspiratorial spin that were obviously fed to it; in that sense *GEE* functioned not unlike *Herald of Freedom* as a leak sheet.[68] Goleniewski also knew *GEE*; in the 3 and 17 April 1968 issues, he posted a notice about a conflict with his landlord, who was threatening his family with eviction.[69]

GEE strongly supported the reinstatement of Otto Otepka as a Security Officer in the State Department. On 15 December 1967, the Senate Internal Security Subcommittee issued a report entitled 'State Department Security – 1963–65.' Pages 39–44 of Part IV of the report ('Michal Goleniewski') focused on Otepka, and the Warsaw Embassy. Otepka may even have inspired the chain of events leading to Congressmen Feighan and Ashbrook's calls for Congressional investigation of the State Department.

Guy Richards was equally aware of Otepka. In a 19 February 1964 *NYJA* story entitled 'New Sex-Spy Scandal' (written a few weeks before the Goleniewski series), Richards reported on the defection of Yuri Nosenko.[70] The defection, however, was a pretext for Richards to complain about the failure of the State Department to act against alleged subversives in the Warsaw Embassy. According to Richards; 'the whole affair is a vindication of the contentions of Otto F. Otepka ... that there were "glaring security deficiencies" at State.'

A career government official, Otto Otepka served as a top lieutenant for Scott McLeod, the pro-Joe McCarthy head of the State Department's Bureau of Security and Consular Affairs from 1953 to 1957. Otepka worked as the chief of the Division of Evaluations of Security Information first under McLeod and then following McLeod's 1957 appointment as US Ambassador to Ireland.

Otepka's troubles began under the new Kennedy administration when he refused to clear Walt Rostow for a government post, claiming he was a security risk.

Otepka was fired in November 1963 for passing classified information to Jay Sourwine, the Senate Internal Security Subcommittee's Chief Counsel. During the leak investigation, Otepka's phone was bugged, his safe was surreptitiously opened with a high-speed drill, and his 'burn bags' were secretly examined. The investigation was believed either authorized or condoned by Justice Department chief Robert F. Kennedy.[71]

To the right, Otepka was a patriot and whistleblower whose warnings about lax security led to his unjust dismissal. The John Birch Society organized a financial support group for his legal case for reinstatement known as the 'American Defense Fund.' The extreme-right Liberty Lobby also turned Otepka's plight into a *cause célèbre*. An article in the 30 April 1969 edition of *GEE* that Rarick inserted into the *Congressional Record* linked Otepka's downfall to a mysterious 'New Team' takeover of the government orchestrated by Bobby Kennedy and liberal foundations:

> A highly secret and unknown American involvement in Yemen was the prelude to major actions by the Central Intelligence Agency's 'New Team' in its November 1963 offensive against President Ngo Dinh Diem of South Vietnam, against Vice President Lyndon B. Johnson, and against Otto F. Otepka, the State Department's former top Security Evaluator, a former Ambassador with close ties to CIA Director Richard Helms, revealed to this newspaper on April 25.
>
> As readers know, the CIA 'New Team' was set up by former Attorney General Robert F. Kennedy following the Bay of Pigs 'fiasco' by the CIA 'Old Team.' Mr. Kennedy recruited into the 'New Team' many officials not only from the CIA (such as Richard Helms) and the Federal Bureau of Investigation (such as Cartha 'Deke' De Loach) but also from the Internal Revenue Service and the National Security Agency. These agencies and their top members were 'knowledgeable' in the exploitation of 'wire taps' and secret informers, the former Ambassador said.

During the 1968 campaign, Richard Nixon indicated that should he win, Otepka would be reinstated. Nixon's new Secretary of State William Rogers, however, wanted nothing to do with Otepka, a decision that outraged Otepka's long-time supporters. Anger over Otepka's treatment now merged with disgust over Nixon's 1969 decision to appoint Jacob Beam as the next US Ambassador to the Soviet Union. After leaving Warsaw in 1961, Beam became acting director of the Arms Control and Disarmament Agency (ACDA). He then was named US Ambassador to Czechoslovakia in 1966. Beam left Prague in March 1969 to accept the Moscow posting.[72]

The public attack on Beam began in January 1968 while he was still in Prague. On 10 January 1968, the *GEE* first suggested that he had betrayed Goleniewski. The *GEE* story (as summarized by a long article in the far-right *Osthe Information Service* newsletter) quoted an unnamed source who presented Myra Michalowski as a Polish Mata Hari who had bewitched Beam.

Born Myra Zandel in Lodz in 1914, Myra became one of Poland's first female foreign correspondents in America. She first married Professor Ignatius (Ignace) Zlotowski, a Polish physicist and nuclear chemistry expert who taught at Vassar during the war. Zlotowski also worked in the Polish Embassy. As for Myra, during World War II she reportedly served in the Polish section of the Office of War Information (OWI).[73]

General Izydor Modelski, who defected to the USA in 1948, identified Professor Zlotowski as most likely a member of a special Communist atomic espionage unit. As Poland's Military Attaché to the USA, Modelski had met Zlotowski. Because atomic espionage matters were above his pay grade, Modelski assumed that a top physics expert like Zlotowski would have been involved in such an effort.

After returning to Poland, Myra next married Zenon Kliszko, the CP's Secretary of Culture and a close Gomulka aide, before her final marriage to Jerzy Michalowski, who became Poland's Ambassador to Washington in May 1967. Previously, he had served in numerous high posts in the foreign service, including as Ambassador to Great Britain and to the United Nations. Myra also became an expert on American literature, and translated Hemingway, Sylvia Plath, and E. L. Doctorow among others before her death in 2007.

According to the *GEE* story, Myra enjoyed a reputation for being 'brilliant in the expertise of the male soul and body.' She almost certainly knew Beam socially since Myra moved in Warsaw's highest cultural and political circles. According to the story, Myra and Beam maintained 'an intimate personal relationship' from 1957 to 1961.

The attack on Beam as an agent and/or dupe of Polish intelligence was also advanced by Michael Jaffe, the General Counsel for the extreme-right Liberty Lobby.[74] Jaffe tried to testify before the Senate Committee on Foreign Relations, but his statement was rejected. On 13 March 1969, Congressman Rarick inserted his statement (which itself quoted from the 10 January 1968 *GEE* article) into the *Congressional Record* with another press release from Liberty Lobby Chairman Curtis Dall. It highlighted Beam's supposed "intimate personal relationship' with Madame Jerzy Michelowski [*sic*], known as the 'Polish Mata Hari.'[75]

The *GEE* story claimed that its source on Beam had over 30 years of career service in the State Department. Otto Otepka spent 36 years working for the government, and it seems obvious that *GEE* wanted to make his identity clear.[76] Shortly before his dismissal from State, Otepka learned of Goleniewski's identity in August 1963 after he read the private bill to grant him American citizenship. Otepka also knew Sidney Goldberg:

Over the years, Otto Otepka told me, he talked to Sidney Goldberg many times. He found Goldberg 'a bit eccentric.' He was a man full of passion, but credible. Had he asked Goldberg for the name of the person who revealed that Walter Sheridan had taken possession of the surveillance tapes? 'You can't ask a newsman for his sources,' Otepka said.[77]

The *GEE* article included this seeming bombshell: In 1960 Myra obtained from Beam details about the dispatches sent by Goleniewski to the West. It was thanks to Beam that Polish intelligence now learned that there was a 'pig' in their spy service. Nor were the charges against Myra new. In *Imperial Agent*, Guy Richards points to Myra, without naming her directly, as Ambassador Beam's enchantress. Richards asks whether Beam has been involved in a honey trap involving a woman who 'possessed beauty and culture,' and who 'might even recall some of the characters in the works of F. Scott Fitzgerald.' All this is a clear reference to Myra.[78]

GEE ran a follow-up article on 7 February 1968 entitled 'Secret Agent's Role in Warsaw Scandals Clarified' that Congressman Rarick reprinted in the *Congressional Record* for 5 February 1969 (E 854). It begins:

> In its January 10 [1968] issue, *The Exchange* reported that Madam Jerzy Michalowski, the 'wife' of the current Polish Ambassador to the United States, has been positively identified as 'one of the chief architects' of the 'Warsaw Sex and Spy Scandals' which disrupted the American Embassy in Warsaw during the incumbency of Ambassador Joseph [Jacob] Beam.... **Madam Michalowski, in 1960, obtained from Ambassador Beam details about the dispatches being sent to the Central Intelligence Agency by a 'Lt. Col. Michael Goleniewski,'** an American 'agent in place' who had first revealed to United States authorities the existence of the sex and spy scandals in Warsaw. [Emphasis added.]

The story continued:

> *The Exchange* report of January 10 intentionally did not indicate how or where 'Lt. Col. Goleniewski' was communicating with American officials or how or where Ambassador Beam learned of his existence or of his report. However, because of certain wrong interpretations or distortions being placed on the January 10 report, a 'witting source' has consented to the publication by *The Exchange* of the fact that Ambassador Beam, who had never met 'Lt. Col. Goleniewski,' first learned of the existence of the 'American agent in place' while the Ambassador was on 'consultation' in the State Department in Washington.
>
> Ambassador Beam's own sources in the State Department 'consultation' were Deputy Under Secretary of State for Administration Loy Henderson and Assistant Secretary of State for Security William Boswell, the source further indicated to *The Exchange* ... Under Secretary Henderson told Ambassador

Beam, the source stated, that the State Department had received its information personally from Richard M. Bissell, Jr., the CIA's Deputy Director for Operations.... While informing Under Secretary Henderson of the details of the dispatches ... Mr. Bissell had requested that none of the suspected American officials in Warsaw be 'alerted' by any personnel actions or transfers without prior approval of such action by CIA.... To prevent any 'inadvertent' personnel actions in Warsaw itself, Mr. Bissell and Under Secretary Henderson had agreed to recall Ambassador Beam for 'consultations' and to have him personally informed about the situation in his Embassy, the source stated.

William Boswell was Otepka's boss at the time, and the *GEE* leak obviously came from Otepka.

Even though Beam never learned Goleniewski's name – indeed the CIA didn't know it – the paper continued:

the information he did receive was sufficiently detailed so that, when Madam Jerzy Michalowski obtained it subsequently in Warsaw from Ambassador Beam, the Soviet intelligence organization was able to identify 'Lt. Col. Goleniewski' as the American 'agent in place,' the source stated. This required 'Lt. Col. Goleniewski' to flee for his life to West Berlin and ended his activities as an American agent in the Soviet camp, the source concluded.[79]

The notion that somehow the Poles knew that Goleniewski was working for American intelligence, and that he fled to West Berlin at the last minute to avoid capture would now appear in stories about Goleniewski by writers like Edward Jay Epstein and Tennent Bagley.

One of the puzzles of the *GEE* story is that it recycles an earlier version dating back to the early 1960s and referenced in *Imperial Agent* but it now names Myra. It also had a few variations. In his 1969 book *The Trial of Otto Otepka*, William Gill cites Beam's reported link to Myra and also references the *GEE* articles. Gill, however, omits the charge that Beam somehow betrayed Goleniewski to Polish intelligence.[80]

Of course, it is always possible that Beam did leak information that led the Russians to become aware that there was trouble in Warsaw. It seems much more likely, however, that when Colonel Raina informed Goleniewski of the 'pig' in Polish intelligence, the KGB's suspicions arose from their monitoring the Embassy. Possibly some new security countermeasures alerted them. Or there could have been a bug, information from a low-level Soviet source, or even a decoded communication intercept.

The Soviets also had one low level agent in the Embassy named Irwin Scarbeck. He was arrested in June 1961 well after Goleniewski defected and he clearly knew nothing about Goleniewski. Some conservatives claimed Scarbeck had been sacrificed by the Poles to protect another 'asset' ('E. S.' in *Imperial Agent*) whose real name was Edward Alan Symans. A long-time diplomat with many foreign postings under his belt, Symans worked for the United States Information Agency (USIA) as a press and cultural attaché. Fluent in Polish, he knew many leading figures in Warsaw. He left the Embassy in 1959. Why Scarbeck would be 'sacrificed' in 1961 to protect an alleged asset who returned to America in 1959 is difficult to grasp. It is possible, however, that the Sniper material did lead to Symans being recalled as there is one report that Symans and his Embassy secretary Dorothy Cwynar were suspected of being spies but that the government was unable to prove the case.[81]

Otepka claimed that he was kept in the dark about Goleniewski by his superior, Under Secretary of State William Boswell. That Otepka knew anything about Goleniewski was a quirk of fate: Otepka was serving as Acting Director of the Office of Security when the CIA first notified State about 'Sniper' because Boswell was on vacation. Once Boswell returned, Otepka was cut out of the loop.[82] If Otepka were the *GEE* source, he presumably did not invent such a serious charge out of thin air. But what could have convinced him to advance such an accusation?

Otepka most likely was guessing that Beam was the source since Beam had been given a security briefing in Washington about problems inside the Embassy. Other sources may have supplied Otepka with the results of an investigation into embassy security. One likely conduit may have been Jay Sourwine. Thanks to a 10 October 1968 memo from the CIA's Office of Legislative Counsel, we know that the CIA was also aware of Sidney Goldberg's connections to Sourwine. The memo reads:

___. Mr. Jay Sourwine, Senate Internal Security Subcommittee staff, called to inquire whether the Agency would have any objection or question concerning the suggested appearance of Mr. Sidney Goldberg, Publisher and Director of *The Government Employee Exchange*, before the Committee. I thanked Mr. Sourwine for his call and advised I would relay the question.[83]

On 5 November 1968, the same Office reported:

___ Talked with Mr. Jay Sourwine ... and advised that the Agency would have no objection to the contemplated appearance of Mr. Sidney Goldberg, publisher of *The Exchange*, before the Committee. I thanked Mr. Sourwine for his consideration in calling us on the off chance that we might in some way have an interest in the matter.[84]

On 1 May 1969, the subject of Sidney Goldberg surfaced in a morning meeting of some top CIA officials:

[Legislative Counsel John H.] Maury called attention to an item inserted in the 30 April *Congressional Record* by Congressman Rarick containing a reprint of an article in the *Government Employees Exchange*. The article alleges the formation of a 'new team' in CIA. [Joseph C.] Goodwin [assistant to CIA Director Richard Helms] briefed on our information pertaining to the ownership and policies of the *Exchange*.[85]

The *GEE* story appears to have been an attempt to recycle old accusations against Ambassador Beam brought back to life to block Beam's nomination to the Moscow post.

The Warsaw Embassy saga is more muddled by the fact that British Intelligence also developed sources in Warsaw in the late 1950s that gave MI6 information about the Embassy.[86] My own guess is that if Colonel Raina did inform Goleniewski about a possible 'pig,' it was because he wanted his help in trying to identify a possible traitor based on information the Poles and Russians had picked up while spying on the Embassy. Something as simple as a slight change in Embassy security protocols may have triggered their suspicion.

It also seems clear that Goleniewski was not suspected of being a spy for the West as Department VI had nothing to do with the American Embassy. It seems far more probable that as the KGB's trusted man in Polish intelligence, Raina simply approached Goleniewski for help. Nor did Goleniewski panic. If Raina had informed him of information that Goleniewski had sent about the Warsaw Embassy, Goleniewski would have known in March 1960 (the usual date given when Raina told him about the 'pig') that his Sniper correspondence had been fatally compromised. If it had been, Goleniewski surely would have defected then and not months later. Once in the West, he also would have demanded to know who leaked the Sniper material to the Russians. Yet he never raised the issue either with the CIA or with his supporters on the right.

Finishing with Feigan

Goleniewski did obtain one gift from the CIA: American citizenship. Yet he now alienated friend and foe alike over his insistence that he was the Romanov heir. He even clashed with Congressman Feighan. In January 1965, Goleniewski (a/k/a 'Aleksei Nicholaevich Romanoff (Goleniewski) Heir to the All-Russian Imperial Throne, Tsarevich and Grand Duke of Russia, etc., etc.') published a statement describing a 5 June 1964 meeting he had with Feighan, Colonel Corso, and Doctor O'Conner.[87] Goleniewski writes in his open letter to Feighan:

1. You visited me in result of your own initiative myself and my wife Irmgard in our apartment together with your aides Dr. O'Connor and Colonel Corso on June 5, 1964, having before visited my sister Grand Duchess Anastasia Nicholaevna Romanoff a/k/a Eugenia Smith and residing in New York City.
2. During this conversation your aide in the US Congress Mr. O'Connor informed me in your presence, and also you informed me yourself, that the Legal Counsel of the CIA, John S. Warner, officially informed you that my assumed identity of 'Michael M. Goleniewski' has been scientifically and legally verified and established by authorized representatives and consultants of CIA as Aleksei Nicolaevich Romanoff, the Heir to the Throne, Tsarevich & Grand Duke of Russia.

3. During aforesaid discussion your second aide Colonel Corso informed me that he is in possession of certain proofs concerning the same verification of my true identity by representatives of the US Central Intelligence Agency.

4. I have legally listed as witnesses to our personal conversation my wife Irmgard M. Romanoff, your aide Dr. O'Connor, and your second aide Colonel Corso.

Just who the 'authorized representatives and consultants of CIA' were remains a mystery, although this may be a reference to a former CIA official and Knight of Malta named Herman Kimsey, who became one of Goleniewski's most loyal defenders. Nor did Corso's 'certain proofs' ever see the light of day, even though Corso was also a Knight of Malta. The most curious reference, however, is Goleniewski's claim that Feighan and his aides also met with Eugenia Smith.

Goleniewski wanted to use Feighan to pressure the US Immigration Service to acknowledge his 'real name' was Romanov and not 'Goleniewski.'[88] He spent years trying to legally change his name since H.R. 5507 naturalized him as 'Michal Goleniewski.' He argued that 'Goleniewski' was as false as the OLDENBURG cover name the CIA assigned him in January 1961.

By 1966, Feighan had enough. He now began ignoring Goleniewski's appeals. In an 'Open Letter to President Johnson and House Speaker John McCormack and members of the U.S. Congress,' Irmgard reported:

> Incidentally, the Congressman, Hon. Michael A. FEIGHAN did not give me any answer to my letter, although I called four times his office and sent him a telegram one week later. To date I am still without the reply of the HON. FEIGHAN.[89]

Goleniewski now reached out for publicity. In a 11 January 1965 interview with the *Long Island Press* headlined 'Czarevich Pretender Eyes Russian Royal Fortune,' he bizarrely claimed, 'I have lived 50 years in full abstinence … one meal a day, no pleasures, no women, no vodka … just five years of my life would kill most Americans.' After telling his interviewer that the Jewish Bolshevik [Yakov] Yurovsky saved the Imperial family, Goleniewski ham-handedly added: 'I believe this will dispel much of the feelings Russians have against Jews because of their supposed connection to the Czar's murder. It would change the situation of Jews, especially in Russia,' a clumsy attempt to appeal to the large Jewish population in eastern Queens and Long Island.[90]

Notes

1 Wang (2015), 50–51.
2 Gill (1969). Chapter XVIII, 'The Defector,' is devoted to Otepka and the Goleniewski case.
3 Mollenhoff, 'Russ Agent Tells of Sex and Spies in U.S. Embassy in Poland,' 12 April 1964 *Indianapolis Tribune*. Also see Mollenhoff (1965) which includes a chapter on the Warsaw Embassy affair.

4 See *Congressional Record*, 11 March 1969, 'Jacob Beam, Our Man in Moscow' (E 1864–67) inserted by Louisiana House member John Rarick. The article by conservative syndicated columnist James Kilpatrick first appeared in the 9 March 1969 edition of the *Washington Evening Star*. The report on the bugging comes from an article in *The Government Employees' Exchange* (*GEE*) entitled 'Power Struggle Looms Over Beam, Otepka, Sonnenfeldt Between Congress, State.'

   When the new US Embassy in Warsaw was being constructed, bugging devices were installed that State Department security experts failed to detect. (Plans were drawn up for a new embassy in 1957 and the new building was occupied on 1 July 1963.) On 3 November 1964, *New York Times* (*NYT*) correspondent Tad Szulc reported on the bugging of the new embassy and that the bugs had been installed during the early stages of construction. The revelations followed the discovery of Soviet listening devices in the US Embassy in Moscow.

5 7 April 1964 *New York Post*, Washington Merry-Go-Round syndicated column written by Jack Anderson.

6 For a look at the controversy, see David Wise, 'HR 5507, a Prize Defector, now the Boomerang,' 8 March 1964 *New York Herald Tribune*. Wise writes the Goleniewski saga is 'cloaked in mystery' and that 'the ending is uncertain.'

7 See https://www.govtrack.us/congress/bills/88/hr5507/text.

8 Robarge (2015), 321. Also see Richards (1966), 195.

9 The CIA statement further noted that Goleniewski enlisted in the Polish army in 1945, and became a lieutenant colonel in 1955.

10 See Congressman Feighan's obituary in the 20 March 1992 *NYT*. Feighan may have been best known to the general public when in 1964 he failed to get Richard Burton banned from entering the USA after Feighan accused him of immoral conduct with Elizabeth Taylor.

11 See the obituary for John Feighan in the 6 August 1953 *NYT*.

12 'Feighan Wary of Peace,' 20 July 1954 *NYT*. Feighan's contempt for the State Department was no secret. In 1955 he attacked Secretary of State John Forster Dulles, who, he said, had 'become the unwitting victim of the tip-toe artists in the Department of State who have for years advocated a policy of delicate diplomacy in dealing with the Russian Communists.' See 'Dulles' Aides Scorned,' 20 June 1955 *NYT*.

13 Drew Pearson column printed in the *Tuscaloosa News*, 29 April 1964.

14 See 'Feighan, Defeated in Ohio, Ending 28 Years in House,' 12 May 1970 *NYT*.

15 Drew Pearson, Washington Merry-Go-Round, 13 January 1967.

16 Robarge (2015), 321, fn. 34. Goleniewski knew enough English to appear on the Barry Farber talk show on WOR radio on 10 August 1964. The WOR show was a joint interview with Goleniewski and the New York publisher Robert Speller (Richards (1966), 241). Speller knew in advance that Goleniewski would go public with his claim to be the heir to the Russian throne. (Recall that in April, Drew Pearson first publicized Goleniewski's claims to discredit him.)

17 Goleniewski, *White Book*, 168.

18 Ibid., 170.

19 Richards (1966), 198–99.

20 Ibid., 168.

21 On Feighan, see 'Pope Receives 4 Congressmen,' 19 October 1947 *NYT*. Also see O'Connor's Obituary in the 27 November 1985 *NYT*.

22 The group was also known as the 'Select Committee to Investigate the Incorporation of Lithuania, Latvia, and Estonia into the U.S.S.R.' After completing its report, it dissolved on 31 December 1954.

23 See https://history.state.gov/historicaldocuments/frus1951v02/d354.

24 Richards (1966), 19.

25 Ibid.

26 Ibid., 19–21.

27 Gill (1969), 215–16.

28 Richards (1966) 22–23. After President Kennedy was assassinated, Corso visited Gole-
niewski a third time to ask if the KGB ran a Department 13 'school for assassins' in
Minsk. Goleniewski said it did not but that the GRU 'did have such an institution in
Minsk.' See Guy Richards, 'CIA Hiding Red Defector from Probers,' 4 March 1964
NYJA. Richards had earlier written articles stating that the KGB had a Minsk assassin
school and linked it to the Stashinsky affair. See Guy Richards, 'Russia's School for
Assassins – and the Oswald Case,' 11 January 1964 *NYJA*.
29 See 'Arends Defends CIA Against Critics,' 27 May 1964 *NYT*.
30 Guy Richards, 'U.S. Secret ...', *NYJA*, 2 March 1964.
31 His then-pregnant wife had a breast cancer scare during this time.
32 They were *Imperial Agent* (1966), *The Hunt for the Czar* (1970), and *The Rescue of the
Romanovs* (1975).
33 His *Social Register* background became clear in a 15 December 1965 background report
by Helene Finan of the CIA's Security Research Staff. She noted that in May 1942 the
wealthy socialite William H. Vanderbilt recommended Richards for possible recruitment
into the OSS. (This was William Henry Vanderbilt, III, who served in the OSS during
World War II.) Another OSS letter of recommendation came from John Hay 'Jock'
Whitney, a Yale grad who worked as an OSS operative in France during World War II.
34 In the Piecuch book, largely a series of edited interview transcripts, the date reads '1959,'
but this is an obvious typo for 1969.
35 Piecuch (1997), 249–51.
36 Richards (1956), 226–27.
37 Ralph Dungan was a long-time aide to JFK. He later became US Ambassador to Chile
during the Johnson administration. The State Department's Edwin Martin, another Latin
American expert, later became the US Ambassador to Argentina. In the 23 March 1964
issue of the *Dan Smoot Report*, Smoot claims that Guy Richards had not identified 19
supposed American traitors but that on March 5, 1964, *Vaba Eesti Sona* (Free Estonian
Word), published out of Estonia House in New York City 'named two of them.' The
article ('*Vene spionaazhi kaastoolised paljastati*'), however, only discusses Martin and
Dungan using information from the 3 March 1964 Richards' article. *Vaba Eesti Sona* was
close to Congressman Feighan and featured him in a 5 March 1964 cover story.
38 'An Inquiry Is Asked on Defector's Story,' an AP article in the 5 March 1964 *NYT*.
39 Ashbrook's interest in Goleniewski was also described in a 4 March 1964 AP story that
the *NYT* ran the next day.
40 Pohl Bang-Jensen was a Danish diplomat who refused to provide the UN with names of
people involved in the 1956 Hungarian Revolution because he feared Russia would use
it against them. Instead, he destroyed the list and was fired from the UN. He committed
suicide in 1959.
41 Thomas Talburt, 'Probers Are Unable to Find Red Defector,' 5 March 1964 *Cincinnati
Post & Times Star*.
42 Gill (1969), 216.
43 Feighan also made a statement in Congress that the CPUSA received $400,000 of the
money the KGB had supposedly conned out of the CIA. See 'Arends Defends CIA
Against Critics,' 27 March 1964 *NYT*.
44 Nor does it appear in *Imperial Agent* outside of one paragraph that repeats the statement
in the original 1964 article. Richards (1966), 19–20.
45 Guy Richards, 'CIA Hiding Red Defector from Probers,' 4 March 1964 *NYJA*.
46 Martin (1997), 108.
47 See Ashley (2004) for a biography of Kisevalter.
48 Goleniewski, *White Book*, 175. This statement appeared in an 'Open Letter' to the head
of the CIA published in the 14 July 1966 *Washington Daily News*.
49 Bagley (2007), 49.
50 Wright (1987), 294.
51 Massie (1996), 153.
52 Richards (1966), 270.

53 Ibid., 188.
54 Goleniewski, *White Book*, 168.
55 Richards (1966), 184–85.
56 A copy of the cover with Dulles's note can be found in the Epstein Archives, Box 26.
57 Heuer (1987), 389.
58 A possible reference to Goleniewski's role in 'Operation Spiders.'
59 Robarge (2003), 32.
60 A transcript of the show can be found on the CIA's Historical Review Program (HRP) website at https://www.cia.gov/readingroom/docs/CIA-RDP75-00149R000300150004-2.pdf.
61 Gontarczyk (2013). Unfortunately, the article does not cite the name of the author of these stories on Goleniewski, or where they appeared in the European press.
62 Richards (1966), 21.
63 Capell (1965).
64 Ibid., 43.
65 See the FBI file on Capell at https://ia800708.us.archive.org/11/items/CAPELLFrankA.HeraldOfFreedomHQMiscSerials/CAPELL%2C%20Frank%20A.-Herald%20of%20Freedom%20-%20HQ%20misc%20serials.pdf.
66 For more on Goldberg, see Hougan (1978). Hougan interviewed both Otepka and Goldberg.
67 In 1954 Goldberg's *GEE* was involved in a legal dispute with a Washington-based distributor named District News Company. A footnote to the legal ruling read:

> At the commencement of this litigation, the publication was owned by Sidney Goldberg, but the publication was later acquired by Government Employees' Exchange, Inc., which was added as a party defendant. The individual and the corporation are both before us as appellees.

http://law.justia.com/cases/district-of-columbia/court-of-appeals/1954/1506-3.html.
68 See http://jfk.hood.edu/Collection/Weisberg%20Subject%20Index%20Files/C%20Disk/CIA%20Foundations%20Fronts/Item%2001.pdf for a reprint of a 27 November 1968 *GEE* article on the conspiracy.
69 The same text ran in the 28 May 1968 *New York Times* as a legal notice.
70 My date for the text, as with a few other *NYJA* stories, comes from a clipping stamped 'FEB 19, 1964' which I am using for the date of publication, although it may be the date the clip was received. In any case, the story appeared sometime in mid-February 1964.
71 See Walter Sheridan's comments at http://www.jfk-online.com/sheridanspook.html. The excerpt is taken from Sheridan's book The *Rise and Fall of Jimmy Hoffa* (New York: Saturday Review Press, 1972). Note Sheridan's confrontation with Sidney Goldberg of the *Government Employees' Exchange*. Also see Hougan (1978). In a 4 September 1968 *GEE* article entitled '"5 Eyes and Doodlegrams" Used for Tapping,' Goldberg linked the tapping of Otepka's phone back to Sheridan and Robert F. Kennedy. Because of his articles, Goldberg ran into legal problems. A famed Louisiana-born Washington lawyer named Bernard 'Bud' Fensterwald volunteered his services on Goldberg's behalf, although it remains unclear how much Fensterwald helped or harmed his client's case. See Peace (1997).
72 After serving in Russia from 1969 to 1973, Beam ended his career as Chairman of Radio Free Europe. See Beam (1978) for more details.
73 See Haynes and Klehr (1999), 421, fn. 14. A 1952 Senate investigation of the Katyn Massacre brings up Myra's name twice but former OWI officials who were asked about her said they could not remember if she worked there or not. See https://archive.org/stream/katynforestmassa07unit#page/n5/mode/2up/search/zlotowski.
74 For the history of the Liberty Lobby, see Coogan (1999) and Zeskind (2009).
75 See https://www.govinfo.gov/content/pkg/GPO-CRECB-1969-pt5/pdf/GPO-CRECB-1969-pt5-4-3.pdf.

76 See http://www.legacy.com/obituaries/news-press/obituary.aspx?page=lifestory&pid=141038768.

77 Joan Mellen, 'Otto Otepka, Robert Kennedy, Walter Sheridan, and Lee Harvey Oswald' at http://joanmellen.com/wordpress/kennedy-assassination/otto-otepka-robert-kennedy-walter-sheridan-and-lee-oswald/.

78 Richards (1966), 155.

79 Presumably the quotes around Goleniewski's name were there to suggest that Goleniewski's real name was Romanov.

80 Gill (1969), 218.

81 Pawlikowicz, 275. On Symans, see Richmond (2008), 45. Richmond was stationed in Warsaw with Symans. On Scarbeck as a KGB-planned diversion from Symans, see Richards (1966), 146–47.

82 Gill (1969), 217.

83 https://www.cia.gov/readingroom/docs/CIA-RDP70B00338R000200180019-7.pdf.

84 https://www.cia.gov/readingroom/docs/CIA-RDP70B00338R000200050013-7.pdf.

85 https://www.cia.gov/readingroom/docs/CIA-RDP80R01284A001800100066-5.pdf.

86 See Appendix I on 'Noddy.'

87 Goleniewski, *White Book*, 250.

88 He and his wife had legally changed their name to 'Romanoff' which is how Goleniewski always spelled 'Romanov'.

89 Goleniewski, *White Book*, 166.

90 In the September 1976 issue of *Double Eagle*, Goleniewski attacked the American Holocaust denier Arthur Butz's book *The Hoax of the Twentieth Century*. Goleniewski, however, was hardly free of prejudice against Jews. He particularly disliked the British Rothschilds as he held them personally responsible for denying him access to Romanov rubles in British banks. He despised the Rockefellers for the same reason.

9

TSAR WARS

Meeting Anastasia

'Was the Czar Really Assassinated? Say Lenin Spirited Royal Family Out of Russia.' With these headlines on 12 September 1964, Guy Richards announced to his *New York Journal-American* readers that Michal Goleniewski publicly proclaimed himself Aleksei, the son of the last Tsar of Russia.[1]

But when did Goleniewski first assert his claim? He said he did so soon after he arrived in the USA. The CIA begged to differ. Eager to provide evidence of his growing mental illness, the Agency claimed he only began his royal quest in the summer of 1963. From Edward Jay Epstein's 17 May 1981 profile of Goleniewski:

> The point at which Goleniewski identified himself as Romanoff is bitterly disputed. He told me that he had identified himself in 1961 after defecting. The CIA officially claims that he did not raise the Romanoff issue until the summer of 1963 when he applied for U.S. citizenship, in a letter to Rep. Michael A. Feighan. But the FBI liaison with the CIA recalled to me that she had heard the Romanoff claim in 1962.[2]

William Clarke quotes a British official involved in one of Goleniewski's debriefings from the early 1960s who recalled that Goleniewski was 'accurate, lucid and particularly fruitful' when it came to intelligence matters. 'The Romanoff material always seemed to emerge at the end of long discussions.' Clarke's source recalled, 'It was as though he had a separate strand of his mind devoted to the Romanoffs.' The source added there was no doubt in his mind that Goleniewski 'actually believed in his Romanoff connection.'[3]

Goleniewski's strange claim doomed him to the dustbin, as well as the loony-bin, of history. He never testified before Congress, and his name disappeared from

DOI: 10.4324/9781003051114-13

mainstream press reports. Our purpose here, however, is to cast light on those who, far from shunning him, now fervently embraced the claim.

Our story begins in the late spring of 1963 when a mysterious woman surfaced in New York and went on to proclaim herself the Grand Duchess Anastasia. On the last day of December 1963, Goleniewski met 'Anastasia' in the West 42nd Street offices of a down-and-out book publisher named Robert Speller. During their encounter, Anastasia broke down and tearfully embraced her beloved long-lost brother, the Grand Duke Aleksei, heir to the Romanov throne!

Outside of a tiny circle of U.S. intelligence officials, no one knew about Goleniewski in the winter of 1963. He lived quietly under a false identity knowing he had a death sentence hanging over him. In contrast, the woman who called herself Anastasia had become a household name. On 18 October 1963, *Life*, a mass circulation magazine with millions of readers and a crown jewel of Henry Luce's *Time-Life* publishing empire, published a cover story entitled 'The Case of a New Anastasia.'[4] The article's centerpiece consisted of excerpts from a book published that November entitled *Anastasia: The Autobiography of H.I.H. the Grand Duchess Anastasia Nicolaevna of Russia* (Volume I) from Robert Speller & Sons.[5] The lengthy article was profusely illustrated with pictures and drawings. In Germany the mass circulation picture magazine *Quick* even ran a 17-installment series on the story as well, priceless advertising for an otherwise smalltime family book firm.[6]

The story's centerpiece, Eugenia Smith, lived in the Chicago area for many years after arriving in America in the early 1920s. In either late February or early March 1963, Smith approached Robert Speller with the manuscript that became the 'autobiography.'[7] Smith first claimed she had been a friend of the Grand Duchess Anastasia, and knew her both in Russia and later in Romania, where Anastasia entrusted her with the autobiographical notes that formed the basis for the memoir. Smith explained that Anastasia had not been murdered by the Bolsheviks in 1918; instead, she had died sometime in 1920, apparently while in exile in Romania.

In the introduction to her book, Smith says that she told a New York friend about Anastasia's manuscript and that friend suggested she contact one of Robert Speller's sons named Jon to arrange a meeting. Another Speller son, Robert Speller, Jr., 'an expert on royal genealogy' to quote *Life*, now realized that Smith knew far too much about the Romanov court to be whom she claimed. He now asked her to take a lie detector test. After Smith agreed, she left Speller's office without giving a forwarding address, but she returned a month later. During this time, the Spellers studied her manuscript to determine its authenticity and realized it contained 'staggering inside knowledge.' When they pressed Smith in their second April 1963 meeting, she suddenly confessed the truth: she was Anastasia!

Smith told the Spellers that after escaping Russia, she had married a Croat named Marijan Smetisko.[8] After the marriage failed, she obtained her husband's permission to emigrate to America; she arrived in New York under the name 'Smetisko.' She relocated first to Detroit and then Chicago where she became a U.S. citizen, officially divorced her husband, and never remarried. While in Chicago, she worked a series of jobs from model to factory worker to manufacturing her own perfume. Since 1945 Smith lived as a guest in the home of Mrs. William Emery, whose family owned a manufacturing company called Chicago Rawhide. Robert Massie reports that:

> Mrs. Emery believed that her houseguest was Grand Duchess Anastasia. She took Mrs. Smith on trips to Europe and always solemnly celebrated her birthday on June 18, Anastasia's birthday. Mrs. Smith lived with Mrs. Emory from 1945 until June 1963, when having inherited money from her benefactress, she moved to New York City to help with the publication of her book.[9]

If this is the truth, it means that the first story that Smith claimed she told the Spellers was false. The Spellers didn't have to force her to 'confess' she was Anastasia since she had been pretending to be Anastasia for years. The only real question was whether or not Smith first lied to the Spellers or that the Spellers and Smith later made up the story of her dramatic 'confession' together to make her sound more believable.

After the Spellers asked her to take a lie detector test, Smith spent '30 hours' over a period of several weeks with a well-known polygraph expert named Cleve Backster, who concluded that Smith was telling the truth. The *Life* article even comes with an enormous picture of Backster administering a polygraph to Smith.[10]

An acknowledged expert who consulted for law enforcement, Backster ran the Academy for Scientific Investigation. He later became famous for his 1966 decision to hook up a plant to his galvanometer. Backster said his test showed that plants had feelings, claims later incorporated into a 1973 best-seller entitled *The Secret Life of Plants*.[11] A close friend of the Spellers, Backster worked with them in a strange group called the Anti-Communist International (ACI) and the pseudo-chivalric group the Knights of Malta which we will explore in more detail later.

Life also assured readers that the Spellers had 'one of the most respected psychiatrists in New York' spend four sessions questioning Smith. He concluded that she was not delusional and was telling the truth. However, 'two anthropologists, Dr. Edward Hunt of Harvard and Dr. Carlton Coon of the University of Pennsylvania' decided independently that Smith was not Anastasia (in Coon's case based on photographic comparisons of her nose). A handwriting expert also thought her claim bogus. Numerous errors in her use of Russian were noted as well.

After the Spellers publicized the book's upcoming release, a woman living in Chicago recalled that she had given Smith Russian lessons in the 1930s and that Smith spoke Russian 'like a Romanian peasant.' Another Russian author named Tatiana Botkin, the daughter of the Tsar's doctor Yevgeny Botkin who was killed along with the Romanovs, drew up a twenty-page list of errors in the purported memoir. She even identified passages from her own book that Smith plagiarized.[12]

And then there was Tatiana's brother Gleb Botkin, who had played with Anastasia as a child. In the 1920s Gleb became a staunch supporter of Anna Anderson's claim that she was Anastasia and he remained committed to Anderson to his dying day. After the Spellers met Smith, they contacted Gleb, He told them that he had already been approached by Smith. He said that 'originally Mrs. Smith submitted a manuscript of her memoirs … in which she … claimed only to have known the Grand Duchess at the time of her stay in Romania.'[13] Informed that Smith had passed a lie detector test, Botkin 'told them their lie detector must have had a screw loose' and warned the Spellers not to publish.

On 26 August 1963, the *Chicago Tribune* ran a front-page article on Smith. The paper reported that Smith had yet another wealthy enthusiast in John H. Chapman, a Chicago businessman. Chapman, in turn, introduced Smith to a local author and ghostwriter named Edward Arpee who recalled that in 1958–1959 he wrote 'an Anastasia story' using material supplied by Smith. 'She was difficult to get along with. I've never received any thanks for my work during those years,' Arpee grumbled. The 'autobiography' Smith gave the Spellers had been written four or five years earlier in draft form by Arpee. None of this information made any difference to the Spellers. Smith, meanwhile, now relocated to a new apartment in Queens, and turned her residence into a shrine to the Romanovs.

Why would *Life* run such a dubious tale, even one sprinkled with a few dollops of skepticism? Did *Life* simply assume this was a great read? Or were there other motives at work as well? *Life's* publisher, after all, was Charles Douglas ('C.D.') Jackson. Jackson resumed his full-time involvement with the Henry Luce empire in 1960 after leaving Washington where he had worked both as a speech writer and special advisor to President Eisenhower.[14] A Princeton grad married to an Astor, Jackson served as President of the Free Europe Committee that worked closely with 'captive nations' émigrés in both the USA and Europe. He also helped found the Bilderberg Group.

As a psychological warfare expert who ran the Operations Coordinating Board (OCB) associated with the National Security Council (NSC), Jackson worked closely with both Colonel Corso and Edward O'Connor.[15] As part of war-planning, the OCB collaborated with the Pentagon to create émigré military units called the Volunteer Freedom Corps (VFC) that would be trained for special operations behind enemy lines in a war. The VFC project, however, would be blocked by other factions in the Eisenhower government and never be realized.

A few months before the 'Anastasia' profile appeared, *Life's* managing editor George P. Hunt used *Time-Life* money to bankroll a plot known as 'the Bayo–Pawley Affair.' The plot was designed to smuggle two alleged Soviet Colonels turned defectors out of Cuba. Once safely in America, the two Russians would be publicly questioned by Jay Sourwine. They would testify that the Russians never abandoned their Cuban missile program; Kennedy had been duped. Hunt provided the plotters with $15,000 of *Time-Life* funds.[16] The Spellers also ran their own private intelligence operation in Cuba. Was there a covert 'Cuban connection' to *Life's* decision to run a huge puff piece featuring both the Spellers and 'Anastasia'?

Whatever *Life's* motives, a strange chain reaction was now set in motion. On 28 December 1963, about a month after the official publication of Smith's Anastasia 'memoir,' Goleniewski – using the cover name 'Burg' – telephoned Robert Speller's New York office. In the call, Goleniewski reportedly convinced Speller that he had important information to share about the Romanovs.[17] The next day 'Burg' and Speller met in Speller's office. Speller then arranged for Goleniewski to encounter Smith on the afternoon of the following day, 31 December 1963, New Year's Eve.[18]

Goleniewski later claimed that just a few days after he arrived in America, he asked the CIA to find his sister Anastasia who, he thought, 'was living in this country, probably somewhere in the Middle West.'[19] For months the CIA said nothing. Then in January 1963 everything changed. Goleniewski told Guy Richards that he had been 'shocked' by 'an almost casual remark' from a CIA official named 'Larsen,' most likely Hal Larsen who worked in the CIA's Reports and Requirements Staff where he helped oversee translations from Polish.[20] From Goleniewski's recollection of the event:

> After two years in the United States, in January of 1963, the CIA representative, Mr. Larsen, informed me in a superficial way that my relative (Anastasia) had at last been found in the United States and that she had emigrated in 1922 to the United States as Anastasia Turynski, the daughter of Raymond Turynski. He also said she was born in 1901 and was living for a long time in Illinois under several different names, including Tatiana Godunova and Eugenia Smith.[21]

Eugenia Smith, however, came to the USA under her married name of Eugenie Drabek Smetisko, as she told Cleve Backster.[22] If Larsen really did tell Goleniewski that 'Anastasia' entered the USA under the name 'Turynski,' he was apparently lying to attract Goleniewski's attention.

Since Goleniewski had been living in New York for some time, did Larsen come to visit him on some pretext to then blurt out this startling news? Or was Goleniewski just making it all up? Or did Larsen really say something along these lines and that somehow the CIA knew about Eugenia Smith. Meanwhile Smith would leave Chicago a few months later and head off to New York to meet with the Spellers? In short, was Eugenia Smith/Anastasia a 'CIA plot'? And if she was, just what was the plot?

Goleniewski continued his story:

> Mr. Larsen informed me that this relative is a 'difficult person' and that it would be better for me never to get in touch with her. I asked the CIA representative, Mr. Larsen, and later Mr. [Edward] Katulski, about the possibilities of my getting in contact with Eugenia Smith by letter. They told me they would do so, but they never did. At this time, I was very well informed that the competent United States officials had spoken with my youngest sister, Anastasia Nicholaevna, about my person and that my identification at the Czarevich Alexei Nicholaevich was completely proven.[23]

As we shall soon see, there was some truth behind Goleniewski's claim about Anastasia.

In a 14 July 1966 'Open Letter' directed 'to the Personal Attention of the Director of the Central Intelligence Agency Headquarters of CIA. Langley, Virginia,' Goleniewski cited Eugenia Smith in an all caps paragraph regarding his contract with the CIA:

SAID CONTRACT WAS BROKEN ON THE PART OF CIA ON JAN. 10. '64, I.E. 10 DAYS AFTER MY MUTUAL RECOGNITION BEFORE WITNESSES WITH MY SISTER, THE GRAND DUCHESS ANASTASIA NICHOLAEVNA OF RUSSIA (A/K/A EUGENIA SMITH WHO IMMI-GRATED INTO THE U.S. IN 1922), IN N.Y.C. ON DEC. 31,'64. (SEE STATEMENTS: *FRANKFURTER ALLG. ZEITUNG* MAY 4 & 6, '65 *NOVOYE RUSSKOYE SLOVO* JUL. 15 '65 ETC.)[24]

As strange as the events leading up to Goleniewski's meeting with Smith were, their first encounter proved even more weird. A former CIA official and devout Goleniewski supporter named Herman Kimsey gave a 14 April 1966 interview with the CIA's Steven Kuhn where he described what transpired. From Kuhn's summary:

a Eugenia Smith, a woman who went to New York and contacted a lawyer who specializes in handling Russian immigrants and their affairs and this lawyer sent Eugenia Smith to Robert Speller & Sons, Publishers. Eugenia Smith alleg-edly had a diary and she alleged that she was the handmaiden to Anastasia. Speller questioned Eugenia Smith thoroughly as her stories were rather confus-ing. Speller then took her to Cleve Backster who operates a polygraph testing service in New York City. The result of this was that Eugenia Smith, herself, was Anastasia. Speller, on being convinced that Eugenia Smith was Anastasia, then organized a party or reception.

Kimsey continued:

Colonel Michal Goleniewski was invited to this reception. At this reception when Eugenia Smith, a/k/a Anastasia, saw Colonel Michal Goleniewski she threw herself to her knees and asked his forgiveness and she introduced him as her brother. To Subject, this was proof that Eugenia Smith was Anastasia and that Colonel Goleniewski was really a Romanov.[25]

In other words, Kimsey confirmed what Goleniewski said and that was the CIA knew about Anastasia as far back as 1963 and that she had confirmed his identity as Tsar. Hence when the CIA portrayed Goleniewski as crazy for making his claim, the CIA was deliberately lying.

But why would 'Anastasia' ask Alexei for 'forgiveness'? The story only makes sense if one accepts Goleniewski's claim that in 1922 Anastasia left for America as part of a plan to help the family but that she was never heard of again.[26] Now seeing her long-lost brother, she begged him for forgiveness. Smith, however, had just claimed both in her memoir and in the *Life* story that she was the sole member of the Romanov family to survive the Bolshevik massacre.

Speller later recounted to Guy Richards the scene on 31 December 1963. Speller, his wife and two sons Jon and Robert, Jr., along with Cleve Backster, were at the office meeting. Speller even arranged for Backster to tape the encounter between 'Mr. Burg' and 'Anastasia.'[27] When Goleniewski and Smith met, Speller recalled, 'it started out quite formally, but it wasn't long before it became very emotional. My sons and I were the only other persons in the room.'

It took about an hour for Smith to be convinced that Goleniewski was her brother, just as it had earlier taken time for the Spellers to make her confess that she was really Anastasia. The transcript of the taped conversation released by the Spellers appeared in the 16 July 1966 edition of *Conservative Viewpoint*; it was also reprinted in the *White Book*.[28] It was released by the Spellers on 17 February 1965 as part of their attempt to discredit Smith after she refused to change her Anastasia story. Guy Richards' highly abridged version in *Imperial Agent* is not accurate to the Speller transcript, although what he does is more paraphrase and abridge than deliberately distort.

Following the Speller transcript, the dramatic moment happened after Goleniewski asked Smith if she knew the name 'Turynski.' As recounted by the press release using Backster's tape recording, she replied:

ANASTASIA: I am so ashamed of myself. (She begins to cry.) Who are you? Who sent you to see me?

BURG: I am a friend and I came to see you, to speak to you. Do you remember the name Turynski?

ANASTASIA: I remember the name.

BURG: And Anastasia Turynska?

ANASTASIA: Anastasia Turynska? I did not come.... Anastasia Turynska I remember. I came as Anastasia Turynska, but my passport is different.[29]

BURG: Do you remember Janina Turynska? The daughter of Raymond Turynski? That was Maria Nicholaevna Romanova.

ANASTASIA: But who told you all that?

BURG: Must I tell you? That you came to America as Anastasia Turynska?

ANASTASIA: Who spoke with you about Janina Turynska? How do you know? How did the family know? I tried to see my Aunt Olga as she came to Toronto. She did not want to see me.... Your eyes. I remember your eyes as if I knew them. I am so afraid. Who sent you to me? ... Maria is alive? (He shows her a snapshot.) Who is that?

BURG: Maria remained with us. I have been looking for you here for two years. They didn't want me to see you. They don't want to recognize you because of the money. Because they got the money.

ANASTASIA: How can you be sure I am Anastasia?

BURG: When I came I began at once to look for you. They did not want me to find you....

After Goleniewski said he would like to speak in Russian, Smith replies: 'I am sorry, but my Russian is not very good. I see very few Russians and I was living for years in Illinois and never had the occasion.' The dialog then resumes:

BURG: I have a photo to show you. This is your sister....
ANASTASIA: I have so many complications....
BURG: But you know that all are alive.

Later Goleniewski says: 'Mashka who was brought through the Red borders in a wash basket. Do you know who Maskha is?'[30] After Smith guesses it could be Maria or her, Goleniewski says 'no.' Smith then says 'Yes, I know' when she obviously does not. Goleniewski answers 'I have to return to my family, but I will always be happy to see you.'

In other words, Goleniewski is ending the conversation. At that point, Smith asks Robert Speller if he has something that could help them. I think Goleniewski wanted her to say that it was he who was brought in the wash basket, and Smith simply missed her cue. Perhaps she did so since 'Maskha' is a female name. 'Mishka,' however, is the Russian diminutive for 'Michael.'

In any case, the dialog then picks up a bit later:

BURG: Do you remember Father said: 'Neskim'?[31]
ANASTASIA: (She cries out): He knows. He knows. He is my brother, Alexei.
  (Crying) My darling, my darling....

The Speller transcript concludes when Cleve Backster enters the room and Smith/ Anastasia says: 'Hello, Mr. Backster. Can I present you to my brother, Aleksei?' Guy Richards now picks up the story: 'This gripping scene was followed by several days in which the newly-reunited brother and sister remained on the warmest terms.'[32]

As for Guy Richards, he now began regularly meeting with Goleniewski sometime in the late spring of 1964. Richards described Goleniewski as

> attractive. He spoke with a foreign accent. He had blue eyes, auburn hair, stood about five eleven, weighed about 180 pounds and walked with a slight limp. He seemed slightly younger than the 60 years he would have to be if he were, indeed, the Grand Duke himself.[33]

Richards now began working on a manuscript for Speller entitled *The Goleniewski Affair*. It was to be published alongside Princess Marina Dmitrievna Kropotkin's *The Reappearance of the Romanovs*, which she was to co-write with Jon Speller.[34] Princess Marina also endorsed Goleniewski's claim.

After Richards and Goleniewski had a bitter falling out, Richards took the project to a Connecticut-based conservative publishing house named Devin-Adair, which issued *Imperial Agent: The Goleniewski–Romanov Case* in 1966. Off the success of *Imperial Agent*, Doubleday published *The Hunt for the Czar* in 1970. Richards final book, 1975's *The Rescue of the Romanovs*, was also issued by Devin-Adair.[35] When it appeared, Goleniewski's name had vanished from the narrative, except for one line on page one where Richards says that Goleniewski definitely was not the Tsar.

Game of thrones

On 30 September 1964 the crowning achievement of Goleniewski's madcap quest for the Russian throne took place: 'Alexei Romanoff' and Irmgard Kampf were officially married by the Russian Orthodox Church Outside of Russia (ROCOR), the White Russian exile institution par excellence.[36] The ceremony was held in Goleniewski's Kew Gardens apartment just over a month after the Guy Richards' *New York Journal-American* article appeared cautiously announcing his monarchical claim. The couple was also married by 'Father Georgi,' Count Georgi Pavlovich Grabbe, the Very Revered Protopresbyter (Archpriest) of the Synod of Bishops of the Russian Orthodox Church.[37] The 35-year-old Irmgard was then whisked off to Manhasset Hospital where a few hours later she gave birth to their only child, a daughter named Tatiana.[38]

Had a leading cleric in the Russian Orthodox Church Outside Russia just given his Church's blessings to something as inconceivable as the Church's recognition of Goleniewski's claim to the throne?

Remarkably, the answer is 'yes.'

The controversy that now erupted around the ceremony lay in the husband's information on the marriage certificate:

Name: Aleksei N. Romanoff
Age: 60
Date of Birth: August 12, 1904
Place of Birth: Peterhof, Russia
Father's Name: Nicholas A. Romanoff
Country of Birth: Russia
Mother's Maiden Name: Aleksandra F. von Hesse
Country of Birth: Germany

News that Goleniewski had been married under the Romanov name touched off outrage in the White Russian community, especially with the followers of the Madrid-based Grand Duke Vladimir Kirillovich Romanov, the son of Grand Duke Kirill (Cyril) and a direct descendent of Tsar Alexander II. Vladimir was supported by the Supreme Monarchist Council (*Vysshe monarkhichekii Soviet*/VMS), the major White Russian monarchist organization in the West.

One of Vladimir's closest supporters was a Tsarist general named Sergei Voitse-khovsky (Voitsekhovskii). Voitsekhovsky helped lead the Russian émigré community in Warsaw in the 1920s in a group known as the Russian Committee. He then became entangled in a famous Cheka penetration of the White Russian exile movement dubbed the 'Trust' (more formally known as the Russian Monarchist

Union).[39] At the end of World War II, Voitsekhovsky organized Vladimir's escape from advancing Russian troops and his safe passage to the West.[40] Voitsekhovsky then established his own monarchist organization devoted to Grand Duke Vladimir that operated out of Ravensburg in Upper Swabia.[41] Voitsekhovsky now issued his own denunciation of Goleniewski entitled *The Russian Orthodox Church Abroad: The Goleniewski Case*.[42]

More ripples of outrage over Father Georgi's actions poured out from the larger White Russian exile community, the vast majority of whom already were sickened by the publicity afforded by the Western media to the two fake Anastasias. But, as Robert Massie explains, their real anger was at Father George:

> The storm raged not so much around Goleniewski – whose claim to be the Tsarevich had long since been dismissed as 'absurd,' 'outrageous,' and 'a stupid Soviet provocation' by the Russian émigré community around America – as around Father George. The priest was ferociously attacked in the Russian-American press; Grabbe's ecclesiastical superiors forbade him to baptize little Tatiana. He was obliged to repeat over and over that the name Romanov was common in Russia, that as a priest he could not refuse to marry a couple who were otherwise qualified, that Goleniewski could not possibly be *that* Alexis Nicholaevich Romanov, and that his performance of the wedding in no way signified church recognition of the groom's claim to identity.[43]

As protectors of the Russian Orthodox Church, the Romanovs occupied an extremely important position theologically; their brutal murders had enshrined them in the aura of martyrdom. For the vast majority of White Russians, then, the reality of what happened to the Romanovs could not be clearer. In June 1918 the Tsar's brother, Grand Duke Mikhail Alexandrovich, was murdered near the city of Perm. One month later, on 16 July 1918, the Tsar and his family were slaughtered in Ekaterinburg. Simultaneously, five Romanov princes and the Empress Alexandra's sister, the Grand Duchess Elizaveta Feodorovna, were thrown down a mine shaft near the Siberian town of Alapaevsk. Hand grenades promptly followed but failed to finish the job; the family starved to death a few days later.

The only immediate direct Romanov survivors were the Tsar's mother, the Dowager Empress, and two of Nicholas's sisters, the Grand Duchesses Xenia and Olga, both of whom lived in total obscurity in Canada and Denmark before they both died in 1950. For Father Grabbe and ROCOR to encourage the fantasy of Goleniewski, a Pole no less, bordered on the obscene.

Surprisingly given this environment, a leading Cossack Monarchist named Colonel Alexis Iosifoyich Toultzeff – a member of the five-man Executive Committee of the Supreme Monarchist Council – on 25 January 1965 reported that he had met with Goleniewski, and he was now convinced that he was Grand Duke Alexei! Resigning from the Council, Toultzeff declared the Bolsheviks lied about the deaths of the Romanov family and that the Tsarevich 'is a man of dignity and one who deserves respect. He is a soldier with a deep faith in God.'[44]

Goleniewski had another defender in Princess Marina Dmitriievna Kropotkin, who lived in Douglas Manor, Queens.[45] Robert Speller knew Princess Marina, and he made sure she listened to the Barry Farber radio show when Goleniewski announced he was Tsar. After Princess Marina heard the show, she wanted to meet Goleniewski, but only in the company of Father Georgi, which is how the priest first met him. Princess Marina's father Dmitri married a daughter of Prince Obolensky. According to Guy Richards, Princess Marina's mother 'born Princess Marina A. Obolensky, had become a by-word as 'Pani' [Lady] Marina among Ukrainian Freedom Fighters in the 1920s for the help she had rendered in their abortive attempts to win Ukraine's independence from Bolshevik rule.'[46]

Goleniewski said that in a 1964 meeting with Princess Marina he asked her if she by chance knew a man named __. Marina told him it was the name her father used in the 'Polish resistance,' and that she never mentioned the name to anyone in the USA.[47] This reported revelation helped convert Princess Marina to his cause.

As for Father Grabbe, he now backpedaled as fast as he could. His claim that he had no clue about Goleniewski's background appeared in the 8 December 1964 issue of *Novoye Russkoye Slovo*. Goleniewski shot back with a statement in the 19 December 1964 *NYJA*. He said he first met Father Grabbe in his Kew Gardens apartment on 18 August 1964 in Grabbe's capacity as a representative of the Orthodox Synod of Bishops and following the WOR radio interview. Grabbe and Princess Kropotkin had been conveyed there by Robert Speller. Although Goleniewski didn't mention it, the meeting also took place shortly after Guy Richards' *NYJA* article on his claim.

During their get-together, Goleniewski said he gave Father Grabbe 23 photocopies of documents 'and many very important letters and statements' proving his Romanov roots. Grabbe, accompanied at times by his son Count Dmitrii and another relative named Vladimir Shishkov, discussed his background on five separate occasions where Grabbe counseled Goleniewski and Irmgard on religious issues. Goleniewski further claimed that Grabbe kept the Metropolitan of the Synod informed of these developments.[48] His statement again put Father Georgi on the spot, so much so that 'Grabbe was asked to resign from all Russian émigré organizations; for a while no one would speak to him.'[49]

In 1994 Robert Massie interviewed Father Georgi, then the retired Bishop Gregory. He claimed that Goleniewski called him on 30 September 1964, told him he had obtained a marriage license, and asked if he could please come quickly because Irmgard was about to give birth. Grabbe went to Goleniewski's apartment listed in the name of Alexis Nicholaevich Romanoff; a court decree also showed that Goleniewski had legally changed his name to 'Romanoff.' Rather than have their child born without a church ceremony, Grabbe said he felt pressured to remarry them in the presence of a handful of witnesses. They included the Spellers as well as 'the Grand Duchess Olga' and 'the Grand Duchess Tatiana.'

Yet Grabbe knew for over two months that Irmgard was pregnant, and that he was tasked with giving them religious instructions before marrying them. That Father Grabbe, himself a high-ranking church official, would do all this on his own knowing Goleniewski's claim that he was the Tsar and not consult with other ROCOR leaders seems preposterous. Grabbe only met Goleniewski after he had gone public with his Romanov proclamation. It seems far more likely that Father Grabbe was following orders from Church higher ups.

The topper to the wedding weirdness was captured in a wedding photograph of two elderly ladies, the 'Grand Duchesses Olga' and the 'Grand Duchess Tatiana,' with Father Grabbe, Goleniewski, and Irmgard. The picture appeared in an article by Maude Files Zimmer in the 28 November 1964 *Hartford Times*, and was almost certainly given to the paper by the Spellers.[50] The Grand Duchess Olga was even to appear at a press conference given by the Spellers.

Of all the strange events surrounding Goleniewski's wedding ceremony, the ghost press conference remains one of the most bizarre. Recall that Guy Richards only told his *NYJA* readers about Goleniewski's royal claim in his 12 September 1964 story. In *Imperial Agent*, however, Richards reports that he first heard about the claim sometime in the late spring of 1964, which means he sat on the news for months. In fact, many in Washington knew about that Spring after the CIA leaked the news to Drew Pearson to discredit Goleniewski.

In August 1964, the Spellers began a public relations rollout to sell the idea of Goleniewski as Alexei. Robert Speller was in the studio with Goleniewski on the 10 August 1964 Barry Farber WOR radio talk show. On 17 August 1964, the journalist Philippa Schuyler published a frontpage story in the rightwing *Manchester Union Leader* entitled 'Russia's Czar Lives!'[51] Schuyler interviewed Goleniewski in Robert Speller's New York office. Her interview was no accident; Schuyler was a member of a news service known as Transglobal that Robert Speller founded in the early 1960s.[52]

In his story announcing Goleniewski's royal claim, Guy Richards also reports that he had been approached by Robert Speller with exciting news. Not only did he learn from Speller that Goleniewski was Alexei; the rest of the Romanovs had survived as well. Even more extraordinary, they were all going to hold a press conference! Alexei, Grand Duchess Tatiana, Grand Duchess Olga, and Grand Duchess Anastasia would now assemble in the same room in New York City! Only the Grand Duchess Maria (a/k/a Janina Goleniewska) would be absent. From Richards' story:

> 'There is no doubt that all the children are alive today,' said Mr. Speller, 'and in a few days at least four of them, including three of the Grand Duchesses, will be together here in New York and ready to tell their stories.'
>
> But the real delayed shocker in Mr. Speller's account concerns the Czar's only son, the Grand Duke and Tsarevich Alexi. Alexi is not only alive and well and a three-year resident of Long Island, Mr. Speller avers. But Alexi is also the highly mysterious and controversial defector and former Polish secret police official, Michael Goleniewski, whose story first appeared in the *N.Y. Journal-American* last March 2.

'One of the reasons Alexi was able to rise so high in the secret police as well as in Communist circles,' said Mr. Speller, is that so many high-placed Poles, many of them members of the clandestine Russian patriotic organization, the White Guard, know his identity. 'My sons and I have checked out this fact in several parts of Europe,' said Mr. Speller. 'We know it to be true.'

Richards' article announcing Goleniewski's claim then appears planned to coincide with the upcoming press conference. The article was a press release dressed up as a news story.

'A few days' now stretched into weeks. After the wedding, the Spellers claimed the press conference was imminent but this time only with 'Grand Duchess Olga' and Goleniewski. Robert Speller, Jr., a 'genealogy expert' per *Life* magazine, now described Olga Nikolaevna and Tatiana Nikolaevna's presence at the wedding this way:

> Also present were two elderly ladies whose faces were familiar to us. They matched perfectly with photographs shown to us some time earlier by the groom-to-be of his two eldest sisters, the Grand Duchesses Olga and Tatiana. The Grand Duchess Olga was white-haired, slender, and stooped, thereby shortening her status. The Grand Duchess Tatiana was dark-haired, quite obviously dyed, and plump, although she held herself quite erect. Both ladies were definitely of the same generation of the groom-to-be, although their degrees of health were quite varied.[53]

Clearly the Spellers went all in to promote the story.

But there was a problem: Anastasia.

Recall that in her 'memoir,' Anastasia/Eugenia Smith asserted that she was sole survivor of her family. Now, not only had Goleniewski/Aleksei returned from the dead but so had two of his sisters. For any of this to make sense, Smith now had to recant her story. She refused; she now accused the Spellers of 'inventing' Goleniewski's claim to the throne. She now used Grand Duchesses Olga and Tatiana as proof that the Spellers were liars.

On 9 July 1965, Robert Speller & Sons issued a press release announcing that the firm intended to take Smith to court to force her to prove that she was not Eugenia Drabek Smetisko, who was born in Bukovina in 1899 and whose relatives, including a daughter, were currently living in Romania. They refused to make any new royalty payments for *The Autobiography of H.I.H. the Grand Duchess Anastasia Nicholaevna of Russia* and demanded Smith return all royalties previously paid. The press release added: 'Mrs. Smetisko has charged that the Speller firm "invented" another heir to the throne, the Czarevich Aleksei Nicholaevich, only son of the Emperor and Empress, in the person of Colonel Michael Goleniewski, a former Polish army intelligence officer....'

Under pressure from Smith, the Speller press statement also includes this wacky comment about 'Olga' and 'Tatiana':

Among those present at the wedding ceremony were Mrs. Luise Henschel Kampf and Mrs. Margarete Kampf Mische, whom the colonel alleges are respectively the Grand Duchesses Olga and Tatiana Nicholaevni. Some months later, Father Grabbe denied that he had recognized the colonel as the Czarevich. The colonel also alleges that Janina Goleniewska is the Grand Duchess Maria Nicholaevna, and that she is at present held in isolation by private persons.

Contrary to Mrs. Smetisko's statement that the Speller firm 'invented' the colonel as Czarevich, she herself introduced him as her brother, the Czarevich, and recognized him as such before witnesses on December 31, 1963. Their mutual recognition scene was recorded on tape.[54]

In other words, two of Kampf's elderly relatives visited New York for her religious marriage and the imminent birth of Kampf's daughter![55] Goleniewski and the Spellers then tried to pretend they were part of the 'royal' family using the photo as proof. Equally weird was the mention of Janina Goleniewska/Grand Duchess Maria Nicholaevna as being 'held in isolation by private persons.' Goleniewski's mother was living in Warsaw so 'held in isolation by private persons' was their oblique way of referring to her living behind the Iron Curtain.

More information on Kampf's relatives emerged in 1966. Irmgard and Goleniewski began taking out notices in the form of open letters in the *New York Herald Tribune* and a few other papers. (Having little money, the notices appeared in very small print.) They complained about their shabby treatment by the CIA and the U. S. government. The letters were addressed to President Johnson, the Speaker of the House of Representatives John McCormack, and to all members of the U.S. Congress. In one February 6, 1966 open letter, Kampf ('Irmgard Margareta Romanoff') wrote:

Because of our departure [from East Germany] 9 members of my family, who were living in BERLIN, found themselves in a very difficult situation, and they were during January 1961, evacuated by the authorized representatives of the U.S. GOVERNMENT from BERLIN into WEST GERMANY, where they are living to this day.[56]

Presumably these relatives included the two elderly women at Goleniewski's marriage ceremony.

On 27 July 1965, a CIA memo reported a conversation with Herman Kimsey, the former CIA agent now helping Goleniewski and the Spellers. According to the report, 'Kimsey inferred that Eugenia Smith is a nymphomaniac, has a daughter and a granddaughter who are living behind the Iron Curtain, and who are blackmailing her not to accept the identity of Anastasia.' Kimsey added that the Smith/Speller court trial was scheduled for that October, although I could find no press report indicating that the case was formally litigated.

There was one other interesting note in the Speller's press release. It cited Goleniewski denying the charge 'that he is the creation of the American secret service,' a claim the statement said was printed in the 14 January 1965 edition of *Red Star* (*Krasnaya Zvezda*), 'the official organ of the Soviet Ministry of Defense, Moscow.' If true, it may have been the first time the Russians publicly acknowledged Goleniewski's existence. It would not be the last. On 27 August 1966, *Komsomolskaya Pravda* claimed that Goleniewski's goal was to get $400 million of Romanov funds deposited in American banks, and that he was 'nothing less than a sinister creation of American intelligence.'[57]

Goleniewski's adventures with the Spellers left him even more bitter. On 17 November 1965, he took out a notice in the *New York Herald Tribune* declaring that he was 'discharging Robert Speller and Company, 10 E. 23rd Street,' the Spellers having recently moved from the Times Square area. Goleniewski added that he would have no connection to the company, and any books planned by it that included the Guy Richards' biography and the one by Princess Kropotkin to be co-written with Jon Speller.

The public break between Goleniewski and the Spellers only underscored the deeper puzzle of their relationship. Eugenia Smith was right: even if they had not 'invented' Goleniewski, the Spellers had gone to enormous lengths to sell him as Tsar, even helping arrange the involvement of at least one high-ranking member of the Russian Orthodox Church Outside of Russia in the hoax.

The news of the wedding, as we have seen, outraged the White Russian community, so much so that there was now a concerted effort to have the Church annul the marriage. On 8 December 1964, Father Grabbe was interrogated about his role in the affair in a meeting at the Russian Immigrants' Representative Association in America office at 349 West 86th Street. The questioners were the Association's President Prince S. S. Belosselskiy, its Secretary General A. W. Rummel, and a Colonel Rogoshyn. Grabbe said that he acted with the full knowledge of the Synod of Bishops.

On 13 January 1965, Robert Speller wrote a letter to the Synod and said that as a witness to the wedding, he and other witnesses would reject any attempt to invalidate the ceremony. The Spellers also issued a statement in the form of a March 1965 Publisher's Preface saying that the Eugenia Smith/Anastasia book was wrong and that the rest of the family had survived.[58] But were the Soviets right as well? Although Goleniewski was arguably 'a sinister creation' of the Spellers, was he also a creation of 'American intelligence'? But that question only raised another: Just who were the Spellers?

Spying by the book

Robert Speller & Sons was an unconventional publishing house to put it mildly. In a 1977 article, the far rightist Revilo P. Oliver described it in the early 1960s as a 'luckless and down-at-the-heels publishing firm' gifted with a 'dingy office' at 33 West 42nd Street.[59] But if the Speller office was shabby, the family's ambition was not. In the early 1960s, Robert Speller launched Transglobal News Service as his own press agency. Transglobal doubled as an intelligence cover organization for its correspondent-agents in countries like Cuba.[60]

Future Watergate burglar Frank Fiorini (Frank Anthony Sturgis) told the FBI that in 1961 he visited Speller's office with a New York socialite turned anti-Castro activist named Alexander Irwin Rorke, Jr.[61] Speller issued Fiorini a Transglobal press card dated 27 April 1961, and told him to use it in case he was captured in Cuba. Speller also introduced Fiorini to an organization called the Anti-Communist International (ACI), and informed Fiorini that 'he was financially backing' the ACI. Fiorini also was told that the ACI 'was supposed to have some influential members in the New York area.'

The ACI's ostensible chairman or General Secretary was Haviv Schieber. A Polish-born Jew and staunch supporter of Ze'ev Jabotinsky's brand of Zionism, Schieber emigrated to British mandate Palestine in 1932. After converting to Christian fundamentalism in the early 1950s, Schieber organized the Anti-Communist League of Israel.[62] He claimed that Israel was suffering under the control of Jewish Marxists committed to doing Russia's bidding. All public disagreements between the Soviet Union and Israel concealed a hidden alliance forged in 1949 when Golda Meir and Mordechai Namir ('the satanic pair') made a secret compact with 'Stalin's right-hand man [Lazar] Kaganovich' for a new strategic alliance.[63]

Schieber also began contacting anti-communist organizations throughout the world. In 1955, he recalled:

> our League had established close contact with the Russian anti-Communist movement headquartered in West Germany. They were sending information to people behind the Iron Curtain in novel ways. One was to put leaflets in helium-filled balloons and release them when the wind was right. Another was to throw bundles of pamphlets into the railroad cars destined for Russia.[64]

Using literature printed in West Germany by Russian émigrés, Schieber's group tried to place propaganda in orange crates destined for the USSR. After they were arrested, the incident was reported in the 20 January 1956 *New York Times*, bolstering Schieber's international reputation. He now began receiving invitations to anti-communist conferences in Latin America, including one in Mexico City 'which would prepare for the formation of a world anti-communist organization.' Schieber said the head of the conference was Charles Edison, the former governor of New Jersey.[65] The attempt to organize the different groups

> resulted in the creation of an international steering committee to coordinate worldwide anti-communist activities known as the World Anti-Communist Congress for Freedom and Liberation (WACCFL), which held a meeting in Mexico City in March of 1958 and included representatives from various east Asian governments, ABN, CIADC, the American Security Council (ASC), and the West German *Volksbund für Frieden und Freiheit* (VFF). This network ... reorganized itself into the World Anti-Communist League in 1966.[66]

WACCFL's secretary general was the former Wisconsin Congressman Charles Kersten, author of the 'Kersten Amendment', and a close ally of Congressman Feighan.[67]

Although Schieber was unable to make the founding WACCFL conclave, he recalled that 'several weeks later another invitation arrived – this time from Guatemala – asking me to participate in the Fourth Inter-American Anti-Communist Conference.' The Guatemala gathering was sponsored by CIADC, the Inter-American Council for the Defense of the Continent/*Confederacion Interamericana de Defensa del Continente*). Historian Jeffrey Bale reports that 'the Fourth Anti-Communist Continental Congress [was] held by CIADC in Antigua, Guatemala, later that same year [as the WACCL meet] also included, for the first time, representatives from Taiwan, ABN, the U.S. and the Middle East.'[68] CIADC was created by the far-right Mexican Tecos (Owls) group; one report claims it received support from the CIA's Howard Hunt.[69] Schieber also recalled meeting an American 'Colonel John Kiefer' there, but does not identify him further.[70]

Schieber now headed north; he entered Miami on 3 March 1959, but quickly relocated to New York City. He now met with a host of American far rightists which included Gerald L. K. Smith, Conde McGinley, and Benjamin Freedman. He networked with other anti-Communist activists such as Eugene Lyons, Bella Dodd, Rabbi Elmer Berger, Rabbi Benjamin Schultz and others. While in New York, he received support from a Mr. Giloni, a stockbroker and staunch Herut Zionist, who helped him rent a small office in Times Square.[71] The American Committee for the First Anti-Communist International (later shortened to the ACI) was now headquartered at 156 West 44th Street in Manhattan.

Schieber reported that the ACI's first 'official gathering' was to protest Nikita Khrushchev's visit to the USA. Schieber also took out a bank loan 'to finance a trip of our committee of three: Rabbi Hershberg, Robert Speller, and ACI's Chairman, retired Colonel Charles Green' to Cuba to investigate conditions there. Through the Cuba visit, the ACI forged ties with anti-Castro exiles and the American adventurers allied with them.

Schieber had been scheduled for deportation to Israel after his visa expired on 18 March 1959. Robert Speller & Sons now sponsored a petition to permit him to stay.[72] Bella Dodd, a former leader of the New York State Communist Party who later converted to militant Catholicism and anti-communist crusading, served as Schieber's lawyer. (Dodd also represented Frank Capell.)

The ACI further cultivated ties to intelligence services in Guatemala and Nicaragua. Both nations supported anti-Castro exiles, and Guatemala allowed CIA-backed Cubans to operate training bases for the projected Bay of Pigs invasion. On 28 May 1962, the *New York Times* reported that some 200 people 'marched outside the house of the Guatemalan United Nations mission' for an hour 'and won the personal thanks of Carlos Gonzales Prado, first secretary of the mission, for the expression of support.' The marchers included 'Dr. Bella Dodd, general secretary of the anti-Communist International' and 'Frank Capell, chairman of the American Education Conference.'

There was something just plain strange about the Anti-Communist International. Along with Schieber, the Spellers collected more curious friends, including Sergius Riis, a mysterious American intelligence agent whose murky trail stretched back into World War I, if not earlier.[73] In a 3 July 2005 story for Falun Gong sect paper *The Epoch Times* entitled 'The Clock is Ticking: The End of Communist Party Rule in China Fast Approaches,' Jon Speller recalled:

> Back in 1959 I was personal secretary to the legendary American intelligence officer, Commander Sergius M. Riis ... [who] felt it was necessary to quietly gather together American and non-American [groups] ... into an infrastructure to coordinate certain types of moral support to resistance to communism in communist-ruled or dangerously penetrated countries. Therefore, the Anti-Communist International (ACI) was organized as a private sector anti-communist organization at arm's length from the U.S. government, and it has been so recognized for many years.... The first Chairperson of the Anti-Communist International was Russian Don Cossack Wasili G. Glaskow, who was also the principal expert on Cossack matters for Radio Liberty and associated institutions.[74] I was Vice-Chairperson (visibly representing Commander Riis as his surrogate initially), from 1959 to 1988, when I succeeded Wasili as Chairperson, a position I continue to hold today.

At the time of the ACI's founding, Riis lived on Staten Island. A longtime member of the Explorers Club, he maintained an office with the American Red Cross. Riis's close ties with the Spellers dated at least to 1935 when Robert Speller published Riis's hoax 'memoir' *Yankee Komisar*.[75] In 1962, the Spellers issued Riis's *Karl Marx: Master of Fraud*.[76]

Yet there is no doubt that Riis enjoyed many intelligence ties, particularly in the Baltic nations from the 1920s to at least the beginning of World War II.[77] Riis was also awarded the Naval Cross for his actions in World War I in the north of Russia and as acting naval attaché to the U.S. Embassy in Archangel. Riis spent considerable time in Poland as well. From 1927 to 1934, he worked in Warsaw for Standard-Nobel Oil Company. The historian Richard Spence comments that:

> This curious company was a remnant of the once immense Russian Nobel Oil Co. and was long the focus of émigré intrigue. Indeed, the man who had helped negotiate the firm's establishment in Poland was none other than Sidney Reilly, who had also been one of its major stockholders. From Poland, Riis made frequent trips to Estonia.... Riis's continued involvement in intelligence gathering focused on Russia is evident by a letter to Washington from the U.S. military attaché in Poland in early 1931. According to this missive, '[Riis] seems to have considerable information on affairs in Soviet Russia ... some of it at variance with all other information ... bits of it are startling.' Riis himself later characterized his work for Standard-Nobel as a cover for his involvement in a 'Polish-British-American network' operating in Russia and the Baltic.[78]

In his preface to *Karl Marx*, Jon Speller states that 'Mrs. Riis and [their son] Earl were in Poland at the start of World War II, they had an exciting escape from the encroaching Nazi and Soviet Armies which crushed that unfortunate country.' In *Karl Marx*, Riis also writes:

> As my records in the Navy Department will show, I have spent many years in Russia and the Far East and know the country inside out, from one end to the other. Ever since I left North Russia, where I was the U.S. Naval Attaché to the American Embassy there, I have kept contact with anti-red underground forces we officially organized there and I know how and what can be done with these forces of loyal Russians, more than just to embarrass the Kremlin, when the time comes…. Later while serving in South Russia … I also built up a nucleus there of patriots, who are still in contact with me, on and off. While serving in the Baltic countries … I participated in organizing another potential underground on the Baltic shores, which is still functioning and with a little encouragement can become a factor to be seriously reckoned with. This was all done prior to our recognition of the Moscow government.[79]

As Richard Spence observes, the possibly Estonian-born Riis 'may have had some connection to the Okhrana, the Russian secret service, prior to his appearance on American shores, a suggestion strengthened by his subsequent association with other ex-Okhrana operatives and informers.'[80]

Whatever Riis was involved with, it seems obvious that Robert Speller & Sons was no ordinary book company. The shabby publishing house sat on top of a para-political fringe intelligence network linked to Latin American reactionaries, Jewish Christian fundamentalists, and aging White Russian exiles.

And then there was the CIA.

The Spellers long helped in the production of *East Europe*, which for decades was published by Free Europe Press, the publishing arm of the Free Europe Committee with support from the CIA. Revilo P. Oliver recalled that the steady income the Spellers received from producing *East Europe* helped keep the firm alive. When the Free Europe Committee finally withdrew its funding and the journal threatened to go out of business, Robert Speller officially assumed editorial control of the magazine in October 1970.[81]

Jon Speller said the new iteration of *East Europe* was now part of the Anti-Communist International network. *East Europe*, however, went out of business in 1977 and back issues of the Speller version of the journal are hard to find. The one issue I did examine from January–February 1973 listed the editor as Herman Singer, the executive editor as Jon Speller, and the publisher as Robert Speller and Sons. However, it was the name of the senior associate editor that was most worth noting. He was Leopold Dende, a/k/a 'Mela,' the cover name Polish intelligence assigned to Dende for espionage operations in America!

Along with the 'Mela' mystery comes an even more puzzling question: were both Goleniewski and the Spellers acting out a pre-existing script? Guy Richards reports that sometime in the late spring of 1964 when he finally met Goleniewski, he told Richards he was the Tsar. Richards said he assumed Goleniewski was insane until

> Days later I learned from a team of American investigators that a mass of evidence supporting his claim was being collected and that it far outweighed the evidence against the claim. I was told, for example, that all four of his sisters had been located. They were reported to be living under rather odd and disarming names in various parts of the world.
>
> Then from independent sources, I was able to establish something which seemed very interesting. I discovered that for a number of years the leaders of the anti-Communist anti-Bolshevik secret organization which has members in Russia, Poland, Czechoslovakia, Germany and elsewhere, were certain that he was the Grand Duke Alexi, Nicholas' son and heir. Their conviction about this was one of the prime reasons why he moved ahead in the Polish Army intelligence network. Was it possible that they, too, could be taken in by a faker?[82]

Rickards also adds, 'I was also warned several times that he could be part of a neatly conceived Soviet plot to gain legal title ... to the overseas wealth of Czar Nicholas – something which the Red Government obviously couldn't do for itself.'

If Richards' report is accurate, how was it possible that by the spring of 1964 'investigators' presumably associated with the Spellers 'confirmed' Goleniewski's claim? Was this a reference to the Knights of Malta? The ACI? Who were the 'independent sources' who reportedly told Richards about the mysterious anti-Bolshevik underground that Richards would label the 'Secret Circle'? As we shall see in a later chapter, the Knights really did have an overseas intelligence network, courtesy of General Charles Willoughby, a Knight of Malta and the former head of Army Intelligence (G-2) for General Douglas MacArthur.

According to the conventional narrative, as we have seen, Goleniewski only approached the Spellers in late December 1963 under his CIA cover name because he wanted to contact Eugenia Smith/Anastasia. On 31 December 1963, they met in person in Speller's office where they dramatically embraced each other as sister and brother. A few months later in the spring of 1964, Richards learned that some mysterious spy network (whose accuracy he never bothers to question) had confirmed Goleniewski's fantastic tale.

Is any of this real? Or are we really watching a play with actors following a pre-arranged script? But if it was a script, who wrote it? And why? What was the point? The notion that somehow the world's leading banks would open their vaults to the long-lost son of Nicholas II sounds ludicrous. Even more ludicrous, if the CIA were orchestrating all this, why would the CIA tell everyone who would listen that Goleniewski went insane when he began claiming he was the Tsar?

Could this then be a strange KGB Russian disinformation 'Trust' ploy? If the KGB's plot to cripple America was to send a false defector loaded with true information that helped break major Soviet espionage rings across Europe, one could only pray for similar false defectors. What possible upside could there be for the Russians?

As long as we are considering strange scenarios, recall General Franciszek Szlachcic's truly weird claim in *The Bitter Taste of Power* when he states, against all known evidence, that Goleniewski defected on a routine business trip to West Germany in 1955. Szlachcic wrote that 'in 1955, he did not return to the country from a business trip to the Federal Republic of Germany. After a few months he revealed himself as a military officer of the U.S. intelligence service.'[83] To make any logical sense of this claim, it is necessary to assume that Szlachcic made a mistake and wrote '1955' when he should have written '1961.'

But what if Goleniewski had been contacted on an intelligence mission in 1955? Another far-fetched scenario might run along these lines. Goleniewski did make initial contact with some anti-communist émigré intelligence network in Germany around 1955. He then agreed to remain a 'defector-in-place' and return to Poland, where he spent almost three years secretly researching East Bloc operations. He was then encouraged to share this information only with the FBI, since this network deeply distrusted the CIA and considered it treasonous. If the Spellers were not flat out lying to Richards, did there exist an underground network that knew Goleniewski and now reconnected with him New York via the Spellers?

Or was it just the CIA all along? Guy Richards reports that the Soviet magazine *Zvesda* (*Star*) in an article on Romanov aspirants singled out Robert Speller and claimed he was a CIA agent, most likely because the CIA funded *East Europe*.[84] Thanks to Mela, presumably Polish intelligence had some insights into the Spellers as well.

But could the mysterious intelligence network that vetted Goleniewski be itself something like a 'Trust' operation? Or was there really some independent network that managed to survive and reconstitute itself after World War II, and functioned independent of any CIA connections? Or did the Spellers and Richards just make it all up?

Notes

1 Just as there were multiple claimants to be 'Anastasia', Goleniewski was only one of numerous people claiming to be 'Alexei'. See Slater (2007), 81–105 for a summary.
2 Epstein (1981).
3 Clarke (1995), 139.
4 The 'new' in the 'New Anastasia' was a reference to the earlier famous claim of Anna Anderson that she was the Anastasia.
5 Grand Duchess of Russia Anastasia. There was no Volume II.
6 Richards (1966), 252–53.
7 Guy Richards says she first approached Speller on 20 February 1963 when she walked into his office out of the blue.
8 Smith said her husband had no idea that she was really Anastasia. When Marijan Smetisko was located, he denied ever knowing her.
9 Massie (1996), 157.

10 Another huge photo shows Smith with 'genealogy expert' Robert Speller, Jr., at a ROCOR ceremony in memory of the Romanovs.

11 Peter Tompkins and Christopher Bird, *The Secret Life of Plants* (New York: Harper & Row, 1973). Tompkins also met Goleniewski, presumably through Backster.

12 Massie (1996), 158.

13 Lovell (1991), 276.

14 For background on Jackson, see O'Gorman (2009).

15 The OCB had been created in the early 1950s on the recommendation of William Harding Jackson (no relation to C.D.), who played a key role in the early organization of the CIA and served as the Agency's first deputy director under General Walter Bedell Smith. President Kennedy abolished the OCB in 1961.

16 Acoca and Brown (1975).

17 The name was a variation of his actual CIA cover name, 'Franz (Frank) Oldenburg.'

18 Richards (1966). 194.

19 Ibid., 192.

20 Weiser, 186–87.

21 Richards (1966), 193.

22 See Cleve Backster's 'Statement about the Russian Imperial Family' published in the 16 July 1965 issue of *Novoye Russkoye Slovo* in defense of both Goleniewski and Smith and in reaction to a 10 July 1965 *NRS* story attacking their respective claims. Backster identifies himself as 'Chairman, Polygraph Research Committee, Academy for Scientific Investigation, 165 West 46th Street' in New York City. See https://www.cia.gov/rea dingroom/docs/CIA-RDP75-00149R000300130027-9.pdf.

23 Richards (1966), 192–93.

24 Goleniewski, *White Book*, 175.

25 See 'Security File on Herman Edward Kimsey' available online at https://ia600702.us. archive.org/25/items/KIMSEYHermanEdwardCIASecurityFile71129/KIMSEY%2C% 20Herman%20Edward%20-%20CIA%20Security%20File%2071129.pdf.

26 In Goleniewski's telling, the Grand Duchesses Olga and Tatiana wound up in Germany while Anastasia went to America. Alexei, his father Nicholas II, and his other sister (the Grand Duchess Maria) remained in Poland. Recall that his 'mother' Empress Alexandra had died in Poland in 1924.

27 Herman Kimsey was not in attendance. As a friend of Backster, he most likely repeated the story Backster told him.

28 Goleniewski, *White Book*, 169–72.

29 She is referring to the fact that her name read 'Smetisko.'

30 In the transcript, the name is spelled four times, twice as 'Mashka' and twice as 'Mushka.'

31 There is no explanation of what 'Neskim' means. I believe it is likely Russian for 'no one' (не с кем/ne s kim) and transcribed incorrectly. In context, I think it is meant to mean something like 'tell no one.'

32 Richards (1966), 255.

33 Ibid., 43.

34 This book never appeared.

35 The transcript released by the Spellers appeared in the 16 July 1966 edition *of Conservative Viewpoint* and is reprinted in the *White Book*, 169–72. It was first released by the Spellers on 17 February 1965 as part of their attempt to discredit Smith after she refused to change her Anastasia story. The Guy Richards' version in *Imperial Agent* (254–55) is not accurate to the Speller transcript, although what he does is more paraphrase than distort.

36 Goleniewski and Kampf had been married in a civil ceremony in the USA in March 1961.

37 Father Georgi was the son of Count Paul Grabbe, who grew up in a highly privileged family in St. Petersburg.

38 Richards (1966), 247–49. Robert Speller, Jr., provides an eye-witness account of the wedding in the text.

39 He later wrote a book about the Trust. See Voitsekhovksy (1974). For the CIA account, see Simpkins and Dyer (1989).

40 Perry and Pleshkov (1999), 317–27. The book documents Vladimir's ties to the Nazis in World War II as well.

41 He apparently shunned the VMS, most likely because the VMS flirted with constitutional monarchy.

42 This document is cited in Voitsekhovsky's papers in his archive at the Hoover Institute. See http://www.oac.cdlib.org/findaid/ark:/13030/tf1z09n52p/entire_text/.

43 Massie (1996), 154–55.

44 'Cossack Exile Shifts Loyalties,' 30 January 1965 *Miami Herald* reprint of a UPI story from New York City. For the full text of the Toultzeff statement, see Capell, *Herald of Freedom*, 25 March 1966 and available at https://www.cia.gov/readingroom/docs/CIA-RDP75-00149R000300130031-4.pdf.

45 Princess Marina had been married to Adolf George Streer Ritter von Streeruwitz of Königssee, Bavaria, and Vienna.

46 Richards (1966), 241–42.

47 Villemarest (1984), 267.

48 Richards (1966), 245–47.

49 Massie (1996), 155.

50 The article was entitled 'WTIC "Americana" Spotlights Romanov' and was meant to promote a program on WTIC radio show hosted by Dick Bertel that was doing to devote an entire week of programs to Goleniewski. For a look at the picture, see https://www.cia.gov/readingroom/docs/CIA-RDP75-00149R000300140032-2.pdf.

51 *The Manchester Union Leader* introduction says the paper could not confirm the story's accuracy but the piece 'makes good reading on a summer day.'

52 Schuyler reports that Goleniewski had to wear braces as a child because he suffered from hemophilia:
    'As a young boy, his crippled legs had had to be in braces for seven years. The indentation left by the constant wearing of the braces can still be seen on his legs. He walks stiffly, often using a cane. But he is tall and well-built now, and his vigorous personality commands your unquestioning respect.'

53 Richards (1966), 249.

54 The press release is reprinted in Lovell (1991), 467–70.

55 It is possible the two women had been brought out of East Berlin by the CIA. Recall that Kampf said in a statement following her defection that the CIA aided in the escape of some of her relatives from East to West Berlin.

56 Kampf open letter reprinted in Goleniewski (1984), 166. In *Mystérieux Survivant*, Villemarest writes (16) that when Goleniewski came to the Americans he asked for asylum for himself, his 'wife,' and 'for two or three people.' Most likely this is a garbled reference to Kampf's relatives.

57 'Soviet Says U.S. Invents Heir to Romanov Throne,' a UPI story from Moscow in the 28 August 1966 *NYT*.

58 The statement was reprinted in the *White Book*, 142–47.

59 Anonymous (1977).

60 Philippa Schuyler worked for Transglobal in the Congo. See Talalay (1995), 201. A brilliant child prodigy pianist, Schuyler was killed in a helicopter crash in Vietnam while covering the war for the *Manchester Union Leader*. Following her death, a foundation was created in her name whose executive vice president was Robert Speller. In July 1967, Schuyler's mother went to Saigon to 'deliver initial grants to the people of South Vietnam.' Former CIA official turned Knight of Malta Herman Kimsey accompanied her. See 'Foundation Formed to Aid Vietnamese, Honors Late Writer,' *NYT* 16 July 1967.

61 Rorke was killed in a plane crash. He had been active in aiding Cuban exile attacks on Castro. In January 1964, the FBI conducted interviews in Miami and New York City to

determine Rorke's fate. His plane appears to have crashed on 24 September 1963 after flying out of Cozumel, Mexico, reportedly on its way to Central America. The FBI wanted to know if the ACI had some involvement in Rorke's activities.

62 Schieber (1987), 28–31.

63 Ibid., 26.

64 Ibid., 30.

65 Schieber (1987), 41.

66 See Bale (1991). The ABN was the Anti-Bolshevik Bloc of Nations.

67 On Kersten's role in the WACCFL, see http://www.marquette.edu/library/archives/Mss/CJK/CJK-bionote.shtml. For a list of some founding members at the WACCFL, see *the Congressional Record*, 23 May 1958, A4918.

68 Bale (1991).

69 Marshall, Scott and Hunter (1987), 65.

70 The Anti-Communist League of the Caribbean (ACLC), founded in 1954, may have been at the Guatemala gathering. The ACLC lists Guatemala, El Salvador, Honduras, Nicaragua, Costa Rica, Panama, Cuba, Dominican Republic, and Haiti as participants in the League. The ACLC's U.S. headquarters was in New Orleans.

71 This was almost certainly Morris Giloni, who headed the 'United Hungarian Jews of America.' Schieber says Giloni introduced him to a famous Hungarian rabbi.

72 Schieber and the INS battled for decades over his legal status. See Andrew Kilgore, 'Haviv Schieber' at http://www.washingtonreport.me/1986-january-27/personality-haviv-schieber.html. On his deportation fight, see the 8 September 1961 *National Jewish Post and Opinion*.

73 Riis died on 14 March 1962. Jon Speller claimed that Riis believed that the entire Imperial Family had escaped from the Bolsheviks, although Riis died before Speller could extensively question him. Speller said that he had known Riis for a long time, but that the subject of the Romanov family never came up in their discussions until the Spellers began to consider publishing Eugenia Smith's Anastasia book. Jon Speller then called him to discuss the matter, but Riis died before Speller could ask any detailed queries. See Richards (1975), 158–59.

74 A Wehrmacht collaborator in the Reichskommissariat Kaukasus, Don Cossack Ataman Glaskow (the name is also transcribed Vasily Glazkov/Vasili Glazkov) later listed himself as 'General Vasily Glazkov, Chief of Political Coordination, Free Cossakia,' a New York-based émigré exile grouping. In 1972, Robert Speller & Sons published Glaskow's book, *History of the Cossacks*.

75 In *Yankee Komisar*, which has no footnotes or solid dates, Riis claims that under the cover name 'Maxim Maximovitch Galinski,' he became the 'Commissar of Kazan Gubernia and was subsequently decorated by Trotsky' according to Jon Speller's preface. Yet official Washington records show that Riis could not have possibly been where he claimed.

76 *Karl Marx: Master of Fraud* includes an introduction by Brigadier General Frank H. Howley, the former head of the U.S. Military Sector in Berlin. The bulk of the book is a reprint of letters Riis wrote to Presidents Truman, Eisenhower, and Kennedy about world affairs. *Karl Marx* is remembered (if it is remembered at all) for Riis's claim that Karl Marx was a devout Jew who regularly attended synagogue. Riis interviewed the Marx family's faithful servant Helene Demuth in a fish and chips shop near Dean Street in 1903. It was during this encounter that he learned about Marx, the 'god fearing Jew' who frequently visited a temple. Helene Demuth died in 1890.

77 On Riis, see Spence (2002a).

78 Ibid., 234–35.

79 Riis (1962), 54–55.

80 Spence (2002a), 224. In *Mystérieux Survivant*, Villemarest (148–49) says Riis was Danish and that he had accompanied his father on business trips to Russia in his childhood where he leaned to write and speak Russian perfectly as well as master different regional dialects. He claims Riis returned to America and graduated from the Naval Academy

and later obtained an engineering degree from Columbia. Spence, however, drew from newly declassified documents to map Riis's enigmatic background.

81 *East Europe* from its founding in 1957 to its close in 1970 was published by the Free Europe Press and backed by the Crusade for Freedom/Free Europe Committee. It was affiliated with American psychological warfare operations such as leaflet drops behind the Iron Curtain. When the Spellers took over, they kept a few of its older staff. On the CIA and *Free Europe*, see Reiser (2013).

82 Richards (1966), 42–43.

83 '*W 1955 roku ze służbowego wyjazdu do RFN nie wrocil do kraju. Po kilku miesaiacach ujawnit sie jako oficer wojskowegeo wywiadu USA.*' Szlachcic (1990), 116.

84 Richards (1975), 40.

10

HATING HENRY KISSINGER

Bessell and 'Bor'

In the early 1970s, Goleniewski's fading star barely flickered in the public mind. On 11 June 1971, the *New York Daily Mirror*, a small newspaper that lasted about two years, reported that it would publish Goleniewski's *Reminiscences and Observations*, although the book never appeared.[1] On 23 March 1973, Goleniewski did meet John Birch Society (JBS) leader Robert Welch, who reportedly invited him to speak at the group's September 1973 National Council Dinner in New York City.[2]

In 1974, however, Goleniewski made public a bombshell claim: Henry Kissinger, Richard Nixon's former National Security Advisor and then US Secretary of State, was a secret Russian agent codenamed 'Bor'! His charge first surfaced in a 20 March 1974 article in the JBS weekly publication *Review of the News*. The author was Knight of Malta Frank Capell, also an associate editor of the *Review*. Capell continued the story in the April 1974 issue of *Herald of Freedom* in a section entitled 'Confidential Intelligence Report.'

Capell wrote that Goleniewski first informed the CIA during his debriefings about Kissinger, then a well-known Harvard academic who did government consulting in the early 1960s. Capell next self-published a 120-page book entitled *Henry Kissinger Soviet Agent* with one section devoted to Goleniewski.[3] In March 1976, the Birch Society's *American Opinion* ran an article by a rightwing author and radio host named Alan Stang further detailing Goleniewski's claims. That same year another leading Bircher, Gary Allen, published *Kissinger: The Secret Side of the Secretary of State*; it too included a chapter recycling Goleniewski's charges.[4]

For Capell and his fellow Birchers, Goleniewski opened up one more flank in their war against Kissinger, the man who orchestrated US ties to Communist China, betrayed Taiwan, abandoned South Vietnam, opened nuclear missile reduction talks with Russia, and embraced détente with the USSR. But why did it

DOI: 10.4324/9781003051114-14

take so long for Goleniewski to attack Kissinger, a highly visible figure whom Gole-niewski said he first warned the CIA about shortly after his January 1961 defection?

The answer probably begins with an April 1970 telephone call to Guy Richards from a British Liberal Party MP named Peter Bessell.[5] Born in 1921 and an MP from 1964–1970, Bessell first met fellow Liberal MP and future party leader Jeremy Thorpe in December 1955. They became long-time friends, confidantes of each other's secrets and political allies. Bessell though led an incredibly dodgy life. His business dealings based in London and New York were extremely shady, with allegations of unpaid debts and dubious practices and he operated in a shadowy world of politicians, bankers, fixers, con men, and criminals.[6]

Bessell told Richards he was now convinced that the Romanovs survived after reading Richards' 1970 book *The Hunt for the Czar*, despite this being a tome obviously written by a historical amateur. Bessell added that Thorpe believed in Richards' book as well.

Bessell said he contacted Richards after learning from a friend in the British Foreign Office that the government knew of a secret codicil to the March 1918 Brest–Litovsk Treaty ending World War I on the Eastern Front. In it, Lenin sup-posedly agreed to let the Imperial Family escape to the West as demanded by Kaiser Wilhelm II. Lenin's agents then faked the Imperial Family's deaths while secretly arranging their passage out of Russia.[7]

Bessell spoke to Richards not from London but from New York where he was on a business trip. After meeting with Richards, Bessell returned to London where on 14 May 1970 he asked in a Parliamentary Question: 'Why Her Majesty's Government have refused to release for research or publication official documents relating to the assassination of Tsar Nicholas II and his family, in view of the thirty-year rule policy on such papers.' The Prime Minister (still Harold Wilson) replied that the government had opened all records on 10 February 1966.[8] Bessell next inquired 'about Michal Goleniewski, the Romanov claimant, and whether or not the Chancellor of the Exchequer held monies from Nicholas II in the "Accounts of the Bank of England."'[9]

On 27 April 1971, Bessell declared in a statement from New York that he was certain the Romanovs had survived. He also said he had been allowed access to classified US State Department documents on the rescue with the help and approval of his friend Henry Kissinger. A Dr. Robert Miller, 'a researcher attached to Secretary of State Henry Kissinger's staff,' let Bessell see these papers.[10] Bessell also published an article entitled 'The Escape of Czar Nicholas and Alexandra' in the June 1971 issue of the Speller family's *East Europe* magazine.

Now no longer an MP, in 1972 Bessell opened a Fifth Avenue office called Peter Bessell, Inc., a boutique financial consulting firm. Richards and his wife gave Bessell some of their money to manage. They also introduced him to a wealthy real estate owner whom Bessell worked with to find European investors in his properties.[11]

Bessell told Richards, whom he saw regularly, that he had done the US gov-ernment a large favor in some financial matter. Using this as leverage, in either late 1970 or early 1971, he approached Kissinger for access to papers on the Romanovs in the State Department's archives. His efforts paid off, or so he told Richards, when a Kissinger aide (presumably Miller) discovered Romanov-related State Department papers in an old White House safe. The 'Chivers Papers' (a codename supposedly used by American officials for the messages) purported to show how US agents in Russia helped arrange the Romanov family's escape.[12]

Bessell stated that while in Washington he examined about one hundred pages of the Chivers Papers and copied the most important ones. It turned out, however, that he only 'copied' notes from the papers. Bessell, however, assured both Richards and BBC reporters Tony Summers and Tom Mangold that the documents would soon be made public under the new Freedom of Information Act (FOIA). As with Richards, he provided them with a hundred pages of 'notes' he had taken from the documents, but he never offered photocopies, much less the original texts.[13]

Bessell's ability to uncover history-changing documents extended to 'the Hardinge letter' that purportedly confirmed the rescue of at least four members of the Romanov family. Bessell's close friend, the Liberal Party leader and MP Jeremy Thorpe, in 1974 asked Sir Alec Douglas-Home, the Heath government's Foreign Secretary, about a supposed letter from Lord Hardinge of Penhurst, who served as Permanent Under-Secretary of State in the Foreign Office from 1916–1920. Thorpe claimed to have seen a letter from Lord Hardinge 'confirming the escape of the Tsar and his family.' Bessell had supplied Thorpe with the letter or a copy of the letter that he said came from the British Foreign Office files. Douglas-Home replied that no such document existed, and the Hardinge letter was later exposed as 'a ludicrous forgery.'[14]

When Summers and Mangold were working on their book *File on the Tsar*, they had a colleague ask Kissinger whether he knew Bessell. Kissinger said he did (Bessell was, after all, a British MP), but that the last time they met socially was in 1969. Questioned about Bessell's claims, Kissinger replied, 'that story is a lot of crap.'[15]

In 1974 Peter Bessell suddenly vanished from New York. Deep in debt with his failed investment firm, Bessell went into hiding in California. He would return to England in the late 1970s as a star government witness in a failed attempt to prosecute Jeremy Thorpe for conspiracy to murder. Thorpe biographer Michael Bloch writes that, like Thorpe

> Bessell was a showman and extrovert, witty and imaginative, an elegant charmer with a theatrical touch who enjoyed intrigue and danger. He indulged in promiscuous heterosexuality hardly less dangerous in terms of career and reputation … than Jeremy's homosexuality: he kept a wife and family in Cornwall and mistress in London and was a compulsive and accomplished seducer of women. He was a fantasist and, in this respect, went further than Jeremy: he developed a habit of telling everyone what they most wanted to hear, causing many to regard him as a liar, hypocrite and mischief maker.[16]

Thorpe had been threatened for years with exposure as a homosexual by a mentally unstable former lover of his named Norman Scott. Bessell spent years managing Scott for Thorpe to keep him silent. Thorpe was then later charged with plotting Scott's murder. Bessell's credibility in court was ruined by the unreliability of his statements and by revelations that he had already sold his story to a newspaper. In the event, Thorpe was controversially acquitted.[17]

Although he never addressed his role in the Romanov caper, in his memoir *Cover-Up* Bessell claims in a long footnote:

> It has been frequently suggested that I had a pecuniary interest in the Tsar mystery, including a fatuous assertion by the *Sunday Times* that I hoped to trace millions of dollars deposited in various banks by the Tsar. I had none and could ill afford the time I expended on the matter. I would have avoided it but for the persistence of Richards, whom I held in affection and regard, and of Mangold and Summers.[18]

In 1975, with Bessell still underground in California, Richards published *The Rescue of the Romanovs: Newly Discovered Documents Reveal How Czar Nicholas II and the Russian Imperial Family Escaped* based on the Bessell 'findings.' In *Rescue*, Richards also states on the first page of chapter one that Goleniewski 'probably is a relative' of the royal family, but that he is not the Tsarevich. Although Richards made his claim in passing, it was a dagger thrust at Goleniewski. Neither Richards nor Bessell could sell their new version of the Romanov saga without first debunking Goleniewski. According to the espionage writer Richard Deacon, Guy Richards offered three different theories as to Goleniewski's real identity:

> He opined then that if Goleniewski was not the Tsarevich there were three other possibilities – that he was the Imperial Family's 'stand-in' for the Tsarevich when it looked doubtful whether the hemophilic son of the Tsar would live to maturity, or a son of the Tsar born out of wedlock, or what he termed 'a ringer hoaxed up by the Russians.'[19]

In August 1976, the Empire struck back. That month Goleniewski published in *Double Eagle* his insane attack on Bessell and Richards entitled 'Double Eagle versus SS Order under Death's Head,' where he accused Guy Richards of being SS General Reinhard Heydrich. Yet Goleniewski also had many genuinely interesting things to report in the article, some of which sound quite believable.

Goleniewski recalled that in July 1970 he met Peter Bessell twice, once in a hotel and once in Goleniewski's apartment. Bessell said he was operating on behalf of a group of British banks interested in gaining access to the Tsarist fortune. Bessell then informed him of a plan to use fake documents to access the money. If Goleniewski cooperated, he could gain at least $40 million in Tsarist money as well as an $8 million advance for a memoir to be published by Dell Books. He even threw in a possible future meeting with the Queen of England.

According to Goleniewski, Bessell said he wanted him to confirm the forgeries 'as original and authentic' under oath in a future court trial.[20] Goleniewski said he told Bessell he absolutely refused to commit fraud. He recalled that 'when I refused Bessell's offer, he threatened me with the planting of the forgeries' in US records and 'making references to his connections with high representatives in the United States government and White House.' Bessell almost certainly invoked the name of Henry Kissinger, as he bragged about his ties to Kissinger to many people, including Guy Richards.

Unable to convince Goleniewski, Bessell left some three hundred pages of documents in Goleniewski's apartment hoping he would change his mind. Goleniewski recalled they were mostly forgeries with a mix of real documents irrelevant to the case. He said the typeface showed that some of the forgeries had been done on typewriters in the possession of Robert Speller & Company, Guy Richards, and a mysterious individual named E. H. Stewart Hill.[21] Goleniewski added that he sent the Bessell forgeries to the FBI.

Were Bessell and Richards, already business partners of a sort, also collaborating on a Romanov scam? Or had Richards no idea that Bessell was shady? Did Richards really believe Bessell had been employed by unnamed British banks to access the Romanov fortune? Goleniewski now suspected BBC journalists Anthony Summers and Tom Mangold as well. When the two journalists tried to approach him for a BBC TV interview, he didn't just reject their request; he told them copies of his rejection letter 'were also going to the President of the General Assembly of the United Nations, the FBI, and lawyers.'

Goleniewski further believed that Gary Null, who interviewed Goleniewski for his book *The Conspirator who Saved the Romanovs*, was corrupt as well. Null inserted the assertion that Goleniewski wasn't 'really' the Tsar; he was instead the illegitimate son of Empress Alexandra and a Russian officer named General Orlov. Goleniewski saw Richards' hand at work. After all, hadn't Null dedicated his book to Richards? (In fact, he had.)

Towards the end of 'Death's Head,' Goleniewski inserted yet another insane claim. Peter Bessell, it turned out, was really Nikolai Yezhov, the former head of Stalin's secret police. As for Richards, Goleniewski knew from '1966' on that he was Heydrich. The fact that Bessell and Richards were forgers sealed the argument. Hadn't Heydrich worked with Yezhov to forge documents to frame Soviet Chief of Staff General Tukachevsky?

Goleniewski also became convinced that Richards had been working with the CIA all along. When Richards wrote his March 1964 *New York Journal-American* articles, it was because the CIA wanted to blow his cover and target him for assassination by the KGB. Richards also wrote his articles when Goleniewski's pregnant wife Irmgard was in the hospital to put even more pressure on him. In short, Richards had 'conspired against myself in the United States for the last 12 years.'

Edward Jay Epstein believed that Bessell's claim that Kissinger was working with him fueled Goleniewski's paranoia. Epstein said that Goleniewski even claimed not only that Bessell was 'really' Nicolai Yezhov, but that Yezhov/Bissell was

Kissinger's Soviet 'case officer.' Bessell's fake link to Kissinger, in short, now 'triggered' Goleniewski.[22] But why did Peter Bessell jump on the Romanov bandwagon? Why did Jeremy Thorpe follow him? What was Guy Richards doing with Bessell? Why did Bessell spend years promoting an elaborate hoax around a futile Romanov claim? What was the payoff? Was the con man conned? But, if so, why? And by whom?

ODRA and Oberammergau

Goleniewski claimed that the key to the Kissinger mystery was a secret Polish–Soviet intelligence operation codenamed 'ODRA' (the Slavic name for the Oder river) based in Legnica, a city in southwest Poland formerly known as Liegnitz. Close both to Germany and Czechoslovakia as well as the Polish city of Wroclaw, Legnica was the headquarters of the Soviet military forces in Poland, the so-called Northern Group. Here is Goleniewski's depiction of ODRA as reported by Capell in *Henry Kissinger Soviet Agent*:

> The story of ODRA and Henry Kissinger's connection with it was disclosed by 'Col. Goleniewski' (Aleksei Romanoff) as follows: The complex known by the code name of ODRA originated with the underground and partisans during World War II and still exists, having begun its own established and controlled operations from Poland after World War II.

Following the end of the war,

> ODRA in Poland was placed under the control of Soviet Intelligence General Zelaznikoff, who headed the directorate of the Soviet Army's north group in Legnica, Poland. Its principal purpose was the infiltration and penetration of military intelligence services in the West, especially those of Great Britain and the United States. Under the leadership of General Zelaznikoff, who was supervised from Moscow, the local chief was Colonel Kujun. Since ODRA operated from Poland, the only representative responsible to the Polish Communist Government was Col. Wozniesienski, who was also a Soviet officer.

Goleniewski was referring to NKVD and SMERSH General Nikolai Ivanovich Zheleznikov, who from 1946 to 1950 was chief of the counter-intelligence section of the Northern Group. 'Colonel Wozniesienski' was Colonel Dmitry Wozniesienski, who had also worked for SMERSH. Wozniesienski helped found Polish counterintelligence out of Polish units in Russia during the war known as Military Information (IW). Wozniesienski then served as a Soviet 'advisor' to Polish intelligence during the reconstruction period.[23] Finally, Colonel Kujun was most likely Lieutenant Colonel Philip (Filip) Kujun. An officer in the Polish Border Protection Army (*Wojska Ochrony Pogranicza*/WOP), Kujun was listed as a WOP Brigade Commander until 24 July 1954.

Capell continues:

> In 1954 an important courier, a woman of Greek–Russian nationality, had been murdered under mysterious circumstances and important material, together with approximately $80,000 of intelligence funds, disappeared. Consequently, the chief of the group who worked with the murdered courier, Col. Kujun (code name Bayan), was ordered to Moscow for questioning.
>
> Anticipating possible liquidation, Col. Kujun shot and severely wounded himself and was placed in a hospital of the GZI (*Glowny Zaraad Informacji* – Polish [Military] Intelligence). Col. Wozniesienski, chief of GZI, personally conducted investigations and interrogated the wounded chief of ODRA, Col. Kujun, who eventually died in July of 1954.
>
> All of the information obtained by Col. Wozniesienski was documented personally in a special dossier. A short time thereafter, Col. Wozniesienski was himself arrested by order of the Polish Minister of Defense and Soviet Marshal Rokossowski. All of his official and personal papers were sealed and deposited in a safe by his deputy, Col. Skulbaszewski of the GZI (who was also a Soviet officer). Col. Wozniesienski was accused of crimes during the Stalin era, was transferred to Moscow and subsequently sentenced to 10 years in prison.[24]
>
> In February 1956, in connection with Col. Wozniesienski's appeal trial and also with the activities of a special commission investigating the crimes of Beria and Stalin, the still-sealed safe of Col. Skulbaszewski was ordered to be opened in the presence of the KGB, and all papers and properties contained therein registered and a memorandum prepared.[25]

Goleniewski said that:

> Among the 1500 pages of documents were 20 hand-written pages in the Russian language by Col. Wozniesienski concerning the interrogation of Col. Kujun. Wozniesienski had a list of the names and code names and short data on the principal agents of ODRA. Under the code name of 'Baraban' there was listed an individual referred to a Bosenhard, a member of the US Military Intelligence headquartered in Oberammergau in West Germany.

Goleniewski was also interviewed by John Birch Society connected journalist Alan Stang for Stang's March 1976 *American Opinion* article on Kissinger.[26] When Stang asked him, 'Were you actually present when the KGB opened Colonel Skulbaszewski's safe?' Goleniewski answered:

> 'Well I opened Colonel Skulbaszewski's safe.'
> 'You opened it yourself?'
> 'Right.'

'And in Colonel Skulbaszewski safe there was a list of Soviet agents – and on that list was the name: Henry Kissinger?'

'Right.'

But did the 'ODRA spy' Baraban/Bosenhard even exist?

My searches in data bases from the *New York Times* to Pro Quest to the *Times of London* and the *Daily Telegraph* to Google have uncovered no mention of Bosenhard, much less that he had been arrested and sentenced to years in jail as a Soviet spy. The *New York Times* regularly reported on Soviet espionage cases in Germany including one of a US solider based in Oberammergau, but the paper never reported on Bosenhard.[27]

Pierre de Villemarest, however, states that when he was working for French intelligence after World War II, he visited Oberammergau, and said he remembered seeing Ernst Bosenhard on occasion.[28] Bosenhard reportedly fled Germany in the late 1930s and began helping the OSS in World War II. He then supposedly began work at Oberammergau as a translator.

In *Henry Kissinger Soviet Agent*, Capell writes:

> Informed Washington sources state that Ernst Bosenhard was born in East Germany and had lived in the United States for 8 years. He was convicted in 1961 [1951] of espionage on behalf of the Soviet Union in the US courts of the Allied High Commission for Germany and sentenced to four years in prison. In his appeal he claimed to have been blackmailed because he was a homosexual. Having failed in his ODRA mission, Bosenhard asked not to be turned over to the Communists because he feared they would send him to Siberia.

There is, as far as I could find, one scholarly or journalistic reference to Bosenhard as a Soviet spy. It comes from the well-known British espionage writer E. H. Cookridge. In his *The Many Sides of George Blake, Esq.*, a book Goleniewski almost surely would have read, Cookridge reports:

> When victory came, plenty of Communist secret agents were still in position.... Their efforts in the Western zones were soon rewarded. One of their master spies, Ernst Bosenhard, managed to obtain an appointment as a clerk at the United States Intelligence HQ at Oberammergau. Before he was caught, Bosenhard sent to Moscow copies of many top-secret documents, including reports from General Lucius D. Clay, director of the US military government in Germany, to President Truman.[29]

In Cookridge's version, 'master spy' Bosenhard was an administrative clerk at Oberammergau. In Villemarest's telling, he was a translator/interrogator. Yet even if Bosenhard did exist and was convicted of spying for Russia in 1951, what did any of it have to do with Kissinger, who left Oberammergau in 1947 to take up his studies at Harvard?[30]

As for 'Bor,' based on Goleniewski's testimony, Kissinger's name never appeared in the files; he simply deduced that Kissinger was 'Bor.' Goleniewski said that he only knew the cover names of agents and not their actual identities. When Stang reported that Goleniewski came across Kissinger's name in the ODRA files, only the 'Bor' code name was there. How then, even assuming there was an agent at the base code-named 'Bor,' could Goleniewski know it was Kissinger?

In the version of the story Goleniewski told Villemarest, he knew an amazing amount about 'Bor' up until 1954, when the Kujun case began, because the ODRA file was so extensive. The file included 'Bor's' date of birth in the town of Fürth, Germany, his rank in the US military, the fact that his mentor was Fritz Kraemer, his position at Harvard, his relationship to the Rockefellers, and his role in the Council on Foreign Relations. All the file lacked was 'Bor's' real name, which had to be Kissinger.

When Goleniewski said he first told all this to his CIA debriefers, Villemarest writes, '*Ses interrogateurs étaient stupéfaits*' as well they might be. Goleniewski had just identified Kissinger – then doing consulting work for the White House – as at a minimum an ODRA spy as late as 1954.[31] What would be even more stupefying is the notion that the CIA would simply ignore this revelation from a man who just helped MI6 catch George Blake.

Kissinger first came to Oberammergau in April 1946 after being stationed in the Hesse town of Bensheim. At Oberammergau, the 23-year-old Kissinger lectured at the European Command Intelligence School along with Fritz Kraemer. Kissinger officially was discharged from the Army in late 1946, but he remained at Oberammergau as a civilian lecturer until the spring of 1947.

As for 'Bor,' Lloyd Shearer wrote a *Parade* Sunday supplement profile of Kissinger that appeared on 24 October 1971. Shearer reports that at age 22, Kissinger became responsible for 'a landkreis [district], Borgstrene' when he worked for Army intelligence (CIC) tracking down Nazis. In *Henry Kissinger Soviet Agent*, Capell writes that the 'Bor' cover name could well have been taken from the first three letters of 'Borgstrene' before he cites Shearer's story on Kissinger.

Shearer's article, however, was based on a typo; there is no 'Borgstrene' landkreis. Kissinger was based in the town of Bensheim in Hesse, which was in the Bergstrasse landkreis. Kissinger was there to investigate the murder of US airmen executed by the Gestapo just a few days before the town surrendered. He did not run the entire district, just the town. It appears likely that Goleniewski concocted 'Bor' based on a spelling mistake in an article in *Parade*. Typo or not, the idea that Kissinger was somehow a Soviet agent codenamed 'Bor' now became an article of faith in prominent sections of the far right, possibly accelerated because of the antisemitism within that milieu. The John Birch Society even sent out thousands of copies of articles repeating Goleniewski's charge.[32]

Goleniewski's claim about Kissinger also entered the intelligence community by another route. On 5 October 1971, a top Middle East expert and former head of the Royal Air Force's intelligence staff named Sir Peregrine Henniker-Heaton went missing. British intelligence feared that he might have been assassinated or that he had even defected to the USSR. From 1973 to 1976, Goleniewski seems to have served as a paid consultant to the British security services, and he was visited a few times by a British intelligence officer who used the name Christopher Fischer. Goleniewski said he believed Sir Peregrine had defected and was now in Moscow planning to write a devastating memoir, although how he claimed to know all this is anyone's guess. He said Henniker-Heaton was most likely recruited by the top Soviet spy Rudolf Abel and Kim Philby's father, St. John Philby, also a leading NKVD operative. The St. John Philby connection stemmed from Henniker-Heaton's work for MI6 in the Middle East during World War II.

Although Sir Peregrine had officially retired in 1958, his family believed he might still have been involved in intelligence-related matters. In June 1974, some three years after he vanished, Henniker-Heaton's son found a skeleton in a locked room in his family's Victorian villa in the London suburb of Ealing. Somehow after his disappearance, this room had never been searched.[33] One question the British asked Goleniewski was whether he knew of any operation where the Soviets had provided a fake skeleton to cover up a defection. Perhaps British intelligence was thinking about the mysterious disappearance of SS General Müller and claims that his skeleton had recently been found in Berlin. If so, asking Goleniewski about Soviet deception operations involving fake skeletons was by no means crazy.

In one of his conversations with Fischer, Goleniewski blurted out that Henry Kissinger was a Soviet agent. Startled, Fisher reported the claim to the CIA, along with Goleniewski's assertion that he had first told the Agency this news after he defected in early 1961.[34] An officer on Angleton's Special Investigations Group (SIG) named Clare Edward Petty now demanded that the CIA open a full investigation on Kissinger.

James Angleton now hired Cordelia Hood, a former retired CIA officer and wife of a CIA officer named William Hood, to reexamine old CIA files to see if there was any documented record of Goleniewski's accusation against Kissinger. Cordelia Hood was a very important CIA officer whose service dated back to World War II when she worked out of the OSS office in Bern with Allen Dulles. As she examined the files, Hood could not find any reference to a claim against Kissinger. Nor did a single CIA officer who had dealt with Goleniewski step forward to verify his charge. While Hood was still pursuing her inquiry, however, William Colby forced Angleton out of the CIA. When Angleton resigned in late December 1974, his investigative unit shut down as well.

ODRA may well have existed, and it may have come under investigation for corruption in the mid-1950s as Goleniewski claimed. As for Bosenhard, although I could find no evidence of his existence outside of one line in Cookridge and Villemarest's claim to have seen him in Oberammergau after the war, he may have been real as well. If so, his espionage activity has left no obvious trace in the historical record.

Goleniewski's charge against Kissinger, however, seems an obvious falsehood for many reasons. Here is just one: Is it really believable that one of the CIA's most valued defectors, a defector who spent close to three years being continually debriefed by experts in the Agency as well as by other intelligence agencies such as

MI5, MI6 and the BND, told the Agency that a top defense intellectual and nuclear strategist like Kissinger was a Soviet spy? Kissinger, after all, was famous in Washington policy circles for a Council on Foreign Relations study on limited nuclear warfare that was turned into a 1957 best-selling book entitled *Nuclear Weapons and Foreign Policy*. He was then doing mid-level consulting work for the Kennedy administration. Yet no one recalled him saying it or even bothered to write his charge down? Or that Goleniewski himself never raised the issue publicly until the mid-1970s? When Goleniewski was threatening to testify to Congress in the early 1960s, he never mentioned Kissinger to Colonel Corso or anyone else.

On the balance of probabilities, it seems most likely that Goleniewski's increasing sense of persecution and paranoia added Kissinger to his roster of supposed traitors after Bessell mentioned knowing Kissinger. His reasons for accusing Kissinger may then be more personal than based on any plausible evidential basis. This interpretation doesn't seem particularly outlandish when we recall that Goleniewski was, as we have seen, contemporaneously accusing Guy Richards of being Nazi Reinhard Heydrich, the chief of the Reich Main Security Office, who was assassinated in 1942!

Yet there was at least one CIA official who might well, at least in spirit, have agreed with Goleniewski: James Angleton. Angleton was deeply suspicious of Kissinger. He also knew that Kissinger maintained his own private 'back channel' to the Russians through a KGB agent named Boris Sedov, who had operated under journalist cover for Novosti Press Agency. Sedov and Kissinger first met during Kissinger's time at Harvard, and they maintained their relationship when Kissinger became National Security Advisor and Sedov worked as a counselor in the Soviet Embassy.[35] After he was fired from the CIA, Angleton would tell any journalist who would listen that Henry Kissinger was 'objectively a Soviet agent.'[36]

Notes

1 Frank Capell reported that the British publisher Weidenfeld and Nicolson had been interested in Goleniewski's memoirs. Goleniewski said that Weidenfeld and Nicolson had paid him $4,000 for his memoir, then dropped the project a few months later. See the *White Book*, 5.
2 See https://sites.google.com/site/ernie124102/golitsyn.
3 Capell (1974). Capell's book was reprinted in different issues of a bizarre far-right New Age publication called *Phoenix Journal* by one 'Gyeorgos Ceres Hatonn.' Hatonn was the name given to transmissions from a channeled space alien. See http://fourwinds10.com/journals/UnPublished/J144.pdf, 101–10.
4 Allen (1976).
5 Guy Richards' *The Rescue of the Romanovs* begins with the phone call from Bessell.
6 See Bessell (1980), and Bloch (2014), and Preston (2018).
7 Bessell made the claim in a Christmas 1970 article in the London *Observer*. Summers and Mangold (1976), 196. On the claim that the Foreign Office suppressed information, see Peter Hopkirk, 'Tsar's Heir Said to be Living in US,' 8 February 1971 *Times of London*.
8 Hansard. https://api.parliament.uk/historic-hansard/written-answers/1970/may/14/czar-nicholas-ii-official-documents.
9 Richards (1975), 6.
10 Bessell (1980), 542.
11 Ibid., 342.

12 One of the Chivers Papers claimed that one of the Americans who 'could have' helped in the rescue was Sergius Riis.

13 Summers and Mangold (1976), 197.

14 Bloch (2014), 359.

15 Summers and Mangold (1976), 197.

16 Bloch (2014), 235.

17 Ibid. and Preston (2018).

18 Bessell (1980), 542.

19 Deacon (1982), 113. Richards actually had four theories as he also entertained the idea that Goleniewski was the illegitimate son of Empress Alexandra and a Russian officer named Orlov. In his 1974 book *The Chinese Secret Service*, Deacon claims (488–89) the Chinese secret service told the Americans that the KGB was behind the idea that Kissinger was 'BOR.' 'Through their Swiss network,' the PRC 'picked up – as early as 1964 – evidence that the KGB was passing on to the CIA, through a double agent, disinformation that Kissinger, as "Bor," – had been an agent of ODRA....' The Chinese 'through another double agent' finally obtained 'the full details of the KGB smear on Kissinger. All this was passed on to the Americans.' In other words, Goleniewski was working for the KGB. Where Deacon got his 'Chinese connection' claim is anyone's guess. In his 1982 memoir, Deacon does not describe Goleniewski as a Soviet agent, and makes no reference to China.

20 Goleniewski was now in a position similar to Eugenia Smith when the Spellers demanded she change her story about being the sole Romanov survivor.

21 Hill, who lived at 1702 Second Avenue on the Upper East Side, was deeply involved with Bessell and Richards and referred to Goleniewski as 'Tsarevich' in a 3 June 1972 letter to the *Spectator*.

22 Edward Jay Epstein comments from the Bagley Archive, Box 11.

23 Born in Russia in 1905, Colonel Dmitry Wozniesienski had a long career in the Joint State Political Directorate (*Obyedinyonnoye gosudarstvennoye politicheskoye upravleniye pri SNK SSSR*/OGPU) and the People's Commissariat for Internal Affairs (*Naródnyy komissariát vnútrennikh del*/NKVD). In 1944, he was sent to work with the Polish Army. As a Colonel in the Polish army, he organized a series of brutal purges and show trials in the Polish military. He was dismissed in 1954 and sent to the Soviet Union where he was arrested, tried, and served a prison sentence for repression against Polish officers. On Wozniesienski, see Wrobel (2014), 339.

24 His recall to Moscow may be related to the Swiatlo radio broadcasts.

25 Born near Kiev in January 1915, Antoni Skulbaszewski began working for the NKVD in Kiev in 1937. He was involved in tracking down Polish anti-communist militants after the war. Skulbaszewski became deputy head of the Main Directorate of Information of the Polish Ministry of National Defense from August 1950 to August 1954. He died in Kiev in 1990. Goleniewski easily could have known him in Poland. On Skulbaszewski, see Roszkowski and Kofman (2008).

26 The interview is on YouTube https://www.youtube.com/watch?v=KNHIL_LMGps.

27 See 'G.I. who is said to have offered services to the Russians goes on trial in Germany,' 15 April 1950 *NYT*. For another story of Germans working as Soviet spies in Oberammergau, see '3 German Spies Jailed,' 20 October 1951 *NYT*.

28 Villemarest (1984), 54.

29 Cookridge (1970), 72. There is also no mention of Bosenhard in Smith. Cookridge briefly mentions Goleniewski, whom he erroneously thinks was head of Polish military intelligence in East Berlin, and who defected on 8 February 1961 with his wife and family whom he brought from Poland.

30 The Bosenhard story was later picked up by the Lyndon Larouche cult which also pushed the story that Kissinger was a KGB agent. In an article in *Executive Intelligence Review*, they mentioned 'Eric [sic.] Bosenhard was sentenced to four years' imprisonment by courts of the Allied High Commission for his role in the 'ODRA Cell.' See Thompson (1989).

31 Villemarest (1984), 62–63.
32 See Hoar (1975).
33 See a 27 June 1974 *NYT* reprint of a Reuters story. https://www.nytimes.com/1974/06/27/archives/spys-skeleton-found-in-british-home.html.
34 Capell first went into print with the Bor story in April 1974, Henniker-Heaton's skeleton was discovered in June. Sometime later Goleniewski told Fisher his already public claim about Kissinger.
35 Kalugin and Montaigne (1994), 111–12.
36 Mangold (1991), 305–06, 426, fn. 34.

PART IV
Knights of Malta

11

SHICKSHINNY SHENANIGANS

In the 1960s, Goleniewski became entangled with a fringe chivalric order known as the Sovereign Order of Saint John of Jerusalem (SOSJ)/Knights of Malta, that we have encountered before and who claimed to trace its origins back to the Crusades.[1] Many of its members became the most vocal supporters of Goleniewski's Romanov claims and several of them, as we shall see, also had links to US military and intelligence agencies.

Because the Order's long-time 'Grand Chancellor' Charles Pichel lived in the small town of Shickshinny, Pennsylvania, the group was often referred to as the 'Shickshinny Knights.'[2] Goleniewski had a strange love/hate relationship with the Knights, and he was even chosen as the Knights 'Imperial Grand Protector' in 1966.

This chapter provides a short introduction to the Shickshinny Knights and explores the various sectarian and ego-driven divisions which often plague such fringe organizations. One of these offshoots from the Shickshinny Knights was the Tennessee Knights which moved even further to the extreme right and linked up with various white supremacist groups. Today the Tennessee Knights exist mostly in cyber-space.[3] Yet their website has posted an extraordinary anonymous history of the Knights entitled *The Sovereign Order of St. John: History and Lineage Charts since 1797* (that I will refer to from now on as the *TN History*) which is useful in unpacking this complex story.[4] My approach to the *TN History* is similar to that of the diplomat and historian George Kennan. He once remarked about a dubious document that it was 'one of those curious bits of historical evidence of which it can only be said that the marks of spuriousness are too strong for us to call it genuine, and the marks of genuineness are too strong for us to call it entirely spurious.'[5]

In the following chapter, we will explore the origins of the mysterious Knights in the interwar far-right antisemitic underground populated by White Russian exiles, Nazi sympathizers and US homegrown rightists, nativists and Jew-haters.

DOI: 10.4324/9781003051114-16

The next chapter examines a network of far-right activists who were promoting the notorious antisemitic forgery *The Protocols of the Elders of Zion* in the USA. It focuses in particular on 'Leslie Fry', author of a widely distributed text supporting the Protocols called *Water Flowing Eastwards* and whose son would be a prominent supporter of Goleniewski's Romanov claims. The final chapter of this section revisits some of the far-right activists – many of them connected to American military and intelligence agencies – who were both active in the Knights and also involved with furthering Goleniewski's claims to be Tsar.

Grand Master Goleniewski

In a 1984 affidavit by Goleniewski in a civil case over control of the Order, he stated that by unanimous vote he was offered the position of 72nd Grand Master of the Knights on 3 May 1966. Goleniewski, however, explained that he could not accept his new role because of Pichel:

> The records of the Order also show that for various reasons at that time I had to refuse this great knightly honor to be the Order's 72nd Grand Master, so closely connected with my Russian Imperial Family, and with some of my activities in the past. One of the key reasons was the person, the past, and some of the activities of the Order's Grand Chancellor, Charles L. T. Pichel, which compelled me to urge him to step aside from his high position in the Order. But despite this confidential request on my part … Pichel refused to relinquish the dictatorial hold he had upon the Order and to remove himself into more administrative areas of the Order and the Delaware Corporation.[6]

Only after Pichel stepped down in 1977 did Goleniewski assume his role as Grand Master. He reports that in mid-1978 Frank Capell, in his new role as head of the American Grand Priory 'and President of the Corporation,' approached him to formally 'extend his Imperial Protection.' Goleniewski was now proclaimed Grand Protector on 27 January 1979. Shortly after Capell's death, Goleniewski was elected to the Knights board of directors on 8 November 1980, replacing the Scandinavia-based Thorbjorn Wiklund. Goleniewski's role as Grand Protector was also memorialized in a public ceremony on 25 March 1981.

The Pichel Knights of Malta is both so strange and so obscure that following its antics can be frustrating. Yet the group played an absolutely central role in Goleniewski's life in America for decades, and the real challenge is to understand just why that was the case.

Pichel's Knights were formally incorporated under Delaware law in August 1957.[7] The American Grand Priory of the Sovereign Order of Saint John of Jerusalem (Knights of Malta) as it called itself now attracted new members, including followers of the Old Catholic Church. The Old Catholic Church traced its origin to its opposition to claims of Papal Infallibility at the first Vatican Council held in 1868 under Pius IX. In 1960, an 'Old Catholic' Wandering Bishop named

Christopher Carl Jerome Stanley (a/k/a 'Christopher Maria') even launched his own version of the Knights dubbed 'the Kentucky Knights' as the group was first headquartered in Louisville.[8] Stanley next created the American Orthodox Catholic Church (AOCC), whose members included David Ferrie and Jack Martin (Edward Suggs), two key figures in New Orleans District Attorney Jim Garrison's probe into the JFK assassination. Stanley, who died in 1967, had a long 'rap sheet' as a grifter. His AOCC/Knights peddled phony 'chivalric' titles, an enterprise that attracted both Martin and Ferrie.

As for Pichel, he seemed blessed with an inexhaustible inventory of odd beliefs. One of his most exotic creations was *Samogitia: The Unknown in History*, a 320-page book published in 1975 by Maltese Cross Press.[9] It portrays a lowland area of modern-day Lithuania called Samogitia/Zemaitija, the last area in Europe to convert to Christianity. The Lithuanian scholar Egidijus Alexandravicius described Pichel's opus as 'an insane fantasy.'[10] The Grand Chancellor's rendition of Lithuanian history, however, was no less fantastic than his demand that *Samogitia* win the 'Nobel Prize for History,' even though there was no such prize.[11]

In September 1976, the Knights then 'Grand Master' Crolian William Edelen announced that the elderly and increasingly erratic Pichel was deposed and replaced as Grand Chancellor by a doctor named James Jacobs. The attempted coup failed when Pichel moved in late October 1976 to appoint 'Roberto Paterno Castello di Carcaci-Ayerbe-Aragona' ('Prince Don Roberto II') as the 73rd Grand Master to replace Edelen.[12] In Europe, Swedish Knights such as Thorbjörn Wiklund and Per Axel Atterbom also opposed Edelen, and acknowledged Pichel's choice of Paterno. Insisting he was still the group's rightful Grand Master, Edelen now formed his own 'American Grand Priory.' Meanwhile, Goleniewski's friend Frank Capell, who wanted Pichel retired but who also opposed Edelen, established his own 'American Grand Priory.'[13]

Sometime in late 1976 or early 1977, Pichel was in a bad car accident and seemed close to death. On 28 February 1977, he sent a letter declaring that he was now 'Grand Chancellor Emeritus.' It was decided that Frank Capell and Thorbjörn Wiklund would run two Grand Priories, one in America and one in Europe. Pichel also received a $5,000 a year pension.[14] The Knights now relocated their headquarters from Shickshinny to Reading, Pennsylvania, although Pichel still maintained physical possession of the group's archive. Pichel, however, unexpectedly recovered from his injuries. He now claimed that his resignation letter was coerced and demanded his old position back. He managed to rally some of his old supporters but without much success, and he would die in 1982 at age 93. Before then, he reportedly destroyed the group's archives.

The strangely intriguing history of the Knights issued by the later faction known as the Association of Family Commanders and Hereditary Knights based in Tennessee describes what happened this way:

> Unfortunately, Grand Chancellor Pichel became increasingly eccentric in his later years. He alienated the members but retained legal control of the SOSJ

by his use of proxy votes. Grand Master Edelen resigned in 1976. The 76th Grand Master elected was Prince Roberto Paterno from Sicily, Hereditary Grand Prior of the ancient Langue of Aragon. Elected in 1976, he served until 1983. Grand Chancellor Pichel, who was 87 years old, was coerced into resigning in 1977, and his duties were divided between Grand Prior Capell of America and Grand Prior Wiklund of Europe. Pichel soon was able to become active again and to work with Grand Prior Capell but both of them were dead by 1982.

American Grand Prior Capell unexpectedly died in October 1980 and when Pichel died in May 1982 several Knights took control of a weakened SOSJ corporation that he had founded in 1956. The loss from old age of many influential members of the SOSJ gave impetus for a few Knights to attempt to seize control of the Order to make legal claim on the legendary lost Romanoff treasure that reportedly lay on the floor of the Sea of Japan.[15]

As for the creation of the Tennessee Knights:

> The leaders of this movement had been expelled from the Order in 1981, prior to the death of Pichel. Regardless, they filed a claim against the Sovereign Council for patent infringement. SOSJ Security General Nicholas Nazarenko was a former Cossack German Waffen SS Intelligence Officer who had been recruited after the war to work in Romania for the US Counter Intelligence Corps. Nazarenko denied the attempt to take control of the Order to the Knights who were shown to be ineligible on several counts and his timely intervention helped the Sovereign Council to form the Association of Family Commanders and Hereditary Knights in 1983. A federal court case filed by the splinter group in an effort to seize control of the Order finally succeeded only in the legal grant to them of a trademarked name from Pichel's 1956 corporation.[16]

In the turmoil following Capell's unexpected death, the Reading-based Salvatore Messineo now took his place. On 25 March 1981, the 'Reading Knights' proclaimed Goleniewski the Order's new 'Grand Protector.'[17] Already under Capell, Goleniewski began to increase his public presence in the group. On 27 January 1979, 'His Imperial Highness' was made a 'Hereditary Bailiff Grand Cross of Justice' by Capell. Following Capell's demise, Goleniewski joined the Knight's legal Board of Directors under Messineo.

On 12 November 1980, the new Goleniewski–Messineo leadership notified Thorbjörn Wiklund by letter that he was now 'retired' from the SOSJ corporation and replaced by 'Imperial Grand Protector' Goleniewski on the board of directors. When Wiklund refused to go quietly, the new leadership voted to withdraw permission by the European members to use the SOSJ corporation's registered membership and trademarks and to expel Wiklund.

In July 1981, the 'Reading Order' issued a 'Knightly Emergency' warning against 'a concerted effort on the part of certain individuals and factions' to usurp control of the Order and place it 'under the direction of Freemasons and the international socialist and communist conspiracy against Christian civilization.' Under that pretext, Goleniewski and Messineo expelled the European wing led by Wiklund.[18] Former Knight William Peters, who quit the SOSJ in the winter of 1982, recalled in an affidavit:

> On July 7, 1981, undoubtedly as a result of collusion between Mr. Goleniewski and Mr. S. Messineo, Mr. Goleniewski, by virtue of his illegal and therefore nonexistent position of Imperial Protector, proclaimed a 'Knightly Emergency,' expelled a number of members and officers of the Order, and appointed his cohort Salvatore Messineo, who only recently had given him his 'recognition' and position as the Acting Lieutenant Grand Master of the Order.[19]

In 1983, Wiklund challenged the Goleniewski–Messineo leadership's denial of the use of the registered trademark and membership lists; Wiklund declared he and his allies were the directors of the SOSJ, not Goleniewski and Messineo. The case now wound up in the US District Court for the Eastern District of Pennsylvania. On 30 August 1983, it ruled in favor of Goleniewski–Messineo. A few years earlier, on 28 December 1981, a Pennsylvania Court rejected Pichel's last legal challenge. The Messineo–Goleniewski control of the post-Pichel Knights appeared complete.

In late 1982–1983, however, yet another faction emerged from the Knights. Its leaders included William Peters, John Grady (who joined the Knights in 1979), Colonel Benjamin F. von Stahl, and Nicholas Nazarenko. They founded the Association of Family Commanders and Hereditary Knights, originally based in Benton, Tennessee. Colonel von Stahl headed the new group's Sovereign Council from 1983 to 1991.[20]

But just what were the Tennessee Knights all about?

Tennessee Knights

Our story begins in Albany, Minnesota, not far from St. Cloud. In 1976 the former Ebenezer Lutheran Church was sold to a small group of Catholic Traditionalists allied with the Shickshinny Knights. The Traditionalists were supporters of the Latin Mass and opposed to Vatican II, although they had no affiliation with the Old Catholics. The Church was now renamed the St. Pius V Priory, and was led by its new 'Grand Prior,' a farmer named LuVerne Hollenkamp. In early 1983, however, a battle broke out over the physical control of the Priory and on Hollenkamp personally. The attack was led by supporters of the Tennessee Knights, who argued that since they were the legitimate Knights, the Albany Priory legally belonged to them. Colonel von Stahl, the former Security General of the Messineo–Goleniewski Knights, now opened discussions with extreme right groups like Posse Comitatus and Christian Identity followers in Minnesota.[21] Nor was von Stahl terribly shy about expressing his beliefs. From an article in the 2 July 1983 issue of the *Panama City [Florida] News*:

Col. Benjamin F. M. von Stahl heads up Harrell's Citizens Emergency Defense System. His bushy gray mustache fairly bristles when von Stahl considers what has happened to his country and the US Army. 'We have 40 million illegal aliens here who should be bounced back to where they came from instead of allowing them to bring their diseases, their poverty, and their revolutionary ideas here,' he says. 'We're in a most perilous position. We're being disarmed all the time, both our military and our personal weapons. Our Army is now 60 percent black.' The only hope for a change, says von Stahl, is to restore all political authority in the country to white Christians. 'Identity is the secret of the whole thing,' he says. 'We have the law (of God). The lesser breeds are without the law.'

Some fifteen supporters of the Tennessee Knights now formed a minority in the Albany congregation. On 29 January 1986, the *St. Cloud Times* published a long story on the conflict. The article cited 'Reading Knight' and Goleniewski ally 'Lieutenant Grand Master Salvatore Messineo' as saying that the Tennessee Knights wished to create paramilitary training camps to fight non-whites and looked to the Christian Identity movement for support. Nor does the *TN History* downplay its connections to the racist right. The Tennessee Knights even highlighted the role of a former Nazi collaborator named Nicholas Nazarenko. According to the *TN History*:

> Nicholas Nazarenko was a former Cossack German Waffen SS Intelligence Officer who had been recruited after the war to work in Romania for the US Counter Intelligence Corps. Nazarenko denied the attempt to take control of the Order to the Knights who were shown to be ineligible on several counts and his timely intervention helped the Sovereign Council to form the Association of Family Commanders and Hereditary Knights in 1983.[22]

Nazarenko was the head of the World Federation of the Cossack National Liberation Movement of Cossackia headquartered in Blauvelt, New York. It, in turn, was part of the Captive Nations Committee of the USA. Nazarenko told author Christopher Simpson that he spent much of World War II working as a POW interrogator for the SS in Romania.[23] He then claimed to have worked for the American Counter-Intelligence Corps (CIC) in Europe until 1949 when he emigrated to America.[24] Nazarenko served as both Grand Marshal for the Tennessee Knights and head of the 'Cossack' wing of the GOP's National Republican Heritage Groups Council. For his part, Goleniewski believed Nazarenko was a fake. In the August 1983 *Double Eagle*, he said Nazarenko claimed repeated escapes from the Vorkuta gulag camp in Siberia that Goleniewski said were impossible. He added:

> Another falsehood is Nazarenko's statement that he was Chief of Cossacks Intelligence in Berlin. Despite the fact that Nazarenko married the daughter of General V. Naumenko, who was member of the Main Cossacks Administration (under Nazi supervision) in Berlin, the supervisor Atman-President

General F. N. Krasnov, never assigned to responsible positions, and especially to intelligence service, former Soviet officers (as Nazarenko claims to be) and other questionable individuals. Chief of Cossacks Intelligence in Berlin was Colonel A. Popov, and his Deputy was Major Dm. Cusev ... Nazarenko is not a Cossack.[25]

Goleniewski said he drew his information on Nazarenko from the Manhattan-based 'Supreme Cossack's Representation ... which is recognizing this Editor, and which many years ago, after investigations, proclaimed Nazarenko's claims as an invention and swindle, and refused to accept him as an original Cossack.'[26] Goleniewski gave this group's mailing address as POB 1095, Grand Central Station. This was the box number for the Cossack–American Citizens' Committee founded in the early 1960s by Vasil Glasgow ('W. Glasgow').[27] The Spellers also published Glasgow's book *A History of the Cossacks* in 1972.[28] Glasgow was also close to the Supreme Cossack Representation in Exile founded in 1947.

The Nazarenko story had a Polish dimension as well as an alleged link to Guy Richards. From the August 1983 *Double Eagle*:

Various facts established ... are clearly identifying a pattern of continuing conspiracy against this Editor which had been initiated during 1964–1966 by Guy Richards in league with several co-conspirators. It is a matter of fact that during 1968–1970, Pichel and his 'Security General' Blazes began to act as Richards' sub-agents, who little by little, in accordance with Richards' instructions, started introducing into the Sovereign Order ... various more than questionable individuals....[29]

In 1973, Richards, operating through another sub-agent in New York City (S-H), made to this Editor a surprising proposition that ... he would arrange by the President of the Republic of Poland in Exile, Juliusz Sokolnicki, residing in London, an official and public recognition of this Editor as Heir, Tsarevich and Grand Duke of Russia.[30] Refusing the proposition at hand, it was also easy to find out that the alleged Polish President Sokolnicki in London, acting in accord with another Polish leader in exile in France, Antoni Zdrojewski, were well known agents of the Division V (Emigration) of the Polish Department of Intelligence in Warsaw, and that their key task had been to subvert and to ridicule the existing in London since W.W. II, Polish Government in Exile, headed by its President Professor Stanislaw Ostrowski.[31]

The London-based exile government led by Juliusz Nowina-Sokolnicki was itself yet another fringe organization. Sokolnicki even called himself a 'Count' or 'Prince,' although he had no royal background. In 1979 he invented his own Ordo Sancti Stanislai and declared himself its Grand Master. Sometime in the mid-1970s, Goleniewski said that Nazarenko became Sokolnicki's 'Adviser for Eastern Affairs' and was given 'a military rank of Lt. Colonel of the Polish Army in Exile.' In 1976, he became a 'Major General' in Sokolnicki's imaginary army.

After the 1981–1982 split in the Knights, Nazarenko helped launch the Association of Family Commanders and Hereditary Knights and began linking them to Sokolnicki. Goleniewski said that Benjamin von Stahl recently learned that 'he is also a Hereditary Baron ... who has been decorated by the Polish "President" Juliusz Sokolnicki with the highest Polish orders and decorations: Order Virtuti Militari, Knight Commander of Polonia Restituta and Cross of Freedom and Independence with Swords.'

Goleniewski devoted another long article in the May 1984 *Double Eagle* to the events in Minnesota. Here he cites at length a story that appeared in the 1 April 1984 issue of the *St. Paul Minnesota Pioneer Press* (now the *Twin Cities Pioneer Press*). From the article (as cited by Goleniewski):

> Salvatore Messineo, worldwide Lieutenant Grand Master of the Sovereign Order of St. John of Jerusalem/Knights of Malta, says the Hereditary Knights are a racist, paramilitary group that has tried to take control of the Knights of Malta for several years. 'We have been attracting people that tend to want to use us.... We seem to be a primary target of racists who want to take over. These people want to put military activity over religion....'
>
> Messineo said the Knights of Malta expelled a number of members in 1981, including Dr. John Grady, who now heads the Hereditary Knights out of Benton, Tenn. Messineo said Grady was expelled because he falsely claimed 'he was authorized by us to set up a paramilitary training base in Benton....' Messineo said Grady formed the Association of Family Commanders and Hereditary Knights in 1982.... Grady established the American Christian Church in Benton, which exists for purposes of tax exemptions. 'Grady runs a rendezvous (in Benton) in which armed fanatics are given paramilitary training,' Messineo said.
>
> Another principal figure in the Hereditary Knights, according to Messineo, is a well-known paramilitary leader. He cited a 1982 article in the Rockford (Ill.) *Register-Star* that Benjamin Stahl, Chairman of the Hereditary Knights, was Director of the Citizens Emergency Defense System – that group is a private militia serving the Christian Defense League....[32] Messineo said the Hereditary Knights believe a subhuman race of people, characterized by Messineo as all non-white people, existed before Adam and Eve. Those 'pre-Adamic' races are the targeted enemy of the Hereditary Knights, according to Messineo.... The Christian Defense League is affiliated with such well-known organizations as the Ku Klux Klan and the Posse Comitatus....

Under Grady, the Tennessee Knights established a para-military training camp in Benton. To do so, Grady first founded an organization known as the American Pistol and Rifle Association (APRA), a more militant version of the NRA that the FBI believed was training and advising extremist super-patriots and white supremacists. APRA and the Tennessee Knights came under scrutiny as part of a larger FBI operation dubbed PATCON ('Patriot-conspiracy'). In July 1993, however, the FBI's Washington headquarters ordered PATCON shut down because it felt PATCON was infringing on individual civil rights without generating significant leads.[33]

By the time Goleniewski became so visibly active in the Knights, the group clearly had moved to the fringe of the fringe. Yet as we shall see in a later chapter, the Shickshinny Knights exerted their most powerful influence on Goleniewski not in the 1980s but in the 1960s.

But before looping back to the rightist political activists, ex-military men and former spooks in the Shickshinny Knights, we must first dive deep into their murky origins among the Tsarist exiles, plotters and Jew-haters in early twentieth-century America. It was from this underground antisemitic milieu that they first emerged.

Notes

1 For a list of the Order's high-ranking Knights, see Pichel (1970), 191–193. Also see Formhals (1979). For more on the Knights, see Coogan (1999), 603–15. Also see Coogan (2004).

2 The town is in northeastern Pennsylvania coal-mining country, close to the Susquehanna river and near cities like Wilkes Barre and Scranton. The name can be misleading because there were no gatherings at Shickshinny; as formal meetings took place in New York City.

3 See http://www.theKnightsofsaintjohn.com/gm.htm. Its current 'Prince Grand Master' is Barry Garland who took the position in 2008.

4 For the text, see http://www.theKnightsofsaintjohn.com/History-After-Malta.htm.

5 Kennan (1971), 167. The *TN History* core text dates most likely to the 1960s or early 1970s, given the use of outmoded spellings for Russian names. It is quite clear that the Romanov family was murdered by the Bolsheviks, and it celebrates Grand Duke Kirill claim to be the rightful heir to the Romanov throne.

6 I rely here on an affidavit Goleniewski gave in a Civic Action in the United States District Court for the Eastern District of Tennessee (Civil Action No. 1–83–369) in 1984 in a dispute over control of the Knights and reprinted in the *White Book*. The *White Book* seems to have been inspired by documents Goleniewski gathered for the legal case.

7 Pichel's name does not appear on the initial incorporation papers, possibly because he had a criminal record and wished to remain behind-the-scenes. The group was incorporated as the Sovereign Order of St. John of Jerusalem, Inc. See https://www.courtlistener.com/opinion/2310593/sov-o-of-st-john-of-jerusalem-knights-v-messineo/.

8 For a brief mention of the 'Ordre de Saint Jean du Kentucky,' see Chairoff (1985), 156. Chairoff gives Stanley's first name as 'Carl,' says Stanley had close relations with certain orders of freemasons, and that Stanley was a 33-degree freemason.

9 Pichel (1975).

10 Alexandravicius (2016), 139–42. Pichel's book was translated into Lithuanian in 1991.

11 See a 13 November 1976 letter from the OSJ's Swedish leader Thorbjorn Wiklund to a Rome-based Knight named Michael Martone reprinted in the *White Book*.

12 On Paterno's background, see http://www.orderofmaltaosj.com/the-grand-master.html. The *TN History* says Edelen 'retired' as Grand Master in 1976.

13 For some background on Edelen's heraldic claims, see Chairoff (1985), 150–52.

14 See Rev. Anthony Cekada, 'Light on the OSJ' at http://www.traditionalmass.org/articles/article.php?id=56&catname=1.

15 See http://www.theKnightsofsaintjohn.com/History-After-Malta.htm.

16 Ibid.

17 Goleniewski had collaborated with different Knights. In the August 1976 issue of *Double Eagle* (August 1976), for example, he mentions a 'Lieutenant General of the Order of St.

John' named Count J. F. Rostworowski, who tried to find him a lawyer. Goleniewski also reports that in the mid-1970s, General Clyde J. Watts, a retired military general turned attorney who had many far-right clients, also wanted to represent him, but that Watts died in a 1975 plane crash.

18 There were two Messineos, Salvatore and Leonard. Leonard became the new Grand Master in 1981 while Salvatore became Lieutenant Grand Master.

19 William Peters is also known as 'William von Peters.' A devout Catholic, he has been a practicing specialist in alternative medicine, natural medicine, and acupuncture in Chattanooga, Tennessee.

20 John Grady then became its new Grand Master and served from 1991 to 2008.

21 The July 1981 *Double Eagle* (VII/7) published a photo of a Knights ceremony that includes Goleniewski, his daughter Tatiana, 'Security General H.E. B. von Stahl,' Salvatore and Leonard Messineo and 'Chaplin Rev. James F. Wathen.' See Goleniewski, *White Book*, 139. (Wathen was a Traditionalist Catholic priest. See his website at http://fatherwathen.com/about-father-wathen/.)

22 See http://www.theKnightsofsaintjohn.com/History-After-Malta.htm.

23 Simpson (1988), 274–75.

24 Bellant (1991), 8. Nazarenko told Bellant he worked in a Cossack SS unit that operated under General Helmuth von Pannwitz until he was relocated to Berlin where he served in a Cossack 'government-in-exile.' For a detailed look at Nazarenko in World War II, see Newland (1991). FBI files indicate he spent five years in a DP camp. See https://www.cia.gov/readingroom/docs/NAZARENKO%2C%20NIKOLAI_0012.pdf.

25 Goleniewski, *White Book*, 24.

26 *Double Eagle*, August 1983, reprinted in the *White Book*, 23.

27 O'Maolain (1987), 285.

28 V. G. Glazkov, *A History of the Cossacks* (NY: Robert Speller, 1972). A report in the CIA files said that Glaskow wasn't a Cossack and that he was suspected of being a Soviet agent. See https://www.cia.gov/readingroom/docs/KORZHAN%2C%20MICHAEL%20%20%20VOL.%201_0142.pdf. This is called the 'Korzhan, Michael' investigation.

29 This was Bernard Benjamin Blazes who is listed in Pichel's history as 'Physicist' and 'Hereditary Grand Duke of Samogitia, Director of Nuclear Research and Development' for the Knights.

30 'S-H' was E. H. Stewart-Hill who lived in Manhattan and knew Goleniewski and Richards.

31 Reprinted in the *White Book*, 22.

32 A key CDL leader was Gordon 'Jack' Mohr, yet another Army Lt. Colonel who retired from the service in 1964. He would almost certainly have known von Stahl. Mohr may also have known Col. Corso as well since they both worked with POWs in the Korean War. As for Stahl, he served as 'military advisor' to the Citizens Emergency Defense System founded by John Harrell, who ran the group out of his large estate in Flora, Illinois. It served as the 'defense arm' of Harrell's Christian Patriot Defense League and ran its 'training camps.'

33 See Berger (2012).

12

WHITE RUSSIANS IN MANHATTAN

Russian Knights

For hundreds of years the Sovereign Military Order of St. John (Knights Hospitallers) was Europe's greatest chivalric order. Formed during the Crusades to fight Muslim infidels and aid Christian pilgrims visiting the Holy Land. Named after St. John the Baptist, the 'warrior monks' took vows of poverty, chastity, and obedience. Driven out of the Holy Land in the 1290s, the Knights regrouped on Cyprus and then Rhodes before finally relocating to Malta, where their headquarters dominated Malta's famed port city of Valetta.

A sovereign state, the Knights' military power now lay in their navy that fought for control over the Mediterranean with the Ottomans, most famously at the famed battle of Lepanto. Following the Reformation, however, the Knights remained exclusively Catholic and in 1774, the Order founded a new Grand Priory in Poland. With Poland's annexation by Catherine the Great in the 1790s, the Knights now found themselves under the sovereignty of the famed Empress.

In 1798 Napoleon seized Malta. The Knights' 71st Grand Master, the Austrian-born Ferdinand von Hompesch, instead of resisting the French, abandoned Valetta without a fight. Hompesch reestablished a new headquarters in Trieste, but he had few supporters. A group of Knights disgusted with Hompesch now sought exile in Russia after being invited there by Emperor Paul I (r.1796–1801).

As a small boy, Paul I had read a book about the Knights and became infatuated with their story. As a child, he loved to dress up as the Order's Grand Master in a lavish uniform decorated with the famed Maltese Cross. Now Emperor, Paul I showered the exile Knights with gifts and declared he was now their Imperial Protector and Grand Master. In 1797 he even gave Knights the great Vorontsov Palace in St. Petersburg; their new headquarters was renamed the Palais de Malte. Nor was Paul's courting of the Knights without larger geopolitical design. The

DOI: 10.4324/9781003051114-17

Russian government was then still part of the First Coalition against France. With the defeat of Napoleon and the return of Malta to the Knights, there was a very real possibility that the Russian fleet could gain a new base there as well.[1]

Under pressure from Tsar Paul I, the Holy Roman Emperor Francis II forced Hompesch's formal abdication on 6 July 1799.[2] On 10 December 1798, Paul I created a separate Grand Priory for non-Catholic nobles. For its part, the Vatican willingly acknowledged Paul's role as 'Protector,' but said the Pope could not acknowledge him as Grand Master since, as a non-Catholic, Paul I could not lead an order of Catholic Knights. Many other Priories in Europe, however, voted for Paul as Grand Master as they too sought Russian help to preserve the Order; only the Priories in Spain and Rome opposed his claim. For all practical purposes, Paul was both the Protector and de facto Grand Master of the Knights until his assassination in 1801.

From the *TN History*:

> Shortly after their arrival in Russia, the exiled Knights of Malta joined with the Catholic Grand Priory of Russia and elected their Orthodox and married Protector, Czar Paul I, as the 71st Grand Master. Grand Master Czar Paul I helped to settle the SOSJ [Sovereign Order of Saint John of Jerusalem] in the Russian capital city. He decreed that their Convent would remain at the Imperial residence of St. Petersburg, and that his successors would continue as its protectors. He created a second Grand Priory principally for his Orthodox nobility. He then invited non-Catholic Europeans, mainly Lutherans, to join this new priory for the purpose of preserving the SOSJ and the Christian monarchies of Europe by perpetual opposition to the Humanist Revolution. His plan to return the Russian Orthodox Church, of which he was the sovereign head, to full communion with the Catholic Church had created enemies among his closest advisors and relatives. Czar Paul I, an unrecognized champion of the Order, was martyred, allegedly by Freemasons, in 1801.[3]

The Knights in exile hoped to return to Valletta after Napoleon's defeat, and in 1800 the British retook Malta. The 1802 Treaty of Amiens ending the First Coalition war with Napoleon stated that Malta should return to the Knights. The Treaty of Amiens, however, quickly collapsed. By the end of the Napoleonic Wars, Britain had been solely in charge of Malta for well over a decade. The Knights were now a distant memory.

If Alexander I, Paul I's son and successor, cared about the Knights he could have raised the issue at the Congress of Vienna. He did not. Alexander despised his father and saw the Knights as Paul's white elephant. On 1 March 1801, Alexander I acknowledged the Pope's role in the Order, and allowed a new Grand Master to be chosen by Rome. On 25 April 1803, the Russian Grand Priory in St. Petersburg recognized the Vatican-endorsed Giovanni Battista Tommasi as the Order's new Grand Master. Then on 5 March 1805, the Russian chapter accepted Tommasi's successor Innico Maria Guevara-Suardo as the new Lieutenant Grand Master of the Order. The Knights chose as their Grand Master the Neapolitan Giuseppe

Caracciolo. As Caracciolo was considered close to England, Pope Pius VII, under pressure from France, refused to confirm him. Alexander I, however, recognized Caracciolo and granted him a 12,000-ruble pension. Guevara-Suardo, however, served as the Order's de facto leader while still technically Lieutenant Grand Master.[4]

On 26 February 1810, Alexander I issued a decree stating that while the government would still pay income to the then-living Knights, there would be no further allocations to their descendants. He also confiscated the Knights' headquarters, the Palais de Malte. Although by this time many exiled Knights had returned to Europe, Alexander I still had to contend with those Russian Orthodox Knights whom Paul I organized into a separate Priory. On 2 December 1811, the Russian government dissolved the Knights' commanderies. Hereditary Commanders could pay funds due from their Commanderies [a district under the control of a commander of an order of Knights] to the government. In return, they would be recognized as the owners of the commanderies, and their payments would be donated to charities.

Alexander I, however, never issued a decree formally banning the Order; he let nobles who wanted to retain some recognition of their past keep their symbols, even though the Knights now ceased to exist as an autonomous Priory. Because the Cavalier Guards Regiment was founded by Paul I in his role as Grand Master of the Order, the Maltese Cross was used for insignias as well as in the Corps des Pages, a military school for young nobles now housed in the Palais de Malte. In short, 'the Order of John was recognized as nothing else but a decoration.'[5]

Most important of all, Alexander I recognized the Vatican-backed Sovereign Military Order of Malta (SMOM) as the Knights' legitimate successor. When Tsars wore the Maltese Cross decoration, it was as a Vatican honor. By a 10 February 1891 decree, for example, SMOM's Grand Master Ceschi a Santa Croce bestowed on Nicholas II SMOM's Bailiff Grand Cross of Honor and Devotion. At the time of his coronation on 30 May 1896, Nicholas II wrote to Ceschi a Santa Croce thanking him for SMOM's good wishes, and underscored the links between the House of Romanov and the 'highly esteemed' Vatican-endorsed Order.[6] How then did the Pichel Knights claim to be the heirs of a non-existent independent Russian Priory?

A partial answer to that question was provided by one of Pichel's off-and-on-again allies inside the Shickshinny Knights named Crolian William Edelen, who also claimed to be the 'Count de Burgh, descendant of Frankish kings of Jerusalem, of the emperors of Byzantium, of Charlemagne, etc. etc.'[7] Born in New Jersey in 1920 and educated at the University of North Carolina, Edelen reportedly served with Signals Intelligence in the India-Burma theater in World War II. In the early 1960s, when protests arose against Pichel's shady financial practices, Edelen allied with the anti-Pichel wing of the Knights associated with the group's new European leader Paul de Granier Cassagnac. Edelen was then elected Grand Chancellor of the Cassagnac Knights, who now looked to King Peter of Yugoslavia as their new Royal Protector. When Cassagnac died in the mid-1960s, King Peter formed his own knightly order.

To lure Edelen back, Pichel made him an offer he could not refuse. In 1967 Edelen became the '72nd Grand Master' of the Shickshinny Knights.[8] After Edelen unsuccessfully tried to depose Pichel in the mid-1970s, he later turned to the Knights allied with Thorbjörn Wiklund and supported their unsuccessful legal challenge to the new Messineo–Goleniewski leadership. As part of that legal effort, Edelen began researching the real origin of the Pichel Knights.

Central to Pichel's claim that the Shickshinny Knights were the direct continuation of the Russian Priory established by Tsar Paul I was a list of top Russian nobles whom Pichel said met at the Waldorf-Astoria in a 1908 gathering that officially transferred the Russian Priory from St. Petersburg to New York. Pichel even circulated a copy of the list of Russian nobles in attendance. He said he 'retyped' the document as the paper from the original list was too old.

In a 1980 letter to the historian Harrison Smith, Edelen explained what he believed was the real origin of those documents:

> My problem with the history is that all seems to be false from 1908 to 1932 as published by Pichel. I know his minutes are false. Dr. Bulloch was never Grand Chancellor of the Order.[9] He was the archivist of the old Scottish American Order of St. John and he kept those records at Lancaster, Pennsylvania. When he was old and blind, in the early 1950s, Pichel went to him with a story that he was writing a history of the Knights of Malta and needed some records from the archives. Dr. Bulloch let him borrow whatever he fancied and then obligingly died while Pichel had the most important records. He took the material, twisted it around, took names of noblemen from the *Times* index and created an order stemming from the Grand Priory of Russia, all a hoax.
>
> The Scottish-American order went out of business in New York in about 1909 following the suicide of the Grand Chancellor, as well as a scandal involving payment (or non-payment) of life insurance policies on the lives of the members. Some members in New Jersey tried to save the situation by securing a charter as 'The Knights of Malta' in Trenton in 1911. Their effort failed and by 1912 was abandoned. Then Pichel came along in the 1950s and claimed to be the duly-elected officer of that corporation to give his order some evidence of antiquity and to substantiate the false minutes from 1908 to 1932.[10]

Edelen now reached out to surviving members of the organization that had incorporated the Knights of Malta in New Jersey in 1911. In a 21 February 1984 letter to Clarence Orth, the Grand Recorder of the Ancient and Illustrious Knights of Malta, Edelen explained:

> My own information about Pichel's activities in connection with your Order is that he seems to have contacted Mr. Bulloch, the Archivist of the defunct Order in New York, the one involved in the insurance scandal. Mr. Bulloch had the Archives in Lancaster, Pennsylvania, being old and blind. Pichel visited

him under the guise of writing a history of the Order, was given free access to all the files. He helped himself to the most important ones and took them home with him. Mr. Bulloch died some time later and he kept the records. Then he took the minutes, doctored them up [to make] himself appear as a member and minor officer, also one or two of his cronies were added, then he transformed Mr. Bulloch into Grand Chancellor, rather than Archivist, so he could succeed him in office.

The important item is that Pichel made oath to secure the patent that the title and insignia had been in continuous use since 1911. That is the year when some survivors of the Order in New York decided to incorporate in New Jersey as the 'Knights of Malta.' This did not last one year, but Pichel came along in the 1950s claiming that he was the successor in office of Mr. Bulloch and secured the Charter for his own use. The charter was issued under old laws and was not tax exempt which did not suit Pichel very well, or his ultimate purpose. He then started a Delaware Corporation of 'Sovereign Order of St. John of Jerusalem' and used this and the New Jersey Charter to secure a patent for 'Sovereign Order of St. John of Jerusalem, Knights of Malta,' including the symbol of the Maltese cross. He was never successful in getting a Federal Tax exemption because of his criminal record [which] was well known....[11]

In a 17 February 1984 letter to Edelen, Orth noted:

In the late 1950s at the request of a Colonel Thourot Pichel, Shickshinny, Pa., I spent a great deal of time and considerable expense in gathering items for what I then believed would be an authentic history of our Order. I forwarded many historical items of history for his pursuance which were never returned to me. After much correspondence I visited Shickshinny and was greatly surprised of his low standing in his community. Some labeled him a cheat and a con man. When his book was finally published, I found that everything he wrote was distorted and untrue.[12]

Edelen's correspondents pointed him to an obscure 1923 book entitled *A History of the Ancient and Illustrious Order Knights Hospitaller of St. John of Jerusalem, Palestine, Rhodes and Malta 1048–1923* by the Rev. George William Welsh, and published by the Malta Book Company located in York, Pennsylvania. Welsh's book is half a history of the actual Knights, and half a history of an obscure Protestant order with masonic overtones founded in Scotland and with branches in both the USA and Canada.[13] Clearly anti-Catholic, it said that membership was extended to 'good Protestants whether they be Orangemen or not.' Edelen believed Pichel used the Scottish Order's history as a partial template to launch his own bogus back history of the Knights when he incorporated the Shickshinny Knights in the mid-1950s.

Edelen's own history, however, overlooked the existence of a strange para-political underground that arose following World War I and that would reincorporate itself in the 1950s as the Shickshinny Knights. That history would now partially emerge thanks in part to the strange *TN History* issued by the Tennessee Knights, who, as we have seen, broke with the Messineo–Goleniewski organization in the early 1980s.

Conspiracy and the enigmatic Count Cherep-Spiridovich

A core myth of the Pichel Order was the assertion that in 1908 Tsar Nicholas II approved the relocation of the (non-existent) Russian Grand Priory from St. Petersburg to New York. All this was supposedly first set in motion in the wake of the 1893 visit of Grand Duke Alexander Mikhailovich to the Chicago World's Fair.

The grandson of Nicholas I, in 1894 Grand Duke Alexander ('Sandro' to his friends) married Grand Duchess Xenia Alexandrovna, the oldest daughter of Emperor Alexander III and Nicholas II's sister. Grand Duke Alexander now became Nicholas II's brother-in-law. A year earlier, however, he visited America for the first time. A devout navy man, Alexander served as a Lieutenant on the *Dmitrii Donskoi*, which sailed into New York harbor in early May 1893. He then traveled to Chicago to represent Russia at the World's Fair and to thank President Grover Cleveland for American aid during a recent Russian famine.

According to the *TN History*, Grand Duke Alexander was accompanied on his visit by 'the Russian Transportation Commissioner Colonel A. Cherep-Spiridovich' (Artemij Ivanovič Čerep-Spiridovič). As Count Arthur Cherep-Spiridovich will play a key role in the events that culminated in the Pichel Knights, he will occupy an important place in our narrative, even though much of his life remains draped in mystery. Reportedly born in 1858, or 1867 and of Lithuanian 'Nordic' descent, he claimed to be related to Rurik, the Viking 'founder' of Russia. Today Cherep-Spiridovich is most remembered, when remembered at all, for his self-published 1926 antisemitic tract *Secret World Government, Or 'The Hidden Hand': The Unrevealed In History: 100 Historical 'Mysteries' Explained*. Published under the imprint of the 'Anti-Bolshevist Publishing Association' of New York City, the book is an insane anti-Jewish text made even more crazed by its continual shift back and forth from regular characters to all upper case letters.[14]

An extensive profile of Cherep-Spiridovich by Frederick Boyd Stevenson was published in the 19 June 1921 *Brooklyn Daily Eagle*. Cherep-Spiridovich stressed that the USA must now lead 'the Great White Race' against its enemies, who included Bolshevik Russia, China, and Germany. Surprisingly, Cherep-Spiridovich did not mention a Jewish conspiracy. In the interview, Cherep-Spiridovich said he came from 'noble Russian and Polish stock': his mother was Polish, and his father was Russian. He claimed that he was descended from the Grand Dukes of Russia and Lithuania and added that the Slavs came from Indo-European and Aryan stock. Stevenson reported that Cherep-Spiridovich spent 17 years as 'managing director of a transport and trade company,' and that he spoke nine languages. At the time of the interview, Cherep-Spiridovich ran the Anglo-Latino-Slav League out of an office at 161 East 23rd Street in Manhattan. Many other reports state that Cherep-

Spiridovich had also been a General in the Russian Army. What seems beyond dispute is that Cherep-Spiridovich worked for many years as a Russian political intelligence operative in Europe, and Paris in particular. His interest in Paris was not surprising given that Tsarist Russia and Republican France were then close political allies.

Cherep-Spiridovich was also an avowed pan-Slavist who, as we are told in the *TN History*:

> became President of the Slavonic Society of Moscow. For five years, he had been Serbian Consul to Moscow, and was a member of the Serbian and later of the Russian Secret Services.[15] The Slavonic Society was an intelligence operation which funneled arms and resources to nationalist elements in the Balkans. The patron of the Society was Grand Duke Sergei Alexandrovich. His wife, Grand Duchess Ella, was the elder sister of the Russian Czarina.

Grand Duke Sergei, Cherep-Spiridovich's Moscow patron, was an extraordinary reactionary even by the standards of the time. He began his tenure as governor of Moscow in 1891 by expelling some 20,000 Jews from the city. His German-born wife Elizabeth of Hesse (Grand Duchess Elizabeth Feodorovna following her marriage) was nicknamed 'Ella.' When infamous antisemitic forgery *The Protocols of the Elders of Zion* was published for the first time in August–September 1903 in a Russian ultra-nationalist 'Black Hundreds' paper called *Znamya* ('Banner') out of St. Petersburg, some accounts state that Ella first called it to the attention of her youngest sister Alix, the Empress Alexandra.

The Protocols of the Elders of Zion may have owed some of its early promotion to Cherep-Spiridovich, Grand Duke Sergei, and Ella. From the *TN History*:

> The late 19th and early 20th century was an era of anarchist activism.... In 1905 Count Alexis Ignatiev, Commander of the SOSJ Chevalier Guards, was assassinated in Russia. Grand Duke Sergei Alexandrovich was also assassi-nated.[16] The Grand Duke was the patron of the Slavonic Society of Moscow, of which Cherep Spiridovich was president.... At the time of his death, Grand Duke Sergei was the Military Governor General of Moscow and had worked to uncover the cells of anarchists who were assassinating government officials which included his own father Czar Alexander II. His wife Grand Duchess Elizabeth, sister of Czarina Alexandra, was involved in the research to unmask the anarchists and this interest brought them both into contact with an Orthodox spiritual writer named Sergei Alexandrovich Nilus. Nilus was one of the earliest men to produce a copy of the *Protocols of the Wise Men of Zion* and Grand Duchess Ella introduced him and the *Protocols* to her sister and to Czar Nicholas II.

Major General Arthur Cherep-Spiridovich, President of the Slavonic Society, was thereby one of the earliest members of any Intelligence Service to see the *Protocols*. He was given the mandate by the Russian Imperial family to investigate the matter fully and to spread the alarm about 'the hidden hand' of international Zionism and its plan to gain global control through the elimination of the Christian Church. He was made a Count of the Catholic Church by Pope Pius X about 1907. He was President of the Catholic Grand Priory and was one of the principal organizers of the American branch of the SOSJ. ... As an intelligence operative, he was handled by the Russian Ambassador to the U.S., Baron Rosen. He was also an agent of the Serbian royal family.[17]

Grand Duke Sergei was assassinated in 1905 by a bomb placed by Socialist Revolutionaries outside the Kremlin. Following his death, Elizabeth became deeply religious and founded her own nunnery where she served as abbess. One of Rasputin's assassins, Prince Felix Yusupov, regarded Elizabeth as a saint; she in turn spiritually consoled him for helping to kill Rasputin, whom she considered evil incarnate.[18]

As for the Slavonic Society (sometimes called the Slavonic Welfare Society or Slavonic Beneficent Society), it first emerged into political prominence in the 1870s when it was chaired by Ivan Aksakov, one of the best-known propagandists of aggressive Pan-slavism. Closely allied with Aksakov was the famously reactionary Director General of Holy Synod Konstantin Pobedonostsev, a top advisor to Tsar Alexander III.[19] Aksakov demanded that Russia occupy Constantinople in the 1877 Russo–Turkish war, and he attacked Alexander II for bowing to British and French pressure at the 1878 Congress of Berlin.[20]

Cherep-Spiridovich had a complicated relationship with pan-Slavism, in part because he said he was a Catholic, possibly as the result of his mother being Polish. In any event, Cherep-Spiridovich said he enjoyed close ties to the Vatican; he claimed the title of 'Count' had been given him by Pope Pius X.[21] His patron Grand Duke Sergei also had maintained ties to Rome:

> At the time of his father's [Alexander II's] death, the Grand Duke Serge was quite a youth and was living in Rome with his younger brother Paul, whose health required a warmer climate than that of Petersburg. From this period dated the paternal kindness of Pope Leo XIII to the Grand Duke Serge. His Holiness treated the young Princes with touching affection. When the news of the Emperor's assassination arrived in Rome, the Pope forbade anyone else to tell them of it, reserving to himself the task of breaking it to them, and of praying with them in their sorrow. The Grand Duke always remembered with gratitude the kindness which the Pope had shown him and never forgot how he had consoled him and his brother in the loss of their beloved father.[22]

Given Cherep-Spiridovich's own Vatican link, it is worth recalling that Hapsburg Austria (along with the Ottomans) controlled 'Slavic' lands in the Balkans. For many pan-Slavists, Austria was therefore as much a problem as Turkey. Around the turn of the twentieth century, however, there arose a form of 'neo-Pan-Slavism' that no longer stressed overt Russian domination of the Balkans. It is possible that

Cherep-Spiridovich held such views because he created an organization first called the Latino-Slav League with branches in Paris and Rome that seems to have promoted a 'neo-Pan Slav' ideology designed to advance a geopolitical understanding between Russia, Catholic Austria, Serbia, and the Vatican against the Ottomans.

By the eve of World War I, however, Cherep-Spiridovich had turned bitterly anti-Austrian. In 1914, he published two books, *Vers la débâcle: le 'Partage' de la France: dangers et remèdes* and *L'union des blancs et le triomphe de la France* denouncing Austria and warning that Austria would cause the next major war. He now proposed a new League of White Nations as well as the dismemberment of the Austrian Empire, although he said the Hapsburgs could still rule Austria proper.

Cherep-Spiridovich also spent much more time in Paris than Moscow before World War I. The scholar Katrin Boeckh notes that the Moscow Slavic Benevolent Society lagged in intensity compared to its St. Petersburg counterpart because Cherep-Spiridovich, 'the former general and general consul in Belgrade' had been living in Paris for some years.[23] Cherep-Spiridovich's Paris operation centered on his 'press service' *Agence Latine* (sometimes labeled as his 'public relations firm in Europe'). It was particularly committed to improving the regime's image in the wake of the infamous 1905 Bloody Sunday massacres when Tsarist forces shot hundreds of unarmed protesters.[24]

An attack on *Agence Latine* at the time of the 1905 Revolution by journalist Alexander Ular begins with his citation of an *Agence Latine* press report that read:

> The Minister of War has received the following dispatch from Paris: 'Our London Correspondent cables that the Japanese government has distributed 18 million rubles to the revolutionaries, liberals, and Russian workmen for the organization of the agitation in Russia. It was intended that the Naval stores should be destroyed, so as to render the departure of the Black Sea and Baltic squadrons impossible, to annihilate General [Alexei] Kuropatkin's army by starvation, and to force the Government to concede the peace which is absolutely necessary to Japan on the verge of her bankruptcy.'[25]

Ular comments:

> Obviously, this confusion between revolution and foreign enmity was not spontaneous.... these dispatches emanated from a contaminated office, the *Agence Latine*, established by the Russian police in Paris, the prime mover in which is an agent of Grand Duke Serge [Sergei], a prime blackmailer, assassin, and avowed swindler named Cherep-Spiridovich, who enjoys an amount of mundane consideration in Paris as the President of a 'Celtic [sic] Slavonic League.'[26]

Russian Foreign Minister Count Vladimir Lamsdorf publicly denounced *Agence Latine* for its attack on Russian Finance Minister Count Witte, who, it claimed, was ultimately responsible for the 1905 disturbances. *Agence Latine* apparently falsely claimed that Witte had fled abroad. Lamsdorf's statement, as cited by Ular, concluded, 'It would be beneath the dignity of any serious Agency to contradict any further announcements emanating from the same source.'

Cherep-Spiridovich used his position to promote Russia's cause not just in Europe but in America as well. On 28 March 1907, the *New York Times* reported that 'Count Jcherep-Spiridovitch':

> a Major General in the Russian Army, and President of the Slavonic Society of Russia and … of the Latino-Slav League of Paris and Rome, gave a luncheon yesterday at the St. Regis to a number of guests, among whom were Samuel L. Clemens (Mark Twain), Gen. Nelson A. Miles, Gen. Grant Wilson, Russian Consul Baron Schilling and Mrs. Schilling.

In his talk, Cherep-Spiridovich praised Nicholas II for instituting a Constitution following the 1905 Revolution, a statement meant to appeal to audience members highly critical of Russia such as Twain.

Cherep-Spiridovich was especially preoccupied with the Balkans. In 1905, for example, he met with Andrew Carnegie in Carnegie's Skibo Castle in Scotland to present him an award from the Latino-Slavic League. During his presentation, reports the 14 October 1905 *New York Times*, Cherep-Spiridovich spoke about 'how he had seen rows of Christians decapitated by Turks in Macedonia and in Armenia. He had seen children impaled upon lances and thrown into fires.' He then asked Carnegie as 'builder of the Temple of Peace' [the Peace Palace Carnegie built in The Hague], to 'lend his moral aid in stopping these shameful massacres. Otherwise the Slavonic nations and Armenia would soon be plunged in a sea of blood.'

Cherep-Spiridovich's pan-Slavist propagandizing in Bulgaria even caught the attention of Leon Trotsky. Trotsky's 'The Balkan Question and Social Democracy' first appeared in the 1 August 1910 edition of (Vienna) *Pravda*. From his essay:

> At the end of June [1910] there was held in Bulgaria's capital, Sofia, the second 'All Slav' Congress.… In meetings held in St. Petersburg and then at the Prague congress of 1908, the new 'Pan-Slavist' movement took the stage to the sound of drums and trumpets: it undertook to reconcile Poles and Russians, Ruthenians and Poles, Serbs and Bulgars, to put an end to friction and enmity between the bourgeois classes of all the Slavonic nations and to set the edifice of the new Slavdom upon a foundation of liberty, equity and fraternity.… Guchkov, Count Bobrinsky, and Cherep-Spiridovich attended as Russia's representatives.[27]

The first All-Slav Congress met in Prague in July 1908 with some 250 delegates. The 1910 Sofia gathering:

> had been prepared by the St. Petersburg conference of the Inter-Slavic Executive Committee set up after the First All-Slavic Congress. Because the

Russian delegation was made up overwhelmingly of Black Hundreds supporters ... such as Count Bobrinsky and Cherep-Spiridovich, 'progressive' Russian pan-Slavists, as well as Polish, refused to participate. In Bulgaria, a special protest committee organized meetings against the Congress.... The Bulgarian socialist newspaper *Rabotnichesky Vestnik* greeted the opening of the Congress with an article titled 'Russian Despotism under the Mask of neo-Slavism.'[28]

Major General Arthur Count Cherep-Spiridovich landed in New York on the *Aquitania* in December 1920. His arrival made news after he was briefly detained by immigration authorities acting on orders from Washington.[29] From a 28 June 1926 *New York World* article about this incident:

> According to the records ... he came here in 1920, and then was taken to Ellis Island for a special inquiry by the Immigration Bureau before being admitted. There was some confusion as to his identity, for the visiting General was denounced in a published letter as the wrong Cherep-Spiridovich. The letter said there were two Cherep-Spiridoviches – one was an enthusiastic amateur of world politics, the other an adventurer who traded on the amateur's name and tried to float large political schemes involving the collecting of money. Yesterday ... the present General was asked about the two Cherep-Spiridoviches. He said the adventurous one was now in Paris and occasionally caused embarrassing confusion.[30]

What letter led the authorities to detain Cherep-Spiridovich? Who wrote it and why? And who was the Count? Was he the 'enthusiastic amateur of world politics' or the 'adventurer who traded on the amateur's name' to 'float large political schemes involving the collection of money' and who was 'now in Paris'?[31]

Before coming to America, Cherep-Spiridovich lived for a time in England. In articles for the British-based *Asiatic Review*, he claimed that the Bolsheviks were nothing more than German agents, of whom 98% were not even 'Slavs.' In 1919 Cherep-Spiridovich pleaded for a close alliance with England against the Bolsheviks, whom he warned were German agents interested in destabilizing India as well as England.[32] He also wrote a series of conspiratorial antisemitic articles for Lord Alfred Douglas's journal, *Plain English*.[33]

The idea of a Bolshevik–German conspiracy was quite common at the time and not limited to those on the far right. In her book *World Revolution*, the *Protocols*-friendly conspiracy theorist Nesta Webster cites reports by the leading German Social Democrat Eduard Bernstein that appeared in the SPD (*Sozialdemokratische Partei Deutschlands*) paper *Vorwärts*. Bernstein, a bitter opponent of Lenin, cited evidence of German funding for the Bolsheviks during the war.[34] The German–Bolshevik link, according to Webster, was further documented in a book by former Okhrana General A. Spiridovich (no relation to Cherep-Spiridovich) entitled *A History of Bolshevism*.[35]

Not long after his arrival in America. Count Cherep-Spiridovich was placed on antisemitic industrialist Henry Ford's payroll.[36] He also published an eight-page pamphlet out of Chicago in 1921. It was entitled *Let Us Prevent the Second World War Already Prepared! (by Revealing Its Causes and All the 'Mysteries')*, a warm-up to his 1926 opus *The Secret World Government*. On page ten of *Secret World Government*, Cherep-Spiridovich relates that he printed thousands of copies of *Let Us Prevent* in both English and Russian.[37] Did Henry Ford help pay the printing bill?

Besides his other activities, had Cherep-Spiridovich also served as Russia's Transportation Commissioner as the *TN History* claimed? What seems clear is that Cherep-Spiridovich had an interest in transportation canals. A 28 July 1929 article in the Sunday Magazine of the *St. Louis Post Dispatch* recalls that in 1907 Cherep-Spiridovich visited the White House to give President Theodore Roosevelt a 'bejeweled cup' as thanks for TR's efforts to end the Russo–Japanese War. The article adds that there were rumors that Cherep-Spiridovich was in America to try to raise $250 million for a proposed transport canal to link the Baltic and Black Seas.[38] Given that the USA was then building the Panama Canal, it would not be surprising if the Russian government wanted to test the financial waters for a similar project.[39] Recall as well the *Brooklyn Eagle* story that said Cherep-Spiridovich spent some 17 years directing a transportation and trade company.

Wherever he went, the conspiratorial Count left an impression. From a 28 June 1926 profile of him in the *New York World*:

> Count Cherep–Spiridovich went everywhere and talked politics with everyone. And at critical moments during the last twenty-five years of European affairs, when Foreign Ministers held their breaths, the Count supplied the press of Europe with explanations and predictions. He claimed at one time to have postponed the World War ten years by intervening at a tense moment.
>
> In 1907 a man arrived here wearing a magnificent uniform with the glittering epaulets of a General, a sash from shoulder to hip and more stars, crosses, medals and decorations – principally Balkan – than ever seen in the United States before....
>
> Arthur Cherep-Spiridovich ... yesterday looked at the reporter for the *World* with unwavering eye and declared he was the man who warned King Alexander of Serbia and Queen Draga in 1902, six months before they were assassinated; who warned the Grand Duke Sergius in Moscow in 1904, several months before he was blown to pieces; who was responsible in 1908 for the war of liberation which freed Romania, Bulgaria and Serbia from the Turks, who foresaw the last World War and now foresees the next. 'Four Emperors who opposed me in 1912 do not exist today,' he said. 'If the Kaiser had known what I knew he would not have entered the war.'[40]

A few months after this interview, Count Cherep-Spiridovich would be found dead under mysterious circumstances.

A strange death in Staten Island

On 23 October 1926, the *New York Times* reported that Major General Count Arthur Cherep-Spiridovich, 'a strange figure who spent considerable time traveling between Europe and America,' had been found dead in his room at Barrett Manor in Staten Island. Barrett Manor was a massive estate owned by Harriet Jean Beauley, who acquired it in a divorce settlement. After becoming infatuated with the White Russian cause, she let many émigrés live on her estate, including Cherep-Spiridovich who in 1926 dubbed Barrett Manor 'Slav Palace.'[41] From Slav Palace:

> Count Cherep-Spiridovich, author of the recently published anti-Semitic book *The Secret World Government*, who is now resident in New York, is planning to become Emperor of an all Slav consolidation, to include Russia, Poland, Czecho-Slovakia, Jugo-Slavia and Bulgaria, the *New York World* of June 28 informs its readers. In this enterprise … the Count is having the financial backing of some Americans, chiefly Mrs. Harriet Jean Beauley and H. Victor Von Broens-Trupp. The general has established his headquarters at Mrs. Beauley's manor at Arrochar, Staten Island, in the old Barrett Manor, which he has renamed Slav Palace. Quoting a 'proclamation' by Cherep-Spiridovich dispatched to the Slavs throughout Europe, informing them that he is convoking an all-Slav convention in New York on October 20….[42]

The initial *Times* report said the Count died on the eve of the All Slav conference he had been organizing for months and that it said was to take place on 25 October. (The Count was found dead on 23 October.) Rumors soon spread that he had been murdered by 'Bolsheviks.' The police, however, attributed his demise to gas poisoning following 'the accidental discharge of a petcock in a gas radiator.'

On 31 October, the *Times* ran a follow-up entitled 'Russian Count Ended Own Life, Police Say.' Now the paper reported that the conference actually took place on 18 October but that only one other person showed up.[43] Upon a reexamination of the evidence, the coroner decided Cherep-Spiridovich's death was most likely a suicide. According to the *Times*:

> The police conducted a second investigation. He was found dead in his room. The windows were down, the door was locked, and the key was on the inside. A gas jet was turned on. The position of the key and windows and other factors which the investigators did not disclose convinced them that the Count had not been murdered…. In his room the police yesterday found a .22 caliber pistol, but no importance was attached to it.

After the *Times* said the penniless Count was to be buried in a potter's field, some 150 White Russians, many of whom contributed funds for his burial, attended his first funeral held in the Greek Orthodox manner in Barrett Manor's private chapel. A 25-member Russian choir sang at his service. Another *Times* story noted that the

Russian Naval Club, the Russian Unity Society, and the Russian Editors Association all contributed funds for the ceremony.[44]

The Count's 'adopted son' Victor von Broenstrupp added that since the Count was Catholic and a member of the Roman Catholic Knight Commandry of St. Gregory the Great, there would be a second ceremony.[45] The Count's body was next taken to a Catholic church in Long Island for a requiem mass before being interned in a vault until it could be shipped back to Poland. Another *Times* story ('Rites of Splendor for Russian Count'), also stated Cherep-Spiridovich's death was still ruled as 'accidental.'[46]

On 27 October 1926, the Jewish Telegraph Agency (JTA) ran this strange piece:

> The circumstance that Count Arthur Cherep-Spiridovich, who was found dead in his room at Barrett Manor, Staten Island, on Saturday was penniless and that an appeal for funds for the burial expenses was made by his foster son was ascribed in well-informed circles to the withdrawal of a certain wealthy American from the anti-Semitic campaign conducted by Spiridovich. It was learned that at one time considerable financial assistance was promised Count Cherep-Spiridovich by a very wealthy American and that the failure of that assistance to come forward caused the collapse of Count Spiridovich's plans.[47]

Who was the 'very wealthy American'?

The JTA report continues:

> Additional information regarding Spiridovich's activities shows that for a time he operated from Chicago, using one of the large hotels as his headquarters, then he travelled to Detroit, Denver, Colorado, and other cities. More recently, various attacks upon Jews were sent out in the name of a printing establishment which called itself the Anti-Bolshevist Association and which operated from 15 East 128th Street. Throughout, this literature was permeated with the most slanderous charges against the Jews, and *The Gentile Review*, a magazine, published for a while, reached perhaps the height of the grotesque in this direction. One leaflet called 'Excerpts from the Talmud' insisted that the sole ambition of the Jew was to kill all Gentiles.[48] An advertisement, which was published in various literary publications, was stopped when the publications learned, through the efforts of the American Jewish Congress, the nature of the books advertised.[49]

Although Cherep-Spiridovich reportedly died penniless, someone was paying rent for his East Harlem Universal Anti-Bolshevist League. As the Count never seemed shy about attacking Jews, the idea that a wealthy American was ready to back him until he turned to antisemitism sounds odd.[50]

There was a potential deeper mystery as well. Although the *New York Times* claimed that Cherep-Spiridovich killed himself just before (or just after) a major conference was to take place in Harlem, the report of his death in the 22 October

1926 *Brooklyn Eagle* is quite different. According to the *Eagle*, Cherep-Spiridovich moved to Barrett Manor in June, and that 'extensive building preparations were underway' at Barrett Manor to house the participants at the expected conference. Perhaps Cherep-Spiridovich renamed Barrett Manor 'Slav Palace' in anticipation of the coming gathering. If the report is true, the story in the *New York Times* was wrong, or there had been some last-minute change in venue and the *Eagle* was incorrect.

The travels of Prince Zevachov

Nor was Cherep-Spiridovich as isolated as he was portrayed in the press. At the time of his death, he was in close contact with Prince Nikolaj Zevachov (Zhevakhov), a personal friend of Sergei Nilus, whose 1905 edition of *Protocols* had now become world famous.[51] Born in 1874, Zevachov studied law in State Service in St. Petersburg, and in 1910 was active in the Imperial Orthodox Society of Palestine. In 1916, at the insistence of the Tsar, Zevachov was appointed as a deputy to the Chief Procurator of the Most Holy Synod.[52]

During the Russian Revolution, Zevachov fled to Ukraine where he met Nilus personally, although he had already been in literary contact with him. Zevachov relocated to Bari, Italy, where he administered a Russian Orthodox Church and hostel for religious pilgrims. The complex was built by assassinated Grand Duke Sergei's widow Elizavesta through the Imperial Orthodox Society of Palestine.[53]

Throughout the 1920s and 1930s, Zevachov traveled regularly to meet members of monarchist, fascist, and antisemitic movements in Germany, Italy, France, the USA, and the Balkans, all in the hope of forming a 'Christian International' against the Jews. In 1922, for example, Zevachov meet in Munich with *Protocols* promoters Vinberg and Shabelskii-Bork.[54]

Zevachov endorsed the claim by antisemitic conspiracy theorist Leslie Fry that the *Protocols* had been composed by an Odessa-based Jewish cultural nationalist named Ascher Ginsberg (Ahad Ha'man). Zevachov and Fry almost certainly knew each other since Fry spent most of her time in London and Paris in the 1930s before permanently returning to America in 1936.[55] Fry – almost certainly with funding from Henry Ford – in 1926 even visited Sergei Nilus when Nilus and his wife Elena Aleksandrovna lived in a suburb of Chernigov in Ukraine.[56]

Cherep-Spiridovich, Fry, and Zevachov all enjoyed ties to the Vatican.[57] We have already seen Cherep-Spiridovich's ties to Rome. As for Fry, her French publisher and collaborator was Monseigneur Ernest Jouin, who in October 1920 introduced the Nilus *Protocols* to France in his journal, *Revue internationale des sociétés secrètes*. In 1921 he published a book that also included a commentary on the *Protocols* entitled *Le Péril Judéo-maçonnique*.

Jouin founded his *Revue* in 1912 under the influence of the 'anti-modernist' movement in the Church centered on a priest, church historian, and Curia official named Father Umberto Benigni.[58] Benigni ran his own press service called *La*

Corrispondenza di Roma from 1909–1912. He further helped found a group called Sodalitium Pianum (Sodality of Pius), which in France was known as La Sapinière (the pine forest). Sodality of Pius referred to Pius V, the Pope who presided over the victory of the Catholic powers over the Ottoman Empire in the famed 1571 battle of Lepanto. A *Protocols* promoter, Benigni regularly appeared at antisemitic international congresses in Europe in the 1920s, where he specialized in promoting 'ritual murder' accusations against the Jews.[59]

In Italy, Zevachov contacted a former priest named Giovanni Preziosi, who in February 1921 introduced the *Protocols* to Italy. He also talked with a Jesuit priest and Vatican Russia expert named Michel d'Herbigny, whom the historian Michael Hagemeister describes as the 'ideologue of the Vatican's "Crusade" against the Soviet Union.'[60]

In the summer of 1926, Zevachov traveled to America. Cesare De Michelis reports that in October 1926, Zevachov moved to New York.[61] Here he met with Cherep-Spiridovich. That very month, Cherep-Spiridovich was found dead under mysterious circumstances. For his part, Zevachov penned an obituary for the Count not long after his death entitled *Pamjati grafa A. Čerep-Spiridoviča* and published in New York.

After Cherep-Spiridovich's passing, his 'adopted son' Howard Victor von Broenstrupp now declared himself his successor. From 1926 until June 1929, he literally held court in the run-down 70 room mansion that was Barrett Manor. The newly minted 'Count H. Victor von Broens-Trupp Tcherep-Spiridovich, Duke of St. Saba' created his own Order of Roses, and appointed Harriet Beauley as Queen of the Order. Broenstrupp also set up his own throne room. Dressed in a royal costume with a black military coat filled with medals presumably taken from the dead Count, Broenstrupp now began 'bestowing decorations and knighthoods on those whose achievements warranted such honors.'

The Duke of St. Saba's kingdom came crashing down in June 1929. Broenstrupp apparently convinced Beauley to take out a $40,000 loan on her mansion that she later claimed was worth $100,000, all in 1929 dollars. When Beauly was unable to maintain payments, she and her tenants were forcibly evicted. Broenstrupp's royal costume and throne unceremoniously wound up on the street in pouring rain.[62]

The *TN History* claims that the Knights emerged around the time of Cherep-Spiridovich's publication of *Secret World Government*:

> The Order was re-organized after the establishment of the Sovereign Council in New York City. The plan centered on strategies to counter the Bolshevist threat to Christendom and was patterned on Major General Arthur Cherep-Spiridovich's Anglo-Latino-Slavic League and on the patriotic organization coalitions. Patriotic organizations in the United States were associated with John B. Trevor's American Coalition of Patriotic, Civic and Fraternal Societies....
>
> In 1925 Captain Sidney G. Reilly, founder of the Anti-Bolshevist League, was lured from the United States into Russia and killed by the Bolsheviks. In

1926 Cherep-Spiridovich incorporated the Anti-Bolshevist Publishing Association of the Anti-Bolshevist League in Albany, N.Y., with H. V. Broenstrupp and G. M. Sykes. This was an SOSJ project of the Kirill intelligence service planned by Captain Reilly and by Cherep-Spiridovich. It was intended to provide propaganda about the danger of the inter-nationalists' agenda and was the continuation of the publishing operation of Cherep-Spiridovich in Paris from 1904 to 1920 known as the *Agence Latine*. It had been continued in 1921 for a few years by Henry Ford and his newspaper the *Dearborn Independent*.

Major General Cherep-Spiridovich, OSJ, was assassinated at his residence on Staten Island, N.Y., a few months after re-starting the publishing operation. Boris Brasol provided the funds to bury this leader of the SOSJ. Cherep-Spiridovich was one of the principal founders of the American Grand Priory of the Sovereign Order of St. John of Jerusalem. H. V. Broenstrupp, OSJ, published *The Hidden Hand* by Cherep-Spiridovich shortly after the assassination of his adoptive father.[63]

Here, perhaps, we now finally arrive at the beginning of the mysterious 'Order of St. John' cited in the 1939 House Un-American Activities Committee (HUAC) hearing.

Grand Duke Alexander

On 10 January 1908, a meeting *that never happened* was held in the Waldorf-Astoria by a non-existent 'Chapter General of the Knights and Descendants of Knights of the Order of St. John' to transfer the imaginary order to New York with the sanction of Nicholas II, who never gave it. The concocted gathering invented decades later by Pichel listed leading members of the Russian nobility at the gathering, which was presided over by Grand Duke Alexander Mikhailovich, the 'Knight Grand Cross of Justice,' who never set foot in America in 1908.[64] Yet the *TN History* fixation with Grand Duke Alexander, similar to its fascination with Cherep-Spiridovich, didn't end there:

> Admiral Grand Duke Alexander Michaelovich, OSJ, was the head of Russian Naval Intelligence. He spent time in the United States developing relation-ships with the wealthiest people in American society. His regular traveling companion became Major Barclay Harding Warburton of the U.S. Army Military Intelligence community. Warburton was a member of the 'East Coast Establishment,' and was closely related to the Wannamaker and Vanderbilt families. The American Grand Priory cooperated with Russian Naval Intelli-gence and the Russian Secret Service directed by Baron Rosen.[65]

Grand Duke Alexander was in New York in September 1913.[66] He also was close to Warburton. A former Rough Rider, Warburton served in the U.S. Embassy in London from 1914–1917. He then became an aide to General Pershing in Paris. Married to Mary Wanamaker from the Philadelphia store fortune, the Warburtons spent part of 1909 in Europe, where they met leading members of the Romanov family, including Tsar Nicholas II and his son Alexei. The Warburtons also owned property in Biarritz, where their close friend and neighbor was Grand Duke Alexander.[67]

Grand Duke Alexander was also connected to Russian Naval Intelligence, as historian Richard Spence notes:

> Alexandr's most important connection ... was with the Russian Navy in which he was a Rear Admiral. Most significantly, Aleksandr was linked to Russian Naval Intelligence, an agency that enjoyed a reputation for great energy and efficiency in the realm of military and technical espionage. In 1906 he went to France in a self-imposed exile but returned to Russia in two years. In addition to supporting AVAK [the Imperial All Russian Aero Club], the Duke arranged for Russian pilots to be trained in France and set up the Empire's first military airfield near his estate in the Crimea.[68]

Grand Duke Alexander even devised war games for the Russian Naval College, and his private library on naval affairs was one of the greatest in the world with some 20,000 books. As a 'modernizer,' he helped develop both the Russian Merchant Marine as well as the modern Russian air force and the aircraft production industry that accompanied it. Although Grand Duke Alexander only visited the USA twice before World War I (in 1893 and 1913), he became intent on acquiring advanced American technology for the Russian military. When Grand Duke Alexander visited America in 1913, for example, he consulted with the Curtis Wright airplane company and toured its factories.[69]

Although an economic 'modernizer,' Grand Duke Alexander was deeply involved in spiritualist practices, although he denied being a spiritualist of the table-knocking type. In Russia, he associated with masonic lodges and Rosicrucian sects. Former Russian Prime Minister Alexander Kerensky in his book *Russia and History's Turning Point* reports that the Barbara Ovchinnikova Organization, a mystical Rosicrucian grouping, had been founded under the auspices of Grand Duke Alexander.[70] In the 1920s, Grand Duke Alexander also gave public talks on spiritual issues and published books on spiritual themes.[71]

For all his interest in modern technology, Grand Duke Alexander remained an absolute monarchist who believed the last thing Russia needed was democracy. In 1905 he stepped down as head of the new Ministry of the Merchant Marine and chose self-imposed exile in France rather than work with the newly created Duma.

The collapse of Russia in World War I deeply embittered Grand Duke Alexander, particularly when it became clear to him that Russia's two wartime allies, England and France, would not commit their forces to the overthrow of Bolshevism and the restoration of monarchical order. As both a military leader and one of the few Russian Grand Dukes still alive after World War I, he attended the Versailles Conference hoping to coordinate with the victorious Allies' new plans to save Russia. Instead, he was now marginalized and ignored by the very Entente politicians who had worked so closely with Russia during the war, a humiliating experience that left him incredibly resentful. After all, how many Russian soldiers had died on the Eastern Front to stabilize the Allied front lines in France?

Alexander's relation with Great Britain turned especially contentious, even though he was rescued by the British cruiser *Forsythe* during an evacuation from Sevastopol. Around this same time, he sought to divorce his wife for an Englishwoman he had meet in the south of France. Xenia, however, refused. She now relocated to England with their six sons and raised them in Windsor at Wilderness House, a cottage given her by King George V, her first cousin. Alexander, however, was now barred from entering England 'probably because of his Germanophilia' reports the historian John Stephan.[72]

Grand Duke Alexander also publicly supported Grand Duke Kirill's claims to the throne, although seemingly with little enthusiasm for Kirill as a person or from a sense that monarchical restoration was a lost cause.[73] A wry sense of world-weary ennui was the impression he conveyed in his memoirs. Or was this too a pose? When Kirill first declared his claim, the Russian naval officers' society *Morskoi Kaiut-kompaniia* (King of the Sea Naval Wardroom) recognized him as Emperor, it would be surprising if Grand Duke Alexander did not play a role in the group's endorsement.

Grand Duke Alexander also knew the far rightist White Russian émigré Anastase Vonsiatsky and there are photographs of one of Alexander's sons named Theodore (Fyodor) playing golf with Vonsiatsky in Los Angeles in 1932. In the photograph, Vonsiatsky is wearing a type of swastika armband. Vonsiatsky, who became a millionaire after marrying an American heiress, had a military background: he had been trained in the elite Emperor Nicholas I Cavalry Academy in St. Petersburg. At the time of his meeting with Grand Duke Alexander and his friendship with Theodore, Vonsiatsky was heading 'the American Branch of the Fund for the Liberation of Russia.' The next year he would cofound the All Russian Fascist Organization.[74]

Although it is easy to demonstrate that Grand Duke Alexander, who died in 1933, had nothing to do with the bogus order whose history Pichel fabricated in the 1950s, the broader question of his involvement in the murky world of Russian émigré and pro-Nazi networks in both America and Europe still remains.

The mysterious Boris Brasol

Did Grand Duke Alexander also know the writer and antisemitic activist Boris Brasol?[75] Brasol was born in Russia in 1885, the son of a doctor, and graduated in law. He was decorated for service in the Imperial Russian army in World War I. He first came to New York in August 1916 to work for the Russian Government Supply Committee based in Manhattan's Flatiron Building.[76] One of his most important tasks was as 'a special investigator charged with ferreting out graft, treason, and subversion in the Supply Committee and related bodies.'[77] In October 1916, he became the Russian representative to the Inter-Allied Conference that coordinated allied purchasing activity in the USA. All these issues were of great concern to Grand Duke Alexander, who looked to America for new weapons technology.

While Grand Duke Alexander remained in Russia, Brasol played an increasingly important role in New York. Brasol also may have been close to Sergius Riis, the strange US naval intelligence operative whose bogus memoir *Yankee Komisar* Robert Speller and Sons published in 1935. In 1908, Riis created a New York-based detective agency, the 'S. M. Riis Confidential Service.' The firm specialized in 'the detection and suppression of radical agitation among employees, and like threats to the security of property and capital.'[78] The historian Richard Spence believes that Riis may have had previous ties to the Okhrana in the Baltics as well. Riis's possible Okhrana connection, plus his knowledge of languages, potentially made his detective firm ideal to protect plants engaged in Russian war contracts against German sabotage and leftist troublemakers. German intelligence was extremely active in New York in World War I. The infamous Black Tom ammunition dump explosion on 30 July 1916, orchestrated by German intelligence, was so powerful that many New Yorkers thought an earthquake had taken place.

In a 22 December 1941 interview with the FBI, Brasol explained that after World War I he

> was appointed to the War Trade Intelligence of the War Trade Board and was assigned to New York City. He stated that he resigned this position in April 1919 and was assigned to a General [Marlborough] Churchill of the MIB, which he stated to be the Military Intelligence Bureau. Brasol advised that during his assignment with the MIB, he engaged in the collecting of information concerning the extreme radical elements in the United States, such as anarchists, etc. He advised that after his services were terminated with the MIB, he became a member of the Luck Committee of New York City, which was a local Committee, where he engaged in the same type of activity, that of exposing extreme radical elements.[79]

General Marlborough Churchill succeeded Ralph van Deman as head of the Military Branch of the War Department from 1918 to 1920. He may have known Barclay Warburton as well. In World War I, Warburton, as US military attaché in Paris under General Pershing, regularly sent reports to the War Department read by Churchill.

The *TN History* explains this critical period in a very interesting way:

> The Order gathered intelligence on the international revolutionary movements. The SOSJ, under Czar Kirill I, engaged in psychological warfare operations including the distribution of anti-Bolshevist information such as the *Protocols of the Elders of Zion....* Because it was an incontrovertible fact that the Communist movement in Russia was dominated by Jews from New York, the American military intelligence community continued to join the ranks of

the SOSJ as sworn enemies of the 'International Conspiracy.' Among those included were the following: Colonel Harris Ayres Houghton, MD, Colonel John Jacob Astor, Major General Ralph Van Deman, Colonel William Sohier Bryant, MD, Major General Frederick Dent Grant, Colonel Nicholas Biddle, Major Barclay Harding Warburton, Major Walter Miller, Colonel Robert R. McCormick, Colonel Theodore Roosevelt, Major John B. Trevor and Captain Sidney Reilly. All of these prominent members of the armed forces have close association with their successors in the Military Affairs Committee of the SOSJ that are found in the Order records well into the 1980s.[80]

The *TN History* adds that the American 'Knights' worked with US military intelligence to keep track of 'subversives' living on New York City's Lower East Side:

On September 15, 1917, J. G. B. Bulloch, MD, first cousin of President Teddy Roosevelt, incorporated the Order of Lafayette in New York City with an international membership as a recruiting front for the SOSJ. An American counter-revolutionary effort became immediately prominent since it became apparent from both government and military intelligence reports that Jewish anarchists were in the majority in the new Bolshevik government in St. Petersburg. The revolutionaries had developed their operational base in the Lower East Side district of New York City and both the American and Russian Imperial secret services frantically worked to prevent an expected Bolshevik revolution in the United States. The American Grand Priory ... remained in the hands of operatives of the anti-Bolshevik intelligence communities. The American Grand Priory of the SOSJ concentrated its activities in NYC, Chicago, Baltimore, Philadelphia and Washington, D.C. It worked to defeat the international anarchist movements and to expose their aligned secret societies.[81]

Brasol further told the FBI that he cooperated closely with Captain Boris Sergievsky, whom he described as working 'for a number of years as a test pilot for the Sikorsky Plant.' The world-famous airplane designer Igor Sikorsky and Grand Duke Alexander worked closely together to develop Russia's military aviation capacity. Sikorsky ran an airplane factory in Kiev, while Grand Duke Alexander created the first Russian naval aviation school in 1909 in the Crimea, where he owned a palace called Ai Todor. Captain Sergievsky, a close friend of Sikorsky, served as a Russian pilot during World War I.[82]

Henry Ford, Sidney Reilly and the Anti-Bolshevik International

Did the American super-patriotic fraternal and heraldic groups that Pichel later tried to fold into the genealogy of the Shickshinny Knights ally with extreme rightwing Russian monarchist networks following World War I? The *TN History* claims that during this time

The OSJ propaganda effort continued both in the United States and in Europe with centers in Belgrade, Paris, Erfurt, Hamburg, Chicago, and New York City. Nicholas Markov II edited in 1920 the White Cross anti-Bolshevik journal in Hamburg and later moved to Paris. Still later, in the 1930s he joined Ulrich Fleischhauer's Welt-Dienst in Erfurt. Henry Ford from the United States published his own literature and financed a detective agency with headquarters in Chicago and New York City to assist in uncovering the global plans of 'The International Jew.' He helped to finance the similar pursuits which came under the direction of Grand Duke Cyril's intelligence service.[83]

Henry Ford's intelligence service was managed by his personal secretary Ernest Liebold, an avowed Hohenzollern restorationist. Liebold also hired former military intelligence officers to help prove that Jewish power was responsible for the world's woes. Ford's detective agency operated out of 20 Broad Street in Manhattan. It included C. C. Daniels, brother of the former Secretary of the Navy, and Harris Ayres Houghton, the former head of New York City's Army Intelligence Gathering Bureau. Jonathan Logsdon notes that Ford's agency was filled with 'ex-cons, amateur detectives, racist fanatics, and, in surprisingly large numbers, exiled White Russians.'[84] According to the historian Leo Ribuffo, throughout this period Liebold 'expanded his contacts with Russian royalists and their dubious documents.'[85]

Liebold also knew Boris Brasol and encouraged Edwin G. Pipp, then the editor of Ford's paper *The Dearborn Independent*, to contact him. The result was an article in the April 12 1919 issue of the paper titled 'The Bolshevik Menace in Russia'.[86] More significantly, Brasol also had in his possession a copy of Sergei Nilus' 1917 (fourth) Russian edition of the *Protocols of the Learned Elders of Zion*. Brasol's copy of the Protocols was passed on to Harris Ayres Houghton an American physician who was also a far-right nativist and antisemite. Brasol had met Houghton in military intelligence circles. Houghton funded the translation of the Protocols into English and his assistant Natalie de Bogory, an American woman of Russian extraction, worked with Brasol on the translation. Brasol's version would be published as *The Protocols and World Revolution* in 1920 by the Boston publisher Small, Maynard & Company.[87] This would be one of the first three English language editions of the Protocols.[88] Henry Ford would later serialise the Protocols in his newspaper *The Dearborn Independent* and in the words of Professor Yaakov Ariel, 'did more than anyone else to publicize the Protocols and promote the notion of a Jewish conspiracy'.[89]

But there were other active antisemitic networks. The Long Island-based Russian monarchist Gleb Botkin heard about an extreme White Russian circle in Chicago after visiting 'a small Russian bookstore' on Columbus Circle to attend a lecture. The bookstore (the Russian National Library) was tied to Boris Brasol's Russian National Society, also headquartered at 5 Columbus Circle. Botkin recalled hearing the chairman of the meeting explain that 'Jews and Masons had united in a drive to exterminate all those who had followed the Imperial Family in exile in Siberia.' The speaker added that all monarchists and anti-Semites had united in a new organization called 'The White Masons,' and that we in our room on Columbus Circle represented the secret headquarters of this formidable organization. The chairman further announced that the British Prime Minister, Balfour, had recently joined the organization and now was begging us for immediate instructions.[90]

After that bit of baloney about Lord Balfour, the chairman turned to Botkin and 'offered to make me head of all anti-Semitic organizations in the West, with headquarters in Chicago.'[91] This may have been a reference to a Chicago network linked to Count Cherep-Spiridovich, who lived for a time in Chicago's Auditorium Hotel after emigrating to America.[92]

For all Cherep-Spiridovich's antisemitic animus, he may even have collaborated with at least one anti-Bolshevik Jew, the Odessa-born Solomon Rosenblum, best known as 'Ace of Spies' Sidney Reilly. In the early 1900s, Grand Duke Alexander first met Reilly in the Russian Far East shortly before the Russo–Japanese War. Grand Duke Alexander was tasked by Nicholas II to economically develop Eastern Siberia. For his part, Reilly/Rosenblum represented Odessa-based business interests hoping to invest in the region. Reilly also helped purchase American war supplies in World War I. For a time in World War I, Reilly lived in an apartment at 260 West 76th Street and worked out of the Equitable Building at 120 Broadway.

After the Bolshevik Revolution, Reilly became involved in countless plots to topple the Soviet Union as well as anti-Bolshevik organizations in Europe including one in Switzerland. On 24 March 1924 an organization was founded in Geneva called the International Entente against the Third International, better known as the International Anti-Bolshevik League.[93] Its ostensible head was a Swiss lawyer named Théodore Aubert. One year earlier, Aubert had defended Moritz Konradi [Maurice Conradi] and Arkadii Poliunin, two White Russians who plotted the murder of the Soviet emissary to Italy Vatslav Vorovskii (Vorovsky). The assassination took place on 10 May 1923, while Vorovskii was attending the Lausanne Conference on Peace in the Near East. Aubert, however, won an acquittal for both men after the jury fell one vote short of the two-thirds majority needed for conviction.[94]

The newly formed *Entente Internationale Anticommuniste* (EIA) now developed affiliates in some 20 countries that included Japan. Its English branch was The Economic League, which before the summer of 1924 was called National Propaganda. It was founded by Sir Reginald 'Blinker' Hall, a former head of British Naval Intelligence.[95]

The EIA also worked closely with a Berlin-based White Russian émigré named Vladimir Orlov, who ran his own intelligence bureau called AB-1 for the EIA even while employed by the German police. Orlov, who owned a castle in Germany, was fired by the police in 1929 after it was discovered that he had forged diplomatic documents that purported to show Idaho Senator William Borah, the Chairman of the Senate Committee on Foreign Relations, and Nebraska Senator George Norris – both of whom supported diplomatic recognition of Russia – took bribes from the communist regime.[96]

The Orlov scandal led back to Henry Ford. From a 10 March 1929 Jewish Telegraphic Agency report:

> The interest of the American government in the case against the forgers of diplomatic documents involving Senators Borah and Norris, which is now being conducted by the Berlin Police Department ... was expressed by the American Embassy to the German Foreign Office....The investigation is of special interest in view of the fact that Vladimir Orloff, who with Michael Sumarakoff was arrested when they attempted to sell forged documents to the *New York Evening Post* linking Senator Borah and the Soviet government, was implicated in the preparation of documents said to have been required by Henry Ford's counsel in the libel suit which Herman Bernstein brought against Henry Ford, subsequently settled out of court. It was declared possible here that Orloff's associates will be examined and it is not unlikely further arrests may be made.
>
> Orloff explained his participation in the Ford–Bernstein trial by saying he had been employed by Henry Ford to pass judgment on certain documentary material which Herman Bernstein intended to introduce into the trial or which Mr. Bernstein had published before the trial. In the negotiations which Orloff said he carried on with 'Attorney Nicol' of New York, Orloff was asked if he could refute the allegations Bernstein had made about the treatment of Jews in Imperial Russia. Orloff asserts that by presenting Ford with evidence of the incorrectness of Bernstein's material he was able to collect a large fee from Ford. The police, however, are not convinced that this is necessarily an accurate description of Orloff's part in the Ford–Bernstein affair.
>
> Delancey Nicoll, of the firm of Nicoll, Anable & Nicoll, attorneys, who represented Henry Ford in the $200,000 libel suit brought against him by Herman Bernstein, in an interview with a representative of the *New York Evening Post* refused to reveal whether he knew Orloff or whether he had met him in Berlin. 'I do not talk about the affairs of my clients,' he said. Told that one New York newspaper had quoted Orloff as saying that he had been paid 31,000 marks for services by representatives of Mr. Ford, Mr. Nicoll again said: 'I do not talk about the affairs of my clients.'
>
> (Mr. Nicoll, who is the senior member of the firm, went to Europe to take depositions from Russian emigres concerning the Jewish problem during the Czarist regime and presented the documents in court.)[97]

The 'Ford–Bernstein matter' was Herman Bernstein's lawsuit against Ford over the *Protocols*. In 1921 Bernstein published a book entitled *History of a Lie* attacking Ford and the *Protocols* hoax. He later sued Ford for slander.[98] Had Orlov been hired to forge documents to add credence to the *Protocols'* supposed veracity? Boris Brasol also worked for Henry Ford in Europe on the Bernstein lawsuit. Brasol said he was hired by a New York law firm representing Ford, and that he traveled to Europe to do research for the Bernstein lawsuit.

Richard Spence reports that Sidney Reilly attended the EIA's 1924 founding meeting. Reilly and Boris Brasol then 'set up an American branch of the International Anti-Bolshevik League,' with Reilly agreeing to serve as its representative in Europe. Reilly and Brasol then decided that the 'nominal head' of the New York operation should be 'the colorful Count Arthur Cherep-Spiridovich, a former Tsarist spy and almost psychotic anti-Semite.'[99] Other members included Alexander Hamilton-Rice, a 'geographer-explorer,' and a lawyer married into the Astor family named Francis Kinnicutt, who headed the Allied Patriotic Societies and the American Defense Society.[100]

Reilly himself would eventually be tricked into visiting Russia in 1925 as part of the OGPU's fake Monarchist organization, Operation Trust, and after capture near the Finnish border and interrogation in Lubyanka prison, he was executed.[101]

Meanwhile even as the EIA without Reilly began to branch out around the world, there was another organization that Brasol supported that focused on White Russian ties to the German radical right. It was called *Aufbau Vereinigung* ('Reconstruction Organization') often shortened just to Aufbau, the name of its journal.

Aufbau

As the far-right White Russians began to organize in America, in Germany the White Russian monarchists and the Nazis now began closely cooperating through a long-forgotten organization called Aufbau. From the *TN History*:

> Walter Nicholai, the leader of German Military Intelligence during WWI, expanded the SOSJ intelligence service for Grand Duke Cyril Vladimirovich in order to closely cooperate with Aufbau. Aufbau was the White Russian monarchical organization which was founded to coordinate the future economic recovery of Russia.[102]

Michael Kellogg reports that Aufbau 'sought to overthrow the Bolshevik regime and to set Grand Prince Kirill Romanov at the head of a pro-German Russian monarchy.'[103] Aufbau further planned to restore the Hapsburg and Wittelsbach dynasties. To help make all that happen,

> General Ludendorff worked to establish an intelligence service for Kirill and his allies under Walther Nicolai in early April 1922. Nicolai had served Ludendorff as the head of the German Army High Command Intelligence Service during World War I.... Nicolai was eminently qualified to lead such an intelligence service. In addition to possessing impressive intelligence credentials from World War I, he enjoyed considerable influence in contemporary right-wing German circles.... He agreed to establish an anti-Bolshevik intelligence agency so that Ludendorff and his allies, including [Max] Scheubner-Richter, Kirill, and Hitler would have a reliable source of information on events in the Soviet Union. The money for the intelligence service, code-named Project S, came from Kirill.[104]

Ostensibly created to develop waterway commerce and industrial production in Ukraine after the anticipated Bolshevik defeat, Aufbau functioned as a political intelligence operation. One French intelligence report said that Aufbau

> sought to detach huge regions from the Soviet Union and to establish friendly governments in the East. Specifically, Aufbau envisioned the creation of a Southern (Ukrainian), Baltic, and Siberian states in addition to a rump Russia. The Southern state was to take the form of a Black Sea League under Ukrainian leadership. This new entity would include the Don, Kuban, and Terek Cossack nationalists. The Black Sea League was to form the most important of the planned successor states to the Soviet Union. The League was to come under the control of [Colonel Ivan] Poltavets-Ostranitsa, the head of Aufbau's Ukrainian faction.[105]

Aufbau even smuggled Kirill's Imperial proclamations into Russia.

The Russians wanted the Nazis, then still seen as extreme monarchists, to endorse the simultaneous restoration of the Hohenzollerns and Romanovs. In the early 1920s, the NSDAP also openly supported a new Russia under Grand Duke Kirill, while Russian monarchists funneled large sums of money to the new party. An NSDAP leader named Max Amann served as Aufbau's second secretary.[106] Nazi ideologue Alfred Rosenberg and General Ludendorff also belonged to the group.[107]

Aufbau's founder Max Scheubner-Richter was one of Hitler's closest friends. Scheubner-Richter died in the failed Munich putsch from a police bullet that could have killed the Nazi leader. As Hitler's biographer, Ian Kershaw, stated, 'Had the bullet which killed Scheubner-Richter been a foot to the right, history would have taken a different course.'[108] In the United States another Aufbau member helped link the White Russians, supporters of the Grand Duke Kirill, and American far right: Boris Brasol.[109]

General Konstantin Sakharov was yet another White Russian Aufbau supporter who visited New York in the early 1920s. From the *TN History*:

> After the defeat of the army in the Baltic campaign, the OSJ essentially became a paramilitary intelligence agency.... Boris Brasol and Cherep-Spiridovich were the principal SOSJ intelligence operatives in the United States. Brasol helped Major General Cherep-Spiridovich redirect SOSJ activities in the West against international anarchism and the globalist agenda. They both championed the validity of *The Protocols of the Elders of Zion*.... General Constantin Sakharov was head of the military division of the Russian Grand Priory. That division came to be known under the front name of the Russian National Society. The Russian National Society worked from offices at 5 Columbia [Columbus] Circle in Manhattan from 1921.[110]

General Sakharov was also described by Michael Kellogg as having 'connections with America,' although Kellogg offered few details. Sakharov first arrived in the

USA from Siberia. He then returned to Germany in 1921 and joined Aufbau.[111] He also participated as an 'American representative' to the First Monarchical Congress held in Bad Reichenhall in Upper Bavaria from 29 May to 5 June 1921.[112] In the early 1930s Sakharov worked with ROND, the Russian émigré National Socialist organization.[113] Explicitly modeled on the Nazi stormtroopers of the *Sturmabteilung* (SA), ROND used the Horst Wessel Song as its hymn, while its uniform included 'a black shirt with a green and white swastika.' Kellogg reports that Sakharov even 'coordinated relations between Kirill's supporters in Germany and abroad, including in the Soviet Union.'[114]

Ataman Grigori Mikhailovich Semenov (Semyónov) also entered the USA in March 1922 and visited New York. Boris Brasol personally lobbied the State Department to grant him a visa.[115] Semenov's circulation of *The Protocols of the Elders of Zion* in Siberia may have especially endeared him to Brasol. Semenov, however, was not allowed to stay long in America as he had committed too many atrocities during the Russian Civil War, including a few reportedly against US citizens.[116] Instead, he permanently relocated to Harbin in Japanese-controlled China. He was captured at the end of the war and was executed by the Soviets in 1946.[117] Yet the most important Aufbau enthusiast would only arrive in New York City in late 1924. This was Grand Duke Kirill's wife, the Grand Duchess Victoria.

Kirill and Victoria

The symbolic leader of the far-right White Russian monarchists was the Grand Duke Kirill. Boris Brasol even served as the Grand Duke Kirill's American representative. As for Kirill, he came from a family with deep roots not just in Russia but in Germany and England as well. Kirill's father, the Grand Duke Vladimir Alexandrovich, was Alexander III's brother. His German mother Marie, the Duchess of Mecklenburg-Schwerin, became the Grand Duchess Maria Pavlovna following her 1874 marriage to Vladimir. Kirill was born two years later in 1876.

During the Russo–Japanese War, Kirill survived a Japanese torpedo attack on his ship the H.I.M.S. *Petropavlovsk*.[118] That same year he married Victoria, his maternal first cousin, who had divorced her husband (Nicholas II's brother-in-law) Ernest Louis, Grand Duke of Hesse.[119] Greatly angered by Kirill's marriage – a union he had expressly forbidden – Nicholas II at first disowned him. The Tsar finally relented and let Kirill return to Russia (and his good graces) in 1910. That same year Victoria became the Grand Duchess Victoria Feodorovna.

Kirill angered many monarchists in 1917 when he sided with the new Kerensky government following Nicholas II's abdication. Kirill served as the Commander of the Naval Guards in St. Petersburg during the February Revolution. He marched his troops to Tauride Palace and publicly pledged his allegiance to the Duma. In June 1917, Kerensky let Kirill and a now very pregnant Victoria escape to Finland where Grand Duke Vladimir, their only son, was born. Kirill's monarchist opponents never forgave 1917; they mockingly labeled him as 'Kirill Égalité.'[120] Gleb Botkin, a leading New York-based Russian monarchist who despised Kirill, recalled:

What further increased the monarchists' skepticism in regard to Emperor Cyril was that he had been among the first to betray his late cousin of radiant memory. Emperor Nicholas hadn't had time to abdicate before Cyril, at the head of the Marines, marched with red banners to the revolutionary headquarters. There he paid an oath of allegiance to the Revolution, proclaiming himself the first free citizen of a free Russia. According to rumors, he hoped that this gracious gesture of his would induce people to make him Emperor then and there. But nothing of the sort happened. Instead, Cyril had soon to seek refuge in Finland, and eventually he proceeded to Western Europe.[121]

Kirill's wife, the Grand Duchess Victoria Melita ('Ducky' to her friends), came from another spectacular royal pedigree as a granddaughter of Queen Victoria and a niece of King Edward VII. Victoria's father was Duke Alfred of Saxe-Coburg and Gotha, the second son of Queen Victoria. Her mother was the Grand Duchess Maria Alexandrovna, the daughter of Alexander II by his first wife, Princess Marie of Hesse and by Rhine (later Empress Marie Alexandrovna, better known as Marie of Hesse).

Following the Romanov inheritance law of primogeniture under the prerevolutionary Fundamental Laws of Empire, Grand Duke Kirill now became the legitimate heir to the throne. To press his claim, Kirill and Victoria relocated from the French Riviera to Coburg in Bavaria, where Victoria had inherited a house called Edinburgh Palace from her mother, the Grand Duchess Maria Alexandrovna.[122] Maria, who died in 1920, had inherited property from her husband Prince Alfred. He, in turn, had acquired the Duchy of Saxe-Coburg following the death of his childless uncle, Ernest II, Duke of Saxe-Coburg and Gotha, who passed away in 1893. Grand Duchess Maria chose to make Coburg her home even after the end of World War I when ducal rule was abolished by the new Weimar state.

Kirill, Victoria, and Victoria's sister Princess Alexandra ('Sandra') of Saxe-Coburg and Gotha now became enthusiastic Hitler supporters.[123] They believed the Nazis were fighting for the restoration of the German monarchy, just as they were fighting for the Romanov restoration in Russia. Kirill and Victoria also became best friends in Coburg with Aufbau founder Max Scheubner-Richter and his wife Mathilde. Scheubner-Richter even arranged for Victoria to serve as honorary president of an Aufbau subsidiary called Renewal. Hitler also visited Coburg in 1922 'to attend a "German Day" rally sponsored by Victoria's family,' even as 'Ducky' graced 'a number of SA rallies.'[124] From May 1923 through 1924, Kirill and Victoria channeled large sums of money to General Ludendorff to aid the radical right. They were reportedly ruined financially when in early November 1923 the Munich Putsch failed.

It has long been asserted that since Kirill gave such large sums of money to the Nazis and that Kirill was poor (having lost almost everything in Russia), the money most likely came from Henry Ford, who used Boris Brasol as his conduit. In *Who Financed Hitler*, for example, James Pool writes that 'it seems apparent' that Ford must have provided Brasol with the funds to give to Kirill who then donated the money to Hitler.[125]

But was Kirill poor? His mother Maria Pavlovna had a world-famous jewelry collection that she successfully smuggled out of Russia.[126] As one student of Kirill's family observed, 'their acquisition of jewelry would have bankrupted more than one nation.'[127] After Maria Pavlovna's death in September 1920, the collection was divided by her children. Victoria also sold some of her famous jewels at a high price to her only sister, Queen Marie of Romania, to raise funds for Kirill's cause.[128] Victoria's mother, the Grand Duchess Maria Alexandrovna, the former Duchess of Saxe-Coburg and Gotha, died on 24 October 1920, only adding to their inheritance.

With the failure of the Munich putsch, Grand Duke Kirill now lost whatever fortune he had invested in Hitler. Eleven months later, on 2 October 1924, the *New York Times* ran an article almost certainly written by Frederick Cunliffe Owen headlined 'Grand Duke Cyril Is Reported to Seek Financiers who Would Make Him Czar.' The report, which wrongly stated that Kirill was planning to visit America in mid-October, continued:

> In Russian circles in Paris it is stated authoritatively that the Grand Duke Cyril has received financial backing from certain American capitalists, who are anxious to assist to bring about a return of a government in Russia, which would make stable trade relations again possible. It is gathered that Cyril's journey is being undertaken with a view to consultation with these backers.
>
> Well-informed Russian diplomats suggest that unknown to the Grand Duke, his attempted self-nomination as Czar is secretly approved by the Bolsheviki, who realize that the Monarchists will be weakened by the creation of factional parties in their midst which might possibly cause a split into two sections. A division of that nature would, of course, greatly weaken the Monarchist hopes of a successful reestablishment of the empire, a fact by which the Bolsheviki must necessarily profit. That is why they are secretly far from hostile to the Grand Duke Cyril's proclamation made in Berlin.[129]

Yet it would be Grand Duke Kirill's wife, the Grand Duchess Victoria Melia, who would come to New York.

Shadow war

Inside the White Russian émigré movement, Grand Duke Nicholas (Nicolai) Nikolaevich, the Commander-in-Chief of the Russian Army in World War I, was perhaps Kirill's harshest critic. Living in exile outside Paris, Grand Duke Nicholas received support from the French government against Kirill and his Aufbau supporters, whom the French saw as allied to the worst revanchists in Germany like Ludendorff and Hitler.[130] Grand Duke Nicholas also enjoyed the backing of the pro-French Supreme Monarchist Council (SMC), initially headquartered in Berlin and then in Paris.[131]

A senior aide to Grand Duke Nicholas named General Alexander Lukomsky on 31 May 1925 told the *New York Times*:

> There is no quarrel between the Grand Duke Nicholas and the Grand Duke Cyril – merely a difference of opinion. This difference of opinion is fundamental: The Grand Duke Cyril considers it possible to reestablish government in Russia from the outside and without the aid of the Russian people; the Grand Duke Nicholas does not and believes moreover that by having himself proclaimed Emperor by a few friends, by holding a miniature court etc., the Grand Duke Cyril is seriously injuring the Russian cause, which is simply to free the majority from their minority oppressors.

Later in the interview, Lukomsky resumed his attack:

> The Grand Duke Cyril considers that it is possible from abroad, and without in any way to obtain an expression of the will of the Russian people, to decide how the Bolsheviki shall be put out and who shall take their place. For this purpose, he had his friends proclaim him a sort of expatriated Czar six months ago. He then sent out agents and issued manifestos to announce this fact. Possibly he and his friends tried to secure material support for it.
>
> What was the result? In Russia it measurably set back the cause of liberation for which his Highness was working, and it strengthened the confidence of the Bolsheviki. It made those ready to strike doubtful and finally convinced them that it was better to wait. But to tell you the truth, the Grand Duke Cyril is practically unknown in Russia. The Bolsheviki made the most of him as a symbol of what was evil in the Czarist regime. Abroad, of course, the aspirations of the Grand Duke Cyril were merely laughed at. In a word, there was a measurable let down everywhere among those who in various ways had been trying to see how we could get rid of the Moscow gang and unite the people so as to discover their will.
>
> As to Grand Duke Nicholas, he has declared many times that everything concerning the future organization of Russia can be established only on Russian soil, and he is also of the opinion that anything predetermined for the Russian people will be rejected by them, that anything forced on them will not be lasting.

Grand Duke Nicholas and his ally General Baron Pyotr Wrangel controlled the Russian All-Military Union (ROVS), which was first headquartered in Serbia and later in Paris. ROVS maintained close ties to the SMC, which began agitating for an invasion of the Soviet Union led by General Wrangel and backed by France in the summer of 1922. This was a time when war, communism, civil war, and famine had brought Russia to near total collapse. A short time earlier in March 1921 the Kronstadt mutiny broke out. The SMC even hoped that if the invasion succeeded, Grand Duke Nicholas would become the next Tsar.[132] As for the

French, they would ally with Polish forces along with ROVS-trained military units during the attack. Poland, however, would prove highly problematic for the Whites.

Aufbau was in such a panic over a French-backed White invasion of Russia that it turned to the Bolsheviks for support! In May 1923 *Aufbau Correspondence* publicly warned about French preparations to attack Russia and made it clear that it was willing to open negotiations with the Bolsheviks. A representative of Aufbau stated that if the 'Jewish finance'-backed Grand Duke Nicholas invaded Russia, nationalist forces would be forced to fight on the side of the Reds. Once the French-backed Whites were defeated, the German-allied Whites would then launch a putsch in the Red Army and bring down the Bolsheviks. Scheubner-Richter also declared, 'we cannot believe that France is serious with the fight against Jewish world Communism.' Aufbau complained the divisions inside the Whites ensured that '"the wise men of Zion" are laughing up their sleeves.'

Finally, there was another player in the secret war, the Bolsheviks. Although our image of White Russian exiles is one of Grand Dukes driving taxi cabs and serving as concierges in elegant hotels, the Cheka didn't see it this way. The Soviet 'Operation Trust' deception which successfully captured Reilly was explicitly designed to destroy Grand Duke Nicholas and General Wrangel's exile network through a fictitious 'monarchist' group headquartered in Moscow.

The Soviet war continued throughout the 1930s. Two ROVS leaders, Generals Kutepov and Miller, were even kidnapped on the streets of Paris and executed. Yet we know far less about Soviet operations against Grand Duke Kirill. Was that because the Cheka and its successor organizations viewed Kirill as a 'useful idiot'? Or was there a deeper connection, one that dated back to Aufbau's pledge to willingly fight with the Reds against 'the wise men of Zion'? In Aufbau do we even see glimpses of Hacke?

The mysteries of the Monday Opera Supper Club

The Grand Duchess Victoria's trip to New York was arranged through the patronage of Julia Loomis, a leader in the Russian Relief Society (RRF).[133] Julia had a home in France, and she first met Victoria in Paris in the summer of 1923.

Shortly before Victoria arrived in New York, the Moscow OGPU (the renamed Cheka) received a report dated 21 September 1924 that said 'a new anti-Bolshevik organization has now been formed in New York' called the Russian-American Financial Syndicate.[134] The Syndicate was meant to serve 'as a link between diverse Russian national organizations – political, cultural-educational, religious and commercial – uniting them in the struggle against the corrupting influences of international communism and the ongoing Bolshevik atrocity in Soviet Russia.' The Syndicate would strive to unite various Russian societies, unions, and associations and funnel 'business support' to them to overthrow the regime.[135] Around this same time, Kirill openly boasted of backing from American capitalists. Was the mysterious Russian–American Financial Syndicate designed as a channel for these funds?

On 29 November 1924, Grand Duchess Victoria left Le Havre on the *Ville de Paris* for a ten-day visit that included stops in New York, Philadelphia, and Washington.[136] When she arrived in New York harbor in early December, Victoria was greeted by Mrs. Loomis. A doyen of New York High Society, Julia Loomis was both President of the New York Chapter of the Colonial Dames of America and Chairwoman of the Metropolitan Opera's elite Monday Opera Supper Club.[137] Born Julia Josephine Stimson in Patterson, New Jersey, in 1861, she was the widow of Dr. Henry Patterson Loomis and the mother of Arthur Lee Loomis, a famous scientist who had his own private laboratory at the family's estate in Tuxedo Park.[138]

Julia Loomis also knew a leading Washington socialite with White Russian ties. This was the Princess Cantacuzene, Countess Spiransky. Julia Dent Cantacuzene Spiransky-Grant was the granddaughter of President Ulysses S. Grant.[139] Julia married Prince Mikhail Cantacuzene and moved to St. Petersburg, where she later witnessed the 1917 revolution. The couple relocated to Washington and maintained close contact with the White Russian community. Julia also served on the Advisory Committee of the Monday Opera Supper Club, which maintained a permanent office at Sherry's, an exclusive restaurant located at 300 Park Avenue.

Victoria told the New York press there was no political motive behind the visit that the Monday Opera Supper Club financed. Few believed her. A headline in the *Jewish Daily Bulletin*, read, 'Monday Opera Club of Exclusive Five Hundred Becomes Center of Monarchistic Restoration Movement.'[140]

After Victoria landed, she went straight to her Waldorf-Astoria suite, and received 'a few important guests.' One was Boris Brasol, described in the press as 'the official representative of the Grand Duke in New York.'[141] That night at Sherry's, 'Ducky' sat at table with 'her retinue, Mrs. Loomis, Mr. Djamgaroff, and Mr. and Mrs. George F. Baker, Jr.' The Baker family co-founded First National Bank. George's father, George, Sr., dubbed 'the Sphinx of Wall Street,' was the third richest man in America behind Henry Ford and John D. Rockefeller. (J. P. Morgan's estimated wealth was one-half that of Baker's.)

Yet the most unusual person at Sherry's may have been George Jamhar Djamgaroff, officially listed as 'Secretary' of the Monday Opera Supper Club. After Hitler took power, Djamgaroff claimed that in 1934 the Nazis offered him $200,000 to be their American PR agent, but that he turned them down. That same year he and his wealthy new American wife Lele Daly spent their summer visiting Kirill and Victoria in France.[142] In 1932 the American Communist Party published a pamphlet by Robert W. Dunn entitled *Spying on Workers* that examined private intelligence outfits used to infiltrate unions. Dunn writes that Djamgaroff

> took credit for calling the mass meeting of patriotic societies in Carnegie Hall on January 9, 1931, in his well-funded drive on Communism. It was likewise Djamgaroff who told newspapermen of his espionage system, his vast knowledge of labor activities, his phony ABC News agency … and his cooperation with the professional patriotic groups of all shades. Later the same Djamgaroff was called in by the police of Flint, Mich., and the General Motors Corp. to

spy on the workers in the Chevrolet and Fisher Body plants and to advise on methods of destroying militant trade union activities in that city. At the same time, he was receiving generous support from Mrs. Henry P. Loomis, the sister-in-law of Secretary of State Stimson.[143]

While Grand Duchess Victoria was touring the East Coast, a 13 December 1924 report appeared in the *Berliner Zeitung am Mittag* claiming that Henry Ford 'and other unnamed Americans' were promising funds to Grand Duke Kirill 'in exchange for Siberian railway and gold-mining concessions once the Bolsheviks were sent packing.' The intermediary was supposed to be the 'banking house of Brasol & Co. of New York.'[144] Yet there was no banking house named Brasol and Company. Could it have been the writer's shorthand for the mysterious Russian–American Financial Syndicate cited in the OGPU file? On 27 December 1924, the German Foreign Office also received a report that while she was in America, Victoria managed to raise a large sum of money for Kirill's cause.[145]

Blue Lamoo

While Grand Duchess Victoria courted New York high society, a radical right network that included 'Colonel' Charles Louis Thourot Pichel now formed in the shadow of the Social Register elite. For decades Pichel flourished in the demi-world of chivalric pseudo-orders, Führer-friendly White Russians, world-class grifters, antisemites, and hyper-patriot nativists obsessed with imaginary Bolshevik–Masonic–Jewish grand conspiracies.

In *The Aryan Order of America and the College of Arms of Canada 1880–1937*, Yves Drolet begins his discussion of Pichel:

> Charles Pichel can best be described as a conman. After serving a jail sentence for drug trafficking in Atlanta, he turned to various money-making schemes, such as setting up a bogus association of chiropractors. In 1928, he found a lucrative scam in the sale of fake coats of arms and incorporated the American Heraldry Society with Dr. William Sohier Bryant, a physician, genealogist, and former US Army officer whom he seemingly used as a screen. This New York-based organization had a questionable character, as it promised that the 'carte cordiale' coming with its (very expensive!) crests would open to their holders the doors of the Court of St. James in London.[146]

Dr. William Sohier Bryant was a leading ear specialist who died in New York on 26 June 1956 at age 95. An 1884 Harvard graduate, he served as a brigade surgeon in both the Spanish–American War and World War I, and retired as a lieutenant colonel in the Army Reserve. Bryant belonged to a host of patriotic societies including the Society of the Mayflower, the Society of the Cincinnati, and the Sons of the Revolution.[147] A genealogist and heraldry buff, he collaborated with Pichel in the American Heraldry Society.

In 1932, Pichel petitioned the Justice Department over his drug trafficking conviction in Atlanta. The government letter rejecting his request explained:

> information was received that various persons had made complaints to the Better Business Bureau, New York City, that the American Heraldry Society was defrauding its members and receiving money on representation that a book entitled *Who's Who in Heraldry* would be published; that you were secretary of the Society and responsible for the publication of the book, that neither you nor the Society was in a position to publish it and you were using the money for your own personal benefit.... It was also reported that you are using the Heraldry Society's rooms in the Waldorf-Astoria Hotel as a sort of rendezvous for yourself and other men where you met women of prominence, and wild drinking parties were held there, in support of which it is alleged that your conduct, as above indicated, was such that you were requested to move out of the hotel.

Pichel proved irrepressible. In 1936, for example, he 'teamed up with Friedrich Hahn, alias Marquis Gugue de Champvans de Farémont, a notorious Paris-based Austrian forger who had become a peddler of nobility diplomas in Europe.'[148] All in a day's work, or so one would imagine.

The *TN History* portrays Pichel's early career more demurely:

> Dr. James Gaston Baillie Bulloch, MD, was the archivist of the Order from 1922 to 1928 and the Grand Chancellor from 1928 until his death in 1934.[149] Bulloch was one of the principals who chartered the American Heraldry Society in 1924 in the District of Columbia from which were recruited candidates for the Order of St. John. Charles Pichel and William Sohier Bryant, MD, operated the American Heraldry Society in New York City out of an office in the Waldorf-Astoria Hotel with which they attempted to provide the necessary noble titles to prospective American Knights from 1925 to 1931.[150]

Omitting Pichel's legal troubles, the *TN History* continues:

> Pichel converted to Catholicism in 1932 and soon became a principal of the SOSJ through his mentor Grand Prior Fr. Joseph Paul Chodkiewicz, a leader of the Polish White Cross in upstate New York. Pichel became Grand Chancellor of the SOSJ in the heyday of the National Socialist Movement after the death of J. G. B. Bulloch, MD, in 1934. The President of the Sovereign Council from 1932 to 1944 was Colonel Dr. William Sohier Bryant, MD, OSJ. After ... Czar Kirill I died in 1938, Dr. Bryant and Grand Chancellor Pichel gained complete control of the Order.[151]

Father Chodkiewicz was a Catholic priest.[152] Born in Zhitomir (Zhytomyr), Ukraine, Father Chodkiewicz helped found the Polish Nobility Association on 27

January 1927 ostensibly to promote the genealogical heritage and chivalric customs of the Commonwealth of Poland and Lithuania.[153] The Polish Nobility Association was incorporated as the Slavic Catholic Club.[154] It also listed 'H. Victor Cherep' as an incorporator. This was Howard Victor Broenstrupp, the 'adopted son' of Count Cherep-Spiridovich and one of the defendants in the 1944 Washington, D.C., 'sedition trials.'[155]

On 15 July 1933, Pichel wrote to Ernst 'Putzi' Hanfstaengl, who ran Hitler's Foreign Press Bureau in Berlin. Declaring himself the director of the American Heraldry Society, Pichel offered to serve as Hitler's personal liaison to America, an offer Hanfstaengl prudently declined.[156] The network around Pichel also functioned as a propaganda outlet for Welt-Dienst (World Service), the German-based far-right network that relentlessly pumped out antisemitic propaganda in eight foreign languages. From the *TN History*:

> In 1933, Pichel contacted Germany through Hitler's friend Putzi Hanfstaengl in an effort to become the German Chancellor's personal representative in the United States. These Russian and American Nationalists were now coordinating their anti-Bolshevik publishing activity with Ulrich Fleischhauer's Welt-Dienst with offices in Erfurt, Germany. German Lt. Ulrich Fleischhauer was in charge of this Welt-Dienst publishing concern which inherited the campaign of the American Anti-Bolshevist Publishing Association of Cherep-Spindovich....
>
> Translated as World Service and known before this time in France as *Service Mondial*, the SOSJ publishing effort had actually been started in 1904 by Cherep-Spiridovich in Paris. At that time it was called *Agence Latine*. When the Paris operation of Cherep-Spindovich was exposed by the Bolshevists in 1919, he was able to convince Henry Ford to succeed him by using the *Dearborn Independent*. The German agency Welt-Dienst had originated in Hamburg where it published a journal called the *White Cross* in 1920. Baltic Germans of the SOSJ to include Fleischhauer and Markov II had originated the anti-Bolshevist journal sharing information with Cherep-Spindovich. Eventually the Welt-Dienst operation came under the administration of Alfred Rosenberg after the death of Czar Kirill I but operations continued in Erfurt.[157]

In America, the *TN History* explains, the White Russian 'Prince Anastase Vonsiatsky and Howard Broenstrupp led the fledgling Russian Nationalist field force.... Paul Winter, OSJ, longtime associate of Grand Chancellor Pichel and former KKK leader from New York and Philadelphia, was involved with the American Nationalists.'[158] The growth of this network

> culminated in a vast propaganda arm which worked against the international conspiracy from government-run offices in the German Third Reich throughout WWII. Beside Markov II, the Baltic Germans Ullrich Fleischhauer, Shabelski-Bork, Alfred Rosenberg, Fedor Vinberg and Eugen von

Engelhardt of the Fichte-Bund were among those active in the information campaign until the closing days of WWII.

All over Europe and the United States, small print shops produced information which was distributed at cost in an effort to stay the spread of militant Socialism. The headquarters for the centralized educational campaign during the lifetime of Czar Kirill I was in Erfurt, Germany. Until his death in 1938, Grand Duke Kirill had been the chosen candidate of Hitler for Czar of Russia when the Soviet Union was defeated.[159]

Mimicking Welt-Dienst, the Americans established their own propaganda operation. One of their leaders was Robert Edward Edmondson, yet another defendant in the Washington Sedition Trials. From the *TN History*:

> The American Grand Priory also restarted this propaganda in the United States in 1936, and it was called Edmondson Economic Service. Pichel operated a similar 'information service' for the SOSJ called 'Crux New Service' from Leonia, New Jersey, from 1939 to 1945. Due to pressure from the government and from the press, both Edmondson and Pichel moved the Order's operations into the Pocono Mountains of Pennsylvania after 1945. The efforts to expose a Jewish-controlled world conspiracy, considered by many as anti-Semitic, were continued by the SOSJ into the 1950s. Thereafter it became politically and economically impossible due to the use of the court system by the liberal establishment.[160]

In the 1930s, Pichel and company also ran a strange-sounding political group called The Ancient and Noble Order of the Blue Lamoo. In 1934 a writer named Pat McGrady wrote a series of exposes of the American far right entitled 'This Fascist Racket,' which was published by the Jewish Telegraph Agency. One of these grouplets struck McGrady as especially strange:

> I have recently come across a manual put out as what might well be called the Protocols of the Learned Elders of Aryandom. Factually the organization is called The Ancient and Noble Order of the Blue Lamoo. The group, I would judge from the type of stuff they advocate, is a super-Aryan cult and may have some slight following in this and other countries. Essentially its tenets are those of all the shirt groups that have sprung up here and elsewhere and they but slightly exaggerate the policies of Nazi organizations.
>
> The Order of the Blue Lamoo is listed as having its 'Stronghold' in the Black Hills of South Dakota and its eastern headquarters at 110–116 Nassau Street in New York. At the latter address, building employees profess to have no knowledge as to the existence of the organization. Its membership is secret. Other asserted headquarters are: North-western, 325 Postal Building, Portland, Ore.; Nordic, Box 3097, Stockholm, Ill.; British, 34, Strand, London; Southwestern, General Delivery, Glendale, Cal.; Latin, Apartado 485, San Juan, Puerto Rico; Slav, 23 Huskisson Street, Liverpool.[161]

110 Nassau Street was the address of an attorney named Clarence E. Sutherland, whom von Broenstrupp (who signed legal documents as 'H. Victor von Broens-Trupp') worked for as a clerk. (Some reports say von Broenstrupp was a former patent lawyer.) Leslie Fry lived in Glendale, California, although up until 1936 she spent most of her time in Europe.

Blue Lamoo also had strange 'New Age' overtones:

> The Black Hills have been chosen for headquarters because, as literature of the order explains, 'Final international sovereign headquarters shall be established at the Stronghold, located near the Home of the Great Spirit, in the Heart of the Black (unmanifested divinity) Hills National Park, in the State of South Dakota, United States of America, as the remnant of the Old Atlantean Continent undefiled by materialistic civilization and reserved by the Spiritual Forces through the Ages past for this purpose.'
>
> The International Sovereign Body 'derives and exercises its powers and authority from the Ancient Immortal Atlantean Initiates of the Sun,' according to the first degree of the order which rambles on for seventeen [pages with] capital and small letters at will.... Membership in the order is limited 'to those of the natural nobility who have proven themselves worthy of the distinction given their forebears, and those of the Aryan People of all classes, who because of greatness of Soul and ardent desire, sink their own personality in and work for the general and common good.'[162]

Blue Lamoo pursued more earthly concerns as well:

> To Maintain the political ascendancy, racial purity and moral ideals of the Aryan Peoples, against all who challenge the former or seek to destroy the latter;
>
> To advocate such an extension in the educational systems as will assure all properly qualified Aryan Youths such instruction and training as will fit them to creditably represent and maintain Aryan Supremacy in the business, professional and scientific worlds, and in the military, naval, air, diplomatic, state and municipal services;
>
> To urge that Aryan Employers, wherever possible without detriment to others, will give preference to and employ Aryan Employees, especially Aryan Ex-Servicemen of Military and Naval establishments, and members of the Order;
>
> To Promote (price, quality and other factors being equal) mutual trading between members of the Order and other Aryans, through advertising, giving of discounts and premiums;
>
> To effect the release of the Aryans from the financial bondage of the Judeo-Mongols and to pay off the interest bearing debt by a proper progressive system of taxation with due regard to the wealth of the individual and in lieu of this 'Gold Standard' to provide the true security, i.e., the Domain, the Culture, the Physical and Mental Working Capacity of the National Aryan Folk;

To Promulgate and encourage the study of those Ancient Aryan Teachings
and Esoteric Sciences which deal with the Mission, Superiority and Responsibility of the Great Aryan Race;

To Unite Science and Religion, whereby the Aryans again may be
Supermen and Superwomen and establish the Aryan Race as the Christ Race
leading the World into the Millennium.[163]

McGrady comments:

The above represents the most rational section of the manual of the Order of
the Blue Lamoo. It is the essence of the order and is shorn of such mysticism
as that of Section VIII, for instance. This section provides for 'Rejuvenation,
New Birth (Freedom from the Second Death).' It explains how to attain
freedom from disease, pain, sin, poverty, and physical death from natural
causes and is available to 'members of the Blue Lamoo who have passed
through the first Four degrees of Sun Initiation.'

I find that the mysticism of the Order of the Blue Lamoo is no less reasonable than that of Silver Shirt Pelley, who can commune with the Great
Beyond in Atlantean and other similar languages by virtue of his possession of
the key to the scriptures of the Great Pyramid; or of White Shirt Christians,
who professes an infallibility and a supernatural ability to 'read between the
lines'; or of [Royal Scott] Gulden [of the Order of 76], whose visions of the
Communist menace and the powers he can (and does, so he says) muster out
of thin air to thwart it.[164]

Blue Lamoo also surfaced in a May 1943 FBI file on Boris Brasol by FBI Special
Agent John Simons.[165] Simons writes that Brasol 'was also described as an anti-
Semite, having reputedly translated *The Protocols of Zion* and to be a power in the
BLUE LAMOO ORDER.' Brasol 'was said … to have been a correspondent of
the FICHTE BUND in 1940 and to have been in close touch with [Vincent]
WALSH, PICHEL, Father PETER DUFFY, and Colonel WILLIAM S.
BRYANT.'[166]

Pichel also claimed that on 13 January 1934, Grand Duke Kirill confirmed the
legitimacy of Pichel's Knights. Then on 24 November 1936, Kirill awarded Pichel
'the Order of Andrew the Apostle, First Class in Gold.' The Order was 'signed by
the President of the Committee of Imperial Orders and the Delegate of the
Emperor in the United States,' in other words, Boris Brasol.[167]

The individual most responsible for calling attention to the Blue Lamoo also had
a close connection to Boris Brasol. This was Casimir Palmer (Pilenas), who had
served as an informant for both the Okhrana and Scotland Yard.[168] Palmer worked
with Brasol in the US Military Intelligence Division (MID) office in New York in
World War I. During this time, Brasol began filing reports arguing that the Bolshevik Revolution was the result of a Jewish banking conspiracy.[169] After his career
with MID ended, Brasol recruited Palmer to work for Ford's intelligence operation

in New York. Palmer may well have been an inside source for Norman Hapgood's 'Henry Ford's Jew Mania' series for *Hearst's International*.

One of Brasol and Palmer's MID colleagues was Captain Nathan Isaacs, who become both a Harvard business school professor and a staunch supporter of Jewish causes. Palmer, who ran his own New York detective agency in the 1930s, began sending Issacs reports on Brasol and his ties to Henry Ford's old operative Ernest Liebold, whom Palmer described as 'a confirmed anti-Semite and supporter of German monarchists.'[170]

In January 1939 Palmer contacted the Anti-Nazi League (also known as the Non-Sectarian Anti-Nazi League) to warn about Blue Lamoo. Palmer told the League that it was led by Pichel, 'said to be an Englishman, alleged drug smuggler, and Nazi spy.' Father Duffy reportedly served as the group's link to Brasol. It seems likely that much information about Blue Lamoo in the FBI file originated from Palmer.

For his part, Brasol regularly visited Europe during the 1930s, where he caught the attention of SS-Leader Heinrich Himmler.

> In the summer of 1938, Brasol, who was by this time an American citizen, helped to organize a clandestine anti-Comintern congress in Germany with the approval of Hitler's secret police, the Gestapo, and Himmler's SS. The assembly included representatives from America, Canada, France, England, and Switzerland. Himmler himself took an interest in Brasol in August 1938 and he commissioned a certain Müller of the SS to write a report on the White émigré's earlier activities.[171]

Another interesting name in the FBI report was Colonel Bryant, Pichel's crony in the American Heraldry Society. Richard Spence reports that 'Bryant served Brasol for years as a front for obtaining subscriptions to various publications, notably the Jewish ones such as the *Forward* and *Jewish Examiner*. Some years down the road, Bryant would become a prominent member of the America First Committee.'[172] Bryant may have come uncomfortably close to being swept up in the 'Great Sedition Trial' since the *TN History* reports:

> Bryant became implicated in the Great Sedition Trial when his name appeared on anti-government correspondence involving William Dudley Pelley and Howard Victor Broenstrupp. Trevor's American Coalition of Patriotic, Civil and Fraternal Societies was also named during the proceedings. Bryant, formerly the personal physician of President Grover Cleveland and a Masonic Knight Templar, found the negative publicity of the trial too controversial, and he dropped out of the Order thereby leaving Grand Chancellor Pichel to name Edmondson as President of the Sovereign Council. As noted earlier, because of liberal governmental and media pressure, Pichel, Edmondson and even Paul M. Winter moved to the Pocono Mountain region of Pennsylvania after 1945.[173]

In September 1942, Brasol went before an Army Exclusion Hearing Board. It recommended that Brasol be banned from the 'entire Eastern Military Area' as a potential security threat. The Exclusion Board, however, could only recommend his banning to the U.S. Attorney General for the Southern District of New York, Matthew Correa. Correa, however, promptly dropped the case, and Brasol stayed in New York.[174]

Blue Lamoo clearly was part of a larger pro-Axis political network. But could it have been a cover for another more secretive organization? On page 3803 of German American Bund leader Fritz Kuhn's 15 August 1939 testimony before HUAC, there is this curious exchange between HUAC Counsel Rhea Whitley and Kuhn:

MR. WHITLEY: . What are your relations with Victor Cherep-Spiridovich [a/k/a Victor Howard Broenstrupp] No. 9 Sheriff Street, New York City, who is connected with organizations known as 'Intelligence,' 'American Tribunal,' and 'Order of the Knights of Saint John of Jerusalem'?[175] Are you acquainted with him, or with those groups?

MR. KUHN: . No.

Despite Kuhn's apparent disavowal of knowledge about The Knights of Saint John of Jerusalem, Pichel would ensure that they continued in the immediate postwar period and that they became ever more intimately involved with Goleniewski from the 1960s onwards. The prewar networks feeding into Blue Lamoo and the Knights consisted, as we have seen, of exiled White Russians, private anti-Bolshevik intelligence groups which overlapped with national intelligence agencies in complex ways, transnational antisemitic and pro-Nazi activists and homegrown American rightists, often with military connections. The postwar networks associated with the Knights shared many of these same features and there were considerable ideological and organizational continuities.

Notes

1 On Paul I and the Knights, see Frendo (2004), Sire (1994), 241–46, and Sainty (1991), 15–16. For the geopolitical side of the story, see Saul (1970).
2 The exiled Knights in Russia had already voted to depose him on 7 November 1798.
3 See http://www.theKnightsofsaintjohn.com/History-After-Malta.htm.
4 Sire (1994), 245–46.
5 Chaffanjon and Flavigny (1982), 207.
6 Ibid., 184.
7 For more on Crolian William Edelen de Burgh's fantastic royal claims, see Chairoff (1985), 150–51.
8 The *TN History* counts Edelen as '75th Prince Grand Master' and says he took the post in 1966. Pichel has Edelen as the 72nd Grand Master.
9 The Virginia-born Dr. Joseph Gaston Baillie Bulloch, an amateur genealogist, was a distant relative of Teddy Roosevelt. He created a host of heraldic and patriotic societies including the Aryan Order of St. George and the Order of Lafayette. The Aryan Order of St. George was a continuation of the Aryan Order of America created in

1880 by 'Frederich Gilman Forsyth de Fronsac'. Although Edelen didn't know it, Pichel knew Bulloch for decades as they both had murky ties to the Aryan Order of America. Drolet (2015), 28–33, 62–63, 68–69.

10 See http://www.theKnightstemplar.org/forums/topic/crolian-william-edelen-1st-grand-prior-of-the-smotj-org/, and http://www.geocities.ws/maltesefakes/stjohn1.html.

11 http://www.theKnightstemplar.org/forums/topic/crolian-william-edelen-1st-grand-prior-of-the-smotj-org/.

12 For the Edelen–Orth correspondence, see http://web.archive.org/web/20160328000746/ http://www.orderstjohn.org/selfstyle/edelen.htm.

13 Welsh (1923), 173. The group even had its own 'Imperial Parent Grand Black Encampment of the Universe.' In the 1920s it was led by Robert Ernest Augustus Land, the Great Commander of America. Land wrote *Fifty Years in the Malta Order*, a two-volume tome published in 1928 and 'privately published by the estate of R. E. A. Land.' The American center of the 'Illustrious Grand Order of the Knights of Malta' was Philadelphia.

14 There is also a profile of Cherep-Spiridovich in the back of the book written by one 'Herjulf Vikingson' and dated 'Chicago, July 4, 1925.' The cover page gives 1926 as the date of publication.

15 Cherep-Spiridovich was Russia's general consul in Belgrade and not the other way around.

16 Grand Duke Sergei was killed on 4 February 1905.

17 See http://www.theKnightsofsaintjohn.com/History-After-Malta.htm.

18 Webb (1976), 260–61.

19 See 'The Russian Mazzini,' 1 June 1881 *NYT*.

20 For an overview of the Pan-Slavists, see Boeckh (2016).

21 See 'Cherep-Spiridovich Dies Here from Gas,' 23 October 1926 *NYT*.

22 From a profile of Grand Duchess Elizabeth written by her former Mistress of the Robe, the Countess Alexandra Olsoufieff (Olsufiev), at http://www.alexanderpalace. org/palace/GDElisabeth.html.

23 Boeckh (2016), 114.

24 Sablinsky (1976), 278.

25 Japanese intelligence did, in fact, fund Russian revolutionaries of all stripes.

26 Ular (1905), 199–200. In 1908, Ular was the American correspondent for *Le Petit Journal* of Paris.

27 Trotsky (1981), 38. Alexander Guchkov was a Moscow industrialist and Octobrist Party leader. He served as chairman of the Third Duma and Minister of War in the Kerensky government. Count Aleksei Bobrinskii, a wealthy landlord and monarchist, headed the Council of United Nobility in St. Petersburg and was Chairman of the Russian-English Bank. In 1916, Bobrinskii became Deputy Interior Minister and Minister of Agriculture.

28 Ibid., 450.

29 The 12 December 1920 *New York Times* article on Cherep-Spiridovich noted that when he visited New York in 1908 he 'became well known in New York society.'

30 https://www.jta.org/1926/06/29/archive/daily-digest-of-public-opinion-on-je wish-matters-108.

31 A high-ranking Okhrana General named Alexander Ivonovich Spiridovich also lived in Paris.

32 Cherep-Spiridovich (1919), 301–304 and 453–456. The *Asiatic Review* editor descri-bed the Count as 'an enthusiastic friend and admirer of England.'

33 See Holmes (1977).

34 Webster (1921), 308–09.

35 This is Istoriia *bol'shevizma v Rossii: ot vozniknoveniia do zakhvata vlasti, 1883-1903-1917; S prilozh. dokumentov i portretov* published in Paris in 1922 by former Okhrana Major General Alexander Spiridovich, not to be confused with Count Cherep-

Spiridovich. Webster referenced this book in her work *The Surrender of an Empire* that appeared in London in 1931.

36 The October 1922 issue of *Hearst's International* carried a section of a long series by Norman Hapgood on Ford's obsession with a Jewish conspiracy. Hapgood reprints a card showing Cherep-Spiridovich's employment by Ford's *Dearborn Independent*.

37 Cherep-Spiridovich said the text was originally written as a special report to President Warren G. Harding and read 'in my presence' by Harding's Secretary George B. Christian.

38 This would almost certainly have been a project to build a Don-Volga canal, a project that the Ottomans first tried to build in 1570. Peter the Great also dreamt of such a canal. It was finally built by Stalin in 1952.

39 The meeting and the cup are mentioned in a 23 October 1926 *NYT* report. It also cites the canal project.

40 https://www.jta.org/1926/06/29/archive/daily-digest-of-public-opinion-on-je wish-matters-108.

41 Cherep-Spiridovich had an office in Harlem. *The Secret World Government* was published by the Anti-Bolshevik Publishing Association at 15 East 128th Street, also the home of his Universal Anti-Bolshevist Association.

42 From a 29 June 1926 Jewish Telegraph Agency (JTA) report.

43 The paper also stated that Cherep-Spiridovich claimed that Queen Marie of Romania, Victoria's sister, was scheduled to appear at his conference.

44 27 October 1926 *NYT*.

45 24 October 1926 *NYT*.

46 1 November 1926 *NYT*.

47 https://www.jta.org/1926/10/27/archive/cherep-spiridovitch-died-penniless-because-his-anti-semitic-campaign-collapsed.

48 Cherep-Spiridovich also published *Slava* for many years in Russian, first in Europe and later in America.

49 Ibid.

50 That said, in his 1919 essays for *The Asiatic Review* Cherep-Spiridovich's main enemy was still Germany.

51 Nilus included the *Protocols* in his book *The Great in the Small and the Antichrist as an Impending Political Possibility. Notes of an Orthodox Christian*. On Zevachov (Prince Nikolai Davidovič Ževachov) and Cherep-Spiridovich, I draw on Hagemeister (2017), 67–67, 584–85, and De Michelis (2004) who transliterates the name as Ževaxov.

52 The Chief Procurator effectively served as the lay head of the Orthodox Church and held a position in the Russian Senate.

53 See De Michelis (2004), 158. Zevachov spent years trying to prevent the Bolsheviks from taking legal possession of the property.

54 For the international impact of the Protocols, see Webman (2011). [For their impact on Nazi Germany see Evans (2020) pp. 13–45. CF.]

55 Hagemeister (2017), 530–31. In London she worked with Lady Queenborough on her *Occult Theocracy* books.

56 Fry's history is discussed in the next chapter.

57 Ibid., 559. The head of the Paris section of the Okhrana, Pyotr Rachkovskii – who has been long linked to the saga of the *Protocols* with much debate over his role in the entire affair – also obtained a special private meeting with Pope Leo XIII in 1901.

58 Jouin founded the *Revue* in connection with the formation of the Ligue franc-cath-olique (1913), and the Fédération antimaçommique, also established in 1913.

59 Hagemeister (2017), 513. Benigni died in Rome in 1934. Jouin passed away in Paris in 1932 but his *Revue* continued publication until 1939. Hagemeister notes that Benigni's Vatican archive remains closed to researchers.

60 Ibid., 66. In the mid-1920s D'Herbigny tried to set up a clandestine shadow hierarchy for the Catholic Church in Bolshevik Russia.

61 De Michelis (2004), 161.

62 See the 29 June 1929 *NYT* where the quote comes from along with the 7 July 1929 *Daily News*, and the 28 July 1929 *St. Louis Post Dispatch*.

63 http://www.theknightsofsaintjohn.com/History-After-Malta.htm.

64 Visits of Grand Duke Alexander were extensively covered in the *New York Times* as high society events. The Grand Duke's visits to New York in 1893 and 1913 generated a series of articles. There is no mention of him being in the USA, much less New York, in 1908. Nor is there any mention of an American visit in Grand Duke Alexander's autobiography *Once a Grand-Duke* or in his sequel *Always a Grand Duke*.

65 http://www.theknightsofsaintjohn.com/History-After-Malta.htm A Baltic German, Baron Roman Rosen in May 1905 became Russian Ambassador to the US. He returned to Russia in 1911 and served on the State Council. An expert on Japan, Ambassador Rosen helped negotiate the Portsmouth Treaty ending the Russo-Japanese War.

66 5 October 1913 *NYT*.

67 https://hsp.org/blogs/fondly-pennsylvania/of-wanamakers-and-romanovs-a-history-mystery-from-the-archives.

68 Spence (2002b), 89.

69 Chavchavadze (1990), 195.

70 Kerensky (1965), 89. Kerensky says that an Okhrana report 'signed by Brune de St. Hyppolite, Director of the Department of Police, is the only document dealing with the Masonic Rosenkreutz Society, which was known to us as the "Barbara Ovchinnikova Organization" and which led to the formation of a society under the auspices of Grand Duke Alexander Mikhailovich that included courtiers and members of the aristocracy.'

71 One of his books, *The Union of Souls*, was printed in New York in 1931 by the Roerich Museum Press. He wrote another book published in London in 1929 entitled *The Religion of Love*. Both were translations.

72 Stephan (1978), 113.

73 See the chapter 'Cyril and His Invisible Empire' in *Always a Grand Duke*.

74 On Vonsiatsky and Grand Duke Alexander, see Stephan (1978).

75 The last name is often spelled 'Brazol' but in the text I'm conforming it to 'Brasol' in quoted material.

76 For biographical details of Brasol, see the invaluable articles by Singerman and Spence (2012a), (2012b).

77 Spence (2012a), 204.

78 Spence (2002a), 224.

79 9 January 1942 report of FBI interview with Brasol on 29 December 1941 by C.C. MacCartee.

80 http://www.theknightsofsaintjohn.com/History-After-Malta.htm.

81 Ibid.

82 https://www.newyorker.com/magazine/1940/11/09/sergievsky. On Brasol, Sergievsky, and Sikorsky, see Spence (2012b), 700.

83 http://www.theknightsofsaintjohn.com/History-After-Malta.htm. The *TN History* also claims that 'Baron Rosen, former Russian Ambassador to the United States, and now head of Grand Duke Cyril's Intelligence operation in the United States, was run down and killed by an automobile in New York City on December 31, 1921.'

84 On Ford and the Jews, see Baldwin (2002); and Logsdon (1999).

85 Ribuffo (1980), 447–48.

86 Baldwin (2002), 81–82.

87 Singerman (1981). Brasol gives his own probably fanciful and typically antisemitic account of the publication of the book in *Which Way Western Man*, a book by neo-Nazi activist, William Gayley Simpson. Simpson (1978), 652.

88 The other ones were *The Jewish Peril* (London: Eyre & Spottiswoode 1920) and Houghton's own version *Præmonitus Præmunitus: The Protocols of the Wise Men of Zion*

(New York: The Beckwith Company, 1920). See Holmes (1977) and Singerman (1981).

89   Ariel (2011), 94.
90   Botkin (1930), 540.
91   Ibid.
92   In the October issue of his *Hearst's International* series on Henry Ford, Norman Hapgood reproduces a wire from a Russian aid organization in the 'White' embassy in Washington sending money to Cherep-Spiridovich at that address. In the November 1922 issue, Hapgood reprints a 10 January 1922 letter from the Embassy to the Count.
93   For brief surveys of the group, see Caillat (2014); and Ruotsila (2010), 26–30.
94   On this incident, see Senn (1981). The League's other leader was a Russian representative to the Swiss Red Cross named Dr. Iurii Lodyzhensky (Lodyzhenskii), who received financial backing from the exiled Russian Octobrist Party leader Alexander Guchkov.
95   For the history of The Economic League, see Hughes (1994).
96   For an overview of the case, see *The American Bar Association Journal*, XV,10 (October 1929), 591–92.
97   https://www.jta.org/1929/03/10/archive/berlin-forgers-implicated-in-publication-of-anti-jewish-documents.
98   See the 9 July 1923 *NYT* for Bernstein's announcement of the lawsuit later settled out of court. Henry Ford also issued an 'Apology to the Jews.'
99   Spence (2002b), 394.
100   As a leader of the Immigration Restriction League, Kinnicutt embraced 'eugenic' arguments. Spence describes Kinnicutt as a banker, but his 4 July 1939 *NYT* obituary states that he was a prominent lawyer. His brother G. Herman Kinnicutt was a banker.
101   See Spence (1995) for an account of his final days.
102   http://www.theknightsofsaintjohn.com/History-After-Malta.htm.
103   Kellogg (2009), 109.
104   Ibid., 152–53.
105   Ibid., 183–84.
106   Ibid., 110.
107   Hagemeister (2017), 66.
108   Kershaw (1999), 211.
109   Yet another Aufbau supporter was Paul Bermondt-Avalov. In his massive 1926 war memoir *Im Kampf gegen den Bolschewismus*, Bermondt-Avalov also devotes a chapter to a laudatory profile of Grand Duke Kirill, written by Rear Admiral H. G. Graf, the Grand Duke's private secretary. Graf later wrote a memoir entitled *In the Service of the Imperial House of Russia, 1917–1941: The Memoirs of H. G. Graf, Commander of the Russian Imperial Navy.*
110   http://www.theknightsofsaintjohn.com/History-After-Malta.htm.
111   Kellogg (2009), 131.
112   Ibid., 146.
113   Ibid., 246. ROND was *Russkoje Osvoboditelnoje Natsionaljnoje Dvizgenije*, the Russian National Liberation movement.
114   Ibid., 249. Sakharov and Hitler maintained a correspondence when Hitler was in jail following the failure of the Munich Beer Hall Putsch.
115   Spence (2012b), 688.
116   Bisser (2005), 347–52.
117   Ibid., 373.
118   Other reports say it was hit by a mine. Kirill was reportedly one of 80 survivors from a crew of 631.
119   Victoria said he was homosexual.
120   A sarcastic reference to Louis Phillippe II, Duc d'Orléans, who supported the French Revolution and was nicknamed 'Phillippe Égalité.'
121   Botkin (1930), 539–40.

122　Maria, who died in 1920, had inherited property from her husband Prince Alfred, the son of Victoria and Albert of Saxe-Coburg and Gotha. He had acquired the Duchy of Saxe-Coburg following the death of his childless uncle, Ernest II, Duke of Saxe-Coburg and Gotha, who passed away in 1893. Alfred died in 1899. Grand Duchess Maria chose to make Coburg her home.

123　Sullivan (1996), 354.

124　Stephan (1978), 13. Max Scheubner-Richter's wife Mathilde sometimes took Victoria to SA exercises outside Munich.

125　Pool (1997), 87–89. This is the revised edition of the original 1978 book.

126　When Cartier's set up in St. Petersburg, she was one of its sponsors.

127　Chavchavadze (1990), 108–09.

128　Sullivan (1996), 348. Kirill reportedly got the pearls, Andrew the rubies, Boris the emeralds, and her daughter Helen the diamonds.

129　This was Kirill's formal claim to the Russian Throne.

130　For an account of Russian exile politics, see Robinson (1992).

131　Kirill's defenders also created the Munich-based Russian Legitimist-Monarchist Council to challenge the SMC.

132　This move might have forced Grand Duke Kirill's hand in publicly declaring his right to the Throne in his August 1922 statement. See Kellogg (2009), 155.

133　Also known as the Russian Relief Society of America. Inc. It lasted from 1924–1928. See its announcement in the 21 May 1923 *NYT*. Based at 350 West 87th Street its chairman was Henry Goddard Leach. As its honorary chair, the RRF chose H. H. Princess Irina of Russia, Princess Yusupov, Grand Duke Alexander's daughter.

134　Alexander Vassiliev, *KGB Yellow Notebook*, #4, p. 44. The *Notebook* is available via the Woodrow Wilson Center Digital Archive at https://digitalarchive.wilsoncenter.org/collection/86/vassiliev-notebooks.

135　Ibid., 45.

136　For details of Victoria's trip, see Nicholson (2014).

137　22 October 1924 *NYT*. Another member of the Advisory Committee was Mrs. Cornelius Vanderbilt.

138　One of Julia's brothers, Louis Atterbury Stimson, was the father of Henry Lewis Stimson, Herbert Hoover's Secretary of State who later headed the War Department for FDR in World War II.

139　Born in 1876, she died in 1975 at age 99.

140　JTA, 11 December 1924.

141　Nicholson (2014).

142　On Djamgaroff, see Gross (2007) who presents Djamgaroff as an Armenian con man.

143　https://www.marxists.org/history/usa/parties/cpusa/international-pamphlets/n17-1930-Spying-on-Workers-Robert-E-Dunn.pdf.

144　Spence (2012b), 683.

145　Kellogg (2009), 249.

146　Drolet, 62.

147　27 June 1956 *NYT*.

148　Drolet (2015), 66.

149　Bulloch was reportedly born in 1852 and he would have been 82 in 1934. According to Edelen, however, Bulloch died sometime in the 1950s. Edelen also says Bulloch was never Grand Chancellor of 'the Order' as he was the archivist of the Scottish-based Order of St. John, an entirely separate grouping.

150　http://www.theknightsofsaintjohn.com/History-After-Malta.htm. In a 1928 brochure entitled *Heraldry in America*, Pichel, who describes himself as the founder of the American Heraldry Society, says that the group was chartered and incorporated in Washington on 16 February 1924. He lists the group's headquarters as located at the Waldorf-Astoria.

151　Ibid.

152 I have also seen him referred to as 'Reverend Joseph Paul, Count Chodkiewicz.' Father Chodkiewicz died of influenza on 27 December 1936 at age 54. He had parishes both in New York and Virginia.

153 The organization advanced Paul Riedelski's claim to be the King of Poland as Riedelski claimed to be a direct descendant of the old Piast dynasty.

154 The Slav Catholic Club was dedicated to 'fighting Bolshevism' and aiding missionary work. See Drolet (2015), 59–61.

155 See http://pnaf.us/pnaf-history.html. The *TN History* consistently misspells Fleischhauer as 'Fleischauer.' I am correcting the spelling.

156 Diamond (1974), 116–17. Pichel also wrote to Hanfstaengl's aide Hans Rolf Hoffmann in the Foreign Press Section.

157 http://www.theknightsofsaintjohn.com/History-After-Malta.htm. Welt-Dienst was founded in Erfurt by Fleischhauer and Georg de Pottere (1875–1951). There may have been a journal called *White Cross* but, if so, it long predated Welt-Dienst. In 1939, Rosenberg moved Welt-Dienst to Frankfurt. Neither Fleischhauer nor Markov were Balt Germans. For more on Welt-Dienst, see Hagemeister (2017), and Plass and Templer (2013).

158 Winter, the Knights 'Security General,' is listed in Pichel's history of the Knights as 'Master of Ceremonies and Lecturer: President of the Law Enforcement League of Pennsylvania; Life Member of the International Police Association.' The Knight's other security chief, Eugene Tabbutt, ran counterintelligence operations for Robert Shelton's KKK. Tabbutt's group was called the Klan Bureau of Investigation (KBI).

159 http://www.theknightsofsaintjohn.com/History-After-Malta.htm.

160 Ibid.

161 https://www.jta.org/1934/08/02/archive/this-fascist-racket-19.

162 Ibid.

163 Ibid.

164 Ibid.

165 (NY File # 100–15704).

166 Father Peter Baptiste Duffy was a Franciscan priest. As for Walsh, he was Vincent Walsh, a former IRA member who reportedly worked for Japanese intelligence. Coogan (1999), 606–07.

167 Ibid., 608.

168 On Palmer/Pilenas, see Spence (2017), 147.

169 Sutton (1974), 186–89.

170 Wallace (2004), 131–32.

171 Kellogg (2009), 249.

172 Spence (2012b), 684.

173 This was Paul M. Winter who lived in Shavertown, PA, and who distributed Nazi literature in the 1930s. See Carlson (1943), 417.

174 Spence (2012b), 703–04.

175 Von Broenstrupp/Cherep-Spiridovich issued a conspiracy leaflet entitled 'The Jewish Attack on Christian Civilization,' which came from 'Intelligence Bulletin 50, American Tribunal.' See Item 66 at https://www.bolerium.com/images/upload/judaica 2016.pdf. Also see the attempt of the American Tribunal to recruit the Mayor of Syracuse to its ranks as an 'honorary member.' See the 15 July 1938 *American Jewish Outlook* at http://digitalcollections.library.cmu.edu/awweb/awarchive?type=file& item=714986. In 1926, *American Tribunal* was published out of 74 West Washington Street in Chicago. 9 Sheriff Street was in the Lower East Side by the Williamsburg Bridge, and no longer exists.

13

PLOTS AND PROTOCOLS

'The English Baby'

In the mid-1950s, Pichel reconstituted sections of the pre-war far-right network driven underground during World War II under the guise of the Knights of Malta, the same group who now tried to shepherd Goleniewski's career. In this enterprise he was helped by the intervention of the Shishmarev family consisting of Prince Kyril Fedorovich de Vassilchikov-Shishmarev (Shishmarióv), the Comte de Rohan-Chandor and his mother Paquita Louise de Shishmarev (Shishmareff) better known as Leslie Fry. Under the pseudonym 'L. Fry' or 'Leslie Fry,' she published a notorious antisemitic book *Waters Flowing Eastward: The War Against the Kingship of Christ* in 1931 which gave further credence to the bogus Judeophobic claims of *The Protocols of the Elders of Zion*. Louise remained active in far right and antisemitic circles until her death in July 1970. She was even indicted by a federal grand jury for the 1944 Sedition Trial and was interned during most of the war on Ellis Island. But in the anti-Communist and antisemitic circles that Goleniewski now frequented, the recognition from established figures and relations in this milieu only served to reinforce his status.

However, Goleniewski's first known encounter with a Knight came in the summer of 1963 when he met Colonel Corso in his Queens apartment. In a 16 February 1967 affidavit in the form of a statement addressed to Congressman Feighan, Goleniewski claimed that when Feighan, O'Connor, and Corso first met him at his home on 5 June 1963, 'MR. CORSO declared that he had certain proofs regarding my identity as the TSAREVICH AND GRAND DUKE OF MOSCOW.' If this were true, it would have meant that Corso was actually encouraging Goleniewski's claim, presumably on behalf of the Knights.

We also know that Knight of Malta Frank Capell contacted Guy Richards sometime in late 1963 or early 1964 to leak Goleniewski's story. Knight of Malta Cleve

DOI: 10.4324/9781003051114-18

Backster was present when Goleniewski encountered Eugenia Smith in Robert Speller's Manhattan office on 31 December 1963. Goleniewski's first known formal connections to the Knights, however, may have taken place on 30 April 1965 when Frank Capell introduced himself as a Knight Commander of Justice and offered Goleniewski his support on behalf of his fellow Knights, who believed he was the Tsar.

Goleniewski's claim to the throne was critically bolstered in the Pichel Order by Prince Kyril Fedorovich de Vassilchikov-Shishmarev (Shishmarióv), the Comte de Rohan-Chandor.[1] Shishmarev, who died in Portugal on 12 May 1975, served as the Order's Lieutenant Grand Master from 1971 until his death. When Shishmarev first investigated Goleniewski, however, he did so as the Knights' Associate Security General; his wife Emilie headed the Order's hospital committee.[2]

Shishmarev first encountered Goleniewski in January 1965 at Robert and Maxine Speller's apartment at 305 East 40th Street. They met at a time of considerable turmoil. On 13 January 1965, Robert Speller sent a letter to the Synod of Bishops of the Russian Orthodox Church Outside of Russia located on 91st and Park Avenue. Speller's letter to ROCOR rejected any attempt by the Church to reverse its earlier marriage of Goleniewski ('Romanoff') and Kampf in late October 1964. Speller told the Synod that he and a list of others witnessed the ceremony conducted by Father Grabbe and there was nothing the Synod could do to invalidate the marriage.[3]

Shishmarev said that he first became aware of the Eugenia Smith 'Anastasia' story in *Life* magazine and her subsequent book. Highly skeptical, he contacted Speller in early January 1964 by letter and told him that any real Romanov would know the name of the 'English baby,' as that was his nickname at the Tsar's compound. Born in Russia 11 April 1907, Shishmarev claimed that as a child he grew up in the Tsarskoye Selo (the Tsar's Village) outside of St. Petersburg, which is where he said he first met the Tsar's son Alexei. Shishmarev said he was nicknamed 'the English baby' because his mother dressed him in clothes from London. Shishmarev then visited Speller's office where he was quizzed in detail by the publisher and his sons, and he was later introduced to Princess Marina Kropotkin. The Spellers and Kropotkin swore that Eugenia Smith was Anastasia. It was also 'during this meeting' that Shishmarev learned the entire royal family 'survived'. Grand Duke Aleksei was even living in New York under the cover name of Colonel Michael Goleniewski:

> Naturally, this was a bombshell and great news to me as a Russian and a monarchist, and I immediately volunteered my personal services to the Tsarevich and his cause, which is the elimination of Bolshevism-Communism in Russia and the world.
>
> At a subsequent conference with Mr. Speller which followed these astounding revelations concerning the Imperial Family, Mr. Speller who had presumably checked my identity and 'English baby' story with both Anastasia and the Grand Duke Aleksei, phoned the Tsarevich from his office and I held a brief conversation with His Imperial Highness, after which a reunion meeting was arranged. However, because of pressing business commitments which took me outside of New York, this meeting did not take place until January 1965.

During this dramatic reunion between the Grand Duke Aleksei and myself which took place in the Speller apartment and was witnessed by the Speller family, the Grand Duke and I reviewed certain incidents of our boyhood.... The Grand Duke's phenomenal memory concerning details which could only be known by us and a few members of our respective families left no doubt whatever in my mind despite the intervening years of separation, trials and exile, that I was once again in the presence of His Imperial Highness, the Tsarevich Aleksei Nicolaevich Romanov. In addition, the Grand Duke revealed for the first time how his father, the Emperor, in the intimacy of the family circle, used to correct anyone who referred to me as 'the English baby' by saying: 'No-No- you mean our Russian-English baby. After all, his father is one of our Guard officers.'[4]

The Grand Duke Aleksei's striking resemblance to his father, the Emperor Nicholas II, his one leg being shorter than the other, his hemophilia from which he still suffers, his manner of speech and Russian sense of humor, his charm, his somewhat autocratic demeanor and behavior, and his phenomenal memory were all factors which led me to the absolute conviction that the personage claiming to be H.I.H., the Grand Duke Aleksei Nicolaevich of Russia, Heir Apparent and Tsarevich, is in fact none other and my boyhood playmate in Tsarakoe Selo.[5]

But who really was Shishmarev?

Shishmarev's mother was an American named Louise Chandor. She was born in Paris in 1882 after her wealthy widowed mother Elizabeth Fry Ralston met John Alfred Chandor, a Harvard-educated American diplomat from a Hungarian background who was then serving as second secretary at the US Embassy in Paris. Chandor later worked for his businessman father in Russia, and Louise spent time growing up in Russia. At least that was the story Shismarev told.

The truth seems much different. Louise apparently was illegitimate; her father was reportedly a notorious bigamist and adventurer who got wealthy women pregnant and took their money.[6] One contemporary expose read: 'Chandor is a Russian Jew, and a naturalized American. His mother was a serf's daughter, and he is illegitimate; his father is an oil merchant and has the lighting of parts of St. Petersburg.'[7] In his affidavit, Shishmarev writes about his mother:

My mother's maiden name was Paquita Louise de Rohan-Chandor, born of American parents in Paris, France. She is a descendant of the ducal and princely ROHAN families of France and Austria, and of the Counts Rohan-Sandor of Hungary.... my mother was one of but two American ladies married to Russian noblemen, and a close personal friend of the Grand Duchess Xenia, sister of Emperor Nicholas II, and the Grand Duchess Elisabeth (Serge), elder sister of the Empress Alexandra Feodorovna.[8]

The Grand Duchess Xenia, as we have seen, married Grand Duke Alexander, while the Grand Duchess Elisabeth of Hesse by Rhine (Grand Duchess Elisabeth

272 Plots and Protocols

Feodorovna) was the wife of the assassinated Grand Duke Sergei. She then founded her own nunnery, and also became a fan of the *Protocols*. She later gave absolution to Prince Felix Yusupov for murdering Rasputin. Arrested by the Cheka, she was murdered on 20 May 1918.

In 1906, Louise reportedly married a Russian nobleman, and they had two sons, Kyril and Misha.[9] Of his father, Shishmarev states:

> My father's name was Feodor Ivanovich Shishmarev. He was head of the senior branch of the Shishmarev family and House, a graduate of the Imperial Corps des Pages Academy, St. Petersburg, an officer of the Imperial Guards Corps, and on the Staff of H.I.H. Grand Duke Nicolai Nicolaevich, CIC Russian Imperial Armies during World War I....
>
> From 1910 to 1915, my family and myself were residents of St. Petersburg and Tsarskoe Selo, in which latter place the Imperial Family had a magnificent Palace and property in which they resided a great deal of the time. During those years, my father was an officer of the 2nd Sharpshooter Regiment of the Guard (a/k/a Chasseurs de la Garde Impériale), a favorite Guards regiment of the Romanov Emperors since Nicholas I. This Regiment had detachments assigned to duty at the Imperial palace, Tsarskoe Selo; my father, a veteran of the Russo–Japan War, and a Chevalier of St. George and wearer of its Cross, was often on duty at Tsarskoe with his Regiment's detachment.

Michael Hagemeister reports that in 1909 Fyodor Ivanovich Shishmarev (Fëdor Šišmarev) served as a First Lieutenant in the 2nd Rifle Regiment (*2-oi strelkovyi polk*) in the provincial town of Plock, now located in Poland. Hagemeister, however, believes that if he held such an exalted position as his son describes – and with the decorations he claimed for his father – there would have been much more mention of him in Russian documents. Hagemeister believes it far more likely that Shismarev simply fabricated the story about being stationed on the Tsar's estate.

Hagemeister reports that Russian Military Archive records show that Fëdor (Fyodor) Ivanovich Shishmarev was born in 1876 and graduated from the 2nd Cadet Corps in Moscow (not the Corps des Pages in St. Petersburg) and the 3rd Alexander Military School. There is nothing in his record to indicate that he had any connection to the Romanov court. Why then did Shismarev decades later lie about his background, and also become a leading promoter of Goleniewski's claim to the throne?

One clue may lie with his mother's remarkable past. After her husband was reportedly killed by the Bolsheviks, Louise and her children fled Russia via the Trans-Siberian Railway and arrived in San Francisco in the late summer of 1917. By this time, Louise's name was Paquita Louise de Shishmarev (Shishmareff). As we have seen, under the pseudonym 'L. Fry' or 'Leslie Fry,' she remained an influential figure within far right and antisemitic circles throughout her life. She remains best known for her book *Waters Flowing Eastward: The War Against the Kingship of Christ*, first published in Paris in 1931 by Father Ernest Jouin's anti-Masonic journal and publishing house, the *International Review of Secret Societies* (*La Revue internationale des sociétés secrètes*/RISS). The RISS had roots in the Sodality of Pius (Sodalitium Pianum), a Vatican 'anti-modernist' organization established in the early 1900s. In *Waters Flowing Eastward*, Fry promoted the legitimacy of the *Protocols of the Elders of Zion*, which is reprinted in *Waters Flowing Eastward*.[10]

From the *TN History*:

> Civilian experts in the early 20th century on the so-called 'Jewish Problem' became involved with the SOSJ. Among them were Paquita de Shishmareff, Fr. Denis Fahey, Lady Edith Starr Miller Queenborough, John B. Trevor, Jr. and Princess Julia Grant Cantacuzene.[11] Much of their knowledge had been gained from the work of Monseigneur Jouin of France, who, with the blessing of the pope, researched and wrote about secret societies involved with the occult and humanist movements. Father Ernest Jouin appears to have been associated with A. Cherep-Spiridovich, OSJ, in this research during the early decades of the last century.[12]

In 1920 Louise reportedly brought Henry Ford a copy of *The Protocols of the Elders of Zion* and was then employed by Ford's Dearborn Publishing Company. In 1921 she argued in the pages of the journal *La Vieille France* that the *Protocols* were written by a Russian Jew named Asher Ginsberg (Ahad Ha'am).[13] After Ford was legally challenged over his promotion of the *Protocols* by Herman Bernstein, Louise was almost certainly funded by Ford on a highly dangerous mission to Russia to try to prove the text's 'authenticity'. (On the trip, she even briefly met Sergius Nilus.) Louise also appears in the August 1922 article of Norman Hapgood's expose of Henry Ford for *Hearst's International*. Hapgood states that 'Fry' ran a far-right paper out of Scranton, Pennsylvania, entitled *The Gentiles' Tribune*.[14] *The Gentiles' Tribune* was the publication of the Universal Gentiles' League established in Chicago by Count Cherep-Spiridovich. He used the League to help finance the publication of *Secret World Government*.[15]

As for Kyril Shishmarev, he reported that after the Bolshevik Revolution, his family lived in 'the United States, England, France, Germany, and other European countries.' After being educated at the Mt. Tamalpais Military Academy in California, he went to the University of London. Kyril said he spent the next five years in the French Foreign Legion and saw action in Morocco. In 1934 he relocated to Hollywood to work for MGM:

> I went to England for my college education at the University of London. Following this, I joined the French Foreign Legion for five years and was on active service in Morocco with the 4th Regiment Etranger, rising to the rank of Lieutenant during campaigns against rebel Berber tribes.
>
> Following my discharge in 1934, [I] had a series of Legion pen-portraits published by a leading Paris daily, and a book on my experiences as a Legionnaire. Both resulted in being offered a contract with Metro-Goldwyn-

Mayer Studios, Hollywood, as a writer, technical director and actor in connection with a film on the Foreign Legion called 'The Bugle Sounds' to be made in cooperation with the French Government.[16]

Shishmarev left his job as a technical director in Hollywood in 1942 and joined the Army where he trained for infantry duty at Fort Benning. He then transferred to intelligence and said he was assigned to 'G-2, SHAEF, Europe, as a combat intelligence officer and deputy chief special intelligence missions.' After returning to civilian life in June 1945, 'I have been a film writer and associate producer in Europe, and a public relations and business executive in the US and Europe.'

With Louise as his mother, one might think her son would know Boris Brasol. In his affidavit in favor of Goleniewski, however, Shishmarev states: 'I had purposely abstained from becoming involved in any Russian monarchist movements and organizations, either in the United States or Europe' due to:

> incontrovertible evidence that some of these monarchist organizations had been infiltrated and subverted by pro-Bolshevik elements and agents, which resulted in the betrayal and slaughter of untold thousands of anti-Bolshevik Russian patriots by the infamous Soviet security agencies.[17]

A more likely explanation, however, is that he avoided these groups because of Boris Brasol. When World War II broke out, Brasol was investigated by the FBI as a possible fifth columnist. Asked about 'Leslie Fry,' he described her as 'a personal enemy' of his.[18] In the 1950s, Brasol launched the 'All Russian Monarchist Front,' whose executive bureau he led.[19] However Brasol died on 19 March 1963, around the time that Eugenia Smith first came to Manhattan from Chicago. Brasol was also fervently committed to the idea that the Jewish Bolsheviks murdered Nicholas II and his family.

Kyril also provided information on Goleniewski to Richard Deacon, the popular British espionage writer. Deacon wrote that Kyril 'had been of some assistance to me when I was researching my history of the Russian Secret Service.' He then stated that Kyril:

> authenticated the claims of Goleniewski to being the Tsarevich, and confirmed this in a letter to me referring to 'The Secret Circle,' headed by the Tsarevich Alexei … given the cover name of 'Heckenschütze' when it contacted the US Intelligence and British Secret Service through the Tsarevich, a/k/a/ Colonel Michal Goleniewski. Curiously, however, this support for Goleniewski's claim did not seem to please the defector colonel, for he appeared to be highly suspicious of Prince Kyril and his motives.[20]

Guy Richards asked Shishmarev about Goleniewski's hostility to him, and if he felt any bitterness. Kyril replied:

None at all…. Better than that, I understand it perfectly. He's playing a game for his life. He's under tremendous pressures, and he has been for years. He knew that the Poles have sentenced him to death. He knows there are others who would love to help the Poles carry out the sentence. He's got one hell of a security problem. He's got to make decisions on a very different frame of reference. That's why I decided to operate independently. His problems are not mine. My obligations are different from his. I think the obligations of the American people are the same as mine. And they can't expect him to see everything their way either.

Kyril then added:

Anyone who decides to help Alexei in a way he doesn't like must be ready for double jeopardy. Not only will Alexei's enemies be arrayed against him; Alexei will be too…. We must take comfort from the fact that it isn't the voice entirely of the real Alexei. Either he's saying something to suit the CIA, which has been paying him a stipend, or he's speaking to the ears of the Heckenschützes ring, or he's speaking to disarm those on whom he must depend for protection until he can speak for himself.[21]

But just what was the 'Heckenschützes ring,' or what Shismarev also called the 'Secret Circle'?

Secret Circle

On 12 February 1968, Count Shishmarev sent 'Knight Commander of Justice OSJ' Frank Capell a memorandum in support of Goleniewski's claims. Shishmarev wrote:

Tsarevich Aleksei had been promoted and proclaimed in a secret underground ceremony on June 24 Old Cal. & July 7, 1929 New Cal., as Bailiff Grand Cross of Justice OSJ in Underground. The ceremony had been solemnized by Metropolitan of Synod of Russian Orthodox Church in Poland (a member of the underground too) Dionizy (Konstanty Waledynski) with a participation of representative of the Polish Prymas Kakowski Aleksander of Warsaw: Kakowski was a former student of the Theology Academy in St. Petersburg, Russia, being a friend of the Imperial Family (allegedly through Emperor's AdC Count Zamcyski), and after the revolution he helped the members of the Imperial Family to hide in underground in Poland….

Tsarevich Aleksei had been in underground in Poland the Imperial Protector of the Sovereign Order of St. John of Jerusalem, Knights of Malta & Russia, approximately since 1948: senior Knights of Underground OSJ had been connected with the mysterious and pro-imperial Polish nationalistic Christian ultra-secret organization known as Kingly Organization of Poland (in Polish *Krolewska Organizacja Polska*), headed mostly by Polish aristocrats who saw in the Russian Empire the only Slavic possibility for survival of the Polish Nation and for maintaining of Poland's Independence.[22] Despite my efforts nothing more could be discovered about the subterranean K.O.P. and its ramifications, with an exception of the fact that this actually anti-Communist movement had been established in secrecy by Polish–Russian nobility in Poland during the reign of Aleksander 1st.[23]

Shishmarev referred to the Metropolitan Dionysius Valedenskii, who led the Orthodox Church in Poland. The Polish government put enormous pressure on him at the time to create a new Autocephalous Church in Poland independent of the Moscow Patriarchate in what was now the Soviet Union.[24] In October 1929, Dionysus suspended negotiations with the Polish government over the church's new status and said the Polish Autocephalous Orthodox Church would continue free from any interference.[25]

Had the White Russians created a secret political network as well?[26] In a 1966 interview with the right-wing radio host Richard Cotten and reprinted in the *White Book*, Goleniewski claimed that 'in 1930 I was introduced by my father … to the All-Russian Imperial Anti-Bolshevik Movement.' In *Hunt for the Czar*, Guy Richards states that Goleniewski was very hesitant to discuss the supposed anti-Bolshevik underground. Yet *Imperial Agent* is filled with claims about a Secret Circle supposedly founded in 1797 by Paul I and leaders of the Church and Army (but not the hereditary nobility) as the Tsar's own private intelligence and security organization. Richards wrote that when Goleniewski was assigned to 'Danzig,' he was warned by the Secret Circle when Stalin died that there could be a crackdown on anyone seen as anti-Bolshevik. The Secret Circle

> strengthened its protective wall around him. He found that members of the White Guard, the underground's MPs and bodyguards, shadowed him as he moved around Danzig's city streets. This was entirely voluntary on their part, and they worked in shifts, standing duty for the most part in their off hours. They were from all walks of life.[27]

To call this claim far-fetched would be kind.

Here the story remained until Pierre de Villemarest's 1984 *Le Mystérieux Survivant d'Octobre*. Villemarest says Frank Capell kept 'secret Russian dossiers' outlining the creation of a new Secret Circle in two Imperial ukases from Nicholas II entitled 'The Obligation of Russian Orthodox Christians to Clandestinely Combat the Bolshevik Antichrist' and 'The Russian Orthodox Church in Clandestineness.' They called for the creation of secret cells centered on Orthodox clergymen to maintain God, the nation, tradition, and combat the Bolshevization of Russia. Working in cells of no more than one leader and two other members, the network would recruit officers, NCOs, former military men, local and regional administrators, bureaucrats, ethnic groups, and religious denominations.

Villemarest remakes that in examining the ukases, 'Nous reconnaissons là, sans erreur possible, l'inspiration de Cherep-Spiridovich.'[28] Villemarest next states that Cherep-Spiridovich headed the Kiev branch of the Okhrana, where he was an expert in countering terrorist activities.[29] In 1916, he convinced Nicholas II to recreate Paul I's old Secret Circle.

Count Arthur Cherep-Spiridovich, however, never headed the Kiev Okhrana, but Colonel Alexander Spiridovich did. Born in 1873, Colonel Alexander Spiridovich (Alexandr Ivanovič Spiridovič) led the Kiev Okhrana from 1903 to 1905.[30] In May 1905, he was nearly assassinated by a Bolshevik named Peter Rudenko, whom he was using as an informer.

Spiridovich became the head of Nicholas II's secret personal bodyguard in 1906, a position he held till 1916. During World War I, Spiridovich was raised to the rank of an Okhrana Major General. Arrested by the Kerensky government, Spiridovich settled in Paris after the Bolshevik Revolution. As a leading Okhrana expert on terrorism, he wrote *Historie du terrorisme russe, 1886–1917*.[31] In exile, Spiridovich strongly backed the Russian Fascist Party, which labeled the Soviet Union 'Jewish state capitalism.'[32]

After the war, General Spiridovich was involved in a controversy over whether Joseph Stalin had collaborated with the Okhrana. In a letter in the 14 May 1956 issue of *Life*, his widow Nina Spiridovich reported that an article by Isaac Don Levine that claimed Stalin had been on the payroll of the Okhrana came partly from her husband's research. Levine visited General Spiridovich in Paris in 1947 to determine whether a document dubbed the 'Eremin Letter' was true. The 'Eremin (Yeremin) Letter' was supposedly written by an Okhrana Colonel named Alexander Eremin, who reportedly signed a July 1913 letter showing that Stalin had been an Okhrana informer. Spiridovich showed Levine a signed silver decanter given him by his colleagues after the failed Kiev assassination attempt; one signatory was Eremin. Levine believed Eremin's signature helped confirm the authenticity of the 1913 letter. Levine also noted that 'General Spiridovich was the outstanding known survivor abroad of the highest echelon in the Czar's secret police.'[33]

Spiridovich and his wife at the time were desperate to relocate to New York where his wife had relatives. Their visa application, however, had been rejected because of reports that Spiridovich visited Nazi Germany in World War II. Told by Spiridovich that this was not true, Levine went to the American Embassy to lobby for him. Spiridovich and his wife were then cleared to emigrate to America, where Spiridovich died in 1952. A decade later, Yale University acquired his archive from his widow.

As an Okhrana Major General who spent a decade running Nicholas II's personal security unit, Spiridovich would have been familiar with a mysterious organization called the Holy Brotherhood that flourished under Nicholas II's father, Tsar Alexander III. Following Alexander II's 1881 assassination, a group of high-ranking Russian aristocrats created their own private intelligence organization/secret society.[34] The historian Alex Butterworth writes of the Holy Brotherhood:

Credulous as to the existence of a vast international terrorist network, comprising myriad small self-sufficient cells in order to inhibit enemy penetration, the progenitors of the Holy Brotherhood structured their own organization on the same model, with an added dash of the Masonic occult. At the apex of the Brotherhood stood a five-strong council of elders, each the designated contact for a subsidiary group of five, and so on, down to the sixth and eighth tiers of more than 3,000 cells, boasting such assertive or esoteric names as Talmud, Success or Genius.[35]

Butterworth estimates that 'at its peak,' the Holy Brotherhood may have had 700 members, many from the wealthy St. Petersburg Yacht Club. Although the Holy Brotherhood is often dismissed as an aristocratic lark that was soon replaced by the professionals in the Okhrana, one of its founders was Grand Duke Vladimir Alexandrovich, Nicholas II's brother, the third son of the assassinated Alexander II, and the man Nicholas II made governor of the St. Petersburg Military District from 1884 until his death in 1909. Grand Duke Vladimir was also Grand Duke Kyril's father.

Villemarest states that in 1905, the year of the first Russian Revolution, Spiridovich and two Okhrana leaders from the Baltics identified a conspiracy to tear down the monarchy. Villemarest also recalled that he 'had known the son of one of these Baltic officers, [who was] a hero of the Resistance (*Armée secrète*) in France from 1940 to 1944.' He adds, 'his father became closely intertwined (*étroitement mêlé*) in the affair called '*Les protocols des Sages de Sion.*''[36] In the 1930s Major General Spiridovich also received money from Ulrich Fleischhauer's Welt-Dienst to research the history of the *Protocols* as part of Welt-Dienst's defense of the *Protocols* in a famous court case in Bern, Switzerland.

Again showing his confusion between Count Cherep-Spiridovich and General Alexander Spiridovich, Villemarest writes: 'According to Aleksei Romanov, Spiridovich remained constantly in liaison with the Tsar up until the moment when in New York, he was assassinated under strange conditions on 21 October 1926,' when, on the very next day, he was to present his latest book and make important revelations before the Pan Slavic Anti-Bolshevik Congress. This, of course, was an obvious reference to Count Cherep-Spiridovich and his book *Secret World Government*.[37]

Was there a 'Secret Circle'?

In 1948, Pierre de Villemarest recalled eating at a famous 'salon rouge' in Baden-Baden, the capital of the French occupation zone in Germany. He struck up a conversation with a young woman who mentioned the 1921 execution of a notorious White general named Roman von Ungern-Sternberg, who had fought alongside the Cossack Atman Semyanov (Semenov). Villemarest's conversation partner was named Egert-Souvorov; her father was an Austrian officer who fought with Ungern-Sternberg.[38] She added that her father had been part of an organization formed in great secrecy under the aegis of Nicholas II that included both Ungern-Sternberg and Semyanov in the Russian Far East. It also enjoyed the backing of the Japanese government, which controlled Pu Yi, the last Emperor of China and Japan's surrogate in Manchuria.[39] Villemarest said she told him all this because she wanted to know what happened to Pu Yi after the World War II.[40]

Goleniewski also reported that in July 1965 he received a photograph from Alexei Govaloff [Alexei Petrovich Govalov], whom he said was chief of information for the South Russian White government in 1918. Govalov later 'became chief of propaganda' of the Vlasov Army that allied with Germany in World War II. In New York, Govalov worked with the Russian Immigrants' Representative Association, which was founded in August 1957 and located at 349 West 86th Street.

Govalov sent Goleniewski a photograph of Tsarevich Aleksei in a military uniform dated 'Perm 1918.' Goleniewski includes on the same page of the *White Book* a copy of a letter written in English and dated 10 September 1918 reportedly from Rostov-on-Don. Written by 'Aleksei,' it was addressed to a General Otani (Kikuzo Otani) in Vladivostok. Here 'Aleksei' thanks the 'Knights of the Rising Sun' for aiding his escape to south Russia. He adds that 'additional messages' will be sent through Baron Ungern-Sternberg, 'an excellent officer of my regiment,' and that Ungern-Sternberg took the photo that Govalov sent him decades later. Next to the fake letter written in his distinctive handwriting, Goleniewski includes a small photo of Ungern-Sternberg with Grand Duchess Olga Aleksandrovna, a Captain Shvedov, and Grand Duchess Olga Nicholaevna reportedly taken during World War I.[41] There may well have existed a network supported by Japanese intelligence that Baron Ungern-Sternberg played a role in. This claim was folded into the 'secret circle' myth of Romanov survival. The real puzzle is why Govalov sent the picture to Goleniewski in the first place.

Notes

1 Shishmarev's either 15 or 25 August (the date is hard to read) 1966 affidavit is reprinted in *The White Book*. It begins 'KYRIL FEODOROVICH SHISHMARIOV (also spelled Shishmarev, Shismarof, Chishmaref, Shishmareff) a/k/a Prince Kyril Vassilohikov-Shishmarev, Count de Rohan-Sandor. Kyril de Rohan-Chandor, Kyril Rohan-Ralston, being duly sworn....' For the full affidavit, see the *White Book*, 222–30.
2 Shishmarev had been married at least once before in the 1930s to a woman named Winifred Jones of Los Angeles.
3 For the letter, see the *White Book*, 119.
4 This was Fëdor Šišmarev. See Hagemeister (2017), 530.
5 *White Book*.
6 See https://www.findagrave.com/memorial/114297387/john-arthur-chandor.
7 See Anonymous (189–), 46.
8 *White Book*, 222–30
9 In 1934 Misha ('Michael Fry') published a pro-Nazi book on life in Germany entitled *Hitler's Wonderland*, which he dedicated to '*ma mère avec reconnaissance*.' He writes about Hitler's anti-Jewish ideas that 'my theory, which is substantiated by a talk with one of Hitler's personal adjutants,' was that Hitler read the *Protocols* before writing *Mein Kampf*. He also says the *Protocols* were first published in Russia in 1901. Fry (1934), 91.
10 On Leslie Fry, see Hagemeister (2014) for an English language essay.
11 Lady Queenborough (Edith Starr Miller) wrote a two-volume book entitled *Occult Theocracy* in 1931–1932. She was a close friend of Fry and Fry may have inherited some of her wealth after Miller died in 1933.
12 http://www.theknightsofsaintjohn.com/History-After-Malta.htm.
13 Ibid., 220.

14 An article in the 20 April 1922 edition of that paper entitled 'Bernard Lazare a Jew' is cited by Cherep-Spiridovich in *Secret World Government*.

15 19 June 1921 *Brooklyn Daily Eagle*.

16 *The White Book*.

17 Ibid.

18 Spence (2012b), 679.

19 Ibid., 705.

20 Deacon (1982), 112.

21 Richards (1970), 219–20.

22 There was a far-right group in Poland founded in the 1920s called the *Organizacja Monarchistow Polskich* and which published a magazine called *Pro Patria*. But this group was Roman Catholic (not Orthodox) and modeled itself on Action Française.

23 Reprinted in Goleniewski, *White Book*, 234–35.

24 Dionysus (in Polish Dionizy) was born Konstanty Nikolajewicz Waledynski, and in Russian Dionisii (Konstantin Nikolaevich Valedinskii).

25 Snyder (2005), 148–51.

26 Shishmarev also points to an article entitled 'Czar and Family Still Alive, Comrade of Royal Aid [*sic*] Asserts' by Frederick Hollowell that appeared in the 21 July 1929 *New York Herald Tribune*. The article is reprinted in the *White Book*, 236. It is based on a statement by Serge Bechtieff (Sergey Bekhtiev), a former cavalry officer in the Imperial Guard then living in a small town in Yugoslavia. He claimed that a former secretary to Grand Duke Michael named N. Jonson visited him unexpectedly on 15 February 1929. Jonson, who was believed executed along with Grand Duke Michael, said the entire royal family survived, except (awkwardly for Goleniewski), Grand Duke Aleksei who died on 17 February 1923 from 'inflammation of the kidneys.' Jonson said the Royal Family survived miraculously 'after having received the benediction of the Patriarch Tichon, who had sent their majesties a relic of the miraculous image of the omnipotent Holy Virgin.' Then Jonson disappeared to return to the royal family which now lived like hermits waiting for God's judgement against the Bolsheviks.

27 Richards (1966), 94.

28 Villemarest (1984), 209.

29 The Social Revolutionary Party conducted assassinations of Tsarist officials.

30 On Alexander Spiridovich, see Hagemeister (2017), 571–72.

31 Villemarest (1984) cites the book in a footnote on page 209 and assumes it was written by Cherep-Spiridovich, even though the book was published in 1930.

32 Stephan (1978), 55–57.

33 Levine (1956), 102.

34 The best introduction to the Holy Brotherhood is Lukashevich (1959) along with Butterworth (2010).

35 Butterworth (2010), 177.

36 Villemarest (1984), 210.

37 Note that in this version, the gathering of the Congress had not yet occurred when Cherep-Spiridovich died.

38 Egert-Souvorov's name does not appear in many books examined by Michael Hagemeister, who has books on Ungern-Sternberg in English, Russian, and German.

39 Japanese intelligence had been extremely active in Eastern Siberia and other parts of Russia dating back to the 1905 War and continuing up to World War II. See Kuromiya and Pepłoński (2009) and Kuromiya and Mamoulia (2009). The NKVD took the threat of Japanese secret networks very seriously. Recall as well that Russia and Japan fought an undeclared war in Manchukuo in the late 1930s.

40 Villemarest (1984), 211–13.

41 Goleniewski, *White Book*, 183.

14

UNCLE SAM AND THE KNIGHTS

General Willoughby's Web

Sometime in the late 1950s or early 1960s, the Pichel Knights assembled a 'Military Affairs Committee' of leading retired top military officers. They included General Pedro del Valle, Gen. Lemuel Shepherd, Lt. Gen. George Stratemeyer, Maj. Gen. Charles Willoughby, Brig. Gen. Bonner Fellers, Admiral Charles M. Cooke, and Rear Admiral Francis T. Spellman among others.[1]

Major General Charles Willoughby, was the longtime head of military intelligence for General Douglas MacArthur who referred to him as 'my pet fascist.'[2] Willoughby retired in 1951 and was especially active in the Pichel Knights.[3] Regular bulletins from the Shickshinny Knights warning about Communism were edited by Willoughby.[4] Willoughby also published the *Foreign Intelligence Digest*, and he was extremely active in the Madrid-based International Committee for the Defense of Christian Culture (ICDCC), reportedly financed in part by the Texas multi-millionaire H. L. Hunt.[5]

The *White Book* also reprints letters from former General Pedro del Valle, head of the Defenders of the American Constitution (DAC), in support of Goleniewski's appointment as Grand Master of the Order. In a 23 May 1966 letter, del Valle states that 'Aleksei' should also become 'head of the Russian Government in Exile.'[6] A 1 June 1966 letter from retired Marine General Lemuel C. Shepherd endorses 'the election of the Grand Duke Aleksei as Grand Master of the Sovereign Order of Saint John of Jerusalem to fill the vacancy caused by the recent demise of the former Grand Master, Count Felix von Luckner.'[7]

The Knights' links to intelligence and the military, however, upset some European members. From the *TN History*,

> The Prussian Prince Wilhelm Karl, the head of the German Order of St. John, visited Grand Chancellor Pichel in Pennsylvania in 1961 after the death of

DOI: 10.4324/9781003051114-19

Grand Duke Cyril's eldest daughter. She was the wife of the Hohenzollern Pretender to the throne of Germany, the Prussian Prince Louis Ferdinand. Prince Louis Ferdinand had been a life-long intimate and employee of Henry Ford and the Ford family. Wilhelm Karl ended Johanniter Orden association with the SOSJ when he learned that there were no charitable activities undertaken by the SOSJ and that most members appeared to be connected to military and government intelligence.[8]

For its part, the *TN History* offers this explanation as to why the Shickshinny Knights attracted high ranking military officers:

> The SOSJ had lost the majority of its Russian and European membership during the last phases of WWI when the Russian Guard Divisions were thrown into battle in tragic fashion. British and French General Staffs directed all battlefield strategy, and therefore, many suspected that the slaughter of the elite of their allied Russian forces was part of the globalists' agenda....
>
> Much later, the intervention of British and Americans on the side of the Soviet Union during WWII culminated in the great victory for international Communism that was the Second World War. The Allies rounded up and incarcerated free White Russians for deportation to Stalin's death camps in Operation Keelhaul, a result of an agreement made between Roosevelt, Churchill, and Stalin at the Yalta Conference. Forced repatriation by the Allies resulted in the deaths of thousands, and perhaps hundreds of thousands, of White Russians by firing squads or deportation to the Gulag archipelago labor camps.
>
> This consistent action during the 20th century in favor of the Communists with the obvious goal of creating high mortality among anti-communists was conclusive proof to the SOSJ that the western governments were controlled by Internationalists and Communists. Because of this, the SOSJ continued to attract patriotic and nationalistic western military men to its membership, and to operate as an anti-Communist intelligence agency. Admiral Barry Domville [sic.], former head of British Naval Intelligence, was a long serving member of the SOSJ. It appeared that General Douglas MacArthur's entire senior staff was in the Order.[9]

Admiral Sir Barry Domvile, interned by the British during World War II for his fascist sympathies, was listed as the Knight's 'Honorary Grand Admiral.'[10] Yet another Knight with far-right connections was Prince Mihail R. Sturdza a former leading member of the interwar Romanian fascist movement Iron Guard who was Foreign Minister under the Antonescu dictatorship.[11] The *TN History* adds that Prince Avalov also played a key role in the creation of the Knights.

A succession of German Lieutenant Grand Masters during the 1950s is evidence of the continued close ties Grand Master Prince Avalov had to the

German Order of St. John. Scipio Baron von Engelhardt-Schnellenstein from the Palatinate contacted Grand Chancellor Pichel during the period 1949 to 1951 with the offer to help reinvigorate the SOSJ. He was an old associate of Prince Avalov from the Baltic Brotherhood and a veteran of the Welt-Dienst and Fichte Bund propaganda services. He served as Lt. Grand Master from 1954 to 1955.

Grand Master Prince Avalov was brought to the United States from Austria by Operation Paperclip in 1952. His stepson, a former German SS officer with the Russian Volunteer Army of Major General Holmston-Smyslovsky, had been captured by the Communists while working behind the lines for the US Counter-Intelligence Corps in 1949. Grand Master Prince Avalov died on September 30, 1954, in the United States and is reportedly buried at Arlington National Cemetery. Many of the remaining members of Avalov's Grand Priory of Columbia were taken onto the rolls of the American Grand Priory in 1955. The Grand Priory of Columbia consisted of most of those Knights of European descent on the rolls of the Russian National Society at 5 Columbia Circle in New York City under the leadership of Brasol and Sakharov.[12]

The Knights may have served as a 'cover' or liaison to émigré groups whom the Army wished to use. In August 1969, the Soviets leaked a NATO war planning document from the early 1960s to journals like *Stern* to show just how destructive a new war would be. The document, which American authorities confirmed as authentic but outdated, stated that 'scattered indigenous individuals and groups will be disposed to take active measures against Soviet bloc forces.' To encourage resistance, 'scores of units' would be dropped 'behind Communist lines to engage in subversion or escape and evasion and guerrilla warfare.' The document included selected drop zones in Albania, Bulgaria, and Romania. These units would then unite with already active cells in the targeted nations.

According to the NATO study, within the first month of operations, 'it was estimated 14,000 such friendly people would emerge in Communist-held areas' to launch 'sabotage, covert propaganda, infiltration into enemy instillations, planned civil disobedience and formation of groups as action nuclei for future guerilla organizations.'[13] Other cells would be active in nations like Italy and Greece. In other words, the NATO document seems to be describing a kind of European-wide 'Operation Gladio', the anti-communist 'stay-behind' network.[14]

When the *New York Times* approached the Pentagon for comment, it was told by an unnamed official:

> The plans alluded to in the documents mailed to *Stern* sounded a lot like the original orders under which the Special Forces had been established. 'That was the mission Special Forces was originally organized to perform,' he said. 'They were created to foment insurgency.' He explained that the Special Forces … were doing an 'about face' in Vietnam by fighting guerrillas instead of leading them, but this was a natural reversal, he added, since the men must know a lot about insurgency and its tactics.

The official added that there was nothing new about plans for Special Forces in Europe to carry on their own brand of warfare in the event of a general ground war and that this fact had been known since the 10th Special Forces, the original unit, was deployed in Bad Tolz, Germany, around 1951.[15]

The Shickshinny Knights, then, may have operated as a cover for sections of the US military who were still committed to a vision of using far-right émigré networks for special warfare operations in spite of strong resistance from the CIA, and OPC (Office of Policy Coordination) in particular. Through the Knights, elements in the military maintained their own off-the-books version of the Volunteer Freedom Corps.

Finally, the Knights' military network may shed light on a puzzling question that dates back to 1964 when Guy Richards first met Goleniewski. Recall that Richards said he assumed Goleniewski was crazy until

> Days later I learned from a team of American investigators that a mass of evidence supporting his claim was being collected and that it far outweighed the evidence against the claim. I was told, for example, that all four of his sisters had been located. They were reported to be living under rather odd and disarming names in various parts of the world.
>
> Then from independent sources, I was able to establish something which seemed very interesting. I discovered that for a number of years the leaders of the anti-Communist anti-Bolshevik secret organization which has members in Russia, Poland, Czechoslovakia, Germany and elsewhere, were certain that he was the Grand Duke Alexi, Nicholas' son and heir. Their conviction about this was one of the prime reasons why he moved ahead in the Polish Army intelligence network. Was it possible that they, too, could be taken in by a faker?[16]

But who were these 'American investigators' and 'independent sources'? Who were the leaders of that 'anti-Communist anti-Bolshevik secret organization'?

Remarkably, the Knights really did have a private intelligence service of a sort centered on Major General Willoughby. The August 1964 edition of the Knights' publication *Maltese Cross* (the one issue I have seen) lists the full array of publications and organizations linked to the Willoughby and the Knights. The *Maltese Cross* reports its associates are 'the *Foreign Intelligence Digest*, Washington, D.C.; the International Committee for the Defense of Christian Culture, Bonn, Germany.'

Under editor-in-chief Willoughby, the *Maltese Cross* lists other Knights such as National Affairs editor Lawrence E. Griswold, International Affairs editor Dr. James G. Jacobs, Bureau and Archives, Dr. Paul M. Winter, and Circulation and Liaison editor Cmdr. Homer Breit, Jr. Other 'associate editors' include Pichel, General Fellers, Prince Vladimir Elctaki, Georgetown historian Charles Callan Tansill, Frank Capell, Tyler Kent, Felix Graf von Luckner, Professor Dr. Burleigh Cushing Roddick, R.W. Formhals, and H. N. Baron von Koerber among others.[17]

The *Maltese Cross* also lists the associate editors for *Foreign Intelligence Digest*. They include Prince Michael Sturdza (Costa Rica), Dr. Emilo Nunez-Portuondo (Cuba), Marquess de Prat de Nantoulliet (Spain), M. Saint Paulien (France), Dr. Walter Becher (Germany), Hilaire du Berrier (France), Dr. Gerald Shelly (Italy), Dr. E. Gehle (German), Freiherr von Braun (Germany), George Brada (Czechoslovakia), Leo M. Petit (Belgium), Admiral E. Heifferich (Holland), Dr. Lazarus Choumanides (Greece), Dr. Sten Forshufvud (Sweden), Vicomte Amaury d'Harcourt (France), Com. Div. Jean Nepote (France), Abbe Pierre Delecambre (France) and many others.

Various 'associated national and international publications' also appear on the *Maltese Cross* list. They include *A.B.N. Correspondence* (Munich, editor Jaroslav Stetzko), *Accion Christiano Ecumenica* (Madrid), *C.I. Information Bulletin* (Bonn), *International Committee for Defense of Christian Culture* (Bonn, Secretary General G. Jaschke), *C.I.A.S. The East of Today* (Bonn), *German News Service* (Munich), *Pressedienst der Heimat Vertriebenen* (Gottingen, editor Freiherr von Braun), *Agencia Informative International* (Havana-Mexico, Madrid), *Das Ostprussen Blatt* (Hamburg), *Free Pacific Journal Association* (Saigon, editor Rev. R. J. de Jaegher), *The Ukrainian Quarterly* (New York, editor Walter Dushnyck), *H. du B. Reports* (Paris), *Pan American Headlines* (New York, editor Harold Lord Varney), *Citizens Foreign Aid Committee* (Washington, editor Brig. Gen. Bonner Fellers), *West und Ost* (Munich, editor Dr. Walter Becher), *The Herald of Freedom* (Staten Island, editor Frank Capell), *The German Bulletin* (Bonn), *The Christian Crusade* (Tulsa, editor E. L. White), *Der Pommern Dienst* (Hamburg), *Voice of the Federation* (Philadelphia, editor Austin App), *National Center for Scientific Research* (editor Charles d'Eszlary), *Japan-American Culture Society* (Tokyo, President Jiuji G. Kasai), *American Business Council* (Chicago, Rev. Ira H. Latimer), *Der Bund der Vertriebenen* (Bonn, Wenzel Jaksch), *The Weekly Crusader* (Tulsa, Rev. Billy James Hargis), *S.I.A. Slovak Information Service* (Schöngau), *Mexican-American Bulletin* (Mexico City, editor Hugo Salinas) and *Interpol Review* (Paris, editor Jean Nepote).

Why did the Shickshinny Knights seek out Goleniewski and promote him as Tsar? Had Goleniewski been recruited by some intelligence/émigré network prior to his official defection? Was there some deeper intelligence connection? Had he been contacted by this network after he relocated to New York City? Goleniewski's decision to break all ties with the CIA took place in early December 1963; just a few weeks later he contacted Robert Speller and declared himself Tsar. Strong claims demand even stronger evidence, but it is hard to shake the feeling that there might still be more to discover.

Colonel Corso

Knight of Malta Colonel Philip J. Corso, a member of the Military Affairs Committee, played an especially key role in the Goleniewski saga. The son of an Italian immigrant father who worked in a steel mill, Colonel Philip Corso grew up in Pennsylvania, not far from Pittsburgh. An engineering student, he was drafted in

1942. After Officer's Training School, Corso was assigned to the 2nd Infantry as an artillery officer but was quickly recruited into Army intelligence (G-2). After training in England by British MI19, Corso interrogated captured enemy troops first in North Africa and then in Italy. After Rome fell, he became the G-2 Assistant Chief of Staff in the Eternal City, and reportedly received the Order of the Crown of Italy before leaving Rome in 1947.[18]

While Corso served in the Far East as chief of G-2's special projects branch for General McArthur during the Korean War, he met General Arthur Trudeau.[19] A 1924 West Point graduate, during World War II Trudeau helped plan the Army's amphibious landing tactics in the Pacific.[20]

General Trudeau served in Korea under General Matthew Ridgeway, and commanded the Army's 7th Infantry Division, which fought the bloody Battle of Pork Chop Hill. On 24 November 1953, Trudeau was appointed Assistant Chief of Staff of the Army for Intelligence.[21] When asked why he was chosen, Trudeau replied:

> I certainly was known as a person who had very great concern about the advance of world communism and the Russians using it as a vehicle for world domination. As a matter of fact, these feelings had come to the surface, I guess, a number of times – even during World War II, when some of us in the Pentagon saw this threat arising, while they were supposedly our great allies. This may have had something to do with it. I never was really told, and I don't really know.[22]

As head of Army intelligence, General Trudeau directed a series of studies on US POWs in the Korean War.[23] Colonel Corso took part in the study group; for the rest of his life he claimed that in 1953 some 500 sick and wounded American POWs held in North Korea were never exchanged.[24] Corso next served on the National Security Council's Operations Coordinating Board (OCB) from 1954 to 1957.[25] The OCB was led by C. D. Jackson, a former OSS veteran who specialized in psychological warfare planning. Among his other tasks, Corso was the OCB's liaison to the plotters of the Guatemala coup. They included the CIA's Frank Wisner, the head of the Agency's Office of Policy Coordination (OPC), the CIA's action wing.[26] Corso said that while at NSC, Eisenhower assigned him the task of creating the Volunteer Freedom Corps (VFC). After Ike had a heart attack, along with strong opposition from both the CIA and State Department, the VFC project was abandoned. In the late 1950s, Corso was assigned to military intelligence operations in West Germany.

Corso developed a deep hatred of the CIA and the OPC in particular. In the mid-1950s a top US Army official named General Lucius Truscott advised against OPC East Bloc operations. A friend of Trudeau, Truscott coordinated CIA activities in Germany first under then-CIA director General Walter Bedell Smith.[27] As CIA Deputy Director for Coordination, Truscott used his Army rank as 'cover' while he oversaw CIA operations in Europe.[28] Truscott had been appointed by Bedell Smith to get the Agency's OPC network led by Wisner under control.[29]

The CIA's Eastern European operations met with repeated failures from the WiN debacle to the swift capture of operatives sent into the Baltic states and Ukraine. Truscott believed the OPC policy was a disaster. If 70 German divisions could not overthrow Stalin, he once asked, what could a handful of agents accomplish?

The Joint Chiefs pushed for 'captive nation' units supplied and trained by the US military on German soil to fight alongside Special Forces operators. From *The Old Boys*:

> On C. D. Jackson's staff at the Operations Coordinating Board, responsibility for salvaging the guard battalions [of émigrés] fell now to the hotspur Colonel Philip Corso – who until 1955 had liaised closely with Nelson Rockefeller, for some months Eisenhower's Special Assistant for Cold War Strategy.... Now Corso plowed vigorously into the planning stages of a proposal to reactivate the fifty surviving garrisons of Eastern European paramilitaries hanging on in Germany, each running to fifty or sixty carbuncular veterans. Corso's working group projected a training nucleus of division strength, liberation's shock troops, rechristened the Volunteer Freedom Corps.[30]
>
> ... One day both Foster [Secretary of State John Foster Dulles] and the Secretary of Defense, Wilson, after passing around the outlines of the proposal, summoned Jackson and explained that Konrad Adenauer had bristled even at a reference to such a naked provocation on German soil. Corso claims the Chancellor was misrepresented, that freedom's last chance was laid to rest as a result of 'lies by our liberal darlings, Kennan and Bohlen.'[31]

The idea of a Volunteer Freedom Corps, it is worth recalling, formed the climatic conclusion to Guy Richards' 1956 novel *Two Rubles to Times Square*. The book ends with the Russian protagonist headed to Spain to begin his new resistance movement. Interestingly, when President Eisenhower flirted with the VFC, Ike 'even considered asking Spain to host future units of the Corps.'[32] The VFC also makes a curious appearance in the *TN Knights* history:

> The Order was engaged worldwide in anti-Communist activities. Former SS Major General Boris Holmston-Smyslovsky, alias Colonel von Reganau, and US Marine Lieutenant General Pedro Del Valle spurred renewed SOSJ activity in opposition to the Communists in Europe after 1948.[33]
>
> Holmston-Smyslovsky was an old associate of Prince Avalov.... As successor to SOSJ Anti-Bolshevik Bloc of Nations operations, Allen W. Dulles, Colonel William J. Donovan, Gen. Reinhard Gehlen and Lt. General Pedro Del Valle initiated NATO's Operation Gladio during the era of the founding of the US Central Intelligence Agency and German BND.
>
> The US Counter-Intelligence Corps, the Gehlen Organization and the Knights of Malta started the Volunteer Freedom Corps otherwise known as Operation Gladio. Ten thousand men were descendants of the secret army of

Czar Kyril I and the fifty garrisons of East European Freikorps mentioned by Cherep-Spiridovich in the 1920's and by Phillip Corso, OSJ, in the 1950's. Even in the United States, some Knights started anti-Communist domestic militias and supported conservative publications to increase public awareness of the agenda of International Socialism.[34]

Since part of the OCB's task was to utilize thousands of displaced persons as potential recruits for the VFC, national defense and immigration policy became intertwined on the planning staff where Corso worked with Dr. Edward O'Connor, who in 1963 accompanied Corso and Congressman Feighan to visit Goleniewski. In *Roswell*, Corso includes a photo of himself, Trudeau, O'Connor and a mysterious intelligence operator named Victor Fediay at Trudeau's office in Gulf Oil Research in Pittsburgh after Trudeau retired to work for the Mellon-owned oil company.[35]

From April 1958 until he retired in June 1962, General Trudeau ran the US Army's R&D unit known as the Army's Research and Development Command.[36] After Corso returned from Germany in 1961, Trudeau offered him the post of deputy chief of the foreign technology division. Corso said that he was then exposed to many incredible proposals that included Project RAINBOW, an attempt to develop artificial intelligence initiated by Princeton's John von Neumann.[37]

In the summer of 1962, some six months before he retired from the Army, Corso claims he was responsible for helping trigger the Cuban Missile Crisis. That summer he said he was shown photos from a top-secret Army unit located deep inside the Pentagon of Soviet intermediate range ballistic missiles in Cuba. Yet the military was not publicly warning Congress about the danger. Corso said that in October 1962 he contacted New York Senator Kenneth Keating and Congressman Feighan to alert them about the missile deployment to force Kennedy's hand. Corso said he went outside channels because he believed the government had been penetrated by KGB agents. He writes that in April 1962, the month General Trudeau officially retired,

> I had already testified to Senator Dirksen's committee on the administration of the Internal Security Act that it was my belief – and I had proof to back it up – that our intelligence services, particularly the Board of Estimates, had been penetrated by the KGB and as a result we lost a war in Korea that we should have won. The testimony was regarded as classified and was never released.[38]

Corso, Keating, and Feighan arranged for Corso to leak the Cuba news to his 'old friend' the newspaper columnist Paul Scott, who ran the story in his syndicated column carried in papers like the *Boston Globe* and *Washington Post*.

South Carolina Senator Strom Thurmond, an arch segregationist, offered Corso a staff position in early 1963. Thurmond was especially angry at the military for punishing conservative generals whose speeches the Pentagon regularly censored.

They included Trudeau, Admiral Arleigh Burke, and General Edwin Walker. Thurmond wanted Corso's help to pursue his investigation.[39] Right before he officially retired, General Trudeau also testified before the Special Senate Preparedness Subcommittee headed by Mississippi Senator John Stennis against any pre-screening or censorship of remarks by military leaders.[40]

In February 1964, Corso worked as an investigator for Warren Commission member and Georgia Senator Richard Russell, a leading skeptic of the 'single bullet' theory and the idea that Oswald acted alone. Corso now enraged the FBI by claiming that Lee Harvey Oswald was an FBI informant. On 10 February 1964, Corso was challenged by the FBI's Cartha de Loach to offer proof and to name his source. In his memo on the meeting, de Loach said that Corso

> gave me the definite impression of being a rather shifty-eyed individual who fashions himself a great intelligence expert. As a matter of fact, it was quite difficult to pin him down with questions inasmuch as he insisted on expounding his theories rather than sticking to specifics.

Corso merely said that he heard that the FBI had been in contact with Oswald prior to the assassination. Corso then suggested that Oswald was an FBI informant. He said unnamed sources 'within CIA' felt that Oswald's activity in the Soviet Union 'represented a State Department operation,' and that Oswald would have submitted reports to three Americans in the Moscow Embassy: 'Angeli, John Vincent Abidian and Hugh Montgomery.' Hugh Montgomery was CIA Deputy Chief in Moscow while John Vincent Abidian, whom Montgomery replaced, was also chief of Embassy security. There was another CIA officer in the Embassy under State Department cover named Russell August Langelle, whose name Corso garbled as 'Angeli.' Corso recalled that when he was in military intelligence, he received 'a tip' that 'the three named individuals had received reports from a double agent within the Soviet Union' and that the double agent 'could have been Oswald.' In fact, there was such an agent, Pyotr Popov, a Major in the GRU, whose case officer was Langelle.[41] It is again hard to know Corso's supposed source as he never identified him. It is striking, however, that Otto Otepka thought that Oswald might have been a 'false defector' run by American intelligence. Was Otepka Colonel Corso's source? In 1965, Corso officially joined Feighan's staff as an investigator despite FBI protests.[42]

Now long retired, Corso became somewhat famous when he published a 1997 bestselling book entitled *The Day After Roswell*. Here he claimed that some of today's most advanced technology came from the Army's 'reverse engineering' of alien technology taken from a UFO that supposedly crash-landed in Roswell, New Mexico, in July 1947.

Corso even claimed he was at Fort Riley, Kansas, in 1947 where he discovered some boxed up remains from the Roswell crash. They included an EBE (Extra Biological Entity) – a real-life space alien! Yet it was only after he returned from Germany in 1961 to work under General Trudeau at the Pentagon's R&D Foreign Technology desk, that Corso began to understand the alien story. Now he learned how the Pentagon supposedly used crashed alien technology to reverse engineer all kinds of cutting-edge scientific innovations.[43]

Curiously, General Trudeau very much had space travel on his mind. The Army R&D Division under Trudeau worked closely with 'Project Paperclip' Nazi rocket scientists at the Army's Redstone missile command base in Huntsville, Alabama. As General Trudeau put it, 'we had a good portion of the men who had been brought over as scientists from Germany under the old "paper clip" program; they had really done the scientific development on much of what we had accomplished.'[44]

Once Trudeau took over Army R&D, he presented a new assignment for the 'Paperclip' scientists: the military occupation of the moon:

> Since 1957 we've seen the race for space go on, and I must say that one of the papers I'm breaking loose shortly is 'Project Horizon'– I might have mentioned it earlier, but in the earliest days when I was chief of Research and Development it was apparent to me, as I've stated before, that there were military implications in space, and that the exploration, and perhaps even – I won't say occupation, but let's say residence – temporary residence on the moon would be important. Between the Ordnance and the Engineers, I directed them to come up with a plan for landing and living on the moon, and this carried it at least as far as the Russians have gone today with their lunar vehicle. In other words, we designed a comprehensive program. When it was submitted to me and sent to higher levels, the project hit the fan. The greatest secrecy was clamped on it, which seemed to indicate military implications in space, and it looked as though we were taking something away from NASA that they didn't have yet. I now have had the two volumes of that project and my letters of instructions unclassified, and I think one of these days this is another story that should be told.[45]

From the mid-1950s on, Trudeau and Corso pursued an even more ambitious project than the military conquest of the moon. They set out to topple the CIA and the Gehlen Organization!

General Trudeau's War

In September 1955, just a few weeks after his dismissal from G-2, General Arthur Trudeau circulated a document on the supposed 'Fabian Socialist' infiltration of the Eisenhower government that included accusations against top officials at both CIA and the State Department.[46] Trudeau explained his long-standing resistance to the CIA this way:

> Unfortunately, the residual capability of Army covert intelligence with cover in Eastern Europe after the war was resented by the Central Intelligence Agency to an alarming degree. I sensed this on many, many occasions; in fact, it always was a factor in any actions that we took and was a real contributing

factor to difficulties that developed in my own relationship, particularly with the covert segment of the CIA....[47]

Trudeau also took aim at the CIA's role in creating the National Intelligence Estimate (NIE) that helped set long-term government policy. Trudeau claimed the CIA's estimate of the Soviet Union was not based on facts but rather on CIA 'ideology' that adopted an apologetic approach to Russia. To convey its views to the President unchallenged, the CIA would give the Army and other agencies the finished NIE draft the weekend before the final version for the Oval Office was finalized, making it almost impossible to challenge its claims. Again from General Trudeau:

> One of the difficulties that developed between myself and the CIA at the US Intelligence Board level was in the insistence by the Director of that agency that a draft on important subjects which had been under study and preparation for four to eight months would be handled by the Army over the weekend preceding a final meeting. After attempting to comply on many occasions at the expense of great demands on key personnel for weekend time, I finally informed the Board that the Army would not respond to any such long-term studies without at least one week of study being available before the meeting. In such cases, and even at best, we were able to get only a footnote to any objections in small print in the report, which seldom counteracted the impact of the desired language as placed into the report by the Agency itself. The subtlety of such actions should be readily apparent when it is considered that these intelligence reports normally form the base for national security policy or actions resulting therefrom.[48]

But why was the CIA so soft on Russia? Why did the Agency suffer from a string of disastrous intelligence failures with CIA agent networks constantly rolled up by East Bloc services. And what about the CIA's German 'crown jewel,' the Gehlen Organization?

In August 1955, the CIA got Trudeau removed from G-2. The next month the intelligence community was rocked by a report from Trudeau and two of his top aides, Corso and Colonel Earle Lerette. The heading of an FBI document gives a summary of their study: 'Allegations of General Arthur S. Trudeau Re: Infiltration of Fabian Socialists into High Policy-Making Areas of the United States Government.'[49] Trudeau submitted the names of 122 top government officials, many from CIA, whom he labeled 'Fabian Socialists' and whose actions contributed to the distorted NIE estimate.[50]

Years later, General Trudeau recalled:

> A report was prepared in some depth by myself and two associates which analyzed the lines of communications between having decision-making or high decision recommending powers in the White House right on back to

agencies who were feeding them material. We plotted these names and their relationships, where they really had an 'in.' We then analyzed the statements made in a large number of national security papers and very frequently would get down to a clause, sentence, or paragraph which changed the meaning or moderated it very materially. We pinpointed these changes. We pinpointed not only these recommendations on papers submitted but also correlated them with resulting national security policy papers and showed the influence and penetration that was made in this regard which, in most cases, was weakening our overall policy. But somebody let it get in the wrong hands of a man so high that they – and I can't explain that too much – started screaming. It resulted in an Assistant Secretary of State's departure from here, was a factor in my departure, and also resulted in the movement out of the State Department of another man. We had the goods. One person handed it to the wrong man who is still in government – in a sensitive position, I believe.[51]

When asked who took the initiative to begin the study, Trudeau replied: 'One other man and myself because I was convinced we were being sold down the river by equivocation and quibbling in national security policy. There were other aspects also.'[52] That 'one other man' was most likely Colonel Corso.

On 8 September 1955, shortly following his dismissal, Trudeau provided the FBI with a copy of the document so the Bureau could conduct its own investigation. Among the names listed by Trudeau as 'Fabian Socialists' were the CIA's Sherman Kent, William P. Bundy, Frank Wisner, a blanked-out name listed as 'in charge of CIA operations in Germany,' Tracy Barnes, Richard Bissell, Richard Helms, and, of all people, James Angleton! From a 7 October 1955 FBI memo from R. R. Roach to Belmont:

Memorandum 10–6-55 indicated there would be a new eruption in relations between Central Intelligence Agency (CIA) and G-2. James Angleton of CIA furnished information on 10–6-55 indicating that __ G-2, has been disseminating derogatory information concerning CIA operations and employees to a 'Mr. X.' described as a Democrat, former Government official, with outstanding reputation. CIA story is that __ went to Mr. X with motive of striking at CIA. Mr. X subsequently came to CIA and related all facts.[53]

The FBI summarized Trudeau's claims as follows:

General Trudeau furnished the Director with charts and memoranda purporting to substantiate charges that certain individuals in and out of Government were influencing the United States to take a soft policy against Soviet Russia and world communism. General Trudeau furnished the names of individuals, some allegedly with Fabian socialist leanings and possibly some with communist leanings, who, he stated, had penetrated certain policy-forming organs of our Government, including State Department, CIA, Operations Coordinating

Board, Planning Control Group, and Planning Board, as well as academic research units at Harvard, Princeton, and Johns Hopkins Universities, Massachusetts Institute of Technology, and the Ford and Rockefeller Foundations which do research work for the government....

Bureau files reflect that Colonel Lerette and a Lieutenant Colonel Philip J. Corso, Operations Coordinating Board, associates of General Trudeau, disseminated information regarding Fabian socialist charges outside the Executive Branch and that G-2 did not handle the matter of Fabian socialists in a secure and prudent manner.... As a result, Colonel Lerette was accused by CIA of releasing false and derogatory information about that agency.[54]

Far-right former Congressman Charles Kersten was also briefed by Trudeau. From a 7 October 1955 FBI memo:

On September 15, 1955, Charles J. Kersten, formerly a member of Congress and now attached to the staff of Nelson Rockefeller at the White House, called on the Director [Hoover]. Kersten stated to the Director that he wanted to discuss matters pertaining to the infiltration into the executive department of individuals with Fabian Socialist philosophy. Kersten stated he had discussed this trend with General Trudeau and with ___ (this is Colonel ___, who is attached to the Operations Coordinating Board).

The FBI reexamined its files and concluded: 'FBI files do not contain any specific, concrete, and conclusive proof that the subjects are Fabian socialists as charged by General Trudeau.'[55]

Trudeau and Corso raised the Fabian specter yet again during the Kennedy administration. A 31 May 1961 FBI memo entitled 'L'Allier-Belmont' lists names of JFK advisors that the Trudeau network previously attacked and states:

In 1955, ___ identified before the Subcommittee the following individuals as 'Fabian Socialists' attached to the White House staff: W.W. Rostow, McGeorge Bundy, Arthur Schlesinger, Jr., J.B. Wisner. ___ recalled that ___ identified the following Senators in attendance during the above testimony: Senators Bridges, Keating, Dirksen and Congressman [Senator] Hill.[56]

As we know that Otto Otepka tried to block W. W. Rostow as a security risk from joining the Kennedy administration, was Otepka also using General Trudeau's list of 'Fabians' as well to block other Kennedy nominees?

The FBI memo suggests that the source was Colonel Lerette, as he is later identified as opposing Trudeau and Corso's attempt to raise the 'Fabian Socialist' red flag yet again. The memo states that Lerette heard that in May 1961 Trudeau began contacting members of Congress and mentions 'the assignment of ___ to his staff,' a reference to Trudeau hiring Corso to the R&D department. The memo continues:

Lerette stated that he warned against his [Trudeau] becoming involved in 'this old issue' again and reminded Trudeau how the 'Fabian Socialists' issue was partly the cause of his problems in 1955 with the 'Dulles family' which caused his transfer from Army Intelligence. According to Lerette, Trudeau has a fetish about security and intelligence work and cannot keep his fingers out of that area even though his present responsibility is that of Research and Development.

Thanks to Trudeau's Congressional connections, 'at some opportune time' the Senate Internal Security Subcommittee 'will hold an open hearing with __ as a witness in order to "smear" the Kennedy Administration.' Corso told Art Bell that he testified before Congress at this time including at a hearing that he claimed remained classified.[57]

Trudeau's despised CIA officials included one 'who went off his rocker' and died. Trudeau meant Frank Wisner as he said the man who 'was most responsible' for opposing Trudeau was 'the individual in charge of covert intelligence operations for the CIA.' In *Roswell*, Corso claimed that during his four years working at the White House, the CIA even put a tail on him. When he returned from Germany to work for Trudeau in 1961

They put the tail back on and I led him down every back alley and rough neighborhood in D.C. that I could. He wouldn't shake. So the next day I led my faceless pursuer right to Langley, Virginia, past a sputtering secretary, and straight into the office of my old adversary, the director of covert operations Frank Wiesner [*sic*], one of the best friends the KGB ever had.

I told Wiesner to his face that yesterday was the last day I would walk around Washington without a handgun. And I put my.45 automatic on his desk. I said if I saw his tail on me tomorrow, they'd find him in the Potomac the next day with two bloody holes for eyes, that is, if they bothered to look for him. Wiesner said, 'You won't do that Colonel.' But I reminded him very politely that I knew where all his bodies were buried, the people he'd gotten killed through his own ineptitude and, worse, his cooperation with the Russians. I'd tell his story to everyone I knew in Congress. Wiesner backed down, Subsequently, on a trip to London, Wiesner committed suicide and was found hanging in his hotel room.[58]

Corso and Wisner knew each other when Corso was on the NSC staff. Yet besides misspelling Wisner's name, the claim that Corso was followed every day for years by the CIA, and the idea that Corso could bully his way into Wisner's CIA office, the fact was that Wisner no longer headed the Directorate of Plans. He suffered a severe nervous breakdown in September 1958 and spent time in a mental hospital while Richard Bissell took over his job. After his recovery, in 1959 Wisner became CIA London station chief. He didn't kill himself on a 'trip to London.' Wisner committed suicide on his farm in Maryland in October 1965, a few years after he retired from the Agency.

Corso's near obsessive hatred of the CIA pours out in the pages of *Roswell*:

> Our own military intelligence personnel told us that the Soviets were traf-
> ficking so heavily in our military secrets that they knew things about us in the
> Kremlin before we knew them in Congress. The army at least knew the KGB
> had penetrated the CIA....
>
> But here's what kept the roof from falling in on all of us. The KGB and CIA
> weren't really the adversaries everyone thought them to be. They spied on each
> other, but for all practical purposes, and also because each agency had been
> thoroughly penetrated by the other, they behaved just like the same organization.
> ... But when it came down to loyalty, the CIA was loyal to the KGB and vice
> versa.... CIA penetration by the KGB and what amounted to their joint spying
> on the military was a fact we accepted during the 1950s and 1960s....[59]

As part of an attempted take down of the CIA, Trudeau tried to discredit the
Gehlen Organization. Corso told Art Bell that during Trudeau's clash with the
CIA, Army CIC (Counter-Intelligence Corps) in Europe gathered intelligence that
proved the Gehlen Org. had been penetrated by the Russians. As G-2 head,
General Trudeau established contact with the first West German Ambassador to
Washington, Dr. Heinz Krekeler after the Embassy opened in May 1955. Trudeau
said that one day in June he visited the Embassy to discuss the need for a German
military attaché to liaison regularly with the Pentagon. Krekeler then invited him
to meet with a high German official who was visiting the Embassy that afternoon.
Trudeau claimed that to his complete surprise, Krekeler then introduced him to
German Chancellor Konrad Adenauer.[60] A short time later, 'Mr. Allen Dulles, the
Director of the CIA, had sent a letter to the Secretary of Defense saying that he
had lost all confidence in me because of this contact I had made with Adenauer.'

Dulles hit the roof for a reason. When Trudeau spoke with Adenauer, he warned
him against relying on the CIA-financed Gehlen Org. From Trudeau's oral history:

> There really could have been some big noises made over this because the CIA
> was not in too good repute anyway, and they were losing an awful lot of
> agents in their German setup who were being exposed – perhaps because they
> built too fast; at least they were penetrated. We were worried about an outfit
> that already was penetrated having charge of German security in Bonn, in the
> area where our war plans and everything else would be exposed. Of course,
> since then those plans were leaked to the Russians, to the East; the things that
> I surmised would happen have happened. They all have happened. There
> have been many serious defections. I have no apologies for what I tried to do
> for American security....
>
> I have no apologies to make at all. What has happened in the way of
> penetration of the West German government and the loss of highly classified
> war plans and intelligence is, to me, still an indication that I was absolutely
> right in what I tried to prevent in 1955. Read the books about Gehlen's

organization. I'm not apologizing to anybody. Nor do I regret that I expended as much effort as I did, even though it put a real crimp in my Army career.[61]

Trudeau's clash with Dulles even reached the New York *Daily News*. In a 1 September 1955 article, *Daily News* writer John O'Donnell reported that Trudeau had been forced out of G-2 by Allen Dulles personally. O'Donnell said that Dulles first sent a letter to the Secretary of Defense; the feud then reached President Eisenhower, who sided with Dulles. In his initial letter, Dulles

> charged that the Army's top intelligence officer 'without consulting the Central Intelligence Agency' had talked with West Germany's Chancellor Adenauer here last June in 'an effort' to 'undermine' the confidence of Adenauer in a hush-hush CIA-bankrolled setup in Germany, headed by … Gehlen. Furthermore, said Dulles, the General has expressed doubt about the reliability of Gehlen as an individual and the security safeguards of the mystery organization.[62]

Just a few years later, Goleniewski would bring down Heinz Felfe and largely prove General Trudeau's fears justified.

Herman Kimsey

One of Goleniewski's most prominent supporters was a former CIA employee turned Knight of Malta named Herman Edward Kimsey, who had been dismissed by the CIA on 20 September 1962 during a purge of Agency personnel known as the '701 Program.'

Goleniewski's supporters claimed that Kimsey was a high CIA official. Part of the confusion stems from an erroneous 20 January 1965 UPI story about Goleniewski.[63] The story states that Kimsey was the 'former chief of the CIA's Analysis and Research Division.' Kimsey, however, actually served as the head of a highly technical section in CIA that specialized in examining documents for evidence of forgery among other things. By the time he met Goleniewski in the mid-1960s, Kimsey was working low-level private security jobs.

Born in 1917 in Gallup, New Mexico, and raised in Oregon and California, Kimsey worked from 1935 to 1939 in the lumber industry. In 1939 he became a forest ranger and studied at the US Forest Service School for Fire Control and Prevention. When World War II broke out, Kimsey was assigned to the US Army Chemical Warfare School for Instructors at Camp Claiborne, Louisiana. He also served in a Combat Intelligence Regiment.

After the war, Kimsey resumed his classes to become a forest ranger. In 1946–1947, however, he decided to make the military his career; he now began studies at the US Army Counter-Intelligence Corps School for Special Agents at Fort Holabird, Maryland. Kimsey also earned a college general equivalency diploma in 1948 via the United States Armed Forces Institute (USAFI). Made a Master Sergeant in the CIC by 1953, Kimsey served on a combat CIC team in Korea. He next became the enlisted Chief of the Technical Laboratory at the CIC Center as well as enlisted Chief of the Special Projects Technical Laboratory (CIC), Far East Command.

After joining the CIA in March 1953, Kimsey's activities included briefing members of police and intelligence agencies from some 50 nations on his expertise in document detection. He worked in some six foreign nations as well. Kimsey would also claim that in January 1962 he had received 'one of the largest individual Monetary Suggestion Awards' from the Agency.

During his CIA career, Kimsey rose to a GS-13 rank in the CIA's Technical Services Division (TSD), specifically in the Graphics Aids Reproduction Division (GARD) of the Agency's Analysis and Research branch. Kimsey served as Section Chief of the Questioned Document Analysis Section (QDS). A 12 April 1961 CIA document describes him as 'Chief of the Analysis and Research Section, Graphic Aids Reproduction Branch, Technical Services Division.' Another CIA document lists Kimsey as 'Section Chief' of the 'Questioned Document Analyst.' It describes his role this way:

> The Analysis and Research Section is responsible for advisory, developmental and service work in the field of Questioned Document Analysis in support of overt and covert activities of the Agency. This includes technical testing and research into handwriting and document evaluation or authentication. The Section Chief directs the assignments of projects, studies developments in scientific fields supporting authentication work, advises Agency officials on the current and long-range capabilities in authentication or evaluation of documents and prepares recommendations for direction of the program.

The Section Chief

> under the policy direction of Staff Chief and administratively reporting to Branch Chief, provides administrative and technical supervision to Questioned Document Analysts in the Section and continually ensures that their technical competence is maintained. The Section Chief reviews requests for analysis of documents and contents, establishes priorities for use of Section Personnel and suggested available external facilities for analysis or research.

Kimsey's dismissal may have been based in part on his Type-A personality that led him to seek help from a Washington-based psychiatrist named James Sheridan. In a 7 October 1960 interview with the CIA, Sheridan said that he had been seeing Kimsey for four years, and that Kimsey initially consulted him because he suffered from high blood pressure. At the time, Sheridan observed, 'Kimsey then [was] alienating associates with "pushing," driving type of approach and with impatience with the work of others.'

Another CIA report from 27 July 1965 comes in the form of an interview with one of Kimsey's old associates in the Questioned Documents Section of the TSD by Curtis M. McSherry, the Chief of the TSD/Liaison Security Staff. The employee told McSherry of her receiving a recent phone call from her former colleague. She reported that

> Kimsey considers himself responsible for all the good work involved in the establishment of the QDS capability of TSD. Kimsey further reiterated that desk officers within TSD had advised him that there is no respect for QDS in TSD, that work they sent to QDS to be done usually was not done in time.... A questioning of Mrs. __ regarding her assessment of the personal characteristics and stability of Kimsey reflects the following. Mrs. __ said that Kimsey, while an Agency employee, had psychiatric problems and at one time had been seeing a psychiatrist. She does not know further details regarding this. When he left the Agency (701), he was visibly shaken and upset, however, his basic pride and personality prevented him from showing outward agony at the decision. He instead covered up by his many references to the many other jobs that had been offered to him in the Agency or made references to the fact that he was not leaving at all but would be working as a consultant on some of the more important Agency problems. Mrs. __ indicates that she considers him to be a paranoiac. He, however, alleges that he has strong loyalties to the Agency and tries to always continue the façade that he is current on matters relating to the Agency and is importantly involved in Agency activities. He continues to live at Vivian Hotel in Washington, basically a very lonely person.

The CIA used the 701 firings to dismiss Kimsey after nine years in the Agency, apparently due to his problem managing his staff.

In *Le Mystérieux Survivant*, Goleniewski states that he first met Kimsey after he arrived in the Washington area. Villemarest writes that Kimsey was assigned to examine Goleniewski's past for the CIA, although there is no obvious reason why Kimsey would be assigned such a task. In the middle of a supposed general conversation about Polish and Russian history in October 1961, Goleniewski suddenly blurted out, 'I am the Tsar: Everything that has been said is false.' Kimsey now began independently investigating Goleniewski's claim only to be fired himself in 1962.

Kimsey, however, never once mentioned that he had met Goleniewski while he was in the CIA. In July 1966, a right-wing commentator named Richard Cotten devoted his radio show to Goleniewski, Kimsey, and Cleve Backster, the Spellers' polygraph expert and the Knights' 'Chief Interrogation Officer.' Cotten asked Kimsey: 'It is my understanding that … the CIA has in its files the documentation needed to establish the identity' of Goleniewski as 'Aleksei Nicholaevich Romanoff,' Cotten then said: 'Could you give us some information on this?'

Kimsey replied:

> Yes, Mr. Cotten! This information which you have just mentioned, and which is in the files of the Central Intelligence Agency, was brought to my attention some time ago. Then early in the stages of this investigation, after my severance of relationship with the Central Intelligence Agency in 1962, I

became interested in this case through the intercession on the part of an old Counter Intelligence Agent friend of mine, Mr. Backster, who felt that there was a development phase of this case which was not within the realm of his technical capacities and which I believe you have discussed in a previous interview. He had asked me to intercede, considering the fact that my background was particularly directed around identification techniques, including personal identification.[64]

Baxter, however, only met Goleniewski on 31 December 1963. Kimsey clearly never met or conducted any research on Goleniewski while he was in the CIA.

On 3 June 1965, Kimsey submitted a 'Confirming Affidavit' in the planned legal action by the Spellers against Eugenia Smith. He swore that he had been quoted accurately in a 19 January 1965 Guy Richards *NYJA* story ('CIA Challenged to Bare Date on Czarevich Case'). After stating later in the affidavit that he had 'terminated my relationship with the CIA on September 20, 1962,' Kimsey added that he was convinced Goleniewski was the Tsarevich.[65] To confirm this, he continued, 'The tests and the affirmative results thereof were as follows according to subject individual.' He then listed such proofs as 'anthropometrical test compared with material from sister and other relatives' and 'fingerprint comparison with those of the Tsarevich taken during his visit in London in 1904' and so on.[66] By reference to Goleniewski's 'sister,' Kimsey could only have meant Eugenia Smith.

Kimsey, however, could never examine the proofs since he based it all on the statements of the 'subject individual' Goleniewski. He never could independently confirm anything. Goleniewski claimed that the CIA and British intelligence – although he said they had the proofs in their files – denied him access to them. According to his own testimony, Kimsey's involvement with Goleniewski began thanks to his friend and fellow Knight G. Cleve Backster.[67]

Kimsey called one of his former CIA colleagues in 1964 about Goleniewski, codenamed BE/VISION by the CIA.[68] His call generated a 9 December 1964 CIA internal memo to the Director of Security by Ralph Tobiassen. The memo was based on a CIA-approved phone call to Kimsey by a CIA employee named Eugene Wintets; the call followed up on a Kimsey call to the Agency to discuss Goleniewski. Tobiassen picked up Kimsey from a Washington hotel and drove him to the meet with Wintets. (Both men used cover names when dealing with Kimsey.) This memo combines both Wintets and Tobiassen's encounter with Kimsey:

KIMSEY began with a rambling dissertation on the VISION story starting back in 1924. There was very little continuity to KIMSEY's statements, and he consistently got away from his subject while talking.

KIMSEY claims to have the confidence of VISION and it finally evolved later in the interview that KIMSEY is attempting to swing a deal with the Agency whereby the Agency would give to VISION some documents which VISION claims he needs to establish his true identity as the Tsarevich.

Specifically, these documents are: a passport, some dental records (on file somewhere in Europe) and a fingerprint card.[69] KIMSEY, throughout the interview, referred to VISION as 'the Tsarevich' and appears to be convinced that VISION's claims are true and also that Eugenia SMITH is in fact the real Anastasia and therefore VISION's sister.

KIMSEY stated that VISION's sole intentions are to establish his name and claim his rightful inheritance for the benefit of his newborn son.[70] He said VISION still wields influence within White Russian circles all over the world and has more information which he has not yet divulged which would be of benefit to this Agency. KIMSEY further stated that if VISION fails to obtain his goals, that there will never be another defector out of Poland.

In the middle of KIMSEY's dissertation, he was interrupted by TOBIAS-SEN and asked how he, that is KIMSEY, fits into this story and what connection did he have with VISION. KIMSEY stated he was recommended by one CLEVE BACKSTER, an old associate who operates a commercial polygraph firm, to one Robert SPELLER, who is the publisher of a book being written or already written by VISION. KIMSEY claims to have co-authored a book, years ago, about systematic formalizing of large volumes of documents and KIMSEY's former employment as a Questioned Document Analyst purportedly made him suitable to help SPELLER and VISION straighten out a large volume of material.

As Goleniewski never did write a book, Kimsey likely was referring to the planned memoir to be written by Goleniewski in collaboration with Guy Richards.

In any case, the memo continues:

He [Kimsey] went on to say that Eugenia SMITH was polygraphed by Cleve BAXTER under contract by Robert SPELLER to establish her bona fides in connection with a book or a magazine article about SMITH's claims to be Anastasia. SMITH at first maintained that at the time of the Russian Revolution she was a lady-in-waiting to the Czarina and had escaped. However, KIMSEY said that BAXTER broke SMITH on the polygraph and got her to admit that she is in fact Anastasia and not a former lady-in-waiting. She claims to have come to the United States about 1924 at the direction of her father, the Czar, with a large amount of money which was to be used in furtherance of White Russian activities. She is alleged to have spent this money instead. In connection with the writing of a book or a magazine article about SMITH's claims to be Anastasia, she is now suing Robert SPELLER for more money. This trial is due to start in New York on 14 December 1964. VISION expects to be subpoenaed to appear at this trial as a witness to establish the credibility of SMITH's story. This subpoena has not been issued yet. VISION feels that he will appear in a very poor position at this trial if his own identity is not established; he needs the documents previously mentioned.

KIMSEY stated that some time ago, *Life* magazine was sued by Robert SPELLER in connection with a story printed in *Life* about the Russian Royal Family and Anastasia. It is not clear just what happened in this situation, however, KIMSEY stated that *Life* settled with SPELLER out of court of over $100,000.00 when SPELLER confronted *Life* with alleged unquestioned documentary proof of his claims.[71]

Kimsey next told the two CIA employees

that a woman by the name of [Anna] Anderson, who lives in Europe, and for twenty years has claimed to be the real Anastasia, is in fact an illegitimate daughter of the Czar by a famous dancer. He also stated that the real Czar did not die until 1952, when he was poisoned.[72] KIMSEY stated that there is an international conspiracy at the highest levels and named Lord MOUNT-BATTEN and the 'French Premier' as part of this conspiracy to deny VISION and 'Anastasia's' claims so that the $400,000,000 lodged in banks in England and France and in the United States will stay there. KIMSEY said he and BAXTER and SPELLER at the moment are not getting any money from VISION, however, should VISION's claim be established, he will no doubt pay them at a later date.... KIMSEY stated that VISION knew that Premier Khrushchev would be out of office six months before it happened and that the present rulers in Russia, KOSYGIN and BREZHNEV, are only temporary and when they leave the Kremlin line will be much harder.

Finally, the CIA report noted of Kimsey, 'he is not currently employed.'

After being dismissed by the CIA, Kimsey worked for Security Associates, a Washington, D.C.-based closed circuit and burglar alarm company run by Leonard Davidov. On 23 September 1983, a long-time JFK assassination researcher named Harold Weisberg wrote a letter to Professor Philip Melanson. In response to an article that wrongly stated that Kimsey served as 'CIA chief of research and analysis under Dulles,' Weisberg remarked:

I very much doubt this. He had no background for it at all and from my knowledge of R&A going back to OSS he was anything but the type for that job. They went in for heavily accredited scholars like Bill Langer.... After the CIA fired Kimsey, he [Kimsey] actually lived in Davidov's offices, which were then in an old apartment house in Washington, the Chas[t]leton. He worked for Davidov's Security Associates, sometimes as a guard.

Kimsey got a temporary job in 1964 working security for the Goldwater campaign. Kimsey and Davidov knew Hugh McDonald, who had taken a 90-day leave from the Los Angeles County Sheriff's Department to work for Goldwater.[73] In 1967 a group called 'Americans Building Constitutionally,' apparently a John Birch Society-friendly front group created for tax purposes, also tried to create a one-man business for Kimsey entitled 'Forensic Science Institute' in a single room located on 17th and G Street. Meanwhile inside the Knights, Kimsey served as its 'Associate Chief of International Intelligence.' (The other associate chief was Kyril de Shishmarev.)

Up until his death in January 1971 during a botched operation, Kimsey was ceaseless in his promotion of Goleniewski. He also used Goleniewski as a pretext to keep in contact with the CIA. Yet his credulity knew no bounds. On 14 April 1966, Steven L. Kuhn, the chief of the CIA's Personal Security Division, wrote a report on an interview he conducted with Kimsey, whom he met on 12 April at the Roger Smith hotel in Washington to hear him talk about Goleniewski. The last two paragraphs of Kuhn's notes about the meeting read:

1. Among other things mentioned by Subject was that another sister of Anastasia [Eugenia Smith] is married to Heinrich Himmler and Subject [Kimsey] said that he has seen Heinrich Himmler in Washington. Subject also said that Colonel Goleniewski is living in an apartment house in New York owned by Martin Bormann.
2. According to Subject, they have sufficient proof that Colonel Michal Goleniewski is a Romanov and that there is a great attempt being made to discredit Colonel Goleniewski.

Another of Kimsey's strange communiqués to the CIA took place on 15 May 1969. It involved a conversation between Kimsey and Harlan Westrell, the Deputy Director of Security for Personnel Security.[74] From the memo:

KIMSEY was alerting the Agency to the 'explosive and dangerous frame of mind' of GOLENIEWSKI as reported to KIMSEY by Cleveland BAXTER in New York. KIMSEY reported that GOLENIEWSKI, among other matters, had told BAXTER that 'he [GOLENIEWSKI] is too old to do anything himself but he had been the restraining element in keeping other people from going ahead here in the United States. He indicated that he was holding some nebulous group "in check."' GOLENIEWSKI had apparently made this statement relative to fourteen Generals, twenty KGB agents, and various other officials who 'have been liquidated' within the past two months.

On 10 August 1970, a CIA official sent a report on Kimsey that involved Baxter. It is unclear who wrote or received it but there are two names, Mr. Donovan E. Pratt and Mr. Edward Kaluski and 'CI/TRCO/GT Stanton/C/CI/R&A' with a hand-written note that reads 'CI/SIG.' Clearly this was Angleton's Special Interest Group. The memo is entitled 'Herman E. Kimsey Shenanigans':

Mrs. __ of TSD just told me in the course of a visit that Herman E. KIMSEY of (BE)VISION fame, a former TSD-nick called her on the phone and tried to get her to have lunch with him, so he could get her to analyze the handwriting of some homosexuals who were the 'real murderers of Martin Luther King.' KIMSEY gives out that he is working to exonerate RAY for this peccadillo.

Mrs. __ said she avoided contact and will report this to Mr. __ TSD Security Officer (previously she told __ but he told her to forget it and evade KIMSEY). I suggested she better tell __ as KIMSEY is capable of any action involving her or the Agency.

KIMSEY also told Mrs. __ that his side-kick E. Cleve BACKSTER has found a way to use a lie detector on plants even to detect people who murder others in the presence of a plant that serves as a witness.... Nothing succeeds like excess....[75]

Kimsey apparently also knew journalist Edward Jay Epstein. A Kimsey affidavit supporting Goleniewski had been published in *Ramparts* and may have caught Epstein's attention. In his 17 May 1981 article in *The Washington Star* on Goleniewski, Epstein writes: 'At least one CIA official whom I spoke with, the late Herman E. Kimsey of the CIA's Office of Security [sic], after leaving the CIA said that various physical tests proved to his satisfaction that Romanoff was indeed the tsarevich.'[76]

Given the complexity of the Goleniewski story, it is hard to know fully what role Kimsey played in the entire affair and why. All one can really do is rely on the known evidence. That evidence strongly argues that Herman Kimsey failed to convince his former CIA associates that Goleniewski was the Tsar; Kimsey did succeed, however, in leaving the impression that after his dismissal from the Agency he had more or less gone insane.

Notes

1 On the Military Committee see Scott (1993), 212–16, and Pichel (1975), 192. Also see Russell (1992), 537. This list of the 'Armed Services Committee of the Sovereign Order of St. John of Jerusalem' in Russell comes from Willoughby's correspondence and includes Lord Malcolm Douglas-Hamilton, who died in a plane crash in 1964.
2 Quoted in Grossman (2014), 257.
3 For a summary of Willoughby's military career, see. Campbell (1998).
4 Formhals (1979), 196.
5 On the ICDCC, see Grossman (2014).
6 Del Valle's letter is reprinted in the *White Book*, 220.
7 Reprinted in the *White Book* on page 221. Shephard was Chairman of the Military Affairs Committee. In the letter, he reports that at a 3 May 1966 meeting of 'the Supreme Council of the Sovereign Order of Saint John of Jerusalem' in Washington, the group voted to accept 'the identity of Colonel Michael Goleniewski as the Grand Duke Aleksei Romanov, only son and heir of HIM Nicholas II.' Shephard, a four-star Marine general, represented the Marines on the Joint Chiefs of Staff until his retirement in 1956. He came out of retirement to run the Inter-American Defense Board (IADB) that promoted 'military solidarity' in Latin America from 1956 to 1959.
8 http://www.theknightsofsaintjohn.com/History-After-Malta.htm.
9 Ibid.
10 On Domvile, see Griffiths (1980).

11 Deletant (2006), 63. Sturdza was dismissed by Antonescu after the failed Legionary Rebellion in 1941. He went into exile for the remainder of the war, fleeing first to Denmark and then later the USA. His autobiography *The Suicide of Europe* was published by Western Islands, the publishing arm of the far-right John Birch Society, in 1968. See Sturdza (1968). The *TN History* reproduces an entry in the *Congressional Record*, 110/42 (9 March 1964) of remarks by Congressman W. J. Bryan Dorn honoring Pennsylvania representative Daniel Flood for his stand on the Panama Canal. In it is reprinted an article from the 16 February 1964 *Sunday Independent* of Wilkes-Barre, Pennsylvania, reporting on a meeting paying tribute to Flood by the Pichel Knights. Presided over by General Willoughby, the gathering included General Pedro del Valle, Prince Sturdza, and Pichel.

12 http://www.theknightsofsaintjohn.com/History-After-Malta.htm. Prince Bermondt-Avalov died in New York City in 1974 at age 96 or 97. (The *TN History* date may be a typo for 1974.) Formhals (1979), 187. Bermondt-Avalov reportedly created his own Order of St. John in Denmark in June 1946 that was formally incorporated in March 1954. He claimed descent from the Knights 'Priory of Dacia' in Denmark, which reportedly shut down in the sixteenth century.

13 See the 26 and 28 August 1969 *NYT* articles on the leaked US plan.

14 The definitive history of Gladio is surprisingly still to be written although British scholar and journalist Stephen Dorril has been working on one for some time. See Nuti and Riste (2007) for a useful overview.

15 28 August 1969 *NYT*.

16 Richards (1966), 42–43.

17 Tyler Kent was a file clerk at the American Embassy in London who was jailed for passing confidential cables to a pro-Axis spy ring in 1940. After his release from jail he married a rich heiress, Clara Hyatt and moved to Florida. He bought a local newspaper *Putnam County Weekly* which he filled with anti-communist, pro-segregationist and anti-Jewish articles. He was also close friends with George Deatherage who ran a KKK-style group called Knights of the White Camellia. Kent was a 'Knight Commander of Justice' in Pichel's knights. For a recent account of his wartime treachery, see Willetts (2015). See also Coogan (1999), 604–5.

18 Corso described his background in a 1997 interview on the Art Bell radio show when Corso was promoting his book *The Day After Roswell*. The 23 July 1997 interview is available on YouTube at https://www.youtube.com/watch?v=IlKffehEsG8.

19 Corso dedicated *The Day After Roswell* to the memory of General Trudeau.

20 It is possible Trudeau met Guy Richards at this time as Richards served in the same theater and studied amphibious landing practices.

21 For background on Trudeau, I draw on *Engineer Memoirs: Lieutenant General Arthur G. Trudeau*. Publication Date: 01 February 1986. This is a lengthy oral history conducted by an Army historian and available at https://web.archive.org/web/20070823024357/http://www.usace.army.mil/publications/eng-pamphlets/ep870-1-26/c-15.pdf. I will refer to it as 'Trudeau.'

22 Trudeau, 232.

23 See a profile of Trudeau in the 15 January 1958 *NYT*.

24 Philip Shenon, 'U.S. Knew in 1953 North Koreans Held American P.O.W.'s,' 17 September 1996 *NYT*.

25 Corso said he obtained his post through General Trudeau. Corso (1997), 38.

26 Hersh (1992), 347.

27 Trudeau mentioned some of his close friends that included OSS founder Bill Donovan, Eddie Rickenbacker, General Mark Clark, and General Truscott. Trudeau, 268.

28 Truscott officially left the CIA in June 1959.

29 Kisatsky (2005), 79.

30 For background on the Volunteer Freedom Corps, see Carafano (1999) as well as Brands (1988). Brands notes that 'the prime mover on the subject of the VFC was C. D. Jackson.'

31 Hersh (1992), 411.
32 Carafano (1999), 34.
33 Recall that General del Valle was a member of the Shickshinny Knights Military Committee. On del Valle and the Knights, see Coogan (2004).
34 http://www.theknightsofsaintjohn.com/History-After-Malta.htm.
35 A Russian émigré, Fediay worked for 20 years in an Air Force Intelligence program called the Aerospace Technology Division. He later joined the staff of Senator Strom Thurmond. On Fediay, see Strasser and McTigue (1978).
36 Trudeau was brought in to manage the Army R&D to prevent it from being eclipsed as the military now found itself in competition with ARPA (the Advance Research Projects Agency, later DARPA). On ARPA, see Corso (1997), 256.
37 Corso said RAINBOW stalled out because the computers were not powerful enough.
38 Corso (1997), 277–78.
39 Trudeau, 311.
40 25 January 1962 *NYT*.
41 The Russians arrested Langelle on 9 October 1959 and expelled him. On 12 March 1963, *Izvestia* ran a long story on American espionage that discussed Langelle at some length. It was translated by FBIS *Daily Report*, issues 51–52.
42 See a 4 April 1965 *Chicago Tribune* profile of Corso available at https://www.cia.gov/library/readingroom/docs/CIA-RDP75-00149R000100960003-6.pdf.
43 Corso's book began as a conventional memoir known as the 'Thousand Battle Memoir.' On Corso, see Cypher (1993).
44 On the 'Paperclip' Germans, see Corso (1997), 283, and Trudeau, 296.
45 Trudeau, 341. In Appendix A of *The Day After Roswell*, Corso (1997) reprints some declassified documents from Operation Horizon.
46 Arguments from that report would echo in attacks on Eastern Establishment 'elites' in Frank Capell's newsletter as well as in Capell's *Treason is the Reason*. The John Birch Society would also promote a book on this theory. See Martin (1966).
47 Trudeau, 259.
48 Ibid.
49 From an 8 March 1957 FBI memo.
50 For some of the Fabian Socialist documents and discussion, see https://ia801708.us.archive.org/33/items/foia_Trudeau_Arthur_G.-HQ-1/Trudeau_Arthur_G.-HQ-1.pdf.
51 Trudeau, 261.
52 Ibid.
53 The memo can be read here: https://documents.theblackvault.com/documents/fbifiles/Trudeau_Arthur_G.-HQ-1_text.pdf.
54 Ibid.
55 8 March 1957 FBI report from William C. Sullivan to A. H. Belmont.
56 The memo and the full FBI discussion of the Trudeau report can be found on the Internet in the Black Vault declassification by Ernie Lazar and available at https://archive.org/details/nsia-a-trudeau/page/n18/mode/2up.
57 Corso (1997), 169.
58 Ibid., 94.
59 Ibid., 92–93.
60 Trudeau, 262.
61 Ibid., 267–68.
62 Cook (1961), 555. (Cook is citing O'Donnell.)
63 The CIA kept a cutting of the story which can be viewed here: https://www.cia.gov/library/readingroom/docs/CIA-RDP75-00149R000300140018-8.pdf.
64 Goleniewski, *White Book*, 153. Goleniewski reprints a 16 July 1966 transcription (Vol. 4, No. 1, Section 28) of 'Script Number 163–166 Broadcast on July 11–14, 1966.'
65 CIA documents say that Kimsey was dismissed from the Agency in July 1962, not September.

66 Alexei Romanov was born in 1904. Most likely this may be a typo for '1909,' as Kimsey claimed Alexei's fingerprints were taken in London in 1909. Alexei, however, never visited London in 1909. Summers and Mangold (1976), 375. They say Alexei never visited England at all.

67 Grover Cleveland Baxter joined the CIA in April 1948 as the Agency's first polygraph expert. In 1949 Baxter left the CIA to head the Keeler Polygraph Institute. Kimsey may have first met him when Baxter worked at an interrogation instructor at the CIC school at Fort Holabird.

68 The 'BE' designation may stand for Baltics/Eastern Europe.

69 This is the passport with the reported microdots. The CIA would only send Goleniewski a copy of his passport and kept the original.

70 Goleniewski's daughter Tatiana, possibly a mistake in the transcription.

71 This is the only reference I know to the alleged suit.

72 Why Kimsey thought Goleniewski's father was 'poisoned' remains a mystery.

73 In 1967 McDonald retired from the Los Angeles County Sheriff's Department as a division chief. He then directed security at the Hollywood Park Racetrack. In 1976 McDonald published *Appointment in Dallas: The Final Solution to the Assassination of JFK*. In it he spun out a tale that he and Kimsey supposedly met 'Saul,' a mercenary who was visiting the CIA, whom McDonald claimed killed Kennedy. For a look at the 'Saul' story as presented by McDonald, see http://jfk.hood.edu/Collection/Weisberg%20Subject%20Index%20Files/M%20Disk/McDonald%20Hugh%20C%20For%20Grove%20Press/Item%2001.pdf.

74 The exchange is cited in a 22 November 1974 'Memorandum for the Record' by Jerry G. Brown of the CIA Security Analysis Group.

75 See https://www.archives.gov/files/research/jfk/releases/104-10120-10597.pdf.

76 Although Epstein makes it sound as if their encounter was relatively recent, Kimsey died in early 1971, a decade before Epstein's profile of Goleniewski.

CONCLUSION

Imaginary Castle

On 1 July 1965, Paul M. Winter, the 'Deputy Security General' of the Knights, sent out an 'International Appeal for Historical Facts' in order 'to conduct a searching investigation with the appointment of appropriate committees to ascertain the true facts and fate of the Russian Imperial Family.'[1] In a 29 November 1966 letter from Pichel to Herman Kimsey, the 'Grand Chancellor' reported that based on the response, 'some time ago' the Knights' Supreme Council had unanimously voted to offer Goleniewski the position of 72nd Grand Master.[2] Pichel then reported that Goleniewski 'refused the offer.' He also

> 'dismissed' Speller as his representative and agent. After months of collaboration in which he consumed days of Speller's time at home and at his office, he neither paid Speller for his services nor returned the books, papers and documents that Speller had obtained for him.[3]

Goleniewski treated Guy Richards the same way.

Why did Goleniewski seem to self-destruct?

Years later Goleniewski would claim that he rejected the Grand Master offer solely because of Pichel. Yet in 1965–1966 he destroyed his connection to the one group that had openly embraced him as well as his other supporters like the Spellers.

One clue to Goleniewski's actions may lie in Hamburg. It too involves yet another 'Anastasia,' not Eugenia Smith but the far more famous Anna Anderson. Although she had been identified as a Polish peasant woman named Franziska Schanzkowska by a German court in the 1930s, Anderson appealed the decision and she kept on appealing. In 1961 a Hamburg court again rejected her claim. In 1964, she filed for a reversal in a different Hamburg court. The new legal battle lasted until March 1967 when she again lost. During Anderson's last Hamburg trial, Goleniewski issued his own statement to the court that was ignored due to its lack

DOI: 10.4324/9781003051114-20

of evidence. Around this same time, Polish intelligence began circulating information about his past.

Goleniewski faced another potential nightmare in the Speller's legal confrontation with Eugenia Smith. If the case went to court, Goleniewski could be subpoenaed and forced to testify. As he was already widely despised by the White Russian community, it would be easy for the Poles and Russians to leak even more personal information to make him look ridiculous. It is also clear that Eugenia Smith was prepared to use her own insider information against him. After all, she already exposed the fact that the two 'Grand Duchesses' that Goleniewski claimed were his sisters, were actually Kampf's elderly relatives.

Did Goleniewski back away from the Knights' offer to become their new Grand Master out of personal fear of facing on the one hand 'active measures' against him by his old colleagues in Polish intelligence and yet more humiliating revelations by Eugenia Smith on the other? Did he make a deal with Polish intelligence to put a stop to whatever was being planned for him?

In August 1966, *Komsomolskaya Pravda* attacked Goleniewski by name and accused the CIA of deliberately manufacturing a pretender to the Romanov throne. 'In reality, this self-appointed man is nothing less than a sinister creation of American intelligence.'[4] Ironically, the charge also came at a time when many White Russians dismissed Goleniewski as 'a stupid Soviet fabrication.'[5] Yet if Goleniewski was not 'a sinister creation' of the CIA, he clearly was a 'fellow traveler' for an extreme right-wing network inside American military intelligence and the Shickshinny Knights.[6] More important, was the fact that *Komsomolskaya Pravda* attacked Goleniewski by name, itself an example of the Soviets sending him a clear warning?

Whatever his reasons, Goleniewski's move baffled the Knights. Their feelings were perhaps expressed in an 8 June 1968 letter from Kyril Shishmarev to Goleniewski when he wrote:

> Your Imperial Highness was several years ago (when Von Luckner was Lt. General of the Order and its Deputy Grand Master) offered the Grand Mastership of our illustrious Order, so closely identified with Your Family, reign and traditions since Emperor Paul I, its first Russian Grand Master and Protector. Had Y. I. H. accepted this great Honor, you might have been saved a great deal of the trouble and problems you have been faced with since your entry into the US as a political refugee from communism.
>
> For the Order is, in a very quiet way, much more powerful and active for Justice than it ever allows the world to know.[7]

At the bottom of the page, Shishmarev added this note: 'Incidentally, Y. I. H. is not the only one who has been at times obliged to use a "cover" name for specific military & personal reasons.'

Yet if even the Knights were baffled by Goleniewski's actions, they were not alone. One of the most important spies of the Cold War, he was also one of the most baffling. Although born and raised in Poland, was he Polish? His birthplace was Polish only by accident of war. His parents came from somewhere in the Russian Empire. Was he raised as a Pole? Or as a White Russian living in exile in Poland?

If Goleniewski's relationship with his former colleagues in Polish intelligence was bitter, at least it was comprehensible. Much stranger was his antagonistic relationship to the CIA, and to James Angleton in particular. For decades Angleton suggested that Goleniewski – perhaps the most productive defector the Agency ever acquired during Angleton's time in the CIA – was somehow in the employ of the KGB. Was there any relationship between Goleniewski and Anatoliy Golitsyn's decision to defect almost exactly one year later?

Angleton's ability to marginalize Goleniewski, however, was no match to Goleniewski's ability to marginalize himself. If the KGB wanted to employ Goleniewski in some diabolical disinformation plan, it could not have chosen a more self-defeating approach than by having him declare himself Tsar. Yet as weird as Goleniewski's claim was, arguably even stranger were his supporters in the pseudo-chivalric Shickshinny Knights of Malta. Why did this bizarre organization embrace Goleniewski's crazy claim to the throne? For that matter, why did the ROCOR apparently legitimate Goleniewski's claim with his religious marriage?

So much of the strange history of the Knights also seems to trace back to the debates in the national security apparatus. The fact that C. D. Jackson who oversaw both Colonel Corso and Dr. O'Connor in the Operations Control Board of the National Security Council was an expert on psychological warfare only adds to the puzzle. It was C. D. Jackson's *Life* magazine that also promoted the Eugenia Smith/Anastasia hoax.

Was Goleniewski an actor in a psychological warfare campaign to somehow rally the 'captive nations'? Is that why the Russian Orthodox Church Outside of Russia let Father Grabbe marry Goleniewski in a church-sanctioned ceremony? And why the Spellers and Shismarev loyally supported Goleniewski's otherwise absurd claim? But why would the CIA and/or military intelligence select such a strange figure as Goleniewski to play the part?

In spite of so much fog, the evidence also suggests at least one simple truth: Goleniewski helped destroy major Soviet operations at a time when the West badly needed a win in the spy game. It is also possible he may well have uncovered a dangerous Soviet intelligence network that worked closely with 'former' Nazis on both sides of the Iron Curtain even if the claims around that network were often exaggerated and conspiratorial.

Vladimir Nabokov once remarked, 'there's nothing abnormal in the fact of a chess player's not being normal.'[8] Goleniewski, however, really was not normal. Had he endured a breakdown after defecting? No doubt his abrasive personality had its deepest roots in Poland. But did his reception in America somehow tip him over the brink? But was that because of something that happened to him after he arrived in America? Or was it that once he was in America, he was now free to openly indulge his Romanov obsession? Or was his imperial claim itself just one more ruse?

What seems undeniable is that Goleniewski more and more retreated into the Imaginary Castle of his mind; his Kew Gardens apartment now his private Imperial Palace. Starting in January 1975, he began issuing ukases in the form of his cheaply produced *Double Eagle* monthly newsletter, each issue filled with one bizarre conspiracy or another. Such was the fate of a man whom the CIA's Tennent Bagley once described this way, 'I considered him to have had the sharpest, most sophisticated C-I mind that ever became available to Western intelligence from the other side. He caused more damage to Soviet Bloc intelligence than any single defector before or since.'[9]

And so it came to pass, that when Goleniewski died, no one in America bothered to take note of the passing of one of the greatest spies of the entire Cold War.

Well, almost no one.

A paid death notice appeared in the *New York Times* on 7 July 1993 announcing the passing of Michal Goleniewski on 2 July at Lenox Hill Hospital after a long illness. After listing his role in Polish intelligence, and his contribution to the security of the USA, the notice concludes: 'He is mourned by his wife Irmgard and daughter Tati and many friends around the world.' Yet the most telling line in the notice comes at the very beginning. It reads: 'GOLENIEWSKI – Michael. Retired Consultant is dead at age 71.'

Notes

1 The appeal is reprinted in Goleniewski, *White Book*.
2 Goleniewski was voted 72nd Grand Master on 3 May 1966. *White Book*, 70.
3 Ibid., 163.
4 28 August 1966 *NYT* story reprinting a UPI dispatch from Moscow.
5 Massie (1996), 154.
6 See Bendersky (2002).
7 Shishmarev letter reprinted in the *White Book*, 130.
8 Interview with Bernard Pivot for *Apostrophes* (1975).
9 8 January 1997 letter from Tennent Bagley to Pierre de Villemarest.

APPENDIX I: NODDY AND THE PIG

Sometime in the late 1950s, three Polish intelligence officers reportedly became MI6 agents in place with the most important spy codenamed "Noddy." Noddy, reportedly a Colonel in Polish intelligence, was said to be MI6's first major penetration into the Iron Curtain since 1945. If so, his recruitment may have been more a result of an ongoing political struggle in Poland than any special competence on the part of MI6.

In the late 1950s, the Polish security services were caught up in a fight inside the Communist Party between the "revisionists," who were viewed as liberals and who wished to continue de-Stalinization. They were dubbed "the Pulawy group." Although they backed Gomulka in his 1956 confrontation with Russia, they felt betrayed as Gomulka sought support from a more authoritarian faction dubbed the "Natolin faction," better known as the "Partisans."[1] Their leader was General Mieczyslaw Moczar.[2] The Partisans were hostile to liberal reformers, many of whom were Jewish. The Partisans now wanted to restrict the number of Jews in government positions.

In 1958, the same year Goleniewski contacted the American Embassy in Bern:

an envelope marked "Secret–Deliver to British Ambassador" had been pushed under the door of a junior British diplomat's apartment in Warsaw. Inside, written in capital letters in English, were three pages describing the structure of the Polish intelligence service, the *Urzad Bezpieczenstwa*, in London, a list and description of Polish intelligence officials based in Britain, and details of the relationship between the UB and the KGB. On the third page, the writer stated that he would supply more information in return for a large payment in Polish currency and a promise of asylum, should that prove necessary.... The Polish intelligence officer was codenamed Noddy.... Noddy's access to senior KGB officers and his regular journeys to Moscow for briefings provided unprecedented information and gossip about both Soviet intelligence and politics.[3]

One of Noddy's MI6 Warsaw case officers was Colin Figures, who later served as MI6's director.

Six months later, "another UB officer approached an embassy secretary and offered his services ... the Pole supplied information about operations against British and American citizens living in Warsaw, especially a blackmail operation against an American diplomat."[4] In other words, the Polish sources were offering inside information about issues inside the American Embassy. In 1960, British intelligence reportedly recruited yet another source.

Polish foreign counterintelligence reportedly spent years working an angle that some of Goleniewski's close colleagues inside Department I had ties with British intelligence. The probe ruined the careers of several officers with one case dragging on until 1980![5]

As previously mentioned, on 13 October 1980, the MI6-friendly journalist Robert Moss wrote an article for the *Daily Telegraph* entitled "Goleniewski: The Anonymous Mole." Moss reported that in March 1960 Goleniewski

> was secretly approached by the top KGB liaison officer attached to the Polish secret service. The KGB told him: "There is a pig in the First Department" and asked for Goleniewski's assistance – as the man most trusted in the UB [*Urzad Bezpieczenstwa*] in tracking down the Polish "traitor."

The CIA's Pete Bagley tells a similar story:

> But then, somehow – it has never been revealed how – the KGB detected Goleniewski's sniping. So sensitive was their source that they didn't even tell the Polish service through routine channels but came just to Goleniewski. His main KGB contact in Warsaw asked him to help them identify a "pig" in the UB's foreign intelligence component whom they had learned was leaking its secrets to the CIA. Goleniewski, of course, recognized the "pig" as himself. In the weeks that followed he felt attention turning in his direction, and when his travel abroad began to be stopped on one excuse or another, he realized that the game was over, and he had to get out before the trap sprang on him.[6]

The story of Noddy and the two other Polish sources, however, suggests, the Russians may well have been put on alert without their suspicion stemming from leaks of Sniper information.

But when did the Russians first get a hint that there might be a "pig"?

The one declassified Heckenschütze report we have is dated 25 January 1960. In it, Goleniewski explicitly states that some information received by Polish counterintelligence (Department II) "did not come from me." He believed that the Poles were not on to him but that other information on UB activities had been picked up by Soviet agents operating in the BND. "Thus," he writes:

there continues to be the very real danger that my information can also be picked up to the degree that it has been or will be turned over to other Western intelligence services…. It is clear that in this situation my activity can only be carried out with the greatest caution. I have restricted it only to the most important and most urgent matters and I hope that you agree with the motto "better a cautious worker than a dead hero."

Goleniewski, of course, did not know about the MI6 network in Warsaw. Instead, he assumed the leak must have come from some Soviet penetration into the BND.

In short, Goleniewski indicates there was some kind of leak back to Polish counter-intelligence in late 1959 or early 1960 of spy information from Western sources in Poland that did not stem from him. Was Raina's mention of the "pig" a few months later simply a follow-up comment about the leak?

In his 17 May 1981 *Washington Star* article, Epstein, like his friend Bagley, believes that Colonel Raina only informed Goleniewski about the "pig" shortly before Goleniewski defected. Epstein writes that in "the next few weeks" before "his departure from Warsaw," a panicked Goleniewski photocopied "thousands of Polish intelligence and KGB documents." In fact, Goleniewski had been copying documents for months if not years. According to Epstein, the fearful spy headed off to Berlin where he and his fiancée "Irma" [*sic*] fled West. Yet there is no record of any suspicion of Goleniewski as a potential traitor in the WOW proceedings. The Russians and Poles were stunned by his defection; Colonel Sienkiewicz lost his job over it.

In his 13 October 1980 *Daily Telegraph* piece, Robert Moss writes that Goleniewski first learned about the pig from Raina sometime "in March 1960" or about a month-and-a-half following his Sniper letter. However Moss's source may have slanted the date since the March 1960 timetable for the KGB's first hint that they had a traitor in Polish intelligence corresponds to dramatic developments with the Sniper material that led to the exposure of the Portland spy ring. Raina's revelation could bolster the claim that the Russians were tipped off to a mole inside Polish intelligence by MI5 Director Sir Roger Hollis. Yet Peter Wright in *Spymaster* claimed that the tip to the Russians could only have come in the last week of July. Bagley and Epstein, however, have Goleniewski being told about the "pig" and realizing the Russians were on to him just a few weeks before his defection. Needless to say, none of these scenarios matches sequence of events in the WOW proceedings.

Finally, if Colonel Raina did tell Goleniewski about a possible "pig," it may have had nothing to do with Goleniewski but rather with leads the Russians and/or the Poles had picked up about Noddy and the two other MI6 spies who became active in Warsaw in the late 1950s.

APPENDIX II: A WEIRD YANK IN WARSAW

In the 1920s, a baffling tale appeared of a Romanov princess living in Poland. The story is recounted in *I Wanted to Write*, the 1949 memoir of Kenneth Roberts, a highly popular writer and journalist from the 1920s to the 1950s. During World War I, Roberts served in Siberia with the American expeditionary forces. While in Siberia, he was much taken with the Romanovs and the rumors swirling around them, so much so that on the boat returning from Siberia to San Francisco, he co-wrote a one act play about the Romanovs' demise entitled *The Brotherhood of Man*. While in Russia, he also heard rumors that one Romanov princess, the Grand Duchess Tatiana Nikolaevna, the second daughter of Nicholas II, had escaped her executioners.

As a roving European correspondent for the *Saturday Evening Post*, Roberts visited Danzig in 1923. Roberts wanted to be close to Russia as he waited for permission by the Soviet authorities to enter, permission that never came. Roberts befriended the US Consul General in Danzig, a Mr. Dawson. Thanks to Dawson, on 16 July 1923 Roberts traveled in a train compartment reserved for the American ambassador from Danzig to Warsaw. While on the train, Roberts met a fellow American named Roy C. Woods from Chicago, a mysterious figure who carried a pearl-handled revolver in his hip-pocket. As Roberts later recalled, Woods "had been moving back and forth between Danzig and Warsaw for the past two months, though nobody could find out what he was doing."

Woods told Roberts that he had been an Assistant State's Attorney for Illinois out of Chicago. He then decided to take a vacation in Poland. Much later in the conversation, Woods explained:

> He had received a call from a New Yorker who represented the Russian royal family. Before the royal family had met its end in the Ekaterinburg well, the Tsar had exported from Russia a nest egg of crown jewels and immensely valuable paintings, all of which were now in a warehouse, crated and ready for

shipment. Furthermore, the representative said, the Tsar's daughter, Tatiana, had been helped to escape from Ekaterinburg by a sympathetic Bolshevik officer and, in peasant garb, made her way over the Urals, across Russia and into Poland, where she was now living as a peasant with a peasant family. The Russian representative, Woods said, had commissioned him to visit Poland and arrange transportation to America for the jewels, the paintings, the girl, the Bolshevik officer who had helped her escape, and three Russian women who had accompanied her from Ekaterinburg.

The name "Tatiana," of course, struck a chord with Roberts:

It was, of course, true that American intelligence officers in Siberia had reportedly reported the rumor that one of the Tsar's daughters had escaped, as Garland and I had set forth in *The Brotherhood of Man*; but Woods's story struck me as fantastic. Why, I wanted to know, should a New Yorker bother to go all the way to Chicago and seek out Woods, when a thousand better-qualified New Yorkers could have been sent on such a mission.

Woods modestly said it was because of his reputation as an astute prosecutor.

Had he seen the girl? I asked.

Certainly he'd seen her. He saw her every week. He took a plane from Warsaw, landing near the village in which she lived, and went secretly by night to visit her.

Roberts then asked Woods how he knew that the girl was really Tatiana:

With that Woods really took down his hair. In his wallet, he had a picture of the Grand Duchess Tatiana, clipped from a magazine. There couldn't be any mistake about it, he insisted. The girl he visited each week was unquestionably the girl in the pictures. He had gifts that she had given him, among them, a gold cigarette case decorated with the double-headed eagle of Russia in white enamel, surrounding a diamond the size of a bean. He had, he insisted, seen the packing cases containing the portraits and the jewels: some had been opened for him: he had handled the jewels, seen paintings, some by great masters, Van Dyck, Rembrandt, Holbein, Titian. If ever he could overcome the girl's fear of Bolshevik reprisal, he proposed to charter a steamer, load all packing cases aboard it, and take Tatiana and her friends to America.

Did she speak English? Certainly she spoke English. All the Tsar's daughters had English governesses.[7]

Roberts continued to pursue the story, although he told Woods he didn't believe a word of it. He thought Woods, then living the high life at the Hotel Bristol in Warsaw, was hiding out in Poland because he needed to escape Chicago.

While Roberts stayed in Warsaw hoping to get his Russian visa, Woods chartered a plane and vanished for three days. Roberts, meanwhile, continued his investigations through Hugh Gibson, our minister to Poland, Consul General Keena and James G. White, a former political editor of *the Boston Herald*, who was representing a Chicago banker in Poland, and by cabling America about him. From these sources I learned that Woods really had been assistant state's attorney for Illinois, that nothing whatever was known about his reasons for being in Poland; that he had made a number of airplane trips toward the Russian border; that he spent money lavishly and seemed to have plenty of it; also that he had applied to Mr. Keena for five passports in blank – an application that Mr. Keena had been forced to refuse.[8]

Woods told Roberts that once Tatiana was on her way to America, he would be granted an exclusive interview with her. After Woods promised to sail back with her and failed to do so, Roberts returned to America in September 1923. He still continued to keep track of Woods back in Warsaw. That November he "asked General Dawes's office in Chicago for a report on Woods."[9]

Three years later, in February 1926, Roberts again met Woods, now back in Chicago. After Roberts said the story was a hoax that had caused him "unnecessary trouble and expense" trying to follow the story, Woods:

insisted that everything he had told him was the simple truth: that he had failed to persuade Tatiana only because he had been unable to persuade her to run the risk of exposing herself to the vengeance of the Bolsheviks, who would leave no stone unturned to murder any surviving member of the Russian royal family. He fully intended, he said, to return to Poland in the following summer and try again to bring the last of the Romanoffs to America. He still had no answer to my insistent queries as to why he should have considered inviting disaster by letting her travel as the Grand Duchess Tatiana when she could have safely claimed to be Ella Svoboda of Vilna – and when he could have purchased a thousand counterfeit passports for just one of those masterpieces in the Tsar's packing case.[10]

Was there a mysterious New Yorker who claimed to represent the Royal Family? Why did Woods take regular plane trips to the Polish–Russian border? What led him to construct such an elaborate story? Had there been a fabulous treasure trove looted after the Revolution and smuggled into Poland? What did the Polish government make of Woods? Was there some attempt to concoct a new myth of Romanov survival?

Pyotr Voykov, the Soviet Ambassador to Poland who would be assassinated in June 1927, had a diplomatic interest in works of art. As part of the Peace of Riga ending the Soviet–Polish War, Voykov negotiated the return of art and other treasures taken by the Soviet Union from Poland in the war and (presumably) treasures taken by the Poles from Russia. He was then appointed Soviet Ambassador to Poland in November 1924. It seems likely that Woods had been involved in some sort of illicit art dealings on the edge of the Polish–Russian border, although for whom remains a mystery.

In the early 1970s, Guy Richards' friend Robert Samborski tracked down Woods, who was extremely sick and living in a nursing home in Scottsdale Arizona. After claiming that he had been sent on a special secret mission for Secretary of State Charles Evans Hughes, Woods refused to discuss what he was doing in Poland with Samborski – or anyone else.[11]

APPENDIX III: SKORZENY

In his 1960 Sniper letter, Goleniewski discussed SS Colonel Otto Skorzeny, whom he claimed was Hacke-connected as well. Skorzeny, known as Hitler's favourite.

> One of the dark and dangerous KGB figures in HACKE is the famous SS Colonel SKORZENY, who presently lives in Madrid and also works for the Spanish IS. SKORZENY was under active deployment by ABAKUMOV as early as 1942. Further details are neither known here, nor have those which are known been checked. He was allegedly (only one source) "doubled" by ABAKUMOV during the war. There was a period, however, when he was suspected by the MVD of playing a "double game." In the opinion of a former high CI chief in Poland who used to work very closely with BESBORODOV, SKORZENY was finally recruited as a collaborator of ABAKUMOV in the middle of 1944, and shortly before the end of the war, through clever maneuvers which exploited the stupidity of the RSHA chief, KALTEN-BRUNNER, appointed chief for a short period of the Nazi military IS.
>
> Through these maneuvers, ABAKUMOV planned above all to catch in time and exploit for himself the Nazi Abwehr agents in America and South America. One of the most dangerous methods of ABAKUMOV was the IS work "under a foreign flag" which has been brought to the point of perfection today by the KGB. To what extent ABAKUMOV succeeded in this plan is not clear, but it is certain that in 1955–1956 the KGB had a few excellent agents in America who had come from the repertoire of the NAZI CI (Ast [branch]) (CANARIS). Naturally SKORZENY has tremendous connections to "old Nazi fighters" and if my facts are true, he is an extremely dangerous boy.
>
> I could only learn two clues which serve as slight confirmation of the assertion that SKORZENY is a KGB agent.

1) One of the clandestine contacts of SKORZENY in the Federal Republic is a certain ROGAL who lived until 1956 in Frankfurt a/M.[12] ROGAL is Lithuanian or comes from Latvia. According to my investigation he is a principle agent of KGB Chief Directorate II. ROGAL formerly (until 1944) (trans: *sic*, presumably 1954 is meant) had contact with an AIS officer, B.O. Mason, Bad Wildungen, Otenbergstarsse 1.[13] MASON allegedly ran an IS section working against the Soviet Baltic countries. A co-worker of ROGAL and at the same time a KGB agent is a certain Colonel JANUINS [Janums] (or something similar) who is Lithuanian.[14] A close connection existed and allegedly exists today between SKORZENY and ROGAL.

2) Karl RADL, around 50 [hard to read the exact number] years old, works for SKORZENY for the Spanish IS in the Federal Republic.[15] A personal friend of SKORZENY. Took part with SKORZENY in the "liberation" of MUSSOLINI. RADL worked a long time for the French, during the time he had to hide under false documents from your service. Yet even before the French, MGB Russians grabbed him by the collar and recruited him – therefore he has played a double role in the French IS.

In 1952 ABAKUMOV learned through RADL of a Vatican plot to free the Hungarian Cardinal [Jozsef] MINDSZENTY from prison and smuggle him to the West.[16] Colonel SKORZENY and RADL were supposed to take part in the plot. ABAKUMOV, however, planned to "liberate" MINDSZENTY through SKORZENY and RADL, to shoot him "during flight" as proof of the connection of the Cardinal and Vatican with the old FASCISTS, to shoot RADL too, and to allow SKORZENY, whom he valued higher, "to escape." Somehow RADL smelled the plot at a contact with ABAKUMOV's special representatives, and to be sure, because of fear of ABAKUMOV, did not warn SKORZENY but did withdraw from the planned action. Since this time the cooperation of RADL with the MGB has "stuttered" and later the contact is supposed to have been broken off for a long time. It is not known whether contact exists at present. Thus the "Cardinal" plan fell through. It is certain that SKORZENY is active in HACKE. Whether today he is currently working for the KGB is absolutely possible, but not certain, according to my investigation so far. In any event, it is certainly worthwhile to take a close look at such bloodhounds as SKORZENY.

It is hard to know how to evaluate Goleniewski's claims. At the very minimum, the Skorzeny story sheds light on the conspiratorial mindset and plots inside plots/ wheels within wheels mindset that helped define Soviet intelligence operations in the early Cold War.

Notes

1 The Pulawy group was named after Pulawska street in Warsaw where some members lived while Natolin referred to a suburban area of Warsaw where some of its leaders resided.

2 Lendvai (1971), 227. Lendvai provides a good overview of the "Partisans" in the late 1960s.
3 Bower (1995), 255–56.
4 Ibid. The diplomat was most likely Irvin Scarbeck, who was compromised by an affair by a Polish young woman named Urszula Maria Discher.
5 Siemiatkowski (2006).
6 Bagley (2015), 29.
7 Roberts (1949), 156–58.
8 Ibid., 158–59.
9 This was the office of General Charles C. Dawes.
10 Ibid., 160.
11 Richards (1975), 47–49.
12 Werner Rogal, who was formerly on the payroll of the US Army's CIC in Germany.
13 Master Sergeant Brooks O. Mason from CIC.
14 Col. Vilis Janums, a leader of the *Daugavas Venagi* (the Daugava Hawks) later awarded the rank of SS Standartenführer. See *Jewish Currents*, November 1966, 24.
15 Born in Austria, Radl was Skorzeny's adjunct in World War II, and surrendered with him in Austria to the Americans in May 1945. There are US intelligence reports on Radl and Skorzeny that include a long interrogation of Radl by the CIC dated 28 May 1945.
16 Cardinal Mindzenty had been arrested on 26 December 1948 and jailed after a show trial. During the Hungarian Revolution, he was freed from prison. After the Soviet invasion of Hungary, he sought refuge in the US Embassy where he stayed for the next 15 years before finally being allowed to leave.

CAST OF CHARACTERS

Goleniewski family (Chapters 1–2 and *passim*)

Michal Goleniewski (1922–1993). Polish spy, defector and claimant to the Romanov throne.

Michal Goleniewski, sr. (1883–1952). Goleniewski's father.

Janina Goleniewski (1891? –?). Goleniewski's mother, whom he later claimed was really his sister 'grand duchess Maria Nicolaevna'.

Irmgard Kampf (1929?–?). Goleniewski's second wife. She defected with him in Berlin in January 1960. They had a civil marriage in 1961.

Tatiana Romanoff (1964–?). Goleniewski's daughter who was born in America.

Polish Intelligence (Chapters 2–3)

Colonel Stefan Antosiewicz (1918–1998). Polish intelligence official who helped promote Goleniewski's career.

Jerzy Bryn (?-?). Polish defector whom the CIA thought was a false defector but whom Goleniewski said was legitimate.

Leopold Dende (1907–1977). Code name 'Mela.' Dende spied for Polish intelligence in America and was involved in the hunt for Goleniewski.

Wladyslaw Mroz (1926–1960). Polish defector murdered in Paris in 1960.

Colonel Witold Sienkiewicz (1920–1990). Head of Department I and Goleniewski's boss.

Colonel Henryk Sokolak (1921–1984). Second in command in Department One of Polish intelligence, took over after Sienkiewicz was dismissed in the wake of the Goleniewski affair.

Jozef Swiatlo (1915–1994). High-ranking Polish intelligence official who defected to the West in 1953 and then worked for the CIA broadcasting propaganda into Poland.

General Franciszek Szlachcic (1920–1990). Leading Polish intelligence official who wrote about Goleniewski.

Marceli Wieczorek (1934–1999). Polish spy in America who was tasked with finding more about Goleniewski.

Soviet Intelligence (Chapters 2–3)

General Oleg Mikhailovich Gribanov (1915–1992). Head of KGB counterintelligence.
Colonel Andrey Ivanovich Raina (1906–1973). KGB advisor to Goleniewski in Section VI of Department I.
General Ivan Serov (1905–1990). Head of the KGB between 1954–1958, then Head of the GRU 1958–1963.

American Intelligence (Chapter 3 and *passim*)

James 'Jesus' Angleton (1917–1987). Legendary controversial chief of CIA counterintelligence (1954–1974). His paranoia about Soviet infiltration meant that he even regarded genuine defectors such as Goleniewski as potentially bogus.
Tennent 'Pete' Bagley (1925–2014). CIA head of Soviet bloc counterintelligence. Close to Angleton.
Allen Dulles (1893–1969). CIA Director (1953–1961) who was in office when Goleniewski defected.
Edward Jay Epstein (1935–). Investigative journalist who disseminated Angleton's version of events.
Anatoliy Golitsyn (1926–2008). Soviet KGB defector whose theories of a 'monstrous plot' influenced James Angleton.
Charles Douglas ('C.D.') Jackson (1902–1964). Psychological warfare expert and head of the operations control board (OCB) of the national security council in the mid-1950s. Later publisher of *Life* magazine.
John McCone (1902–1991). CIA Director (1961–65) who had to deal with Goleniewski after Dulles.
Howard Roman (1926–1998). Goleniewski CIA case officer close to James Angleton.
Frank Wisner (1909–1965). CIA Deputy Director of Plans.

British Intelligence (Chapter 5)

George Blake (1922–2020). MI6 officer and Soviet spy exposed by Goleniewski. Later escaped from prison and died in Moscow in 2020.
Morris Cohen (1910–1995) and Lona Cohen (1913–1992). Two 'illegal' Soviet spies (aka Peter and Helen Kroger) that were arrested as part of the Portland spy ring on the basis of information derived from Goleniewski.
Michael Hanley (1918–2001). MI5 official wrongly suspected of being a Soviet agent based on information from Goleniewski. Later Director General of MI5 (1972–1978).
Sir Roger Hollis (1905–1973). MI5 Director General (1956–1965) who was controversially accused of being a Soviet 'mole' by Chapman Pincher, Peter Wright and James Angleton.
Harry Houghton (1905–1985). Polish/Soviet spy in England, part of the Portland spy ring exposed by Goleniewski.
George Leggett (?–2012). MI5 official and expert on Eastern Europe who was forced into early retirement following an investigation into information provided by Goleniewski.
Gordon Lonsdale (1922–1970). Cover name for Konon Molody, a top Soviet 'illegal' exposed by Goleniewski.
William John Vassall (1924–1996). British admiralty spy exposed in part by Goleniewski.
Peter Wright (1916–1995). Principal scientific officer for MI5 and controversial right-wing hawk who believed MI5 Director General Sir Roger Hollis was a Soviet mole. His publication of his memoirs Spycatcher was a major embarrassment for the Thatcher government.

Hacke (Chapters 6 and 7)

General Viktor Abakumov (1908–1954). Head of SMERSH, later executed. Believed to have played an important role in Hacke.

Frantisek August (1928–?). Czech defector who knew Barak.

Rudolf Barak (1915–1995). Former Czech interior minister who reportedly kidnapped General Müller on behalf of the KGB.

Ladislav Bittman (1931–2018). Czech intelligence officer and master of disinformation who knew Barak and later defected to the USA.

Peter Deriabin (1921–1992). Former KGB agent who defected to the USA in 1954 and believed SS General Müller was captured by the Russians.

Gregory Douglas (?-?). Publisher of a series of books purporting to be memoirs of General Müller.

Albert Foerster (1902–1952). Former Nazi leader in Danzig. Reportedly revealed the existence of Hacke to Goleniewski. Executed in Poland for war crimes.

Josef Frolik (1928–1989). Czech intelligence officer who defected to the USA in 1969.

Aleksandr Korotkov (1909–1961). Head of the Special Directorate (Illegal Intelligence) who supposedly knew Müller.

SS Sturmbannführer (Major) Jacob Löllgen (?-?). Reported key Hacke agent whose case was never fully investigated.

SS Gruppenführer (Major General) Heinrich 'Gestapo' Müller (1900–1945). Director of the Gestapo presumed to have died in Berlin in 1945. But Goleniewski claimed that he survived the war.

SS-Obersturmbannführer (Lieutenant Colonel) Otto Skorzeny (1908–1975). 'Hitler's favourite paratrooper' who led the daring rescue of Fascist dictator Mussolini in the Gran Sasso raid in 1943. Postwar he was involved with various neo-Nazi networks including Hacke according to Goleniewski.

Peter Stähle (?-?). West German journalist who wrote articles about Müller living in Albania and South America.

Pierre Faillant de Villemarest (1922–2008). French journalist, writer and far-right activist who wrote a 1984 book on Goleniewski to try to prove aspects of Goleniewski's Hacke story.

Goleniewski's American allies and the Tsar wars (Chapters 8 and 9)

Anna Anderson (1896–1984). The most famous of several impostors who claimed to be Grand Duchess Anastasia of Russia. Rival to Eugenia Smith.

Dr. Edward O'Connor (?-?). Immigration expert and former OCB member who worked for congressman Michael Feighan. Also worked with Colonel Corso.

Congressman Michael Feighan (1905–1922). Longtime Democratic Congressman from Ohio and a Goleniewski supporter.

Sidney Goldberg (?-?). Owner of a small Washington paper who claimed that former US ambassador to Poland Jacob Beam betrayed Goleniewski because he was having an affair with a Polish communist named Myra Michalowski.

Otto Otepka (1915–2010). Former State Department security official fired by the Kennedy administration.

Count Georgi Pavlovich Grabbe (Father Georgi) (?-?). Married Goleniewski and Irmgard Kampf under the Romanov name in 1964.

Guy Richards (1923–1979). Reporter and editor of the *New York Journal-American* and writer of books on Goleniewski and the Romanovs.

Eugenia Smith (1899–1997). Claimed to be the Grand Duchess Anastasia, youngest daughter of Nicholas II, the last Tsar of Imperial Russia. One-time supporter of Goleniewski's Romanoff claims who later turned against him.

Robert Speller (?-?). New York publisher who promoted Goleniewski's claim to the Romanov throne. The Speller family was also close to a mysterious American intelligence agent named Sergius Riis.

The Kissinger saga (Chapter 10)

Peter Bessell (1921–1985). British Liberal politician and MP for Bodmin. Tried to get Goleniewski to cooperate with him on a plan to access the Romanov fortune.

Jeremy Thorpe (1929–2014). Liberal party leader (1967–1976) and close Bessell ally.

Antony Summers (1942–) and Tom Mangold (1934–). BBC Reporters who covered Bessell and the story of the possible survival of the Romanovs for their book *The File on the Tsar* (1976).

White Russian exiles (Chapters 12 and 13)

Gleb Botkin (1900–1969). Son of the Tsar's court physician Yevgeny Botkin who was murdered by the Bolsheviks along with the Russian royal family. White Russian monarchist who was highly critical of Eugenia Smith's claim to be Anastasia.

Boris Brasol (1885–1963). Leading White Russian figure in New York closely connected to the far right in both America and Europe.

Major General Arthur Count Cherep-Spiridovich (1867–1926). Russian Count who operated in underground, antisemitic and chivalric networks in both America and Europe. Best known for his crazy antisemitic (1926) book *Secret World Government*. His 'adopted son' was the American far right activist Victor von Broenstrupp.

Grand Duchess Victoria Melita (Grand Duchess Victoria Feodorovna) (1876–1936). Grand Duke Kirill's wife whose trip to New York was arranged by Julia Stimson Loomis (Mrs. Henry Patterson Loomis), a leading New York socialite and head of the Monday opera supper club.

Grand Duke Alexander Mikhailovich (1866–1933). A leading Russian aristocrat with close ties to America.

Grand Duke Nicholas (Nicolai) Nikolayevich (1856–1929). Russian general and bitter opponent of Grand Duke Kirill.

Sidney Reilly (1873–1925). Dubbed 'the ace of spies,' the Russian-born Reilly lived in New York for part of World War I and worked for various intelligence agencies including MI6. He was reportedly a leader of an anti-Bolshevik group founded in Switzerland after the war that had an affiliate in America. He was tricked into visiting Russia in 1925 and executed.

Paquita Louise de Shishmarev (Shishmareff) aka 'L. Fry' or 'Leslie Fry' (1882–1970). American woman who married a Russian military officer. She played a key role in the radical right and was known for her promotion of the *Protocols of the Elders of Zion* in her conspiratorial antisemitic book *Waters Flowing Eastward*. She had ties in America to Henry Ford and in Europe to Monseigneur Ernest Jouin, another leading *Protocols* supporter.

Kirill de Shishmarev/'Prince Kyril Fedorovich de Vassilchikov-Shishmarev (Shishmariëv), the Comte de Rohan-Chandor.' (1907–1975). Louise's son, and a Pichel Knight of Malta, he strongly promoted Goleniewski's claim to be the Tsar.

General Alexander Spiridovich (1873–1952). Leading Okhrana expert on terrorism who lived in exile in Paris. Often confused with Major General Arthur Count Cherep-Spiridovich.

Grand Duke Kirill Vladimirovich (1876–1938). Leading claimant to the Romanov throne.

Prince Nikolaj Zevachov (?-?). A leading White Russian reactionary who spent many years in Italy following the Bolshevik revolution and who worked to promote the *Protocols*.

Shickshinny Knights of Malta (Chapters 11 and 14)

Cleve Backster (1924–2013). CIA Polygraph expert and friend of both Robert Speller and Herman Kimsey.

Frank Capell (1907–1980). Longtime far-right anti-communist activist and editor of *The Herald of Freedom*.

Colonel Philip J. Corso (1915–1998). Long time Knight and member of the military committee of the Knights. Worked closely with Goleniewski as an aide to Congressman Feighan. Best known for his 1997 book *The Day after Roswell* where he claims he saw a dead alien from a flying saucer.

Herman Kimsey (1917–1971). Former chief of the CIA's special analysis and research section (1953–1962) who backed Goleniewski's claim. Also, a friend of Cleve Backster.

Salvatore Messineo (?-?). Took over leadership of the Knights with Goleniewski after Pichel was forced out of the organization.

'Colonel' Charles Louis Thourot Pichel (1890–1982). Long time far-right activist and convicted criminal. Con man extraordinaire, and creator of the Shickshinny Knights. In the 1920s ran the American heraldry society with Dr. William Sohier Bryant. In the 1930s he was a member of yet another bizarre right-wing group with new age overtones called Blue Lamoo.

(Selected members) Military Committee of the Knights of Malta (Chapter 14)

General Pedro del Valle (1893–1978). Former three-star US Marine Corps general and leader of the fanatically antisemitic organization, the Defenders of the American Constitution (DAC).

General Lemuel Shepherd (1896–1990). Four-star US Marine Corps general and former member of the Joint Chiefs of Staff.

Lieutenant General George Stratemeyer (1890–1969). Three-star US Air Force general.

Major General Charles Willoughby (1892–1972). Two-star general who ran G-2 (military intelligence) for his patron and close friend General Douglas MacArthur during World War II and in the Korean War. Was tied to numerous far-right groups in the 1950s and 1960s.

Brigadier General Bonner Fellers (1896–1973). One-star general who served under General MacArthur, where he served as chief of psychological operations. Also served under MacArthur during the occupation of Japan. Tied to numerous right-wing groups including the John Birch Society.

Admiral Charles M. Cooke (1886–1970). Four-star admiral in US Navy who also worked closely with the KMT government in Taiwan before retiring.

Rear Admiral Francis T. Spellman (1895–?). US Navy Rear Admiral who fought in the Pacific in World War II.

Ex-Knights (Chapter 11 and Chapter 14)

Paul de Granier Cassagnac (?-?). Leader of the European branch of the Shickshinny Knights in the early 1960s who broke with Pichel and created his own order.

Crolian William Edelen (1920–2006). Former Pichel ally who later exposed Pichel's fraudulent creation of the Shickshinny Knights.

John Grady (?–?). Leader of the association of family commanders and hereditary Knights (the 'Tennessee Knights').

Nicholai Nazarenko (1911–1992). Head of the World Federation of the Cossack National Liberation Movement of Cossackia and Nazi collaborator in World War II.

Colonel Benjamin F. von Stahl (?–?). Extreme rightist and former long-time member of the Pichel Knights.

Thorbjörn Wiklund (?–?). Swedish-based leader of the Knights who unsuccessfully tried to legally challenge the Messineo–Goleniewski leadership in court.

CHRONOLOGY: POLAND (1922–1961)

16 August 1922 Goleniewski is born in Nieswiez.

Mid-1920s The family relocates to western Poland near the town of Wolsztyn in the Lubusz Voivodeship (Province).

September 1939–1945 With the outbreak of war, Goleniewski leaves high school. During the German occupation, he works as a clerk for the German state company Reichsland.

22 February 1945 'Festung Posen' (Fortress Posen) falls to the Red Army. The city is renamed Poznan.

8 May 1945 V-E Day in Europe.

13 August 1945 Goleniewski begins his career as a guard for the PUBP facility in the town of Nowy Tomysl, 34 miles west of Poznan.

26 June 1946 Appointed clerk at Zielona Gora, the former German city of Grünberg. Goes from sergeant to warrant officer ensign in one year. Becomes an officer at Zielona Gora PUBP. Then senior clerk and acting deputy head of PUBP. Awarded Bronze Cross of Merit (*Brazowy Krzyz Zaslugi*).

1 May 1947 Goleniewski becomes head of Zielona Gora PUBP.

1 June 1949 Appointed chief of MUBP (*Ministerstwo Urząd Bezpieczeństwa Publicznego*/Ministry Office of Public Security) in Poznan.

June 1950 Assigned to Gdansk (formerly Danzig) as new head of Dept. 1 of WUBP (*Wojewódzki Urząd Bezpieczeństwa Publicznego*/Provincial Office of Public Security).

1950 Promoted to Captain.

1951 Promoted to Major

17 May 1952 Goleniewski's father dies in the town of Ciosaniec, some 14 miles south of Wolsztyn.

1 June 1953 Appointed head of Department IX (study and analysis) of Department I of (Counterintelligence) of MBP (*Ministerstwo Bezpieczeństwa Publicznego*/Polish Ministry of Public Security). Relocates to Warsaw.

15 March 1955 Made Vice Director of Counterintelligence (Dept II) of *Bezpieczeństwa Publicznego* (Office of Public Security/BP).

14 December 1955 Reassigned from civilian to military intel to head the GZI (*Glowny Zaraad Informacji*/Central Information Board) of the Ministry of National Defense (*Ministerstwo Obrony Narodowej*/MON) where he is engaged in Counterintelligence. He described his role as Deputy Chief of the Main Department of Military Counterintelligence.

1956 Made Lt. Colonel

1 Feb. 1957 Transferred to MSW (*Ministerstwo Spraw Wewnętrznych*), the successor organization to the MBP.

November/December 1957 Appointed the director of Section VI in charge of scientific and technological matters.

1 April 1958 First Sniper letter arrives at the US Embassy in Bern, Switzerland.

25 December 1960 Goleniewski leaves Warsaw for a planned operation in Berlin.

4 January 1961 Goleniewski appears at the American Consulate in West Berlin with Irmgard Kampf.

5 January 1961 Arrives at the USAF base in Wiesbaden, West Germany, for initial debriefings by CIA.

12 January 1961 Goleniewski lands at Andrews Air Force base in Maryland on a military plane. Taken to a CIA safe house in Maryland to begin his full debriefing.

BIBLIOGRAPHY

Archives

Tennent Bagley Collection, Howard Gotlieb Archival Research Center, Boston University, USA.

Central Intelligence Agency Reading Room https://www.cia.gov/library/readingroom/home.

Edward Jay Epstein Collection, Howard Gotlieb Archival Research Center, Boston University, USA.

Books and articles

Acoca, Miguel and Brown, Robert K. (1975). 'The Bayo-Pawley Affair: A Plot to Destroy JFK and Invade Cuba,' *Soldier of Fortune*, I/3 (February).

Alexander Mikhailovich, Grand Duke of Russia (1932). *Once a Grand-Duke* (New York: Farrar & Rinehart).

Alexander Mikhailovich, Grand Duke of Russia (1933). *Always a Grand Duke* (New York: Farrar & Rinehart).

Alexandravicius, Egidijus (2016). *Lithuanian Paths to Modernity* (Kaunas: Vytautas Magnus University).

Allen, Gary (1976). *Kissinger: The Secret Side of the Secretary of State* (Seal Beach, CA: '76 Press).

Andrew, Christopher (2009). *The Defence of the Realm: The Authorized History of MI5* (London: Allen Lane).

Andrew, Christopher and Gordievsky, Oleg (1990). *KGB: The Inside Story* (New York: Harper Collins).

Andrew, Christopher and Mitrokhin, Vasili (2000). *The Mitrokhin Archive: The KGB in Europe and the West* (London: Penguin).

Andrews, Geoff (2020). *Agent Molière: The Life of John Cairncross, the Fifth Man of the Cambridge Spy Circle* (London: IB Tauris).

Anonymous (189–). *Concerning the man John Arthur Chandor, alias Count Chandor, alias Captain Chandor, alias Montagu Chandor, alias Captain Carlton, &c.* (London: The Private Vigilante Society).

Anonymous [Revilo P. Oliver]. (1977). 'The Reincarnations of Col. Goleniewski', *Instauration*, Vol. 2 no. 5, April.

Anonymous (2011). 'James J. Angleton, Anatoliy Golitsyn, and the "Monster Plot": Their Impact on CIA Personnel and Operations,' *Studies in Intelligence*, 55/4 (December) pp. 39–55.

Applebaum, Anne (2012). *Iron Curtain* (New York: Doubleday).

Ariel, Yaakov (2011). 'Philosemites embracing the Protocols? American fundamentalist Christians and The Protocols of the Elders of Zion,' in Esther Webman (ed.), *The Global Impact of the Protocols of the Elders of Zion: A Century-Old Myth* (London: Routledge) pp. 89–100.

Ashley, Clarence (2004). *CIA Spymaster* (Gretna, LA: Pelican).

August, Frantisek and Rees, David (1984). *Red Star Over Prague* (London: Sherwood Press).

Bagieriski, Witold (2014). 'Afera kurierska' w wywiadzie i MSZ,' *Pamiec i Sprawiedliwosc*, 1/23.

Bagley, Tennent (2007). *Spy Wars: Moles, Mysteries, and Deadly Games* (New Haven: Yale University Press).

Bagley, Tennent (2013). *Spymaster: Startling Cold War Revelations of a Soviet KGB Chief* (NY: Skyhorse).

Bagley, Tennent (2015). 'Ghost of the Spy Wars: A Personal Reminder to Interested Parties,' *International Journal of Intelligence and CounterIntelligence*, 28:1, pp. 1–37.

Baldwin, Neil (2002). *Henry Ford and the Jews: The Mass Production of Hate* (New York: Public Affairs).

Bale, Jeffrey M. (1991). '"Privatising" Covert Action: The Case of the Unification Church,' *Lobster* (May).

Barnes, Trevor (2020). *Deadly Doubles: The Extraordinary Worldwide Hunt for One of the Cold War's Most Notorious Spy Rings* (London: Weidenfeld & Nicholson).

Beam, Jacob D. (1978). *Multiple Exposure: An American Ambassador's Unique Perspective on East-West Issues* (New York: W. W. Norton & Company).

Beckett, Andy (2002). *Pinochet in Piccadilly: Britain and Chile's Hidden History* (London: Faber & Faber).

Beevor, Anthony (2004). *The Mystery of Olga Chekhova* (New York: Penguin).

Bellant, Russ (1991). *Old Nazis, the New Right, and the Republican Party* (Boston: South End Press).

Bendersky, Joseph (2002). *The 'Jewish Threat': Anti-Semitic Politics of the U.S. Army* (New York: Basic Books).

Berger, J. M. (2012). 'Patriot Games: How the FBI Spent a Decade Hunting White Supremacists and Missed Timothy McVeigh,' *Foreign Policy* (18 April).

Bessell, Peter (1980). *Cover-Up: The Jeremy Thorpe Affair* (Oceanside, CA: Simons Books, Inc.).

Bezymenskii, Lev (1966). *Tracing Martin Bormann* (Moscow: Progress Publishers).

Bezymenskii, Lev (2000). 'Müller's Three Lives,' *Novoye Vermya*, 33.

Bisser, Jamie (2005). *White Terror: Cossack Warlords of the Trans-Siberian* (London: Routledge).

Bittman, Ladislav (1972). *The Deception Game* (Syracuse University Research Corporation).

Blake, George (1990). *No Other Choice: An Autobiography* (London: Jonathan Cape).

Bloch, Michaël (2014). *Jeremy Thorpe* (London: Little Brown).

Boeckh, Katrin (2016). 'The Rebirth of Pan-Slavism in the Russian Empire, 1912–13', in Katrin Boeckh and Sabine Rutar (eds.), *The Balkan Wars from Contemporary Perception to Historic Memory* (London: Palgrave) pp. 105–137.

Botkin, Gleb (1930). 'The Czar of Shadowland,' *The North American Review*, 229/5 (May).

Bourke, Sean (1970). *The Springing of George Blake* (London: Viking).

Bower, Tom (1995). *The Perfect English Spy: Sir Dick White and the Secret War 1935–90* (London: Heinemann).

Brands, Jr., H. W. (1988). 'A Cold War Foreign Legion? The Eisenhower Administration and the Volunteer Freedom Corps,' *Military Affairs*, 52/1 (January), pp.7–11.

Brandt, Karl and Shiller, Otto (1954). *Management of Agriculture and Food in German-occupied and Other Areas of Fortress Europe. A Study in Military Government* (Stanford: Stanford University Press).

Breitman, Richard and Goda, Norman J. W. (2011). *Hitler's Shadow: Nazi War Criminals, U.S. Intelligence and the Cold War* (Washington: National Archives).

Brisard, Jean-Christophe and Parshina, Lars (2019). *The Death of Hitler: The Final Word on the Ultimate Cold Case: The Search for Hitler's Body* (London: Hodder & Stoughton).

Brysac, Shareen Blair (2000). *Resisting Hitler: Mildred Harnack and the Red Orchestra* (Oxford: Oxford University Press).

Bułhak, Władysław and Pleskot, Patryk (2014) *Szpiedzy PRL-u* (Kraków: Znak Horyzont).

Bury, Jan (2017). 'Operation Spiders: Fighting an Early Cold War Ukrainian Subversion behind the Iron Curtain', *International Journal of Intelligence and CounterIntelligence*, 30/2, pp. 241–268.

Butterworth, Alex (2010). *The World That Never Was* (New York: Pantheon).

Caillat, Michel (2014). 'Théodore Aubert and the Entente International Anticommunist: An Unofficial Anti-Marxist International,' *Twentieth Century Communism: A Journal of International History*, 6, pp. 82–104.

Cairncross, John (1997). *The Enigma Spy: An Autobiography – The Story of the Man Who Changed the Course of World War Two* (London: Century).

Campbell, Kenneth A. (1998). 'Major General Charles A. Willoughby: General Macarthur's G-2,' *American Intelligence Journal*, 18/1–2, pp. 87–91.

Campbell, Kenneth J. (2009). 'Colonel Walter Nicolai: A Mysterious but Effective Spy,' *American Intelligence Journal* 27/1, pp. 83–89.

Capell, Frank (1965). *Treason is the Reason: 847 Reasons for Investigating the State Department* (Zarephath, NJ: Herald of Freedom).

Capell, Frank (1966). 'The Strange Case of 'Col. Goleniewski," *The Herald of Freedom*, XI/1 (11 February).

Capell, Frank (1974). *Henry Kissinger Soviet Agent* (Zarephath, NJ: Herald of Freedom).

Carafano, James Jay (1999). 'Mobilizing Europe's Stateless: America's Plan for a Cold War Army', *Journal of Cold War Studies*, 1/2 (Spring), pp. 61–85.

Carlson, John Roy (1943). *Undercover: My Four Years in the Nazi Underworld of America* (New York: E.P. Dutton).

Carr, Barnes (2016). *Operation Whisper: The Capture of Soviet Spies Morris and Lona Cohen* (Lebanon, NH: University Press of New England).

Carter, Miranda (2001). *Anthony Blunt: His Lives* (New York: Farrar Straus Giroux).

Chaffanjon, Arnaud, and Flavigny, Bertrand Galimard (1982). *Ordres et Contre-Ordres de Chevalerie* (Paris: Mercure de France).

Chairoff, Patrice (1985). *Faux Chevaliers, Vrais Gogos* (Paris: Jean Cyrille Godefray).

Chapman, Robert D. (2006) 'Remembering the Polish Underground', *International Journal of Intelligence and CounterIntelligence*, 19/4, pp. 746–752.

Chavchavadze, David (1990). *The Grand Dukes* (New York: Atlantic International Publishers).

Cherep-Spiridovich, Arthur, Count (1919). 'Russia: An Appeal to the Anglo-Saxon World and England and Slavia,' *The Asiatic Review*, XV (January-October 1919).

Cherep-Spiridovich, Arthur, Count (1926). *The Secret World Government: or, 'The Hidden Hand': The Unrevealed in History: 100 Historical 'Mysteries' Explained* (New York: The Anti-Bolshevist Publishing Association).

Clarke, William (1995). *The Lost Fortune of the Tsars* (New York: St. Martin's Press).

Coogan, Kevin (1999). *Dreamer of the Day: Francis Parker Yockey and the Postwar Fascist International* (Brooklyn, NY: Autonomedia).

Coogan, Kevin (2004). 'The Defenders of the American Constitution and the League of Empire Loyalists: The First Postwar Anglo-American Revolts Against the 'One World Order,' a paper presented at the International Institute for Social History in Amsterdam.

Coogan, Kevin (2015). 'Tokyo Legend? Lee Harvey Oswald and Japan,' *Lobster*, 70 (Winter).

Cook, Fred (1961). 'The CIA,' *The Nation* (24 June).

Cookridge, E. H. (1970). *The Many Sides of George Blake, Esq* (Princeton: Brandon/Systems Press).

Corera, Gordon (2018). *The Illegal: The Hunt for a Russian Spy in Post-War London* (Seattle: Amazon Publishing).

Corn, David (1994). *Blond Ghost: Ted Shackley and the CIA's Crusades* (New York: Simon & Shuster).

Corso, Charles (1997). *The Day After Roswell* (New York: Pocket Books).

Cram, Cleveland (1993). *Of Moles and Molehunters: A Review of Counterintelligence Literature, 1977–92* (CIA/Center for the Study of Intelligence), October, pp.129–137.

Cypher, James (1993). 'Introducing Lt. Col. Philip J. Corso, Army Intelligence,' *The Third Decade*, 9/2 (January).

Daly-Groves, Luke (2019) *Hitler's Death: The Case Against Conspiracy* (Oxford: Osprey).

Davenport-Hines, Richard (2019). *Enemies Within: Communists, the Cambridge Spies and the Making of Modern Britain* (London: William Collins).

Deacon, Richard (1974). *The Chinese Secret Service* (London: Frederick Muller).

Deacon, Richard (1982). *With My Little Eye* (London: Frederick Muller).

Deletant, Dennis (2006). *Hitler's Forgotten Ally: Ion Antonescu and His Regime, Romania 1940–44* (Basingstoke: PalgraveMacmillan).

De Michelis, Cesare G. (2004). *The Non-Existent Manuscript: A Study of the Protocols of the Sages of Zion* (Lincoln, NE: University of Nebraska Press).

Diamond, Sandor (1974). *The Nazi Movement in the United States 1924–1941* (Ithaca, NY: Cornell University Press).

Dorril, Stephen and Ramsay, Robin (1991). *SMEAR! Wilson and the Secret State* (London: Fourth Estate).

Douglas, Gregory (1995). *Gestapo Chief: The 1948 Interrogation of Heinrich Müller* (San Jose, CA: R. James Bender Publishing).

Drolet, Yves (2015). *The Aryan Order of America and the College of Arms of Canada 1880–1937* (Montreal: Self-Published).

Dulles, Allen (1963). *The Craft of Intelligence* (New York: Harper & Row).

Duns, Jeremy (2014). *Dead Drop: The True Story of Oleg Penkovsky and the Cold War's Most Dangerous Operation* (London: Simon & Schuster).

Epstein, Catherine (2010). *Model Nazi: Arthur Greiser and the Occupation of Western Poland* (New York: Oxford University Press).

Epstein, Edward Jay (1978). *Legend: The Secret World of Lee Harvey Oswald* (New York: McGraw Hill).

Epstein, Edward Jay (1980). 'The Spy Wars,' *The New York Times Magazine*, (28 September).

Epstein, Edward Jay (1981). 'An Incredible Mole Who Would Be Tsar,' *Washington Star* (17 May).

Epstein, Edward Jay (1989). *Deception: The Invisible War between the KGB and the CIA* (New York: G. P. Putnam).

Epstein, Edward Jay (2014). *James Jesus Angleton: Was He Right?* (New York: Fast Track Press/EJE Publications).

Evans, Richard J. (2001). *Lying About Hitler: History, Holocaust, and the David Irving Trial.* (New York: Basic Books).

Evans, Richard J. (2020). *The Hitler Conspiracies* (New York: Oxford University Press).

Fitzpatrick, Sheila. (2015). *On Stalin's Team: The Years of Living Dangerously in Soviet Politics* (Princeton: Princeton University Press).

Formhals, Robert Sanguszko (1979). *White Cross: Story of the Knights of Saint John of Jerusalem* (Camarillo, CA: Sanghals Publishers).

Frendo, Henry (2004). 'Czars, Knights and Republicans: The Malta Question in Paul I's Time,' *Storja 2003–2004.*

Frolik, Josef (1975). *The Frolik Defection* (London: Leo Cooper).

Fry, Michael (1934). *Hitler's Wonderland* (London: John Murray).

Gehlen, Reinhard (1972). *The Service: The Memoirs of General Reinhard Gehlen* (New York: World Publishing).

Gill, William J. (1969). *The Ordeal of Otto Otepka* (New Rochelle, NY: Arlington House).

Glazkov, V. G. (1972). *A History of the Cossacks* (New York: Robert Speller).

Gluchowski, L. W. (1999). 'The Defection of Jozef Swiatlo and the Search for Jewish Scapegoats in the Polish United Workers Party, 1953–1954,' *Intermarium*, 3/2.

Goleniewski, Michal (1984). *White Book: Volume I, Interlocking Interlopers* (Route 3, Box 120-P, Huntsville (Clifty), AK: Ducerus) (November).

Goleniewski, Michal (1985). *Selected Analysis of Dissemination of Soviet Disinformation Through Western Publications in Result of Arrangements, Participation and/or Nonfeasance on the Part of the United States Government* (s.l.: s.n.).

Golitsyn, Anatoliy (1984). *New Lies for Old* (New York: Dodd, Mead).

Gontarczyk, Piotr (2013). 'Agent, kyory chcial byc carem,' ('The Agent who would be Tsar'), *Do Rzeczy* (26 December).

Grand Duchess of Russia Anastasia (1963) *Anastasia: The Autobiography of HIH the Grand Duchess Anastasia Nicholaevna of Russia* (New York: Spellman).

Granville, Johanna (2002). 'Why Hungary and Not Poland?' *The Slavonic and East European Review*, 80/4 (October), pp. 656–687.

Griffiths, Richard (1980). *Fellow Travellers of the Right: British Enthusiasts for Nazi Germany, 1933–39.* (London: Constable).

Gross, Michael (2007). *740 Park: The Story of the World's Richest Building* (NY: Broadway Books).

Grossman, Johannes (2014). 'The Comité International de defense de la Civilization chrétienne and the Transnationalization of Anti-Communist Propaganda in Western Europe after the Second World War', in Luc van Dongen, Stéphanie Roulin, and Giles Scott-Smith (eds.), *Transnational Anti-Communism and the Cold War: Agents, Activists, and Networks,* (New York: Palgrave Macmillan), pp. 251–262.

Hagemeister, Michael (2009). 'Fry, Leslie (Louise Chandor-Shishmareff),' in Wolfgang Benz (ed.), *Handbuch des Antisemitismus 1. A-K* (Munich: Saur).

Hagemeister, Michael (2011). 'The Protocols of the Elders of Zion in Court: The Bern Trials, 1933–1937,' in Esther Webman (ed.), *The Global Impact of the Protocols of the Elders of Zion: A Century-Old Myth* (Abingdon: Routledge) pp. 241–253.

Hagemeister, Michael (2014). 'The American Connection: Leslie Fry and the Protocols of the Elders of Zion,' in Marina Ciccarini, Nicoletta Marcialis, and Giorgio Ziffer (eds.), *Kesarevo Kesarju. Scritti in onore di Cesare G. De Michelis* (Florence: Florence University Press).

Hagemeister, Michael (2017). *Die 'Protokolle der Weisen von Zion' vor Gericht: Der Berner Prozess 1933–1937 und die 'Antisemitische Internationale'* (Zurich: Cronos).

Hart, John L. (1997). 'Pyotr Semyonovich Popov: The Tribulations of Faith', *Intelligence and National Security*, 12/4, pp. 44–74.

Haslam, Jonathan (2015). *Near and Distant Neighbours: A New History of Soviet Intelligence* (New York: Farrar, Straus & Giroux).

Haynes, John Earl and Klehr, Harvey (1999). *Venona: Decoding Soviet Espionage in America* (New Haven: Yale University Press).

Haynes, John Earl, Klehr, Harvey, and Vassiliev, Alexander (2010). *Spies: The Rise and Fall of the KGB in America* (New Haven: Yale University Press).

Hermiston, Roger (2014). *The Greatest Traitor: The Secret Lives of Agent George Blake* (London: Aurum).

Hersh, Burton (1992). *The Old Boys* (New York: Charles Scribner's Sons).

Heuer, Jr., Richards J. (1987). 'Nosenko: Five Paths to Judgment,' *Studies in Intelligence*, 31/3 (Fall), pp. 71–101. Reproduced in H. Bradford Westerfield, (ed.) (1997) *Inside CIA's Private World: Declassified Articles from the Agency's Internal Journal, 1955-1992* (New Haven: Yale University Press).

Hoar, William (1975). 'Henry Kissinger: This Man is on Their Side,' *American Opinion* (June).

Höhne, Heinz and Zolling, Hermann (1972). *Network: The Truth about General Gehlen and his Spy Ring* (London: Secker & Warburg).

Holmes, Colin (1977). 'New Light on the "Protocols of Zion"', *Patterns of Prejudice*, 11/6, pp. 13–21.

Holzman, Michael (2008). *James Jesus Angleton, the CIA, and the Craft of Counterintelligence* (Amherst, MA: University of Massachusetts Press).

Hougan, Jim (1978). *Spooks: The Haunting of America: The Private Use of Secret Agents* (New York: William Morrow).

Houghton, Harry (1972). *Operation Portland* (London: Robert Hart-Davis).

Hughes, Mike (1994). *Spies at Work* (Bradford: 1 in 12 Publications).

Hylozoic Hedgehog (2009). *Smiling Man from a Dead Planet: The Mystery of Lyndon LaRouche.* Available online at: http://laroucheplanet.info/pmwiki/pmwiki.php?n=Library.UnityNow.

Hylozoic Hedgehog (2012). *How It All Began: The Origins and History of the National Caucus of Labor Committees in New York and Philadelphia (1966–1971).* Available online at: http://laroucheplanet.info/pmwiki/pmwiki.php?n=Library.HIAB.

Jackson, Paul (2017). *Colin Jordan and Britain's Neo-Nazi Movement: Hitler's Echo* (London: Bloomsbury Academic).

Jens, Erik (2017). 'Cold War Spy Fiction in Russian Popular Culture: From Suspicion to Acceptance via Seventeen Moments of Spring,' *Studies in Intelligence*, 61/2 (June), pp. 31–41.

Kalugin, Oleg and Montaigne, Fen (1994). *The First Directorate: My 32 Years in Intelligence and Espionage against the West* (New York: St. Martin's Press).

Kellogg, Michael (2009). *The Russian Roots of Nazism: White Émigrés and the Making of National Socialism* (Cambridge, UK: Cambridge University Press).

Kennan, George (1971). 'The Historiography of the Early Political Career of Stalin,' *Proceedings of the American Philosophical Society*, 115/3 (June), pp. 165–169.

Kerensky, Alexander (1965). *Russia and History's Turning Point* (New York: Duell, Sloan & Pearce).

Kershaw, Ian (1999). *Hitler: 1889–1936 Hubris* (New York: W.W. Norton).

Kisatsky, Deborah (2005). *The United States and the European Right* (Columbus, OH: Ohio State University Press).

Koch, Peter-Ferdinand (2011). *Enttarnt: Doppleagenten: Namen, Fakten, Beweise* (Salzburg: Ecowin Verlag).

Kochanski, Janusz/'Mr. X.' (1979). *Double Eagle: The Autobiography of a Polish Spy who Defected to the West* (New York: Bobbs-Merrill).

Kuromiya, Hiroaki, and Pepłoński, Andrzej (2009). 'The Great Terror: Polish-Japanese Connections,' *Cahiers du Monde Russe*, 50/4 (October–December), pp. 647–670.

Kuromiya, Hiroaki, and Mamoulia, Georges (2009). 'Anti-Russian and Anti-Soviet Subversion: The Caucasian-Japanese Nexus, 1904–1945,' *Europe-Asia Studies*, 61/8 (October), pp. 1415–1440.

Le Carré, John (2016). *The Pidgeon Tunnel: Stories from my Life* (New York: Viking).

Lendvai, Paul (1971). *Anti-Semitism without Jews* (New York: Doubleday).

Nuti, Leopoldo and Riste, Olav (2007). 'Preparing for a Soviet Occupation: The Strategy of "Stay-Behind",' Special Issue of *Journal of Strategic Studies*, 30:6.

Levine, Isaac Don (1956). *Stalin's Great Secret* (New York: Coward McCann).

Lingen, Kerstin von (2008). 'Conspiracy of Silence: How the "Old Boys" of American Intelligence Shielded SS General Karl Wolff from Prosecution,' *Holocaust and Genocide Studies*, 22/1 (Spring), pp. 74–109.

Lingen, Kerstin von (2013). *Allen Dulles, the OSS, and Nazi War Criminals: The Dynamics of Selective Prosecution.* (Cambridge: Cambridge University Press).

Lipstadt, Deborah E. (2005). *History on Trial: My Day in Court with David Irving* (New York: Harper Collins).

Logsdon, Jonathan (1999). 'Henry Ford and the Jews,' *The Hanover Historical Review*, 7 (Spring).

Lovell, James Blair (1991). *Anastasia: The Lost Princess* (New York: St. Martin's Press).

Lownie, Andrew (2015). *Stalin's Englishman: The Lives of Guy Burgess* (London: Hodder & Stoughton).

Lukashevich, Stephen (1959). 'The Holy Brotherhood 1881–1883', *The American Slavic and East European Review*, 18/4 (December), pp. 491–509.

Macintyre, Ben (2015). *A Spy Among Friends: Philby and the Great Betrayal* (London: Bloomsbury).

Macklin, Graham (2020). *Failed Führers: A History of Britain's Extreme Right* (Abingdon: Routledge).

Mangold, Tom (1991). *Cold Warrior: James Jesus Angleton: The CIA's Master Spy Hunter* (New York: Simon & Schuster).

Marnham, Patrick (1971). 'The Czar of Russia is Alive and Living on Long Island,' *Daily Telegraph* (14 February).

Marshall, Jonathan, Scott, Peter Dale, and Hunter, Jane (1987). *The Iran-Contra Connection* (Boston: South End Press).

Martin, David C. (1980). *Wilderness of Mirrors* (New York: Harper & Row).

Martin, Rose L. (1966). *Fabian Freeway: High Road to Socialism in the USA 1884–1966* (Belmont, MA: Western Islands Press).

Massie, Robert (1996). *The Romanovs: The Final Chapter* (New York: Random House).

Matthews, Owen (2019). *An Impeccable Spy: Richard Sorge, Stalin's Master Agent* (London: Bloomsbury).

Mazower, Mark (2009) *Hitler's Empire: Nazi Rule in Occupied Europe* (London: Penguin).

McDonald, Hugh (1975). *Appointment in Dallas: The Final Solution to the Assassination of JFK* (New York: Zebra Books).

Meinl, Susanne and Krüger, Dieter (1994). 'Der politische Weg von Friedrich Wilhelm Heinz,' *Vierteljahrshefte für Zeitgeschichte*, 42/1, January pp. 39–69.

Metelmann, Henry (1990). *Through Hell for Hitler* (London: Patrick Stephens).

Mitrokhin, Vasili (2002). *KGB Lexicon* (London: Frank Cass).

Modin, Yuri (1994). *My Five Cambridge Friends: Burgess, Maclean, Philby, Blunt and Cairncross* (New York: Farrar, Strauss & Giroux).

Mollenhoff, Clark (1964). 'Russ Agent Tells of Sex and Spies in U.S. Embassy in Poland,' *Indianapolis Tribune* (12 April).

Mollenhoff, Clark (1965). *Despoilers of Democracy* (New York: Doubleday).

Moorhouse, Roger (2014). *The Devil's Alliance: Hitler's Pact with Stalin, 1939–1941* (New York: Basic Books).

Morley, Jefferson (2017). *The Ghost: The Secret Life of CIA Spymaster James Jesus Angleton* (New York: St. Martin's Press).

Morley, Jefferson (2018). 'Wilderness of Mirrors,' *The Intercept* (1 January).

Moss, Robert (1980). 'Goleniewski: The Anonymous Mole', *The Daily Telegraph*, October 13.

Mulloy, Darren (2014). *The World of the John Birch Society: Conspiracy, Conservatism and the Cold War* (Nashville, TN: Vanderbilt University Press).

Murphy, David, Kondrashev, Sergei, and Bailey, George (1997). *Battleground Berlin: CIA vs. KGB in the Cold War* (New Haven: Yale University Press).

Naftali, Timothy and Goda, Norman and Breitman, Richard and Wolfe, Robert (2001). 'The Mystery of Heinrich Müller: New Materials from the CIA', *Holocaust and Genocide Studies*, 15/3, Winter, pp. 453–467.

Newland, Samuel (1991). *Cossacks in the German Army 1941–1945* (London: Frank Cass).

Nicholson, Nicholas (2014). '"How Lovely a Country this is": The 1924 Visit of the Grand Duchess Victoria Feodorovna to the United States,' *Royal Russian*, 6 (Summer), pp. 71–96.

Null, Gary (1973). *The Conspirator who Saved the Romanovs* (New York: Pinnacle Books).

O'Gorman, Ned (2009). '"The One Word the Kremlin Fears": C. D. Jackson, Cold War "Liberation" and American Political-Economic Adventurism,' *Rhetoric & Public Affairs*, 12/3 (Fall), pp. 389–427.

O'Maolain, Ciaran (1987). *The Radical Right: A World Directory* (Santa Monica, CA: ABC-Clio).

Paczkowski, Andrzej (2007). 'Civilian Intelligence in Communist Poland, 1945–1989 An Attempt at a General Outline,' *InterMarium*, 10/1.

Page, Bruce, Leitch, David, and Knightley, Phillip (1968). *The Philby Conspiracy* (New York: Doubleday).

Parrish, Michael (1996). *The Lesser Terror: Soviet State Security, 1939–53* (Westport, CT: Praeger).

Pawlikowicz, Leszek (2004). *Tajny Front Zimnej Wojny: Uciekinierzy z polskiech stuzb specjalnych 1956–1964* (Warsaw: KRTM).

Peace, Lisa (1997). 'What Did Otto Otepka Know About Oswald and the CIA?' Probe, 4/3 (March–April).

Pearson, John (2002). *The Cult of Violence: The Untold Story of The Krays* (London: Orion).

Perry, John Curtis, and Pleshkov, Constantine (1999). *The Flight of the Romanovs* (New York: Basic Books, 1999).

Perry, Roland (1994). *The Fifth Man* (London: Sidgwick & Jackson).

Philipps, Roland (2018). *A Spy Named Orphan: The Enigma of Donald Maclean* (London: Bodley Head).

Pichel, Charles (1970). *History of the Hereditary Government of the Sovereign Order of St. John of Jerusalem* (Shickshinny, PA: Maltese Cross Press).

Pichel, Charles L. Thourot (1975). *Samogitia: The Unknown in History* (Shickshinny, PA: Maltese Cross Press).

Piecuch, Henryk (1997). *Imperium Sluzb Specjalnych od Gomulki do Kani* (Warsaw: Agencja Wydawn).

Pincher, Chapman (1984). *Too Secret Too Long* (New York: St. Martin's Press).

Plass, Hanno and Templer, Bill (2013). 'Der Welt-Dienst: International Anti-Semitic Propaganda,' *The Jewish Quarterly Review*, 103/4 (Fall), pp. 503–522.

Platt, Roger H. (2010). 'The Soviet Imprisonment of Gerald Brooke and Subsequent Exchange for the Krogers, 1965–1969', *Contemporary British History*, 24/2, pp. 193–212.

Plokhy, Serhii (2016). *The Man with the Poison Gun* (New York: Basic Books).

Pool, James (1997). *Who Financed Hitler: The Secret Funding of Hitler's Rise to Power, 1919–1933* (New York: Simon & Schuster).

Powers, Thomas (2004). *Intelligence Wars: America's Secret Wars from Hitler to Al-Qaeda* (New York: New York Review of Books Collection Series).

Preston, John (2018). *A Very English Scandal: Sex, Lies and a Murder Plot at the Heart of Establishment* (New York: Other Press).

Pringle, Robert W. (2006). *Historical Dictionary of Russian and Soviet Intelligence* (Lanham, MD: Scarecrow Books).

Randle, Michael and Pottle, Pat (1989). *The Blake Escape: How We Freed George Blake and Why* (London: Harrap).

Reiser, Alfred (2013). *Hot Books in the Cold War* (Budapest/New York: Central European University Press).

Ribuffo, Leo (1980). 'Henry Ford and the "International Jew,"' *American Jewish History*, 69/4 (June), pp. 437–477.

Richards, Guy (1956). *Two Rubles to Times Square* (New York: Duell, Sloan and Pearce).

Richards, Guy (1966). *Imperial Agent: The Goleniewski-Romanov Case* (New York: Devin-Adair).

Richards, Guy (1970). *The Hunt for the Czar* (Garden City, NY: Doubleday).

Richards, Guy (1975). *The Rescue of the Romanovs* (Old Greenwich, CT: Devin-Adair Co.).

Richmond, Yale (2008). *Practicing Public Diplomacy: A Cold War Odyssey* (New York: Berghahn Books).

Rid, Thomas (2020). *Active Measures: The Secret History of Disinformation and Political Warfare* (London: Profile).

Riehle, Kevin P. (2020) 'Russia's Intelligence Illegals Program: An Enduring Asset', *Intelligence and National Security*, 35/3, pp. 385–402.

Riis, Sergius (1935). *Yankee Komisar* (New York: Robert Speller).

Riis, Sergius (1962). *Karl Marx: Master of Fraud* (New York: R. Speller).

Riley, Morris and Dorril, Stephen (1988). 'Rothschild, the Right, the Far-Right and the Fifth Man', *Lobster* 16 (June).

Robarge, David (2003). 'Moles, Defectors, and Deceptions: James Angleton and CIA Counterintelligence,' *Journal of Intelligence History*, 3/2, pp. 21–49.

Robarge, David (2015). *John McCone as Director of Central Intelligence 1961–1965* (CIA/Center for the Study of Intelligence).

Roberts, Kenneth (1949). *I Wanted to Write* (New York: Doubleday).

Robinson, Paul (1992). *The White Russian Army in Exile 1920–1941* (New York: Oxford University Press).

Rosenfeld, Gavriel D. (2019). *The Fourth Reich: The Specter of Nazism from World War 2 to the Present* (Cambridge, UK: Cambridge University Press).

Roszkowski, Wojciech, and Kofman, Jan (eds.) (2008). *Biographical Dictionary of Central and Eastern Europe in the Twentieth Century* (London: Routledge).

Ruotsila, Markku (2010). 'International Anti-Communism before the Cold War: Success and Failure in the Building of a Transnational Right,' in Martin Durham and Margaret Power (eds.) *New Perspectives on the Transnational Right* (London: Palgrave Macmillan) pp. 11–37.

Russell, Dick (1992). *The Man Who Knew Too Much* (New York: Carroll & Graf).

Sablinsky, Walter (1976). *The Road to Bloody Sunday: The Role of Father Gapon and the Petersburg Massacre of 1905* (Princeton, NJ:Princeton University Press).

Sainty, Guy Stair (1991). *The Orders of St. John* (New York: American Society of the Most Venerable Order of the Hospital of Saint John of Jerusalem).

Saul, Norman (1970). *Russia and the Mediterranean 1997–1807* (Chicago: The University of Chicago Press).

Schellenberg, Walter (1971) [1956]. *Hitler's Secret Service* (New York: Pyramid).

Schenk, Dieter (2000). *Hitlers Mann in Danzig. Gauleiter Forster und die NS-Verbrechen in Danzig-Westpreussen* (Bonn: Dietz Verlag J.H.W. Nachf).

Schieber, Haviv (1987). *Holy Land Betrayed* (Boring, OR: CPA Books).

Schrader, Del (1975). *Jessie James Was One of His Names: The Greatest Cover Up in History by the Famous Outlaw Who Lived 73 Incredible Lives* (Arcadia, CA: Santa Anita Press).

Schuyler, Philippa (1964). 'Russia's Czar Lives!' *Manchester Union Leader* (17 August).

Scott, Peter Dale (1993). *Deep Politics and the Death of JFK* (Berkeley: University of California Press).

Senn, Alfred Erich (1981). *Assassination in Switzerland* (Madison: University of Wisconsin Press).

Shackley, Ted (2005). *Spymaster: My Life in the CIA* (Dulles, VA: Potomac Books).

Shekhovtsov, Anton (2018). *Russia and the Western Far Right: Tango Noir* (Abingdon: Routledge).

Siemiatkowski, Zbigniew (2006). 'Agenci I dezerterzy,' *Wyborcza* (6 April).

Sikora, Miroslav (2014). 'Wirtschaftliche Innovation durch Spionage. Forschung, Entwicklung und der Geheimdienst in der Volksrepublik Polen 1970–1990,' *Jahrbücher für Geschichte Osteuropas*, Neue Folge, 62/4.

Simpkins, Pamela K. and Dyer, K. Leigh (eds.) (1989). *The Trust* (Arlington, VA: The Security and Intelligence Foundation (CIA) Reprint Series).

Simpson, Christopher (1988). *Blowback* (London: Weidenfeld & Nicolson).

Simpson, William Gayley (1978). *Which Way Western Man?* (Washington DC: National Alliance).

Singerman, Robert (1981). 'The American Career of the "Protocols of the Elders of Zion,"' *American Jewish History*, 71/1 (September 1981), pp. 48–78.

Sire, H. J. A. (1994). *The Knights of Malta* (New Haven: Yale University Press).

Sisman, Adam (2015). *John Le Carré: The Biography* (New York: Harper).

Slater, Wendy (2007). *The Many Deaths of Tsar Nicholas II: Relics, Remains and the Romanovs* (Abingdon: Routledge).

Smith, Christopher (2019). *The Last Cambridge Spy: John Cairncross, Bletchley Codebreaker and Soviet Double Agent* (Cheltenham: The History Press).

Smith, Daniel (2020). *The Peer and the Gangster: A Very British Cover-up* (Cheltenham: The History Press).

Smith, Jean Edward (1990). *Lucius D. Clay: An American Life* (New York: Henry Holt).

Smith, Simon (2018). *Otto Skorzeny: The Devil's Disciple* (Oxford: Osprey)

Snyder, Timothy (2005). *Sketches from a Secret War* (New Haven: Yale University Press).

Speller, Jon (2005). 'The Wheel of History Counts: The End of the Chinese Communist Party's Dominant Power is Fast Approaching,' *The Epoch Times* (3 July).

Spence, Richard (1995). 'Sidney Reilly's Lubianka 'Diary' 30 October – 4 November 1925,' *Revolutionary Russia*, 8/2, pp. 179–194.

Spence, Richard (2002a). 'The Strange Case of Sergius Riis,' *International Journal of Intelligence and Counterintelligence*, 15/2, pp. 222–242.

Spence, Richard (2002b). *Trust No One: The Secret World of Sidney Reilly* (Los Angeles: Feral House).

Spence, Richard B. (2008). *Secret Agent 666: Aleister Crowley, British Intelligence and the Occult* (Port Townsend, Washington: Feral House).

Spence, Richard (2012a). 'The Tsar's Other Lieutenant: The Antisemitic Activities of Boris L'vovich Brasol, 1910–1960 Part I: Beilis, the Protocols, and Henry Ford,' *Journal for the Study of Antisemitism*, 4/1 (June).

Spence, Richard (2012b). 'The Tsar's Other Lieutenant: The Antisemitic Activities of Boris L'vovich Brasol, 1910–1960 Part II: White Russians, Nazis, and the Blue Lamoo,' *Journal for the Study of Antisemitism,* 4/2 (December), pp. 679–706.

Spence, Richard (2017). *Wall Street and the Russian Revolution, 1905–1925* (Walterville, OR: Trine Day).

Stephan, John J. (1978). *The Russian Fascists: Tragedy and Farce in Exile, 1925–1945* (New York: Harper & Row).

Stephan, Robert (2004). *Stalin's Secret War: Soviet Counterintelligence against the Nazis, 1941– 1945* (Lawrence: University Press of Kansas).

Strasser, Fred, and McTigue, Brian (1978). 'The Fall River Conspiracy,' *Boston Magazine* (I November).

Sturdza, Michel (1968). *The Suicide of Europe* (Belmont, MA: Western Islands).

Sullivan, Michael John (1996). *A Fatal Passion: The Story of Victoria Melita, the Uncrowned Last Empress of Russia* (New York: Random House).

Summers, Anthony, and Mangold, Tom (1976). *The File on the Tsar* (New York: Harper & Row).

Sutton, Anthony (1974). *Wall Street and the Bolshevik Revolution* (New Rochelle: Arlington House).

Sweet, Matthew (2019). *Operation Chaos: The Vietnam Deserters who Fought the CIA, the Brainwashers, and Themselves,* (London: PanMacmillan).

Szlachcic, Franciszek (1990). *Gorzki smak wladzy* (Warsaw: FAKT).

Talalay, Kathryn (1995). *Composition in Black and White: The Life of Philippa Schuyler* (New York: Oxford University Press).

Tate, Tim (forthcoming, 2021). *The Spy who was Left Out in the Cold: The Secret History of Agent Goleniewski* (London: Transworld).

Thompson, Scott (1989). 'BORing from within U.S. Intelligence', *Executive International Review,* 16/10, March 3.

Tompkins, Peter, and Bird, Christopher (1973). *The Secret Life of Plants* (New York: Harper & Row).

Trotsky, Leon (1981). *The Balkan Wars 1912–13* (New York: Pathfinder Press).

Trudeau, Arthur (1986). *Engineer Memoirs: Lieutenant General Arthur G. Trudeau* (Publication Number: EP 870–871-26).

Ular, Alexander (1905). *Russia from Within* (London: Heinemann Books).

Vassall, John (1975). *The Autobiography of a Spy* (London: Sidgwick & Jackson).

Villemarest, Pierre de (1984). *Le Mystérieux Survivant d'Octobre* (Geneva: Crémille et Farnot).

Villemarest, Pierre de (2002). *Le Dossier Saragosse: Martin Bormann et Gestapo-Müller après 1945* (Panzol: Lavauzelle).

Villemarest, Pierre de, and Kiracoff, Clifford (1988). *GRU: Le plus Secret des Services Soviétiques 1918–1988* (Paris: Stock).

Vogel, Steve (2019). *Betrayal in Berlin: The True Story of the Cold War's Most Audacious Espionage Operation* (New York: Custom House).

Voitsekhovksy, S. L. (1974). *Trest: vospominaniia i dokumenty* (London, Ont: Zaria).

Wallace, Max (2004). *The American Axis: Henry Ford, Charles Lindbergh, and the Rise of the Third Reich* (New York: St. Martin's Publishing Group).

Wang, Chi (2015). *The United States and China Since World War II: A Brief History* (New York: Routledge).

Webb, James (1976). *The Occult Establishment* (Chicago: Open Court).

Webman, Esther (ed.) (2011). *The Global Impact of the Protocols of the Elders of Zion: A Century-Old Myth* (London: Routledge).

Webster, Nesta (1921). *World Revolution* (London: Constable and Company).

Weglinski, Marcin (2010). *Aparat Bezpieczenstwa gdanskim w latach 1945–1990* (Gdansk: Instytut Pamieci Narodowej).

Weiser, Benjamin (2004). *A Secret Life: The Polish Officer, His Covert Mission, and the Price He Paid to Save His Country* (New York: Public Affairs).

Welsh, George William (1923). *A History of the Ancient and Illustrious Order Knights Hospitaller of St. John of Jerusalem, Palestine, Rhodes and Malta 1048–1923* (York, PA: The Malta Book Company).

West, Nigel (1983). *The Circus* (New York: Stein and Day).

West, Nigel (1987). *Molehunt* (London: Weidenfeld and Nicholson).

West, Nigel (1988). *The Friends: Britain's Post-War Secret Intelligence Operations* (London: Weidenfeld and Nicolson).

West, Nigel, and Tsarev, Oleg (1998). *The Crown Jewels* (London: Harper and Collins).

White, Carol (1980). *The New Dark Ages Conspiracy* (New York: New Benjamin Franklin House).

Whiting, Charles (2000). *The Search for 'Gestapo' Müller: The Man without a Shadow* (Barnsley: Leo Cooper).

Widen, J. J. (2006). 'The Wennerström Spy Case: A Western Perspective,' *Intelligence and National Security*, 21/6, pp. 931–958.

Willetts, Paul (2015). *Rendezvous at the Russian Tea Rooms: The Spyhunter, the Fashion Designer and the Man from Moscow* (London: Constable).

Williams, Andrew (2019). *Witchfinder* (London: Hodder & Stoughton).

Wise, David (1964). 'HR 5507, a Prize Defector, now the Boomerang,' *New York Herald Tribune* (8 March).

Wise, David (1992). *Molehunt* (New York: Random House).

Witak, Robert (2014). 'Szpieg, ktory podawal sie za carewicza,' *Internal Bulletin of the Institute for the Study of Terrorism*, 11/35, pp. 57–61.

Wolton, Thierry (1986). *Le KGB en France* (Paris: Grosset).

Wright, Peter (1987). *Spycatcher: The Candid Autobiography of a Senior Intelligence Agent* (New York: Viking).

Wrobel, Piotr (2014). *Historical Dictionary of Poland, 1945–1996* (London: Routledge).

Zeskind, Leonard (2009). *Blood and Politics: The History of White Nationalism from the Margins to the Mainstream* (New York: Farrar, Straus & Giroux).

Zietara, Pawel (2015). 'Troubles with "Mela" a Polish-American Reporter, the Security Services of the People's Poland and the FBI,' *Polish-American Studies*, 72/1 (Spring), pp. 11–40.

KEVIN COOGAN BIBLIOGRAPHY

Published works

Books

Dreamer of the Day: Francis Parker Yockey and the Postwar Fascist International (Brooklyn, NY: Autonomedia, 1999).

The Spy Who Would be Tsar: The Mystery of Michal Goleniewski and the Far-Right Underground (Abingdon: Routledge, 2021).

(With Claudia Derichs) *The Secret History of the Japanese Red Army* (Abingdon: Routledge, forthcoming, 2022).

Articles

'The Importance of Robert Gayre,' *Parapolitics/USA*, no. 2, 30 May 1981, pp. 44–51.

'Jackboots and Sporrans: The Strange World of Robert Gayre,' *Anarchy* no. 38, pp. 10–13. Available online at: http://libcom.org/files/anarchy-38.pdf. [NB This was reproduced from *Parapolitics* without KC's permission].

'The Friends of Michele Sindona,' *Parapolitics/USA* no. 3/4, 15 August 1981, pp. 71–103.

'The Men Behind the Counterreformation,' *Parapolitics/USA* no. 6, 31 March 1982.

Co-authored with Martin A. Lee, 'The Agca Con', *Village Voice*, 24 December1985.

Co-authored with Martin A. Lee, 'La croisade des chevaliers de Malte', *Le Monde Diplomatique*, Octobre 1986, p.6. Available online at: https://www.monde-diplomatique.fr/1986/10/COOGAN/39569.

Co-authored with Martin A. Lee, 'Killers on the Right: Inside Europe's Fascist Underground,' *Mother Jones*, May1987 pp. 40–46, 52–54. Available online at: https://books.google.co.uk/books?id=recDAAAAMBAJ&printsec=frontcover&redir_esc=y#v=onepage&q&f=false.

'Introduction' to Dwight MacDonald, *The Root is Man* (Brooklyn, NY: Autonomedia, 1995). [Autonomedia republication of the 1953 update of the 1946 original]. Available online at: https://theanarchistlibrary.org/library/dwight-macdonald-the-root-is-man.pdf.

'How "Black" is Black Metal? Michael Moynihan, Lords of Chaos, and the "Countercultural Fascist" Underground', *Hit List*, 1/1 (February–March 1999), pp. 32–49. Available online at: https://ia800306.us.archive.org/6/items/HitListVol.1No.1/hit_list_v01n01_part1.pdf.

'Kevin Coogan Responds', letter reproduced in *Hit List*, 1/3, June–July 1999, pp. 5–7. Available online at: https://ia801908.us.archive.org/8/items/hit_list_1.3_1999/hit_list_1.3_1999.pdf.

'International Action Center – "Peace Activists" with a Secret Agenda?' *Hit List*, vol. 3, no. 3 November–December2001, pp. 159–168. Available online at: https://ia801904.us. archive.org/27/items/hit_list_3.3_2001/hit_list_3.3_2001.pdf.

'Lost Imperium: the European Liberation Front (1949–54)', *Patterns of Prejudice*, 36:3, 2002, pp. 9–23. Available online at: https://doi.org/10.1080/003132202128811466.

'The Mysterious Achmed Huber: Friend to Hitler, Allah… and Ibn Ladin?' *Hit List*, vol. 3, no. 4, April–May2002, pp. 120–127. Available online at: https://alexanderreidrossnet. files.wordpress.com/2020/03/coogan_articles.pdf.

'The League of Empire Loyalists and the Defenders of the American Constitution', *Lobster Magazine*, no. 46, Winter 2003. [This was an abbreviated version of the next entry focusing more on the LEL].

'The Defenders of the American Constitution and the League of Empire Loyalists: The First Postwar Anglo-American Revolts Against the "One World Order",' 2004. [This was based on a paper presented at the Institute for Social History in Amsterdam that was originally due to appear in an edited book but that fell through]. Available online at: https://web. archive.org/web/20060823103720/http://www.iisg.nl/research/coogan.doc.

'Tokyo legend? Lee Harvey Oswald and Japan,' *Lobster Magazine*, no. 70, Winter 2015. Available online at: https://www.lobster-magazine.co.uk/free/lobster70/lob70-oswald-a nd-japan.pdf.

'Lee Harvey Oswald's Address Book: A Follow-Up Note,' *Lobster Magazine*, no. 78, Winter 2019. Available online at: https://www.lobster-magazine.co.uk/free/lobster78/lob78-le e-harvey-oswald.pdf.

'Lost Imperium? Yockey: 20 Years Later.' Review of *Yockey: A Fascist Odyssey* by Kerry Bolton, *Lobster Magazine*, no. 78, Winter 2019. Available online at: https://www.lob ster-magazine.co.uk/free/lobster78/lob78-lost-imperium.pdf.

Published pseudonymously as 'Hylozoic Hedgehog'

How It All Began: The Origins and History of the National Caucus of Labor Committees in New York and Philadelphia (1966–1971), 2012. Available online at: http://laroucheplanet. info/pmwiki/pmwiki.php?n=Library.HIAB.

Smiling Man from a Dead Planet: The Mystery of Lyndon LaRouche, 2009. Available online at: http://laroucheplanet.info/pmwiki/pmwiki.php?n=Library.UnityNow.

Unpublished manuscripts

Red Swastika [A manuscript on post-Cold War Russian politics including Pamyat and their conflict with other Russian Nationalist groups.]

Marx, Russia and the Great Game [A manuscript reinterpreting Marx's writing on imperialism and Russia.]

Publications that Kevin Coogan contributed research to

Joe Conason, 'To Catch a Nazi', *Village Voice*, 11 February1986. Available online at: https:// www.villagevoice.com/2020/02/26/to-catch-a-nazi/.

Dennis King, *Lyndon LaRouche and the New American Fascism* (New York: Doubleday, 1989). Available online at: http://laroucheplanet.info/pmwiki/pmwiki.php?n=Library.LyndonLa RoucheAndTheNewAmericanFacism.

Martin A. Lee, *The Beast Reawakens* (Boston: Little, Brown and Co., 1997).

Nicholas Goodrick-Clarke, *Black Sun: Aryan Cults. Esoteric Nazism and the Politics of Identity* (New York: New York University Press, 2003).

Arthur M. Eckstein, *Bad Moon Rising: How the Weather Underground Beat the FBI and Lost the Revolution* (New Haven and London: Yale University Press, 2016).

Matthew Sweet, *Operation Chaos: The Vietnam Deserters who Fought the CIA, the Brainwashers, and Themselves* (London: PanMacmillan, 2019).

INDEX